Child Law

The International Library of Essays in Law and Legal Theory
Series Editor: Tom D. Campbell

Schools

Natural Law, Vols I & II *John Finnis*
Justice *Thomas Morawetz*
Law and Economics, Vols I & II *Jules Coleman and Jeffrey Lange*
Critical Legal Studies *James Boyle*
Marxian Legal Theory *Csaba Varga*
Legal Reasoning, Vols I & II *Aulis Aarnio and Neil MacCormick*
Legal Positivism *Mario Jori*
American Legal Theory *Robert Summers*
Law and Language *Fred Schauer*
Sociological Theories of Law *Kahei Rokumoto*
Rights *Carlos Nino*
Law and Psychology *Martin Levine*
Feminist Legal Theory, Vols I & II *Frances Olsen*
Law and Society *Werner Krawietz*
Contemporary Criminological Theory *Francis Cullen and Velmer Burton*

Areas

Criminal Law *Thomas Morawetz*
Tort Law *Ernest Weinrib*
Contract Law, Vols I & II *Larry Alexander*
Anti-Discrimination Law *Christopher McCrudden*
Consumer Law *Iain Ramsay*
International Law *Martti Koskenniemi*
Property Law, Vols I & II *Elizabeth Mensch and Alan Freeman*
Constitutional Law *Mark Tushnet*
Procedure *Denis Galligan*
Evidence and Proof *William Twining and Alex Stein*
Company Law *Sally Wheeler*
Privacy, Vols I & II *Raymond Wacks*
Administrative Law *Denis Galligan*
Child Law *Harry Krause*
Family Law, Vols I & II *Harry Krause*
Welfare Law *Peter Robson*
Medicine and the Law *Bernard Dickens*
Commercial Law *Ross Cranston*
Environmental Law *Michael Blumm*
Conflict of Laws *Richard Fentiman*
Law and Religion *Wojciech Sadurski*
Human Rights Law *Philip Alston*
European Community Law, Vols I & II *Francis Snyder*
Tax Law, Vols I & II *Patricia White*
Media Law *Eric Barendt*

Legal Cultures

Comparative Legal Cultures *Csaba Varga*
Law and Anthropology *Peter Sack*
Hindu Law and Legal Theory *Ved Nanda*
Islamic Law and Legal Theory *Ian Edge*
Chinese Law and Legal Theory *Michael Palmer*
Socialist Law *W. Butler*
Japanese Law and Legal Theory *Koichiro Fujikura*
Law and Development *Anthony Carty*
Jewish Law and Legal Theory *Martin Golding*
Legal Education *Martin Levine*
Civil Law *Ralf Rogowski*

Future Volumes

Labour Law, African Law and Legal Theory, Postmodernism and Law, Law and History, Law and Ethics and Cumulative index.

Child Law

Parent, Child, and State

Edited by

Harry D. Krause

Max L. Rowe Professor of Law
University of Illinois

NEW YORK UNIVERSITY PRESS
REFERENCE COLLECTION

First published in the U.S.A. in 1992 by
NEW YORK UNIVERSITY PRESS
Washington Square
New York NY 10003

Library of Congress Cataloging-in-Publication Data
Child law : parent, child, and state / edited by Harry D. Krause.
p. cm. — (The International library of essays in law and legal theory. Areas ; 13)
"New York University Press reference collection."
Includes bibliographical references.
ISBN 0-8147-4631-4
1. Children—Legal status, laws, etc. 2. Parent and child (Law)
I. Krause, Harry D., 1932– . II. Series.
K639.Z9C43 1992
346.01'35—dc20
[342.6135] 92-33417
CIP

Contents

Acknowledgements

The editors and publishers wish to thank the following for permission to use copyrighted material.

Boston University Law Review for the essay: Richard A. Posner (1987), 'The Regulation of the Market in Adoptions', *Boston University Law Review*, **67**, pp. 59–72.

Brigham Young University Law Review for the essay: Bruce C. Hafen (1976), 'Children's Liberation and the New Egalitarianism: Some Reservations About Abandoning Youth to Their "Rights"', *Brigham Young University Law Review*, pp. 605–58.

Columbia Law Review for the essay: Strauss & Strauss (1974), 'Review of Joseph Goldstein, Anna Freud and Albert J. Solnit "*Beyond the Best Interests of the Child*"', *Columbia Law Review*, **74**, pp. 996–1015. Copyright © 1974 by the Directors of the Columbia Law Review Association, Inc. All Rights Reserved. This article originally appeared at **74** Colum. L. Rev. **996** (1974). Reprinted by permission.

Henry H. Foster, Jr and Doris Jonas Freed (1972), 'A Bill of Rights for Children', *Family Law Quarterly*, **6**, pp. 343–75. Copyright © Harry H. Foster, Jr. and Doris Jonas Freed.

Harvard Law Review for the essay: Peggy C. Davis (1987), '"There is a Book Out...": An Analysis of Judicial Absorption of Legislative Facts', *Harvard Law Review*, **100**, pp. 1539–1604. Copyright © (1987) by the Harvard Law Review Association.

Harvard Women's Law Journal for the essay: Martha Minow (1986), 'Rights for the Next Generation: A Feminist Approach to Children's Rights', *Harvard Women's Law Journal*, **9**, pp. 1–24. Permission granted by the Harvard Women's Law Journal. Copyright © 1986 by the President and Fellows of Harvard College.

Robert J. Levy (1987), 'Custody Investigations as Evidence in Divorce Cases', *Family Law Quarterly*, **21**, pp. 149–67. Copyright © Robert J. Levy.

Michigan Law Review for the essay: David L. Chambers (1977), 'Men Who Know They Are Watched: Some Benefits and Costs of Jailing for Nonpayment of Support', *Michigan Law Review*, **75**, pp. 900–40.

Oxford University Press for the essay: John Eekelaar (1986), 'The Emergence of Children's Rights', *Oxford Journal of Legal Studies*, **6**, pp. 161–82. Copyright © Oxford University Press 1986. Reprinted from the Oxford Journal of Legal Studies by permission of Oxford University Press.

Sweet & Maxwell for essays: Bernard M. Dickens (1981), 'The Modern Function and Limits of Parental Rights', *The Law Quarterly Review*, **97**, pp. 462–85 and M.D.A. Freeman (1983), 'Freedom and the Welfare State: Child–Rearing, Parental Autonomy and State Intervention', *Journal of Social Welfare Law*, pp. 70–91.

Syracuse Law Review for the essay: Andrew S. Watson (1969), 'The Children of Armageddon: Problems of Custody Following Divorce', *Syracuse Law Review*, **21**, pp. 55–86. Reprinted by permission of the Syracuse Law Review.

University of California Davis Law Review for the essay: Michael S. Wald (1979), 'Children's Rights: A Framework for Analysis', *University of California Davis Law Review*, **12**, pp. 255–82. Copyright © 1979 by the Regents of the University of California. Reprinted with Permission.

University of Illinois Law Review for the essay: Harry D. Krause (1989), 'Child Support Reassessed: Limits of Private Responsibility and the Public Interest', *University of Illinois Law Review*, pp. 367–98. Copyright © by the Board of Trustees of the University of Illinois.

John Wiley & Sons, Ltd for the essay: Judith S. Wallerstein (1986), 'Child of Divorce: An Overview', *Behavioral Sciences and the Law*, **4**, pp. 105–18. Copyright © 1986 John Wiley & Sons Ltd. Reproduced by permission of John Wiley and Sons Limited.

Every effort has been made to trace all the copyright holders, but if any have been inadvertently overlooked the publishers will be pleased to make the necessary arrangement at the first opportunity.

Editor's Apologia and Acknowledgements

Early in this project, any hope of completeness became the first casualty. After many levels of reading and sifting, these volumes contain what remains of the enormous number of essays that are credible candidates for inclusion in the collection here attempted. Each work selected caused another to lose out. The space available to the family and children, even when it was – at my urging – expanded to three volumes, cannot accommodate a representative overview of even the best of the vast new literature on family law in the common law world.

In short, the selection is incomplete and, ultimately, arbitrary. It is the product of attempting to resolve conflicts between the relatively modest length prescribed by the publisher for each volume (350–500 pages), the great length of many excellent pieces which collided directly with the publisher's desire to accommodate as many as 20–35 essays per volume and *not* to allow editing. It was important to achieve a reasonable balance of subject matter coverage, as well as to emphasize 'hot spots' in the legal debate. Accordingly, I did not attempt systematic coverage of all subjects. Recognition was due a few older 'landmark' essays that, despite or because of their age, remain relevant to illuminate the foundation on which reform was subsequently built.

Finally, I strove for some measure of geographic diversity throughout the common law countries. Even with that attempt, 'commonwealth' representation may seem a little sparse, reflecting not only this editor's greater familiarity with US writing, but also the fact that, in terms of family law, the United States represents not one, but more than 50 jurisdictions, each with its own body of family law. This has resulted in an overwhelming US output. A large number of authors – Commonwealth and US – whose splendid works had to be omitted are recognized in the bibliography. Even when the process of selection was all but completed, new essays appeared on the scene. A single grouping of essays that will have impact is in a symposium issue of the Brigham Young University Law Review, Volume 1991, No. 1.

Numerous exciting articles have recently sought to place family law in a broader philosophical perspective, drawing on a wide spectrum of current trends. Many noteworthy contributions come to mind and are included in the bibliography. While the importance of attempts to develop broad new philosophical approaches to family law is clear, this literature is relatively new.* Approaches vary, political preferences often dominate, and tangible results are difficult to predict. What will survive is not yet evident. This is as it should be in an emerging line of thinking. It was clear, however, that only a broad sampling would have yielded a fair result and, since there is no space for a fourth volume on the 'post-modern'

* But see Carl Llewellyn (1932), 'Behind the Law of Divorce', *Columbia Law Review*, **32**, 1281; (1933), *Columbia Law Review*, **33**, 249.

philosophy of the family, I again was forced to choose. In the main, I chose essays dealing with specific subject matter, preferably on a 'grand scale', thus many of my selections do echo the broader, ongoing philosophical debates.

My sincere thanks go to many colleagues who generously shared with me their ideas on the best and most durable of common law family law literature. From their participation I gained not only inspiration, but also a sense of security. Often I found my own preferences confirmed and sometimes my choices made. Particular thanks go to Frank Bates, Margaret Brinig, Homer Clark, Eric Clive, Mary Coombs, Douglas Cusine, Samuel Davis, John Eekelaar, Jane Ellis, Aidan Gough, Dieter Giesen, Mary Ann Glendon, Kathy Graham, Brenda Hoggett, Joseph Kelly, Charles Kindregan, Mary Kay Kisthardt, Paul Kurtz, Sylvia Law, Robert Levy, Frederica Lombard, Kathryn Venturatos Lorio, Marygold Melli, Ross Nankivell, Mary O'Connell, Frances Olson, Sarah Ramsey, Sheryl Scheible, Pedro Silva-Ruiz, Serena Stier, J. Neville Turner, John Wade, Lynn Wardle, Mary Wenig, Walter Weyrauch, Judith Younger and Reinhard Zimmerman.

Special gratitude and recognition are due to Sally Waters whose expertise, as librarian at Stetson University College of Law, provided material for the non-US bibliography; to Carrie May whose clerical assistance throughout this project was invaluable; and to Scott Shipplett who helped to assemble and sort out the bibliographies.

Preface

In most Western countries, women have achieved *legal*, if not always full *de facto* equality. Everywhere, they have made notable legal and economic progress. This is the central fact in the cultural and socio-economic revolution that has brought unprecedented change in family life and law. This 'revolution' gathered speed in the liberal 1960s and was consolidated in the 1970s. The conservative 1980s did not turn back the clock, even if the pace of change has slowed.

In the common law world, the move to no-fault divorce is all but complete. True, in 1986 63 per cent of Irish voters defeated a constitutional amendment to allow divorce, but in 1992 they are reconsidering divorce, along with abortion. Elsewhere, even if traditional fault grounds remain on the books, they typically constitute only an option to no-fault divorce. Most divorce now is consensual or even unilateral. Rates remain high, even if they are levelling off.

The goal of modern divorce is finality. This is reflected in the emphasis on property division. The treatment of separate property on divorce has undergone fundamental change, favouring the economically weaker spouse, typically the wife. Too often, of course, there is no significant property. Contrasted with the new willingness to divide property, long-term spousal maintenance after divorce – traditionally 'alimony' – is granted less often and in lower amounts. When post-divorce maintenance is provided, the new theme is 'rehabilitation'. From what? From motherhood. To what? To self-support, but all too often without adequate concern for the dependent spouse's lack of adequate or appropriate economic opportunity.

It should be noted that the word 'rehabilitation' implies pathology. In turn, this implies that marital role-division to allow full-time parenthood is now considered pathological. This may go a little far, even if it is obvious that the tradition of full-time motherhood, as an exclusive track for women, was not a fair societal response to the *joint* parental responsibility of child rearing. Answers are needed, and needed fast. The needs of our children should remind 'post-modern' social theorists of unchanging, 'traditional' practicalities.

Partly in response, children born to unmarried parents have obtained improved legal rights that often are equal to those of children with married parents. Unmarried fathers are gaining custodial rights to their non-marital children. New concepts of children's rights have weakened age-encrusted notions of parental prerogatives. Instead, the emphasis is on parental and societal obligations, even while both fall short in practice.

New beginnings of pregnancy, ranging from artificial insemination to *in vitro* fertilization, embryo transplants and 'surrogate motherhood', have spawned ethical and legal questions without precedent and, so far, without universally accepted answers. On the opposite end of the 'wish list', modern medicine helps potential parents not to parent children. While the age-old dispute over abortion ('life begins at conception' vs. 'life begins at viability') is more alive than ever, abortion has become a widely accepted alternative to birth control – as well as to pregnancy and childbirth. Compounding the problem, the risk of tort liability has forced leading United States manufacturers of birth control devices out of business. The US Supreme

Court has begun to vacillate on the abortion issue – the very issue that has determined the fate of recent candidates for that Court.

Domestic violence directed against women and children has garnered attention, much sympathy, if few solutions. On divorce, joint custody of children is a new idea that must still prove itself to be a workable alternative to having *one* final decision-maker for the child. Grandparents are gaining rights to visit their grandchildren, sometimes against the parent's will.

Disillusionment with the role of law and lawyers in divorce has given rise to a wishful search for non-adversarial alternatives. 'Mediation' is the preferred approach, on the sometimes mistaken notion that 'no-fault' divorce implies a non-adversarial situation. The reality remains that where important rights are at stake, there must be rules. And there must be those who are trained to interpret the rules. Divorcing ex-partners will continue to need law and lawyers, even as both are becoming more 'user-friendly'.

New attitudes towards sexual companionship, marriage and family formation have become socially and legally acceptable. Marriage itself may be on the decline. To the middle class, 'role division' poses risks that reasonable women and men may soon consider unacceptable: the likelihood of divorce is high and, for a homemaker-spouse, inadequate economic provision after divorce is predictable. Bad as traditional marriage thus sounds for the economically weaker spouse, the cost of post-divorce economic provision for children and ex-spouse may also bring the 'earner-spouse' to a financial breaking point.

Many modern couples thus think that the commitments and burdens of marriage outweigh its advantages. One very practical attraction of unmarried cohabitation is that potentially costly procedures are not needed to end the relationship. More importantly, the financial consequences of divorce – though not child support – are avoided. For the sophisticated couple, unmarried cohabitation seems to afford an opportunity to define the terms of their relationship individually and precisely – an opportunity still largely denied them by traditional marriage which often overrides contractual variation of essential rights and duties that the law deems inherent in marriage. For two-earner couples who are conscious of tax law and social welfare benefits, cohabitation may bring financial advantages over marriage. For the feminist, cohabitation promises freedom from traditional male dominance that is perpetuated in antiquated marriage and family laws. For the 'unemancipated' recipient of alimony derived from a first marriage or of welfare benefits, remarriage or marriage may be costly if, as is often the case, these benefits are thereby terminated.

Ironically, many of the same 'progressives' who widely applauded the 'deregulation' of the legal family now call for the regulation of the informal family. Indeed, it is a good question whether this movement is 'progressive' or quite the opposite. If 'free love' is to be legally regulated, why is so little concern expressed about the resultant decrease in freedom of sexual and lifestyle choice? Traditionalists fear that formal marriage is depreciated if legal incidents similar to those of marriage are bestowed on unmarried cohabitation. Pragmatists are concerned about the legal uncertainties that are created if, typically retrospectively, informal relationships are judicially held to be endowed with legal rights and obligations that, at best, were thoroughly unclear during the ongoing relationship. Historians see a replay of developments that, in 1753 in England, led to the abrogation of common law marriage. Cynics think of the old-time semi-legal status of the 'concubine'.

The legal ramifications of unmarried cohabitation are thus at the 'cutting edge' of current developments. The old family is no more, but the new family is not yet. The revolution is not over, but the debate has shifted from asking whether cohabitation without marriage may produce legally sanctioned partnerships with legal and financial consequences, to what these consequences should be. In that sense, the cohabitation debate is subtly turning into a modern redefinition of 'marriage'.

Most of the discussion, however, has emphasized the rights of the parties *vis-à-vis* each other, and sometimes their legal relationship to their children. The equally important issue of what judicial or legislative recognition should be given to the relationship between the unmarried couple and the 'welfare state' has fallen short of thoughtful commentary. What, if any, 'public' legal consequences should attend unmarried cohabitation? For instance, should cohabiting partners be permitted to pay income tax at rates favouring married partners? Should they be required to pay marital rates if that would be to the advantage of the tax authorities? If unmarried cohabitants are allowed to waive mutual support liability, should the welfare authorities (taxpayers) be bound by such a contract? Should a dependency relationship based on unmarried cohabitation trigger welfare eligibility when the 'provider' leaves? Should welfare and similar benefits be terminated when a *de facto* 'provider' enters the picture? Should cohabitants have standing to sue for loss of consortium and wrongful death benefits? So far, these issues have not received much attention, even while the cohabitation relationship has sometimes been extended to include 'third-party-effects'. For instance, the City of San Francisco provides employee insurance to homosexual lovers who play the role of stay-at-home spouse, and the City of Berkeley adopted an ordinance assimilating marriage and cohabitation in terms of social and welfare benefits.

For the 1990s, the AIDS catastrophe, the continuing herpes epidemic and the increasingly bitter abortion debate may herald a return to more traditional lifestyles. After only two decades, history's first sexual revolution may be over, the casualty of *physical* causes. This was a revolution that had become *physically* possible only with scientific birth control and legal abortion. So much for the power of the ideology of sexual liberation!

What next? Piecemeal law reforms of the past two decades have not met the challenge of the redefinition of family lifestyles and relationships that is still taking place in Western society and culture. To most observers, the 'family' – whatever that may or should be – is continuing to disintegrate. In some areas, the rules of the game have not kept pace, in others the rules may have been adapted too much too soon and may indeed have accelerated social phenomena with which the law might have been better advised to continue to differ.

In the United States, legislators are generally unwilling to face up to sensitive issues. In consequence, too much of the clash between past and future has had to be resolved in the courts. This has caused uncertainty, because the judiciary is not equipped to make comprehensive law – sweeping though its edicts may be – especially if those edicts are based on implicit, sometimes vague, constitutional mandates. When compared with advanced Western European (civil law) democracies (which also have not distinguished themselves in coping with similar and equally unprecedented social and cultural changes), common law countries seem to have been very slow to formulate a deliberate social and legal focus on children. This is true particularly in the US which faces a cultural diversity on which – when it prided itself as a melting pot – it used to thrive, but which, unamalgamated, now threatens to throttle civil society.

The number of non-marital births and the creation of long-term 'single parent families' have caused concern, with non-marital births in the US and the UK exceeding 25 per cent of all births, up from 5 per cent in 1960.[1] This is eclipsed by a newer phenomenon, the 'no-parent family', which may now have reached 10 per cent of all children in the US. As far back as 1980, the US Census Bureau found nearly 5 per cent of all children to be 'true no-parent children, up from 3.5% ten years before'.[2]

Comprehensive welfare reform with attention to a national pro-family policy, one that would emphasize parental responsibility over state intervention or subsidy has become a goal. A variety of enactments focuses on the increasing incidence of poverty among children. But it is understood only vaguely that welfare laws often affect family behaviour and thus are intimately related to family legislation.

In the social welfare arena, the guiding force has long been modern liberalism, which replaced the 'charity'-mould and 'altruism'. The 1960s and 1970s spawned a 'welfare rights' and 'entitlements' philosophy, but after the conservative 1980s, the trend is back to a 'work ethic' approach. The 1990s emphasis on self-sufficiency is reminiscent, for better or for worse, of the much-maligned old English 'poor laws'. To illustrate, in 1992, New Jersey enacted a controversial welfare package that denies welfare benefits to more than one child of one mother, along with encouraging the mother to work.

If welfare legislation has been the product of compassion mixed with ideology, legislation dealing with the family, by contrast, has traditionally been the product of intuitive value judgments. Religious tradition has dominated the family sphere. As increasing interdependence of the members of our complex society has brought increased dependence on laws and government, a coordinated and deliberate approach to dealing with social problems has become a necessity – albeit one that generally has not been well served.

Important family policy issues arise in relation to social assistance laws. Without the understanding that welfare law influences family behaviour, social reform will not succeed. We need look no further than the negative effect on family stability of 'welfare' programmes assisting only unmarried mothers. In effect, these laws *require* the responsible but impecunious father to absent himself in order to make his family eligible for assistance. Other correlations are less visible, such as the interdependence of social insurance programmes and traditional, intergenerational 'relative responsibility' laws. Obvious side-effects on the family result from laws regarding women's rights in the work-place, from the provision of public day care designed to free parents for work (if not to improve the 'quality' of child rearing), from public provision of means of birth control and abortion, from the grant of maternity or paternity leaves and so forth. Even the tax laws – income, inheritance and gift taxes and especially the deduction and tax credit framework – are an important aspect of 'family' legislation. Tax laws grant or deny benefits or impose burdens on the basis of marital status or family-related dependency. Indeed, in some circumstances, the state provides greater tax and social security incentives to unmarried working couples or individuals than to traditional families. Witness, in the US, the so-called 'marriage tax penalty'[3] as well as a mix of other intended or coincidental incentives and disincentives to marriage and parenting. Such factors have contributed to the increase in unmarried cohabitation and child rearing, as well as to many married couples' decision not to have any or only a few children. At the same time, many wealthy states provide inadequate financial support for a climbing rate of births to single mothers. While there is only a low work force participation rate of mothers 'on welfare', efforts to improve the collection of child support from fathers have been a qualified success, but – due to many fathers' lack of adequate means – this source cannot fulfil all children's needs.

Conversely, the enactment of family legislation may affect welfare facts. For instance, liberal divorce laws and the concomitant relaxation of economic ties that in the past survived divorce have left their marks in terms of increased dependency statistics. The liberalization of abortion laws may have had the opposite tendency. The point to note is that the predictable effect on public welfare burdens of these changes in 'private' family law typically has not been a conscious factor in the making of these laws.

Even when family concerns are on the legislators' minds, side-effects are not always obvious. Consider only the 'pro-family' idea to grant working mothers or fathers paid leave upon the birth of a child. Or look at taxpayer-supported day care for working parents. While intended to aid families, such legislation specifically subsidizes *working* parents, and thus produces a relative financial disadvantage for the traditional role-divided marriage. Whether that may be a good idea for the future remains at issue, but it is not an idea that has been a conscious factor in the making of these laws.

Presidents and legislators speak of the importance of a new policy for families and children. Unfortunately, rhetoric has been buried in budget problems and political disagreement. Little has been done. In the US, the federal Congress is divided as sharply as the public. Fractured state legislatures are torn between tradition and the 1980s' appeal for *laissez faire* deregulation. Ironically, it seems that the political 'right' would deregulate business and re-regulate the family, whereas the 'left' would re-regulate business and support the continued deregulation of the family. The taxpayer, however, is neither ready nor willing to pick up the pieces.

Despite widespread misperception to the contrary, these problems are not issues of 'right' or 'left' politics, even if some proposed 'solutions' are. The problem is driven by fact – by a confluence of facts. The principal forces are (1) the realization of equality for women in the market place (which has led to the participation in the US labour force of some 70 per cent of mothers with children aged 6–17); (2) unmarried cohabitation and parenting (sometimes for the specific purpose of escaping the legal and financial consequences of traditional marriage); (3) single parent child rearing (post-divorce or non-marital); and (4) the social security, welfare and tax network of the modern state.

In its own way, each of these forces contributes to – even while it may be a result of – the unsuitability to current conditions of traditional concepts of legal marriage and family. Pointed questions arise: is the legal and economic incentive structure now so loaded against the traditional family that an intelligent woman or man no longer has a rational choice to forego market participation in favour of family role division? If marriage and procreation are fundamental human rights, have legal/economic circumstances rendered these rights less meaningful by making the cost of their exercise all but prohibitive? Is it even possible for law to define a fair compromise between career and child rearing? Can legislation provide parents (fathers *or* mothers) a 'more equal' choice between participation in the market place or dedicating themselves to their families? Do the partners or society want an equal choice?

In any event, maternity leaves, child support collection from absent parents, subsidized day care, free health care or welfare assistance are ultimately ineffective in dealing with the deeper structural challenges the family faces. To accommodate the radical redefinition of family behaviour witnessed at this time, we need a radical rethinking and restructuring of the legal framework for parent and child, and of the relationship between child and state. Certainly, populist calls for a return to the past are likely to be ineffective. In any event, that past may not have been quite so 'nice' as it is made out to be.

To reestablish social stability, the legal system must balance modern 'family facts' and society's legitimate needs. This should be understood to include both *regulatory* enactments and thoughtfully targeted and adequately funded intervention mechanisms – as well as outright subsidies where those are most effective. All this, of course, must remain in line with surviving social values that, in the common law world, prominently include the parents' right to autonomy and privacy, even if its corollary, parental responsibility, seems to have slipped. Given the latter, it is time to affirm that our respect for parental rights must not be carried to the point of harming the child – as I think it has been of late.

'Neutrality' is a misleading slogan when no matter how it is defined, it favours one side or the other. To illustrate, if 'neutrality' spells non-intervention when intervention is needed – to protect a child, for instance – 'neutrality' is an illusion. Let us in any event be sure to recognize that 'neutrality' cannot mean inattention.

Beyond that, I conclude that somewhere, sometime soon, the modern social contract must return to a set of basic value judgments, and I see one that should not be open to opposition: Each child should have the right to a decent opportunity in life! This must include at least minimally adequate parents or state services. I think it is cause for concern that recent trends decisively favour adult autonomy in matters of procreation and child rearing. Very little regard is given to the child. While I hasten to emphasize that the private sphere must indeed be free of state intrusion, the 'private sphere' has been wrongly defined to include areas that are of major public, of societal, consequence and thus of legitimate public concern.

A child-oriented restructuring of our family and social laws should redefine the scope of individual parental authority over children as well as family-based financial obligations (parent to child and child to parent). The active, supportive role of the state, through agencies and appropriate intervention, needs to be rethought. On a less direct but equally important level, the question is how welfare or social security and tax legislation should be devised to affect family behaviour 'positively' – however that may be defined.

In one paragraph, if social crisis is to be relieved in our lifetime, radical reform is needed. Such reform must identify, accommodate and redefine social and economic incentives and disincentives affecting child-related family behaviour – all in the light of a rational, tolerant and forward-looking redefinition of the kind of constructive 'family behaviour' society wants to evoke. The task must start with a rational definition of modern society's legitimate interests in children and parents, in the family. In the light of that, a legal redefinition of marital and parental relationships as an economic and social community will follow.

It is my hope that the essays here selected may begin to light the way forward on these issues.

Notes

1. US Department of Commerce, Bureau of the Census, *Statistical Abstract of the United States 1991*, at 838.
2. *New York Times*, 31 March 1992, p. 1, col. 2.
3. See Bittker, Chapter 11 in Volume I.

Series Preface

The International Library of Law and Legal Theory is designed to provide important research materials in an accessible form. Each volume contains essays of central theoretical importance in its subject area. The series as a whole makes available an extensive range of valuable material which will be of considerable interest to those involved in the research, teaching and study of law.

The series has been divided into three sections. The Schools section is intended to represent the main distinctive approaches and topics of special concern to groups of scholars. The Areas section takes in the main branches of law with an emphasis on essays which present analytical and theoretical insights of broad application. The section on Legal Cultures makes available the distinctive legal theories of different legal traditions and takes up topics of general comparative and developmental concern.

I have been delighted and impressed by the way in which the editors of the individual volumes have set about the difficult task of selecting, ordering and presenting essays from the immense quantity of academic legal writing published in journals throughout the world. Editors were asked to pick out those essays from law, philosophy and social science journals which they consider to be fundamental for the understanding of law, as seen from the perspective of a particular approach or sphere of legal interest. This is not an easy task and many difficult decisions have had to be made in order to ensure that a representative sample of the best journal essays available takes account of the scope of each topic or school.

I should like to express my thanks to all the volume editors for their willing participation and scholarly judgement. The interest and enthusiasm which the project has generated is well illustrated by the fact that an original projection of 12 volumes drawn up in 1989 has now become a list of some 60 volumes. I must also acknowledge the vision, persistence and constant cheerfulness of John Irwin and the marvellous work done by Mrs Margaret O'Reilly and Mrs Sonia Bridgman.

TOM D. CAMPBELL
Series Editor
The Faculty of Law
The Australian National University

Introduction

Part I Children's Rights

Not long ago, the male-female, role-divided nuclear family took its strength from centuries of unquestioned, and unquestionable, tradition. The family's primary social role was the bearing and nurture of children. The 'bad news' was that in the eyes of traditional law, only adults were persons. Children were wards – almost comparable to chattels, nearly owned by their parents. By and large, however, parents were required by social constraints and law to be responsible and, by and large, most were.

Today's rapidly evolving 'liberated' lifestyles are at variance with the continuing social need for a functioning 'infrastructure' to raise our young. To the extent the family has abdicated that role, there is need for a considered and responsible policy and legislative approach to children outside the family process. If the family is to remain in the picture, the law should abandon 'neutrality' and affirmatively support family formation and stability. 'Neutrality' is appropriate *vis-à-vis* 'consenting adults', but children are not adults and not consenting.

Legitimate family law must look to children as the 'socially relevant' and therefore principal actors in the family process. Legislation should take a hard look both at children within the family and those without one. Outdated 1930s and 1960s social legislation needs to be carefully adapted to current family models.

The United Nations 'Convention on the Rights of the Child' of 20 November 1989 is being considered by many countries. The Convention seeks to define a worldwide consensus on what society expects from and for its own future – even if there is disagreement on specific substantive mandates of the Convention, as well as on the manner in which it was adopted by the General Assembly or influenced by various social and political interest groups. The Convention asks society, the State, to recognize the child as an independent actor, breaking with a past that put children under the sole control of their parents. In that sense, the Convention mirrors developments in social programmes, tax policies and protective legislation of leading countries. It is not possible to include here the full text of the Convention, which is generally available for reference, in any event more so than other writings in this collection.

Ironically, the high rate of international acclaim that has accompanied the Convention may be due to the acceptability in many countries of a wide gulf between public, especially international, pronouncements and their realization in practical terms. In the United States, by contrast, a ratification of the Convention would force real change because a federal treaty would supersede state laws in an area traditionally reserved to the latter. Since that would strike at the heart of US federalism, chances for ratification are not great.

Preceded by the United Nations Convention on the Rights of the Child and its earlier Declaration on Social and Legal Principles Relating to the Protection of Children, the United Nations issued yet another Declaration on Children in September 1990, at the World Summit for Children. This latest document calls (1) for political action 'to promote earliest possible ratification and implementation of the Convention on the Rights of the Child', as well as setting forth goals for child survival, development and protection, as follows:

(2) We will work for a solid effort of national and international action to enhance children's health, to promote pre-natal care and to lower infant and child mortality in all countries and among all peoples. We will promote the provision of clean water in all communities for all their children, as well as universal access to sanitation.

(3) We will work for optimal growth and development in childhood, through measures to eradicate hunger, malnutrition and famine, and thus to relieve millions of children of tragic sufferings in a world that has the means to feed all its citizens.

(4) We will work to strengthen the role and status of women. We will promote responsible planning of family size, child spacing, breastfeeding and safe motherhood.

(5) We will work for respect for the role of the family in providing for children and will support the efforts of parents, other care-givers and communities to nurture and care for children, from the earliest stages of childhood through adolescence. We also recognize the special needs of children who are separated from their families.

(6) We will work for programs that reduce illiteracy and provide educational opportunities for all children, irrespective of their background and gender; that prepare children for productive employment and lifelong learning opportunities, i.e. through vocational training; and that enable children to grow to adulthood within a supportive and nurturing cultural and social context.

(7) We will work to ameliorate the plight of millions of children who live under especially difficult circumstances – as victims of apartheid and foreign occupation; orphans and street children and children of migrant workers; the disabled and the abused, the socially disadvantaged and the exploited. Refugee children must be helped to find new roots in life. We will work for special protection of the working child and for the abolition of illegal child labor. We will do our best to ensure that children are not drawn into becoming victims of the scourge of illicit drugs.

(8) We will work carefully to protect children from the scourges of war and to take measures to prevent further armed conflicts, in order to give children everywhere a peaceful and secure future. We will promote the values of peace, understanding and dialogue in the education of children. The essential needs of children and families must be protected even in times of war and in violence-ridden areas. We ask that periods of tranquility and special relief corridors be observed for the benefit of children, where war and violence are still taking place.

(9) We will work for common measures for the protection of the environment, at all levels, so that all children can enjoy a safer and healthier future.

(10) We will work for a global attack on poverty, which would have immediate benefits for children's welfare. The vulnerability and special needs of the children of the developing countries, and in particular the least developed ones, deserve priority. But growth and development need promotion in all states, through national action and international cooperation. That calls for transfers of appropriate additional resources to developing countries as well as improved terms of trade, further trade liberalization and measures for debt relief. It also implies structural adjustments that promote world economic growth, particularly in developing countries, while ensuring the well being of the most vulnerable sectors of the populations, in particular, the children. (New York Times, 11 October 1990 at A10, col. 2.)

Speaking more to the situation in well-off countries, Henry H. Foster, Jr. and Doris Jonas Freed advocate a 'Bill of Rights for Children' in Chapter 1 that would accord children enumerated rights, extending beyond the very basic goals of the UN Declaration. Their 1972 essay, radical in many ways, reflects the better side of 1960s idealism, showing distrust of authority whether exercised by parents or by the state. Foster's and Freed's 'Bill of Rights' is especially concerned with older children, in situations in which the state is involved for one reason or another. Their ten-point 'Bill of Rights' is used as a foil against which the authors test traditional law and suggest reform:

> Our emphasis has been upon the rights rather than the duties of children. That has been so because children's rights have been sadly neglected, not because children have no duties or responsibilities. Moreover, unless children are treated fairly and their rights are respected, it is idle to speak down to them about duty and responsiblity (p. 35).

John Eekelaar examines the 'Emergence of Children's Rights' in terms of two decisions of the House of Lords. Eekelaar delves deeply into history, tracing the change of attitudes and values of society:

> [O] ne might summarize the position in Blackstone's day as being that the legal apparatus protected a father's relationship with his legitimate children not primarily because the children's interests were thought worth protecting in themselves but because it was in one way or another deemed beneficial to the father. Injuries to the children were injuries to the father; that their interests might conflict with his was perceived, but protection was given only where his failure to regard their interests sufficiently threatened other people (p. 43).

Eekelaar is concerned about the child on divorce:

> [T] he very question: to what is a child entitled when assets and incomes are distributed, has never even been openly posed. Our learning has been centred on grappling with the problem of what a former *spouse* should be allocated after divorce. The interests of children have been quite submerged in the course of this debate (p. 50).

Relying on Lord Scarman, Eekelaar moves on to 'autonomy':

> [W] here a child has reached capacity, there is no room for a parent to impose a contrary view, *even if this is more in accord with the child's best interests*. For its legal superiority to the child's decision can rest only on its status as a parental right. But this is extinguished when the child reaches full capacity. More importantly, the argument catches the court itself. Should the child be warded, custody of the child vests in the court. The inherent jurisdiction of the High Court to intervene in the lives of children rests on the doctrine of the Crown's role as *parens patriae*. But on what principle can the Crown retain the parental jurisdiction when the parent himself has lost it, not through deprivation, but due to the superior right of the child? The primary question in wardship cases involving older children can no longer be: what is in the best interest of the child? It must be, has the child capacity to make his own decisions? ... Children will now have, in wider measure than ever before, that most dangerous but most precious of rights: the right to make their own mistakes (pp. 57–8).

Martha Minow discusses 'Rights for the Next Generation' in terms of 'A Feminist Approach':

> Yet the topic presents conceptual, practical, and political difficulties. What exactly is a right that can be exercised by a five-year-old, or a two-year-old – and does it rest on different premises than rights for adults? How are rights for children to be enforced: do they require adult supervision, and if so, by which adults (p. 59)?
>
> Children's rights owe some portion of their origins to struggles for women's rights, and the conceptual and practical problems raised by children's rights help to illuminate obstacles encountered by women's rights as well. In addition, the historic roles played by women as advocates for children's needs and interests closely link women's own political struggles with political reforms on behalf of children. Finally, rights for children, as developed later in this Essay, epitomize feminist concerns about the importance of connection, care-taking, and social relationships; pursuing a theory of

children's rights holds promise for a wider feminist approach to new forms that rights could take (p. 61).

Should a woman be free to choose whether to work in a workplace hazardous to any child she might conceive and bear? Should a woman's pregnancy entitle her to special work-leave benefits unavailable to a man – or should a workplace designed without pregnancy in mind disadvantage her when she chooses to bear a child? A woman's relationships, or potential relationships, with her children challenge the premise that she is a separate, autonomous person; and yet treating her as connected to others could disadvantage her in the workplace or seem to justify restrictions on her own choices. Is the woman to be treated 'the same' as a male employee – with no attention to her private relationships? Or is the woman entitled to special treatment – potentially curbing her choices and her success in a work world that uses the autonomous person as the model (p. 75)?

Michael Wald's essay, 'Children's Rights: A Framework for Analysis',

does not attempt to delineate what specific rights, if any, children should be given. Instead, it tries to provide a framework for analyzing the concept of 'children's rights' and to isolate some of the issues that must be resolved in order to make sound policy decisions (p. 87).

Wald's analysis proceeds in terms of the child's

(A) generalized claims against the world, e.g., the right of freedom from discrimination and poverty; (B) the right to greater protection from abuse, neglect or exploitation by adults; (C) the right to be treated in the same manner as an adult, with the same constitutional protections, in relationship to state actions; (D) the right to act independently of parental control and/or guidance (p. 88).

Wald understands that

[t]he questions are difficult ones; their resolution requires data about child development which are not available currently. Far more articulation of the assumptions underlying the positions of both opponents and advocates of children's rights also is necessary before we can begin to intelligently define the appropriate scope of both the rights and protections to which children should be entitled. The need for an interdisciplinary approach is critical. ... Finally, it must be recognized that the proposed analysis ... assumes that the capacity of children for decision-making and the impact of autonomy on family structures are relevant to deciding whether children should have more rights. These assumptions need not be accepted. Other commentators have approached the subject as a moral issue. They believe children should have autonomy because they are independent individuals. Giving parents control of children can be viewed as treating children as property. As one commentator concluded 'in the final analysis the ... justification ... for ... honoring children's rights is that it is right and fair.' One must wonder, however, whether such an approach is, in effect, a case of abandoning children to their rights (p. 110).

Part II Parental Rights, Society's Responsibility?

With his last phrase, Wald invokes Bruce C. Hafen's 'Children's Liberation and the New Egalitarianism: Some Reservations About Abandoning Youth to Their "Rights"'. As Hafen sees it, the tradition of family and parental authority is 'on a collision course' with the emphasis on individualism that has arisen out of the civil rights movement. Hafen cautions that serious risks are involved in an uncritical transfer of egalitarian concepts from the contexts in which they developed to the unique context of family life and children. The family life context has a history all its own – a history replete with psychological, economic, sociological, and political implications. The use of 'children's rights' language in this day of rights movements offers a way to leap over that history and its implications into the realm of abstract ideology. Whether that leap is the result of strategy or ignorance, its consequences are the same. The most harmful of the potential consequences is that the long-range interests of children themselves may be irreparably damaged as the state and parents abandon children to their 'rights' (p. 115).

Hafen analyses US Supreme Court jurisprudence involving children and discusses history, social science and philosophy from the Roman Empire to the Middle Ages, from Ariès to Sir Henry Maine, from Goldstein, Freud and Solnit to John Locke and John Rawls. Hafen concludes:

The individual tradition is at the heart of American culture. Yet the fulfillment of individualism's promise of personal liberty depends, paradoxically, upon the maintenance of a set of corollary traditions that require what may seem to be the opposite of personal liberty: submission to authority, acceptance of responsibility, and the discharge of duty. The family tradition is among the most essential corollaries to the individual tradition, because it is in families that both children and parents experience the need for and the value of authority, responsibility, and duty in their most pristine forms. When individualism breaks loose from its corollaries, however, its tendency to destroy personal fulfillment and human relationships is exposed (p. 164).

Bernard Dickens discusses 'The Modern Function and Limits of Parental Rights' and disagrees with Goldstein-Freud-Solnit's essentially 'neo-conservative' position:

The idea that children and their futures should be at the disposal of their parents' discretion, and that the courts should be entitled to intervene in the exercise of discretion only when parents are clearly and convincingly shown by due process of law to be at fault, may appear an overreaction to instances of children being placed at disadvantage by judicial and administrative insensitivity and oppression of parental choice. However much as the concept of parental autonomy may appeal to adherents of family solidarity and privacy, and to those sympathetic in principle to the prevalence of parental authority, the risk of injury and disadvantage to which this principle leaves children exposed may compel the harshness of the principle to be mitigated in practice (p. 174).

Dickens explores the issue 'primarily in the context of decisions concerning the medical care of children':

The issue to be critically addressed is the point at which an exercise of parental choice over a child's management and future is so potentially harmful to the welfare or interests of the child as to require state intervention and possibly a countermanding of parental choice (p. 176).

He concludes

The modern function of parental rights is to prepare children and adolescents for maturity, and as minors come to achieve maturity and to exercise autonomy, this may be seen not as a limitation or defeat of parental control, but as a successful discharge of parental responsibility (p. 190).

Part III The Best Interest of the Child? (Concerning the Freud-Goldstein-Solnit Theory)

Michael Freeman deliberates on 'Freedom and the Welfare State' in the context of 'Child-Rearing, Parental Autonomy and State Intervention'. He puts Goldstein, Freud and Solnit into the context of libertarian political philosophy, observing that

> Nozick makes only a cursory reference to the family and Goldstein, Freud and Solnit, whose *Before the Best Interests of the Child* is to be the pivot of this article, make absolutely no reference to the philosophy of Nozick or Hayek. Nozick's is true 'grand theory'; the Goldstein *et al.* project is a micro-study. Though less extreme than Nozick, *Before the Best Interests* belongs very much to the same tradition of libertarianism as *Anarchy, State and Utopia*. Goldstein *et al.* are most typical of a powerful lobby today which advocates parental autonomy in child-rearing. They argue for strict limitations upon state intervention in matters which intimately concern parent-child relations. Such interventionism is a characteristic of the growth of the Welfare State (p. 193).

Freeman argues

> [a]t the crudest the case for non-intervention is that intervention does not work. (p. 196). ... A second argument supportive of non-interventionist policies concerns the vagueness of the standards conventionally used to measure parent conduct. Vague language invites unwarranted and arbitrary intervention. ... A cognate point is that vague standards can all too easily be employed to impose the standards of one section of the population on another. (p. 197). ... The danger is that intervention will be grounded on vague concepts such as 'proper parental love' or 'inadequate parental affection'. As Michael Wald has argued, language like this (and it is commonly found in social welfare literature) 'invites unwarranted or arbitrary intervention. It could be applied to parents who travel a great deal, leaving their children with housekeepers, who send them to boarding school to get rid of them, or who are generally undemonstrative people'. Another critic is Harry Krause who insists that 'emotional neglect' is hardly 'susceptible to legally acceptable proof'. He is another to emphasize the difficulty of separating prejudices regarding lifestyles from it (p. 201).

Freeman tests Goldstein-Freud-Solnit's thesis on four well selected, provocative cases from both sides of the Atlantic. The cases involve parental decision-making ranging from issues concerning their child's sterilization or commitment to a mental hospital, to ultimate questions regarding their defective child's life. Freeman concludes

> that there are considerable problems in leaving the family alone. Victory for the family often means defeat for the children. It is, as I have indicated, a line-drawing exercise. Goldstein and his colleagues have erred in drawing the line too close to the parents' interests and too far from the children's. But the picture is not all black and white. Goldstein *et al.* seem to think in polar positions (you are, for example, either an adult or a child): I hope I do not. I recognize that intervention has its problems but I do not ignore its benefits. Intervention must be properly controlled. This requires an activist, committed judiciary capable of forging principles with the collaboration of other disciplines involved. One detects a laissez-faire attitude in our judges as well: this is the world of 'social administration', not a 'legal-battlefield', said Lord Scarman in a recent case. ... The judiciary must be prepared to control the controllers if intervention is ever to be acceptable. This, it may be thought, leads inevitably to one of the most commonly posed questions of all: *quis custodiet ipsos custodes* (p. 214)?

Peggy Davis, herself formerly a judge,

investigates the effects of judicial liberty in the determination of legislative facts. The investigation centers around analysis of judicial decisions that were influenced by a particular set of legislative 'facts' – the psychological parent theories espoused by Joseph Goldstein, Anna Freud and Albert Solnit. It was undertaken to identify the ways in which judges find and use legislative facts; to discover whether there are patterns of misuse; and to document the effect of legislative facts upon the development of law. The investigation reveals that legislative facts do have a dramatic and broad effect upon the development of law. Yet, their legal enshrinement is casual and unselfconscious, and their assessment often superficial and skewed by litigation imbalances. These results cast serious doubt upon Professor Morgan's view that judicial lawmaking should be unrestrained in the investigation and incorporation of factual predicates. The Article addresses the deeply problematic nature of permissive legislative fact-finding and seeks to offer a more constrained method by which judges may take notice of legislative facts (p. 218).

Davis concludes:

The litigator or judge who senses that judicial notice of a disputable proposition may figure significantly in a pending matter should have an acknowledged method of addressing the issue. This, too, could be accomplished by simply codifying an authority that no one disputes: the authority of a court to entertain or solicit special briefs, argument, affidavits or depositions of experts, or, in the rare case, hearings, as to the propriety of taking judicial notice of a disputable fact. A trial court's decision whether to exercise this authority should be reviewable and informed by standards. The rules themselves might provide such standards, or standards might evolve as acknowledgment and enhanced visibility of the process lead to its review and discussion in judicial opinions. But legislative controls should in either event be loose – in acknowledgment of, and without complaint against, the 'creative nature of the judicial function' (p. 279).

By now, the reader may wish that Goldstein-Freud-Solnit would be permitted to appear here in their own words. That is not possible, both in terms of the strictures of this collection – no books – and the authors' foresight not to reveal their ideas in an article, royalty-free.[1] However, Peter and Joanna Strauss provide a fairly detailed exposition of Goldstein-Freud-Solnit in their thorough book review:

[W]e think that the authors introduce political premises which receive no support from the findings of psychoanalysis or psychiatry when they insist that the natural parent has no claim independent of his child's interests, that he has no 'right.' The point is strikingly made by repetitive characterization of the birth certificate as an 'allocation', as if it were more than an (optional) record-keeping device and as if placement at birth involved a social judgment that *could* be made in any way. This characterization is effective only as a rhetorical device. The parents' claim is honored, not only out of concern for the child or even diffidence regarding present ability to determine its interests, but also in recognition of interests that the biological parents enjoy, which must somehow be compromised before any intervention can be justified. The failure to acknowledge this independent parental, perhaps more properly custodial, claim flaws the analysis (p. 285).

Strauss and Strauss conclude:

In sum, we view much of what the authors say as extraordinarily helpful. The exhortation that courts would ordinarily do best to leave well enough alone – to distrust their capacities for bettering even apparently harmful family situations, and consequently to follow a policy of repose – is forcefully grounded and long overdue. But lawyers who understand and accept the authors' imperative concerns, whose highest value now in custody matters is keeping their clients out of court, may come to question this book for its failures to consider both the values – values *to children* as well as to their parents –

> of planning and compromise, and the impact of changed law upon behavior that does not presently come to court or find reflection in trouble cases. The book takes only the first, creative step towards important legal growth. So understood, its insights may mark the spot from which further analysis will occur. But initial creativity, the bold shift of perspective, must be channeled and refined before effective legal regimes can be shaped from it. That job remains to be done (pp. 299–300).

Part IV Judge Posner's Proposition and the Economics of Adoption

In the full range of human endeavours, some issues defy wholly rational, coldly economic solution. Human sexual, procreative and family behaviour is one such area. Family *law* tends to respect emotion and caters to non-rational cultural values in this arena. Similar respect, however, is not extended by prominent proponents of the law-and-economics persuasion. Indeed, it may fairly be said that no position taken by advocates of the economic approach to law has caused as much consternation as Richard Posner's proposals on the 'Regulation of the Market in Adoptions'. Posner is quite aware of this: 'Whenever critics of the law-and-economics movement want an example of its excesses they point to what is popularly known as the "baby selling article" which Dr. Elizabeth Landes and I wrote almost a decade ago.'[2] In his ground-breaking book on law and economics,[3] Posner carried the baby-selling debate forward.

Despite the ridicule the idea generated for the marriage of law and economics,[4] Posner saw fit to reassert that he was serious and sought to justify himself in 1987.

> Some critics of our article apparently believe we wrote it as an exercise in mechanical extrapolation from the economic analysis of conventional markets. According to one of the least controversial concepts in normative economics – Pareto superiority – a transaction that makes at least one person better off and no one worse off increases social welfare, and is therefore efficient. A voluntary exchange is such a transaction, since the parties would not make it if they did not think it would make both of them better off. Therefore (it might seem) the exchange of money for a baby is efficient. But this last step does not follow from the first two. A baby is a member of society too. If the transaction diminishes its welfare, the transaction is not Pareto-superior. If it diminishes the baby's welfare by more than it increases the transactors' welfare, the transaction is not efficient even under a less demanding definition of efficiency. These points are fundamental to an economic analysis of family law, but they do not establish the irrelevance of economics to adoption. Economics is not just about the exchange of objects. Labor economics, and more recently family or household economics, are important fields of economic inquiry even though they deal with the exchange of, and not merely between, human beings. The purpose of our article was not to make an extrapolation at once mechanical and unsound from the market in goods to the market in babies but to use the analytical tools of economics to explore a pressing social problem – the imbalance between the demand for and supply of babies for adoption (p. 304).

Referring to aspects of adoption and to 'surrogate' motherhood, Posner argues: 'So we have legal baby selling today; the question of public policy is not whether baby selling should be forbidden or allowed but how extensively it should be regulated'.

Space limitations prevent reproduction of a variety of responses by Roland Cass, Tamar Frankel and Frances Miller, and Jane Cohen that follow Posner's piece in the same issue of the 1987 *Boston University Law Review*.[5] Moreover, the prohibition on books forbids more than a reference to what may be Posner's ultimate riposte – the economic analysis of sex.[6]

Recent events in Eastern Europe and elsewhere substantiate the need for repudiation of the apparently growing international 'baby market' and emphasize the urgency of proper regulation of international adoptions in the best interest of the children. The good news is that the Hague Conference on Private International Law is sponsoring the negotiation of a treaty to govern international adoption. By 1993, that treaty is expected to be ready for ratification by interested countries.

Important developments are also occurring in the areas of interracial and subsidized adoption. The new idea of subsidizing the adoption of children, often those that are handicapped, has provided homes for children not otherwise likely to be adopted. In the United States, finally, the Uniform Laws Commissioners are preparing a comprehensive new Uniform Act that seeks to reconcile modern views of the 'pros' and 'cons' of adoption and produce a consensus that will be acceptable to legislators, adoptive and biological parents and will also safeguard the children involved.

Part V Child Custody on Divorce

In 'Child of Divorce', Judith Wallerstein presents data estimating

> that 45% of all children born in the early 1980's will experience their parents' divorce, 35% will experience a remarriage, and 20% will experience a second divorce. In 1981, approximately 22.5 million young people, or 36% of all American children under 18, were living in a family other than the traditional two-parent family. This group included 11.4 million children living with their mothers only; 1.2 million living with fathers only; 6.4 million living with one biological parent and one stepparent; and the remainder living with adoptive parents, grandparents, or in foster homes. For black children, living with two parents is already less common than living with one parent. Although many children weather the stress of marital discord and family breakup without psychopathological sequelae, a significant number are identified within a troubled population. Children of divorce are significantly over represented in outpatient psychiatric, family agency, and private practice populations compared with children in the general population. The best predictors of mental health referrals for school age children are parental divorce or parental loss as a result of death. A significant survey of adolescents whose parents had separated and divorced by the time the children were seven-years old found that 30% of these children had received psychiatric or psychological therapy by the time they reached adolescence, compared with 10% of adolescents in intact families. Several studies suggest that children of divorce show lower achievement and experience greater difficulty in learning than do their classmates from two-parent families. Several large scale surveys report a higher incidence of disrupted learning, erratic attendance, higher dropout rates, increased tardiness, and deteriorated social behavior among boys from single-parent families. Another survey revealed that 15% of teenagers living with divorced mothers had been expelled or suspended from school at some time between elementary school and high school, whereas only 3% of teenagers from low-conflict, intact families had sustained a similar experience. At the other end of the developmental ladder, a study of kindergarten children shows that single-parent status resulting from divorce predicts significantly lower academic and lower social competence at school entry independent of socioeconomic status. Also relevant to the children's experience is the fact that divorced adults use inpatient and outpatient mental health services at a significantly higher rate than adults in intact marriages (pp. 321–2).

Differing from the assertive self-assurance of other social scientists, Wallerstein concludes pessimistically:

> Although policy makers, legislators, and judges have increasingly sought support from the findings of behavioral science and guidance from the mental health professions, the accumulation of psychological knowledge has not kept up with the rapid evolution of family law. Knowledge about children and parent-child relationships in the post-divorce family is still fragmentary and insufficient to support many of the legislative changes in family policy that have found powerful adherents. The subtleties of psychological thinking and shadings of individual difference that are so critical to the perspective of the behavioral scientist translate poorly into the arenas of court and legislature. The several years of follow up required to assess the impact of changed circumstances or altered family structure are ill suited to the pressured agendas of the political and judicial process. Despite the widespread acknowledgment given to the important interface between family law and mental health, the major task of building cooperation and mutual understanding on a firm basis of empirical knowledge and shared values still lies ahead (p. 331).

The last word has not been found, much less spoken. The debate goes on.

Andrew Watson, M.D. and psychiatrist turned law professor, concludes this segment with his classic 'Children of Armageddon: Problems of Custody Following Divorce'. Watson concurs that social science has far to go before it can be trusted, but he finds predictable factors in the typical situation and develops specific recommendations. Putting the lack of certainty in social science data in perspective, Watson counsels:

> Though the literature is replete with studies of the various factors which relate to a child's successful maturation, none of it is without the vulnerability of methodological inadequacy. These inadequacies are not due necessarily to the naivete of the observers although that is sometimes the case. They are caused both by the complexity of the subject, as well as by the fact that we do not experiment with human beings. For this reason, any view put forward by the behavioral scientist can be speedily set aside on the ground that it lacks 'scientific certainty'. Let us hasten to note, however, that this kind of information is considerably more 'hard' than the hunches of philosophers or the theoretical predilections of judges (p. 351).

Watson is concerned that

> [L]awyers have a conspicuous lack of understanding of the behavioral sciences. This is not attributable to neglect on their parts, for legal education and training do little to facilitate the gaining of such knowledge. As I have said elsewhere, legal education tends to blunt native ability so far as psychological sensitivity is concerned. Together with this functional 'blindness', there is a strong inclination for lawyers to be oblivious to the emotional results of their procedures. They appear to believe that they can conduct a vigorous adversary contest and then have the contestants return to some kind of working rapport. Such contests in child custody cases will most surely produce wounds which do not heal adequately to assure a good subsequent working relationship between the parents. If judges are to handle custodial disputes effectively, they must give very careful consideration to the techniques they use. The not uncommon and often inviting temptation to moralize with one or the other parent must be avoided if the contestants are to be assisted in fulfilling their ongoing parental duties. For many judges this will be an almost insurmountable task (p. 343).
>
> ... There is a similar need on the part of psychiatrists, social workers, and psychologists working in this area of law to be educated about some of the fundamental legal matters which arise in family law cases. While there have been occasional courses offered to these professionals, nowhere do they learn enough to assure that they will come into court or write their opinions with adequate legal knowledge about how their information will be used. This, too, should be remedied, since failure of communication between these two professional groups can only increase the hazards for children (pp. 362–3).

From the lawyer's point of view, Robert Levy writes about 'Custody Investigations as Evidence in Divorce Cases':

> Judges have enthusiastically relied upon out-of-court caseworker custody investigations in divorce cases for a complex of reasons which they have often identified in appellate decisions and in the trade literature: custody decisions are too important to be treated in the same fashion as ordinary adversary litigation – in which the parties have uncontrolled discretion as to what testimony is presented to the decision maker; a neutral expert, removed from the emotional turmoil of the dispute and the partisan advocacy of the lawyers, can provide more reliable information to the judge than the embattled spouses are likely to provide; the information essential to custody decision making tends to be more psychological than in other litigation contexts and therefore more suited to written reports by psychological experts than to testimony in a courtroom (pp. 367–8).

Levy's concern is not only about unpredictable and possibly arbitrary criteria for child custody, but also about the proper presentation of non-legal data in an appropriate forum. He cautions:

> [W]hen we examine the quality of custody investigations and devise procedural techniques to regulate their use, we should be attentive to the risks to children and to family privacy and autonomy posed by their interventionist potential (p. 369).

Levy concludes:

> Perhaps more important than any procedural safeguard is the message to attorneys these data convey: beware of nonadversary experts bearing fact-finding gifts. Be prepared to doubt, to question, to investigate, and, if necessary, to cross-examine. That custody investigations appear often to be unreliable is not a reason to settle fewer custody cases; but it is a reason to protect your client by developing the facts of the case thoroughly (p. 383).

Part VI The Child Support Obligation and One Paragraph on 'Illegitimacy'

Great progress has been made in equalizing the legal rights of the non-marital child with those of the child whose parents are married to each other. In the US, this ideal has become a constitutional principle.[7] The issue of 'illegitimacy', it should be noted, now encompasses far more than ascertaining the traditional 'casual progenitor' and holding him financially responsible. Birth out of wedlock has taken on a different social meaning with the vast increase in stable and long-term, though unmarried, relationships that have produced children. Today, the principle of equal legal rights for children regardless of their parents' marital status – even the notion that some unwed fathers may themselves have certain custodial rights – seems so obvious that no more need be said than that sweeping reforms are being implemented in some and stand quite complete in other countries.

The issue of defining an appropriate child support obligation for absent parents and the collection of that support, however, is one that remains under serious scrutiny, even while major reforms are being put in place in Australia, the UK, the US and elsewhere. The last word has not been spoken on the proper balance between private and social responsibility for the support of children.

David Chambers describes his study of the 'Benefits and Costs of Jailing for Non-Payment of Support'.[8] Chambers concludes that jail is indeed effective in coercing the payment of child support, but considers jailing a poor choice in comparison to other techniques. He proposes mandatory deduction from paychecks of support owed and, for most practical purposes, his proposal now is law in the United States:

> If a federal system were established under which withholding occurred from the first moment of an order and traveled with a person wherever he took work within the country, the need for much of the current enforcement system would largely disappear. To effectuate this network, the federal government would need to create a national computerized system tied to the man's Social Security number. Employers would be required to make a check on a new employee through a Social Security office to learn whether support payments were to be withheld from his wages. Under such a system, the frequency of payments would be nearly perfect except by the unemployed, the self-employed, and those able to evade the floating wage assignment by falsifying their Social Security numbers or by colluding with the employer (p. 421).

Throughout this 3-volume collection and their respective Introductions, I have had my share of difficulty *not* to inject my own ideas – expressed in my articles and books on most of the subjects covered – into the discussion and, with an exception or two, to stay clear of predisposing the reader in one direction or another. At this point the reader may fairly wonder who I am and perhaps I owe an answer in the form of adding one essay to this collection. My 'Reassessment' of 'Child Support' is that piece.

Harry D. Krause

Notes

1. But *cf.* Comment, (1963), 'Alternatives to "Parental Right" in Child Custody Disputes Involving Third Parties', *Yale Law Journal*, **74**, 151.
2. E. Landes and R. Posner (1978), 'The Economics of the Baby Shortage', *Journal of Legal Studies*, **7**, 323. Anyone seeking a more compelling illustration of how an excess of reason will produce nonsense will enjoy Gary Becker's economic analysis of the institution of of polygamy in his '*Treatise on the Family*' (1981), especially his formula at pp. 58–65.
3. R. Posner (1986), *Economics of Law*, 3rd edition, 139–43.
4. For instance, D. Farber (1986), 'An Economic Analysis of Abortion', *Constitutional Commentary*, **3**, 1.
5. *Boston University Law Review*, **67**, 73, 99, 105.
6. See Wohl (1992), Book review of *Posner, Sex and Reason* in *American Bar Association Journal*, April, at 95.
7. Krause (1967), 'Equal Protection for the Illegitimate', *Michigan Law Review*, **65**, 477; for other countries, see Krause (1976), 'Creation of Kinship Relations', Ch. 6 in Vol. IV, *Persons and Family, International Encyclopedia of Comparative Law*, J.C.B. Moor; Tübingen.
8. David Chambers' study is presented more fully in his well-known book, *Making Fathers Pay: the Enforcement of Child Support*, 1979.

Selected Bibliography

This bibliography lists recent articles on selected child law topics. To stay within a manageable size, almost no articles written prior to 1980 are included; more recent work was given priority but, even then, only a fraction of the available literature could be listed. Given the overwhelming quantity of US publications and the sometimes closer legal relationships among the other common law countries, it seemed useful to list US publications and those of other common law jurisdictions separately. The broad headings follow those used in the text and are only a general guide for quick access. Numerous entries fit more or less equally well under several headings, but as they are listed only under one, related topical headings should also be examined.

Children's Rights (Part I)

United States

Coons, Mnookin, and Sugarman, (1991), 'Puzzling Over Children's Rights', *Brigham Young University Law Review*, **1991**, 307.

Geimer, (1988), 'Juvenileness: A Single-Edged Constitutional Sword', *Georgia Law Review*, **22**, 949.

Meyer, (1984), 'Protecting the Best Interests of the Child: Is the State the Necessary Blunt Instrument?', *Arizona State Law Journal*, **1984**, 601.

Minow, (1987), 'Are Rights Right for Children?', *American Bar Foundation Research Journal*, **1987**, 203.

Rush, (1985), 'The Warren and Burger Courts on State, Parent, and Child Conflict Resolution: A Comparative Analysis and Proposed Methodology', *Hastings Law Journal*, **36**, 461.

Symposium, (1987), 'Juvenile Law' (Ambler, Edwards, Roche, Patton), *Santa Clara Law Review*, **27**, 197–329.

Teitelbaum, (1980), 'Foreword: The Meanings of Rights of Children', *New Mexico Law Review*, **10**, 235.

Youth Law Center, (1981–82), 'Legal Rights of Children in the United States of America', *Columbia Human Rights Law Review*, **13**, 675.

Common Law Countries, Other than the United States

Blown, Nerys and Milliken, Susan (1989), 'The failure of the legal system to protect the economic rights of children' (Canada), *Canadian Journal of Family Law*, **7** (2), 367–82, Spring.

Duncan, William R. (1986), 'Family law – the child's right to a family – parental rights in disguise' (Ireland), *Dublin University Law Journal*, **8**, 76–86, January, Annual.

Gamble, Helen and Weeks, Phillipa (1982), 'The right of a child to take independent action for maintenance under the Family Law Act 1975' (Australia), *Australian Law Journal*, **56** (2), 68–76, February.

Goodman, Ellen (1983), 'A child's "right" to access – a problematic postulate' (Australia), *University of Tasmania Law Review*, **7** (3), 308–18, January, Annual.

Heffey, Peter G. (1984), 'Dennis the Menace, and the wonderland of children's torts: children's torts and parental responsibility' (Australia), *Law Institute Journal*, **58** (6), 660–3, June.

Laudau, Barbara (1988), 'Children's rights to visitation, support and the home' (Canada), *Canadian Family Law Quarterly*, **3** (1), 55–70, April.

Ray, Alan (1988), 'Parents' and children's rights: Family Law Act perspectives' (Australia), *Legal Service Bulletin*, **13** (1), 12–15, February.

Ruoff, Theodore B.F. (1981), 'Links with London' (Downs Syndrome baby's right to life), *Australian Law Journal*, **55** (11), 826–7, November.

Sutherland, Elaine E. (1987), 'Petition by natural sister for access to two sisters' (Scotland), *Journal of the Law Society of Scotland*, **32** (7), 274(2), July.
Sutherland, Elaine (1990), 'Scotland: financial provision, the status of children and child protection' (Annual Survey of Family Law), *Journal of Family Law*, **28** (3), 588–99, May.
Sutherland, Elaine E. (1991), 'The United Nations Convention on the Rights of the child: does Scots law measure up?' (Scotland), *Scots Law Times*, No 17, 198(4), May.
Turner, J. Neville (1982), '"Hey mum, mum's on the phone for you": some legal aspects of foster care' (Australia), *University of Tasmania Law Review*, **7** (2), 174–90, January. Annual.

Parental Rights, Society's Responsibility? (Part II)

United States

Annas, (1984), 'Refusal of Lifesaving Treatment for Minors', *Journal of Family Law*, **23**, 217.
Apollo, (1989), 'The Biological Father's Right to Require a Pregnant Woman to Undergo Medical Treatment Necessary to Sustain Fetal Life', *Dickinson Law Review*, **94**, 199.
Atwater, (1989), 'A Modern-day Solomon's Dilemma: What of the Unwed Father's Rights?', *University of Detroit Law Review*, **66**, 267.
Bartlett (1984), 'Rethinking Parenthood as an Exclusive Status: The Need for Legal Alternatives When the Premise of the Nuclear Family Has Failed', *Virginia Law Review*, **70**, 879.
Benshoof, (1988), 'The Chastity Act: Government Manipulation of Abortion Information and the First Amendment', *Harvard Law Review*, **101**, 1916.
Bernstein, (1991), 'Termination of Parental Rights on the Basis of Mental Disability: A Problem in Policy and Interpretation', *Pacific Law Journal*, **22**, 1155.
Blair, (1989), 'Parent-Initiated Termination of Parental Rights: The Ultimate Weapon in Matrimonial Warfare', *Tulsa Law Journal*, **24**, 299.
Burrell, (1989), 'Parental Consortium: A House Built on Sand', *UMKC Law Review*, **58**, 145.
Byrd, (1988), 'Relative Responsibility Extended: Requirement of Adult Children to Pay for Their Indigent Parent's Medical Needs', *Family Law Quarterly*, **22**, 87.
Eveleigh, (1989), 'Certainly Not Child's Play: A Serious Game of Hide and Seek with the Rights of Unwed Fathers', *Syracuse Law Review*, **40**, 1055.
Fanshel, (1983–84), 'Urging Restraint in Terminating the Rights of Parents of Children in Foster Care', *New York University Review of Law and Social Change*, **12**, 485.
Gallagher, (1989), 'Prenatal v. Parental Rights: What a Difference an "a" Makes', *St. Mary's Law Journal*, **21**, 301.
Garrison, (1983), 'Why Terminate Parental Rights?', *Stanford Law Review*, **35**, 423.
Geis, Binder, (1991), 'Sins of their Children: Parental Responsibility for Juvenile Delinquency', *Notre Dame Journal of Legal Ethics and Public Policy*, **5**, 303.
Griffin, (1989), 'Death of the Family: What's Become of the Parents and the Children', *Akron Law Review*, **22**, 303.
Guggenheim, (1984), 'State Intervention in the Family: Making a Federal Case Out of It', *Ohio State Law Journal*, **45**, 399.
Guthrie, (1990), 'Should Pennsylvania Recognize a Cause of Action for Loss of Parental Consortium?', *Duquesne Law Review*, **28**, 697.
Hayman, (1990), 'Presumptions of Justice: Law, Politics, and the Mentally Retarded Parent', *Harvard Law Review*, **103**, 1201.
Hill, (1990), 'Putative Fathers and Parental Interests: A Search for Protection', *Indiana Law Journal*, **65**, 939.
Koropp, (1989), 'Setting the Standard: A Mother's Duty During the Prenatal Period', *University of Illinois Law Review*, **1989**, 493.
Lawton, Carder and Weisman, (1985), 'Recent Governmental Action Regarding the Treatment of Seriously Ill Newborns', *Journal of College and University Law*, **11**, 403.

Mangel, (1988), 'Licensing Parents: How Feasible?', *Family Law Quarterly*, **22**, 17.
McCarthy, (1988), 'The Confused Constitutional Status and Meaning of Parental Rights', *Georgia Law Review*, **22**, 975.
Mlyniec, (1986), 'Lifelines to Biological Parents: Their Effect on Termination of Parental Rights and Permanence', *Family Law Quarterly*, **20**, 233.
Monopoli, (1991), 'Allocating the Costs of Parental Free Exercise: Striking a New Balance Between Sincere Religious Belief and a Child's Right to Medical Treatment', *Pepperdine Law Review*, **18**, 319.
Olsen, (1985), 'The Myth of State Intervention in the Family', *University of Michigan Journal of Law Reform*, **18**, 835.
Parness, (1991), 'Prospective Fathers and their Unborn Children', *University of Arkansas at Little Rock Law Journal*, **13**, 165.
Paul, (1989), '"You Get the House. I Get the Car. You Get the Kids. I Get their Souls." The Impact of Spiritual Custody Awards on the Free Exercise Rights of Custodial Parents', *Pace Law Review*, **138**, 583.
Polikoff, (1990), 'This Child Does Have Two Mothers: Redefining Parenthood to Meet the Needs of Children in Lesbian-mother and Other Nontraditional Families', *Georgetown Law Journal*, **78**, 459.
Prygoski, (1983), 'When a Hearing is not a Hearing: Irrebuttable Presumptions and Termination of Parental Rights Based on Status', *University of Pittsburgh Law Review*, **44**, 879.
Runner, (1989–90), 'Protecting a Husband's Parental Rights When His Wife Disputes the Presumption of Legitimacy', *Journal of Family Law*, **28**, 115.
Secor, (1990), 'Michael H. v. Gerald D.: Due Process and Equal Protection Rights of Unwed Fathers, *Hastings Constitutional Law Quarterly*, **17**, 759.
Stenger, (1980–81), 'Expanding Constitutional Rights of Illegitimate Children, 1968–1980', *Journal of Family Law*, **19**, 407.
Trahan, (1990), 'Constitutional Law: Parental Denial of a Child's Medical Treatment for Religious Reasons', *1989 Annual Survey of American Law*, 307.
Waldrop, and Waldrop, (1990), 'Making and Breaking Connections Between Parents' Duty to Support and Right to Control Their Children', *Oregon Law Review*, **69**, 689.
Weinstein, (1991), 'Visiting the Sins of the Child on the Parent: The Legality of Criminal Parental Liability Statutes', *Southern California Law Review*, **64**, 859.
Wheeler, (1987), 'A Father's Right to Know His Child: Can it be Denied Simply Because the Mother Married Another Man?', *Loyola of Los Angeles Law Review*, **20**, 705.
Wintjen, (1990), 'Make Room for Daddy: A Putative Father's Rights to his Children', *New England Law Review*, **24**, 1059.
Wright, (1990), 'Fetus vs. Mother: Criminal Liability for Maternal Substance Abuse During Pregnancy', *Wayne Law Review*, **36**, 1285.

Common Law Countries, Other than the United States

Atkin, William R. (1988), 'New Zealand: children versus families – is there any conflict?' (Annual Survey of Family Law 1987), *Journal of Family Law*, **27** (1), 231–42, November.
Atkin, W.R. (1990), 'The courts and child protection – aspects of the Children, Young Persons, and Their Families Act 1989' (New Zealand), *Victoria University of Wellington Law Review*, **20** (4), 319–42, November.
Bates, Frank (1989), 'The children of Mansoul – adopted children and natural parents: some comparative developments' (Australia), *Australian Law Journal*, **63** (5), 314–26, May.
Cusine, Douglas J. (1985), 'Contraceptive advice to the under-sixteens' (Great Britain), *Journal of the Law Society of Scotland*, **30** (6), 217(4), June.
Devereux, John (1991), 'The capacity of a child in Australia to consent to medical treatment – Gillick revisited?', *Oxford Journal of Legal Studies*, **11** (2), 283–302, Summer.
Downey, P.J. (1986), 'Parents, rights and responsibilities' (New Zealand, Great Britain), *New Zealand Law Journal*, 217(3), June.

Freeman, Michael D.A. (1986), 'England: the trumping of parental rights' (Annual Survey of Family Law 1985), *Journal of Family Law*, **25** (1), 91–102, October.
Greif, Judith Brown (1980), 'Access: legal right or privilege at the custodial parent's discretion?', *Canadian Journal of Family Law*, **3** (1), 43–56, January.
Johnston, Ian D. (1981), 'Standards and pre-adjudication procedures for state intrusion in the family' (New Zealand), *New Zealand Universities Law Review*, **9** (3), 217–46, June.
Kerr, Gillian (1982), 'Judicial review and parental rights' (Northern Ireland), *Northern Ireland Legal Quarterly*, **33** (4), 378–88, Winter.
Kovacs, Dorothy (1986), 'The child under the Family Law Act: recent developments' (Australia), *Monash University Law Review*, **12** (3–4), 133–60, September.
Lucas, Brian (1982), 'Legal intervention in the care of children' (Australia), *Criminal Law Journal*, **6** (3), 119–30, June.
Magnet, Joseph Eliot (1980), 'Withholding treatment from defective newborns: a description of Canadian practices', *Legal Medical Quarterly*, **4** (4), 271–92, Winter.
Payne, Julien D. (1981), 'Parenting rights on marriage breakdown or divorce' (Canada), *Family Law Review*, **4–6**, 71–91, Summer–Winter.
Simpson, Jim (1989), 'Judges at odds; who should decide whether an intellectually disabled girl should be sterilized?' (Australia), *Legal Service Bulletin*, **14** (3), 102–4, June.
Somerville, Margaret A. (1984), 'Governing professional intervention in the family: achieving and maintaining a delicate balance' (Canada), *Revue du Barreau de Quebec*, **44** (4), 691–718, September.
Thomson, George (1981), 'Confidentiality and the compulsory reporting of child abuse' (Canada), *Health Law in Canada*, **2** (1), 15(3), Spring.
Thomson, George (1981), 'Minors and medical consent' (Canada), *Health Law in Canada*, **2** (4), 76–8, Winter.
Ullrich, Vivienne (1981), 'Parents at law' (New Zealand), *Victoria University of Wellington Law Review*, **11** (2), 95–122, May.
White, Walter G.W. (1980), 'A comparison of some parental and guardian rights' (Canada), *Canadian Journal of Family Law*, **3** (2–3), 219–49, June.

The Best Interest of the Child? (Part III)

United States

Bowen, (1987–88), 'Cultural Convergences and Divergences: The Nexus Between Putative Afro-American Family Values and the Best Interests of the Child', *Journal of Family Law*, **26**, 487.
Charlow, (1987), 'Awarding Custody: The Best Interests of the Child and Other Fictions', *Yale Law & Policy Review*, **5**, 267.
Cochran, (1983), 'Child Protective Divorce Laws: A Response to the Effects of Parental Separation on Children', *Family Law Quarterly*, **17**, 327.
Elster, (1987), 'Solomonic Judgments: Against the Best Interest of the Child', *University of Chicago Law Review*, **54**, 1.
Perry, (1990–91), 'Race and Child Placement: The Best Interests Test and the Cost of Discretion', *Journal of Family Law*, **29**, 51.
Salthe, (1990–91), 'Would Abolishing the Natural Parent Preference in Custody Disputes be in Everyone's Best Interest?', *Journal of Family Law*, **29**, 539.
Sorkow, (1991), 'Best Interests of the Child: By Whose Definition?', *Pepperdine Law Review*, **18**, 383.
Taub, (1983–84), 'Assessing the Impact of Goldstein, Freud, and Solnit's Proposals: An Introductory Overview', *New York University Review of Law and Social Change*, **12**, 485.
Van Deusen, (1991), 'The Best Interest of the Child and the Law', *Pepperdine Law Review*, **18**, 417.
Waters and Noyes, (1983–84), 'Psychological Parenting vs. Attachment Theory: The Child's Best Interests and the Risks in Doing the Right Things for the Wrong Reasons', *New York University Review of Law & Social Change*, **12**, 485.

Common Law Countries, Other than the United States

Davidson, G.P. (1980), 'Counsel for the child and psychological expert witness in custody and access cases' (New Zealand), *New Zealand Law Journal*, No 8, 177–8, May.

Day, David C. (1983), 'Counsel for Christopher: representing an infant's best interest in the Supreme Court of Canada', *Reports of Family Law*, **33** (1), 16–34, June.

Dickey, Anthony (1988), 'Right of a child's guardian to decide where the child shall live (Australia), *Australian Law Journal*, **62** (12), 1026–8, December.

Schlosser, M. Joyce (1984), 'Third party child-centered disputes: parental rights v. best interest of child' (Canada), *Alberta Law Review*, **22** (3), 394–416, Summer.

Waters, Brent (1985), 'Psychiatric considerations in preserving the best interests of the child' (Family Law) (Australia), *University of New South Wales Law Journal*, **8** (1), 137–51, January, Annual.

White, Kevin H. (1989), 'In the best interests of the child? Lingering doubts echo through the courts' (Australia), *Law Society Journal*, **27** (3), 66(7), April.

Adoption (Part IV)

United States

Ali, (1989), 'Homosexual Parenting: Child Custody and Adoption', *University of California Davis Law Review*, **22**, 1009.

Bartholet, (1991), 'Where Do Black Children Belong? The Politics of Race Matching in Adoption', *University of Pennsylvania Law Review*, **139**, 1163.

Carlson, (1988), 'Transnational Adoption of Children', *Tulsa Law Journal*, **23**, 317.

Carroll, (1985), 'Abrogation of Adoption by Adoptive Parents', *Family Law Quarterly*, **19**, 155.

Dickson, (1991), 'The Emerging Rights of Adoptive Parents: Substance or Specter?', *UCLA Law Review*, **38**, 917.

Gustafson, (1990), 'Regulating Adoption Intermediaries Ensuring that the Solutions are No Worse than the Problem', *Georgetown Journal of Legal Ethics*, **3**, 837.

Hollinger, (1989), 'Beyond the Best Interests of the Tribe: The Indian Child Welfare Act and the Adoption of Indian Children', *University of Detroit Law Review*, **66**, 451.

Howard, (1984), 'Transracial Adoption: Analysis of the Best Interests Standard', *Notre Dame Law Review*, **59**, 503.

Howe, (1983), 'Adoption Practice, Issues, and Laws 1958–1983', *Family Law Quarterly*, **17**, 173.

Jonet, (1990), 'Legal Measures to Eliminate Transnational Trading of Infants for Adoption: An Analysis of Anti-infant Trading Statutes in the United States', *Loyola of Los Angeles International and Comparative Law Journal*, **13**, 305.

McCormick, (1989–90), 'Transracial Adoption: A Critical View of the Courts' Present Standards', *Journal of Family Law*, **28**, 303.

Miller, (1987), 'The Inapplicability of Market Theory to Adoptions', *Boston University Law Review*, **67**, 99.

Samuels, (1985), 'Draft ABA Model State Adoption Act', *Family Law Quarterly*, **19**, 103.

Selun, (1985), 'The ABA Model State Adoption Act: Agency Perspective', *Family Law Quarterly*, **19**, 131.

Silverman, (1989), 'Regulating Independent Adoptions', *Columbia Journal of Law and Social Problems*, **22**, 323.

Strong-Amlung, (1990), 'Conflicts of Interest in Independent Adoptions: Pitfalls for the Unwary', *University of Cincinnati Law Review*, **59**, 169.

Watts, (1989), 'Voluntary Adoptions Under the Indian Child Welfare Act of 1978: Balancing the Interests of Children, Families, and Tribes', *Southern California Law Review*, **63**, 213.

Common Law Countries, Other than the United States

Johnston, Iain D. (1981), 'Adoption by parent and stepparent: infants and children' (New Zealand), *New Zealand Law Journal*, No 11, 349–54, August.

McGillivray, Ann (1985), 'Transracial adoption and the status Indian child' (Canada), *Canadian Journal of Family Law*, **4** (4), 437–67, November.

Prichard, J. Robert S. (1984), 'A market for babies?' (Symposium: Economic Perspectives on Issues in Family Law) (Canada), *University of Toronto Law Journal*, **34** (3), 341–57, Summer.

Sclick, Karen (1991), 'The case for baby buying' (Canada), *Canadian Lawyer*, **15** (1), 44(1), March.

Williams, Catherine (1982), 'Step-parent adoptions and the best interests of the child in Ontario', *University of Toronto Law Journal*, **32** (2), 214–30, Spring.

Wilson, J. (1982), 'Adoption and parental consent' (Canada), *Supreme Court Law Review*, **3**, 465–77, January, Annual.

Child Custody (Part V)

United States

Bargamian, (1989), 'Intentional Infliction of Emotional Distress in the Child Custody Context: Proposed Guidelines', *Wayne Law Review*, **36**, 125.

Baron, (1986), 'The Texas Statutory Right to Jury Trial in Child Custody Cases: Its Constitutionality Remains Unresolved', *Texas Tech Law Review*, **17**, 1399.

Baron, (1987), 'A Parent's Constitutional Right to Possession of His Children', *Probate Law Journal*, **7**, 251.

Baron, (1988), 'The Good, the Bad, and the Ugly: A Supreme Look at the PKPA', *Probate Law Journal*, **8**, 339.

Bartlett, (1986), 'Joint Custody, Feminism and the Dependency Dilemma', *Berkeley Women's Law Journal*, **2**, 9.

Benson, (1989), 'The Child Dependency Exemption and Divorced Parents: What is "Custody"?', *Capital University Law Review*, **18**, 57.

Beschle, (1989), 'God Bless the Child?: The Use of Religion as a Factor in Child Custody and Adoption Proceedings', *Fordham Law Review*, **58**, 383.

Chambers, (1984), 'Rethinking the Substantive Rules for Custody Disputes in Divorce', *Michigan Law Review*, **83**, 477.

Crippen, (1990), 'Stumbling Beyond Best Interests of the Child: Reexamining Child Custody Standard-setting in the Wake of Minnesota's Four Year Experiment with the Primary Caretaker Preference', *Minnesota Law Review*, **75**, 427.

Davis, (1985), 'Family Evaluation and the Development of Standards for Child Custody Determination', *Columbia Journal of Law and Social Problems*, **19**, 505.

Dooley, (1989–90), 'Immoral Because They're Bad, Bad Because They're Wrong: Sexual Orientation and Presumptions of Parental Unfitness in Custody Disputes', *California Western Law Review*, **26**, 395.

Elrod, (1987), 'Hearsay and Custody: The Twice Told Story', *Family Law Quarterly*, **21**, 169.

Erickson, (1984), 'The Feminist Dilemma Over Unwed Parents' Custody Rights: The Mother's Rights Must Take Priority', *Law & Inequality*, **2**, 447.

Fineman and Opie, (1987), 'The Uses of Social Science Data in Legal Policymaking: Custody Determinations at Divorce', *Wisconsin Law Review*, **1987**, 107.

Harmer, (1990), 'Limiting Incarceration for Civil Contempt in Child Custody Cases', *Brigham Young University Journal of Public Law*, **4**, 239.

Hyde, (1984), 'Child Custody in Divorce – Generally', *Juvenile and Family Court*, **35**, 1.

Ingulli, (1984–85), 'Grandparent Visitation Rights: Social Policies and Legal Rights', *West Virginia Law Review*, **87**, 295.

Kelly, (1983), 'Further Observations on Joint Custody', *University of California Davis Law Review*, **16**, 739.

Korzec, (1991), 'A Tale of Two Religions: A Contractual Approach to Religion as a Factor in Child Custody and Visitation Disputes', *New England Law Review*, **25**, 1121.

Levy, (1985), 'Custody Investigations in Divorce Cases', *American Bar Foundation Research Journal*, **1985**, 713.

Levy, (1985), 'Custody Investigation in Divorce Cases: The New York Law Revision Commission Proposal in Perspective', *Columbia Journal of Law and Social Problems*, **19**, 485.

Levy, (1987), 'Custody Investigations as Evidence in Divorce Cases', *Family Law Quarterly*, **21**, 149.

Lombard, (1984), 'Judicial Interviewing of Children in Custody Cases: An Empirical and Analytical Study', *University of California Davis Law Review*, **17**, 807.

Magid, and Oborn, (1986), 'Children of Divorce: A Need for Guidelines', *Family Law Quarterly*, **20**, 331.

Neely, (1984), 'The Primary Caretaker Parent Rule: Child Custody and the Dynamics of Greed', *Yale Law and Policy Review*, **3**, 168.

Note, (1989), 'Custody Denials to Parents in Same-Sex Relationships: An Equal Protection Analysis', *Harvard Law Review*, **102**, 617.

Radin, (1983), 'The Psychological Parent Concept in Contested Custody Cases', *Journal of Psychiatry and Law*, **11**, 503.

Raines, (1986), 'Joint Custody and the Right to Travel: Legal and Psychological Implications', *Journal of Family Law*, **24**, 625.

Reidy, Silver, Carlson, (1989), 'Child Custody Decisions: A Survey of Judges', *Family Law Quarterly*, **23**, 75.

Singer and Reynolds, (1988), 'A Dissent on Joint Custody', *Maryland Law Review*, **47**, 497.

Solnit, (1983–84), 'Psychological Dimensions in Child Placement Conflicts', *New York University Review of Law and Social Change*, **12**, 485.

Spitzer, (1985), 'Moving and Storage of Postdivorce Children: Relocation, the Constitution and the Courts, *Arizona State Law Journal*, **1985**, 1.

Stone, (1989), 'The Moral Dilemma: Child Custody When One Parent is Homosexual or Lesbian – An Empirical Study', *Suffolk University Law Review*, **23**, 711.

Strauss, (1986), 'The Myth of Colorblindness', *1986 Supreme Court Review*, 99.

Susoeff, (1985), 'Assessing Children's Best Interests When a Parent is Gay or Lesbian: Toward a Rational Custody Standard', *UCLA Law Review*, **32**, 835.

Vasterling, (1989), 'Child Custody Modification Under the Uniform Marriage And Divorce Act: A Statute to End the Tug-of-war?', *Washington University Law Quarterly*, **67**, 923.

Wexler, (1985), 'Rethinking the Modification of Child Custody Decrees', *Yale Law Journal*, **94**, 757.

Common Law Countries, Other than the United States

Abella, Rosalie Silberman (1983), 'Procedural aspects of arrangements for children upon divorce in Canada', *Canadian Bar Review*, **61** (2), 443–70, March.

Bates, Frank (1983), 'Joint custody in Australian law: a broad perspective', *Australian Law Journal*, **57** (6), 343–53, June.

Bates, Frank (1984), 'Welfare and reality in custody disputes: some new developments in Australian law', *International and Comparative Law Quarterly*, **33** (3), 701–11, July.

Boyd, Susan B. (1990), 'Potentialities and perils of the primary caregiver presumption', *Canadian Family Law Quarterly*, **7** (1), 1–30, November.

Broomfield, Anne Maree (1984), 'Discrimination in custody within the Family Court' (Australia), *Legal Service Bulletin*, **9** (3), 127–30, June.

Burns, Fiona (1983), 'The Commonwealth marriage power and third parties in custodial proceedings', *Sydney Law Review*, **10** (1), 193–204, January.

Chisholm, Richard and Catanzariti, Joe (1980), 'Preference for mothers in custody cases' (Australia), *University of New South Wales Law Journal*, **3** (3 and 4), 339–44, March.

Clancy, Patricia (1990), 'Custody – sharing the responsibility' (Australia) (The Contemporary Face of Family Law), *Law Institute Journal*, **64** (7), 607–8, July.

Colman, Gene C. (1989), 'Joint custody: recent developments' (Canada), *Canadian Family Law Quarterly*, **4** (1), 1–38, January.

Crawford, Elizabeth (1990), 'International child abduction', *Journal of the Law Society of Scotland*, **35** (7), 277–82, July.

Curtis, Lindsay (1989), 'The Hague Convention on the Civil Aspects of International Child Abduction: the Australian experience', *Commonwealth Law Bulletin*, **15** (2), 627–34, April.

Davidson, G.P. (1984), 'Custody and access – a brief overview of psychological research on custody and access in the separating family', *New Zealand Law Journal*, 61–3, February.

Delorey, Anne Marie (1989), 'Joint legal custody: a reversion to patriarchal power', *Canadian Journal of Women and the Law*, **3** (1), 33–44, January.

Devine, Susan and Murray, Elizabeth (1989), 'Some implications of equal time-sharing arrangements: new directions in parenting' (Canada), *Canadian Family Law Quarterly*, **4** (1), 47–55, February.

Dickey, Anthony (1990), 'Applicable law in custody cases involving residents of different states' (Australia), *Australian Law Journal*, **64** (7), 428, July.

Dickey, Anthony (1990), '"Rights of custody" under the Child Abduction Convention', *Australian Law Journal*, **64**, (1–2), 85–6, January.

Duff, David G. and Mykitiuk, Roxanne (1989), 'Parental separation and the child custody decision: toward a reconception' (Canada), *University of Toronto Faculty of Law Review*, **47**, 874–938, Autumn.

Ehrcke, Ann (1987), 'Limiting judicial discretion in custody proceedings on divorce' (Canada), *Canadian Journal of Family Law*, **6** (2), 211–46, Fall.

Elterman, Michael F. and Ehrenberg, Marion F. (1991), 'Sexual abuse allegations in child custody disputes', *International Journal of Law and Psychiatry*, **14** (3), 269–86, June.

Goodman, Ellen (1980), '"Fault" notions in custody adjudication under Australian "no fault" matrimonial law', *Canadian Journal of Family Law*, **3** (1), 27–41, January.

Goodman, Ellen (1981), 'The relevance of religion in custody adjudication under the Family Law Act' (Australia), *Monash University Law Review*, **7** (3–4), 217–24, June.

Irving, Howard H. and Benjamin, Michael (1986), 'Shared parenting in Canada: questions, answers and implications', *Canadian Family Law Quarterly*, **1** (1), 79–103, August.

Johnston, Iain D. (1982), 'Shared custody after parental separation' (New Zealand), *New Zealand Law Journal*, 8–12, January.

Lehmann, Geoffrey (1984), 'Legal craftsmanship in custody cases or a joint custody presumption?' (Australia), *Melbourne University Law Review*, **14** (3), 442–67, June.

Lyon, Christina M. (1989), 'The redefinition of parental rights – recent English developments relating to joint custody, custodianship and adoption in England' (Children and the Law: Anglo-Australian Developments), *Journal of Social Welfare Law*, No 3, 138–47, May.

Mackinnon, V.J. and Groves, J.R. (1988), 'Some proposals to reform custody litigation' (Canada), *Canadian Family Law Quarterly*, **3** (3), 287–314, October.

Marshall, Audrey, Grant, Joyce and Nasser, Jill (1980), 'Children's wishes in custody and access disputes' (Australia), *Law Society Journal*, **18** (1), 49–52, February.

McInnes, J.C. (1988), 'Family law – divorce; on the warpath for custody' (Scotland), *Journal of the Law Society of Scotland*, **33** (8), 281–3, August.

Nicholls, Lee (1984), 'Ex-nuptial custody disputes' (New South Wales), *Law Society Journal*, **22** (7), 483(1), August.

Pask, E. Diane (1989), 'The effect on maintenance of custody sharing' (Canada), *Canadian Journal of Women and the Law*, **3** (1), 155–81, January.

Payne, Julien D. and Edwards, Brenda (1989), 'Co-operative parenting after divorce: a Canadian perspective', *Advocates' Quarterly*, **11** (1), 1–30, August.

Quansah, E.K. (1991), 'Custody of children: customary principles in Ghana and Nigeria', *Commonwealth Law Bulletin*, **17** (1), 347–55, January.

Ryan, Judith P. (1980), 'The overlapping custody jurisdiction: Co-existence or chaos' (Canada), *Canadian Journal of Family Law*, **3** (2–3), 95–139, June.

Saunders, Elisabeth B. and Melville, Catherine (1987), 'Custodial father, custodial mothers and their former spouses in protracted custody disputes: clinical opinions and data' (Canada), *Journal of Psychiatry & Law*, **15** (4), 555–70, Winter.

Wilson, Bertha (1985), 'Children: the casualties of a failed marriage' (address delivered to the Vancouver Institute at the University of British Columbia, September 1984), *University of British Columbia Law Review*, **19** (2), 245–70, Spring.

Zemans, Frederick H. (1983), 'The issue of cultural diversity in custody disputes' (Canada), *Reports of Family Law*, **32** (1), 50–75, February.

The Child Support Obligation (Part VI)

United States

Benson, (1990–91), 'Can a Case Be Made for the Use of the Uniform Child Custody Jurisdiction Act in Child Support Determinations?', *Gonzaga Law Review*, **26**, 125.

Brackney, (1988), 'Battling Inconsistency and Inadequacy: Child Support Guidelines in the States', *Harvard Women's Law Journal*, **11**, 197.

Bruch, (1985), 'The Economic Consequences', *Juvenile and Family Courts Journal*, **36**, Fall, 5.

Burt, (1985), 'Coercive Freedom: A Response to Professor Chambers', *University of Michigan Journal of Law Reform*, **18**, 829.

Czapanskiy, (1989), 'Child Support and Visitation: Rethinking the Connections', *Rutgers Law Journal*, **20**, 619.

Garland, (1991), 'Second Children Second Best? Equal Protection for Successive Families Under State Child Support Guidelines', *Hastings Constitutional Law Quarterly*, **18**, 881.

Goldfarb, (1987), 'Child Support Guidelines: A Model for Fair Allocation of Child Care, Medical, and Educational Expenses', *Family Law Quarterly*, **21**, 325.

Horan, (1988), 'Post-Minority Support for College Education – A Legally Enforceable Obligation in Divorce Proceedings?', *New Mexico Law Review*, **18**, 153.

Krause, (1983), 'Reflections on Child Support', *University of Illinois Law Review*, **1983**, 99; also *Family Law Quarterly*, **17**, 109.

Krause, (1990), 'Child Support Reassessed: Limits of Private Responsibility and the Public Interest', *Family Law Quarterly*, **24**, 1; also *University of Illinois Law Review*, **1989**, 367.

Mnookin, (1981), 'Review: Using Jail for Child Support Enforcement', *University of Chicago Law Review*, **48**, 338.

O'Donnell, (1990–91), 'Title I of the Family Support Act of 1988 – The Quest for Effective National Child Support Enforcement Continues', *Journal of Family Law*, **29**, 149.

Pearson and Thoennes, (1988), 'Supporting Children After Divorce: The Influence of Custody on Support Levels and Payments, *Family Law Quarterly*, **22**, 319.

Schuele, (1989), 'Origins and Development of the Law of Parental Child Support', *Journal of Family Law*, **27**, 807.

Smithburn, (1989–90), 'Removing Nonconforming Child Support Payments from the Shadow of the Rule Against Retroactive Modification: A Proposal for Judicial Discretion', *Journal of Family Law*, **28**, 43.

Thurman, (1980), 'Contempt for Nonsupport in Florida – Civil or Criminal Proceeding', *Stetson Law Review*, **9**, 333.

Common Law Countries, Other than the United States

Burtch, Brian E., Pitcher-LaPrairie, Carol and Wachtel, Andy (1980), 'Issues in the determination and enforcement of child support orders', *Canadian Journal of Family Law*, **3** (1), 5–26, January.

Chesterman, Michael and Waters, Peter (1985), 'Contempt and the disobeying spouse' (Australia), *University of New South Wales Law Journal*, **8** (1), 106–36, January, Annual.

Diamond, Robyn Moglove (1989), 'Enforcement of custody and access orders' (Canada), *Canadian Family Law Quarterly*, **4** (3), 303–34, October.

Eades, John (1989), 'Arrears of child maintenance: is the 12 month rule now dead?' (New South Wales), *Law Society Journal*, **27** (3), 40(2), April.

Edwards, Meredith (1986), 'Child support: assessment, collection & enforcement issues & possible directions for reform' (Australia), *Windsor Yearbook of Access to Justice*, **6**, 93–140, January, Annual.

Eekelaar, John (1991), 'A child support scheme for the United Kingdom; an analysis of the White Paper' (Great Britain), *Family Law*, **21**, 15–21, January.

Farquhar, Keith B. (1982), 'The variation, enforcement and interpretation of maintenance orders in Canada – some new aspects of an old dilemma', *Canadian Bar Review*, **60** (4), 585–618, December.

Farquhar, Keith B. (1986), 'Variation and enforcement of maintenance orders: Ruttan revisited' (Canada), *Canadian Bar Review*, **64** (3), 534–49, September.

Fodden, Simon R. (1980), 'Poor relations: The effect of second families on child support' (Canada), *Canadian Journal of Family Law*, **3** (2–3), 207–18, June.

Fogarty, John (1988), 'Property and child support reforms' (Family Law in Australia, part A), *Queensland Law Society Journal*, **18** (3), 161–70, April.

Goodman, Wolfe D. and Eng, Susan (1981), 'Education trusts and other provisions for education expenses' (Canada), *Estates and Trusts Quarterly*, **5** (3), 246–76, February.

Heron, Alex (1987), 'Child support; making fathers pay?' (Australia), *Legal Service Bulletin*, **12** (1), 17–20, February.

Kay, Joseph (1990), 'The child support scheme' (Australia) (The Contemporary Face of Family Law), *Law Institute Journal*, **64** (7), 604–6, July.

Mossip, Nancy M. (1989), 'Interim spousal support – to pay or not to pay?' (Ontario), *Canadian Family Law Quarterly*, **5** (1989), 157–77, January, Annual.

Sachs, Elisabeth (1989), 'Support and custody enforcement programme: the experience of two years' (Canada), *Advocates' Quarterly*, **11** (1), 31–42, November.

Samuels, Alec (1981), 'Refusal or failure to observe access order – the remedy for the aggrieved party' (England), *Family Law*, **11** (5), 156–8, September.

Part I
Children's Rights

[1]

A Bill of Rights for Children*

HENRY H. FOSTER, JR.**
DORIS JONAS FREED***

Introduction

Children are *persons* and the law should recognize that fact, although it will take some doing. The status of minority is the last legal relic of feudalism and the arguments for and against perpetuation of that status have a familiar ring. In good measure they are the same arguments that were advanced over the issues of slavery and the emancipation of married women.

The liberation movements of the past hundred or more years have succeeded in establishing the principle, earlier proclaimed in our Declaration of Independence, that there is a moral right to be regarded as a human being and not to be treated as a thing. Gradually this moral principle is being implemented into law. The opposing argument for retention of the status quo, or gradualism in emancipation, may be summed up in the word "paternalism." Today paternalism is out. It has been thoroughly discredited. It no longer is true that "children are to be seen but not heard," even though sometimes it also is true that "no one will lissen."[1]

It is curious that parents, judges, police, and teachers, in their

*This article appeared in the NEW YORK LAW JOURNAL, July 28, August 25 and September 22, 1972.

**Professor of Law, New York University, School of Law.

***Member of the Maryland and New York Bars. Professor Foster and Dr. Freed are co-authors of FOSTER AND FREED, LAW AND THE FAMILY, (Vol. I, 1972, and Vol. II, 1967, Lawyers Cooperative Publishing Co., New York) and of PLOSCOWE, FOSTER AND FREED, CASES AND MATERIALS ON FAMILY LAW, (Rev. ed. 1972, Little, Brown & Co.).

1. *See* FORER, NO ONE WILL LISSEN (1971), for a strong and bitter criticism of the failure of police and juvenile authorities to listen to children.

relations with children, often behave in authoritarian fashion, no matter how respectful they may be in coping with adults. Lord Acton's famous maxim that power corrupts and absolute power corrupts absolutely may have some relevance to this phenomenon. Children are scapegoats for adult frustrations. But the worst of it is hypocrisy—a vice readily discernible by our youth. They are specialists at detecting it. Hypocrisy, we say, because invariably adults dispense denials and punishments in terms of its-for-your-own-good, no matter what the circumstances and in many cases where it's really a case of "might is right."[2]

Authority carries with it added responsibility and in the case of adults dealing with minors there are obligations of fairness and empathy. The relative helplessness and lack of autonomy of children require self-restraint and legal checks on parental and other authority.[3] Moreover, if children are persons, their points of view should be considered, adult decisions should be reasoned, and their true best interests should always be reckoned with in terms of reality rather than fantasy. In addition to love, children are entitled to respect.

The ideal for adult behavior does not carry with it the inference that as persons children are incapable of wrong conduct or should be immune from accountability for their actions.[4] On the contrary, the more self-determination and responsibility accorded to minors, the greater the accountability. To stipulate a "Bill of Rights for Children" does not rid them of moral and legal obligations but on the contrary is intended to enhance their sense of responsibility.

---

2. *See, for example,* Roberts v. State, 82 Neb. 651, 118 N.W. 674 (1908), where the court affirmed a commitment to an industrial school for an indeterminate sentence (possibly until age 21) because a 16-year-old boy swore at a church meeting. The penalty for blasphemy for an adult was a fine of 25 cents to a dollar. The court said: "Our industrial school is not a place of punishment nor is it in any sense a prison, no more than our public schools. It is a place of education, reformation, refinement, and culture. It is a beneficent provision for the uplift of boys who by reason of their surroundings and condition are deprived of an educational and moral training which are so essential to their well-being and good citizenship. . . . The action of the court . . . is to avoid a 'conviction' and change the prospective punishment into a blessing."

3. *Compare* the common law duty of a captain to his crew or a gaoler to prisoners.

4. The point is, children should be treated fairly and when the occasion calls for it firmly and in a consistent fashion. We are not here advocating that Dennis the Menace should get off "tot free."

Of course, there are practical difficulties in trying to devise a "Bill of Rights for Children." Technically, terms such as "children," "minors," and "infants" apply to all those under 21-years-old. The specific age set is purely arbitrary, a carry over from feudal times,[5] and perhaps anachronistic. Reduction in voting age, the age for emancipation, and the varying ages set for divers functions, indicate the arbitrary character of such classification. There is a consensus, however, that the age line must be drawn some place, and legislatures and courts are not unreasonable in taking an average age as regards a particular function as long as the age set is not completely out of kilter with custom and mores. With regard to the 10 principles that follow, obviously some pertain with greater force and some with lesser force depending upon the maturation factor. Although marriage is "a basic civil right of man" we would not argue that a child of three has a constitutional right to marry. The child of three, however, should not be treated as an object or thing, and in a custody proceeding between his parents, it is our contention that he should receive legal protection and representation.

Sweeping declarations aside, there is a paucity of legal authority for the general proposition that children (as well as corporations) are persons under the law.[6] The most significant court decision that is relevant to our philosophical base is *In re Gault.*[7] Since that landmark decision, in legal theory, there are checks upon arbitrary exercises of either parental or public authority and the welfare of children no longer should be determined by gratuitous assumptions. The spirit of *Gault* is that we must have regard for reality—for pragmatic consequences—and pious hopes or good intentions are not good enough. The child's point of view, what's fair to him, not merely the *mens rea* of the one who wields the rod, must be taken into account. Otherwise

5. *See* James, *The Age of Majority,* 4 AMER. J. LEG. HIST. 22 (1960).

6. The most relevant Supreme Court decisions include: Kent v. United States, 383 U.S. 541 (1966); *In re* Winship, 397 U.S. 358 (1970); Levy v. Louisiana, 391 U.S. 68 (1968); Prince v. Massachusetts, 321 U.S. 158 (1944); Meyer v. Nebraska, 262 U.S. 390 (1923); and Pierce v. Society of Sisters, 268 U.S. 510 (1925).

7. 387 U.S. 1 1967. *Compare,* McKeiver v. Pennsylvania, 403 U.S. 528 (1971) (no right to jury trial in juvenile court).

the whole system is a fraud and delusion. *Parens patriae* power is not a blank check.[8]

It took *Gault* to dispel hypocrisy about juvenile justice. The decision forces us to look at what is being done. In addition to *Gault* and its implications there is *Loving v. Virginia*.[9] If the marital relationship is constitutionally protected from unreasonable state regulation, the parent-child relationship may enjoy a similar, albeit more limited, advantage.

Professor Sanford N. Katz has pointed out, most effectively, that the greatest intrusion of government into family life has been with reference to the parent-child relationship which most often occurs in the case of the poor.[10] Increasingly, a challenge will be made where government intervenes, and courts will be forced to look at the consequences of state intervention or maintenance of the family's status quo and to realistically evaluate goals, policies, and programs.[11] Due to the confusion that exists wherever there is an assertion of *parens patriae* power or a concern over the best interests of the child, it may be helpful to express the rights and expectations of minors in our contemporary society. The generalizations that are made in the following "Bill of Rights for Children" will be particularlized seriatim in an attempt to give the basic framework for analysis, rather than a detailed blueprint for decision. The premise behind the following principles is that children are people; they are entitled to assert individual interests in their own right, to have a fair consideration given to their claims, and to have their best interests judged in terms of pragmatic consequences.

---

8. *See* ALLEN, THE BORDERLAND OF CRIMINAL JUSTICE (1964), and REPORT BY THE PRESIDENT'S COMMISSION ON LAW ENFORCEMENT AND ADMINISTRATION OF JUSTICE, TASK FORCE ON JUVENILE JUSTICE, JUVENILE DELINQUENCY AND YOUTH CRIME (1967), for a detailed analysis of abuses of the *parens patriae* power and how the juvenile system operates when there is a lack of resources.

9. 388 U.S. 1 (1967). For a discussion of limitations upon state regulation of marriage, *see* Foster, *Marriage: A "Basic Civil Right of Man,"* 37 FORDHAM L. REV. 51 (1968).

10. S. KATZ, WHEN PARENTS FAIL (1971).

11. *See* Rubin, *Children as Victims of Institutionalization*, 60 CHILD WELFARE 6 (1972), and for a documented study, *see* THE COMMITTEE ON MENTAL HEALTH SERVICES INSIDE AND OUTSIDE THE FAMILY COURT IN THE CITY OF NEW YORK, JUVENILE JUSTICE CONFOUNDED: PRETENSIONS AND REALITIES OF TREATMENT SERVICES (1972).

A Bill of Rights for Children

A child has a moral right and should have a legal right:

1. To receive parental love and affection, discipline and guidance, and to grow to maturity in a home environment which enables him to develop into a mature and responsible adult;

2. To be supported, maintained, and educated to the best of parental ability, in return for which he has the moral duty to honor his father and mother;

3. To be regarded as a *person,* within the family, at school, and before the law;

4. To receive fair treatment from all in authority;

5. To be heard and listened to;

6. To earn and keep his own earnings;

7. To seek and obtain medical care and treatment and counseling;

8. To emancipation from the parent-child relationship when that relationship has broken down and the child has left home due to abuse, neglect, serious family conflict, or other sufficient cause, and his best interests would be served by the termination of parental authority;

9. To be free of legal disabilities or incapacities save where such are convincingly shown to be necessary and protective of the actual best interests of the child; and

10. To receive special care, consideration, and protection in the administration of law or justice so that his best interests always are a paramount factor.

Principle One

The need of a child for parental love and affection is so thoroughly documented by clinical and common experience and the literature of behavioral science that it may be accepted as an established fact.[12] It is also agreed, but not so evident, that

12. For a relatively recent discussion, *see* Watson, *The Children of Armageddon: Problems of Custody Following Divorce,* 21 SYRACUSE L. REV. 55 (1969). *See also,* Note, *Alternatives to "Parental Right" in Child Custody Disputes Involving Third Parties,* 73 YALE L.J. 151 (1963). *See also,* the United Nations Declaration of Rights of Children, adopted unanimously on November 20, 1959. Principle 6 provides: "The child, for the full and harmonious development of his personality, needs love and

children need discipline and guidance. Difficulty arises when we try to apply such generalizations. Whose standards are applicable?

Until quite recently, the law presumed that children in the home received love and affection and that cases of child abuse or emotional deprivation were rare. It is now known that the presumption is a dangerous one to make and that many parents are brutal, indifferent, or rejecting. The "battered child" syndrome has received extensive publicity and most if not all states have enacted legislation to cope with the phenomenon.[13] The majority of such statutes, however, relate to the reporting of physical abuse and except in the most flagrant cases the law shies away from mere psychological abuse of children, even though the medical facts are clear.[14] Unless parental cruelty is attested to by physical damage, courts hold back from a determination of neglect.

There are several reasons for judicial reluctance to recognize and act on emotional deprivation. Among them is a common suspicion of psychiatric and psychological testimony, its intangible quality, personal guilt, and the conclusive character of a termination of parental rights. More important, there is the problem of reasonable alternatives and the lack of assurance that placement out of the home would be any better for the unhappy child.[15] Unless physical injury or death is threatened, it may be practical to leave the child where he is and to induce the family into counseling.

In the case of the parent's right to give and the child's right to receive discipline and guidance, we again have the problems of standards. One danger is that courts, or case workers, will inflexibly apply middle class mores without regard to the cir-

---

understanding. He shall, whenever possible, grow up in the care and under the responsibility of his parents, and, in any case, in an atmosphere of affection and of moral and material security . . ."

13. *See* Foster and Freed, *The Battered Child*, 3 TRIAL 33 (1967), and Article 10 of the NEW YORK FAMILY COURT ACT.

14. *See*, however, Application of Mittenthal, 37 Misc. 2d 502, 235 N.Y.S.2d 729 (Fam. Ct. 1962).

15. For critiques on foster care, *see* Lewis, *Foster-Family Care: Has it Fulfilled Its Promise?*, THE ANNALS OF THE AMER. ACAD. OF POL. AND SOC. SCI., September 1964, and MASS AND ENGLER, CHILDREN IN NEED OF PARENTS (1959).

cumstances of the particular family.[16] Obviously, methods of discipline differ, and parents tend to repeat those they were subjected to in their youth. Beyond that, however, the more recent cases have diminished the parental privilege of corporal punishment and pass upon its necessity as well as excessiveness.[17] As is true of the obsolete privilege of wife chastisement, modern thinking does not condone the philosophy expressed in "spare the rod, spoil the child." At the same time, both courts and behavioral scientists agree that firm and consistent discipline is essential for maturation and socialization.[18] Although the lack of appropriate moral guidance may constitute one form of child neglect,[19] it is interesting to note that only an egregiously unfit mother will be deprived of custody and there is no practical way to impose legal guidelines for guidance. Again referral for counseling may be the sensible alternative.

The application of this first principle should be particularly beneficial in cases where placement of a child is at issue in a custody or adoption proceeding. By "parental love" is meant the affectionate relationship between those who stand in the positions of parent and child. This does not necessarily mean the biological parents and child, but may mean those who have such a psychological relationship.[20] It is the on-growing nurturing care and attention, not biological birth, which gives rise to real mother love, as distinguished from fantasy. The development of such a bond of attachment between de facto parents and child should always be a crucial factor in resolving difficult cases as to custody or adoption. As New York public policy now provides, despite lamentable decisions to the contrary, foster parents should have preference or priority if they choose to petition for adoption.[21] And a natural mother should not be

16. For example, *see In re* Rinker, 117 A.2d 780 (Pa. Super. 1955).

17. *See* PROSSER, LAW OF TORTS, 140 (3d ed.), and State v. Straight, 347 P.2d 482 (Mont. 1959).

18. An extensive sampling of various theories as to the causes of juvenile delinquency may be found in GLUECK, THE PROBLEM OF DELINQUENCY (1959).

19. *See* Family Court Act § 312.

20. *See In re* Adoption of Child by P, 114 N.J. Super. 584, 277 A.2d 566 (1971), and Revocation of Appointment of a Guardian of a Minor Surrendered for Adoption, 271 N.E.2d 621 (Mass. 1971).

21. *See* Laws 1969, ch. 1080, amending Social Services Law § 383, which modified

permitted to belatedly revoke her formal surrender for adoption once the child is in a loving home and bonds of attachment have developed.

It is patent nonsense *to presume* that the best interests of a child will be served by being taken out of an adoptive home and returned to a natural mother.[22] On the contrary, assuming a satisfactory mutual adjustment, it is adverse to the child's best psychological, developmental, and physical interests to precipitously remove him from the security and warmth he has known and to deprive him of his psychological parents. In such cases, legal fictions should not be permitted to obscure the reality that factors other than the child's welfare are regarded as decisive. The 1972 session of the legislature recognized this when it placed strict limitations upon a natural mother's alleged privilege to revoke a surrender for adoption, thus overruling some of the reasoning in the "Baby Lenore" case.[23]

Principle Two

The child's right to support, maintenance, and education usually has been expressed in terms of the parental duty to provide the same. Blackstone enumerated three duties owed by parents to a child, namely to provide maintenance, protection, and education.[24] Chancellor Kent referred only to the duty to maintain

the policy expressed in Matter of Jewish Child Care Association, 5 N.Y.S.2d 222, 156 N.E.2d 700 (1959), which was criticized by Katz, *Foster Parents Versus Agencies*, 65 MICH. L. REV. 145 (1966), and by Foster and Freed, *Children and the Law*, 2 FAM. L.Q. 40, 54–56 (1968). *See Also* Katz, when parents fail 96–100 (1971).

22. *See* Foster, *Revocation of Consent to Adoption: A Covenant Running With the Child?* 166 N.Y.L.J. No. 26, Aug. 6, 1971, p. 1, cols. 4–5, p. 4 cols. 1–3, commenting upon Scarpetta v. Spence-Chapin Adoption Service, 28 N.Y.S.2d 185, 321 N.Y.S.2d 65, 269 N.E.2d 787 (1971), the so-called "Baby Lenore" case where the Florida courts ignored the New York decision and awarded the baby to the would-be adoptive parents because it would best serve the baby's welfare.

23. Laws 1972, ch. 639, amending Social Services Law §§ 383, 384 and DOM. REL. LAW § 115-b, so that the natural mother will have no preference; custody will be awarded "solely on the basis of the best interests of the child;" and revocation of a surrender for adoption (absent fraud, duress, or coercion) may not occur after placement of the child in the adoptive home for 30 days or more. It should be noted that it is not here advocated that the "best interests" test should apply to deprive a parent of a child unless there has been a formal surrender, an abandonment, or sufficient cause for termination of parental rights.

24. BLACKSTONE'S COMMENTARIES ON THE LAW 194 (Gravit Ed. 1941). Maintenance is the obligation to provide for offspring; protection is not defined except as a natural duty; education is said to be of great importance, but it is noted that there was no legal sanction. *See* Speca and Wehrman, *Protecting the Rights of Children in Divorce Cases in Missouri*, 38 U.M.K.C. L. REV. 1 (1969).

and the duty to educate.[25] The tragedy, however, is that these parental duties, or rights of children, were not backed up by effective legal sanctions. In large measure, it was up to ecclesiastical courts or the clergy to persuade a devout believer, under pain of penance, to do his duty. The parish might recoup for handouts doled to an abandoned family, and the common law provided only an uncertain action by creditors to recover the price of necessaries given to the family.[26] Today, however, most if not all states have alternative remedies to enforce the obligation of child support, ranging from criminal, quasi criminal, to civil actions.[27] Quite recently, illegitimate children have achieved some, if not most of such rights as are accorded to legitimate children.[28]

The general principle here involved is not disputed. However, it should be noted that as worded the right exists against both parents and each parent has a duty to support, maintain, and educate the children of the family. What is meant is that such parental duty should be joint and several, or to put it differently, the measure of the mutual duty is their joint ability, and each parent has the duty to contribute thereto to the extent of his or her respective ability.[29] If the mother has greater resources or income, under this principle, she could be called upon to contribute more than the father to the children's support, maintenance, and education. This merely treats parents equally and without discrimination.

It is only fair that something in return be given for the sometimes onerous duty of child support. We have phrased that reciprocal duty in the traditional terms of "honor thy father and thy mother." We have labeled it a "moral duty" because an attempt at specific enforcement or other legal remedy might be doomed to failure. However, indirect recognition may be given, as in the case where the father was excused from supporting his

25. KENT, COMMENTARIES ON AMERICAN LAW 260–267 (Browne's Ed. 1894).

26. *See* Foster, *Dependent Children and the Law*, 18 U. PITT. L. REV. 579 (1957).

27. *Id.*

28. *See* Levy v. Louisiana, 391 U.S. 68 (1968), and Glona v. American Guarantee & Liability Ins. Co., 391 U.S. 73 (1968), but compare Labine v. Vincent, 401 U.S. 532 (1971). *See also*, KRAUSE, ILLEGITIMACY: LAW AND SOCIAL POLICY (1971).

29. *Compare* Family Court Act §§ 413–14, which imposes a child support duty on the mother where the father is dead, incapable of support, or cannot be found within the state.

daughter at a university unless she complied with his reasonable conditions as to life style.[30] Rebellious children should not have it both ways, especially where they are rebels without cause. Obviously, this point also involves the duty to give and the right to receive parental guidance. Again, courts must be wary, otherwise they will be called upon to write codes of behavior for internecine conflicts.[31] As a moral duty or exhortation, we are tempted to add that children should be more tolerant of their elders, but that runs against the new conventional wisdom that "no one over 30 is to be trusted" and presumably would fall on deaf ears. We also considered a reciprocal duty on children to comply with the fair and reasonable demands of parental and other lawful authority, but we are at a loss at how to back it up with an effective sanction and we therefore conclude that it might detract from an enumeration of the rights of children.

Principle Three

The child's right to be regarded as a *person* is basic to the other rights which follow. If this fundamental concept were accepted, appreciated, and implemented, the other principles would fall neatly into place. A great deal of the difficulty with minors derives from the refusal to accept them as individuals, with their own needs, interests, and desires. It does not take a good memory to recall the communication and attitudinal problems youth encounter when dealing with adults. Despite any and all evidence to the contrary, the inferiority of youth is assumed by those who "speak with the voice of experience." An authoritarian adult not only swings his weight around, he makes explicit the inferior status of minority.

Authoritarian behavior by adults is not limited to the home.

---

30. *See* Roe v. Doe, 324 N.Y.S.2d 71, 272 N.E.2d 567 (1971). ". . . while the duty to support is a continuing one, the child's right to support and the parent's right to custody and services are reciprocal: the father in return for maintenance and support may establish and impose reasonable regulations for his child."

31. *Compare* the reluctance of courts to enforce a husband's duty to support while the wife is still in the home for fear of having to take over the writing of the family budget. McGuire v. McGuire, 157 Neb. 226, 59 N.W.2d 336 (1953), is a leading case in point.

Some but not all teachers and school administrators are martinets and some judges have been known to have a "Jehovah's complex." And then there are case workers and bureaucrats. Such personalities, for a variety of reasons, treat minors as inferiors, show them little or no respect, and wield authority with heavy hands. Children may become scapegoats for frustrated adults who relieve their own sense of inferiority by treating children as things.

The Judeo-Christian belief in the dignity of man does not have a cut-off point based on age. Neither does a belief in the sacredness of man and the integrity of the individual. To fail to treat a minor as a person, at home, in school, or before the law, is to deny his humanity. Thoughtful adults presumably will accept this general principle.

Principle Four

A juvenile's right to receive fair treatment is what *Gault* was all about.[32] The facts of that case were outrageous and it is to our discredit that a trial judge and a state appellate court permitted such a decision to be made and to stand until reversed by the Supreme Court. The distasteful thing about *Gault* however, is not that the minor was deprived of numerous constitutional rights, but that he was treated so unfairly while being subjected to a process which supposedly was geared to his own welfare. The Arizona courts never looked at the matter of essential fairness from the standpoint of young Gault.

In many places, juvenile court procedures have been so unfair that the whole system has come under attack.[33] More moderate critics, however, have not given up on the hope for reform.[34] It is a false hope unless the essentials of fairness are

32. *In re* Gault, 387 U.S. 1 (1967). A 15-year-old boy was picked up and taken to the police station while his parents were at work. No notice or specification of charges were given to young Gault or his parents. He was not represented by counsel until after the adjudication. No record of the hearing was made; there was no confrontation of the witness against him; and hearsay statements were accepted. He got an indeterminate sentence (possibly until age 21) for allegedly having made a "lewd phone call," a misdemeanor for which an adult (who received due process of law) might be fined from five to fifty dollars or serve up to two months in jail.

33. *See* Forer, No One Will Lissen (1971); and Rubin, *Children as Victims for Institutionalization*, 60 Child Welfare 6 (1972), for recent comments.

34. *See* Midonick, Children, Parents and the Courts (1972).

observed throughout the process and juveniles are treated as people. For example, it is unfair to the juvenile, from his point of view, if as in the Nebraska case previously referred to,[35] or as in *Gault,* a more severe sentence is visited upon a juvenile than would be imposed upon an adult for the same offense. It also is unfair to be denied the privilege against self-incrimination, the right to notice, right to counsel, the right to confrontation, and other matters of essential fairness on the theory that he is receiving help rather than punishment.

But the right to fair treatment is not limited to the forensic area. Kangaroo courts may be set up at home or school. In part, arbitrary adults may fail to appreciate that fair procedure and rules are essential for a just determination of controversies and that the lawyer's "red tape" is not hypertechnicality but a reasoned approach to fact finding when facts are disputed.[36] Guilt by association, a presumption of guilt, and the denial of an opportunity to be heard, or to confront and to refute, all too often are the indicia of lay procedure. And such laxity is not to be excused because the penalty is not deemed to be severe. Any judgment or penalty imposed upon a human being is unjust and is likely to be resented if it was arrived at unfairly. Speaking pragmatically, it is self-defeating.

Principle Five

One of the most frequent complaints children make with regard to adult behavior is that grown ups won't listen to them. Admittedly, it takes patience to be a good listener, and it is difficult to cultivate the art, especially if one regards the speaker as an intellectual inferior or as immature. To the extent that the generation gap is a communications problem, adult inability to listen is a major source of difficulty.

The tendency of youth and adults to be on different wave lengths extends beyond intra-family communication. It is conspicuous in our schools and churches, and in most areas where there is communication between different age groups. Unfortu-

35. *See* Roberts v. State, *supra* note 2.

36. *See* Foster, *Social Work, the Law, and Social Action,* in SOCIAL CASEWORK, July 1964, pp. 383, 386.

nately, stereotypes of the young and the old block free exchange of ideas and each side may seek to confirm preconceptions. Even where they are heard, youth may not be listened to. As persons, our young people deserve a better audience than they ordinarily are given and they are entitled to reasoned argument rather than ultimatums. Understanding is promoted if not achieved when reasons are given for decisions, as is attested by our judicial tradition of written opinions.

The right to be heard includes the right to have standing in legal proceedings to assert one's claims of interest. It is anomalous that under the procedure in most states children are unrepresented when parents seek divorce.[37] The major disputed issue may be their custody and visitation rights, and in a very real sense, they may be the principal parties in interest since the ultimate issue, according to theory, is their welfare and best interests. Unless specific statutes or rules prohibit, there is ample authority or inherent power to appoint counsel or to grant leave to intervene so that the children of divorce may have their day in court.[38]

In Wisconsin, pursuant to statute and court decision,[39] a guardian *ad litem* may be appointed to represent minor children when parents seek a divorce. The guardian may introduce evidence, have investigations made, and cross-examine witnesses with reference to the custodial issue. Moreover, a so-called "Bill of Rights of Children in Divorce Actions" is handed to parents before trial in order to remind them of their parental obligations. States which recently have reformed divorce law and procedure, such as California, Iowa, Oregon, and New York,[40] have enacted various devices in an effort to safeguard the interests of children. In addition, several states require welfare or probation department investigations when custody is

37. *See* Speca and Wehrman, *supra* note 24.

38. *Id.*

39. *See* WIS. STAT., ch. 245.001(2), and ch. 247.15(1) (Supp. 1971–72); Kritzik v. Kritzik, 21 Wis. 2d 442, 124 N.W.2d 581 (1963); and Wendland v. Wendland, 29 Wis. 2d 145, 138 N.W.2d 185 (1965). *See also*, Hansen, *The Role and Rights of Children in Divorce Actions*, 6 J. FAM. LAW 1 (1966).

40. *See* Dom. Rel. Law § 215-c which authorizes the appointment of a guardian to represent the interests of children in divorce cases. Such authority has been but rarely exercised.

disputed[41] and still others require that the district attorney or some other public official be notified when the parties seeking divorce have children under a certain age.[42] In Michigan, for example, the prosecuting attorney is directed by statute to appear at the hearing and to introduce evidence opposing the divorce if the interests of children and the public good so require.[43] As previously stated, independent of statute, several states have held that a divorce court has inherent power to appoint counsel to represent the welfare of children when it is at issue.[44]

This matter of independent representation by counsel, so that children have their own lawyer when their disposition or welfare is at stake, is the most significant and practical reform that can be made in the area of children and the law. Given our predilection for the adversary format and the small likelihood that it will be abandoned in the foreseeable future, no matter how procrustean it may be in child welfare cases, it is clear that reform should be directed at making the process functional, and to permit all interested parties—including children—to have independent counsel. Proponents of the system can hardly object to measures aimed at making it work.

Again, children have individual interests apart from and sometimes in conflict with parental interests or those of society. Their interests are entitled to be heard and under the established system the only way that can be done is through independent representation. Counsel for either parent owes a paramount duty to his client and cannot and should not be relied upon to promote the interests of children unless they coincide with those of his client. Moreover, courts faced with a backlog of cases do not have the time or usually the inclination

---

41. In Colorado and certain counties in Texas such reports are mandatory.

42. This requirement exists in Delaware, the District of Columbia, Georgia, Hawaii, Indiana, Kentucky, Massachusetts, Michigan, Nebraska, Washington, West Virginia, Wisconsin, and Wyoming.

43. MICH. STAT. ANN. § 25.121 (1969). *See also* 5 HARV. J. LEGIS. 563 (1968), which contains a "Divorce Reform Act" containing the concept that children whose parents seek divorce are parties to the action who should be represented by counsel so that their interests will be protected.

44. *See* Speca and Wehrman, *supra* note 24 for citations. Leading cases include Wendland v. Wendland, 29 Wis. 2d 145, 138 N.W.2d 185 (1965); Barth v. Barth, 12 Ohio Misc. 141, 225 N.E.2d 866 (1967); and Zinni v. Zinni, 238 A.2d 373 (R.I. 1968).

to sort out the evidence and the issues from the child's point of view.

Placement of a child, whether the issue arises in a custody, adoption, or neglect proceeding, is a matter of crucial importance to the child. Quite literally, his life and his future may be at stake. The consequences may be as traumatic or dire as commitment to an institution. The same reasons that extended due process principles to delinquency proceedings also apply to the placement issue, and in real life the need for independent counsel may be even greater because only about 20 percent of adjudicated delinquents are instutionalized.[45] In the past, many if not most courts have not been sensitive to the child's need for independent counsel. This may be due to tradition, a desire to conserve time or to duck difficult issues, or because lawyers usually have not represented the interests of children. More probable, however, is the likelihood that such lack of representation is a hangover from feudalism and the notion that children are not people but things subjected to parental ownership and rights. Be that as it may, there are no valid arguments against having *Gideon's* right[46] extended to children, and there is a fresh crop of young lawyers at hand who may be eager to serve their interests. The child should have his day in court.

Principle Six

Perhaps it is not too important, except to a child, that at common law he has no right to keep his own earnings. Under feudalistic principles, his father was entitled to his services and earnings in exchange for the father's duty of support.[47] Wives were under a similar onus at common law but Married Women's Property Acts of the last century emancipated them from

45. Judge Midonick, *supra* note 34 at 82, reports that the Family Court of New York City handles about 9,000 delinquency and 7,000 PINS cases a year, but that there are only 40-50 cases each year involving murder, first-degree rape or first-degree arson. The dismissal rate in delinquency cases is about 40% *Id.* at 98. Of the cases proceeding to disposition in 1969, 15% had judgment suspended, 6% involved discharge with warning, 56% were placed on probation, 8% were placed in a private facility, and 10% in a state training school, and 3% entailed "other placement." *Id.* at 91.

46. The reference is to Gideon v. Wainwright, 372 U.S. 335 (1963), which securely established the right to counsel.

47. *See* MADDEN, PERSONS AND DOMESTIC RELATIONS 439 (1931).

the system. Except for occasional statutes designed to cover the child prodigy in sports or entertainment,[48] the status of children as property owners or income producers remains much the same as it was in medieval times.

The common law rules are obsolete and contrary to prevailing mores. It may come as a surprise to many parents to learn that they are legally entitled to their son's earnings from his paper route or baby sitting money saved by their daughter. It would be natural to assume that the laborer is worthy of his hire. Another anachronism is that what is given to the child by way of support and maintenance and for purposes of education, such as clothing, school books, etc., belongs to the parent who may reclaim it or recover damages for its injury.[49] Moreover, property purchased with the earnings of the child, which has not been given to him, belongs to the parent.

The right to earn and keep his own earnings is tied in with the problem of emancipation which will be discussed under Principle Eight *infra*. The rule itself is objectionable because it denigrates minors and relegates them to an inferior status and at the same time does not reflect current values or our sense of justice. Since the rule may be abridged by agreement or subject to an estoppel, its abrogation would have little practical effect, although it would be a gesture of good will towards minors.

Principle Seven

One would suppose that a genuine concern for the welfare of children would be expressed most positively when their physical and mental health was at stake. Of course they should receive, as needed, medical care and treatment and should have a right on their own to seek professional counseling. But here again autonomy is denied and it follows from the status of minority that minors lack legal capacity to give valid consent. Such is the common law or general rule, but fortunately there are broad exceptions, and recently many state legislatures have changed the rule.

48. *See* N.Y. GEN. OBLIG. LAW § 3-105 *et seq.*
49. MADDEN, *supra* note 4 at 440.

Unquestionably, the usual rule which requires parental consent for medical treatment deters large numbers of young people from seeking and obtaining medical attention when needed or as early as is desirable. Moreover, doctors who generally are aware of the rule, customarily refuse to accept minors as patients without parental consent. Statutes are needed to permit minors with health problems to receive medical and professional services, as needed, without parental consent. This does not mean, however, that parental consent should be ignored or by-passed in a normal situation where such consent ordinarily would be given and the parents are expected to pay the bill. Authority to suspend the usual requirement for parental consent is needed for exceptional situations, as where the family no longer is intact or there is a problem which the minor is unwilling or emotionally unable to communicate to the family.

The point is that an assumed parental power of a proprietary character should not operate to the detriment of children, and an individual right to treatment should be recognized for sensitive problems. Pregnancy, contraceptive information, drug abuse, and emotional disturbance are among the sensitive problems where a rule requiring parental consent for treatment may be counter-productive. Unfortunately, it cannot be assumed that such sensitive problems are rare or virtually non-existent. The appalling statistics show the contrary. Moreover, minors with such problems are not getting the medical care needed.

In 1964, in New York City, 19.6 percent of all out-of-wedlock babies were premature as compared to only 7.7 percent of in-wedlock babies.[50] Fetal deaths were almost twice as great in out-of-wedlock pregnancies, and maternal deaths were four times as great in that category. Approximately 43–44 percent of unmarried mothers are under 20-years-old.[51] Good

50. Wiss, Position Paper on Medical Care and the Minor (1971), an unpublished paper compiled for the Conference on the Rights of Minors, at the New York University Law School, made possible by a grant from the W. T. Grant Foundation and held in October 1971.

51. *Id.*

early pre-natal care and nutrition could eliminate the disparities between the above categories.

Although it is true that under existing law a neglect proceeding may be ordered if a parent unreasonably withholds consent for necessary medical care and treatment,[52] and also that in some circumstances welfare officials may act *in loco parentis*,[53] the mere statement of such ultimate remedies shows that they are unsatisfactory for the "sensitive problems" of minors. Litigation or the involvement of strangers may not be practicable.

The question of the right to autonomy becomes even more controversial and perhaps complicated when we consider the minor's interest in contraceptive information and services. Realistically, sexually active adolescents should have access to counseling and contraceptive services on demand, because usually they already have rejected parental control and advice and the practical consequence of withholding counseling and services unless parental consent is obtained is likely to be more disastrous than a fancied usurpation of parental authority. It also is realistic to concede that sex experimentation by teen-agers quite properly is a sensitive area for parents as well as minors and that prudent legislators and judges are well advised to be reluctant to enter this thicket. Nonetheless, the welfare of minors and of the community concur and take precedence over parental authority, for to hold otherwise is to vindicate an ineffectual power at the expense of social reality.

A similar question, but one which is even more complicated, arises in connection with the right of teen-age girls to procure a medical abortion. The existing statutes in New York provide that under enumerated circumstances the female's consent to the abortion is legally effective.[54] No age is specified. California has held that under their law, parental consent is unnecessary and that a teen-age girl may give an effective consent to an abortion.[55] With reference to decision-making authority, on the

---

52. *See* Note, *Judicial Power to Order Medical Treatment for Minors Over Objections of Their Guardians*, 14 SYRACUSE L. REV. 84 (1962).

53. *See In re* Seiferth, 309 N.Y. 80, 127 N.E.2d 820 (1955).

54. *See* Laws 1970, ch. 127, effective July 1, 1970.

55. Ballard v. Anderson, 95 Cal. Rptr. 1, 484 P.2d 1345 (Sup. Ct., 1971).

one hand it may be argued that the decision to have an abortion is precisely the kind of problem a distraught young girl should not make on her own due not only to immaturity of judgment, but to the emotional dimension of the decision. It may be argued that she is incapable of an informed consent. On the other hand, from the standpoint of the pregnant girl, involvement of the parents may be the thing she most dreads, or the pregnancy itself may be a rebellion against parental authority. To the extent that the new abortion law is based on a policy of providing an alternative to criminal abortions, it may be practical to urge the involvement of parents where feasible but where the pregnant girl has left home, or communication with the parents would be harmful to her, to dispense with any need for parental consent. Admittedly, the particular age of the pregnant girl, and the total circumstances, must affect any decision. A hard and fast rule would be difficult if not impossible to administer.

The case is much clearer for a suspension of the need for parental consent where minors have health problems such as venereal disease. A legitimate concern over public health dictates that treatment be given with or without parental consent, although it may be sound medical judgment to warn those subject to possible contagion.[56] Any requirement of parental consent to the treatment of a minor for a venereal disease is medically and psychologically absurd and not in the public interest. At least 39 states presently have statutes permitting minors to give a valid consent to examinations and treatment for venereal disease.[57] This has been a dramatic legislative change because only three years ago there were but eight states having such statutes.

Counseling and psychiatric care and treatment is another area where the need for parental consent should be suspended, at least under some circumstances. Since such problems often are associated with intrafamily diffculties and conflicts, if the individual child is to be counseled or treated it may be neces-

56. *See* Simonson v. Swenson, 177 N.W. 831 (1920).

57. Wiss, *supra* note 50.

sary to do so without parental involvement. It should be left to the professional to determine at what stage, if any, the parents should be brought into the picture. The need of the minor for confidentiality may be very intense, especially when the immediate problem relates to matters of sex or drug abuse. Again, the combination of the interests of the minor and concerns of public health and welfare together outweigh parental prerogatives. Moreover, long term parental interests coincide with confidentiality for the minor.

We have been discussing situations where it would be contrary to the best interests of children and society to require parental consent to medical care and treatment. Admittedly, these are exceptional circumstances and ordinarily family involvement is desirable. The law itself recognized this when it created exceptions to the general rule that a minor lacked capacity to consent to medical treatment. The most important exception is that for emergency treatment, where there appears to be an imminent danger of death or impairment of health in the absence of immediate treatment. In some states, this exception is codified, while in others a person *in loco parentis* may be given authority to consent.[58] The rule also does not apply to emancipated minors who do have capacity to consent, and a few states have adopted a "mature minor" exception which permits such a juvenile to consent to medical treatment where the procedure is for his benefit and he understands the nature and consequences of the proposed course of treatment.[59] *Bach v. Long Island Jewish Hospital*[60] held that the consent of a 19-year-old married minor was effective, and the "mature minor" exception has been given statutory recognition in Mississippi. The difficulty with this exception revolves around the problem of what constitutes an "informed consent" by a minor.

There are numerous other statutory modifications of the general rule that a minor lacks capacity to consent to medical procedures. A few states, both before and after the change in

58. *See* MASS. GEN. LAWS ANN. ch. 112, § 12D (1970); MD. ANN. CODE art. 43, § 135 (1971); MISS. CODE ANN. § 7129–81 (1966); and Pa. Stat. tit. 35, § 10104 (1969).

59. *See* Smith v. Selby, 431 P.2d 719 (Wash. 1967).

60. 267 N.Y.S.2d 289, 49 Misc. 2d 207 (Sup. Ct. Nassau Co. 1966).

voting age, have lowered the age for an effective consent to medical treatment.[61] In Oregon, any person 15 or over may give such consent, in Washington the age of 18 is set as the age of consent for all purposes, and in Maryland, North Carolina, and Pennsylvania, any person 18 or over, and in Hawaii, any person 19 or over may consent to medical treatment.[62] In other states the age for attaining majority usually is set at 21. As previously stated, 39 states now give minors capacity to consent to treatment for venereal disease. Fourteen states by statute provide that minors may consent to treatment related to pregnancy, six states have statutes authorizing physicians to provide birth control information and services to minors without parental consent; still other statutes authorizing such services have no restrictions as to age.[63] There also are specific statutes permitting minors to consent to treatment for drug addiction and for blood donation.[64]

Perhaps the most comprehensive recent statute is that of Pennsylvania which allows medical treatment to be given to minors of any age, without parental consent, if an attempt to obtain consent would cause delay which would increase the risk to the minor's health or life or if it is for examination and treatment of venereal disease.[65] The Pennsylvania statute also codifies the common law exceptions to the general rule by permitting a minor who is of age 18 or older, who has graduated from high school, or who has become pregnant, to receive medical services without parental consent. The statute also provides that physicians may not be held liable if they in good faith treat minors who profess that they do not need their parents' consent.

A different approach has been taken in California and Minnesota where minors are given the capacity to consent to medical treatment where they are living separate and apart from their parents, however short the duration, and managing their

61. Wiss, *supra* note 50.
62. *Id.*
63. *Id.*
64. *Id.*
65. *See* Pa. Stat. tit. 35, § 10104 (1969).

own financial affairs.[66] Minnesota also specifically permits the treatment of minors for alcohol or drug abuse without parental consent. Maryland, in substance, repeats the common law exceptions, but also provides that a minor may consent to advice or treatment relating to drug abuse, venereal disease, pregnancy, or contraception not amounting to sterilization, and emotional or mental disorders. Immunity against civil suit is accorded to doctors who honor such consent of minors.[67]

This brief citation of common law authority and recent statutory developments should be sufficient to show that a minor's right to medical care and treatment is an individual interest backed up by a social concern for his welfare. In the ordinary situation the lack of capacity of the minor and the need for parental consent to medical procedures does no harm. But there are exceptional circumstances where the claim of parental authority should be rejected because it conflicts with the best interests of the child. Statutory authority is needed to permit counseling, medical care and treatment, without parental consent, if the procedure is for the benefit of the minor, and it would be unreasonable to withhold consent. There is existing law which permits this to be done after legal proceedings[68] but what is needed is authority in advance to make the minor's consent effective where his individual interests may conflict with those of his parents. Rather than setting up an arbitrary age of consent, a more flexible standard probably is to be preferred, and in addition to repeating the common law exceptions, another should be added to cover situations where the minor has left home or for satisfactory reasons refuses to bring his parents into the picture.

Principle Eight

The common law status of a minor child could be terminated by emancipation which has the legal consequence of relieving the minor of parental control and from the duty of rendering filial services and terminating the parental duty of support, mainte-

66. *See* Minn. S.F. No. 1496, ch. 544, §§ 144, 344 (1971).
67. MD. ANN. CODE art. 43, § 135 (1971).
68. For example, by a neglect petition under Fam. Court Act § 312.

nance and education. But emancipation was a one way street in that it occurred with the express or implied consent of the parents. Emancipation, as such, was not an option open to the minor, rather it was a unilateral parental privilege. More recently, however, some states have seized upon the concept of *implied* consent to emancipation as a means of safeguarding or promoting the best interests of children.

Implied emancipation originally covered such situations as where a minor left home for good (runaway or not) and was completely on his or her own. A daughter by marriage emancipated herself from parental control,[69] although some courts have insisted that the marriage must have been with parental consent for emancipation to occur.[70] Most commonly, a son emancipated himself by taking a job and moving out of the parental home or by joining military service.[71] In addition, some courts faced with the doctrine of immunity for parental torts, have held that an implied emancipation occurs whenever a parent is guilty of outrageous behavior, wilful misconduct, or even gross negligence. A leading Maryland case held that children were emancipated and could sue their father's estate where he had killed the mother in their presence and then committed suicide.[72] Other cases held that emancipation took place and a father who was a reckless driver incurred liability when his children were injured.[73]

Termination of parental rights, as by court order after a neglect petition, also emancipates a child from the control of his parents. In New York, this may occur where it is shown that there is inadequate care, maintenance and protection, lack of supervision or moral guidance, or abandonment of the child.[74] Understandably, there must be strong and convincing evidence

69. *See* Commonwealth v. Graham, 157 Mass. 73, 3 N.E. 706 (1892), and Austin v. Austin, 167 Md. 164 (1911).

70. *See* Wolf v. Wolf, 194 App. Div. 33, 185 N.Y.S. 37 (1920), 58 A.L.R.2d 355 (1958).

71. *See* 20 A.L.R.2d 1414 (1951), but *compare* Wack v. Wack, 74 N.Y.S.2d 435 (Sup. Ct. 1947), and Harwood v. Harwood, 49 N.Y.S.2d 727, *aff'd* 52 N.Y.S.2d 573 (First Dept. 1944), *with* Craig v. Craig, 24 A.D.2d 588, 262 N.Y.S.2d 398 (2d Dept. 1965).

72. Mahnke v. Moore, 197 Md. 61, 77 A.2d 923 (1951).

73. For example, *see* Cowgill v. Brock, 189 Or. 282, 218 P.2d 445 (1950).

74. Family Court Act § 312.

for such drastic action and it also should be noted that it is quite common for the fact pattern to be such that either a neglect petition or a delinquency proceeding may be brought and that family problems overlap. Different quanta of proof may be required depending upon the label given to the proceedings, the disposistion of the case, and the permanent or temporary character of the termination of parental rights.

It should not be assumed that the status of childhood subjects minors to the equivalent of a Roman *patria potestas*. Especially during the last century, courts increasingly have asserted *parens patriae* power to intervene into family affairs and to check harmful exercises of parental prerogatives.[75] Parents are not permitted to oust courts of jurisdiction over the welfare of children by their private agreement. Child custody, visitation, and support arrangements are subject to judicial control and scrutiny, which may be another way of recognizing that the rights of children are paramount in legal theory. The child's welfare or best interests may be at issue in numerous kinds of proceedings and where asserted become a matter of special concern. There is some authority that a child may purchase necessities not provided by parents and that the latter are liable therefor to suppliers, or that the child himself may sue a parent for support.[76] Moreover, where a minor is an heir, a guardian is appointed to protect his interests, and guardianship of a child's property may arise in other connections. In short, there is inherent judicial power under the *parens patriae* doctrine to support intervention into the parent-child relationship and to subject parental authority to legal safeguards.

As a common law matter, an infant or minor achieves majority at age 21, *i.e.*, at the beginning of the day before his twenty-first birthday.[77] Thus, a person born on December 3, 1950, would become twenty-one for legal purposes at 12:01 a.m. on December 2, 1971. The fixing of the age of majority at 21, except for the sovereign, who attained majority at 18 and for legislative purposes never was in minority, was purely arbi-

75. *See* Speca and Wehrman, *op. cit., supra* note 24, at 3–4.
76. *Id.*
77. *See* CLARK, LAW OF DOMESTIC RELATIONS, 230 (1968).

trary and probably related to the ability to bear arms and the completion of training in knighthood.[78] Before and after age 21 was settled upon as the age for majority there were numerous exceptions for special functions or purposes. Thus, today, there are differing ages for emancipation in general, and for majority for voting, drinking, smoking, employment, etc. As is true with regard to tests of mental competence in civil litigation there is a general test and a specific test related to a particular function. The impractical and unsatisfactory character of general tests as to competence or capacity is shown by the special adaptations to specific functions. In a sense, the exceptions all but eat up the rule. Moreover, the extreme variance between ages set for specific purposes and the diversity of the ages set in different states for the same functions permit the inference that legislative hunch rather than reason has been at work.

Even though it is conceded that any age selected for the attainment of majority or for participation in various so-called adult activities inevitably is arbitrary classification, it does not follow that all attempts at age differentials should be abandoned. Rather, what is needed is a periodic review of the ages set and re-examination in terms of function and efficacy. It is necessary and reasonable to establish age limitations on driving automobiles, induction into the military draft, purchase of intoxicating liquors or cigarettes, the age of consent, the right to vote or marry, etc., but it is only fair to set the specific age in terms of current realities. The differentiation should have a reasonable basis in terms of the general maturity and behavior of youth with reference to the particular activity.[79]

The legal consequences of emancipation from parental authority should reflect de facto situations. Although it is not new it is an increasing phenomenon that thousands of minors have become alienated from their families and have left home. Nomadic minors by the dozens if not thousands drift into Greenwich Village, Haight-Asbury, Harvard Square, and other supposedly hospitable or "groovy" places. In legal theory they

78. *See* James, *The Age of Majority*, 4 AMER. J. LEG. HIST. 22 (1960).

79. *Compare* the discussion of the equal protection problem in Foster, *Marriage: A "Basic Civil Right of Man,"* 37 FORDHAM L. REV. 51 (1968).

still are unemancipated and subject to parental control; as minors they lack capacity to give a valid consent to medical care and treatment, or for counseling and guidance; and they are subject to treatment as runaways by the legal authorities.[80] The common law or traditional rules simply do not work insofar as effective handling of their problems is concerned. The status of minority may inhibit or bar their care and protection. Litigation to have them declared wards or to have guardians appointed usually is not practical.

Perhaps it might be of some value to have a public guardian designated who would have the authority of a surrogate parent, empowered to consent to welfare, medical, and other services for minors who have left home. The primary obligation of such a guardian would be to serve the best interests of the child, and, where proper, to preserve confidentiality with reference to communications made to him. The responsibility would be to deal with the minor as a person, to help solve problems, and to see that the minor received proper care and protection. To be effective, such a guardian would counsel and advise, and by persuasion rather than orders, would seek to reunite the family where that was feasible. Where impossible, he would seek to provide such security as was available for the minor's life on his own. An emphasis would be placed on social services rather than upon legal rights and remedies, and the guardian of minors might have branch offices at community or legal aid centers.

A statute will be necessary to create the office of such a guardian and in addition legislative authority will be needed to redefine "emancipation." It is suggested that the child should have a right to emancipation from the parent-child relationship when that relationship has broken down and the child has left home due to abuse, neglect, serious family conflict, or other sufficient cause, and his best interests will be served by a termination of parental authority. Depending upon age, there

80. Family Court Act § 712(b) defines a "person in need of supervison" (PINS) as "a male less than sixteen years of age and a female less than eighteen years of age who does not attend school . . . or who is incorrigible, ungovernable or habitually disobedient and beyond the lawful control of parent or other lawful authority." Running away from home is covered by this section and there also is a model act in effect in several states for the handling of runaways without resort to usual extradition laws.

may or may not be any need for the protection of a guardian. There also may be a need to relax compulsory school attendance laws and child labor laws for emancipated children. Laws, rules, and regulations pertaining to unwed mothers and drug abuse, in particular, should be reviewed in terms of a revised concept of emancipation.

Principle Nine

The women's liberation movement has raised and confirmed the suspicion that some legal disabilities have been imposed under the guise of protective measures for ulterior purposes.[81] The same may be true of some of the disabilities of minority. Paternalistic measures may be more protective of parental prerogatives than of the best interests of minors. Moreover, the occasion or need for a particular measure may no longer exist or may no longer justify the restriction.

Perhaps the most obvious example of currently questionable regulation and restriction is to be found in compulsory school attendance and child labor laws. With some exceptions, minors between 6 and 16 in New York must attend school for full time instruction. There is no need to comment here upon drop-out rates or the traditional orientation of secondary schools towards preparation for college entrance. It is sufficient to note that we are doing an inadequate job of providing a bridge between school and life work for many of our young people. Whatever the cause or the blame, the fact remains that the primary function of some schools is a warehousing or custodial one to keep kids off the streets. Many of these teen-agers might be better off on job training or apprenticeship work, but due to compulsory attendance and child labor laws are frozen into a meaningless routine.

The general pattern is that all wage employment is barred to children under 14, all employment during school hours is barred to those under 16, and hazardous jobs to those under 18.[82]

81. *See* KANOWITZ, WOMEN AND THE LAW, THE UNFINISHED REVOLUTION (1968). *See also*, MILLETT, SEXUAL POLITICS (1970), and *Symposium on Women and the Law*, 4 FAM. L.Q. 1 (1970).

82. *See* position paper on Education and Employment and the Minor, an unpub-

There may or may not be justification for a particular classification of "hazardous," and it should be remembered that 16-year-olds are deemed old enough to get learner's permits to drive and 17-year-olds may be permitted to enlist. There also is an artificial barrier in that a high school diploma may be required for certain jobs. The state, generally effectively, regulates age requirements by the issuance of employment certificates, which are difficult to obtain where a minor is under age 18. To be a caddy, in New York a boy must be 14-years-old, and the same age is set for girls who wish to serve as babysitters. Interestingly, no employment certificate is required for household chores or casual work. The state Minimum Wage Act authorizes lower rates for minors, as does the law pertaining to farm workers.[83]

It is no exaggeration to say that for many minors in New York the combination of compulsory school attendance and child labor laws is an intolerable burden that forces them into becoming "drop outs" and bars access to meaningful work. The human and social cost of the system is exorbitant. Unless flexibility is achieved, the system itself is bound to fail.

There are many other indicia of a status as a non-person, some of which have been previously discussed. In addition to limitations on ownership of property, and the traditional family immunity doctrine, there is the area of contract law where we start with the rule that an infant lacks capacity to contract, and that infancy persists until age 21. Again the impracticality of the rule is attested by numerous exceptions. The infant may validly contract for "necessaries."[84] If he disavows the contract, the infant may be required to make a good faith effort to return the goods. His privilege of disaffirmance must be exercised within a reasonable time after reaching majority. If he is a child prodigy or athelete, those concerned have induced legislatures to suspend the minor's incapacity.[85] Depending upon his age, the minor may contract a valid marriage even though statutes pro-

lished paper compiled for the Conference on the Rights of Minors, New York University Law School, held in October, 1971.

83. *Id.*

84. *See* Panza v. Panza, 112 N.Y.S.2d 262 (Dom. Rel. Ct. Bronx Co. 1952).

85. *See* New York Gen. Oblig. Law §3-105 *et seq.*

vide for parental consent until majority.[86] The public policy basis for the usual incapacity of an infant to contract is said to be his lack of mature judgment and the vulnerability of the minor to overreaching.

Although there has been substantial statutory modification of the notion that a minor should not be bound by his contracts, as by lowering the age at which he is bound or by exempting certain occupations, the usual attacks on the rule have been in terms of the hardship that may be occasioned to sellers. The rule also does harm to the minor. Behavioral science assures us with confidence that one does not promote responsibility by making people irresponsible. The minor who is able to welch on his commitments due to his privilege to disaffirm may also find that sellers or suppliers won't sell or supply to him for that reason, so that the supposed protection boomerangs. In theory he may own the money in his pocket but he is limited as to what he can do with it. In real life, however, transactions are carried on by minors and, except as to serious matters, the question of infancy is not raised.[87]

It would make good sense to adopt a general rule that infants (those below age 21) have full capacity to contract and are bound by their agreements, but that those dealing with them are subject to rules as to fraud, duress, and mistake which take into account the maturity of the minor, the experience of the other party, and the nature of the bargain. Such a rule for contracts would be more analogous to the tort rule that an infant is liable for his torts but that his "negligence" may be judged in terms of a "reasonable infant."

The parent-child immunity doctrine, which had a relatively brief span in New York,[88] still exists in many states. The two factors which led to an abandonment of the doctrine are the belated conviction that the rule was not in the best interests of

86. *See* FOSTER AND FREED, LAW AND THE FAMILY—NEW YORK § 2:7 (Rev. 3d. 1972), and Dom. Rel. Law § 15, subd. 2.

87. *See* CLARK, LAW OF DOMESTIC RELATIONS 235 (1968).

88. The parent-child immunity to negligence actions was established by Hewlette v. George, 68 Miss. 703, 9 So. 885 (1891), and New York abolished the immunity doctrine in Gelbman v. Gelbman, 23 N.Y.2d 434, 297 N.Y.S.2d 529, 245 N.E.2d 192 (1969).

children or the family, and the assumed presence of insurance. Those states still adhering to the immunity doctrine purport to do so to save domestic tranquillity and to prevent fraud. Fortunately, New York has rejected both the doctrine and its rationale.

It follows from the above brief discussion of disabiliites and incapacities that such incidents of status have given way with changing times. It is not enough, however, to chisel away at hardship instances; what we need is the philosophical base that children are persons and that there must be justification in terms of current social reality for denying them the rights of persons. It is naïve to assume that rules derived from feudalism actually serve their best interests or are protective, and in the spirit of requirements for classification under the equal protection clause, the burden should be on the proponent of differentiation.[89]

Principle Ten

Thus far we have been concerned for the most part with removing bars, barriers, and inhibitions to a humanizing of the treatment of youth. There also is a positive obligation to act affirmatively to better the lot of children. This is especially evident when minors are institutionalized. It is not enough to say that public schools and compulsory attendance are for their own good, or that an industrial school will rehabilitate or build character. If youth are to be captives, at home, school, or before the family court, they are entitled to special care, consideration, and protection.[90]

It is difficult if not impossible to legislate proper etiquette for the parent-child relationship at home. But order out of chaos may be achieved if school administrators are forced to adopt fair procedures and the rudiments of due process for disciplinary hearings at school. The starting point is that children have a right to an education, and since they are a captive audience, there is a duty to provide a meaningful educational

89. *See* and *compare* Levy v. Louisiana, 391 U.S. 68 (1968).
90. *See* Rubin, *supra* note 11.

experience. All too often school administrators and teachers have operated on the assumption that school attendance is a privilege the enjoyment of which is conditioned upon unquestioning compliance with whatever regulations they handed down. Only recently has there been a belated recognition that students have any standing to participate in making decisions which affect their lives at school. It is now established that arbitrary or unreasonable school regulations are a nullity, that at least an expurgated version of the Bill of Rights applies to students *qua* students, and that disciplinary procedures and especially expulsion or suspension proceedings must satisfy the basic requirements of due process of law.[91]

Before a student may be suspended for behavioral or medical reasons, he must be accorded a fair hearing by the principal, and the principal's decision is subject to appeal.[92] The student has a right to counsel of his choice at any hearing where suspension or expulsion may be ordered.[93] Students and their parents have a right to know in advance the school rules, and parents have a right to group statistical records concerning the school and a right to inspect their child's full school record at any time.[94] A principal has no legal authority to withhold a diploma if the student has successfully completed his course of study. Subject only to reasonable regulations, students have the right to free speech, freedom of the press, and freedom of assembly.[95] Again, subject only to reasonable limitations, students have a right to determine their own appearance as to dress and hair, to form political and social organizations, and to

91. *See* Breen v. Kahl, 296 F. Supp. 702 (W.D. Wis. 1969).

92. *See* N.Y.C.L.U., STUDENT RIGHTS HANDBOOK FOR NEW YORK CITY. *See also* Wright, *The Constitution on the Campus*, 22 VAND. L. REV. 1027 (1969).

93. *See* Madera v. Board of Ed. of City of New York, 386 F.2d 778 (C.A.2d, 1967) (dicta); and Dixon v. Alabama State Bd. of Education, 294 F.2d 150 (M.D. Ala., 1960).

94. N.Y.C.L.U., *supra* note 92.

95. *See* Note, *Developments in the Law—Academic Freedom*, 81 HARV. L. REV. 1045 (1968). For conduct found to be outside the bounds of academic freedom, *see* Grossner v. Trustees of Columbia University, 287 F. Supp. 535 (S.D. N.Y. 1968); Zanders v. La. State Bd. of Education, 281 F. Supp. 747 (W.D. La., 1968); *In re* Bacon, 240 Cal. App. 2d 34, 49 Cal. Rptr. 322 (1966); and Buttny v. Smiley, 281 F. Supp. 280 (D.C. Colo., 1968). *See also* Van Alstyne, *The Judicial Trend Toward Student Academic Freedom*, 20 U. FLA. L. REV. 290 (1968).

use school facilities.[96] A pregnant student has a right to remain in school as long as physically possible.[97] Finally, there are uncertain limitations on police work at school and intrusions into the privacy of students.[98]

The above examples of student's rights show the substantial change that has occurred and is occurring in teacher-student relations. The status of being a student no longer is a subservient or servile one insofar as the law is concerned, no matter what the attitudes of individual teachers or officials may be in real life. Hopefully, there will be at least a grudging acceptance of students' rights. Students must be dealt with fairly and teachers must have sound reasons for restrictions upon student conduct and freedom of action which are justified in terms of the larger interest of students as a whole. Most significantly, students will demand and receive the right to participate in decision-making as it affects their life at school. The Board of Education has recognized the right of students to "be involved in the process of developing curriculum and of establishing disciplinary policies" and "in the formulation of school student policies."[99]

The most practical and effective way to make sure that children receive special care, consideration, and protection at school or before adult authority is to provide for the implementation of the right to counsel. In a sense, the so-called "establishment" itself is an adversary system, as much so as our administration of justice, and the system requires representation for all parties concerned. Youth advocacy programs are being developed for and by students in order to supply spokesmen and spokeswomen for youth's point of view. Adults will have to listen and eventually may be compelled to reexamine many old assumptions that no longer hold water. It may be helpful to such a burdensome undertaking if adults start with an acknowledgement that children are people, not objects, or things, and that to acquire respect, one must give it.

96. *See* Tinker v. Des Moines School District, 393 U.S. 503 (1969); Richards v. Thurston, 424 F.2d 1281 (C.A. 1st, 1970).

97. *See* N.Y.C.L.U., STUDENT RIGHTS HANDBOOK.

98. *Id.*

99. *Id.*

Conclusion

We have tried to give, as Karl Llewellyn used to say, the bare bones for a bill of rights for children. Doubtlessly, we have overlooked equally important rights and interests but we have tried to stress those matters which seem to be of immediate importance. Our emphasis has been upon the rights rather than the duties of children. That has been so because children's rights have been sadly neglected, not because children have no duties or responsibilities. Moreover, unless children are treated fairly and their rights are respected, it is idle to speak down to them about duty and responsibility. As noted at the outset, of course the several principles here advanced may apply with varying degrees depending upon individual circumstances and the age of the child. The general proposition should be, perhaps, that children should be granted individual freedom commensurate with their maturation and development and the burden should be on those who abridge the freedom of children to show that such abridgement is necessary and actually in their best interests.

With the aid of poor memories adults often look back on their youth as happy carefree days. We tend to forget that children usually have a highly developed sense of fairplay and honor and are sensitive to injustice and bullying. Their relative helplessness may intensify what to us are minor wrongs or errors of adult judgment. To the child, to be treated unfairly is a double wrong, for in addition to any other error, there is an abuse of authority. And the crowning insult is when the adult says it's for the child's own good. The lessons of *Gault* should be studied with care for the adult world needs to reflect not only upon behavior but to search conscience as well. We profess a dedication to the best interests of children but do we serve them well? Adult hypocrisy, as distinguished from their own, no longer is tolerable to our youth. To win their respect, we will have to earn it, and the first order of business is to make the heartfelt concession that children are people. From that concession will come recognition of the rights and principles which we have referred to in this discussion.

[2]

THE EMERGENCE OF CHILDREN'S RIGHTS

JOHN EEKELAAR*

Two decisions of the House of Lords in recent years[1] have significant implications for assessing the current status, in English law, of any concept of children's rights. The purpose of this article is to attempt such an assessment within the context of these decisions and an historical overview of the emergence of such a concept within our social organization.

PRIVATE BEHAVIOUR AND PUBLIC PERCEPTIONS

Until recently, social historians held the surprising consensus that parents of old felt little affection for their children.[2] This opinion is sometimes thought to be derived from the thesis expounded by Philippe Aries that, in medieval times, there was no concept of childhood as a period with a character distinct from adulthood. While, as Aries himself admits, this fact (if fact it be) does not necessarily imply that there could be no affection for them, nevertheless his assumption is that it indicated actual indifference.[3] But how do we define, and measure, affection? Aries argues that the growth of the idea of childhood was related to increasing perception of the importance of education as the agrarian economy declined, which, as then understood, imposed rigorous, often cruel, regimes upon children. To inquire whether parents in any period loved their children more, or less, than in another, is to examine the nature of love. This did not deter Lloyd de Mause, who claimed that 'it is, of course, not love which the parent of the past lacked, but rather the emotional maturity needed to see the child as a person separate from himself'.[4]

The thesis that parental affection has only recently been acquired in European civilization (it was not claimed that it did not exist in the ancient world) has now

*Fellow of Pembroke College, Oxford.

1 *Richards* v *Richards* [1984] AC 174; *Gillick* v *West Norfolk and Wisbech Area Health Authority* [1984] QB 581 (Woolf J), [1985] 2 WLR 413 (CA), [1985] 2 WLR 830 (HL).

2 See Lawrence Stone, *The Family, Sex and Marriage in England 1500–1800* (1977): 'In such a society relations with one's own children were not particularly close' (of the sixteenth century) (p 6); 'parent-child relations were anyway often exploitative and authoritarian rather than affective and nurturant' (of the seventeenth century) (p 58). Some affection might arise for children aged between two and seven, but at some time between seven and fourteen most would leave home 'usually for good' (p 116). Edward Shorter, *The Making of the Modern Family* (1976) 'we note little of the affectionate concern ... that characterize the modern mother' (of peasantry in early nineteenth century) (p 171). See the discussion in Linda M. Pollock, *Forgotten Children: Parent-Child Relations From 1500 to 1900* (1983), ch 1.

3 P. Aries, *Centuries of Childhood* (1962), p 134.

4 L. de Mause (ed) *The History of Childhood* (1976), p 17.

 Oxford Journal of Legal Studies Vol. 6 No. 2

been subjected to serious criticism.[5] Without purporting to adjudicate on that debate, two observations are offered. First, four years' research into the institutional response to child abuse and neglect revealed cases of apparent indifference and cruelty by parents towards their children which I would not have thought possible in the world around us. But I would hesitate long before concluding that all these parents did not love their children. Indeed, the restraint against intervening within a parent-child relationship in the face of such apparent love is one of the most important inhibitors against decisive response to child abuse and neglect.[6] Second, we may add the evidence of Sir William Blackstone to the historical record. When discussing a parent's duty to protect his children, he observes that, because of a parent's 'natural affection' towards his child, the law needs rather to restrain a parent's protective impulses than to encourage them, and cites as an example of the law's recognition of these impulses a case 'where a man's son was beaten by another boy, the father went near a mile to find him and there revenged his son's quarrel by beating the other boy, of which beating he unfortunately died; it was not held to be murder, but manslaughter merely. Such indulgence does the law show to the frailty of human nature and the workings of parental affection'.[7] It is true that some social historians claim to detect a transition to more affective parent-child relationships at the time Blackstone was writing, although Stone confines this to the middle, professional and landed classes and the upper artisans.[8] But it is unlikely, if we remember Kahn-Freund's strictures on his lack of perception of contemporary changes in employment relationships,[9] that Blackstone was representing a particularly modern turn in the law. Of course, the statement cannot be regarded as a reliable guide to the actual state of family relationships; but it does seem to reflect an assumption about human behaviour in general which looks very similar to one which might be made today, and which Blackstone did not expect his audience to contradict.

For the present purposes, I wish to place greater significance on how the relationship is perceived *externally* than on the true nature of the sentiment held by parents towards their children. A system of law which recognizes in *patria potestas*, a father's power to execute (or, as in later Roman times, expose) his children clearly perceives the structure and role of family life very differently from one which enacts a Bill of Rights for children similar, say, to the one advocated by Foster and Freed, which includes the rights to receive

5 Linda Pollock op cit, n 1. Ferdinand Mount, *The Subversive Family: An Alternative History of Love and Marriage* (1982), ch 7.

6 The research is reported in Robert Dingwall, John Eekelaar and Topsy Murray, *The Protection of Children: State Intervention and Family Life* (1983).

7 *Commentaries on the Laws of England* 1.16 (7th ed, 1775, p 450). See also text to n 20, below.

8 Stone, op cit, ch 9.

9 O. Kahn-Freund, 'Blackstone's Neglected Child: the Contract of Employment' (1977) 93 *LQR*. 507.

love and affection and to be treated as a person.[10] Of course, such proclamations do not necessarily describe social reality. Rather, they present public images about what social reality should be. They may influence people's behaviour, although how far that influence extends beyond the official institutions of a society into personal relationships may be peculiarly difficult to discover. Goody's account of the assault upon the familial systems of Western Europe by the early medieval church (increasingly severe restrictions on marriages within close degrees of kindred, prohibitions on marriages with the widow of a dead brother or sister of a dead wife, outlawry of adoption and of concubinage), which he attributes to a strategy of cutting down systems of succession which kept property within families in favour of its passage into ecclesiastical ownership, also refers to the persistence of the original practices, frequently surfacing in open resistence.[11] Our interest lies primarily in the public posture, because it is here where the language, indeed, the very concept, of rights is located.

Therefore we need to examine how relationships within the family, in particular, between parents and children, are characterized by statements of law. Not surprisingly, early law viewed children primarily as agents for the devolution of property within an organized family setting. The law, wrote Pollock and Maitland:

> never laid down any such rule that there is or ought to be a guardian for every infant. It had been thinking almost exclusively of infant heirs, and had left other infants to shift for themselves and to get guardians as best they might from time to time for the purposes of litigation. The law had not even been careful to give the father a right to the custody of his children; on the other hand, it had given him a right to the custody of his heir apparent, whose marriage he was free to sell. It had looked at guardianship and paternal power merely as profitable rights, and had only sanctioned them when they could be made profitable.[12]

It might not be an exaggeration to say the the social role of children was primarily seen as furthering the interests of the family group as a whole and over time by maintaining and perhaps extending the family's land-holding. While he was alive, the father can be taken to represent these interests. The remedies given to heirs against guardians (for negligent conduct of litigation, mostly concerning land or for account regarding the care of their property) reflect these concerns.[13] In the case of socage tenants, these interests were recognized by assigning the guardianship of an heir's lands to relatives on the side of the family who would be least likely to have a claim to the property themselves, producing perhaps the earliest form of the trust. But if the children owned no land, the law was uninterested. 'We may suppose,' wrote Pollock and Maitland, 'that in the common

10 Henry H. Foster and Doris J. Freed, 'A Bill of Rights for Children' (1972) 6 *Fam Law Quarterly* 343.

11 Jack Goody, *The Development of the Family and Marriage in Europe* (1983).

12 F. Pollock and F. W. Maitland, *The History of English Law* (1968 edition) vol. ii, p 444.

13 Holdsworth, *A History of English Law*, vol. iii, pp 63, 517.

case the sisters and younger brothers of the youthful heir dwelt with their mother in the dower house – often she purchased the wardship of her first born son—***but we know of no writ which would have compelled her or anyone else to maintain them***, or which would have compelled them to live with her or with anyone else. Probably the ecclesiastical courts did something to protect the interests of children by obliging executors and administrators to retain for their use any legacies or "bairns' parts" to which they had become entitled.'[14]

Was the lack of any articulated legal duty, and, of course, corresponding remedy, compelling a parent to support his children or even to act generally in their interests, significant as an indicator of the ideological conception of family relations? It seems that it must be. We may perhaps illustrate this by reference to ancillary rules dealing with third party intrusions into this relationship. The writ of wardship was an early adaptation of the writ of trespass for the purpose of protecting a father's or a guardian's rights if he lost the benefits of a potentially attractive marriage into the family by the ravishment of the ward. Hence it was that the action for abduction was based upon the injury to the father's proprietary interest, not in the child (for he had none) but in the child's marriage, and was accordingly restricted to his heirs. It followed that when this became obsolete, the remedy was allowed to a father only on the basis that the injury to the child had deprived him of his pecuniary interest in the child, represented by the child's services. So injury to a child of two would not justify compensation because a child so young was manifestly unable to perform any services.[15] Yet there were no rules which recognized a child's interest in receiving support from a parent. A child could not sue a third party who wrongfully killed his parent (we needed to wait until the first Fatal Accidents Act of 1846 before such claims were allowed) and to this day the law will not grant any action to a child who loses the benefits of his breadwinner by that person's injury or enticement (whether by a woman, an employer, or even the church).[16]

Was the fact that the law viewed this relationship in so one-sided a fashion indicative of the general public view of the position of children? Surely, it might be said, the early church, while weakening the claims of wider kin on the family, would have strengthened and supported the claims of children to support by their parents. Yet Gibbon, writing of the earliest days of the Church, remarked: 'The Christians of Rome were possessed of a very considerable wealth . . . many . . . had sold their lands and houses to increase the public riches of the sect, at the expense, indeed, of their unfortunate

14 Pollock and Maitland, op cit, n 12, p 444, (emphasis supplied).

15 *Hall* v *Hollaender* (1825) 4 B & C 660.

16 The incongruity was not unnoticed, even in the seventeenth century. In 1657, William Shepherd wrote: '. . . it is an hard law that no recompense is given to a man's wife or children for killing of him, whereas for the beating and wounding of him while he was still alive, he should have had recompense for the wrong': Holdsworth, op cit, n 13, vol. iii, p 333.

children, who found themselves beggars because their parents had been saints.'[17] In the fifth century, writes Goody, Salvian castigated those who left their property to relatives or to strangers and neglected the Church. 'A father should not love even his own children more than his Lord, and therefore he should leave the same share of his property to God as to his own children.'[18] Later, in England, the church achieved monopoly over the execution of wills and administration of estates. Under this monopoly, earlier practices which imposed restraints on the freedom of testation in favour of widows and children, seem to have faded away.[19] It does not, of course, follow that this conflict of interest between church and near relatives which arose on a man's death would undermine perception of the man's duty to his children during his lifetime. Yet it remains that the church courts notably failed to develop any means for implementing it.

The common law, too, failed to create any legal duty that parents support their children. That children had an interest to receive such support was obvious, but the law, both religious and secular, it seems, was content to rely on the natural moral sense of parents to fulfil it. As Blackstone remarks:

> this moral duty is laid on them by their own proper act, in bringing them into the world: for they would be in the highest manner injurious to their issue if they only gave their children life, that they might afterwards see them perish. By begetting them, therefore, they have entered into a voluntary obligation to endeavour, as far as this lies, that the life which they have bestowed shall be supported and preserved. And thus the children will have a perfect right of receiving maintenance from their parents.

Fortunately, Blackstone observes, providence has implanted in every parent that 'insuperable degree of affection which not even the deformity of person or mind, not even the wickedness, ingratitude or rebellion of children, can totally suppress or extinguish'.[20] Here there is certainly a recognition of an interest of a child, separate from those of its parents, for at least some degree of support. Blackstone even uses the word 'right'. But it seems that the perception of this interest was clouded with ambiguity. Observe, for example, Blackstone's comments on the fact that the law failed to enforce a parent's moral duty to educate his children. 'Perhaps', he writes, 'they thought it punishment enough to leave the parent who neglects the instruction of his family to labour under those griefs and inconveniences which his family, so uninstructed, will be sure to bring upon him.' The father's interest in educating his children is but an extension of his own

17 E. Gibbon, *The Decline and Fall of the Roman Empire* (1880) vol. ii, p 132.

18 Goody, op cit, n 11, p 100.

19 '. . . the canonist himself was not greatly interested in the maintenance of the old restraints. He could not regard them as outlines of the church's ius commune; at best, they could be but customs of English dioceses or provinces. His training in Roman law might indeed teach him that the claims of children should set limits to a father's testamentary power; but 'wife's part', 'bairn's part' and 'dead's part' cannot be found in the Institutes; besides, the church had legacies to gain by ignoring the old rules' (Pollock and Maitland, op cit, n 14, p 355).

20 Blackstone, op cit, n 7, 1.16.

self-interest. This projection might even be seen in his (moral) duty to support them. It was on this basis that the dissenting judge in *Barham* v *Dennis*[21] thought that the action for abduction should be extended beyond the protection of a father's pecuniary interest in the marriage of an heir. The father, said Glanville J 'has an interest in every one of his children, to educate them and to provide for them and he hath his comfort by them; wherefore it is not reasonable that any should take them from him, and to do him such an injury, but that he should have his remedy to punish it'. This view seems to have had Blackstone's support,[22] and was also championed by Holdsworth[23] and Pollock[24] who argued that it would have been better if the law had based its remedy against third parties who injure children not on the father's assumed loss of services, but on outrage or injury to the parent as head of the family. On this view, the sustaining of a child may indeed be thought of as a moral duty, but worth protecting only insofar as infractions on its performance may be thought to injure the present or long-term interests of the parent. We shall see that probably until at least the end of the nineteenth century, the protection given to a father's relationship of guardian to his children was almost certainly conceived of in this way.

INTERESTS AND RIGHTS

Joseph Raz has argued that 'a law creates a right if it is based on and expresses the view that someone has an interest which is sufficient ground for holding another to be subject to a duty'; and, again, that 'to be a rule conferring a right it has to be motivated by a belief in the fact that someone's (the rightholder's) interest should be protected by the imposition of duties on others'.[25]

The reference to the 'beliefs motivating' the rule-creators requires, in this context at any rate, a subtle examination of the public perception of the purpose of the law. Blackstone may indeed have appreciated the 'interests' of children in this context, but when we look at the private law, we see that it makes no direct attempt to protect them. Rather, it is the interest of the father to which the legal remedies are related. It is true that their enforcement may *incidentally* benefit the children, but that is not their aim and purpose. This distinction is even clearer when we look at public law. The first *legal* expression of a father's duty to support his children can be found in the poor laws of the sixteenth century. Here the law would step in and indirectly enforce the father's obligation to educate his children by putting them out to apprenticeship. But the purpose of this, as Blackstone remarked, was so that they might 'render their abilities in their several stations, of

21 (1600) Cro Eliz 770.

22 W. Blackstone, op cit, n 7, 3.8.3.

23 Op cit, n 13, vol. ii, p 428.

24 Pollock, *The Law of Torts* (1929), p 231.

25 J. Raz, 'Legal Rights' (1984) 4 *Oxford J Legal Stud* 1, 13–14.

the greatest advantage to the commonwealth'.[26] The circumstances in which apprenticeship was frequently undergone bore sufficient witness to that. As far as support is concerned, I have elsewhere[27] indicated the coincidence between the introduction of the legal enforcement of the parental support obligation and the growth of mass unemployment and labour mobility in the sixteenth century when the assumption that economic benefits would be distributed naturally throughout the family no longer held, bringing about the consequential threat to social stability. The imposition of a duty upon the father might appear to follow from a conceptualization of rights in the children that their interests should be safeguarded, but the reality was different. Once again, the enhancement of those interests was only incidental to the gains to others (reduced claims on the parish funds; social stability) of enforcing support.

We shall return to the question of support later. At this point one might summarize the position in Blackstone's day as being that the legal apparatus protected a father's relationship with his legitimate children not primarily because the children's interests were thought worth protecting in themselves but because it was in one way or another deemed beneficial to the father. Injuries to the children were injuries to the father; that their interests might conflict with his was perceived, but protection was given only where his failure to regard their interests sufficiently threatened other people. To this subsumption of children's interests to those of their father, there soon grew some exceptions. The criminal law had always protected children, at least in theory, against severely injurious or life-threatening acts perpetrated against them by their parents.[28] But this covered only a small segment of a child's exposure to danger. The early legislation controlling the employment of children in factories and mines was conspicuously motivated by a wish to protect the interests of children. These controls were not, however, conceived (as they might be today) as operating against the children's own claims to independence, but against the interests of their parents to profit from their labour as much as of the employers.

> They were going to interfere, not between the master manufacturers and the children, but between the master manufacturers and the parents of the children. The children in question were not of age, but were under the care of parents who, it was to be supposed, knew best their interests, and were the most feeling judges of the extent to which they should be worked. But they were overworked.[29]

The controls operated only with regard to the severest depredations of child labour. We can find a similar willingness to abrogate the parental interest emerging at the same time where a father was claiming possession of his child and

26 W. Blackstone, op cit, n 7, 1.16.1.

27 John Eekelaar and Mavis Maclean, *Maintenance after Divorce* (1986), ch 1.

28 See the newspaper reports of trials of parents held between 1785 and 1860 cited in Linda Pollock, op cit, n 1, pp 92–5.

29 Hansard, HC Deb., February 28, 1833, cols. 1294–5 (Mr Cobbett); in like fashion, see Hansard, HC Deb, June 1842, cols. 1353–4 (Mr Lambton).

the court considered that to hand the child over put him in bodily danger.[30] This was the origin of the 'welfare principle' of the Chancery courts. But it should be said that the way it was applied during the nineteenth century did not greatly differ from the approach which characterized other areas of law. Unless he seriously threatened the child's well-being, the father's rights were paramount. They were, however, subordinated to the perceived wider interests, not of the child, but of the community. Immorality, profligacy, impiety and radical social views, all of which might undermine the child's commitment to the dominant social values, were frequently the bases for denying custody to fathers (and sometimes to mothers).[31] The welfare of the child was thus routinely equated with the transmission of conventional social norms; and, of course, one of the most powerful of these norms was that the interests of parents (in practice, of fathers) should be enforced. So, in *Wellesley* v *Duke of Beaufort* (1827),[32] it was said to be in the *children's* interest that the 'filial affection and duty towards their father (should) operate to the utmost'. In *Symington* v *Symington* (1875)[33] Selborne LC declared that it was 'in the material and moral interest of the boys to leave them in the care of their natural and legal guardian'. In *re Agar-Ellis* (1883)[34] it was stated that 'when by birth a child is subject to a father, it is for the general interest of families, and for the general interest of children, and really for the interest of the particular infant, that the Court should not, except in very extreme cases, interfere with the discretion of the father but leave to him the responsibility of exercising that power which nature has given him by birth of the child'.

By the end of the nineteenth century, then, when a parent (usually the father) was seeking to use legal machinery to enforce his own interest in the possession of his child, the courts had articulated an interest which children might have which was distinct from that of the father, although the inclination was to see that interest as coincident with it. In life-threatening cases, it could be detached from the parental interest, and where the child was likely to receive from the parent habits or modes of thought which were deemed inimical to society as a whole, the parental interest might be overborne. On those occasions where the state actively intervened and removed children from parental control (or lack of it) into state institutions, the object was similarly to protect society from the threat they posed, whether they had offended or were merely neglected. The earliest measures for dealing with child neglect were activated by concerns about social cohesion rather than the implementation of the children's interests in their own right.[35] Yet, as the century drew to a close, we can detect the beginnings of a different appreciation of

30 *R.* v *De Manneville* (1804) 5 East 221.

31 See *R.* v *Dobbyn* (1818) 4 Ad & El 644n.; *ex P. Bailey* (1838) 6 Dowl 311; *Wellesley* v *Duke of Beaufort* (1827) 2 Russ 22; *Shelley* v *Westbrooke* (1817) Jac 266; *re Besant* (1879) 11 ChD 508.

32 See n 31.

33 (1875) L.R. 2 Sc & Div 415; see Maidment, *Child Custody and Divorce* (1984), p 95.

34 (1883) 4 ChD 317.

35 See J. M. Eekelaar, R. W. J. Dingwall and T. Murray, 'Victims or Threats? Children in Care Proceedings' (1982) *Journal of Social Welfare Law* 68.

children's interests. Maidment[36] has drawn attention to the formulation of the 'welfare' test in *re McGrath*[37] in which Lindley LJ said:

> The word 'welfare' must be taken in its widest sense. The moral and religious welfare of the child must be considered as well as its physical well-being, *nor can the ties of affection be disregarded.*

The reference to the child's affectional ties focuses upon an interest which pertains to the child and to no other. It might now become possible to disentangle perceptions of the child's interests from the promotion of other interests, to which the child's welfare may relate only incidentally. A few years earlier, the first Prevention of Cruelty to and Protection of Children Act 1889 created an offence if anyone over sixteen who had custody, control or charge of a boy under 14 or a girl under 16 wilfully ill-treated, neglected or abandoned the child in a manner likely to cause unnecessary suffering or injury to its health. It is not possible yet to say that the concern was solely with the children's interests, despite the language. The impetus for this legislation may have equally lain in the concerns for the moral health of the nation expressed in the Christian evangelical movement, or in more straightforward worries about secular order associated with the economic depression of the 1880s.[38] But the idea that children should not undergo 'unnecessary' suffering, wilfully inflicted, can again be seen as an important concentration of attention on the interests of the child alone, derivable from the humanitarian tradition of the reformers of the factory system.

We might usefully at this point reflect on how we might characterize the position thus reached in terms of children's rights. We may accept that the *social perception* that an individual or class of individuals has certain interests is a precondition to the conceptualization of rights. But these interests must be capable of isolation from the interests of others. I might believe that it is in my infant daughter's interests that I (and not she) take decisions concerning her medical welfare. This may even be supportable by objective evidence. But my interest, or right, to take such decisions is not identical with her interests. I might make stupid or even malicious decisions. Her interest is that I should make the best decisions for her. I am no more than the agent for fulfilling her interests. Hence we should be careful to understand that when we talk about rights as protecting interests, we conceive as interests only those benefits which the subject himself or herself might plausibly claim in themselves. This point is of great importance in the context of modern assertions of the right to parental autonomy. This has been advanced as a fuller enhancement of children's rights. Goldstein, Freud and Solnit[39] construct the concept of 'family integrity' which is a

36 Op cit, n 33, p 100.

37 [1893] 1 Ch 143 (italics supplied).

38 Nigel Parton, *The Politics of Child Abuse* (1985), p 32; R. Dingwall, J. M. Eekelaar and T. Murray, 'Childhood as a Social Problem: A Survey of the History of Legal Regulation' (1984) 11 *Jo. Law & Soc.* 207–32.

39 J. Goldstein, A. Freud and A. J. Solnit, *Before the Best Interests of the Child* (1979), p 9.

combination of 'the three liberty interests of direct concern to children, parental autonomy, the right to autonomous parents and privacy'. But can we say the children might plausibly claim any of these things in themselves? If they are claimed (which they may be) it will be because they are believed to advance other desirable ends (perhaps material and emotional stability) which are the true objects of the claims. Observe that the formulation refers to claims children might plausibly make. Not, be it noted, what they actually claim. We here meet the problem[40] that children often lack the information or ability to appreciate what will serve them best. It is necessary therefore to make some kind of imaginative leap and guess what a child might retrospectively have wanted once it reaches a position of maturity. In doing this, values of the adult world and of individual adults will inevitably enter. This is not to be deplored, but openly accepted. It encourages debate about these values. There are, however, some broad propositions which might reasonably be advanced as forming the foundation of any child's (retrospective) claims. General physical, emotional and intellectual care within the social capabilities of his or her immediate caregivers would seem a minimal expectation. We may call this the 'basic' interest. What a child should expect from the wider community must be stated more tentatively. I have elsewhere[41] suggested the formulation that, within certain overriding constraints created by the economic and social structure of society (whose extent must be open to debate), all children should have an equal opportunity to maximize the resources available to them during their childhood (including their own inherent abilities) so as to minimize the degree to which they enter adult life affected by avoidable prejudices incurred during childhood. In short, their capacities are to be developed to their best advantage. We may call this the 'developmental' interest. The concept requires some elaboration.

It seems plausible that a child may expect society at large, no less than his parents, to ensure that he is no worse off than most other children in his opportunities to realize his life-chances. Could a child also plausibly claim that he should be given a *better* chance than other children, for example, by exploitation of his superior talents or a favoured social position? As an expectation addressed to the child's parents, such a claim might have some weight. A child of rich parents might retrospectively feel aggrieved if those resources were not used to provide him with a better chance in life than other children. On the other hand, such an expectation is less plausibly addressed to society at large, except perhaps with respect to the cultivation of singular talents. But from the point of view of a theory of rights, it does not much matter whether we decide that a privileged child has an interest in inequality favourable to himself. For, if the interest is to become a

40 Discussed in M. D. A. Freeman, *The Rights and Wrongs of Children* (1983), ch 2; and see D. N. MacCormick, 'Children's Rights: A test case for theories of right'. *Archiv für Rechts und Sozialphilosophie*, vol. 62, p 305, (1976).

41 See John Eekelaar, 'Parents and Children—Rights, Responsibilities and Needs: An English Perspective' (1984) *Human Rights Annual*, vol. ii, 81–93.

right, it must be acknowledged in the public domain as demanding protection for its own sake. As far as the 'developmental' interest is concerned, therefore, societies may choose to actualize it in harmony with their overall social goals, which may (but not necessarily) involve creating equality of opportunity and reducing socially determined inequalities, but encouraging diversity of achievement related to individual talent.

There is a third type of interest which children may, retrospectively, claim. A child may argue for the freedom to choose his own lifestyle and to enter social relations according to his own inclinations uncontrolled by the authority of the adult world, whether parents or institutions. Claims of this kind have been put forward on behalf of children by Holt[42] and by Farson.[43] We may call them the 'autonomy' interest. Freeman[44] has argued that such interests might be abridged insofar as children also have a right to be protected against their own inclinations if their satisfaction would rob them of the opportunity 'to mature to a rationally autonomous adulthood . . . capable of deciding on [their] own system of ends as free and rational beings'. This may be no more than a version of the developmental interest defined earlier. The problem is that a child's autonomy interest may conflict with the developmental interest and even the basic interest. While it is possible that some adults retrospectively approve that they were, when children, allowed the exercise of their autonomy at the price of putting them at a disadvantage as against other children in realizing their life-chances in adulthood, it seems improbable that this would be a common view. We may therefore rank the autonomy interests subordinate to the basic and the developmental interests. However, where they may be exercised without threatening these two interests, the claim for their satisfaction must be high.

Let us now consider how far we can say, in the late twentieth century, that any of the interests outlined above have assumed the character of 'rights'.

THE BASIC INTERESTS

These interests are served insofar as a society promotes the more extensive developmental interests, a matter to be discussed later. However, there is one provision which seems to focus expressly on the basic interests, and to translate them into rights. Section 1 of the Children and Young Persons Act 1969 permits state intervention if a child's 'proper development is being *avoidably prevented or neglected* or his health is being *avoidably impaired or neglected* or he is being *ill-treated*' and he is 'in need of care and control which he is unlikely to receive unless the court makes an order'. The duty is to refrain from the actual prevention or neglect of proper development or natural health rather than the maximum promotion of these qualities, and thus the interest falls short of the wider

42 John Holt, *Escape from Childhood* (1975).

43 R. Farson, *Birthrights* (1978).

44 Op cit, n 40, p 57.

developmental interests. It is imposed primarily upon the child's parents, to whom the interests of the children in these matters are normally entrusted. But it extends also to the state, because local authorities are under a *duty* to inquire into information suggesting breaches of the duties, and to bring enforcement proceedings if they reasonably believe that grounds exist for making an order.[45] The term 'avoidably' allows for flexibility in application of the standard to take into account 'unavoidable' effects of social inequality: the statute does not confer rights to be free of deprivations suffered by parents which are reflected on the children. But it does, as applied in practice, seem to give children rights to be removed from the adverse consequences of care by parents who suffer social or personal inadequacy. The imposition of these duties is primarily perceived by the enforcement agencies as directed at advancing the interests of the rightholders, and represents a total reversal of earlier characterizations of the child-parent relationship.[46] This reflects not only the social recognition of the basic interests of the rightholders as ends in themselves, but also a societal decision of the priority to be applied where those interests conflict with the interests of others, in this case, the parents. Even if respect for these rights may be conceived by the parent to be contrary to the parent's own interests, those interests must give way to those of the child. The extent to which compromises are made in practice[47] is, of course, another question.

DEVELOPMENTAL INTERESTS AND *RICHARDS* v *RICHARDS*

When we turn to the developmental interests, there is more difficulty. The requirement to allocate resources so that an individual child does not suffer such deprivations during childhood that he is disadvantaged disproportionately, when compared to children generally, in the outset of his or her adult life, can for large part be met only by the community at large. The cost appears in such areas as children's medical services and education. The duties lie primarily in the political domain and therefore become enmeshed in still broader considerations of public policy.[48] Their legal articulation is at a very broad level of generality. The Secretary of State for Health and the Social Services is under a legal duty to promote a national health service designed to ensure 'the improvement . . . in the physical and mental health of the people' in England and Wales and to provide such facilities 'for the care of expectant and nursing mothers and young children as he considers appropriate as part of the health service'.[49] The Secretary of State

45 Children and Young Persons Act 1969, s 2.

46 See Dingwall, Eekelaar and Murray, op cit, n 6.

47 For a general discussion of the 'liberal compromise' in the enforcement of these rights, see Dingwall, Eekelaar and Murray, op cit, n 6, where it is argued that the ethos and structure of the relevant agencies are systematically biased against intervention.

48 The extent to which they may presently be satisfied may owe something to general articulation of children's claims to 'welfare rights': see Freeman, op cit, n 40, pp 40–3.

49 National Health Services Act, 1977, ss 1(1)(*a*) and 3(1)(*d*).

for Education is under a duty to 'promote the education of the people of England and Wales'.[50] Such duties may be satisfied by providing coverage for the basic interests, although in the case of education, the additional duties placed upon local authorities to provide special education for children with a learning difficulty[51] suggests the conception of a right held by such children which would be accurately described in the terms used for the developmental interest described here.

While children are resident with their parents, the law imposes no duty on the parents to fulfil the developmental interests, apart from ensuring their education.[52] This is the legacy of the vacuum left by the common law which has been referred to earlier. We can, perhaps, safely assume that while the family remains intact, family resources will be used as far as possible to satisfy them, and that compromises will be fairly arrived at. Or, if we are unhappy about making such an assumption, we may believe that legal intrusion over the disposition of the resources of the intact family is inappropriate, at least if the basic interests are not threatened. However we may justify it, the developmental interest for the vast majority of children is not protected as a right, but owes its satisfaction to the natural workings of the economies of families which are themselves dependent on the wider social and economic mechanisms of the community. Where, however, the family is split apart, the regulation of the distribution of resources between the families is thrown into the public domain. Failure to ensure some such distribution carries the risk of visible impoverishment of the mother and child, with attendant threats to social stability and community welfare funds.[53] The developmental interests of children are also threatened in these circumstances, so it is of interest to discover how far the legal regulation of income distribution after family separation can be characterized as the protection of that interest. The interests of parents are in strong contention here: their interests in releasing themselves from a disliked marriage and in entering a new one (with sufficient resources); their interests in using their resources, capital and income, as they think fit; their interests in freedom of movement; their interests in pursuing new relationships free from the influences of the past; their interests in salvaging a relationship with their children. It is important to realize that separation and divorce do give rise to serious conflicts between the interests of parents and children. Martin Richards[54] has suggested that failure to recognize such conflicts is the source of much of the guilt which surrounds divorce. But it is not enough simply to recognize the conflicts. They need resolution. The

50 Education Act 1944, s 1.

51 Education Act 1981.

52 Education Act 1944, s 36, extended to special education by the Education Act 1981, s 17.

53 *Supra*, n 27.

54 Martin Richards, 'Developmental Psychology and Family Law: A Discussion Paper', *Brit J Dev Psychology*. (In press).

children's interests cannot be characterized as rights if they are equated with, or subservient to, those of the adults. Nor can they be so treated if the resolution of such conflicts is abandoned to the uncontrolled discretion of adjudicators.

The principle that the child's welfare is the 'first and paramount' consideration when determining custody disputes was given statutory form for the first time in the Guardianship of Infants Act 1925. The earlier Act of 1886 had merely stated that the court should make 'such order as it may think fit . . . having regard to the welfare of the infant, and to the conduct of the parents, and to the wishes as well of the mother as of the father'. As Maidment has shown, the statutory enshrinement of the paramountcy of the child's welfare was a result not so much of a desire to elevate the children's interests above those of the parents, but to stave off feminist demands for equality of parental rights.[55] The Government argument was that, if it was indeed in the child's interests to be entrusted to the mother, this provision would protect her relationship. It was therefore unnecessary to meet the women's demands to be given equal parental rights during marriage and thus risk (so it was thought) undermining the family unit by subverting the father's status as its head. Yet as the century progressed, despite real problems in separating a child's interests from those of one or other of its parents, and even from the imagined interests of society in controlling the manner of reproduction and form of family life, it is probably true to say that the recognition of the paramountcy of the children's welfare has by and large enabled their interests to prevail over competing adult interests in the resolution of custody disputes.

As regards other questions which arise on divorce, the picture is not so clear. Indeed, the very question: to what is a child entitled when assets and incomes are distributed, has never even been openly posed. Our learning has been centred on grappling with the problem of what a former *spouse* should be allocated after divorce. The interests of children have been quite submerged in the course of this debate. However, the Matrimonial and Family Proceedings Act 1984 now requires courts, when dealing with financial provision after divorce, to give 'first consideration' to the welfare of children of the marriage who are under eighteen. The circumstances in which this provision was introduced bear an uncanny resemblance to those in which the paramountcy test was introduced in 1925; in this case, the purpose seems to have been to try to placate those women's groups who opposed other provisions in the enactment, in particular those which seemed to cut down a former wife's entitlement to maintenance. However, it is noticeable that the children's welfare is not stated as being 'paramount', so it is unclear whether they will prevail over adult interests in a conflict. Nor has any serious attempt been made to determine how children's interests in these situations may be assessed and evaluated. The degree of protection of the developmental interest in these circumstances remains obscure.

55 See Maidment, op cit, n 33, pp 131–40.

As regards occupancy of the home, the final arrangements will be made according to the principles of the 1984 Act. However, if a dispute arises before final decree (which is very likely), even if divorce is contemplated, the House of Lords held in *Richards* v *Richards*[56] that decisions on this issue must not be based on the paramountcy of the child's interests. The House found a technical reason for coming to this conclusion. Applications for ouster injunctions, which regulated the occupation of the home prior to divorce, had, for at least the previous twenty years, been made under what the matrimonial courts considered to be their inherent jurisdiction to protect the interests of parties to pending matrimonial litigation. In exercising this jurisdiction, the courts paid particular attention to the interests of children. But clashes between their interests and those of the expelled adult (if one was to be expelled) were seldom acute because in most cases the adult could be considered to have forfeited the right to protection of his interest on account of his (violent, or otherwise unreasonable) behaviour. But what if the children's interests conflict with those of a perfectly innocent adult, as in *Richards* v *Richards*, where, without offering any substantial justification, the wife withdrew the children from the home into a very inferior environment, and refused to take them back unless her husband was required to leave? The judge and the Court of Appeal, applying the jurisprudence of the inherent jurisdiction, held that the father's interests must give way to those of the children. The House of Lords, however, argued that that jurisdiction had been abolished by the Matrimonial Homes Act 1967, and that all such applications should have been, and in future must be, made under the rubric of that Act as consolidated in 1983, which directs courts to consider all the circumstances in coming to a decision, but notably fails to place the interests of the children in a superior position.

There is little doubt that this decision involved a misreading, whether intentional or otherwise, of the purposes for which the Matrimonial Homes Act of 1967 was enacted. There is no indication in that Act that it was intended to supplant the 'inherent' jurisdiction. In fact, its whole thrust was to deal with occupation rights between spouses outside the divorce context, by conferring such rights on entry into marriage.[57] Why, then, did the House of Lords re-write history and distort the flow of the development of the jurisprudence on matrimonial injunctions into the straight-jacket of the 1967 (now 1983) Act? The answer, it seems, lies in the political climate regarding the effects of divorce on the interests of divorced men at the time the case arose. In 1982, as a result of the activities of a pressure group for divorced men (the Campaign for Justice in Divorce), a Private Member's Bill had been introduced into Parliament aimed at

56 [1984] AC 174.

57 The legislation was prompted by the decision of the House of Lords in *National Provincial Bank* v *Ainsworth* [1965] AC 1175, where it was held that a deserted wife had no property interest *qua* wife in the house in which she was living. The Act therefore created 'rights of occupation', vesting in each spouse automatically upon entering marriage or acquiring a home, which bound third parties if registered.

removing what was seen to be the injustice caused to divorced men by the perpetuation of the marital maintenance obligation after divorce. The Bill failed on the dissolution of Parliament, but a similar Bill (which subsequently became the 1984 Act) was introduced as a Government measure in 1983. The Lord Chancellor, Lord Hailsham, who promoted it, had earlier acknowledged the pressure to which he had been subjected by the Campaign.[58] It was he who presided over the House in its judicial capacity in the *Richards* appeal in April 1983. The Court of Appeal's decision had been given on 6 December 1982 and the reaction of an editorial in *The Times* on 7 January 1983 summarizes the indignation that had been raised by this elevation of the interests of children over those of an adult (and the incidental advantage gained by the mother over the father).

> . . . there is the question whether the courts should not restrain their understandable inclination to further above all else the interests of the children (and thus of their mother) in situations of family breakdown. Should the children's needs be allowed to override all other considerations? . . . The requirements of justice to the family as a whole may not always coincide with what appear to be the children's immediate needs.

The final result of this litigation creates a severe anomaly in court practice in dealing with children's interests on divorce. When granting the divorce, and making arrangements for the family's post-divorce lives, the courts are now required, by the 1984 Act, to give 'first' consideration to the children's welfare. But in dealing with such questions at an earlier stage, there is no such principle and, furthermore, it would be wrong for a judge to purport to base his decision on any principle.[59] But it is not simply the deficiencies of the decision as a matter of legal doctrine which is of concern in this context. The decision, and the political context in which it was taken, illustrate the process that takes place when a new set of rights is struggling to emerge. The set-back to children's rights represented in *Richards* may be thought to be curious in the light of its apparent success in the 'first' consideration clause in the 1984 Act. In fact, it may be more significant as showing the fragility of the statutory principle when faced with strongly opposed adult interests. In the divorce context, contemporary society has still to determine the full extent of what the interests of children are and the degree to which, by restraining the fulfilment of conflicting interests of adults, the children's interests should be promoted to the status of rights.[60]

58 See 401 HL Deb, col 1459; 405 HL Deb, col 148.

59 It is arguable that the position reached is incompatible with the fundamental character of judicial decision-making which ought to be of a principled rather than *ad hoc* character: see Neil MacCormick, *Legal Reasoning and Legal Theory* (1978), ch 4.

60 For a normative theory as to how such rights might be determined, see John Eekelaar and Mavis Maclean, op cit, n 27.

THE AUTONOMY INTERESTS AND THE *GILLICK* CASE

The exercise of autonomy by children can conflict not only with the child's own basic or developmental interests, but also with the interests of the child's parents. In view of the history of legal intervention in family relations outlined earlier, we shall not be surprised to discover that early law curtailed children's autonomy where its exercise threatened the interests of the parent, or the family, rather than those of the child. An important example is the statute of 1557[61] entitled 'An Act for the Punishment of such as shall take away Maydens that be Inheritors, being within the age of sixteen years, or that marry them without the Consent of their Parents'. It was enacted that 'Where Maydens and Women, Children of Noblemen, Gentlemen and others, as well such as be Heirs Apparent to their Ancestors, as others, having left with them by their Father or other Ancestor or Friends, Lands, Tenures and Heriditaments, or other great Substances in Goods and Chattels moveable, for and to the Intent to advance them in Marriage . . . be oftentimes . . . by Flattery, trifling Gifts and fair Promises, of any unthrifty and light Personages . . . allured and won to contract Matrimony with the said unthrifty and light Personages . . .' such enticers would commit a criminal offence if the woman was under sixteen; her property would pass to her next-of-kin. This anticipation of the concerns which eventually led to the Marriage Act 1757 was patently directed at the interests of property holders over the devolution of their wealth. It was, however, used as the basis for the doctrine, later developed, that the courts would enforce a parent's right to possess his child by issue of the writ of habeas corpus if the child was under sixteen. It was said to represent the legislature's view of the age at which a child 'attained an age of sufficient discretion to enable it to exercise a wise choice of its interests'.[62] But the legislature of 1557 was not concerned with the child's interests. Nevertheless, this authority underlay the Court of Appeal's decision in the *Gillick* case[63] that a child under sixteen could give no valid consent to any act against it which would otherwise constitute an assault.

The issue in *Gillick* concerned the lawfulness of a notice issued by the Department of Health and Social Security to the effect that, while it was desirable to consult the parent of a person under sixteen who sought contraceptive counselling and treatment, the relationship between doctor and (child) patient was confidential, and the doctor retained the right to exercise his clinical judgment not to make such consultation when, in exceptional circumstances, he thought it against the child's interests to do so. Reversing the original decision, the Court of Appeal concluded that the notice was unlawful on the ground that a child under that age could not validly consent to such treatment without parental approval. Parker LJ drew the logical conclusion from the premise that such consents were a

61 4 & 5 P and M, c 8.
62 *R.* v *Howe* (1860) 3 El and El 332.
63 [1985] 2 WLR 413.

nullity: acts which apart from such consent would constitute assaults on the child would retain their tortious character. Although the decision applied to non-emergency medical procedures, its logic extends, and was seen to extend, to all touchings of children not otherwise authorized. Fox LJ, while accepting the premise, did not draw the conclusion expressly, but the logic remains. Eveleigh LJ avoided the question of the validity of the child's consent. He held the notice to be unlawful on the simpler ground that, at least in this case, it contravened a parental right pertaining to the upbringing of a child.

The public debate which accompanied the litigation tended to revolve around the competing claims of parents and doctors to determine children's interests. In this way it could be presented as an issue between the family and the state. Thus it was reported that, shortly after the first decision found in favour of the Department, over two hundred MPs petitioned Ministers to review the notice so as to require consultation with parents,[64] and when the Court of Appeal found in favour of the plaintiff, it was reported that 'A national campaign to protect the family from interference from officialdom' had been set up by the plaintiff and another mother.[65] This presentation forms part of a general phenomenon of the 1970s which manifested itself in generalized opposition to state intervention in family life. There were at least two strains to this movement. One was born from disillusion with the apparent failure of the rehabilitative and preventive policies of the 1960s. It was argued that too few resources had been directed to these goals and that interventionist policies represented bureaucratic control over the poor by an increasingly conservative state intent on removing the threats to the social order created by poverty without removing its causes.[66] The other follows the general move to the political right in extolling the advantages of the private over the public sphere.[67] The *Gillick* decision is certainly enmeshed within this debate.

Yet it is evident that if a child were to be disabled from entering legally effective relationships with another person without his parent's consent in each case, his social capability would be severely circumscribed. Furthermore, all dealings with the child would be fraught with danger. This has been long recognized by the law of contract. Lord Mansfield observed in 1765 that:

> Miserable must the condition of minors be; excluded from the society and commerce of the world; deprived of necessaries, education, employment and many advantages; if they could not do binding acts. Great inconvenience must arise to others if they were bound by no act.[68]

64 *The Times*, 11 November 1983.

65 *The Times*, 28 May 1985, under the headline 'Mothers fight for family life'. An important exception to this perception is to be found in *Childright* (a publication of the Children's Legal Centre), February 1985.

66 See Nigel Parton, *supra* n 38, especially ch 8.

67 See for example, Ferdinand Mount, *The Subversive Family* (1982).

68 *Zouch* v *Parsons* (1765) 3 Burr 1794.

The law therefore held a child bound by transactions entered into for his benefit and also for 'necessaries'. While this might be represented as yielding to the child's interests, the outcome is equally consistent with protecting the interests of the adult world. We are not concerned here with very young children, with whom transactions are unlikely to take place (unless cash is handed over simultaneously), but with children who are capable of acting independently of their parents to whom credit might be granted. To bind them for necessaries supports trading interests, a point well illustrated by the wide interpretation given to the concept of necessaries by nineteenth century juries (of tradespeople) in cases arising out of dealings with young people.[69] It is also significant that contracts of apprenticeship and employment were considered necessaries. This was an age when this type of employment was controlled as well by the criminal as the civil law, creating, in Kahn-Freund's analysis, a status akin to serfdom.[70] If a young person, still under the age of minority, is capable of consenting to these transactions, it must follow that his consent is effective to any invasions of his body which they may entail. *Doyle* v *White Stadium*[71] furnishes an excellent example. A minor was held bound by his contract as a professional boxer. There is no suggestion that the consent of his parents was given, or considered relevant. As Harland observes, he could surely not sue his opponents for battery.[72]

Contracts for the provision of medical treatment and education were also classed as necessaries.[73] It is hard to believe that touchings forming part of the treatment or instruction constitute assault in the absence of parental approval. Yet if a child is so young as not to understand the nature of the act (nor to enter any contractual relationship), how could physical treatment escape the taint of trespass? The solution has been to permit parents or guardians to supply the requisite consent, although, as has been pointed out,[74] it might be more logical to allow the treatment on the principle of necessity. This would be true with respect to unconscious persons or persons otherwise incapable of consenting. The argument nevertheless succeeded in *Gillick* in the Court of Appeal that a parent is in a special position with regard to his child so that not only does he have a right physically to possess the child, which will be enforced to the age of sixteen, but that right implies that the child is incapable of consenting to legal dealings, at least for the purposes of the law of torts, while under that age, unless supported by parental approval.

The conceptual flaw in this argument lies in its failure to distinguish between the role of parental consent when supplied to overcome the factual incapacity of a

69 See Hansard, vol 219, col. 1225 (1874).

70 *Supra*, n 9.

71 [1935] 1 KB 110.

72 David Harland, *The Law of Minors in relation to Contracts and Property* (1974), p 190.

73 *Dale* v *Copping* (1610) 1 Bulst 39; *Huggins* v *Wiseman* (1690) Carth 110; *Walter* v *Everard* [1891] 2 QB 369.

74 Winfield and Jolowicz on Tort (1984), p 708.

child to enter legal relations and the character of the power given to parents to determine matters relating to their children. The distinction is well understood in the law of marriage. The consent of a parent is a preliminary requirement to the marriage of a child aged over sixteen and under eighteen years.[75] But if the marriage takes place without this consent, it is nevertheless valid.[76] The breach of the parent's 'right' to prohibit the marriage does not negate the consent of the child; intercourse with the child after the marriage cannot be battery. In the same way, even if it were true that a doctor, or any other person wishing to have dealings with a minor needed to obtain the consent of the parent, if would not follow that failure to obtain it would negate the effectiveness of the child's consent to such transactions. Sir Frederick Pollock stated the position clearly in relation to the tort of seduction (now abolished):

> It is equally plain that on general principle a daughter or servant can herself have no civil remedy against the seducer, though the parent or master may; . . . She cannot complain of that which took place by her own consent. Any different rule would be an anomaly.[77]

The contrary conclusion, which the Court of Appeal reached, effectively annihilates any scope for the legal recognition of autonomy interests in children. It would have been extraordinary had such a conclusion been reached in the late twentieth century. The House of Lords however, reached a very different conclusion.[78] But it did so only by a majority of three to two. Of the nine judges who gave a decision in this litigation, five were in favour of the plaintiff. This perhaps illustrates the ambiguity in current perceptions of the proper scope of children's autonomy interests. But the majority decision of the House of Lords has implications which extend beyond the parent-child relationship and into the scope of state power over the lives of children themselves.

Both Lord Scarman and Lord Fraser adopted the major premise that once a child had attained sufficient understanding and maturity, he had full capacity to enter legal relationships without the consent of his parents. The consistency of this position with authority and principle has already been demonstrated. Lord Scarman then concluded that as soon as a child reached this position, any parental right within the relevant area, terminated. The parental right 'yielded' to the child's right. Lord Fraser, however, was less clear about this. In the medical context, he seemed to say that a doctor would only be 'justified' in treating a child without parental consent if this was in the child's best interests, and, as far as contraceptive treatment was concerned, this would normally entail involvement of the parents, although this could be avoided if the child refused to permit it, and the protection of (her) physical and mental health required such treatment despite

75 Marriage Act 1949, s 3.

76 Marriage Act 1949, s 48(1).

77 Pollock, *The Law of Torts* (1929), p 231.

78 See *Gillick* v *West Norfolk and Wisbech Area Health Authority* [1985] 3 WLR 830.

lack of parental knowledge and consent. This might mean that, in certain situations, the parental right survives the minor child's acquisition of capacity and, with judicial support, could prevent such a child from acting according to her wishes if her interests demanded such restriction. But an alternative interpretation of the speech is possible. This would permit anyone to deal lawfully with a minor child who had acquired capacity, and restrict the requirement to consult parents (outside exceptional situations) to a rule of good practice applicable only in medical matters and enforceable only through professional discipline. No help is obtained from Lord Bridge, who simply agreed with both Lord Scarman and Lord Fraser. Lord Templeman, who dissented on the issue as far as it related to *contraceptive* treatment, seemed to express a view close to that of Lord Scarman as far as other medical matters were concerned.[79]

The significance of Lord Scarman's opinion with respect to children's autonomy interests cannot be over-rated. It follows from his reasoning that, where a child has reached capacity, there is no room for a parent to impose a contrary view, *even if this is more in accord with the child's best interests.* For its legal superiority to the child's decision can rest only on its status as a parental right. But this is extinguished when the child reaches full capacity. More importantly, the argument catches the court itself. Should the child be warded, custody of the child vests in the court. The inherent jurisdiction of the High Court to intervene in the lives of children rests on the doctrine of the Crown's role as *parens patriae.* But on what principle can the Crown retain the parental jurisdiction when the parent himself has lost it, not through deprivation, but due to the superior right of the child? The primary question in wardship cases involving older children can no longer be: what is in the best interest of the child? It must be, has the child capacity to make his own decisions?

This recognition of the autonomy interests of children can be reconciled with their basic and developmental interests only through the empirical application of the concept of the acquisition of full capacity. This, as Lord Scarman made clear, may be no simple matter. The child must not only understand the nature of the transaction, but be able to evaluate its implications. Intellectual understanding must be supplemented by emotional maturity. It is easy to see how adults can conclude that a child's decision which seems, to the adult, to be contrary to his interests, is lacking in sufficient maturity. In this respect, the provision of the simple test of age to provide an upper limit to the scope of a supervisory, paternalistic power has advantages. We cannot know for certain whether, retrospectively, a person may not regret that some control was not exercised over his immature judgment by persons with greater experience. But could we not say that it is on balance better to subject all persons to this potential inhibition up to a defined age, in case the failure to exercise the restraint unduly prejudices a

79 Ibid at p 869: 'I accept also that a doctor may lawfully carry out some forms of treatment with the consent of an infant patient and against the opposition of a parent based on religious or other grounds. The effect of the consent of the infant depends on the nature of the treatment and the age and understanding of the infant'. In Lord Templeman's (minority) view the position was different regarding contraceptive treatment because sexual intercourse with a girl under sixteen is a criminal offence: Sexual Offences Act 1956, s. 6.

person's basic or developmental interests? It avoids judgments in which question of fact and value will be impenetrably mixed. But the decision, it seems, has been taken. Children will now have, in wider measure than ever before, that most dangerous but most precious of rights: the right to make their own mistakes.

[3]

RIGHTS FOR THE NEXT GENERATION: A FEMINIST APPROACH TO CHILDREN'S RIGHTS

MARTHA MINOW*

And though one says that one is part of everything,
There is a conflict, there is a resistance involved;
And being part is an exertion that declines:
One feels the life of that which gives life as it is.
—WALLACE STEVENS[1]

"Children's Rights" is a new, but recognizable topic. Law schools offer courses on the subject; casebooks and other publications herald its arrival.[2] Yet the topic presents conceptual, practical, and political difficulties. What exactly is a right that can be exercised by a five-year-old, or a two-year-old—and does it rest on different premises than rights for adults? How are rights for children to be enforced: do they require adult supervision, and if so, by which adults? Won't many adults politically oppose suggestions that children—perhaps their own children—should have legal liberties and powers that constrain the liberty and authority of adults?

Behind the answers to these questions—and behind the issue of children's rights generally—lie assumptions about the differences between children and adults. Although societies throughout time have drawn distinctions between children and adults, the specific line drawn has shifted; in our culture and legal system, there is no one line or single characteristic commonly understood

---

* Assistant Professor, Harvard University. The author thanks Bill Rubenstein, Kathleen Sullivan, and Sarah Walzer for their help, and Mary Joe Frug for her inspired and constant conversations. An earlier version of this Essay was a background paper for the Harvard Executive Sessions on The Future of Juvenile Justice at the John F. Kennedy School of Government.

[1] Wallace Stevens, *The Course of a Particular*, in THE HARVARD BOOK OF CONTEMPORARY AMERICAN POETRY 39 (H. Vendler ed. 1985).

[2] *See, e.g.*, R. MNOOKIN, CHILD, FAMILY, AND STATE: PROBLEMS AND MATERIALS ON CHILDREN AND THE LAW (1978); W. WADLINGTON, C. WHITEBREAD & S. DAVIS, CHILDREN IN THE LEGAL SYSTEM: CASES AND MATERIALS (1983).

to signify adulthood. Different demarcations result from focusing on age, behavior, biological development, indications of mental status, and relationships between the individual and other persons, not to mention any combination of such factors.

Critics and reformers concerned with children's legal status have drawn on these competing theories about childhood in both defending and challenging separate treatment for children. Yet no theory specifically resolves the practical—and political—issues about when to treat a given individual as a child or as an adult. Whatever a chosen theory may point to as the distinguishing characteristics of childhood, the choice to label an individual as a child or as an adult often entails sharp differences in the treatment that individual will receive. In a powerful sense, the debate over where to draw the line between childhood and adulthood represents a debate over the kind of relationship any given individual should have with the larger community.

The current pattern of drawing lines between childhood and adulthood in our society is marked by inconsistencies and contradictions. These inconsistencies, I will argue, arise not from anything intrinsic to children, but instead from legal conceptions affecting children—legal conceptions insensitive to the relationships children have and those they need. The inconsistencies cannot be rationalized by a notion of variable competence that would adjust legal status in light of a range of competencies demanded for contrasting situations. Variable competence is an idea toward which the varied legal treatment of children might aspire, but this Essay offers an explanation of why this aspiration has not been achieved, practically and theoretically. Nor can the inconsistencies be explained as expressions of an incomplete march toward children's independence, for competing legal trends invoke children's dependencies. I suggest that we need to develop a perspective on children's rights that refrains from comparing the abilities of children and adults and instead addresses their mutual needs and connections.

In Part I, I show how the current legal lines drawn between children and adults have little rationale and I offer explanations of why that is: first, because the lines we presently draw seldom focus on children at all; and second, because when we do focus on children, legal rules embody competing principles about how the state should treat them. I then turn to consider how this line-drawing task misses the challenge of children's rights. In Part II, I provide a more complex conceptual framework, one that goes beyond merely drawing lines according to competency notions. The starting point for this framework is a recognition of the relationships children have with parents and with the state—and the relations also arising between parents themselves and the state. Pursuing the preconditions for these relationships, the framework offers a basis for understanding what children's rights have meant and could entail.

This exploration offers special importance for those interested in women's rights. Children's rights owe some portion of their origins to struggles for women's rights, and the conceptual and practical problems raised by children's rights help to illuminate obstacles encountered by women's rights as well. In addition, the historic roles played by women as advocates for children's needs and interests closely link women's own political struggles with political reforms on behalf of children.[3] Finally, rights for children, as developed later in this Essay, epitomize feminist concerns about the importance of connection, care-taking, and social relationships; pursuing a theory of children's rights holds promise for a wider feminist approach to new forms that rights could take. By thinking through steps toward a jurisprudence of children's rights, this Essay seeks to clarify not only what rights could mean for a new generation, but also what a new generation of rights could mean.

I. CONTRADICTIONS IN THE LEGAL TREATMENT OF CHILDREN

How does our society draw the line between childhood and adulthood? An overview of the legal treatment of children reveals what seem to be patterns of inconsistency. In many places, an eighteen-year-old may consent to her own abortion without telling her parents, but the truancy laws and school regulations require that she obtain parental permission to miss school to see the doctor. A seventeen-year-old may be treated as an adult on

[3] *See* Minow, *"Forming Underneath Everything That Grows": Toward a New History of Family Law*, WIS. L. REV. (1986) (forthcoming).

charges of committing a violent crime; he may even be subject to the death penalty; but the same person could well be treated as a child for purposes of employment and other contractual relations, including marriage. A six-year-old may not consent to her own medical care, but she may be forced to testify in court against her parents. The law may compel the payment of child support for an individual past the age of eighteen who is still attending school, but allow nonpayment if school attendance ceases. What accounts for these varied legal treatments of young people?

A. Rational Line-Drawing Gone Awry?

An initial explanation of these seemingly inconsistent treatments could build on a notion of rational line-drawing based on assessments of varied kinds of competencies any given child may have. Thus, legal rules may treat children variously because lawmakers recognize that a child may have developed some, but not all, of the competencies society deems relevant to a range of tasks or responsibilities. From this vantage point, children need custody and care when they are incompetent, and rights and autonomy when they are competent. Variations in legal treatment could be justified on the basis that each individual progresses through stages of development. At any given time in a child's development, he or she may be competent for some purposes and incompetent for others.

However appealing this view may be as a normative theory,[4] it fails to describe the current legal universe. It seems bizarre to justify the variable treatment of young people currently manifested in the patchwork of legal regulations as though it expressed careful judgments about their competencies for various tasks and responsibilities. Why would an eighteen-year-old be competent to consent to her own abortion but not be entitled to miss school for her doctor's appointment without parental permission? Why would the seventeen-year-old be competent to be treated as an adult in criminal court but not competent to sign a contract at that age? A theory of variable competence may make theoretical

[4] *See* Gaylin, *Competence: No Longer All or None*, in WHO SPEAKS FOR THE CHILD: THE PROBLEMS OF PROXY CONSENT (W. Gaylin & R. Macklin eds. 1982).

or programmatic sense, but it does not supply the rationale for the particular choices the law has made up to this point.

Besides descriptive failure, this effort to understand the current legal universe in terms of rational line-drawing presents a theoretical defect: it pretends that competency is the only issue, and that there are knowable boundaries between competence and incompetence for any given societal task. Instead, it is more honest to disclose that competence and incompetence are used here as proxies for a variety of concerns about what societal decision-makers think children may need, and about what they simultaneously think allows adults to choose for themselves. Additionally, competence and incompetence are a crude set of proxy ideas. There are no uncontroversial principles to pinpoint the kinds of competencies crucial to accord an individual independent decision-making power and to relinquish paternalist control. Granting someone independence is a political or moral choice made by each society to fulfill its own purposes—not a rational decision gauged by psychological or other scientific measures. Moreover, competence to act with "independence" as a political or moral status is quite distinguishable from the psychological, physical, and social involvements that connect any individual to others. Legal rules that imply that only independent people may enjoy rights fictionalize the actual grant of rights to people who remain dependent in many ways.

From this perspective, the inconsistent legal treatment of children cannot be attributed solely to the general problem of drawing boundaries. Even though there seems no obvious line between childhood and adulthood, the many, and many inconsistent, lines drawn by this society to signify legal distinctions between children and adults invoke competing conceptions of the individual's relationship to the community and the state, not merely competing definitions of adulthood versus childhood. A more candid and comprehensive analysis, then, should turn to the conceptions of the child's relationship to the state—and to adults—that govern our legal system.

B. Children Neglected in the Public Sphere

Locating children within the larger legal system, I suggest, yields the conclusion that children simply are not the real focus of the varied laws that affect them. Instead, other powerful social goals are the focus of these laws. Traffic safety, control of violent crime, and regulation of abortion, for example, are social goals in which children may have incidental roles, and the laws affecting children in these areas actually play out political and practical debates which make children quite beside the point. Law reformers may in fact mix some concern for children with these other concerns. Yet it is noteworthy that laws against child labor, for example, did not pass legislatures until organized labor joined in their support—and realized that child labor laws could improve the ability of adult workers to command higher salaries by constricting the available labor pool. Children here were only one of many social concerns, and perhaps not even a central one. Because children are not the dominant focus of many legal reforms, it should not be surprising that laws treat them inconsistently.

Put somewhat more contentiously, let me suggest that the inconsistent legal treatment of children stems in some measure from societal neglect of children. The needs and interests of children, difficult enough to address when highlighted, are too often submerged below other societal interests. The dominance of these other interests helps to explain the inconsistent treatment of children.

It may seem odd to talk about societal neglect of children, given the occasional outpourings of rage over particular problems confronting them.[5] Yet here are some facts. Despite the wealth of this nation, twelve countries do better than we do in keeping their infants alive.[6] Over twenty percent of all children in this country live in families whose incomes fall below the poverty line.[7] The same point, put another way: nearly forty percent of people in poverty in this country are children.[8] Over one million children come to the attention of public authorities each year as victims of serious abuse by adults—and these are just the children

[5] *See, e.g.*, Recent Development, *The Insurance Crisis: Who's Looking After Day Care?*, 9 HARV. WOMEN'S L.J. 199 (1986) (discussing magnitude of response to child abuse in day-care centers).

[6] CHILDREN'S DEFENSE FUND, A CHILDREN'S DEFENSE BUDGET: AN ANALYSIS OF THE PRESIDENT'S FY 1986 BUDGET AND CHILDREN 4 (1985) [hereinafter cited as CHILDREN'S DEFENSE BUDGET].

[7] CHILDREN'S DEFENSE BUDGET, *supra* note 6, at 18.

[8] My calculations from CHILDREN'S DEFENSE BUDGET, *supra* note 6, at 33, make it approximately 37.8% (13.3 out of 35.2).

whose abuse becomes known by others.[9] Massachusetts spends about the same daily fee for a child in foster care as a kennel charges per day to house a dog.[10] Only thirty-five percent of all mothers raising children alone receive any child support from fathers.[11] Nearly one million children under age five have no adult supervision during the day.[12]

Adolescent suicide for children aged eighteen to nineteen increased from three out of one hundred thousand in 1950 to ten out of one hundred thousand in 1977.[13] The risks of injury and violence for fifteen- to twenty-four-year-olds has grown more serious in recent years. The issues for children in this country are especially severe for racial minorities: about fifteen percent of white children suffer some nutritional deficit—compared with about one-third of all Black children.[14]

Why might these problems facing so many children seem so unfamiliar in public debate? What set of beliefs could permit social conditions placing children at such risk while allowing legal rules that instrumentally use children to achieve other social goals? Here, the basic legal framework governing children deserves another look. That basic framework rests on a sharp distinction between public and private responsibilities for children. Using this public/private distinction, the framework assigns child-care responsibilities to parents, and thereby avoids public responsibility for children. Public power becomes relevant only in exceptional circumstances, when parents default. The government is not supposed to "intervene" in the private realm of the family, where children's needs and interests are managed by their parents.[15] At a societal level, the basic framework essentially

[9] BETTER HEALTH FOR CHILDREN: ACTION FOR THE EIGHTIES 76 (S. Buka, M. Peck & J. Gardner eds. 1982) (proceedings of a conference sponsored by the Student Comm. Dept. of Maternal and Child Health and Aging, Harvard School of Public Health, April 17, 1982) [hereinafter cited as BETTER HEALTH FOR CHILDREN]. The CHILDREN'S DEFENSE BUDGET, *supra* note 6, at 38, says 1.5 million.

[10] MASSACHUSETTS ADVOCACY CENTER, MASSACHUSETTS: THE STATE OF THE CHILD 82 (E. Vorenberg ed. 1982).

[11] S. LEVITAN & R. BELOWS, WHAT'S HAPPENING TO THE AMERICAN FAMILY? 73 (1981).

[12] U.S. COMMISSION ON CIVIL RIGHTS, DISADVANTAGED WOMEN & THEIR CHILDREN 13 (1983) (32,000 pre-schoolers caring for themselves, 2 million between ages of 7 and 13 unsupervised).

[13] BETTER HEALTH FOR CHILDREN, *supra* note 9, at 75.

[14] *Id.* at 76.

[15] From another vantage point, however, the state is always "intervening" in the sense

authorizes public neglect of children while assigning duties to parents entrusted with children's care.

Children's rights—in contrast simply to laws affecting children—represent a challenge to this basic framework of governance. The proponents of rights for children may seek to direct governmental attention to what children say they want for themselves, or to secure specific governmental rules restraining parents, teachers, and other authority figures from imposing their wills on children. These very different forms of governmental attention that reformers may seek suggest a new explanation for the pattern of inconsistent legal treatments of children. Indeed these inconsistencies could be understood in part as clashes between policies erected by Progressive Era reformers, and those created by more recent advocates for children's independence.

C. Children Spotlighted in the Public Sphere: A Short History of Children's Rights in America

Reformers advocating rights for children have cut against the basic legal framework that assigns responsibility for children to the private sphere. Yet sharp contrasts arise between claims of public protections—initiated by the Progressives—and claims of publicly conferred autonomy for children, advanced more recently. Both kinds of claims now compete for legal enforcement and complicate the meaning of children's rights.

1. Progressive Protections

The Progressive Era reforms implemented protective notions—compulsory schooling, child labor laws, and the juvenile court system—which furthered children's dependence on adults and legally removed children from the adult spheres of the market-

---

that its noninvolvement in family matters expresses its approval, or at least its lack of disapproval, of what goes on in the private realm. Further, public norms governing compulsory schooling, child employment, and indeed marriage, child support, and child abuse establish governmental rules about what children need and deserve. *See* Minow, *Beyond State Intervention in the Family: For Baby Jane Doe*, 18 MICH. J.L. REFORM 933, 951–53 (1985); Olsen, *The Myth of State Intervention in the Family*, 18 MICH. J.L. REFORM 835, 836–37, 855–58 (1985).

place and the civic community.[16] Progressive reformers offered a variety of reasons for these early efforts to concentrate public attention on children. Some expressed revulsion at the risks to children in industrial labor settings; others identified the economic and political needs of an industrial society for people with formal educations, and at minimum, literacy.[17] In effect, the reformers helped to invent adolescence—a new stage after infancy but before adulthood—and thereby prolonged childhood.

Contemporary commentators have observed how the child became the focus for humanitarian reforms that otherwise occupied the Progressives. Many women reformers—with Jane Addams, Lillian Wald, and Grace and Edith Abbott among the most famous—advocated humanitarian concerns and paternalist measures that became more politically palatable when focused on children. The child in this sense "united the campaigns for health, education, and a richer city environment; and he dominated much of the interest in labor legislation."[18] Similarly, the child served as a symbol of the human who could be redeemed or changed, and who then could help change society.[19]

Notions of the child as a creature different from adults occupied the inventors of the juvenile court as well, but the child's differences, according to those reformers, ranged from the child's innocence and impressionability to the child's dangerousness to society. Thus, alongside an environmental analysis that attributed children's crimes in the 1890's to their inhumane treatment by parents and society, arose a Freudian theory about the child who seethed with tensions and impulses, and lacked moral sensibility.[20] Environmental and psychological theories supported ex-

---

[16] Even these turn-of-the-century rules for children trace back to earlier innovations, according to historians who claim that childhood was created by late Medieval society, and adolescence by industrial society. *See* P. Aries, Centuries of Childhood: A Social History of Family Life (R. Baldick trans. 1962); J. Demos, A Little Commonwealth: Family Life in Plymouth Colony (1970); J. Kett, Rites of Passage: Adolescence in America—1790 to the Present (1977).

[17] *See* V. Zelizer, Pricing the Priceless Child: The Changing Social Value of Children 56–137 (1985) (attitudes about work and education figure in transformation of conceptions of child's worth).

[18] R. Wiebe, The Search for Order 169 (1967).

[19] *See* B. Wishy, The Child and the Republic (1968). *See also* Skolnick, *The Limits of Childhood: Conceptions of Child Development and Social Context*, 39 Law & Contemp. Prob. 38 (1975) (contrasting ideas of child as innocent and child as evil). *See generally* E. Ryerson, The Best-Laid Plans: America's Juvenile Court Experiment (1978) (rationales for juvenile court).

[20] *See* Skolnick, *supra* note 19.

cuses for a child's deviant conduct and promoted social service programs to assist both child and family. Such developments, along with the social rules excluding children from adult activities, made ambiguous what exactly children were to be held accountable for, and what enforceable duties children should have.

2. Independence Movement

The Progressive legal reforms offered a world of separate protections for children—and that very separation struck later observers as discriminatory and likely to expose children to adult indifference or abuse. Social critics starting in the mid-1950's attacked the creation of adolescence in particular for stigmatizing and excluding young people from adult worlds and responsibilities.[21] Thus, these recent reformers urged recognition of children's sameness or similarity to adults, rather than emphasizing children's differences. Like the civil rights movements extending rights to Blacks and women, children's rights advocates pushed to expand the definition of who is a self-determining person, who can make claims recognized by law, and who can assert entitlements to change how he or she otherwise would be treated. These movements of the mid-twentieth century proceeded on a conception of each individual's right to be treated the same as other individuals, and to be protected against unwarranted intrusions by the state.[22]

Notable decisions in the field of children's rights can be fitted within such a narrative. Perhaps the starting point for this story

---

[21] *See* R. FARSON, BIRTHRIGHTS (1974); E. FRIEDENBERG, THE DIGNITY OF YOUTH & OTHER ATAVISMS (1965); P. GOODMAN, GROWING UP ABSURD (1956). *See generally* B. GREENLEAF, CHILDREN THROUGH THE AGES: A HISTORY OF CHILDHOOD (1978) (summarizing research on history of childhood).

[22] One conception of the history of Western civilization locates these civil rights movements in the deeper context of the liberal tradition. Under this conception, liberal ideology challenged feudal hierarchies that established fixed patterns of social obligations and dependence and introduced notions of individual autonomy, freedom, and equality through the vehicle of individual rights. *See* Kennedy, *The Structure of Blackstone's Commentaries*, 28 BUFFALO L. REV. 209 (1979). The French and American Revolutions adopted such notions as their watchwords, but this historical narrative could locate the liberal transformation even earlier. *See* S. SEIDMAN, LIBERALISM & THE ORIGINS OF EUROPEAN SOCIAL THEORY (1983) (assessment of Enlightenment's consequences for liberalism).

is its convergence with the movement for racial justice: *Brown v. Board of Education*[23] accorded equal treatment to children regardless of race, and in so doing, granted children the status of rights-bearing individuals. Next, in 1967, came the landmark juvenile justice case, *In re Gault*,[24] which required that delinquency proceedings use certain procedural protections much as adult criminal courts do—notably, procedural rights to a hearing, cross-examination, and access to legal counsel. Beyond specifically requiring these procedures, the decision announced children's entitlement to be treated as rights-bearing persons rather than subjects of paternalism. Because an institution ostensibly devoted to children's best interests could hurt them, the Supreme Court concluded that children need and deserve the kinds of rights against the exercise of state power that adults enjoy.

Similarly, the Court's decisions in *Tinker v. Des Moines Independent Community School District*[25] and *Planned Parenthood of Central Missouri v. Danforth*[26] recognized rights for children that approximated the rights of adults. In *Tinker*, the Court declared unconstitutional a school rule that prevented children from expressing their political views at school by wearing black armbands. Although the Court ruled that students' free speech rights are limited—their exercise cannot disrupt the school's daily operations—the Court announced that children enjoy rights and do not lose them when they enter the schoolhouse gate. In *Danforth*, the Court rejected a statute requiring parental consent to a minor's abortion. The Court ruled that the minor has a right, just as an adult woman does, to determine in consultation with medical personnel whether to terminate her pregnancy, and this right permits autonomy from both state intervention and the intervention by other persons—including parents.[27]

---

[23] 347 U.S. 483 (1954).

[24] 387 U.S. 1 (1967). The reasoning in the decision has little to do with any assessment of juveniles' actual competence. Rather, it grew from a critique of the kind of institution that the juvenile court had become, an institution marked by abusive discretion. Justice Fortas concluded that "the condition of being a boy does not justify a kangaroo court." *Id.* at 28. *Gault* itself contains an undertow of commitment to children's custody and control by parents. *See infra* text accompanying note 41.

[25] 393 U.S. 503 (1969).

[26] 428 U.S. 52 (1976).

[27] This right may have some basis in an asserted competence of the child: the Court suggested that any girl old enough to get pregnant is old enough to decide whether or not to continue the pregnancy. *Id.* at 75. Yet the basis for the minor's right has as much to

3. Counter-Principles

These cases suggest a legal march away from the conception of the child as a dependent person, toward the view of the child's independent enjoyment of legal rights. Pushed as much by practical assessments of the abusive institutions and unrealistic hopes for parental authority as by theories of individual competency, advocates for these kinds of children's rights have transformed the legal landscape. Yet understanding this historical narrative as simply the march toward children's independence ignores some of the most recent legal developments that in fact curtail the rights of children and subordinate them to adults.

A Supreme Court decision in 1971, four years after *Gault*, denied children in juvenile court the same right to trial by jury assured to adults.[28] In 1984, the Court decided that a state can authorize detention for juveniles who pose a serious risk of committing a crime, because "juveniles, unlike adults, are always in some form of custody."[29] Accordingly, the Court reasoned that the state may subordinate whatever interests a child has in liberty to actions made in the name of the child's interests. Precisely opposite to the dominant reasoning in *Gault*, the Court revived a notion of custody, rather than liberty, as children's due and thereby legally enforced a difference between children and adults.

These are not simply two aberrant decisions. The Court has also ruled that unlike adults, children are not entitled to an adversarial hearing when they face commitment to an institution for the mentally ill.[30] Instead, the Court concluded that parents can be trusted to act in their child's interest when they seek such commitment decisions, and any doubt about this can be resolved by the admitting medical personnel, rather than by a legal proceeding.[31] The Court also countered an initial declaration of children's rights to hearings before facing school suspensions with a

do with a pragmatic view that the minor is in fact a separate person, and the state cannot expect to force the child's submission. The Court reasoned that "where the minor and the unconsenting parent are so fundamentally in conflict and the very existence of the pregnancy already has fractured the family structure," then the "veto power [would not] enhance parental authority or control." *Id.*

[28] McKeiver v. Pennsylvania, 403 U.S. 528 (1971).

[29] Schall v. Martin, 467 U.S. 253, 265 (1984).

[30] Parham v. J.R., 442 U.S. 584 (1979).

[31] *Id.* at 604.

subsequent ruling that children have no right to a prior hearing when threatened with corporal punishment in the school setting.[32] Again, pitted against the rights theory is a view of children's essential difference from adults. Their liberty interests are made subordinate to their dependence on adults.

These counter-principles of child dependency and custody animate legislative as well as judicial action. Several states have enacted laws requiring minors who seek abortions to notify their parents, and the Supreme Court has approved at least one of these statutes.[33] Although this is not a reversal of the *Danforth* decision, which struck down a consent requirement for minors seeking abortions, it is a resurgence at least in part of a legal use of children's custodial relationships with parents as a curb on children's independent rights. In another trend, many states recently have raised the legal age for drinking or driving, or both, to combat the high risks of drunk driving among teenagers.[34]

4. Competing Notions in Public Discourse

In each of these developments, state and parental interests in controlling and guiding children counter or constrict notions of individual rights for children. The legal treatment of children from this perspective expresses the results of a contest between two competing principles: the principle of individual rights, and the principle that the care and custody of children by adults serves the interests of both. This second principle—shared interests—indeed suggests that individual rights are not just unnecessary, but may actually damage the relationships between parent and child, teacher and child, and even judge and child, because children need authority, not rights. There is a real risk that this asserted identity of interests between children and adults will cancel out the intended effect of the public focus on children—and yet again subordinate children's interests to those of the adult society.

[32] *Compare* Goss v. Lopez, 419 U.S. 565 (1975) *with* Ingraham v. Wright, 430 U.S. 651 (1977).

[33] H.L. v. Matheson, 450 U.S. 398 (1981) (rejecting challenge by unemancipated minor to Utah statute requiring parental notification before the minor could obtain an abortion).

[34] *See Drinking Limit—State Impact*, U.S. NEWS & WORLD REP., July 9, 1984, at 14; *Ahead: Minimum Drinking Age of 21*, U.S. NEWS & WORLD REP., June 25, 1984, at 8.

Contributing to the confusion in public debate over children's rights is the availability of rights rhetoric to both those who would preserve the Progressive Era reforms and those who challenge them. "Rights" may be claimed to underscore children's similarity to adults—but rights may also be invoked to call attention to children's differences. The notion of "Children's Rights" could—and has—been seized by advocates of both separate, protective treatment and identical, equal treatment for children and adults. This confusion bears a striking parallel to the special versus equal treatment debate about women's legal rights.[35] For women, too, a legacy of legal protections—and restraints—encounters challenges in the names of rights and autonomy. Arguments about the enduring value of special protections, however, complicate the meaning and shape of rights sought by advocates for women.[36]

Like the contest between special and equal treatment claims for women, the contest between rights and custody as principles for children's legal treatment hints at a choice between seeing the child as basically the same as or basically different from adults. Moreover, the debate about children contrasts a view of the child as independent of adults with a view of the child as totally dependent. Both of these choices obscure the child's relationship with the state under either principle. These choices also ignore the real possibility that the same child may need custody and care for one purpose, and rights of autonomy or self-determination for another. The next Section seeks to create a framework large enough to expose the significant features of relationships embedded in contrasting notions of children's rights.

II. RIGHTS IN RELATIONSHIPS

Part I suggested that underlying some of the inconsistencies and confusion about legal treatment of children is the significance, too often ignored, of children's relationships with adults and with

[35] *See* Foster & Freed, *A Bill of Rights for Children*, 6 FAM. L.Q. 343, 343 (1972) (arguments for children's rights resemble arguments over slavery and over women's emancipation).

[36] *See* Williams, *Equality's Riddle: Pregnancy and the Equal Treatment/Special Treatment Debate*, 13 N.Y.U. REV. L. & SOC. CHANGE 325 (1984–85).

the state. In this Section, I will suggest that accounting for these relationships among child, parent, and state not only challenges simplistic conceptions of rights, but also offers an avenue for developing richer notions of rights. I first look at how integrating children's relationships into a theory of children's rights draws support from a particular understanding of adult's rights; then I will view children's rights through the relational frame. I offer one instance—through the example of juvenile court history—of what an application of this relational conception of rights would look like, given existing institutional arrangements. My analysis is informed by three feminist concerns: appreciation of relationships, a commitment to a vision of the self forged in connection with—not just through separation from—others, and a preference for glimpses of complexity, contextual detail, and continuing conversation.[37]

A. The Concept of Rights as Problematic

The rhetoric of rights dominant in legal discourse poses a choice between persons under the law being treated either as separate, autonomous, and responsible individuals entitled to exercise rights and obliged to bear liabilities for their actions, or else as dependent, incompetent, and irresponsible individuals denied rights, removed from liabilities, and subjected to the care and protection of a guardian—or the state. In a sense, these two tracks of legal treatment for persons could themselves be located in different historical points of origin.[38] The modern, post-feudal

[37] For illuminating discussions of emerging feminist concerns and methodologies, see C. GILLIGAN, IN A DIFFERENT VOICE: PSYCHOLOGICAL THEORY IN WOMEN'S DEVELOPMENT (1981); N. NODDINGS, CARING: A FEMININE APPROACH TO ETHICS & MORAL EDUCATION (1984); M. Frug, *Re-reading Contracts: A Feminist Analysis of a Contracts Casebook*, 34 AM. U.L. REV. 1065 (1986); Scales, *The Emergence of Feminist Jurisprudence: An Essay*, YALE L.J. (1986) (forthcoming); *The 1984 James McCormick Mitchell Lecture: Feminist Discourse, Moral Values and the Law—A Conversation*, 34 BUFFALO L. REV. 11 (1985); Schneider, Rights and Politics, (unpublished manuscript) (on file at HARV. WOMEN'S L.J.).

[38] Though my rendition is in no way a comprehensive account of these sources, my thinking about this history has been influenced by, among others, M. GILMORE, *Individualism in Renaissance Historians*, in HUMANISTS AND JURISTS: SIX STUDIES IN THE RENAISSANCE 38 (1963); M. GLENDON, THE NEW FAMILY AND THE NEW PROPERTY (1981); P. LASLETT, THE WORLD WE HAVE LOST (3d ed. 1984); S. SEIDMAN, *supra* note 22; W. ULLMANN, THE INDIVIDUAL AND SOCIETY IN THE MIDDLE AGES (1966); R.

state challenged traditional notions of a social organism that submerged each individual in the community and required obedience by each individual to the authority of the religious and political authorities. The modern state, at least according to some accounts, introduced ideas of the consent of the governed, and therefore, the autonomy of individuals to grant or withhold consent. This new set of ideas thus created an opening wedge for what has become the dominant set of conceptions about the relationship between the individual and the society: notions according rights to autonomous individuals against a state and notions imposing responsibilities on individuals for their willed actions. As applied to children, this simplistic view of rights would envision a program of drawing an exact line between incompetence and competence, childhood and adulthood.

These ideas co-exist, however, with earlier and persistent uses of law to facilitate interpersonal relationships. Feudal relationships themselves embodied a contractual dimension, a notion of chosen affiliation, permitted and enforced by law. Liberal freedoms in some measure retained the purpose of enabling affiliations between people. Freedom of association, freedom of religion, rights to marry, rights to procreate, and rights to preserve contact with family members are all current versions of this kind of rights conception—one at odds with the claim that rights protect autonomy rather than human relationships or connections.

Of course, for some individuals and some circumstances, the earlier feudal notions of status-based relationships and mutual obligation endured. Especially for people who continued to occupy special statuses even under the liberal order—persons like children, women, and the mentally incompetent—the dependency track of legal treatment remained in force. It is possible to see these people in special statuses as solely the exceptions to the liberal legal order. Yet it is also possible to see them as people for whom legal rules foster relationships: relationships of care, protection, and perhaps, at times, chosen affiliation. The tensions between rights to autonomy and rights to connection may seem

UNGER, KNOWLEDGE AND POLITICS (1975); R. UNGER, LAW IN MODERN SOCIETY: TOWARD A CRITICISM OF SOCIAL THEORY (1976); Kennedy, *supra* note 22; Strayer & Coulborn, *The Idea of Feudalism*, in FEUDALISM IN HISTORY 3 (R. Coulborn ed. 1956).

most vivid and poignant with people like children, but these tensions arise for adults as well.[39]

Such tensions are evident in issues concerning women in the workplace. Should a woman be free to choose whether to work in a workplace hazardous to any child she might conceive and bear? Should a woman's pregnancy entitle her to special work-leave benefits unavailable to a man—or should a workplace designed without pregnancy in mind disadvantage her when she chooses to bear a child? A woman's relationships, or potential relationships, with her children challenge the premise that she is a separate, autonomous person; and yet treating her as connected to others could disadvantage her in the workplace or seem to justify restrictions on her own choices. Is the woman to be treated "the same" as a male employee—with no attention to her private relationships? Or is the woman entitled to special treatment—potentially curbing her choices and her success in a work world that uses the autonomous person as the model?

Behind these doctrinal issues are deeper ones: Who is responsible to care for this woman in the workplace—to restructure the workplace if necessary to alleviate the tensions between her connections to her family and her own individual chances for success and self-determination? What collection of rights can be designed to permit her exercise of choices in favor of connections to her family as well as choices advancing her job success? It may be that the adult woman's interest in relationships arises most vividly when pertaining to children, yet relationships between adults pose similar complications for rights premised on autonomy.

These questions challenge a conception of rights that fits people into a slot labelled, "the individual," on a game board with the state as the only other player. These questions also implicitly reject the view that rights necessarily run only between an individual and the state, and that rights only mark and preserve distances between people. Instead, rights could be part of legal arrangements that permit, not to mention promote, relationships for adults—while also combatting hierarchy and fixed assign-

[39] This may be why the legal framework often seems inadequate for dealing with questions of inclusion and exclusion in group membership. The problem of inclusion and exclusion has come before the Supreme Court recently, *see* Roberts v. U.S. Jaycees, 468 U.S. 609 (1984), but it has not reached a stable resolution.

ments of status. This conception remains problematic given a regime of rights that emphasizes individual autonomy to the exclusion of duty and interpersonal connection. These problems with traditional rights for adults mirror, but also compound, the difficulties in devising rights for children that can promote relationships while protecting autonomy.

B. Conceptions of Children's Rights

To the extent that the dominant conception of rights presumes both autonomy and a direct relationship between the individual and the state, rights for children are even more problematic than rights for adults. Conceptually and practically, children in our society are not autonomous persons but instead dependents who are linked legally and daily to adults entrusted with their care.[40] Children are doubly dependent. Their dependency is constructed by legal rules and also is in their lives as lived. This double dependency situates children outside the sphere of rights-bearing persons in a system that makes independence a premise for the grant of rights. Children's dependencies specifically situate them within the sphere of the private family, where parents stand between children and the state.

Yet a choice between rights of self-determination on the one hand, and custody on the other, is too simplistic to capture the relationships among children, parents, and the state as embodied in legal rules and rights. Given the critical role of relationships with adults in children's lives, rights for children could take several forms. First, children's rights could represent efforts by the state to protect children from the neglect or abuse by the adults entrusted with their care. Perhaps better named "child protections," such rights appear in state statutes defining child abuse and authorizing state proceedings to evaluate, help, or punish parents on this basis. Child protective rights also arise in rules restricting child labor, and even rules restricting drinking and driving by children. Such rules cut in the opposite direction of adult rights that enable individuals to exercise autonomous

[40] For a thoughtful sketch of this problem, see Rodham, *Children Under the Law*, 43 Harv. Educ. Rev. 487 (1973).

choices. Yet the rhetoric of rights can, and has, been applied to child protection: these instances of state action penetrate the traditionally private sphere of the family and construct a direct relationship between child and state. The state thereby has obligations that can be invoked by or in the name of the child.

Alternatively, rights for children could protect children from state power but do so in a way that reinforces the privacy of the family, and indeed, the authority of the parents. A hint of this possibility appears in *Gault*, where the Court articulated the child's right to consult legal counsel in the context of juvenile court proceedings as a right of the child and parents, together.[41] The conception of the child's right here joins the child with the parent rather than either stationing the state with the child against the parent or offering the child state assistance to pole-vault over parental authority.

A more direct example of this form of children's rights appears in *Wisconsin v. Yoder*,[42] where the Supreme Court allowed Amish children to avoid the compulsory schooling requirement due to its asserted infringements on their religious beliefs and way of life. There, too, the Court's grant of protection to children from a state requirement strengthened parental authority, for it was parents who asserted the children's claims. Indeed, it was parents who faced sanctions for failing to assure their children's attendance at the public high school. This form of legal rule could be called "family protection," but family protection itself is a particular conception of the best way to advance the rights of children.[43]

Justice Douglas's dissenting opinion in *Yoder* formulated a contrasting, third form of children's rights by arguing that the chil-

---

[41] 387 U.S. 1, 41 ("the child and his parents must be notified of the child's right to be represented by counsel retained by them, or if they are unable to afford counsel, that counsel will be appointed to represent the child."). The *Gault* Court also rejected the claim that neither the juvenile nor his parents should be advised of the juvenile's right to remain silent. *Id.* at 51. Here, though, the Court acknowledged potential conflicts between parents who might urge confession, and children who might react with hostility if punished after confessing. *Id.* at 52.

[42] 406 U.S. 205 (1972).

[43] Another example of this form of children's rights is the standard law of child support that entrusts a custodial parent or guardian with the power to assert the child's right to support, whether or not such assertion is what the child wants, or is even fully in the child's interest. *See* Sugarmen, Roe v. Norton: *Coerced Maternal Cooperation*, in IN THE INTERESTS OF CHILDREN: ADVOCACY, LAW REFORM, AND PUBLIC POLICY 366–447 (R. Mnookin ed. 1985) (examining litigation challenge to such a rule).

dren themselves should be allowed to voice their views about attending the public high schools.[44] In this form, children's rights involve the state in suspending its usual reinforcement of parental power. Indeed, this form of children's rights involves the state in lifting children from their usual dependence on and subjection to parental authority. Thus, under *Danforth*, the state gives minors the right to consent to their own abortions and thereby rejects parental demands to have their power reinforced by the state. The grant of the right also draws the state into authorizing doctors and other medical personnel to enter into treatment directly with the minor, without the parental consent customarily required. Further, the state's curtailment of paternalism entails a self-restraint: the state empowers adolescents to consent to their own abortions even where that decision departs from a judge's assessment of the minor's best interests.

These possible permutations of children's rights offer some analytic clarity. They may also shed light on why the same "Children's Rights" banner can be raised by sharp opponents over the role of the child's own voice, the parents' authority, and the responsibilities of the state. Consider, for example, a case where parents oppose medical treatment for their child. A state agency may bring suit to order such treatment over the parents' objections, and do so in the name of the child's rights. Yet a lawyer for the child, perhaps hired by the parents, may assert that the child has a right to determine whether she, herself, wants the medical treatment.[45] All sides have a fair claim to the assertion of "rights" for the child, because rights represent the coinage of opposition to two kinds of power: the power of the parents and the power of the state. Freedom from parental power could be achieved in some measure if the state asserted power over the child, but a very different sort of freedom would arise if the state accorded the child freedom to choose for herself. Even this latter form of freedom requires state involvement and state enforcement; and freedom for the child's own choice-making may be unimaginable or impossible in many situations facing children. Still, the double layers of parental and state control supply the

[44] 406 U.S. 205, 241 (1972) (Douglas, J., dissenting).
[45] *See* In re Green, 448 Pa. 338, 292 A.2d 387 (1972).

bases for rights arguments on behalf of children that point in opposite, or contrasting directions.

C. The Dilemma for Juvenile Court

The juvenile court offers a vivid instance of the problems presented by these complex notions of rights for children. Not until 1899 did this country offer any special legal institution for adjudicating criminal charges against children; by the 1960's, however, the sprawling courts, social service agencies, and corrections facilities comprising the juvenile justice treatment institutions came under attack for unfairness and for exposing the minors under their supervision to abuse. The history of the rise and fall of the juvenile court could be understood as an experiment in restricting the liberal rights tradition and reviving the dependency and care track for juveniles. In this light, it was an experiment tried and rejected.

The initial effort called for carving out legal territory to remove juveniles from the realm of rights and responsibilities. The explicit rationale for this experiment drew from claims of children's incompetence and actual dependency, as well as from optimistic predictions about their ability to learn and grow into responsible, autonomous persons if helped toward that end. Creating a set of institutions that looked to the juvenile's needs entailed denying juveniles rights accorded to those already autonomous and responsible. Instead, the juvenile would enter into a dependency relationship with the state, much like the feudal orders of guardian and ward, and other hierarchical relationships.

Absent the disciplining focus of individual rights rhetoric and procedures to enforce it, the needs of society and bureaucracy rather than the needs or obligations of the individual took precedence. Without ascertainable rights to autonomy and liberty—not to mention rights to counsel, rights against self-incrimination, and other protections accorded *adult* criminal defendants—minors in juvenile court risked long detentions in hostile or abusive institutions.[46] The disillusionment with such results invited an

[46] *See* K. WOODEN, WEEPING IN THE PLAYTIME OF OTHERS (1976). The Supreme Court

obvious cure, the same cure developed for the defects of feudalism more generally: liberal rights to autonomy. Thus, *Gault* and subsequent developments prescribed rights for juveniles, in part to constrain the power of the state, and in part to fulfill the very educational function animating the initial juvenile court experiment. This time, juveniles were to learn the norms of a liberal order that metes out justice through the interplay of rights and restraints on governmental power. As a result, the differences in treatment of children have diminished somewhat in the criminal justice context.[47] Juveniles may now be tried in adult courts under some circumstances, and may receive adult punishments for crimes committed as juveniles.[48]

There is, however, a serious shortcoming in this rendition of the juvenile court as a failed attempt to revive the dependency and care track for juveniles. This analysis obscures the degree to which the juvenile court experiment borrowed only some features of the rights to care, connection, and indeed custody. The juvenile court does recognize some of these rights: it originally offered rights in the form of child protection against parents, in situations such as charges of abuse; it currently offers some forms of family protection against state power; and at times it affords juveniles power to assert their own wishes. Nevertheless, the court has not taken as its task the articulation or promotion of rights of care and connection or rights to affiliative relationships—or the preconditions for such relationships.

This omission would have been cured in part had the juvenile court spelled out not just rights, but duties—including both the duties of adults upon whom the juvenile is dependent, and duties of the juvenile to those entrusted with his or her care, as well as to the state and the larger community.[49] The notion of duty begins

---

in *Gault* reviewed the original justifications for, and ensuing disillusionments with, the juvenile court. 387 U.S. 1, 14–31.

[47] Many differences remain to distinguish the juvenile justice process from criminal law for adults. Fourth amendment protections, for example, have not been granted to minors in the same form or degree as those accorded to adults. *See* New Jersey v. T.L.O., 105 S. Ct. 733 (1985).

[48] *See Killing Young Killers*, N.Y. Times, Jan. 9, 1986, at A22, col. 1; *South Carolina Executes Killer: Age Stirs Protest*, N.Y. Times, Jan. 11, 1986, § 1, at 6, col. 1 (South Carolina case imposing capital punishment for crimes committed while defendant was a juvenile).

[49] To some extent, the general substantive law defining offenses for which a juvenile

to introduce a bilateral dimension to rights that gives them content. Under this approach, difficulties in articulating the duties of parents, children, and state officials would certainly arise, but at least the task of formulating these duties would direct people's attention to aspects of rights committed to facilitating interpersonal connections. In this sense, rights would represent not only a social commitment to preserve individual freedom from the injuries and intrusions of others, but also individual freedom to form relationships with others.

This rhetoric of duty is only a first step, though. The critical need for the juvenile court, and other institutions addressing children's rights, is to focus on the preconditions for relationships. Treating children as though they already had working relationships with parents or other adults, and as though enforcing rights and duties alone would fix the problems brought to the court, could miss what those problems are truly about. What legal rules governing child custody, education, and child support would promote settings where children thrive? Similarly, what rules would promote adults' abilities to create these settings? To pose such questions and provide working answers to them, the juvenile court should be authorized to commandeer resources such as public support benefits, homemaker assistance, day-care volunteers, and job-training for both youths and their care-takers. Although it would be difficult theoretically, practically, and politically to empower the juvenile court to promote the preconditions for relationships in these ways, I suggest that pursuing this line of inquiry holds promise of breaking out of patterns of disillusionment. Reforms in the past at first treated children differently from adults, then treated them like adults, and in each instance, built bureaucratic institutions and a public sense of futility. The goal for the future is to devise reforms that help people help themselves—reforms that acknowledge the public as well as private influences on and preconditions for human relationships.

could be punished defines such duties, but its terms are too general and courts usually lack the ability to make real for the adolescent the mutual social pact. That pact maintains that if the individual obeys the law, the individual will be accepted by the society, yet no such acceptance has been guaranteed for poor, minority youth.

III. A NEW GENERATION OF RIGHTS AND A CONCLUDING HOPE FOR CHILDREN

Children lack the autonomy presumed under one version of what rights mean. But so do adults. Children need environments where they can learn what is just, learn what it means to have their needs met, and learn what it means to have and fulfill obligations and to meet the needs of others. Adults need this too—from other adults, and from children as well. Debating whether children should be treated like adults for one purpose but not for another misses these points. So does debating whether children are entitled to liberty or custody, although both of these norms contain hints of an important line of inquiry. That inquiry addresses the interrelationships and tensions between rights for children that constrain abuses of power by their parents and by the state, and rights for children that promote their abilities to form relationships of trust, meaning, and affection with people in their daily lives and their broader communities.[50]

My hope is that efforts to bring the talk about children's rights in greater accord with the facts of children's double dependency on parents and on the state could begin to build a jurisprudence of children's rights of some use in current debate. Further, I believe that there remains a role for an institution, perhaps still called a juvenile court, that engages in efforts to educate parents, children, and the broader community about their interdependent needs, duties, and yes, rights. Someday, such a court could serve as a mender of a social fabric in which it is safe for children and adults to craft trusting relationships. Meanwhile, a richer debate over the rights for children—a debate joining goals of autonomy and goals of affiliation—would challenge social patterns that permit public neglect, assign private responsibility for children, and also perpetuate public failures to develop the preconditions for that private responsibility. Through that debate, people may exert pressure for autonomy—but the debate may also demonstrate how public and private realms, and indeed, children and adults, are potentially part of one another.

---

[50] *See* Schneider, *supra* note 37 (describing dialectical development of women's rights through theory and practice and through communal activity).

[4]

CHAPTER ONE — CHILD, PARENT AND STATE

Children's Rights: A Framework for Analysis*

Michael S. Wald**

The Article identifies four different types of claims being made under the rubric of "children's rights" and explores the questions that need to be answered in deciding whether to expand the "rights" of children in each area. Some of the claims involve providing children with more protection, others involve giving them more autonomy. These claims may be inconsistent or conflicting. The author argues that a separate framework is needed in analyzing each category of rights.

The question of what rights should be given children is now being debated in courts, legislatures and scholarly and popular journals.[1] Increased societal concern over individual rights, the

---

* This research was supported, in part, by funds from the Boys Town Center on Youth Development at Stanford.

I wish to thank Cheryl French, Tom Grey, Charles Halpern, Susan Halpern, John Kaplan and Catherine Lewis for their helpful comments on earlier drafts.

** A.B. 1963, Cornell University; M.A., LL.B., 1967, Yale University. Professor of Law, Stanford University; Member Boys Town Center on Youth Development at Stanford.

[1] Among the most important court cases are In re Gault, 387 U.S. 1 (1967) (juvenile court procedures); Ginsberg v. New York, 390 U.S. 629 (1968) (first amendment); Tinker v. Des Moines School Dist., 393 U.S. 503 (1969) (first amendment); Goss v. Lopez, 419 U.S. 565 (1975) (school expulsion); Erznoznik v. City of Jacksonville; 422 U.S. 205 (1975) (first amendment); Bellotti v. Baird, 428 U.S. 152 (1976) (abortion); Carey v. Population Services, Int'l, 428 U.S. 132 (1976) (access to contraceptives); Ingraham v. Wright, 430 U.S. 651 (1977) (corporal punishment); In Re Roger S., 19 Cal. 3d 921, 569 P.2d 1286, 141 Cal. Rptr. 298 (1977) (civil commitment). The literature is becoming quite extensive. Among the most influential works are R. Farson, Birthrights (1974); H. Foster, A Bill of Rights For Children (1974); J. Holt, Escape From Childhood (1974); IJA-ABA Juvenile Justice Standards Project, Standards Relating to Rights of Minors (Tent. Draft 1977); Geiser, *The Rights of Children*, 28 Hast. L. J. 1027 (1977); Goldstein, *Medical Care for the Child at Risk: On State Supervision of Parental Autonomy*, 86 Yale L. J. 645 (1977); Hafen, *Children's*

recognition of child abuse as a major problem, the loss of faith by many in juvenile courts, schools and other institutions dealing with children, and the changing structure and role of families have all played a part in the emergence of a movement to give children more "rights."[2]

The idea of children having rights is, in many ways, a revolutionary one. Historically, children have been under the control of their parents, and to a lesser degree, the state.[3] Presumed by law to lack the capacity of adults, children are denied full participation in the political, legal and social processes.[4] In lieu of most rights, the state affords children special protection.[5]

Today, however, many people consider this control, and the special protection that accompanies it, to be harmful, even op-

---

Liberation and The New Equalitarianism: Some Reservations About Abandoning Youth to Their Rights, 1976 B.Y.U.L. REV. 605; *The Rights of Children,* Special Issue (p 131-2), 43 HARV. EDUC. REV. 481, 44 HARV. EDUC. REV. 1 (1973-74).

The issue has received a good deal of press as well. *See, e.g., Children's Rights: The Latest Crusade,* TIME, Dec. 25, 1972, at 41; *Drive For Rights of Children,* U.S. News & World Rep., Aug. 5, 1974, at 42.

[2] *See* Margolin, *Salvation v. Liberation: The Movement For Children's Rights In A Historical Contest,* 25 SOC. PROB. 441 (1978), for a discussion of the forces leading to the "children's rights movement." *See also* Geiser, *supra* note 1.

[3] The discussion in this article focuses on the status of children in the United States. The degree of autonomy given to children and the relative role of state and parent varies from society to society. Unfortunately, the anthropological and historical literature provide relatively little information about children's rights in different cultures or times.

[4] Jeremy Bentham stated the traditional view of the law over 100 years ago:

> The feebleness of infancy demands a continual protection. Everything must be done for an imperfect being, which as yet does nothing for itself. The complete development of its physical power takes many years; that of its intellectual faculties is still slower. At a certain age, it has already strength and passions, without experience enough to regulate them. Too sensitive to present impulses, too negligent of the future, such a being must be kept under an authority more immediate than that of the laws . . . . . .

1 J. BENTHAM, THEORY OF LEGISLATION 248 (Boston 1840).

[5] It is questionable whether children actually get special protection. Adult treatment of children has always been a mixed bag. While children are thought of as special, deserving of extra help and care, they have also been viewed and treated as chattels. Infanticide, severe misuse of children in factories, selling of children into marriage are just some examples of the ways children have been treated like property. Institutions, like juvenile courts, designed to protect children have often harmed them instead. *See* E. RYERSON, THE BEST LAID PLANS (1978).

pressive,[6] to children. At the extreme, some children's rights advocates call for a total change in policy. For example, teacher and author John Holt advocates that children of any age be given the right to vote, to work for money, to choose what type of education they want, and to be free from corporal punishment.[7] Psychologist Richard Farson goes even futher. He argues that the issue of self-determination is at the heart of "children's liberation."[8] To Farson, children's rights can only be realized when all children have total freedom to decide for themselves what is best for them, including the right to sexual freedom, financial independence, and the right to choose where they shall live. Therefore, he argues for the elimination of both state and parental control of children.[9]

While most advocates do not go this far, respected experts from many disciplines argue that we need to adopt a "Bill of Rights" for children to assure their well-being. The type of rights suggested range from broad claims such as the right to grow up free from poverty and discrimination, to be born a wanted child, and to grow up nurtured by affectionate parents, to more specific rights, such as the right of children to choose their custodians upon divorce, to decide whether or not to have an abortion, to get medical care without parental consent or knowledge and to live on their own if they can support themselves.[10] Some advocates

---

[6] Even the media uses the term oppression. *See* Finefrock, *Our Last Oppressed Minority—Children*, San Francisco Examiner, Nov. 30, 1978, at 1.

[7] Holt, *supra* note 1, at 18 *passim*.

[8] Farson, *supra* note 1, at 27.

[9] *Id. passim.*

[10] One of the first Children's Bill of Rights is found in the United Nations Declaration of the Rights of the Child reprinted in B. Gross & R. Gross, The Children's Rights Movement 333 (1977). *See also* H. Foster, *supra* note 1. A constitutional amendment to assure children's rights has been proposed by S. Soman, Let's Stop Destroying Our Children (1975). The amendment would include the right to

—Physical safety and health care before and after birth;
—The basics of life itself, including love;
—Learn and be educated;
—Enjoyment, play, laughter;
—The same constitutional protections as anyone else;
—Understanding, tolerance, acceptance on the part of all adults;
—Adult models demonstrating consideration, integrity, ethics and, most especially, compassion;
—A peaceful, nonracist world where violence, massacres and wars are considered obsolete;
—His or her own identity;

Even the children have joined in. A recent conference of educators, held at Columbia Teachers College, invited a group of 9 to 16-year-olds to address them

make distinctions by age; many do not.[11] Most advocates also assert that children must have access to counsel to effectuate their rights. A number of legal organizations funded to provide free legal services to children are already raising issues of children's rights.[12]

Not everyone shares the views of children's rights advocates, however. Among the most prominent proponent of limited rights and expanded parental control is Yale Law Professor Joseph Goldstein. He argues that:

> To be a *child* is to be at risk, dependent, and without capacity to decide what is "best" for oneself.
> To be an adult is to be a risktaker, independent, and with capacity and authority to decide and to do what is "best" for oneself.
> To be an *adult who is a parent* is to be presumed in law to have the capacity, authority, and responsibility to determine and to do what is good for one's children.[13]

Others, who fear that expansion of the notion of children's rights will undermine the family structure to the detriment of children and society as a whole, have expressed similar views.[14]

To date, neither legislatures nor courts have developed a coherent philosophy or approach when addressing questions relating to children's rights.[15] Different courts and legislatures have been willing to give some new rights to children, while denying them others, without explaining the difference in outcome.[16]

---

on the issue of children's rights. The children made more limited claims than their elder advocates. They asked for freedom from corporal punishment, the end of placement of children in large penal or mental institutions, and the end of child pornography. Their position was summarized by 9-year-old Cristy, who said, "Children should have civil rights, just like women and other people get, because, you know, civil rights isn't only for grownups, it is for children, too." *Last Oppressed Minority Speaks Up*, N.Y. Times, June 17, 1977, A at 24.

[11] *Cf.* FARSON *supra* note 1 and IJA-ABA STANDARDS, *supra* note 1.

[12] Among the organizations suing on behalf of children are the National Youth Law Center, the ACLU Juvenile Rights Project, and the Children's Defense Fund. *See* Campbell, *Children's Rights Drive Is Centered In Courtroom,* N.Y. Times, Oct. 31, 1976, at 26.

[13] Goldstein, *supra* note 1, at 645.

[14] *See, e.g.,* Hafen *supra* note 1.

[15] For example, many states allow minors the right to abortion without parental permission or guidance, while others demand such permission. For a summary of various state laws relating to children's rights, *see* A. SUSSMAN, THE RIGHTS OF YOUNG PEOPLE (1977).

[16] *See* SUSSMAN, *supra* note 15, for a comparison of which rights each state gives to, and denies, to children. *Compare* Bellotti v. Baird, 428 U.S. 152 (1976) *with* Ingraham v. Wright, 430 U.S. 651 (1977).

The absence of a coherent theory is not surprising. The status of children in society raises extremely perplexing issues. The demand for children's rights calls into question basic beliefs of our society. Implementation of many of the rights being claimed for children could involve substantially altering the role of the state towards parents and children and the role of parents towards children. Most legal and social policy is based on the beliefs that children lack the capacity to make decisions on their own and that parental control of children is needed to support a stable family system, which is crucial to the well-being of society.[17] These views are widely held and, at least for young children, seem intuitively correct.[18] On the other hand, our society is unwilling to treat children merely as the property of adults. Given our commitment to individual liberty, there needs to be substantial reason for treating any class of individuals in a special way. Therefore, it is necessary to examine closely the claims of children's rights advocates in order to see whether the existing legal structure should be altered.

This article does not attempt to delineate what specific rights, if any, children should be given. Instead, it tries to provide a framework for analyzing the concept of "children's rights" and to isolate some of the issues that must be resolved in order to make sound policy decisions.[19] In order to assess the need for further extension of children's rights, it is first necessary to separate the various type of claims beings made on behalf of children. By lumping a wide range of claims under the heading "children's rights," proponents of expanded rights broaden their appeal while masking significant differences in the desirability or undesirability of granting specific rights to children.[20] In addition, assuming that children should have some additional rights, the means of achieving and enforcing various rights depends on the type of "right" being advocated.[21]

---

[17] Statements about the importance of family are commonplace in judicial opinions regarding family or children's rights. *See, e.g.*, Wisoncsin v. Yoder, 406 U.S. 816, 844 (1977). However, the reasons why our family structure is critical to the well-being of the state are rarely articulated.

[18] These intuitive views are supported by child development research. *See* notes 71-76 *infra*.

[19] The article addresses policy decisions at both the legislative and judicial level. Although much of the activity concerning children's rights has focused on the courts, it may well be that legislative, rather than judicial, resolution is more appropriate for many issues.

[20] Many advocates do lump the classes together, without distinction. *See* SOMAN, *supra* note 10.

[21] Means of enforcement are of particular concern to lawyers, who think in

I. Categories of Rights

There are four different types of claims under the general rubric of children's rights. While there is some overlap among the categories, each has special characteristics relevant to analyzing whether children should be given such rights. The categories are: (A) generalized claims against the world, e.g., the right of freedom from discrimination and poverty; (B) the right to greater protection from abuse, neglect or exploitation by adults; (C) the right to be treated in the same manner as an adult, with the same constitutional protections, in relationship to state actions; (D) the right to act independently of parental control and/or guidance.

A. *Rights Against the World*

The first category, claims for rights such as the right to freedom from poverty, to adequate health care, to adequate housing and to a safe community are frequently found in proposed "Children's Bills of Rights."[22] In many respects, these type of claims are the most important "rights" that could be given to children. They lie at the heart of a child's well-being. It is now well-established that factors such as nutrition and medical care can greatly affect a child's physical and mental development from the time of conception onward.[23] In addition, poverty, neighborhood conditions and discrimination seem to contribute to delinquency, school and mental health problems.[24] To the extent that children are denied equal access to adequate nutrition, housing, medical care and schooling they may be effectively denied equal opportunity in our

---

terms of legal remedies. Many non-lawyer proponents of children's rights have not given much thought to implementation. *See, e.g.,* S. Soman, *supra* note 10. The failure to think about implementation is not limited to non-lawyers, however. *See* Foster, *supra* note 1.

[22] This type of protections can be thought of as "welfare" or "positive" rights. *See* Michelman, *In Pursuit of Constitutional Welfare Rights: One View of Rawls' Theory of Justice,* 121 U. Pa. L. Rev. 962, 966, 997 (1973).

[23] *See generally* K. Keniston, All Our Children (1977); U.S. Dept. of HEW, 200 Years of Children, chs. 2 & 3 (E. Grotberg ed. 1977). This does not mean that nutrition or medical care are dispositive, just that they can have a big influence. Children are quite resilient and often can overcome deficits. *See* Werner, Bierman, & French, Kauai's Children Come of Age (1977).

[24] We do not know the "causes" of these problems, but there is a high correlation between the factors enumerated and these problems. Other factors are certainly important as well. *See* Pierce, *Poverty and Racism as They Affect Children* and Berlin, *It Can be Done: Aspects of Delinquency Treatment and Prevention* in Advocacy for Child Mental Health (I. Berlin ed. 1975).

society. In a society committed to both equal opportunity and individualism, the moral force of such claims is very great.

On the other hand, these claims are not of great significance in terms of reordering the legal and social status of children. First, the rights in this category are not meant to benefit only children; they are not claims for legal rights now given adults but denied children. These are rights that would and should benefit all people if they were available to children.[25]

Moreover, making the world a better place for children will not alter the status of children in the manner Holt, Farson or the numerous lawsuits attempting to establish legal rights for children seek. Providing children with adequate income or health care does not entail giving them more autonomy or self-determination. Quite the opposite. Demands for such rights recognize that children cannot provide for themselves and need the care and guidance of adults. Thus, these claims might be better thought of as protections due, rather than rights of, children.[26]

In fact, these claims generally are not for things traditionally though of as legal "rights," i.e., entitlements enforceable by court order. Courts cannot order that the world be free of poverty or that all children have adequate health care.[27] Only the legislative process can provide all children with these goods and it cannot guarantee a "right" to them.

Properly classifying these "rights" as protections tells us where to focus claims and how to defend them. Because the claims are basically moral and social goals, they should be addressed to legislatures, not courts. The debate should center in defining the obligations society has towards both adults and children, not on questions of the status of children and parents or on the capacity of children for independent decision-making.

B. *Protection from Inadequate Care*

The second category of rights encompasses claims that the

---

[25] Some of these "rights" could be given solely to children, through special medical programs, school breakfast and lunches, etc. It may be that children should have a special claim to such goods since they are more dependent than adults, and perhaps more likely to be affected by deprivations. They are also a more politically appealing group for redistribution purposes. However, by not giving adults such goods as well, we impair their ability to care for their children.

[26] *See* Geiser, *supra* note 1, at 1039-1044.

[27] Courts can give children some such rights, especially if there is any legislative basis. *See* Michelman, *supra* note 22, at 991-997, 1003-1015.

state should more actively protect children from harm by adults, especially their parents. Over the past fifteen years, concern over child abuse, plus increased evidence that early child rearing can affect a child's school readiness and performance, has led many commentators to advocate, in the name of children's rights, increased state monitoring of the adequacy of the parental care.[28] In general, these commentators have argued for broadening the definition of child neglect, in order to insure that parents rear their children properly. The most expansive definition would include "any act of commission or omission by individuals, institutions, or society as a whole . . . which deprive children of equal rights and liberties, and/or interfere with their optimal development."[29]

In many respects, this category of "rights" is closely analogous to the category of general rights just discussed.[30] The need for more "rights" is based on the premise that children lack the capacity to care for themselves and therefore need adult protection, care and guidance. Our society, as most societies, has given the power and duty to rear children primarily to their parents.[31] The power is great, although it has never been without limits. Because society assumes that children cannot raise themselves, that the type of rearing they receive will affect their life chances, and that children, as individual human beings, are not merely chattels subject to total parental control, all states have established some minimal standards for parental conduct[32] and have assumed some child rearing activities, most notably schooling.[33]

[28] These trends and the issues they raise are discussed in Wald, *State Intervention on Behalf of "Neglected" Children: A Search For Realistic Standards*, 27 STAN. L. REV. 985 (1975).

[29] D. GIL, VIOLENCE AGAINST CHILDREN 202 (3d ed. 1973). Insofar as definitions like Gil's apply to "society as a whole" they are addressing category one as well as category two "rights."

[30] The rights in both groups are designed to insure that children receive adequate care from adults until such time as they can care for themselves. The distinction lies in the fact that the first category requires the state to directly provide goods to the child to insure the child a given quality of life, while the second category only requires the state to monitor whether adults, especially parents, are actually harming children.

[31] A few countries or cultures have adopted more communal child-rearing methods, such as the kibbutz in Israel. While the relative role of state and parent must be addressed in deciding how to cope with child abuse, it is unlikely that the U.S. will move in any significant way towards communal child-rearing, although some subgroups in society may do so.

[32] *See* Wald, *supra* note 28.

[33] Given our society's commitment to parental freedom, the state has not

Those advocating more rights for children would require a higher level of minimum parental care than current standards require,[34] just as they would require the state to provide a higher level of state services to children and help to parents through expansion of the rights included in category one.

Again, however, claims in this area are of a very different nature than the assertion that children should have more autonomy or independence. They do not change the status of children. The intervention advocated entails substituting one adult decision-maker for another, rather than giving children the choice of deciding whether they like the conditions in which they find themselves. Generally, it is adults, not children, who invoke the protection process.[35]

In fact, children's views often are disregarded when giving them more protection.[36] Thus, if parents allowed their children to appear in pornographic movies, few children's rights advocates, let alone legislators or the general public, would allow the situation to continue, even if the child said, "I'm enjoying myself and making good money. Leave me alone." They would "protect" children in spite of their "rights" or "autonomy." Neither do we ask physically abused children whether they want to remain with their parents if we cannot protect them from further physical harm. We assume that children in these situations are not capable of protecting their own long-range interests.

---

assumed total control of schooling. Although all parents must insure that their children receive a certain amount and type of education, they can do so in schools of the parents' choice, if they are able to pay for them. Some parents may even be able to limit the amount, as well as influence, of education. *See* Wisconsin v. Yoder, 406 U.S. 205 (1972) (Amish parents can end their children's formal schooling at eighth grade).

[34] One group of children's rights cases has focused on the adequacy of care given to children under state care. *See, e.g.*, New York State Ass'n for Retarded Children v. Rockefeller, 357 F. Supp. 752 (E.D.N.Y. 1973). Conceptually these are not a separate class of rights; instead they can be seen as an extension of abuse and neglect laws to the state, when it assumes guardianship of a child. The key issue is the level of such care. The greater resources available to the state make it appropriate to demand a higher level of care than we demand of parents.

[35] Older children do sometimes initiate abuse proceedings.

[36] Courts often solicit older children's views in abuse or neglect proceedings. Young children usually are not consulted. Even when children have lawyers to represent them, the lawyers frequently see their role as deciding what is best for the child, not advocating the child's position. *See* Areen & Mlyniec *Representing Juveniles In Neglect, PINS, and Delinquency Cases* in DISTRICT OF COLUMBIA (DC Bar Assoc. 1975).

In addition to protection from parental abuse or inadequate care, a number of other claims for increased protection of children come within this category of "rights." For example, those adults who advocate, in the name of children's rights, putting controls on television violence or on the quality of children's food are not asking whether children like violent programs or enjoy eating Captain Crunch Chocolate Flakes; they are asserting that such fare is not in a child's interest, regardless of the child's views.[37] At least in my family, my children would consider this a significant interference with their rights. Implementation of such controls would actually reduce, rather than increase, the rights of choice many children now have.

Thus, these claims, like those in category one, are appropriately viewed as protections, not rights. Because the protections in this category are more specific and generally focus on whether parents are harming a child, the claims are more easily subject to judicial, as well as legislative, resolution.[38] The critical questions for debate should center on the appropriate role of parents and the state in child rearing.[39] It is necessary to decide what level of adult care is essential for children and how this can be best provided. This is an issue that divides "children's rights" advocates, since some people who work with children believe that less, rather than more, state interference is the way to best protect children.[40] It must also be decided what role the child should have in defining an acceptable environment.[41]

---

[37] Opponents of regulation of commercials or cereal makers usually are defending parents' rights, not children's. They argue that control of television watching and food buying should be in the hands of parents, not government.

[38] Social work agencies and courts are responsible for protecting children from inadequate parental care. They are expected to apply specific standards in evaluating the adequacy of parental care. Through the use of services to the parents or foster care, these agencies are supposed to insure that children receive adequate care.

[39] *See* Wald, *supra* note 28, for a discussion of the various issues that must be considered in this debate.

[40] *Cf. e.g.*, Bourne & Newberger, *Family Autonomy or Coercive Intervention? Ambiguity and Conflict in the Proposed Standards For Child Abuse and Neglect*, 57 BOSTON U. L. REV. 670 (1977); Wald, *supra* note 28.

[41] The question of the role of the child in defining abuse or neglect is a very troublesome one. The problem can arise even in cases where society in general believes the parent to be abusive, such as in cases of incest. The child may not view the relationship as harmful. How much weight should be given the child's views? Protectionists would protect; it is not clear what liberators would say.

Even more difficult are instances where older children want to leave their home because of parent-child conflict or because they find the home a difficult

While there has been some increase, in the past few years, in the "rights" afforded children with regard to state services and parental care—or more accurately put, there has been some effort to better protect children's interests—implementation of these rights has not affected the status of children in society. If these claims were the full extent of the children's rights movement, the debate over children's rights would be relatively limited. Since 1967, however, the children's rights movement has focused on two other categories of rights. These categories—the right of children of certain ages to be treated similarly to adults with regard to constitutional claims and the right to act independently of parents—do raise fundamental issues regarding the role assigned to children in our society.

C. *Adult Legal Status*

The third category of rights, i.e. the right of children to fuller adult legal status in terms of state policies, has been the focus of the greatest amount of legislative and judicial activity. Historically, age alone has been accepted as a sufficient basis for withholding certain privileges from children.[42] Among the adult rights they lack are the right to vote, marry, drive, drink alcoholic beverages, work, express themselves and read what they please. Children are subject to compulsory education, a form of coercion that would be unconstitutional if attempted with adults. In addition, children have been denied due process protections in proceedings

---

place to live. Home environments can be bad for children without falling into the abuse or neglect range. If the child is able to earn a living and is willing to be independent, emancipation is possible. However, emancipation is unrealistic for most people under 18, since they are unemployable. It must then be asked whether the state would provide them with state supported alternative living arrangements.

When the home situation does not amount to abuse or neglect but the child finds the situation intolerable, the policy questions involve category four disputes, i.e. parent-child conflicts.

It may be difficult to draw the line between neglect and family conflict in many instances. Thus, the two categories overlap.

[42] Throughout this article I use the term children rather than minors. The term obviously lumps a disparate group. While it may be reasonable to lump all persons falling below the age of majority for purposes of providing children protection, issues of autonomy generally involve older children, primarily adolescents. In fact, the term "minors" is often used in discussing the type of issues raised in categories three and four. The semantic difference may reflect real differences in how we perceive young people depending on the issue under consideration.

where adults would be entitled to such protections.[43] The special treatment of children has been justified on the basis of the minor's incapacity or lack of maturity or because of special protections children purportedly receive.[44]

Beginning with the U.S. Supreme Court decision in *In Re Gault*,[45] which provided due process procedural protections to minors charged with crimes in a juvenile court, the right of minors to adult legal status or protections has gradually increased. For example, the U.S. Supreme Court has ruled that children have a right to some due process protections before being expelled from school[46] and that school children are entitled to some first amendment freedoms, such as the right to wear armbands or distribute literature.[47] Among the legislature reforms are new juvenile court codes which give children rights similar to adults in delinquency and school expulsion proceedings.

In granting children these rights, the courts and legislatures have not arrived at any consistent theory of why they should grant children some rights and not others. In many instances the courts also have stopped short of placing the minor on equal footing with an adult in the same situation. For example, children still do not have full adult rights in delinquency proceedings and may be subjected to corporal punishment at school.[48]

It is in this area that children's rights advocates make their strongest claim. The special treatment of children rests on assumptions about their incapacity to act in an "adult" manner or on the necessity to protect them from factors that might impair their growing into autonomous, productive citizens. To the extent that the assumptions of incapacity are invalid or that changes in our social structure and in the rate of development of adolescents call into question constraints placed on children, these constraints should be eliminated.[49]

---

[43] For example, children do not enjoy full adult rights in proceedings which deprive them of liberty, such as juvenile delinquency or civil commitment proceedings.

[44] *See* RYERSON, *supra* note 5.

[45] 387 U.S. 1 (1967).

[46] Goss v. Lopez, 419 U.S. 565 (1975).

[47] Tinker v. Des Moines School Dist., 393 U.S. 503 (1969).

[48] Ingraham v. Wright 430 U.S. 651 (1977).

[49] Children now reach puberty earlier than in the past. *See* Tanner, *Physical Growth* in MANUAL OF CHILD PSYCHOLOGY, vol. 1 at 146-47 (P. Mussen ed. 1970). Children are exposed to television which may provide them with more information (and misinformation) than they have had in past times. On the other hand, people started full time work much earlier in the past, which may have prepared

Such an action has already taken place, on an immense scale, by the lowering of the age majority from 21 to 18 in most states. In so doing, the legislatures determined that people at 18 have the capacity to exercise all rights of citizenship and/or do not need the special protections given younger people.[50] Eighteen, however, should not be a magic age. Various states already use widely disparate standards in granting rights to children at different ages. For example, the minimum age for marriage ranges from 14 to 21; for driving the age range varies from 13 to 17.[51] Similar disparities exist in other areas—such as contract law, work laws and compulsory schooling ages.[52] Different conditions among the states may, in some instances, justify disparities. For example, it may be that younger people can drive more safely in primarily rural states. In many instances, however, states have adopted age constraints arbitrarily, without any basis in developmental or sociological differences.

The question of age discrimination should be examined from both a constitutional and a legislative perspective. At the constitutional level, the basic question is whether a given discrimination based on age is rationally related to differences in the capacities of people under a certain age or to the special needs of children.[53] In deciding this question the courts must also determine whether age is a "suspect classification," which would require states to meet a high burden of proof in order to justify differential treatment of children.[54]

In determining the rationality of a given restriction, it must be recognized that any given age will be arbitrary to some degree.

(entitled?) them for adult roles earlier. There is virtually no literature describing the capacities of children at different times in history. *But see* P. ARIES, CENTURIES OF CHILDHOOD (1962).

The rationale for given restrictions can also change. *See, e.g.*, the discussion of child labor laws in R. MNOOKIN, CHILD, FAMILY, STATE 646-667 (1978).

[50] Not all legislatures have lowered the age of majority and some "rights," such as the right to drink alcoholic beverages, still may be withheld even after a person reaches the age of majority. *See* SUSSMAN *supra* note 15, at 220-223.

[51] *See* SUSSMAN, *supra* note 15, at 229-230.

[52] *Id.* at 245-46.

[53] *Id.* at 220-246.

[54] Advocates of total liberation argue that no age-related disabilities are rational. *See* FARSON, *supra* note 1; HOLT, *supra* note 1. However, the evidence from developmental psychology belies their assertions. *See* note 59 and accompanying text *infra*. While it is therefore tempting to dismiss their claims outright, this should not be done. Instead their claims should be treated as a challenge to prove the basis for existing restrictions and to abandon those that do not withstand scrutiny.

People mature at different times so that not all 13 year olds are the same. The difficulty of making decisions on a case-by-case basis may justify selection of some age as a cut-off point for granting specific rights.[55] However, the courts should determine both whether any age restriction is necessary in order to achieve a legitimate state interest and whether the specific classification chosen is reasonable in light of existing data of the capacities of children at different ages.[56] Since most restrictions were enacted years ago, the courts should determine whether their rationales remain valid.[57]

Depending on the standard of review employed by courts, a number of present restrictions may be unconstitutional. Courts have already invalidated many restrictions. For example, courts have struck down school regulations limiting speech by students, as well as school hair and dress codes. Other decisions provide children with the right to counsel and other constitutional protections when the state is seeking to deprive them of liberty, and the right of access to contraceptive devices and to abortions.[58] The rationality of the present age limits on the exercise of other rights, such as the right to contract, marry, or vote also may not withstand judicial scrutiny.

Legislative reevaluation of existing restrictions is needed also. Such review should extend into areas that may be outside the realm of judicial review. Given society's commitment to equality under law, legislatures should examine closely the accuracy of prevailing assumptions about the capacities of children and should analyze the skills needed for specific rights, e.g. voting, marrying, or reading "obscene" literature. It should be determined whether existing age lines continue to make sense (if they ever did) in light of changes in children's development and our social structure. Only through such an analysis can the claim of Holt, Farson and other children's liberators be confidently rejected or accepted.

Such review is not likely to totally eliminate the incapacities

---

[55] A specific cut-off age, even if somewhat arbitrary, may be preferable to a system which requires case-by-case determination of "maturity" or "capacity." Case-by-case determination is only viable if there are objective ways to measure capacity. Otherwise there is too great a possibility of discrimination. Case-by-case determination can also be very costly.

[56] For a discussion of some of the constitutional law considerations *see*, Garvey, *Child, Parent, State, and the Due Process Clause: An Essay On The Supreme Court's Recent Work*, 51 So. Cal. L. Rev. 769 (1978).

[57] *See* note 49 *supra*.

[58] *See* cases cited in note 1 *supra*.

of childhood. Many restrictions are undoubtedly sound. Children are not adults in their mental abilities, judgment, or work capacity.[59] Adequate preparation for participation in society may require a period of forced learning. This does not mean, however, that existing age lines are sensible. While the reasons for disenfranchising a one year old are clear, the justification is less obvious with regard to sixteen year olds.[60] Upon analysis, a legislature may conclude that a different age line is appropriate in some areas and that age resrictions should be abandoned and new criteria adopted in other areas.[61]

For some rights it may be sensible to give control to parents, rather than the state. Many states already make some rights contingent upon parental approval, for example the right of children to marry. Requiring parental guidance or approval can alleviate concerns about a child's capacity to make wise decisions.[62]

In deciding whether to give children more rights, it also must be recognized that the notions of rights and responsibilities are closely related. There is currently a growing movement to hold children more responsible for their criminal actions.[63] If children

---

[59] Most researchers interested in child development have not examined the capacities of children to make decisions with regard to such activities as voting, marrying, driving or reading "obscene" material. A thorough review of the literature on adolescent decision-making is found in C. Lewis, Three Studies of Adolescent Decision-Making (unpublished Ph.D. dissertation, Stanford Univ. 1979).

Of course, criteria for "good" decision-making in these areas must be established before we can examine whether children of various ages are capable of making "good" decisions.

[60] *See* Schrag, *The Child's Status In The Democratic State*, 3 POLITICAL THEORY 441 (1975) for an analysis of the capacities required for voting.

[61] This analysis should be on a "right" by "right" basis.

[62] The fact of parent-child unity in asserting a claim for rights is significant since in such situations family privacy and autonomy is being preserved. Deference to parents is especially justified in cases where the "right" is denied on the theory that it is good for the child (e.g. limits on access to contraceptives), as opposed to cases where the right is denied for the good of society (driving? voting?). The Supreme Court seems to have indicated that in some areas state limitations are unreasonable but parental control may be acceptable. *See* Carey v. Population Services, Int'l, 431 U.S. 678 (1977).

Legislatures have made the same decision with regard to some rights, e.g., marriage. Children under a certain age are allowed to exercise these rights only with parental permission.

However, some rights might be the minors' regardless of parental views, e.g., the right to counsel in delinquency proceedings.

[63] *See* IJA-ABA JUVENILE JUSTICE STANDARDS PROJECT, STANDARDS RELATING TO DISPOSITIONAL PROCEDURES (Tent. Draft 1977).

are to be held responsible for their acts, perhaps they should be given rights commensurate with their responsibilities. On the other hand, those arguing for additional rights must decide whether they are willing to accept the imposition of responsibility on children as well.

D. Rights Versus Parents

Perhaps the most controversial and the most complex questions make up the fourth category of claimed rights, i.e. the right of children to act independently of their parents prior to emancipation.[64] It is one thing to argue, for example, that a school, without compelling reasons, should not be able to dictate to children and their parents the length of children's hair. It is quite another to argue that children who want long hair should have a right, enforceable by court order, not to cut their hair if their parents want it cut.[65]

In order to develop a framework for analyzing claims in this category, it is useful to examine the types of claims currently being asserted. Again, the extreme view asserts that all children, of any age, should be free to make their own decisions, ranging from what to eat and when to go to bed to whether to have an operation. Fortunately, most court cases have involved issues of greater magnitude than bedtime. The major questions center on whether a parent should be able to control the medical care a child receives, including whether a child should have an abortion, whether the parent should be able to determine what school the child attends, the material the child reads or views, and the place where a child shall live.

---

[64] The issue of emancipation involves both category three and four rights. By selecting an age of majority each legislature determines the general age of emancipation. However, it may be that certain children are ready for emancipation, i.e. freedom from parental control, prior to the general age of majority. Such freedom, however, may not be accompanied by full adult status, e.g. emancipation does not entitle the minor to vote. Emancipation may even be partial, i.e. for specific rights, such as access to medical care.

In deciding whether to allow case-by-case emancipation the legislature must formulate standards for determining that a minor is ready to be emancipated and decide what institution should make the determination. It must also decide whether emancipation only involves freedom from parental control or should entail complete adult status.

[65] The question of rights versus parents has been an especially troublesome and devisive issue among people concerned with children's rights. *See* Uviller, *Children Versus Parents: Perplexing Policy Questions for the ACLU* in HAVING CHILDREN 214 (O. O'Neill and W. Ruddick eds. 1979).

Historically, all such decisions were within the parents' domain, unless a given decision endangered the child in a manner covered by abuse and neglect laws. Recently, however, courts and legislatures have altered the extent of parental control. For example, a number of legislatures have granted children the right to get medical care, especially care related to pregnancy or contraception, without parental permission or knowledge.[66]

The expansion of rights can take several different forms. The right to act independently can be given solely to the child or the child may be required to seek approval for his or her action, or to challenge the parental decision, in a court or other agency. For example, some states have given a child the right to have an abortion whenever the child wants, without parental consent or even knowledge. Other states do not leave the final decision to the child. Instead, the child may petition a court to order the abortion in cases of parent-child dispute. In other instances, children must inform their parents of given actions, even if the children have the ultimate decision.

Thus, if decision-making authority is removed from the realm of parental discretion, it must be decided who will be given the authority—the child or an adult other than the parents. In determining whether to remove the decision-making authority from the parents, five factors must be considered: (a) whether the child can make such decisions adequately; (b) if not, whether other decision-makers, or decision-making processes, are likely to arrive at better decisions than the parents; (c) whether the state can really remove the decision-making power from the parents; (d) the costs of removing the decision from the parents in terms of family autonomy and family privacy (both valued goals in our society); and (e) the costs of *not* giving the decision to the child. For some specific issues, it also must be considered whether there are parental interests, such as in being able to visit a child not in one's custody, which may equal or exceed the child's interest in autonomy. In addition, if the decision is given solely to the child, it must be decided whether the parents should be informed of the child's actions.

Analyzing claims from this perspective, it is apparent that it is unrealistic to treat certain claimed rights, designed to give children autonomy, as legally enforceable rights. Children, as members of family units, cannot enjoy total autonomy over their lives, even if they are capable of making all decisions. While a

[66] *See* SUSSMAN, *supra* note 15, at 24-38.

legislature could declare that children, while living with their parents, have the right to decide when to go to bed, when to bathe and what to eat, it would not be realistic to expect such a declaration to have operative consequences. Allowing courts to enforce such rights would be enormously costly, and not very effective. It would be a waste of resources for courts to hear such disputes. Moreover, it would be very difficult to enforce such orders. For example, if a parent orders a child to bed and the child refuses, can a court order the parent to let the child stay up? If the parents do not follow the court order, will they be sent to jail? Will the parents be forbidden from enforcing their request by cutting off allowance, setting a curfew, not buying Christmas presents, or giving the child a spanking? With regard to these decisions, Farson's concept of total independence is just unrealistic unless we are prepared to place an outside monitor in every home to eliminate the authority parents have stemming from their greater strength and economic power.[67]

Of course, analysis need not stop at this level. One could ask whether children are capable of making such decisions without harming themselves. Clearly infants cannot. We know little about how older children would make such decisions. As a practical matter most older children probably enjoy substantial autonomy in many such areas, anyway. The impact of total autonomy on parental willingness to provide and sacrifice for children might also be explored. But such analysis seems unnecessary in light of the practical reasons militating against giving children total autonomy in these areas. Debate over such issues can be left in the philosophical or rhetorical arenas.

Most children's rights advocates do not go as far as Farson or Holt, of course. Instead of focusing on minor decisions like bed time or clothing, they argue that some types of decisions, such as

---

[67] Giving children such rights might have substantial symbolic value. Husbands and wives each can act independently in such matters but they could not enforce these "rights" in a court. Adults either use power or negotiation to do what they want or get a divorce. While some people advocate allowing children to divorce their parents, *see Expert Proposes Child "Divorce" of Parents,* Los Angeles Times, Nov. 17, 1978 Pt. 1-B at 7, this is unrealistic unless the child can be independent. It is not very likely that a large number of children can do so.

The symbolic value may be important if we want to alter family power relationships. Of course, many children are able to obtain such rights from their parents without legal backing. Parents may go along willing or grudgingly. It is probably best to leave the internal workings of families to "power politics" and to reserve state action for only very serious situations.

whether to have an abortion, to receive drug, alcohol or medical care, to go to a certain school or participate in religious exercises, to use contraceptives, or to enter a mental hospital, either should be entirely in the hands of the child or, at least, be subject to the ultimate control of a court, rather than the parents.[68]

There are a number of good reasons for giving children additional rights in these areas. First, such rights are most likely to be exercised by older children, who have the greatest claim to individual autonomy. Moreover, failure to give children certain rights might be harmful to them. For example, parents may place a child in a mental hospital because they do not like his or her behavior or may refuse to allow a daughter to receive an abortion although she may be psychologically damaged by bearing the child. Similarly, requiring parental involvement in some of these decisions may lead some children to forego actions that would benefit them. For example, teenagers with a drug or alcohol problem or who are sexually active may refuse to seek out counseling or contraceptive information if their parents must learn of their actions.[69]

Giving children the right to make such decisions does not entail the same problems as giving them the right to decide on bedtime or bathing. It would not involve courts in the minutia of day-to-day living decisions. Some rights, for example the right to receive certain medical care, if given exclusively to the child, could be exercised without parental knowledge. Monitoring of a limited class of conflicts, e.g. conflicts over civil commitment, would not place undue burdens on the courts or other agencies and generally would not require on-going involvement with the family.[70]

However, there are many countervailing considerations. Before giving children a specific right it is necessary to determine whether children are likely to have the capacity to make the decision for themselves. For example, do we believe that a child of a given age (or maturity level if we can develop a means of

---

[68] The ability to exercise category three's "rights," e.g., voting, driving, counsel, also fall in this more significant area of rights.

[69] It is unclear whether teenagers are, in fact, discouraged by parental consent requirements. *See* Torres, *Does Your Mother Know. . . .?*, 10 FAMILY PLANNING PERSPECTIVES 280 (1978).

[70] Spelling out children's rights in the medical or contract area may be extremely important in terms of giving guidance to third parties, such as doctors or merchants, who deal with children. Their actions often are constrained due to the uncertain legal status of children. *See* IJA-ABA JUVENILE JUSTICE STANDARDS PROJECT, STANDARDS RELATING TO RIGHTS OF MINORS 1-6, 50-85, 104-119 (Tent Draft 1977).

determining maturity levels) is capable of deciding whether to have an operation (including abortions?), to go to one school rather than another, or to use contraceptives? To analyze this question we must determine what types of skills a person needs to make a given decision and to what degree children of any given age possess the requisite abilities.

The exploration of these questions should begin with the research regarding the intellectual, social and moral development of children.[71] This research documents, contrary to the assertions of total liberators, that younger children, generally those under 10-12 years old, do lack the cognitive abilities and judgmental skills necessary to make decisions about major events which could severely affect their lives.[72] These limitations are developmental, not just a result of more limited experience or social expertise. Younger children are not able to think abstractly, have a limited future time sense, and are limited in their ability to generalize and predict from experience.

The research regarding older children is more limited and therefore offers less guidance for legislation. In both moral and cognitive development, many people seem to reach adult levels between 12 and 14.[73] However, there is little evidence regarding adolescents' decision-making capacity with regard to issues such as abortion, use of medical care, or choice of education.[74] It does appear that the ability to reason improves throughout adolescence. This may reflect greater social experience, but there may be biological reasons as well.[75]

---

[71] This research is summarized in Lewis, *supra* note 50. Among the major works are W. DAMON, THE SOCIAL WORLD OF THE CHILD (1977); CONTEMPORARY ISSUES IN ADOLESCENT DEVELOPMENT (J. Conger ed. 1975); J. CONGER, ADOLESCENCE AND YOUTH: PSYCHOLOGICAL DEVELOPMENT IN A CHANGING WORLD (1973); E. DOUVAN & J. ADELSON, THE ADOLESCENT EXPERIENCE (1966); E. ERIKSON, CHILDHOOD AND SOCIETY (1963); J. PIAGET, THE MORAL JUDGMENT OF THE CHILD (1932); MORALIZATION, THE COGNITIVE DEVELOPMENT APPROACH (L. Kohlberg & E. Turiel eds. 1973).

[72] *See, e.g.*, DAMON, *supra* note 71.

[73] *See* PIAGET, *supra* note 71; KOHLBERG & TURIEL, *supra* note 57. With regard to some types of moral development the age may be much earlier. *See* Darley, Klosson & Zanna, *Intentions and Their Contexts in the Moral Judgments of Children and Adults*, 49 CHILD DEV. 66 (1978).

[74] Lewis, *supra* note 59, in her dissertation, interviewed pregnant girls ages 13 to 18 who were faced with the decision whether to have the child. She found that older girls did tend to consider a larger number of factors and consult more people but no clearcut decision-making differences emerged along age lines.

[75] It may well be that children's problem solving capacities reflect the limited role they are given in society and that if they were given more responsibility they

Some researchers and clinicians assert that the decision-making capabilities of adolescents are limited in other ways. It is argued that adolescents must struggle with both dependence and independence needs, which may cause an adolescent to act in a way which meets some immediate psychological needs, but which may be adverse to long-term interests, as the child would define those interests.[76] For example, a 12-year-old may wish to keep a baby in order to feel more "grown-up" or to compensate for rejection by parents or peers, without any realistic assessment of her capabilities at childrearing or the impact that having a child would have on her development. Similarly, teenagers may resist necessary psychiatric treatment because they feel it is an imposition of adult values.

Clinicians also claim that adolescents benefit from having parental restraints available. Such restraints allow adolescents to challenge authority and to explore new areas with the realization that "wise" parents will stop them if they act in harmful ways.[77] While parents often do not act wisely, removing the authority structure may be more detrimental than unwise parental actions.

This brief summary is not meant to be exhaustive. Moreover, it is unlikely that developmental psychology can provide any firm conclusions about adolescent decision-making at this time. However, in deciding whether to give adolescents more autonomy, it is necessary to utilize the best existing data and to assess the likely costs of giving adolescents greater autonomy.

Even if adolescents could make some (or all) decisions without harming themselves significantly, we still might not give autonomy to children because of its disruption of the family system.[78]

---

would have the ability to make sound decisions. *See* Skolnick, *The Limits of Childhood: Conceptions of Child Development and Social Context*, L. & CONTEMP. PROB., Summer 1975, at 66.

[76] *See* D. ELKIND, CHILDREN AND ADOLESCENTS: INTERPRETIVE ESSAYS ON JEAN PIAGET 101 (1970).

[77] These views have been expressed to me in conversations with a number of mental health professionals.

Even when autonomy is presumably given directly to the child, the effect may be to turn the decision over to an adult, such as a lawyer, doctor or counselor. Young children, and even adolescents, often have great difficulty acting independently. In many cases where I have represented children, my clients wanted me to make the decisions for them. Unlike adult clients, children rarely tell you what they want. Instead, they ask "What should I do?" In fact, decision-making authority may be extremely traumatic for children.

[78] Home and family disruption are not the only concerns. Children are unable to utilize some rights because they lack money. For example, the right to medi-

The loss of family harmony and the potential destruction of family autonomy are major concerns of those opposed to more children's rights in the family context.

These concerns need careful scrutiny, however. Opponents of children's rights fail to explain how giving children some autonomy to make major decisions threatens our family system.[79] As discussed below, the family system may be threatened if courts are given authority to intervene in cases of family disputes.[80] However, if the ultimate authority to decide on an abortion, on other medical care, on schooling[81] or religion resides in the child, no outside intervention is necessary. Family privacy remains.

What is the threat to the family then? Giving children decision-making power could generate family conflict, thereby worsening the situation for all family members. Since "divorce" by either side often is impossible or undesirable,[82] such conflict can con-

---

cal care is only valuable if it is provided free or for the limited number of children with income.

[79] The impact of the law on changing social attitudes and customs is highly debatable. The law generally follows changes in values rather than generates them. All discussions about the impact on our family system is highly speculative and no data are presented documenting changes caused by the recent grants of autonomy to children.

[80] *See* notes 100-101 and accompanying text *infra*.

[81] Choice of school could become a major issue if proposals to use school vouchers in lieu of compulsory attendance at a given school are adopted. School vouchers could be used to buy a variety of kinds of education. It would then have to be decided who has the right to use the voucher—parent or child. *See* J. Coons & S. Sugarman, Education By Choice: The Case for Parental Control (1978).

[82] Divorce, by emancipation, is impossible because most children do not have the resources, and ability, to live independently. This would still be true even if we eliminated child labor laws, since most children do not have marketable skills.

"Divorce" would only be feasible if the state were willing to assume care of children or the state compelled parents to pay for their children to live elsewhere. Historically laws dealing with "status" offenders, i.e., children beyond control of their parents, did allow parents to divorce their children by turning them over to the state. This approach is now being widely rejected. *See* IJA-ABA Juvenile Justice Standards Project, Standards Relating to Noncriminal Behavior (Tent. Draft 1977).

Whether the state should provide alternative living situations for children who cannot get along with their parents is an extremely troubling one. There is no problem if both the parent and child agree to an alternative living situation and are willing to pay for it.

Even if children were allowed to divorce their parents prior to emancipation, they would still have to remain under adult supervision, until they were capable of living on their own and supporting themselves.

tinue for long periods or may lead to the child's running away. On the other hand, children resentful of parental decision-making may also generate family conflict.

Parental retaliation is also possible. We cannot prevent parents from cutting allowances, setting curfews, etc., as a means of enforcing their authority even if the child has the legal right to autonomy. This may be a cost children are willing to pay for exercising autonomy, especially since parents already exercise such powers, and children have no legal redress.

Perhaps the most legitimate concern is that if parents lose ultimate authority they will be less willing to assume responsibility for the child. Among the major reasons for supporting family-based child rearing is the substantial evidence that children thrive best in an environment where a small number of adults strongly committed to their well-being nurture and guide them.[83] Among the commitments of parenthood is the willingness to put the child's well-being ahead of the parents'. There is evidence that an increasing number of parents feel unwilling or unable to make this commitment.[84] For example, in a recent survey of American families a large number of parents expressed the belief that parents should not sacrifice in order to give their children the "best."[85] Many of these parents expressed doubts about their capability of controlling or guiding their children.[86] If such commitment is deemed important, it must be determined whether giving children more autonomy will affect adults' willingness to assume parent functions.[87] It must be recognized, however, that the legal system and the granting or withholding of legal rights may have little to do with how parents view their role. Other forces in society are likely to be far more important.[88]

Finally, it must be decided whether in some situations the costs of not giving the child autonomy exceed any costs in terms of weakening families. For example, forcing a girl to have (or not

---

[83] *See* J. GOLDSTEIN, A. FREUD & A. SOLNIT, BEYOND THE BEST INTERESTS OF THE CHILD 9-52 (1973) [hereinafter cited as GOLDSTEIN, FREUD & SOLNIT].

[84] *Raising Children In a Changing Society* in GENERAL MILLS AMERICAN FAMILY REPORT 1976-77 (1977).

[85] *Id.* at 10.

[86] *Id.* at 16.

[87] Traditionally families have played a central role as a stabilizing and socializing force in our society. This role is said to be critical to the development of the child. While the "decline of the family" has been blamed for many of society's ills, there is little research supporting such assertions. Assertions of autonomy by children need not necessarily result in less parental commitment.

[88] *See* note 79 *supra*.

have) an abortion or discouraging children from getting drug counseling or birth control information by requiring parental permission before the child can obtain such services may be very harmful to some children. It has been argued that if children faced with such problems are unwilling to talk with their parents, there is not much of a family relationship to preserve anyway.[89]

These concerns may be decisive, especially for specific issues, such as abortion. An analysis much more thorough than the courts or legislatures have made so far is necessary, however, before we can conclude that children should have greater autonomy.

The preceding analysis focuses on claims that autonomy ought to be given to the child. This is not the only option, however. It may be that in cases of parent-child conflict a court or other agency should have to resolve the dispute. The Supreme Court seems to have supported this approach with regard to teenagers' abortions.[90] Other courts have become involved in disputes ranging from whether a parent can place a child in a psychiatric hospital[91] to whether a teenager should have to accompany her parents on a round-the-world trip.[92]

The option of referring such disputes to courts or to "child development experts"[93] is attractive to many legislators. "Experts" frequently are involved in deciding whether a child is abused or neglected, who should have custody of a child and what to do with delinquents. In all these instances they have to decide what is in a child's best interest; so why not let them decide cases of parent-child conflict?

There are many reasons not to allow court intervention in such cases, however. In fact, many commentators question whether courts should continue to have authority even in areas such as custody disputes.[94] First, disputes between parents and children

---

[89] *See, e.g.*, P. Wald, *Making Sense Out of the Rights of Youth*, 55 CHILD WELFARE 379, 383-84 (1976).

[90] *See* Bellotti v. Baird, 428 U.S. 132, 147 (1976).

[91] *See* In Re Roger S., 19 Cal. 3d 921, 569 P.2d 1286, 141 Cal. Rptr. 298 (1977).

[92] The Hennepin County, Minn. Juvenile Court was willing to intervene in this dispute and arrange to have the girl stay with an aunt. In re Lee Anne G., (Hennepin County Dist. Ct.—Juv. Div. Aug. 11, 1972).

[93] The legal system relies heaviliy on professionals from other disciplines, especially psychiatry, psychology and social work—in making decisions about children. While these professionals have expertise in treating children with problems, it is questionable whether they are expert in determining what is best for a child. *See* Wald, *supra* note 28, at 992.

[94] *See* GOLDSTEIN, FREUD & SOLNIT, *supra* note 83, at 63 n.12; Mnookin, *Child-*

cannot be settled by reference to any existing statutes or principles of law. Instead, they involve making value judgments about appropriate family relationships. Inevitably, such decisions will be based on the personal values and biases of the decision-maker, not on legal grounds. In other areas where judges have such discretion, they often make decisions based on their own moral or social values or life style preferences.[95] Personal predilections, which vary from judge to judge, would undoubtedly become decisive in a court's views regarding whether to grant an abortion, to allow a child to use contraceptives, or to attend a particular school. Moreover, since judges are not trained in child development, are not chosen from a wide cross section of racial, ethnic or cultural backgrounds,[96] and frequently are not subject to public control, it must be questioned why they should be allowed to make decisions about a child's best interest or about how a family should function.[97]

Similar concerns may dictate against giving these decisions to other professionals. Except in extreme situations, there is no scientific method for determining a child's best interest. We get no consistent answers from Drs. Spock, Ginott, Salk or Brothers. Most experts have not even faced questions of the sort raised by children's rights issues. We could expect value judgments to play just as large a role as in the decisions of judges, regardless of the profession involved.

Moreover, courts, doctors, lawyers and other professionals frequently just drop in and then drop out of the child's life. Yet the child's problems may be ongoing. For example, a girl who gets an abortion may need counseling after the abortion, either with regard to the psychological impact of the abortion or to future sexual behavior. No professional can insure that the child will continue to consult them.[98] So long as the child continues to function

---

Custody Adjudication: Judicial Functions In the Face of Indeterminancy, 39 L & CP 226 (1975).

[95] *See* Mnookin, *supra* note 79, at 260-61. One widely known example is the Iowa Supreme Court decision in Painter v. Bannister, 258 Iowa 1390, N.W.2d 152, 154, 156 (1966) where the court opted for grandparents who provided "a stable, dependable, conventional middle-class midwestern background," rather than the father, whose home would be "unstable, unconventional, arty, Bohemian and probably intellectually stimulating."

[96] Females are not well represented either.

[97] It is questionable whether any type of training exists which would enable judges to make such decisions, in any case.

[98] Some proposals would have the professional decide whether the child is a "mature minor" capable of giving "informal consent." *See* Amer. Academy of

as part of the family, it will still be the parents who bear primary responsibility for providing help, guidance and support for the child. Parents may not be able to perform these roles adequately if they do not know about critical events in the child's life—such as abortions or psychiatric counseling.[99] Even a helpful professional who is willing to make the kind of commitment to a child that most parents are willing to make cannot be certain that the child will remain available, since either the parents or the "helper" may leave the area.

Finally, we must again consider the broader implications for the family system if courts or experts become the ultimate decision-makers. As discussed previously, this might deter parents from assuming important parental roles. While many factors influence the role a parent assumes, one of these factors might well be society's view of the role of parents. At least one commentator has argued recently that turning over major decision-making to professionals is extremely detrimental to society.[100] He claims that parents will not be able to act autonomously, and children will be harmed as a result, if parents are made to believe that only professionals know what is best for children. If we want to bolster the family, parents have to want to perform traditional functions, and they must be able to feel confident that they can perform these functions. While no data are provided to support such claims, we might want to search for evidence and analyze the logic of the claims before abandoning traditional structures.

One other cost of court intervention is also relevant. Just the fact of turning over such disputes to courts or agencies outside the family may, in and of itself, have negative implications. Our society is already very litigious. We have, in recent years, placed a great deal of emphasis on protecting individual rights. One benefit of staying out of such disputes may be in the message that family problems should be worked out within the family.

Of course, all these supposed advantages of family decision-making assume that parents will be willing to make such deci-

---

Pediatrics, *A Model Act Providing for Consent of Minors For Health Services,* 51 PEDIATRICS 293 (1973). Obviously, this isn't giving autonomy to children; it's being given to the professional. Can professionals make better judgments than parents?

[99] Difficulties like unwanted pregnancies are frequently recurring problems for the child. Yet, doctors who perform an abortion may do little to prepare the girl for avoiding future unwanted pregnancies.

[100] *See, e.g.,* C. LASCH, HAVENS IN A 'HEARTLESS' WORLD (1978). *See also* Goldstein, *supra* note 1 for a strong condemnation of court involvement.

sions.[101] Perhaps we have passed the point where this can be assumed to be true of most parents. If large numbers of parents are disinterested in their children, that circumstance may justify giving more autonomy to children, or even to other institutions. Recent changes in family structure, which result in parents being less available to their children, may also affect the ability of parents to perform these roles.[102]

In addition, some decisions by parents may have such potentially negative consequences for almost all children that we should subject such decisions to review. The decision to place a child in a mental hospital may be one such decision.[103] Requiring such review would alter the roles of the state and parents in control of child rearing. Requiring review is analogous to expanding the definition of abuse and neglect, and proposals to require review should be analyzed in the manner recommended for category two cases.[104] Instead of viewing state review of commitment decisions as protecting a child's right to liberty, it is more appropriate to see the state acting in its protective functions, ensuring that parents are providing adequate care.[105]

Conclusion

The foregoing analysis raises, rather than resolves, questions.[106]

---

[101] A policy protecting family (parental) autonomy does not mean children should be totally excluded from decision-making. Parents should be encouraged to include their children in the decision-making process. The findings from researchers like psychologist Diana Baumrind indicate that including children in family decisions contributes to their positive growth in areas such as the development of autonomy, flexibility and self-esteem. *See* Baumrind, *Some Thoughts on Children* in CHILD DEVELOPMENT CONTEMPORARY PERSPECTIVES (S. Cohen & T. Comiskey eds. 1977).

[102] *See* NATIONAL ACADEMY OF SCIENCES, TOWARD A NATIONAL POLICY FOR CHILDREN AND FAMILIES Ch. 2 (1976).

[103] This is the argument being made in cases of civil commitment. *See* Bartley v. Kremens, 402 F. Supp. 1039 (E.D. Pa. 1975) *rev'd on other grounds*, 431 U.S. 119 (1977). Similar decisions might be the decision to sterilize a child or to force an abortion.

[104] It is also possible to leave the decision to the child, of course.

[105] Questions of appropriate medical care, including hospitalization in a psychiatric facility, are among the most difficult for courts to handle. *See* Wald, *supra* note 28, at 1028-33; Goldstein, *supra* note 1.

[106] Moreover, not every type of children's right claim falls within one of the four categories. The most significant exception involves the role of children in the custody process. Among the issues are: should children have a right to choose their custodian upon divorce? Does it have to be one of the parents? Should this differ depending on whether the parents are in agreement or disa-

The questions are difficult ones; their resolution requires data about child development which are not available currently. Far more articulation of the assumptions underlying the positions of both opponents and advocates of children's rights also is necessary before we can begin to intelligently define the appropriate scope of both the rights and protections to which children should be entitled. The need for an interdisciplinary approach is critical. At present persons from different disciplines often talk past one another. Common framing of questions and attempts at data gathering should help significantly in clarifying and resolving issues.

Finally, it must be recognized that the proposed analysis, especially the analysis of parent-child conflicts, could be rejected entirely. The analysis assumes that the capacity of children for decision-making and the impact of autonomy on family structures are relevant to deciding whether children should have more rights. These assumptions need not be accepted. Other commentators have approached the subject as a moral issue. They believe children should have autonomy because they are independent individuals. Giving parents control of children can be viewed as treating children as property. As one commentator concluded "in the final analysis the . . . justification . . . for . . . honoring children's rights is that it is right and fair."[107] One must wonder, however, whether such an approach is, in effect, a case of abandoning children to their rights.[108]

---

greement about custody? Should children have to visit a non-custodial parent?

At least in cases of parental disagreement these issues do not fit any category. [Where the parents agree it then becomes a parent-child dispute.] The key questions turn on the child's capacity to make such decisions and, in the case of visitation, the balancing of the adult's needs with the child's. In these latter cases it should be recognized that we do not require adults to visit their children. Why should it be different for children, (perhaps because the adult is paying support?).

[107] *See* P. Wald, *supra* note 89, at 392.

[108] This term is borrowed from Hafen, *supra* note 1.

Part II
Parental Rights, Society's Responsibility?

[5]

FAMILY LAW SYMPOSIUM

Children's Liberation and the New Egalitarianism: Some Reservations About Abandoning Youth to Their "Rights"

Children have a very special place in life which law should reflect. Legal theories and their phrasing in other cases readily lead to fallacious reasoning if uncritically transferred to determination of a state's duty toward children. Frankfurter, J., concurring in *May v. Anderson,* 345 U.S. 528, 536 (1953).

*Bruce C. Hafen**

After the type for this article had been set, the U.S. Supreme Court decided two cases having potential implications for the constitutional rights of minors—Bellotti v. Baird, *44 U.S.L.W. 5221 (July 1, 1976) and* Planned Parenthood of Central Missouri v. Danforth, *44 U.S.L.W. 5197 (July 1, 1976). In* Belloti, *a unanimous Court held that the lower federal court should have abstained from determining the constitutionality of a state statute requiring parental consent to an unmarried minor's abortion but providing for judicial order of consent "for good cause shown" after parental consent is refused. The Court found the statute susceptible of an interpretation by the appropriate state court that would not impose an absolute "parental veto" power. Because such an interpretation would "avoid or substantially modify the federal constitutional challenge to the statute," abstention was held to be appropriate.*

The Planned Parenthood *case struck down a state statute imposing an "absolute" parental veto power over minors' abortion decisions; however, the majority opinion represented the views of only three of the nine Justices. There were four dissenters and the concurring opinion by Justice Stewart (joined by Justice Powell) implied that a statutory imposition of parental "consent or consultation" requirements short of an unconditional veto (such as the* Belloti *statute might be) could well be "constitutionally permissible."*

---

* Professor of Law, Brigham Young University, B.A., 1966, Brigham Young University; J.D., 1967, University of Utah. The author acknowledges the valuable assistance of Eric G. Andersen, Steven G. Johnson, Bruce T. Reese, and George R. Ryskamp, students at the J. Reuben Clark Law School, Brigham Young University; James Lucas, a student at Columbia Law School, and Lisa Anne Bolin, an undergraduate student at Brigham Young University.

The meaning of these decisions is unclear because of the uncertainty created by such a split among the members of the Court and the variety of potential approaches to parental consent requirements short of an absolute veto power. However, some of the language in Mr. Justice Blackmun's majority opinion in Planned Parenthood, *while representing the views of but one-third of the Court, illustrates the serious lack of perspective on children's rights issues already reflected in a variety of lower court decisions and in other literature. It is that lack of perspective that gave rise to this article.*

Current court decisions and law-related writing reflect a growing concern with the subject of children's rights, in contexts ranging from juvenile courts and child custody disputes to matters of minors' rights to abortions and other forms of medical treatment. Some interest in the topic is attributable to recent Supreme Court decisions establishing procedural due process standards for proceedings involving minors and establishing First Amendment rights for public school pupils. Many of the philosophical underpinnings of this development, however, do not have their origins in the traditional domains of juvenile and family law; rather, policies developed and articulated in the civil rights movement and other egalitarian movements it has spawned are now being applied to situations involving children. Race, sex, and age being three of the most obvious traditional categories of discrimination, it has been only natural to assume that if one form of obvious discrimination is unfair, other obvious forms of discrimination may be equally unfair. Thus, the momentum of recent antidiscrimination movements has provided a running start for a children's rights movement.

This article suggests that serious risks are involved in an uncritical transfer of egalitarian concepts from the contexts in which they developed to the unique context of family life and children. The family life context has a history all its own—a history replete with psychological, economic, sociological, and political implications. The use of "children's rights" language in this day of rights movements offers a way to leap over that history and its implications into the realm of abstract ideology. Whether that leap is the result of strategy or ignorance, its consequences are the same. The most harmful of the potential consequences is that the long-range interests of children themselves may be irreparably damaged as the state and parents abandon children to their "rights."

I. Introductory Illustration: *In re Snyder*

Agents of the state, including juvenile court judges, are restricted in their power to invoke jurisdiction over family disputes unless one of a few well-known situations arises: divorce and related custody matters; adoption; parental neglect, abuse, or abandonment; and juvenile law violations by minors—either delinquent acts or status offenses such as ungovernability. Although many families have voluntarily accepted the advice of juvenile court authorities in circumstances approaching one or more of these traditional categories, juvenile court judges and court-appointed professionals are not viewed as arbitrators empowered to intervene unless the particular circumstances rise to the serious level of one of the mentioned categories. The advisory intervention that has occurred short of that level has typically been at parental request (often at the suggestion of a social worker), and has virtually never been at the request of children unless serious parental fitness questions were invoked. Recently, however, the merits of parental decisionmaking on general life-style subjects have attracted the attention of juvenile court judges in new ways.

A recent case in Washington, for example, raises the possibility that children may now be able to secure significant judicial intervention into traditional parental prerogatives—including the termination of parental custody rights—when there are parent-child conflicts over lifestyle preferences. In this case, *In re Snyder*,[1] a bright, independent 15-year-old girl who had never had trouble with the law, but who was antagonistic toward her parents, asked a juvenile court to declare her "incorrigible" and place her in a foster home. She had lived all her life with her natural parents, who were fairly typical middle-class people with traditional ideas about the role of parents in disciplining and rearing their children. The family had experienced friction because of differences of opinion between the parents and the girl concerning her dating, her friends, and her desire to smoke. In an early phase of the case, the parents were found to be "fit" in the statutory sense, so that neither their conduct nor their competence was technically at issue when the incorrigibility question subsequently arose. After hearing the basis for the girl's incorrigibility claim, the juvenile court judge initially thought that it would be "improper" for him to "simply accommodate her [the girl] by her just saying 'I am incorrigible and I want out.' " He went on to state, "I do not think it works that way yet. I think these parents are responsible for this girl and I think that it is their duty to try to raise her."[2] After further consideration, however, the judge granted the girl's request, apparently concerned that she might otherwise run away from home. On appeal to the Supreme Court of Washington, his decision was upheld.

The *Snyder* result seems to imply that, even when a family problem does not reach the level of traditional juvenile court jurisdictional requirements, a dissatisfied child should be permitted to leave the family at her own request when her discontent is serious enough to indicate that jurisdictional levels may soon be reached and when some stress can be avoided if the court simply

1. 85 Wash. 2d 182, 532 P.2d 278 (1975), *noted in* Comment, *Status Offenses and the Status of Children's Rights: Do Children Have the Legal Right To Be Incorrigible?* 1976 B.Y.U.L. Rev. 659.

2. Record, vol. 1, Statement of Facts, at 82, *In re* Snyder, 85 Wash. 2d 182, 532 P.2d 278 (1975).

moves in. This theory is essentially an argument for the proposition that a child should be able to "divorce" (or at least achieve separation from) his or her parents on grounds of incompatibility.

Although *Snyder* is arguably just another family breakdown case, the lawyers for the state acknowledged that they had been unable to find "applicable case law" governing the facts of the case.[3] They argued that *In re Gault*[4] suggests the new idea that "children are autonomous individuals, entitled to the same rights and privileges before the law as adults."[5] They also cited Foster and Freed's proposed "Bill of Rights for Children"[6] for the proposition that a child should have the legal right to emancipation from the parent-child relationship when that relationship has broken down and the child has left home due to . . . serious family conflict."[7]

One may wonder just how great a step it is from traditional variations on the family breakdown theme to a child-initiated request for divorce on simple incompatibility grounds. The step requires little stretching if one assumes that, since children are people too, they should have some right to choose their own living environment. On the other hand, the step becomes a quantum leap if one assumes that family life is fundamental and, therefore, that state intervention in the parent-child relationship must be a last resort. Perhaps only questions of degree are involved, but as Justice Holmes once wrote, questions of degree are the only ones worth arguing about in the law. Further, these are potentially watershed questions, representing differing assignments of priorities between two significant American traditions—individualism and the family. Recent legal and social developments suggest that these two traditions may be on a collision course. Certain modern conceptions of children's rights, if carried through to their logical implications, assure that collision. Resolving the effects of the collision may be one of the critical legal problems of our time.

3. Brief for State Respondent at 23, *In re* Snyder, 85 Wash. 2d 182, 532 P.2d 278 (1975) [hereinafter cited as Brief for State Respondent].

4. 387 U.S. 1 (1967).

5. Brief for State Respondent at 23, *In re* Snyder, 85 Wash. 2d 182, 532 P.2d 278 (1975).

6. Foster & Freed, *A Bill of Rights for Children*, 6 FAMILY L.Q. 343 (1972).

7. *Id.* at 347.

II. Two Traditions on a Collision Course

A. The Individual Tradition

1. The Enlightenment and American democratization

The writers of the European Enlightenment argued that sound political theory must begin with the individual in the idealized "state of nature." Government was thought of as the contractual creation of a collection of such individuals. This notion was a revolutionary departure from prevailing ideas about man as a creature of the state. Although at least one writer made a belated attempt to demonstrate that the "state of nature" concept was nothing more than a clever rhetorical device that hardly reflected the legal and cultural origins of Western society,[8] these beginnings of the philosophy of the individual tradition so captured the imagination of European and American thinkers that the philosophy became for many a set of self-evident truths.

Nowhere was that philosophy more influential than in the United States. Notions about the natural rights of man, about the right of revolution, and of men being created equal may have been derived from the a priori reasoning of Europeans, but they were not therefore less significant to Americans like Thomas Jefferson. The philosophical context in which the American Republic was created assumed at a most fundamental level an individual tradition.

The assumption, however, was not unqualified:

> The eighteenth century republicans who founded the nation understood equality in terms of equality among those having equal status. Like the constitutionalists of antiquity, they were, in the main, not democrats in the sense of extending the rights and privileges of citizenship to *all* persons.[9]

Even the significant democratization attributed to the Jacksonians did not extend to "the abolition of slavery, the emancipation of women from legal and political subjection, or the eradication

---

8. H. Maine, Ancient Law (1st American ed 1870). Maine pointed out that under the ideal theory of Roman law, the propositions that "all men are equal" or men are entitled to equal protection of the laws had a purely legal (as distinguished from political) meaning: to the extent that Roman civil law coincided with a natural law of equality, Roman tribunals would have to apply the same law to citizen and foreigner, freeman and slave. *Id.* at 89. Maine observed that beginning in the 14th century and continuing through the revolutions in France and England, the concept of equality took on the more political meaning that "all men ought to be equal." *See id.* at 89-90. The concept then became an assumption underlying the hypothetical state of nature. "This," wrote Maine, "is the enunciation not of a legal rule but of a political dogma; and from this time the equality of men is spoken of by the French lawyers just as if it were a political truth which happened to have been preserved among the archives of their science." *Id.* at 90.

9. 1 B. Schwartz, Statutory History of the United States: Civil Rights 3 (1970).

of all constitutional discriminations based on wealth, race, or condition of servitude."[10] Only after the Civil War was "equality" introduced into the Constitution in the form of the equal protection clause of the Fourteenth Amendment.

Gradually, the voting franchise was extended, women's rights were more widely recognized, and American political institutions were increasingly democratized. But the Reconstruction statutes did not guarantee equality in fact, and from 1875 until 1957 there was no new federal civil rights legislation—perhaps because there was little public concern with equality for disadvantaged classes. Then, given great impetus by *Brown v. Board of Education*[11] in 1954, a serious movement for racial equality was born. That movement grew into an irresistable appeal to the national conscience that culminated in the Civil Rights Act of 1964. The relative success of the civil rights movement generated other movements seeking greater equality for women and minority groups. The current high level of interest in these movements makes it easy to forget how recently they have come to the nation's attention. Nevertheless, the individual tradition in America has seldom been more broadly alive than it is today.

2. *The exclusion of children from the individual tradition*

In 1861, Sir Henry Maine observed that the movement toward individualism was changing the role of both slaves and women.[12] Children, however, had not been included in the theoretical formulations that gave birth and growth to democratic concepts; nor were they included in any pre-1960 applications and extensions of those concepts. Some of the early writings about individual liberty were explicit about the reasons for excluding children. Viewing their position as a matter of legal theory, Maine noted that "[children] before years of discretion" were classified with "the adjudged lunatic" because "they do not possess the faculty of forming a judgment on their own interests; in other words . . . they are wanting in the first essential of an engagement by Contract."[13]

For John Locke, limited capacity necessarily excluded minors from participation in the Social Contract. He explained in some detail why "[c]hildren . . . are not born in this state of equality, though they are born to it."[14] Although Adam was "cre-

10. *Id.* at 5.

11. 347 U.S. 483 (1954).

12. H. MAINE, *supra* note 8, at 163-64.

13. *Id.* at 164.

14. J. LOCKE, THE SECOND TREATISE OF GOVERNMENT § 55 (1952).

ated" as a mature person, "capable from the first instant of his being to provide for his own support and preservation . . . and govern his actions according to the dictates of the law of reason,"[15] children lacked a "capacity of knowing that law."[16] Parents were therefore under an obligation of nature to nourish and educate their children to help them attain a mature and rational capacity, "till [their] understanding be fit to take the government of [their] will."[17] "And thus we see how natural freedom and subjection to parents may consist together and are both founded on the same principle."[18]

John Stuart Mill later addressed the topic in conjunction with his classic statement of the libertarian principle:

> It is, perhaps, hardly necessary to say that this doctrine is meant to apply only to human beings in the maturity of their faculties. We are not speaking of children or of young persons below the age which the law may fix as that of manhood or womanhood. Those who are still in a state to require being taken care of by others must be protected against their own actions as well as against external injury. . . . Liberty, as a principle, has no application to any state of things anterior to the time when mankind have become capable of being improved by free and equal discussion.[19]

In this same passage, Mill acknowledged that authoritarian guidance for the incapacitated was justifiable only as a means of bringing them to the necessary point of maturity.

Locke and Mill did not discriminate arbitrarily on the basis of age but rationally on the basis of capacity. Neither would have justified discrimination against children once capacity had been attained, and Locke particularly saw the parental role (as well as the duty of children to their parents) as designed precisely to develop mature capacities.

---

15. *Id.* § 56.

16. *Id.* § 59.

While Locke may have reference to the law of England, his thesis is that children are born "ignorant and without the use of reason" and therefore are not "under the law of reason." *See id.* § 57.

17. *Id.* § 59.

18. *Id.* § 61. Locke was convinced that there was no alternative for children but to be subject to their parents. "From this obligation no state, no freedom can absolve children." However, he clearly saw that the parental role was an educational one designed for the benefit of the children, and, as such, it did not give parents "a power of command over their children, or an authority to make laws and dispose as they please of their [children's] lives and liberties." *Id.* § 66.

Locke also saw the capacity problem as the source of limitations on the freedom of lunatics and idiots. "And so lunatics and idiots are never set free from the government of their parents." *Id.* § 60.

19. J. MILL, ON LIBERTY 13-14 (1956).

The law has long assumed the necessity of capacity. The assumption is reflected in restrictions on the freedom of children to vote, hold office, marry, drive automobiles, shoot firearms, gamble, enter into contracts, consent to sexual acts, and to make many other binding decisions about their own lives. The presumption of minors' incapacity has been so strong that the growth of democratic ideals in American society, rather than encouraging the "liberation" of children from limitations upon their liberty, has encouraged even greater discrimination on the basis of age—to protect children from the excesses of their immature faculties and to promote the development of their ability ultimately to assume responsibility. The juvenile court movement and the expansion of compulsory public education are obvious examples of the way American democratization has reflected the views of Locke and Mill about protecting and developing the capacities of the young.[20]

B. *The Family Tradition*

1. *Origins*

Philippe Ariès' classic work on the history of the Western family—more particularly the history of childhood[21]—is frequently cited for the idea that childhood is a relatively recent social invention. Thus, it has been argued that a family tradition which includes a legal concept of minority status does not reflect a natural condition, and that assumptions about the limited capacities of minors may represent vested parental interests rather than a fact of nature.[22] Primarily by reference to iconographic sources, Ariès documents that medieval children were typically absorbed into the working world of adults at about the age of seven.[23] The concept of a longer childhood emerged gradually with the coming of the Renaissance, the Enlightenment, and the Industrial Revolution.

One is not justified, however, in concluding from Ariès' work

20. Even with the American commitment to shielding children from their own immaturity, American sociologist Seymour Lipset has documented some revealing accounts reflecting the influence of egalitarian principles on child-rearing in the early history of the United States. He notes that foreign visitors have often been shocked by the extent to which American children have been "treated like rational beings," to the creating of a "dictatorship of the young" in which parents "avoid to the utmost the exercise of authority, and . . . make children friends from the very beginning." S. LIPSET, THE FIRST NEW NATION 119-20 (1963).

21. P. ARIÈS, CENTURIES OF CHILDHOOD (1962).

22. R. FARSON, BIRTHRIGHTS 17-25 (1974).

23. P. ARIÈS, *supra* note 21, at 411.

that childhood has been only recently invented. It has, rather, been rediscovered. Ariès himself notes, in an offhand way, that medieval society had lost sight of established Greek and Roman concepts about education and childhood:

> Medieval civilization had forgotten the *paideia* of the ancients and knew nothing as yet of modern education. . . .
>
> . . . The age groups of Neolithic times, the Hellenistic *paideia*, presupposed a difference and a transition between the world of children and that of adults, a transition made by means of an initiation or an education. Medieval civilization failed to perceive this difference and therefore lacked this concept of transition.
>
> The great event was therefore the revival, at the beginning of modern times, of an interest in education.[24]

Both family life and the prolonged education of children flourished during the high points of ancient Greek and Roman cultures.[25] Indeed, it was usually the family that took chief responsibility for educating the young. In these greatest of the ancient societies, childhood was viewed as a time for obtaining the education necessary for responsible entrance into the adult community. As the glories of the Roman Empire gave way to the Middle Ages, childhood, family, and education all took on drastically reduced importance. When Western civilization gradually emerged from the darkness of that period, the ancient concept of childhood, with its concomitant emphasis on prolonged education, returned. This reappearance was not remarkable in an age that sought to emulate the art forms, law, political institutions, and philosophy of the Greeks and Romans.

Sir Henry Maine's *Ancient Law* attempts to demonstrate that ancient Western society began with a primary focus on the group, not the individual. According to Maine, the primal group was the family.

> [S]ociety in primitive times was not what it is assumed to be at present, a collection of individuals. In fact, and in the view of the men who composed it, it was an aggregation of families. The contrast may be most forcibly expressed by saying that the unit of an ancient society was the Family, of a modern society the Individual.[26]

---

24. *Id.* at 411-12.

25. *See generally* J. Carcopino, Daily Life in Ancient Rome (1940); H. Johnston, The Private Life of the Romans (1903); J. Mahaffy, Social Life in Greece from Homer to Menander (1902).

26. H. Maine, *supra* note 8, at 121.

Maine then hypothesizes that the movement of Western society has been from Status to Contract, arguing that while the ancient societies attached legal and social significance to individual action primarily as a function of the group or family to which the individual belonged, modern society has attributed increased significance to individual action.[27] Maine's generalization suggests the steady growth of the individual tradition and its separation from the family tradition. The continued movement from Status to Contract is reflected in the democratic egalitarianism of modern times and the diminished influence of extended family kinship ties in today's highly mobile, industrialized society. Still, the concept of the nuclear family has continued to influence modern thinking to such an extent that children have not yet been fully included in the individual tradition.

Recognition of the family tradition by English and American law occurs primarily in cases involving parental rights. Several tributaries contribute to a mainstream judicial attitude historically favorable to protecting parents' interests in their children. The common law and certain constitutional doctrines have developed along similar lines.

2. *The common law view*

The common law has long recognized parental rights as a key concept, not only for the specific purposes of domestic relations law, but as a fundamental cultural assumption about the family as a basic social, economic, and political unit. For this reason,

---

27. Maine explains his "Status to Contract" theory as follows:

> The movement of the progressive societies has been uniform in one respect. Through all its course it has been distinguished by the gradual dissolution of family dependency and the growth of individual obligation in its place. The individual is steadily substituted for the Family, as the unit of which civil laws take account. . . . Nor is it difficult to see what is the tie between man and man which replaces by degrees those forms of reciprocity in rights and duties which have their origin in the Family. It is Contract. Starting, as from one terminus of history, from a condition of society in which all the relations of Persons are summed up in the relations of Family, we seem to have steadily moved towards a phase of social order in which all these relations arise from the free agreement of individuals. . . .
>
> The word Status may be usefully employed to construct a formula expressing the law of progress thus indicated . . . . All the forms of Status taken notice of in the Law of Persons were derived from, and to some extent are still coloured by, the powers and privileges anciently residing in the Family. If then we employ Status . . . to signify these personal conditions only, and avoid applying the term to such conditions as are the immediate or remote result of agreement, we may say that the movement of the progressive societies has hitherto been a movement from Status to Contract.

Id. at 163-65.

both English and American judges view the origins of parental rights as being even more fundamental than property rights.[28] Parental rights to custody and control of minor children have been variously described as "sacred,"[29] as a matter of "natural law,"[30] and as "inherent, natural right[s], for the protection of which, just as much as for the protection of the rights of the individual to life, liberty, and the pursuit of happiness, our government is formed."[31] These judicial word choices imply that the parent-child relationship antedates the state in much the same sense as natural individual rights are thought to antedate the state in American political philosophy. It has been said:

> Our political system is superimposed on and presupposes a social system of family units, not just of isolated individuals. No assumption more deeply underlies our society than the assumption that it is the individual [parent] who decides whether to raise a family, with whom to raise a family, and, in broad measure, what values and beliefs to inculcate in the children who will later exercise the rights and responsibilities of citizens and heads of families. . . .
>
> . . . [T]he family unit does not simply co-exist with our constitutional system; it is an integral part of it. In democratic theory as well as in practice, it is in the family that children are expected to learn the values and beliefs that democratic institutions later draw on to determine group directions. The immensely important power of deciding about matters of early

---

28. Much children's rights literature argues that children should no longer be regarded as the "property" of their parents. For example, Pilpel, *Minors' Rights to Medical Care*, 36 ALBANY L. REV. 462, 463 (1972), states that "the common law regarded children largely as the property of their parents," and implies that this view prevailed even until *In re* Gault, 387 U.S. 1 (1967). A similar statement is made by the Fifth Circuit Court of Appeals in Poe v. Gerstein, 517 F.2d 787, 789 (5th Cir. 1975): "The [common] law did not distinguish between the infant and the mature teenager, treating them both as the property of their parents, who could make all decisions affecting them." The court also implied that this view continued until *Gault* and *Tinker v. Des Moines Independent Community School District*. *Id.* at 789-90. The "children-as-chattels" view, however, has not in fact been taken seriously for many years, as suggested not only by the cases cited in this section, but also by the limitations that have long existed on the exercise of parental rights. *See* notes 89-91 and accompanying text *infra*.

29. *In re* Hudson, 13 Wash. 2d 673, 685, 126 P.2d 765, 771 (1942).

30. People *ex rel.* Portnoy v. Strasser, 303 N.Y. 539, 542, 104 N.E.2d 895, 896 (1952).

31. Lacher v. Venus, 177 Wis. 558, 569-70, 188 N.W. 613, 617 (1922); *cf. In re* Adoption of Anderson, 235 Minn. 192, 200, 50 N.W.2d 278, 284 (1951), which states:

> Parents who faithfully discharge their parental obligations with assiduity and to the full extent of their means and abilities are entitled to the custody of their children. Parental rights, however, are not absolute and are not to be unduly exalted and enforced to the detriment of the child's welfare and happiness.

socialization has been allocated to the family, not to the government.[32]

Parental power is thought to be plenary—prevailing over the claims of the state, other outsiders, and the children themselves unless there is some compelling justification for interference.[33] Such compelling justifications have been recognized for centuries where natural parents have abandoned, neglected, or abused their children in some way that required state intervention to avoid serious harm to the children.[34] Although judicial percep-

32. Heymann & Barzelay, *The Forest and the Trees;* Roe v. Wade *and Its Critics*, 53 BOSTON U.L. REV. 765, 772-73 (1973).

33. The Supreme Court of Rhode Island, in Matarese v. Matarese, 47 R.I. 131, 132-33, 131 A. 198, 199 (1925), stated the following concerning the law's regard for parental authority:

> Immemorially the family has been an important element of our civil society, one of the supports upon which our civilization has developed. Save as modified by the legislature, in domestic affairs the family has remained in law a self-governing entity, under the discipline and direction of the father as its head. . . . These fundamental principles are traceable to ancient customs and usages and are fixed by tradition and evidenced by the decisions of the courts. Anything that brings the child into conflict with the father or diminishes the father's authority or hampers him in its exercise is repugnant to the family establishment and is not to be countenanced save upon positive provisions of the statute law.

Similarly, the Supreme Court of Mississippi stated:

> The kind and extent of education, moral and intellectual, to be given to a child and the mode of furnishing it are left largely to the discretion of the parents . . . . Unless shown to the contrary, the presumption is that natural parents will make the best decisions for their offspring.
>
> . . . .
>
> . . . [T]his important parental right is protected by common-law principles. It is also a right protected by the due process clauses of the Federal and State Constitutions. . . .
>
> . . . .
>
> The family is the basis of our society. [The parent in this case] has an interest in [the education of his children] which lies on a different plane than that of mere property. Moreover, a child has no higher welfare than to be reared by a parent who loves him and who has not forfeited the right of custody. The agencies of our democratic government are obligated to preserve that right, which is not recognized in a totalitarian society.

In re Guardianship of Faust, 239 Miss. 299, 305-07, 123 So. 2d 218, 220-21 (1960).

34. Blackstone mentioned England's historical limitations on parental authority in the following statement:

> The ancient Roman laws gave the father a power of life and death over his children; upon this principle, that he who gave had also the power of taking away. But the rigor of these laws was softened by subsequent constitutions
>
> . . . .
>
> The power of a parent, by our English laws, is much more moderate; but still sufficient to keep the child in order and obedience. He may *lawfully* correct his child, being under age, *in a reasonable manner;* for this is for the benefit of his education.

tions of abuse and neglect have varied over time, American courts and legislatures have expressed increasingly lower tolerance for serious physical harms inflicted by parents on their children.

Some authorities have suggested that in more modern times (the 20th century) the interests of parents in claims to custody and control have been limited by increased emphasis on "a social interest in the protection of dependent persons."[35] Similarly broad statements have been made about "the waning of parental rights"[36] in British Commonwealth countries; however, such statements actually refer to increased limitations on the rights of biological parents in situations where the normal parent-child relationship has already been interfered with by the application of traditional criteria giving rise to custody disputes or parental neglect claims. The criteria themselves have undergone no significant change. The domain of parental discretion has also been modestly limited within the last century by increased state concern with such specific subjects as child labor and public education, attention to various categories of child behavior classified under juvenile delinquency laws, continued extension of the circumstances under which emergency medical treatment may be given to children, and a greater judicial commitment to the best interests of children involved in custody disputes.

---

1 W. Blackstone, Commentaries *451 (emphasis added).

A 19th century English court enunciated the justifications for judicial interference in parental authority:

> A father has a legal right to control and direct the education and bringing up of his children until they attain the age of twenty-one years . . . and the Court will not interfere with him in the exercise of his paternal authority, except (1) where by his gross moral turpitude he forfeits his rights, or (2) where he has by his conduct abdicated his paternal authority.

In re Agar-Ellis, [1883] 24 Ch. D. 317 (C.A.).

35. Pound, *Individual Interests in the Domestic Relations*, 14 Mich. L. Rev. 177, 182 (1916).

36. J. M. Eekelaar begins his article, *Deprivation of Parental Rights: Legislative Contrasts in England, Wales, Australia, and Canada*, 7 Family L.Q. 381 (1973), with this statement: "One of the outstanding features of the twentieth century development of the law relating to children has been the emergence of the doctrine which promotes the child's welfare over parental rights." As support for this premise, Eekelaar refers to an article by Hall, *The Waning of Parental Rights*, 31 Cambridge L.J. 248 (1972), which briefly documents that a gradual erosion of parental rights during this century is due to "the ever-increasing concern of society for the well-being of its youngest members." An examination of the cases cited by Hall reveals, however, that the only changes he identifies are modifications in judicial attitudes when the custody of a child or the rights of parents have already been called into question. At this point the "best interests of the child" standard has been given increasing recognition over the bare legal claim of a natural parent who may have relinquished practical custody in some obvious way. There is no evidence from these authorities that there has been any recognizable change in the criteria initially giving rise to an inquiry about child custody, such as parental neglect, abandonment, divorce, or other custody disputes.

Still, the most fundamental legal aspects of the parent-child relationship, including the basic presumption favoring custody and control by parents in relatively normal family situations, have remained unchanged. Indeed, many aspects of the juvenile court movement have probably strengthened traditional assumptions favoring parental custody rights.[37] One authority has recently stated, "[t]he truth of the matter is that there has been no radical change in the child's situation in American law or indeed in the thinking about his condition for over a century."[38]

3. Constitutional rights of parents

A series of Supreme Court opinions has addressed the subject of parental prerogatives in a number of contexts and appears to have established a strong presumption favoring parental control, at least as against intervention from the state. Because the Supreme Court has not yet dealt directly with a conflict between parental rights and alleged children's rights, however, it is unclear whether the pro-parent decisions arise from concerns about protecting children from the excesses of state interference with their lives or from efforts to affirm a constitutional doctrine that there is some separate parental right.[39]

Many of the cases state clearly that parental rights warrant constitutional protection based upon established cultural preferences for parent-directed family life. The effect of these cases is to create both constitutional protections for parents and constitutional limitations on the state's role in child-rearing. In *Pierce v. Society of Sisters*,[40] a case striking down an Oregon compulsory

---

37. Relatively recent modernizations of state juvenile court statutes typically contain statutory-purpose sections stating explicit legislative preferences for parental custody and family support. For example, the Illinois Juvenile Court Act states the following purpose:

> The purpose of this Act is to secure for each minor subject hereto such care and guidance, preferably in his own home, as will serve the moral, emotional, mental, and physical welfare of the minor . . . ; to preserve and strengthen the minor's family ties whenever possible, removing him from the custody of his parents only when his welfare or safety or the protection of the public cannot be adequately safeguarded without removal. . . .

ILL. REV. STAT. ch. 37, § 701-2 (1973). *See also* CAL. WELF. & INST'NS. CODE § 726 (West 1972); UTAH CODE ANN. § 55-10-63 (1953).

38. S. KATZ, THE LEGAL RIGHTS OF CHILDREN, Introduction (1974).

39. Thus, the question has recently been asked whether Wisconsin v. Yoder, 406 U.S. 205 (1972) and other cases discussed in this section of the text "mean that parents have a constitutionally sanctioned role in their children's lives; or does it mean that the state has a constitutionally limited role in child-rearing that typically, but not necessarily, is enforced by deference to the parents?" *See* Burt, *Developing Constitutional Rights of, in and for Children*, 39 LAW & CONTEMP. PROB. 118 (1975).

40. 268 U.S. 510 (1925).

education statute which in effect precluded attendance at private schools, Justice McReynolds expressed what was later called in *Wisconsin v. Yoder* "a charter of the rights of parents to direct the religious upbringing of their children."[41] He stated that "[t]he child is not the mere creature of the State; those who nurture him and direct his destiny have the right, coupled with the high duty, to recognize and prepare him for additional obligations."[42] The Court in *Yoder* then made this broad statement:

> The history and culture of Western civilization reflect a strong tradition of parental concern for the nurture and upbringing of their children. This primary role of the parents in the upbringing of their children is now established beyond debate as an enduring American tradition.[43]

In *Meyer v. Nebraska,* a 1923 decision invalidating a state statute that prohibited foreign language instruction to young schoolchildren, the Court said that a teacher's right to teach a foreign language "and the right of parents to engage him so to instruct their children" are protected by the due process clause of the Fourteenth Amendment.[44] *Meyer* rejected the state claim that patriotism and good citizenship would be advanced by ensuring that English would be the mother tongue of all children raised in the state. Acknowledging the right of German-speaking parents in an American community to have their children taught German, the Court referred expressly to the social structure discussed in Plato's *Republic,* in which family life was to be replaced entirely by state child-rearing activities so pervasive that "no parent is to know his own child, nor any child his parent."[45] Regarding this system, the Court stated:

> Although such measures have been deliberately approved by men of great genius, their ideas touching the relation between individual and State were wholly different from those upon which our institutions rest; and it hardly will be affirmed that any legislature could impose such restrictions upon the people of a State without doing violence to both letter and spirit of the Constitution.[46]

41. 406 U.S. 205, 233 (1972).
42. 268 U.S. at 535.
43. 406 U.S. at 232.
44. 262 U.S. 390, 400 (1923).
45. 262 U.S. at 401-02.
46. *Id.* at 402. Because *Meyer* involved the prosecution of a private schoolteacher rather than a parent, this language might be regarded as dicta. However, the case also involved the larger question of how much liberty foreign-born parents should have to influence their children with the customs, attitudes, and language of their native culture.

In stating that the ideas of those who would have removed the interposition of the family between the individual and the state were "wholly different from those upon which our institutions rest," the Court seems to have acknowledged that our culture presupposes a system of family units, not just a mass of isolated individuals.[47]

In *Ginsberg v. New York*,[48] the Court upheld a New York statute making it unlawful to sell pornographic magazines to persons under 17 years of age. The Court identified two justifications for the statutory restrictions. First, "Constitutional interpretation has consistently recognized that the parents' claim to authority in their own household to direct the rearing of their children is basic in the structure of our society."[49] Second, "[t]he state also has an independent interest in the well-being of its youth."[50] Because parental control cannot always be provided, the Court acknowledged that the second rationale justified regulation of the availability of pornographic materials to juveniles on standards more stringent than those that govern distribution to adults. Since the Court might have disposed of *Ginsberg* solely by reference to the state's interest in protecting the welfare of its youth, the explicit recognition of parental authority as a separate justification suggests that the Constitution contemplates a direct role for parents in the lives of their children—a role distinct from the state-child relationship.

One of the strongest statements about independent parental interests was made in *Stanley v. Illinois*,[51] in which the Court struck down a state statute providing that illegitimate children, upon the death of their mother, become wards of the state without a hearing on the parental fitness of the father. In holding that the Fourteenth Amendment entitled the father to a hearing, the Court stated:

> The private interest here, that of a man in the children he has sired and raised, undeniably warrants deference and, absent a powerful contervailing interest, protection. It is plain that the interest of a parent in the companionship, care, custody, and

47. Contrary to this conclusion, Professor Burt seems to think that the Court's reference to "the relation between the individual and State," together with the fact that a parent was not a party to the litigation in *Meyer* suggests that the Court was talking about the relationship between the state and individuals, not the relationship between the state and parents or families. Burt, *supra* note 39.

48. 390 U.S. 629 (1968).

49. *Id.* at 639.

50. *Id.* at 640.

51. 405 U.S. 645 (1972).

> management of his or her children "come[s] to this Court with a momentum for respect lacking when appeal is made to liberties which derive merely from shifting economic arrangements."[52]

The authorities cited for this proposition included *Meyer* and *Prince v. Massachusetts*,[53] from which the following language was cited: "It is cardinal with us that the custody, care and nurture of the child reside first in the parents, whose primary function and freedom include preparation for obligations the state can neither supply nor hinder."[54] The Court recognized in *Stanley* that the children would suffer from uncertainty and dislocation under the arrangement proposed by the state, but it was to the interest of the parent, not to the interest of the children, that the Court directed its attention.

An authority cited by the *Stanley* Court contrasting a parent's interest in his children with an "economic" interest offers some rebuttal to the oft-cited but inaccurate statement that, until the *Gault* case in 1967, children were regarded as the "property" of their parents.[55] The *Stanley* Court quoted the 1953 decision of *May v. Anderson*, which referred to parental custody rights as "[r]ights far more precious . . . than property rights."[56]

A similar distinction elevating the right of parental custody and control beyond the level of property rights was also made in Justice Goldberg's concurring opinion in *Griswold v. Connecticut*:[57]

> Certainly the safeguarding of the home does not follow merely from the sanctity of property rights. The home derives its preeminence as the seat of family life. And the integrity of that life is something so fundamental that it has been found to draw to its protection the principles of more than one explicitly granted Constitutional right . . . .
>
> The entire fabric of the Constitution and the purposes that clearly underlie its specific guarantees demonstrate that the rights to marital privacy and to marry and raise a family are of similar order and magnitude as the fundamental rights specifically protected.

52. *Id.* at 651.
53. 321 U.S. 158 (1944).
54. 405 U.S. at 651.
55. *See* note 28 *supra*.
56. 345 U.S. 528, 533 (1953)(custody dispute between divorced parents of minor children).
57. 381 U.S. 479, 495 (1965) (right of access of married persons to contraceptive information and devices given constitutional protection).

This language from *Griswold* introduces another line of Supreme Court cases that construes the right to marital privacy and the right to raise a family as "fundamental." This line of cases includes *Skinner v. Oklahoma*,[58] in which a state statute providing for the sterilization of habitual criminals was struck down because it threatened the right of "marriage and procreation," which the Court found to be "one of the basic civil rights of man," and "fundamental to the very existence and survival of the race."[59] and in *Eisenstadt v. Baird*,[60] the Court extended to unmarried persons the privacy protection given married persons in *Griswold* by holding unconstitutional a state statute that prohibited the distribution of contraceptives to single persons. The *Eisenstadt* Court explicitly acknowledged that the right to be free from governmental intrusion on matters as private as the decision whether to have a child is the right of an *individual,* married or single, rather than a right granted to a married couple as an independent entity.[61]

One additional line of Supreme Court cases helpful in defining the nature and limits of constitutionally protected parental rights is that dealing with state attempts to regulate the education and religious activity of children. Both *Meyer* and *Pierce* arose within this subject area. The general principles established by these cases[62] were limited somewhat in *Prince v. Massachusetts,*[63] wherein the Court sustained the conviction of an adult member of a Jehovah's Witness family for violating a state law prohibiting street solicitation by certain minors. The Court rejected Mrs. Prince's claim that the conviction violated her due process rights to raise the children for whom she was responsible as well as the freedom of religion claim exerted on behalf of the child involved, a 9-year-old girl who had enthusiastically volunteered to go with her guardian to assist in selling religious literature on a public street. The Court acknowledged the conflict between the state's claims and the "sacred private interests" associated with the parental claim, but held that, under its *parens*

---

58. 316 U.S. 535 (1942).

59. *Id.* at 541.

60. 405 U.S. 438 (1972).

61. *Id.* at 453. Of course the marital privacy cases involved considerations other than the right to bear children and have their custody once they are born. These cases also provided basic authority for the abortion decisions, Roe v. Wade, 410 U.S. 113 (1973) and Doe v. Bolton, 410 U.S. 179 (1973), which extended the "fundamental right" of privacy to women confronted with a decision whether to submit to an abortion.

62. *See* notes 40-47 and accompanying text *supra.*

63. 321 U.S. 158 (1944).

patriae authority, the state had a duty to limit parental control by requiring school attendance, regulating child labor, and otherwise protecting children against the evils of employment and other activity in public places.[64] The gist of the Court's view is captured in its statement that "[p]arents may be free to become martyrs themselves. But it does not follow [that] they are free . . . to make martyrs of their children before they have reached the age of full and legal discretion when they can make that choice for themselves."[65]

Prince makes it clear that there are limits (unrelated to basic parental fitness) to the authority of parents to control the educational and religious activities of their children. Nonetheless, *Prince* was significantly narrowed in 1972 by *Wisconsin v. Yoder*,[66] which upheld parental claims, based on grounds of both religious freedom and parental rights, to exempt children from state compulsory education laws as applied to children beyond the eighth grade. Writing for the *Yoder* majority, Chief Justice Burger noted that prior case law had limited the *Prince* doctrine substantially.[67] *Yoder* indicated that the state may not interfere with First Amendment freedoms of parents unless there is "harm to the physical or mental health of the child or to the public safety, peace, order, or welfare."[68] *Yoder* thus circumscribes state interference with parental control considerably more than *Prince*. The removal of children from obligations imposed by compulsory education laws (even if only after the eighth grade) would seem to portend a greater impact on youthful minds and choices than an afternoon of selling religious literature on a streetcorner.

The freedom of parents to impose their values upon their children as part of their overall discretion in child-rearing was enunciated in both *Meyer* and *Pierce*, limited in *Prince*, and then broadly reaffirmed in *Yoder*, at least when the parental preference is associated with a religious belief.[69] The religious freedom claim was explicitly buttressed by *Yoder's* references to *Pierce* and to the "history and culture of Western Civilization [which] reflect a strong tradition of parental concern for the nurture and upbringing of their children."[70]

64. *Id.* at 166.

65. *Id.* at 170.

66. 406 U.S. 205 (1972).

67. *Id.* at 230.

68. *Id.*

69. Chief Justice Burger implied that he might have taken another view of the situation in *Yoder* if the Court had not been persuaded that the claims of the Amish parents were genuinely religious. *Id.* at 235-36.

70. *Id.* at 232.

Under the *Yoder* test, parental discretion will be interfered with, not when parental choices deviate from the mainstream of public opinion or the views of state authorities, but only "if it appears that parental decisions will jeopardize the health or safety of the child, or have a potential for significant social burdens."[71] As an example of the kind of fact situation in which such jeopardy might arise, *Yoder* cites the *Georgetown College* case,[72] where a federal court of appeals upheld a lower court order that a blood transfusion be given to a Jehovah's Witness patient who, along with her husband, had been unwilling to consent to the transfusion. It may be noted that this limitation on parental authority is consistent with the common law limitations discussed earlier.[73]

The dissent of Justice Douglas in *Yoder* has been widely quoted by children's rights advocates because of Douglas' concern that *Yoder* imposed the religious views of parents upon their children.[74] The majority opinion dealt specifically with the questions raised by Justice Douglas and concluded that it was in fact the right of the parents that was at stake in the case.[75]

The common law and constitutional developments concerning parental rights are mutually reinforcing and arrive at the same basic posture—children should be subject to the custody and control of their natural parents until the parents' conduct falls below the minimum standards established in such areas as neglect and abandonment, or until the parents propose to subject the child to some action that would interfere with his or her

71. *Id.* at 234.

72. Application of the President and Directors of Georgetown College, 331 F.2d 1000 (D.C. Cir. 1964).

73. *See* notes 33-34 and accompanying text *supra*.

74. Douglas stated:

> On this important and vital matter of education, I think the children should be entitled to be heard. While the parents, absent of dissent, normally speak for the entire family, the education of the child is a matter on which the child will often have decided views. . . .
>
> . . . It is the student's judgment, not his parents', that is essential if we are to give full meaning to what we have said about the Bill of Rights and of the rights of students to be the masters of their own destiny.

406 U.S. at 244-45 (Douglas, J., dissenting).

75. Chief Justice Burger, speaking for the majority, stated:

> Contrary to the suggestion of the dissenting opinion . . . our holding today in no degree depends on the assertion of the religious interest of the child as contrasted with that of the parents. It is the parents who are subject to prosecution here for failing to cause their children to attend school, and it is their right of free exercise, not that of their children, that must determine Wisconsin's power to impose criminal penalties on the parent.

Id. at 230-31.

health or safety. The pro-parent presumption is rebuttable. But its rebuttal is not dependent upon the relative quality of parents' child-rearing practices, at least not until that quality reaches some almost obvious extremes. Our society and its children are not infrequently required to bear difficult burdens as part of the price we pay for this degree of parental leeway. To this point in our history, the price has not seemed too high.

4. *Parental rights: in whose best interest?*

In spite of the widespread agreement on general principles that emerges from the common law and constitutional decisions, few of the cases shed much light on the reasons why parental rights have been recognized for so many years.[76] A question that naturally arises is whether these principles protect some interest of parents independent of the social, psychological, or other interests of children that flow from the family autonomy tradition. This question is relevant because, if all that matters is what is most advantageous to a particular child, perhaps state intervention in parent-child relationships should be more readily allowed than it is under existing law and practices.

The language chosen by many of the judges who have dealt with parental interest issues, however, suggests that more is at stake than the welfare of children.[77] The Supreme Court in *Meyer v. Nebraska* selected the right "to establish a home and bring up children" along with "the right[s] . . . to contract, to engage in any of the common occupations of life . . . [and] to worship God

76. Some relatively obvious social interests are served by the general discharge by parents of their duties toward their children as a concomitant of their rights to control and care for them. Whether viewed as parental rights or simply as family autonomy, some sense of parental sovereignty has been thought necessary in order to reinforce the responsibility that must be assumed by parents for maintenance of the social order. Roscoe Pound pointed out that the law should refrain from securing too vigorously the interests of children against their parents because of what would follow if any incentive were available to minors to abandon their family home rather than submit to necessary parental discipline. Thus, "a child impatient of parental authority might be incited to set at naught all reasonable domestic control by holding over his father's head the alternative of allowing him his way at home, or of paying for his support abroad. Accordingly it has been said that no one shall take it upon him to dictate to a parent what clothing a child should wear, at what time it shall be purchased, or of whom. All that must be left to the discretion of the father or mother." Ramsey v. Ramsey, 121 Ind. 215, 217, 23 N.E. 69, 70 (1889), *quoted in* Pound, *supra* note 35, at 186-87.

In addition to ensuring domestic control, our assumptions about parental authority have been thought necessary to ensure the fulfillment of basic functions served by the family that are necessary for the continuance of our culture. Such functions include the processes that involve socializing children as well as providing for their biological, psychological, and economic needs. *See* S. KATZ, WHEN PARENTS FAIL: THE LAW'S RESPONSE TO FAMILY BREAKDOWN ch. 1 (1971).

77. *See* notes 28-31 and accompanying text *supra*.

according to the dictates of [one's] own conscience" as a few of the most obvious illustrations of the meaning of "liberty," as the term is used in the due process clause of the Fourteenth Amendment.[78] Similarly, the Court in *Stanley v. Illinois* included within the protections of the due process clause "the interest of a parent in the companionship, care, custody, and management of his or her children."[79]

The right of parents to bring suits against third parties for alienation of the affections of their children has been recognized within the limited categories of relational interests protected by common law tort actions.[80] Parents may also recover for injuries to that relational interest under most wrongful death statutes, just as children may recover under those statutes for the death of a parent.[81] The existence of a significant economic interest does not satisfactorily explain these statutes. Corporations, for example, do not have a protected relational interest in their "key men" sufficient to justify a wrongful death action, even though the economic damage to a corporation through the loss of a key man may be of greater economic detriment than the loss by a family of its breadwinner. Similarly, the associational or companionship interest within families is valued in common law tort actions while that same interest is not protected as between close friends. That particular distinction may be influenced somewhat by the difficulties inherent in proving who one's friends are, but it is still a meaningful way of demonstrating the peculiar recognition given by the law to the uniqueness of intrafamily relational interests.

A recent Eighth Circuit decision acknowledges interests of this kind in recognizing the standing of a father to bring a civil rights action against police officers who had shot and killed his son.[82] In concluding that the killing invaded the father's "constitutionally protected rights under the due process clause of the Fourteenth Amendment,"[83] apart from the father's claims under wrongful death statutes, the court cited *Meyer* and *Griswold*,

---

78. 262 U.S. at 399.

79. 405 U.S. at 651. The Court cited three of its earlier decisions as authority for protecting the parental interest—a due process case, an equal protection case, and a Ninth Amendment case.

80. W. PROSSER, THE LAW OF TORTS § 124 (4th ed. 1971).

81. *See, e.g.*, UTAH CODE ANN. § 78-11-6 (1953): "[A] father, or in case of his death or desertion of his family, the mother, may maintain an action for the death or injury of a minor child when such injury or death is caused by the wrongful act or neglect of another . . . ."

82. Mattis v. Schnarr, 502 F.2d 588 (8th Cir. 1974).

83. *Id.* at 593.

saying: "The familial relationship between parent and child is fundamental to our civilization," and "[t]he practical effect of [the shooting by the policeman] was to deny the plaintiff the fundamental right to raise his son."[84]

It is quite possible that when family life is involved, some natural law attitudes linger, even in this age of sociological jurisprudence. Thomas Aquinas wrote that one of the most obvious examples of the operation of natural law is the education of one's own offspring.[85] Men and women in most cultures have long viewed their offspring as somehow being an extension of themselves, and as more than mere "property." The bearing and raising of children has probably brought people into contact with some sense of the Infinite, the mysteries of the universe, or Nature—however one may express it—more than any other human experience. Thus, it is not surprising that common law judges refer to parental interests as "sacred," "natural," or "fundamental" rights, especially when the constitutional standard for a "fundamental" right is whatever judges find when they

> look to the "traditions and [collective] conscience of our people" to determine whether a principle is "so rooted [there] . . . as to be ranked as fundamental." The inquiry is whether a right involved "is of such character that it cannot be denied without violating those 'fundamental principles of liberty and justice which lie at the base of all our civil and political institutions' . . . ."[86]

This search for fundamental rights is thought by some scholars to be in the nature of a search for natural law.[87]

Some special interest of parents (distinct from the welfare of their children) has been and should be the subject of legal and constitutional protections. What the parental interest may mean—especially where it is pitted against the interests of children—remains to be developed more fully. Nevertheless, the well-established cultural assumption favoring parental interests re-

84. *Id.* at 594, 595. The court added, "We believe that 'parenthood is a substantial interest of surpassing value and protected from deprivation without due process of law'—a fundamental legal right." *Id.* at 595.

85. T. AQUINAS, SUMMA THEOLOGICA, TREATISE ON LAW, Question 94, in THE GREAT LEGAL PHILOSOPHERS 67 (1959).

86. Griswold v. Connecticut, 381 U.S. 479, 493 (Goldberg, J., concurring) (citation omitted).

87. *See* Dixon, *The "New" Substantive Due Process and the Democratic Ethic: A Prolegomenon*, 1976 B.Y.U.L. REV. 43; Kauper, The Higher Law and the Rights of Man in a Revolutionary Society (AEI's Distinguished Lecture Series on the Bicentennial 1974).

quires that the interests of children not be the only factor weighed when considering the state-family relationship.

Furthermore, as discussed more fully below,[88] the evidence suggests that the maintenance of parental interests within a family tradition is also in the best interests of children.

5. *Protection for children within a family tradition*

As suggested above, the family tradition has not been insensitive to the need for protecting children against potential abuse by parents or others who might be in a position to exploit their limited capacities. Although there is some dispute about the philosophical origins of the common law right of children to be protected from parental neglect, abuse, or abandonment,[89] the beginnings of such rights were recognized—at least theoretically—in Blackstone's day.[90] Protections against child abuse and other forms of parental unfitness have grown until today they represent fundamental limitations on parental rights. Statutes proscribing various forms of parental misconduct are found in every state,[91] with remedies ranging from supervision of parental custody to criminal prosecution and permanent termination of parental rights.

Significantly, protections against parental unfitness exist as part of the family tradition. Parental authority per se is not questioned, but only its abuse. Forms of protection for children consistent with, or part of, the family tradition may be found in such developments as child labor laws, the growing breakdown of intrafamily tort immunity, statutory recognition for the preferences of minors involved in custody disputes, the emergence of favorable tort doctrines applicable to child trespassers, and the maintenance of rights entitling minors to inherit and own property and to be parties to litigation (albeit through adult representatives). Such developments reflect continuing awareness of the special needs of children.

The family tradition has developed its own balance between

88. Notes 146-58 and accompanying text *infra*.

89. *Compare* Kleinfeld, *The Balance of Power Among Infants, Their Parents and The State*, 4 FAMILY L.Q. 410, 411-12 (1970) (Aristotle is the source for the theory that the purpose of parental control is the welfare of the child rather than the welfare of others in society or benefit to the parent) *with* Kelly, *On Some Changes in the Legal Status of the Child Since Blackstone*, 13 INT'L REV. 83, 90, 91 (1882) (protection of the child is a natural right inherent in the child), in THE LEGAL RIGHTS OF CHILDREN (1974).

90. 1 W. BLACKSTONE, COMMENTARIES *450.

91. *See* Katz, Howe & McGrath, *Child Neglect Laws in America*, 9 FAMILY L.Q. 1 (1975).

the rights of parents and the rights of children; its purpose is to support the family as an institution and at the same time provide state protection for children where parental authority is abused. The juvenile court system, which has had the responsibility of balancing children's and parents' rights, has produced its share of disappointments, but even after the close scrutiny given it in *Gault* and its progeny, its unique contributions are still highly valued. This system, together with the common law and constitutional doctrines that have been developed in the family law context, contain at least the conceptual tools for accommodating the competing claims and needs of parents and children. Thus, the notion of "children's rights" is neither as original nor as recent as it may sound.

C. *When Traditions Collide: The Abolition of Childhood?*

As indicated above, children have not been part of the individual tradition. They have, however, been very much a part of a family tradition intended to prepare them for entry into the individual tradition. The fairness of maintaining that relationship between the two traditions has gone unquestioned for years. However, since the civil rights movement and recent Supreme Court decisions giving constitutional dimensions to certain rights for children, new questions have been raised.

1. *The effect of other rights movements*

One significant fact about the civil rights movement of the 1950's and '60's is the extent to which it involved students and other concerned citizens from all parts of the country. Such participation contributed materially in bringing the concerns of the movement to the nation's attention. It also exposed a large number of people already characterized by a strong social conscience to the plight of disadvantaged groups. Thus, many of the same persons who cut the teeth of their social activism in the civil rights movement were later attracted to other social action causes. It was no coincidence, then, that rising concern about poverty and discrimination against ethnic minority groups and women followed so closely on the heels of the civil rights movement.[92]

Civil rights workers recognized early that poverty was a sig-

92. *See generally* Freeman, *The Origins of the Women's Liberation Movement*, 78 Am. J. Sociology 792 (1973).

nificant impediment in the path toward equality of opportunity. The effects of poverty and racial discrimination seemed especially harsh when visited upon the children of disadvantaged families. As a result, a specific concern about the needs and rights of those children emerged within the context of larger concerns.[93] The peculiar needs of disadvantaged children were more a function of the widespread impact of racial discrimination and poverty than of discrimination against children per se. Nevertheless, the social and political powerlessness of disadvantaged families seemed especially poignant when considered from the viewpoint of the children within those families, who lacked ability to change their circumstances not only because of their minority or economic status, but also because of their childhood.

Increased public awareness of the damage caused to members of minority groups by cultural deprivation and other forms of discrimination also increased public concern about child abuse and neglect. The inability of children to defend themselves against such parental failures has made it logical to view them as another class of victims being harmed by the exploitation of those holding a position of relative power and advantage.

The recognition of disadvantage and discrimination in these circumstances has made irresistible the inclination to lump children together with other disadvantaged classes who are struggling for their own kind of liberation. It has been said that the civil rights movement and the various liberation efforts that have followed it have made the nation begin "to see the necessity for children's liberation."[94] One advocate of a general children's liberation movement has written that "the arguments for and against perpetuation of [minority] status have a familiar ring. In good measure they are the same arguments that were advanced over the issues of slavery and the emancipation of married women."[95] Another has echoed, "[t]he child's subjugated status was rooted in the same benevolent despotism that kings, husbands, and slave masters claimed as their moral right."[96]

As a result of this conceptual consolidation, many of the arguments for granting greater rights to children proceed from

93. *See The Rights of Children—A Statement by Senator Walter F. Mondale*, 43 HARV. EDUC. REV. 483 (1973); Polier, *Myths and Realities in the Search for Juvenile Justice*, 44 HARV. EDUC. REV. 112, 121 (1974) ("the denial of services to children from minority groups [has] shadowed every aspect of child care and juvenile justice"). *See generally* CHILDREN AND POVERTY (N. GLAZER & C. Creedon eds. 1968).

94. R. FARSON, BIRTHRIGHTS 2 (1974).

95. Foster & Freed, *supra* note 6, at 343.

96. Wald, *Making Sense Out of the Rights of Youth*, 4 HUMAN RIGHTS 13, 15 (1974).

general premises of philosophical egalitarianism rather than from evidence that children as a class are damaged in some demonstrable way by existing constraints upon their liberty or that removal of such constraints would benefit them in some way. A sociologist who advocates full abolition of legal and social concepts of minority status from compulsory education laws to laws restricting sexual activity, voting, marrying, divorcing, and contracting has stated:

> In another sense, asking what is good for children is beside the point. We will grant children rights for the same reason we grant rights to adults, not because we are sure that children will then become better people, but more for ideological reasons, because we believe that expanding freedom as a way of life is worthwhile in itself.[97]
>
> . . . .
>
> If all this sounds too open and free, we must recognize that in this society . . . we are not likely to err in the direction of too much freedom.[98]

2. *Supreme Court decisions*

Within the last decade, the Supreme Court has begun to address children's rights in constitutional terms. There does not

97. FARSON, *supra* note 94, at 31.

98. *Id.* at 31, 153. The a priori justification advanced by Farson for his point of view is shared by other children's liberation advocates who are unable to offer much support for their "radical version of children's rights"—"[I]ts most convincing justification is simply that it is right." Wald, *supra* note 96, at 29. Farson's views have received wide and provocative press coverage. Note, for example, the leading article by Joan Nassivera, *Get Ready for Kids' Lib*, National Observer, Sept. 14, 1974, at 1, col. 1. Also, see Farson's treatment of the same topic in the L.A. Times, Oct. 19, 1975, part IV, at 5, col. 2.

A point of view similar to Farson's is outlined in educator John Holt's ESCAPE FROM CHILDHOOD (1974), which outlines and then treats at length a proposed list of rights that, it is argued, should be made available "to any young person, of whatever age, who wants to make use of them." *Id.* at 18. The list includes the right to vote, the right to financial independence and responsibility, the right to choose where one lives, how one is educated—"the right to do, in general, what any adult may legally do." *Id.* at 19. *See also* CHILDREN'S LIBERATION (D. Gottlieb ed. 1973); CHILDREN'S RIGHTS (1971); M. GERZON, A CHILDHOOD FOR EVERY CHILD: THE POLITICS OF PARENTHOOD (1973).

Such sources contain criticisms of the public school systems, assumptions about family life, and the effect of modern technological society upon children, with occasional reference to some legal issues. The prevailing tone of this literature is that of disappointment and frustration with American institutions. Consider, for example, the statement by child psychiatrist Paul Adams that "the family's vital role in authoritarianism is entirely repugnant to the free soul in our age." Adams, *The Infant, the Family and Society*, in CHILDREN'S RIGHTS 51, 52 (1971). Adams asks for a restructuring of society in favor of children, but states that the conditions necessary to achieve the goals to which children are entitled are "to end war as an institution; then to eliminate poverty; then racism; and finally to put an end to the meaninglessness of living in a bureaucratized society." *Id.* at 76.

seem to be any necessary relationship between these cases and the country's heightened equality consciousness, at least not in the language of the decisions, but the coincidence in timing suggests that the two developments are not unrelated. Still, the Court's concerns have been confined to much narrower contexts than the large-scale legal and social changes advocated by those who would reject the concept of minority status. The possibility that the Court's decisions may improperly be cited as authority for implications well beyond the Court's intent is no small risk in the current climate. It is therefore important to read the cases closely in search of both legal effects and underlying intentions. What follows is a descriptive summary of relevant recent cases. Further classification and analysis of these cases is offered in a subsequent section.[99]

In re Gault[100] established the principle that minors may not be denied basic prodecural due process in juvenile court proceedings. Drawing upon prior cases in which "restricted aspects" of procedural due process protection for minors had been acknowledged, Justice Fortas wrote that whatever the precise impact of the prior cases, "neither the Fourteenth Amendment nor the Bill of Rights is for adults alone."[101]

Gault was an especially compelling case. A 15-year-old boy had been committed to a state industrial school for a period up to 6 years on charges arising out of a lewd phone call. The facts indicated flagrant abuse of the simplest procedural protections, from lack of notice about the nature of the charge to absence of the complaining witness from the hearing. The opinion expressly rejects the idea that a child's only right is to custody, not liberty,[102] thereby expressing the clearest idea to emerge from *Gault*—that there is nothing about minority status that requires the courts to exclude ideas about due process protections from proceedings involving juveniles. What the case meant for the juvenile court philosophy of protecting minors against the full-blown formality of criminal proceedings, however, was less than clear in 1967.

The meaning and implications of *Gault* have been developed in subsequent cases, many of which are summarized in *McKeiver v. Pennsylvania*,[103] wherein the Court rejected a claimed right to

99. Notes 130-45 and accompanying text *infra*.
100. 387 U.S. 1 (1967).
101. *Id.* at 13.
102. *See id.* at 17.
103. 403 U.S. 528 (1971).

trial by jury in the juvenile courts. In *McKeiver*, the Court explained that its collective decisions on due process requirements for juveniles arose from a special need to remedy what had become an inadequate fact-finding process in delinquency proceedings, rather than from a rejection of the basic philosophy of the juvenile justice system. The Court stated that *Gault* and its progeny "do not spell the doom of the juvenile court system or . . . deprive it of its 'informality, flexibility, or speed.' "[104] Further, the Court made it clear that it "has not yet said that all rights constitutionally assured to an adult accused of crime . . . are . . . available to the juvenile . . . ."[105] Rather, said the Court, denial of the right to a jury trial in fact promotes a desirable preferential treatment of minors accused of crimes:

> The imposition of the jury trial on the juvenile court system would not strengthen greatly, if at all, the factfinding function, and would, contrarily, provide an attrition of the juvenile court's assumed ability to function in a unique manner. It would not remedy the defects of the system. Meager as has been the hoped-for advance in the juvenile field, the alternative would be regressive, would lose what has been gained, and would tend once again to place the juvenile in the routine of the criminal process.[106]

---

104. *Id.* at 534, *quoting In re* Winship, 397 U.S. 358, 366 (1970).

105. *Id.* at 533.

106. *Id.* at 547. The Court continued:

> We are reluctant to disallow the States to experiment further and to seek in new and different ways the elusive answers to the problems of the young, and we feel that we would be impeding that experimentation by imposing the jury trial.
>
> . . . .
>
> . . . Concern about the inapplicability of exclusionary and other rules of evidence, about the juvenile court judge's possible awareness of the juvenile's prior record and of the contents of the social file; about repeated appearances of the same familiar witnesses in the persons of juvenile and probation officers and social workers—all to the effect that this will create the likelihood of pre-judgment—chooses to ignore, it seems to us, every aspect of fairness, of concern, of sympathy, and of paternal attention that the juvenile court system contemplates.

Id. at 547, 550.

The disappointments of the juvenile court movement are hardly unique. The same report on which the Supreme Court relied so heavily in summarizing some of its negative conclusions about the juvenile courts also stated that to "say that juvenile courts have failed to achieve their goals is to say no more than what is true of criminal courts in the United States. But failure is most striking when hopes are highest." THE PRESIDENT'S COMM'N ON LAW ENFORCEMENT AND ADMINISTRATION OF JUSTICE, TASK FORCE REPORT: JUVENILE DELINQUENCY AND YOUTH CRIME 7 (1967), *quoted in* McKeiver v. Pennsylvania, 403 U.S. 528, 545 (1971).

In the juvenile justice context, then, the Court has evidently not rejected the validity of a legal minority status, although it is willing to provide constitutional protection against the abuse of that status.

The public school setting is the second major area in which the Supreme Court has acknowledged minors' rights of constitutional dimensions. In *Tinker v. Des Moines School District,*[107] the Court found that the First Amendment rights of three students had been violated when school authorities suspended them from school for wearing black armbands to protest the government's policy in Vietnam. Writing for the majority, Justice Fortas stated that, "[s]tudents in school as well as out of school are 'persons' under our Constitution. They are possessed of fundamental rights which the State must respect . . . ."[108] The Court did not elaborate on the meaning of "fundamental rights," leaving the reader uncertain whether the Court had in mind the introduction of any new principles broader than necessary to achieve the result of the case. This lack of clarity prompted Justice Stewart's concurring opinion, in which he stated that he could not "share the Court's uncritical assumption that, school discipline aside, the First Amendment rights of children are co-extensive with those of adults." Continuing, he stated that: "Indeed, I had thought the Court decided otherwise just last Term in *Ginsberg v. New York*."[109]

Tinker, like *Gault,* demonstrates the Court's willingness to recognize constitutional protections for minors. It is far from

107. 393 U.S. 503 (1969).

108. *Id.* at 511.

109. *Id.* at 515 (citation omitted). For a summary of *Ginsberg* see notes 48-50 and accompanying text *supra*. In an emotional dissent by Justice Black, whose record in support of First Amendment freedoms needs no explanation, great concern was expressed about the implications of the *Tinker* decision:

> [I]f the time has come when pupils of state-supported schools, kindergartens, grammar schools, or high schools, can defy and flout orders of school officials to keep their minds on their own schoolwork, it is the beginning of a new revolutionary era of permissiveness in this country fostered by the judiciary. The next logical step, it appears to me, would be to hold unconstitutional laws that bar pupils under 21 or 18 from voting, or from being elected members of the boards of education.
>
> . . . .
>
> . . . The original idea of schools, which I do not believe is yet abandoned as worthless or out of date, was that children had not yet reached the point of experience and wisdom which enabled them to teach all of their elders.

Id. at 518, 522. As pointed out more recently by Justice Powell in Goss v. Lopez, 419 U.S. 565, 600 n.22 (dissenting opinion), some of Justice Black's fears have been realized since *Tinker* through a "flood of litigation" by children alleging violations of their constitutional rights by school officials.

clear, however, that the *Tinker* Court intended directly to address the question of minority status.

One of the cases apparently spawned by *Tinker* reached the Supreme Court in *Goss v. Lopez*,[110] a 1975 decision holding that students facing temporary disciplinary suspensions from a public school are entitled to such due process protections as prior notice and an opportunity for a hearing. The *Goss* majority opinion, written by Justice White, also said nothing about the larger question of minority status raised by the concurring opinion in *Tinker;* however, Justice Powell's dissent in *Goss* did briefly address the larger question:

> [T]he Court ignores the experience of mankind as well as the long history of our law, recognizing that there *are* differences which must be accommodated in determining the rights and duties of children as compared with those of adults. Examples of this distinction abound in our law: in contracts, in torts, in criminal law and procedure, in criminal sanctions and rehabilitation, and in the right to vote and to hold office. Until today, and except in the special context of the First Amendment issue in *Tinker,* the educational rights of children and teenagers in the elementary and secondary schools have not been analogized to the rights of adults or to those accorded college students. Even with respect to the First Amendment, the rights of children have not been regarded as "co-extensive with those of adults."[111]

Justice Powell's statement accurately summarizes statutory and common law attitudes as well as the prior opinions of the Court, all of which have consistently recognized differences between adults and children—both by express acknowledgment and by assumptions of the obvious.

Because the *Goss* majority did not explicitly deal with the historic distinction between the legal statuses of adults and minors, it is doubtful that the Court intended to address that question by mere implication. It is more reasonable to expect that issues of that significance would be dealt with explicitly if the Court intended to deal with them at all. Perhaps the most that is intended by *Goss* is found in Justice Powell's suggestion that minors' rights in the school context have now been "analogized" to the rights of adults.

The Court has not yet addressed the issue of minor's constitutional rights in a case where a minor's claim was pitted against

110. 419 U.S. 565 (1975).

111. *Id.* at 590-91 (Powell, J., dissenting) (emphasis in original).

the alleged constitutional rights of parents. In rejecting Justice Douglas' dissenting argument that the desires of the Amish children were relevant to the resolution of the case, the majority in *Wisconsin v. Yoder*[112] did come close to dealing with that kind of conflict:

> Our holding in no way determines the proper resolution of possible competing interests of parents, children, and the State in an appropriate state court proceeding in which the power of the State is asserted on the theory that Amish parents are preventing their minor children from attending high school despite their expressed desires to the contrary. Recognition of the claim of the State in such a proceeding would, of course, call into question traditional concepts of parental control over the religious upbringing and education of their minor children recognized in this Court's past decisions. It is clear that such an intrusion by a State into family decisions in the area of religious training would give rise to grave questions of religious freedom . . . .[113]

This view reflects obvious concern with the family tradition and the implications for that tradition of a child's constitutional claim against the interests of his parents. Also, in such circumstances it is the "claim of the State" that would create the conflict, rather than the claim by a child. The assumption that the child's claim would be asserted by the state rather than by the child may arise out of the compulsory school law context of *Yoder*, but it may also reflect the implicit assumption that minors would lack the capacity, legally, and perhaps practically, to assume responsibility for evaluating and asserting their own position. A further attempt to classify and evaluate the Court's children's rights decisions is made below.[114]

3. *Lower court interpretations of Supreme Court decisions*

The failure of some key Supreme Court majority opinions to respond to invitations for clarification made by concurring and dissenting opinions may have left the impression that perhaps the Court has intended to make the constitutional rights of minors coextensive with those of adults. At least, the scarcity of clear statements on the general validity of a legal minority status has allowed some lower courts to conclude that they may, consistent

112. 406 U.S. 205 (1972).

113. *Id.* at 231.

114. Notes 130-45 and accompanying text *infra*.

with Supreme Court precedent, severely limit the effect of that status, if not abandon it completely.[115] *State v. Koome,*[116] a 1975 Washington case, illustrates such an interpretation. The significance of the case arises not only from its language, but also from the possible effect of its reasoning in a later Washington case, *In re Snyder.*[117]

Koome involved an appeal by a physician who had been convicted of violating a state criminal statute by performing an abortion on a woman under the age of 18 without the consent of her legal guardian. In holding that the statute unduly infringed on minors' constitutional right of privacy, the Supreme Court of Washington reasoned that: (1) *Roe v. Wade*[118] established that state regulation of abortions in the early stages of pregnancy violates a pregnant woman's fundamental constitutional right of privacy; (2) minors are people and, therefore, have a fundamental constitutional right to privacy; and (3) statutory parental consent requirements constitute state interference with personal privacy to an extent not justified by any compelling state interest. Some equal protection arguments were also dealt with regarding the failure of any asserted state interest to justify age classifications affecting the fundamental right of privacy. Four of the nine judges in *Koome* dissented on the grounds that, even assuming the existence of a fundamental right of privacy for minors, the state had a sufficiently compelling interest in the "quality" of a minor's abortion decision and in the mental health of minors to justify the consent requirement.[119]

A major difference between the reasoning of the majority and dissenting opinions is the extent to which each recognized the legal status historically given to minors. The dissent defended the distinction between minors and other persons with broad, general arguments, citing authorities ranging from Supreme Court cases acknowledging the legitimacy of the classifications to the introductory section of *American Jurisprudence 2d's* treatment of "infants." The majority view deeply undercut the distinction:

115. *See* Poe v. Gerstein, 517 F.2d 787, 789 (5th Cir. 1975).

116. 84 Wash. 2d 901, 530 P.2d 260 (1975).

117. 85 Wash. 2d 182, 532 P.2d 278 (1975).

118. 410 U.S. 113 (1973).

119. The dissenting opinion was influenced by the statute's requirement of consent by a "legal guardian" rather than by the minor's "parent," because the "guardian" language would permit a juvenile court to intervene in the parent-child relationship under its neglect statute and appoint a guardian who could consent to an abortion in circumstances where parental refusal amounted to neglect. 84 Wash. 2d at 921, 530 P.2d at 272.

> Prima facie, the constitutional rights of minors, including the right of privacy, are coextensive with those of adults. Where minors' rights have been held subject to curtailment by the state in excess of that permissible in the case of adults it has been because some peculiar state interest existed in the regulation and protection of children, not because the rights themselves are of some inferior kind.[120]

The majority's choice of language betrays the contradiction inherent in its reasoning. By acknowledging that a "peculiar state interest" in "the regulation and protection of children" has justified differential treatment, the court disproves its premise that "prima facie, the constitutional rights of minors . . . are coextensive with those of adults." The pattern has not been to presume "coextensive rights" or coextensive capacities; rather, the law has presumed the existence of basic differences between the capacities and needs of children and adults.

Because of this presumption, the basic inquiry in contexts involving minors has been the extent to which their peculiar limitations and needs justify or require greater flexibility, supervision, protection, and the like. In addition, the law has consciously considered relevant parental claims in order to foster the long-range preference of our system for the family.

Consider, for example, the common law's concern about the need for parental consent prior to the performance of surgery on a minor. The cases have long recognized that a child has a "right" to essential medical treatment. But the legal authority recognized in parents has always been carefully balanced against that right. In contrast, after suddenly concluding that a "constitutional right" may be involved in the abortion context, the Washington court only casually and inaccurately addresses the common law background. The court relies more heavily on two recent Washington statutes that authorize minors 14 years of age and older to receive treatment for drug abuse and venereal disease without parental consent.[121] Although the court does not discuss the policies represented by these statutes, they appear to involve two special situations that have been singled out for legislative treatment because of the unusually strong and recent interest in assisting youth afflicted by drug addiction and venereal disease to obtain confidential nonsurgical treatment for problems that pose serious permanent threats to their physical health.

120. *Id.* at 904, 530 P.2d at 263.

121. *Id.* at 910-11, 530 P.2d at 266-67.

The court then cites and quotes at length from a 1967 Washington case which held that a jury could appropriately evaluate the capacity of a married, 18-year-old father to give an informed consent to sterilization surgery. Further, the court refers to Washington's basic age-of-majority statute, which authorizes persons 18 years of age and older to marry, consent to surgery, and otherwise act as adults. These latter two references are irrelevant to the common law positions of minors because they deal with adults, not with unemancipated minors.

The court's only other statement about parental consent requirements is a surprising misstatement of authority:

> A doctor competently performing any other type of surgery [than abortion] on a consenting minor runs virtually no risk of even civil liability because of the absence of parental consent. *See* Pilpel, Minor's Rights to Medical Care, 36 Albany L. Rev. 462, 466 (1972).[122]

Many cases have established the prevailing common law rule that liability may be imposed upon a physician in such circumstances, and Ms. Pilpel does not dispute the existence of the cases or the rule. Rather, she simply observes that "no case has been found in any jurisdiction in which liability has been imposed on a physician or health facility on the basis of failure to secure parental consent for any kind of medical treatment where the minor was over the age of 15 years." She points out that despite this fact, doctors remain fearful of treating minors without parental consent, and therefore she favors the adoption of statutes altering current consent requirements. With this as its sole authority, the *Koome* court concludes that a statute requiring parental consent for abortions is inconsistent with the common law. Existing case law, even in Washington, seems to be quite the opposite.[123]

This brief treatment of the Washington court's lapse of both perception and judgment is not presented merely to criticize its statement of the law, but, more importantly, to illustrate the extent to which the apparent magic of a child's alleged constitutional right can desensitize a generally competent court to the real context in which a parent-child conflict arises. Any adequate discussion of the constitutionality of statutes requiring parental consent for abortions must take into account the origins and purposes of the common law rules on parental consent to surgery on

122. *Id.* at 913, 530 P.2d at 268.

123. *E.g., In re* Hudson, 13 Wash. 2d 673, 126 P.2d 765 (1942). *See also In re* Green, 448 Pa. 338, 292 A.2d 387 (1972); W. PROSSER, THE LAW OF TORTS § 18 (4th ed. 1971).

children, just as the United States Supreme Court has taken into account the context of the juvenile court in its juvenile due process decisions and the public school context in the school discipline decisions. The involvement of a constitutional right for minors by no means lifts a case above the practical and policy problems of minority status into some abstract sphere in which an abandonment of that special body of law that has always applied to children is justified. When both parents and children are involved, as in *Koome,* the law must concern itself even more with that special context, since a court must then confront the unique legal and social role of parents.

It is doubtful whether the children's rights decisions of the United States Supreme Court warrant the conclusion that, by interjecting concerns of constitutional dimension into state processes involving minors, the Court has intended to say that the presumptions justifying the treatment of minors as a special class have become outmoded. None of the relevant cases imply that the actual capacities of minors have changed in any way that requires a change in the legal rules or assumptions that grew out of the traditional view that the competence of minors to exercise adult rights is limited. The oversimplified reasoning of courts that believe recent constitutional case law has made the "rights" of minors "prima facie . . . co-extensive with those of adults" is especially dangerous, since such reasoning permits a shift in the crucial presumptions about the status or capacity of minors. Indeed, just such a shift seems to occur in *State v. Koome* because of the heavy presumptive effect of placing the claim of a minor behind the barricades of the compelling state interest test.

This shift in presumptions in the laws dealing with minors can come legitimately only after a strong factual showing that there is no longer any basis for the premises underlying traditional treatment of minors. That there has been such a showing regarding the factual premises underlying certain limited aspects of the procedures employed by the juvenile courts or the public schools may illustrate the process by which specific, case-by-case changes in the law's treatment of minors will and should come about; but the showing in those narrow areas dealt primarily with certain procedural issues, not the general question of the capacity of minors. These cases offer no rational justification for abandoning an established, factually based presumption, the disappearance of which would have almost limitless consequences for American law.

The use of "children's rights" terminology in *Koome* not only teased the court away from dealing adequately with established presumptions about minority capacity, but it also precluded any serious attempt at dealing with established presumptions about parental roles and rights. The purpose and history of either presumption is sufficient to place the problem of minors' abortions on a different plane from the matter of adult abortions. Taken together, the two presumptions demand a broad and sophisticated judicial inquiry into both evidence and policy. No such inquiry was supplied by the Washington court, perhaps because it believed that the introduction of terms used in the individual tradition somehow made the family tradition irrelevant.

In *Poe v. Gerstein,*[124] another case dealing with parental consent requirements for abortions performed on minors, the Fifth Circuit showed a similar tendency to place what is characterized as a child's constitutional right ahead of parental and familial interests. One wonders what the logical extensions of the following reasoning might mean for the myriad other sources of normal parent-child confrontation:

> [M]erely facing one's parents with the problems of unwanted pregnancy would present a considerable deterrent to abortion among teenage girls and, in fact, may adversely affect their mental and physical health and thereby arguably infringe upon the minor's constitutional rights.[125]

This point of view carries overtones of an important theme in the egalitarian ethic as it applies to the parental role: "[T]he family's vital role in authoritarianism is entirely repugnant to the free soul in our age."[126]

The Washington court's opinion in the *Snyder* case, discussed as the introductory illustration of this article, was handed down just 1 month after that court's decision in *Koome*. Although the court in *Snyder* avoided reference to a children's rights theory in upholding the juvenile court's finding of incorrigibility, the record and the briefs filed in the case make it clear that the parties favoring the lower court action were influenced by a broad reading of *Gault* and general literature arguing for a broad extension of the traditional rights of minors.[127] The "right" of a child to effect termination of parental custody as a means of perma-

124. 517 F.2d 787 (5th Cir. 1975).

125. *Id.* at 793 n.11.

126. Adams, *The Infant, the Family and Society*, in CHILDREN'S RIGHTS 51, 52 (1971).

127. *See* notes 4-7 and accompanying text *supra*.

nently leaving home when there is a "serious family conflict" has been advocated in various ways in recent literature.[128] However, *Snyder* may be the first case in which legal proceedings have resulted in a child-initiated termination of parental rights in the express absence of any finding of parental unfitness.

Although the *Snyder* court may not have believed it was breaking new ground, its uncritical acceptance of what amounts to a children's rights position on a matter as basic as parental custody is worthy of some attention. Under both the theory and the result of *Snyder*, there is little to prevent any other dissatisfied and "resolute" child from taking the same position and achieving the same outcome as the teenager in that case.[129] It is at least reasonable to wonder to what extent the philosophy of constitutional rights for minors made explicit in *Koome* may have influenced the court's assessment of the issues in *Snyder*.

Perhaps the courts involved in *Gerstein*, *Koome*, and *Snyder* were unwittingly influenced by the modern winds of egalitarianism; perhaps they were conscientiously trying to follow the leadership of the Supreme Court; perhaps the impact those decisions would have on the family tradition was not adequately pointed out by counsel; perhaps that impact was pointed out, understood, and rejected. Whatever their basis, cases like these convey the impression that, in the aftermath of *Gault*, the nation has suddenly awakened to the supposedly startling idea that children are people.

With that awakening comes embarrassment and an impulse to right all the wrongs ever committed against children. The vehi-

---

128. J. Holt, Escape from Childhood 206 (1974) (establishment of "secondary guardians" to which children could turn if they desire to leave their natural parents); Farson, *supra* note 94, at 42-62 (1974) (Kibbutz-type cooperative arrangements to take children away from possible conflicts at home); Foster & Freed, *supra* note 6, at 368 (1972) (appointment of a public guardian to serve the best interests of children).

129. The following excerpts characterize the view taken by the state of the child's position in *Snyder*:

> [C]o-respondent is a bright, able and resolute young woman who . . . knowingly and intelligently admitted the facts of the petition.
>
> . . . .
>
> . . . The petitioner's contention seems to be that . . . only in cases of extreme physical abuse or neglect should the state be allowed to intervene. Cynthia Snyder is a person who has apparently made a decision about her life. That decision is that she will not go home and be treated like an inanimate possession by her parents.
>
> . . . .
>
> . . . [C]hildren are autonomous individuals, entitled to the same rights and privileges before the law as adults.

Brief of State Respondent at 5, 11, 23.

cle for this penance is a series of judicial pronouncements that seem to incorporate by reference and thereby misapply massive amounts of constitutional law and other legal doctrines developed painstakingly over the generations in cases involving adult litigants and the classes they represent. These pronouncements also tend to ignore another large group of legal concepts already developed to meet the special needs and problems of children in families.

III. Abandoning Children to Their "Rights": The Risks of Uncritical Liberation

A. *Rights of Protection vs. Rights of Choice*

When children are involved, a significant distinction can be drawn between legal rights that protect one from undue interference by the state or from the harmful acts of others and legal rights that permit persons to make affirmative choices of binding consequence, such as voting, marrying, exercising religious preferences, and choosing whether to seek education.[130] For purposes of this discussion, the first category will be referred to as rights of protection; the second, rights of choice.

Rights of protection include the right not to be imprisoned without due process, rights to property, and rights to physical protection. The protection category seems to embrace most, if not all, of the legal doctrines that have been developed to date for the benefit of minors in both the constitutional context and the juvenile law context. *Gault,* for example, was expressly concerned only with procedural protections applicable to the adjudicatory

130. A general distinction of this type has been suggested in Kleinfeld, *The Balance of Power Among Infants, Their Parents, and The State,* 4 Family L.Q. 320, 321-22 (1970).

The Supreme Court has construed the "liberty" rights of the due process clause broadly and has in recent years rejected the distinction between "rights" and "privileges" which was once thought applicable to procedural due process rights. Board of Regents v. Roth, 408 U.S. 564, 571 (1972). The liberty concept has been defined to include "not merely freedom from bodily restraint but also the right of the individual to contract, . . . to marry, . . . [and] to worship God according to the dictates of his own conscience . . . ." Meyer v. Nebraska, 262 U.S. 390, 399 (1923). The elimination of the rights-privileges distinction and the use of such expansive language may appear to suggest that there is no room for a distinction between protection rights and choice rights. However, the rights-privileges distinction focuses on the form of liberty in question, while the protection-choice distinction argued for here focuses on the individual's capacity to benefit from the liberty in question. Moreover, the flexibility inherent in the broad approach to due process liberty actually encourages giving attention to factual distinctions as meaningful as capacity, so that instead of being bound by purely monolithic theories about "rights," the courts may evaluate "the significance of the state-created or state-enforced right and . . . the substantiality of the alleged deprivation." Goss v. Lopez, 419 U.S. at 599-600 (Powell, J., dissenting).

stage of juvenile delinquency proceedings in which incarceration may be a consequence of the adjudication.[131] *McKeiver* noted that all of the Court's juvenile delinquency decisions had been limited to the application of certain procedural constitutional protections to the adjudicative aspects of juvenile proceedings.[132] Nevertheless, the *McKeiver* Court refused to grant the right to trial by jury to juveniles precisely because that particular right did not provide a form of protection beneficial to minors, given the Court's continuing commitment to the "paternal attention that the juvenile court system contemplates."[133]

Goss v. Lopez proceeds from the due process principle of protection against the procedurally unfair deprivation of a state-created right to education. The *Goss* Court identified this right as "a property interest . . . which may not be taken away for misconduct without adherence to the minimum procedures required by the [due process] clause."[134] The due process guarantees applied in *Goss* were also intended to protect students against the arbitrary deprivations of liberty thought to be inherent in the damage to their personal reputations caused by suspension.

Tinker is less clearly in the protection category than are the due process cases. The First Amendment rights involved in that case are probably closer, as a matter of pure theoretical categories, to choice rights than protection rights. It was this theoretical aspect of *Tinker* that caused Justice Stewart to enter a concurring opinion in which he wrote that "[a] State may permissibly determine that, at least in some precisely delineated areas, a child—like someone in a captive audience—is not possessed of that full capacity for individual choice which is the presupposition of First Amendment guarantees."[135] Justice Stewart's reasoning suggests that it is reasonable to conclude (as he did) that the school authorities in *Tinker* could be legally limited in restricting the right of students peacefully to wear black armbands without also concluding that such an outcome imputes "full capacity for individual choice" to public school students. This position flows in part from the observation that the exercise of free speech rights

131. 387 U.S. at 13.

132. 403 U.S. at 550.

133. *Id.*

134. 419 U.S. at 574.

135. 393 U.S. at 515 (1969) (Stewart, J., concurring), *quoting* Ginsberg v. New York, 390 U.S. 629, 649-50 (1968). Justice Powell, who dissented in *Goss*, would also have joined in the *Tinker* conclusion, had he been on the Court, because it was "a narrowly written First Amendment opinion which I could well have joined on its facts." 419 U.S. at 600 n.22 (Powell, J., dissenting).

in the *Tinker* context did not involve the assumption of binding and permanent responsibility that would be involved in such choice rights as voting, contracting, or marrying. It can also be argued that the rights of parents to free expression and control of their children may have been an important subject of protection in *Tinker* since the parents of the children involved had encouraged their children to wear the armbands and were obviously instrumental in bringing the litigation that ensued.[136] In that sense, *Tinker* might be considered another in the long line of cases protecting parental rights to teach and influence their children against state claims that would limit the exercise of such parental prerogatives. Thus, *Tinker* is not an obstacle to the assertion that none of the Supreme Court's children's rights cases provide authority for upholding the exercise of minors' choice rights—particularly against contrary parental claims.

The statutes creating juvenile court jurisdiction over parents are also in the "protection" category, being designed to protect children against harmful abuse, neglect, or abandonment by their parents. Moreover, the entire juvenile justice system is based upon the premise that children who are yet in the developmental stages of becoming mature adults should be protected against the long term implications of their own decisions made at a time when they lack sufficient capacity and experience to be held as responsible as an adult would be for the same decision. Thus, legal limitations on the effect of minors' choices are in fact "rights" designed for minors' protection. That basic philosophy has not been repudiated by the Court's recent juvenile due process cases, which have criticized specific inadequacies of modern juvenile court factfinding procedures, but not the concepts about the peculiar capacities and needs of children that underlie the juvenile court system.[137]

More broadly, it has been of profound importance in all legal inquiries involving children that minors are presumed by all phases of the law (and by the culture reflected by our law) not to

---

136. *See* Burt, *supra* note 39, at 122-23.

137. In addition to the language from *Gault* and *McKeiver* quoted in the text accompanying notes 100-106 *supra*, consider this language from Justice White's concurring opinion in *McKeiver*:

> Reprehensible acts by juveniles are not deemed the consequence of mature . . . choice but of environmental pressures (or lack of them) or of other forces beyond their control. Hence the state legislative judgment not to stigmatize the juvenile delinquent by branding him a criminal; his conduct is not deemed so blameworthy that punishment is required to deter him or others.

403 U.S. at 551-52 (White, J., concurring).

have the same basic capacities as adults. That presumption is so obvious that it has not been the subject of any discussion in the Supreme Court cases on the constitutional rights of children. Of course, nothing about the capacity presumption precludes the Court from considering whether, either in spite of the presumption or because of it, certain circumstances warrant a definition of the precise ways in which the legal position of a minor in a given situation should be protected, for constitutional or other reasons. Indeed, the presumption that minors lack adult capacity has remained preeminent in cases involving juveniles, to the extent that the Court has specifically refused to consider the "totality of the relationship of the minor and the State."[138] Rather, the Court has preferred to leave intact the basic presumption of the legal incapacity of minors, making specific, narrow adjustments on a case-by-case basis.

The presumptions arising from the limited capacities of minors account in large part for the general limitation on their exercise of rights that are in the "choice" category, because the law assumes, as suggested by Justice Stewart's concurring opinion in *Tinker*, that a basic capacity to make responsible choices is a prerequisite to the meaningful exercise of choice rights. For example, the age limitation on voting rights has been thought to fix the level above which citizens "are capable of intelligent and responsible exercise of the right to vote."[139] This restriction has persisted even though the right to vote may be the most fundamental of citizenship rights because it is "preservative of other basic civil and political rights."[140] Presumably, also for general reasons of capacity, the Constitution expressly limits membership in the House of Representatives and the Senate on the basis of age, and lists age as a qualification for the Presidency.[141] Other illustrations abound, from statutes fixing the age below which one may not marry without parental consent to longstanding common law and statutory rules presuming lack of capacity to make a legal contract or to consent to sexual or tortious acts.[142]

The serious question about the capacity limitation is where to draw the age line above which a given right or activity may be

138. Ginsberg v. New York, 390 U.S. 629, 636 (1968).

139. Oregon v. Mitchell, 400 U.S. 112, 240 (1970) (Brennan, White & Marshall, JJ., concurring).

140. Reynolds v. Sims, 377 U.S. 533, 562 (1964).

141. U.S. CONST. art. I, §§ 2, 3; art. II, § 1.

142. For a discussion of limitations on the right to vote in the context of other legal restrictions based upon age see Kleinfeld, *The Balance of Power Among Infants, Their Parents and The State*, 5 FAMILY L.Q. 64 (1971).

permitted. Children develop from incapacity toward capacity. That incontrovertible natural pattern is consistent with the presumption that capacity does not exist for children as a class until the general weight of evidence shows that a given level of capacity does in fact exist.[143] To presume, to the contrary, that rational and judgmental capacities exist until the evidence demonstrates otherwise is to defy both logic and experience, because the evidence already demonstrates from the outset that such capacities among infants are negligible. Thus, the presumption of incapacity to make certain choices is compelled by nature.

The effect of the protection-choice distinction may be illustrated by reference to two specific situations. The first is where a minor desires state support of a decision to have an abortion. If the physical health of a pregnant minor were in danger in a given case, existing rights to physical protection would prevent parents from legally resisting the abortion. Otherwise, however, no right to protection from serious harm is involved, leaving the right to make the decision in the choice category. The long-range psychological implications of the decision present the young woman with formidable difficulties in trying to make a mature assessment of her ability to live with the consequences of either an affirmative or a negative abortion decision. There is no reason to assume that she would have greater capacity to evaluate the implications of an abortion than she would the consequences of voting or marrying. It can be argued, of course, that certain parents may be in no better position to evaluate those risks than are their children—and may be even less likely to provide a better evaluation than a physician or a trained social worker. Whether the adult advice received by a pregnant minor comes from a parent or a professional, however, raises larger questions than who knows more about abortions, since once children are allowed to decide whose advice about abortions they will accept, there is little reason not to extend the right to parental noninterference to many other subjects, ranging from a minor's lifestyle choices to adolescent marriage. Thus, to bar a parent's right to prevent a minor child from having an abortion when no serious danger to health exists is to provide precedent for abrogating traditional parental control over the entire range of minors' choice rights.

In spite of some lower court decisions that statutes requiring parental consent for minors' abortions are unconstitutional,[144] it

143. See p. 605 *supra*.

144. *E.g.*, Poe v. Gerstein, 517 F.2d 787 (5th Cir. 1975); Baird v. Bellotti, 393 F. Supp. 847 (D. Mass. 1975); State v. Koome, 84 Wash. 2d 901, 530 P.2d 260 (1975). *See also* Note, *The Minor's Right to Abortion and the Requirement of Parental Consent*, 60 VA. L. REV. 305 (1974).

is not clear that any general judicial change has been intended in the common law's historic recognition of parental control over children's decisions to submit to surgery, especially when such surgery is not medically necessary to their physical health. If that rule is to be overturned in the abortion context simply because the right to have an abortion has been said to be "fundamental" for adult women, a court would have difficulty refusing a minor the affirmative right to make choices that control more about her life than her body.

The *Snyder* case illustrates the second situation, where a child desires a familial separation against the wishes of legally fit parents on grounds tantamount to incompatibility. In such a case, there is no parental abuse, neglect, or abandonment involved, so the child's rights to protection are not at stake. This is, therefore, a relatively extreme minor's choice matter. Acknowledgement of a child's right successfully to make such a choice necessarily assumes mutuality of capacity between parents and children, both in the formal legal sense and in the substantive sense of individual capacity to assume total responsibility for one's decisions. To conclude that children have the capacity to participate in or initiate a legal severance of family ties requires that the present legal presumption about the incapacity of minors be reversed. This reversal requires not only a flick of the legal wrist, but also a clear evidentiary demonstration that children as a class are not characterized by actual limitations upon their capacity to form judgments, assume economic responsibility, and otherwise act independently in their own behalf.

In the absence of such a reversal, a child would require representation in such a proceeding by some adult who could assert the best interests of the child, even though some such assertions may differ from the child's preferences. But when the parents are legally fit, who is to say that a nonparental guardian or a juvenile court judge is better able to interpret the child's interests than are the child's parents? It is precisely that question that has made most students of the subject argue strongly in favor of retaining support for the protection of natural family ties, because experience has shown that to do so is a better alternative for the children involved,[145] even though the children themselves are not yet in a position to appreciate fully why that may be so.

145. *See, e.g.*, Wald, *State Intervention on Behalf of "Neglected" Children: A Search for Realistic Standards*, 27 STAN. L. REV. 985 (1975).

The term "choice rights" as it has been used here applies to minors' decisions having serious long term consequences that have traditionally required either legal or parental approval (or both) in order to be enforceable. To suggest that legal rights of this special character should not be given premature approval is, however, not to argue for increased state-supported parental interference with the vast variety of less solemn choices that arise daily in the lives of children. Indeed, the availability of gradually increasing freedom to live with the consequences of one's own decisions is a critical element in the development of mature judgmental capacities. Still, the development of the capacity for responsible choice selection is an educational process in which growth can be smothered and stunted if unlimited freedom and unlimited responsibility are thrust too soon upon the young. Moreover, the lifelong effects of binding, childish choices can create permanent deprivations far more detrimental than the temporary limitations upon freedom inherent in the discipline of educational processes.

The development of the capacity to function as a mature, independent member of society is essential to the meaningful exercise of the full range of choice rights characteristic of the individual tradition. Precisely because of their lack of capacity, minors should enjoy legally protected rights to special treatment (including some protection against their own immaturity) that will optimize their opportunities for the development of mature capabilities that are in their best interest. Children will outgrow their restricted state, but the more important question is whether they will outgrow it with maximized capacities. An assumption that rational and moral capacity exists, when in fact it does not exist, may lead to an abandonment of the protections, processes, and opportunities that can develop these very capacities. In this sense, the concept of restricting certain choice rights is in fact an important form of protection rights. For these reasons, some distinction between rights of protection and rights of choice must be preserved. As suggested above, the existing children's rights decisions of the Supreme Court could reasonably be categorized as cases involving rights of protection only. It would be both inappropriate and contrary to the ultimate interests of children to construe those decisions as encouraging the removal of traditional constraints upon minors' exercise of choice rights.

B. *The Right of a Child Not To Be Abandoned to His "Rights": The Most Basic Right?*

The influences of some parental authority and responsibility are inevitable in view of the natural dependence of children. Rather than inhibiting optimal child development, however, this element of the parent-child relationship may be the child's most valuable source of developmental sustenance. Psychological evidence indicates that children "are not adults in miniature, they are being per se, different from their elders in their mental nature, their functioning, their understanding of events, and their reactions to them."[146] Children have many special needs that must be met in their quest for maturity and independence. The most critical of these needs is a satisfactory and permanent psychological relationship with their parents. Thus, even assuming the highest policy priority for fulfilling the actual needs of children, the worst possible results would be visited upon children by "liberating" them from the crucial psychological matrix of true family relationships. That kind of liberation would constitute the most ironic adult treatment of children—"abandoning them to their 'rights.' "[147] As stated by Goldstein, Freud, and Solnit:

> Psychoanalytic theory . . . [and] developmental studies by students of other orientations [establish] the need of every child for unbroken continuity of affection and stimulating relationships with an adult.
>
> . . . .
>
> To safeguard the right of parents to raise their children as they see fit, free of government intrusion, except in cases of neglect and abandonment, is to safeguard each child's need for continuity. This preference for minimum state intervention and for leaving well enough alone is reinforced by our recognition that law is incapable of effectively managing, except in a very gross sense, so delicate and complex a relationship as that between parent and child.[148]

This thesis suggests that parental authority must be regarded as a sovereign right if the psychological needs of children are in fact to be met. If there is insecurity or lack of commitment in the relationship, either because of governmental intrusion or because a parent has substantial doubts about the extent of his

---

146. J. Goldstein, A. Freud & A. Solnit, Beyond the Best Interests of the Child 13 (1973).

147. Panel discussion remarks of Albert Solnit, Child Advocacy Conference, Madison, Wisconsin, Sept. 26, 1975.

148. J. Goldstein, A. Freud, & A. Solnit, *supra* note 146, at 6, 7-8.

or her personal authority, serious psychological deficiencies are more likely to exist in the relationship. For this reason, these authors resist the use of temporary foster parents in child-placement decisions, because foster parents "find themselves deprived of the position on which parental tolerance, endurance, and devotion are commonly based, namely that of being the undisputed sole possessor of the child and the supreme arbiter of his fate." In that kind of relationship, insecurity and lack of emotional constancy "[defeat] the very intentions of the decision to move from professional institutional care to family care."[149]

This understanding of the needs of children enables a more long-range interpretation of what children may well "prefer" under the most theoretical views of egalitarian fairness. In *A Theory of Justice*, John Rawls would include children within the class of beings protected by his principles of justice, because children possess innate (although unrealized) moral capacity.[150] He maintains that guardians should be "guided by [the child's] own settled preferences and interests insofar as they are not irrational."[151] He acknowledges, however, that children generally lack the rationality to act for themselves[152] and therefore suggests that adults in a guardian role should try to obtain for a child "the things he presumably wants, whatever else he wants."[153] Rawls has been interpreted to mean that no one (including parents) should be permitted to act on behalf of children until the absence of a child's "full ability to decide" for himself has been affirma-

149. *Id.* at 24-25.

New York Family Court Judge Nanette Dembitz has expressed her concern that *Beyond the Best Interests of the Child* focuses too exclusively on the interests of children while ignoring basic parental rights: "The doctrine of the biological parent's natural rights, which continues to appear in numerous New York decisions, reflects a deeply held ethic." Dembitz, Book Review, 83 YALE L.J. 1304, 1306 (1974). Judge Dembitz may be among others who have seen the Goldstein-Freud-Solnit work as advocating premature interference with biological parent-child relationships. However, close reading of the book as well as conversations with its authors confirms that the authors favor parental autonomy as a general rule, as indicated in the text, except in cases of neglect, abandonment, or other recognized circumstances that give rise to custody disputes. They have not advocated new intervention standards, but merely new standards for evaluating custody dispositions once existing standards have put custody into issue.

150. J. RAWLS, A THEORY OF JUSTICE 509 (1971) states:

> [T]he minimal requirements defining moral personality [those entitled to equal justice under his theory] refer to a capacity and not to the realization of it. A being that has this capacity, whether or not it is yet developed, is to receive the full protection of the principles of justice. [This includes] . . . infants and children . . . ."

151. *Id.* at 249.

152. *See id.* at 209, 244.

153. *Id.* at 249.

tively demonstrated in a given situation[154]—in other words, that the existing presumptions about minors' lack of capacity should be reversed. But Rawls has offered no new proof about the capacities of children, nor does he purport to know what children "presumably" want, especially when that presumed wanting is to be evaluated, under his theory, according to the view a child would have if he enjoyed adult capacity at the time a decision affecting him is made. It is arguable under Rawls' theory, given the evidence showing the critical psychological value of secure, parent-directed family relationships, that the encouragement of parental authority is the most likely means of satisfying the long-range needs of children. When imagining themselves as children, persons who accept that evidence would "presumably" prefer subjection to parental control up to the point of actual abuse or neglect, even if that meant their expressed preferences as children would frequently be overridden.

There is a group of legal scholars in the family law field who recognize the need for family autonomy, but whose commitment to the individual tradition leaves them idealogically uncomfortable with the thought that state policies should encourage parental authority over children. Consider, for example, this statement from a student treatment of problems arising from statutory parental consent requirements as a condition to the availability of contraceptives to minors:

> Moreover, it is a misconception to equate the preservation of family structure with reinforcement of parental control. Maintaining the integrity of the family is not only a reflection of interests of the parents. It also mirrors a distinguishable, relational privacy interest, arguably rooted in first amendment associational values, the thrust of which is not merely to protect parental authority, but also to safeguard from state encroachment the intimacy and autonomy of the family relationship. Where, as in the contraceptive context, individual interests of parent and child are likely to collide, protection of their shared relational interest assumes independent importance and should not be directed at reinforcing the values of parents alone, which results when a parental consent requirement is imposed, but rather at fostering autonomous intrafamilial resolution of controversies.[155]

This comment reflects the merit of encouraging the autono-

154. Worsfold, *A Philosophical Justification for Children's Rights*, 44 HARV. EDUC. REV. 142, 156 (1974).

155. Note, *Parental Consent Requirements and Privacy Rights of Minors: The Contraceptive Controversy*, 88 HARV. L. REV. 1001, 1017-18 (1975).

mous resolution of family differences, but it necessarily assumes a degree of equality in capacities and roles within the family relationship that is neither realistic nor in the ultimate interests of children. The psychological value of autonomy in the family relationship cannot truly be accomplished if parental authority is not ultimately authoritative. While authority may be most effectively used when based upon patient persuasion rather than only upon brute force, the family that operates as a true democracy is less likely to provide the security, the role-modeling, the leadership, the socializing, the growth, or many of the other interests preserved by a basic policy decision that parental authority is worthy of some state support. That has been the premise underlying much juvenile court law, and, in spite of the abuses that have been generated in extreme cases by inept caseworkers and insensitive parents, the concept retains a soundness that is still preferable to the anarchy that would result from state support of some kind of democratic egalitarianism among all family members. The failure of the state to provide some support for parental authority—even if as a last resort—is likely to diminish the power of parent-child relationships to provide the psychological matrix necessary to optimize the preparation of children for independent participation in adult society.

It has nevertheless been argued[156] that concerns about state intervention into family life should apply not only to direct acts by state agents, but also to the use of state resources as supports for parental authority. This view of opposition to state intervention seems to derive from a philosophical position that opposes not only governmental action but also any authoritarian interference with the lives of children. Ironically, limiting parental authority is likely to require some kind of state intervention on behalf of children, perhaps in the form of more far-reaching recognitions of children's rights in contexts where their actual needs for protection are not at stake. It is not possible for the state to remain truly neutral, particularly when parents begin with a position of authority over their children within the inherent status quo. Denying a portion of parental authority necessarily adds to the authority of children. Such an addition may be appropriate when the circumstances make it clear in an individual case that children have some special need. But, as long as the limited capacities of children make it either impossible, unrealistic, or un-

156. Burt, *supra* note 39, at 132.

fair to them to let them assume full responsibility for their own lives, ultimate control over their conduct must and will necessarily rest either with their parents or with the state. Thus, reducing parental authority simply creates increased state involvement. That, it is submitted, would be the worse of two potential evils.

Professor Michael Wald has advanced a compelling series of arguments for a reduced level of state intervention in parent-child relationships. He maintains that a desirable diversity of views, lifestyles, and attitudes is encouraged by parental autonomy; that since our society is unsure of the best methods or even the objectives of child-rearing in any event, children should be protected only from the more obvious harms upon which policymakers can agree; and that state intervention has a long record of placing children in more detrimental positions than they would have been without such intervention.[157] These observations, particularly the extensive documentation related to the frequent failure of state intervention, suggest additional reasons why the maintenance of parental autonomy is, when compared to the alternatives, in the best interests of children. After an exhaustive analysis of a set of proposals designed to cope with presently inadequate standards, Professor Wald concludes:

> The approach suggested in this Article might be viewed by some readers as more solicitous of parents' rights than of children's rights. As such, it may be interpreted as a defense of the "old system" against the mounting calls for emphasis on children's rights and greater state protection for children; but, to me, such charges are unwarranted. Aiding children through coercive intervention has not proven to be a success.[158]

Filtering through the lines in this statement is a certain reluctance to acknowledge explicitly the position that seems to have been advocated, and it needs no apology: preservation of the parental authority that is a prerequisite to meaningful family autonomy is in fact in the interest of children and their most vital long-range rights.

To the extent that governmental policies foster noncommittal attitudes on the part of parents—either because parents believe they have no right to give direction to their children, or because they fear that in giving them direction they might meet the kind of state-supported resistance encountered by the parents of Cynthia Snyder—both the children of those families and the larger society will suffer.

157. Wald, *supra* note 145, at 992-1000.

158. *Id.* at 1038.

For most parents, the "rights" of parenthood leave them no alternative but an assumption of parental responsibility, because that responsibility, both by nature and by law, can be assumed by no one else until the parent has failed. But when state-enforced policies undermine traditional parental rights, those same policies will inevitably undermine the assumption of parental responsibility. To undermine parental initiative would not be wise because our society has found no realistic alternative to it. The encouragement of parental responsibility for children is certainly less detrimental than a pervasive state assumption of child-rearing. Indeed, the development of policies that encourage parental responsibility is probably the best thing we could do for our children. One might even say that children have a right to such policies.

IV. Conclusion

The individual tradition is at the heart of American culture. Yet the fulfillment of individualism's promise of personal liberty depends, paradoxically, upon the maintenance of a set of corollary traditions that require what may seem to be the opposite of personal liberty: submission to authority, acceptance of responsibility, and the discharge of duty. The family tradition is among the most essential corollaries to the individual tradition, because it is in families that both children and parents experience the need for and the value of authority, responsibility, and duty in their most pristine forms. When individualism breaks loose from its corollaries, however, its tendency to destroy personal fulfillment and human relationships is exposed. This result was anticipated in the infancy of the American democratic experiment by Alexis de Tocqueville:

> As social conditions become more equal, the number of persons increases who, although they are neither rich nor powerful enough to exercise any great influence over their fellows, have nevertheless acquired or retained sufficient education and fortune to satisfy their own wants. They owe nothing to any man, they expect nothing from any man; they acquire the habit of always considering themselves as standing alone, and they are apt to imagine that their whole destiny is in their own hands.
>
> Thus, not only does democracy make every man forget his ancestors, but it hides his descendants and separates his contemporaries from him; it throws him back forever upon himself

> alone, and threatens in the end to confine him entirely within the solitude of his own heart.[159]

Perhaps it is no coincidence that the recent period of expansive egalitarianism is also the period of the most widespread loneliness and alienation Western culture has known. It may also be that the tendency of democracy to make men forget both their ancestors and their descendants is causing some adults to seek the liberation of children as a way of liberating themselves from the duties, the ambiguities, and the self-denial that are necessarily required of parents and communities committed to the pattern of family life.[160]

But individualism must remain embedded in the context of its corollary obligations to family and community if the individual tradition itself is to survive in a meaningful form. Family life, rather than subjecting the young to the permanent disadvantages caused by certain unfair discriminations against other classes, has served to nurture children's readiness for responsible participation in the individual tradition. The natural need to prepare children for entry into the fray of individualism, with its risks and obligations as well as its opportunities, has, until the last decade, kept children within the walls of the family tradition. We may now be on the verge of seeing a rejuvenated egalitarian movement break down those walls. To date, however, there is no serious evidence that society has outgrown the need for the preparatory role of the family tradition, nor has industrial society discovered substitute institutions or relationships adequate to fulfill the functions historically performed by the family.

Because of its preparatory role, maintenance of the family tradition is in fact a prerequisite to the existence of a rational and productive individual tradition. John Locke concluded his discussion of the role of children in the individual tradition with this statement: "And thus we see how natural freedom and subjection to parents may consist together and are both founded on the same principle."[161] The principle upon which both freedom and subjection to parents are founded has to do with the most fundamental human processes of learning. Locke believed that parents were obliged by "Nature" to "nourish and educate" children in developing the minimal capacities one must possess before the liberty

159. A. de Toqueville, Democracy in America 194 (R. Heffner ed. 1956).

160. Novak, *The Family Out of Favor*, Harper's, April 1976, at 37.

161. Locke, *supra* note 14, § 61, at 35.

to make binding choices can be meaningful. The related obligation of children is to submit to some degree of parental authority; otherwise, little significant learning can take place. In his important work on the development of individual knowledge, philosopher Michael Polanyi has pointed out that neither basic nor sophisticated skills can be learned without the kind of personal master-apprentice relationship Locke saw as existing between parents and children:

> An art which cannot be specified in detail cannot be transmitted by prescription, since no prescription for it exists. It can be passed only by example from master to apprentice. . . . To learn by example is to submit to authority. You follow your master because you trust his manner of doing things even when you cannot account in detail for its effectiveness. By watching the master and emulating his efforts in the presence of his example, the apprentice unconsciously picks up the rules of the art, including those which are not explicitly known to the master himself. These hidden rules can be assimilated only by a person who surrenders himself to that extent uncritically to the imitation of another. A society which wants to preserve a fund of personal knowledge must submit to tradition.[162]

It is more than coincidental that for the ancient Greeks and Romans, as well as for Western society in the post-1500 period, a strong commitment to the idea of childhood and lasting family relationships grew parallel with a strong commitment to the idea of education.[163] Childhood, as a time of life and as a frame of mind, is intimately related to educational development.

Ardent advocates of children's rights may believe that "in this society . . . we are not likely to err in the direction of too much freedom,"[164] but too much freedom can undermine and finally destroy the most fundamental learning processes and the human relationships that sustain them. To the extent that these relationships and processes are undetermined, it is ultimately the tradition of individual liberty that will be damaged.

162. M. Polanyi, Personal Knowledge: Towards a Post-Critical Philosophy 53 (1964).

163. *See* notes 25-27 and accompanying text *supra*.

164. Farson, *supra* note 94, at 153.

[6]

THE MODERN FUNCTION AND LIMITS OF PARENTAL RIGHTS

In discussing parental rights without first undertaking to apply to the word "rights" Hohfeld's techniques of analysis explained in his book *Fundamental Legal Conceptions*,[1] one takes the risk of seeming to use language loosely. A "right" is taken for the present purpose to refer to a parental discretion to act regarding a child in a way others have a co-relative duty to permit, or a duty to forbear from preventing. By "others" bound by this duty or forbearance are meant particularly officers of different levels of government and of quasi-public child protection and welfare agencies. The difficulty with applying Hohfeld in this setting, however, is that while such public and quasi-public officers may be required to tolerate an exercise of parental rights within the sense of this paper, the children regarding whom such rights are exercised may not necessarily be bound by a duty of tolerance or compliance. They may at times lawfully resist the impositions and constraints upon them by which parents seek to make their rights effective. As Lord Denning M.R. observed in *Hewer* v. *Bryant*,[2] a parental right is: "a dwindling right which the courts will hesitate to enforce against the wishes of the child, the older he is."[3]

To suggest that parental rights have a legal function, and to go further and suggest that the function sets limits upon the ambit and exercise of rights, is to invoke utilitarian language in an area long governed by concepts of natural rights: rights seemingly as natural as the biology that generates children and makes parents of their progenitors. In his *Commentaries on the Laws of England*, Sir William Blackstone observed that the most universal relation in nature, is that between parent and child.[4] The common law view that parental rights arise by nature reflected a cultural emphasis upon duties owed to parents by their children. The fifth of the Ten Commandments[5] is "Honour thy father and thy mother," a Commandment apparently enjoying priority over the sixth Commandment "Thou shalt not murder."

A late nineteenth-century commentator drew upon Blackstone's *Commentaries* to conclude that: "The power of a parent over his

---

1 (1919), reprinted in 1964. For a more developed application of Hohfeld's analysis, see J. M. Eekelaar, "What Are Parental Rights?" (1973) 89 L.Q.R. 210

2 [1970] 1 Q.B. 357.

3 At p. 369.

4 (1765), Bk. I, Chap. 10.

5 Exodus xx 1–17.

children is derived from their duty to him." [6] No general emphasis can be said to exist in modern common law that minor children owe their parents duties,[7] although their duty to render domestic services in the home has afforded parents the power to sue third parties interfering with the parent-child relation.[8] The tort of harbouring a child against parental wishes, even with the child's consent, was abolished in England in 1970,[9] however, and the contrived action for a daughter's seduction based upon a parental right to her domestic services, whether rendered in fact or not,[10] was terminated at the same time. Criminal offences continue to exist of abduction of young children, and of taking unmarried girls out of their parents' possession without parental consent, and they may be understood against the background of parental custodial rights, since they are not dependent upon an intention of sexual exploitation.[11]

Modern legislation is designed to achieve protection of children and the promotion of their welfare. It therefore tends to lay emphasis upon parental duties to children and underplays the role of parental rights. In this, the legislation reflects a trend observed in case law. Professor Bromley has noted that:

> "Whilst equity left untouched the common law duties of parents, its attitude towards the exercise of their rights underwent a fundamental change during the nineteenth century. Earlier cases indicated that effect would always be given to the father's legal rights unless he had forfeited them by his immoral or cruel conduct or was seeking to enforce them capriciously or arbitrarily. . . . On the other hand there was a growing view, which ultimately prevailed, that the welfare of the child was the first consideration and equity would not hesitate to deprive a father of his rights if it would clearly be contrary to the child's best interests to give effect to them." [12]

Criminal laws punish parents who have abandoned their children or denied them necessaries of life, including medical treatment.[13] The State may also intervene in parent-child relations by civil proceedings when children are found to be in need of care or protec-

[6] Robert M. Kerr, *The Students' Blackstone: Commentaries on The Laws of England by Sir William Blackstone: Abridged and Adapted to the Present State of the Law* (1880), p. 100.

[7] For a contrast with Civil law jurisdictions, see S. M. Cretney, *Principles of Family Law* (3rd ed., 1979), p. 427.

[8] See P. M. Bromley, *Family Law* (5th ed., 1976), p. 348.

[9] Law Reform (Miscellaneous Provisions) Act 1970, s. 5.

[10] See *Terry* v. *Hutchinson* (1868) L.R. 3 Q.B. 599.

[11] See Bromley, note 8 above, at p. 347.

[12] *Ibid.* at p. 299.

[13] See the Canadian cases *R.* v. *Brooks* (1902) 5 C.C.C. 372 and *R.* v. *Lewis* (1903) 7 C.C.C. 261 interpreting the present s. 197 of the Criminal Code.

tion. Such a need may arise because the parents have defaulted in the legally mandated provision of education,[14] health services, food, shelter or clothing, or because parents have failed to guard their children against unsuitable companions, surroundings or influences.[15] The function of parenthood may appear to be the protection of children against physical, psychological, social and moral harm.

It may appear obvious that parents possess legal powers and rights to discharge the duties they owe their children. It may be equally obvious that no right exists to act positively or negatively, so as to violate duties, since criminal and civil protective rights exist in the courts, and in others to invoke the process of the courts, to prevent parental breach of duty. It is interesting to observe, however, that in the United States, principles of parental immunity are still widespread, so that children generally cannot sue parents for breach of duty.[16] Whether enforceable by children or not, however, parental duties and related rights appear to be defined by reference not to the positive standard of achieving good for children, but by reference to the negative standard of protecting children from harm. This leaves open, therefore, a parental discretion to employ control over children for purposes not violating children's interests, but equally not advancing their welfare or best interests. A non-beneficial but not unreasonable exercise of parental power may be illustrated by, for instance, medical experimentation which is non-invasive and of minimum risk.[17]

This region of the law between not harming children and not advancing their welfare requires more detailed scrutiny, since it concerns an area where the existence of legal means of intervention may appear oppressive of family integrity and autonomy, but where children may become exposed to risk, and to pre-emption by an exercise of parental authority of the rights to autonomy they would otherwise acquire upon subsequent maturity and adulthood. Recourse will be made for illustration to experience in the United States, whose legal developments tend somewhat to anticipate those in Canada, and whose jurisprudence and legal literature may be influential in England.

The year 1979 was International Year of the Child, reflecting

---

14 See *Re S. (A Minor) (Care Order: Education)* [1978] Q.B. 120.

15 For a comparison of English, Canadian and United States approaches, see Bernard M. Dickens, "Legal Responses to Child Abuse," in John M. Eekelaar and Sanford N. Katz (eds.) *Family Violence* (1978), Chap. 23, p. 338.

16 Immunity is, however, in visible decline. In *Gelbman* v. *Gelbman* (1969) 245 N.E. 2d 192, for instance, intrafamilial immunity from tort proceedings was abolished in New York.

17 See Bernard M. Dickens, "The Use of Children in Medical Experimentation" (1975) 43 Medico-Legal J. 166.

an emphasis in recent times upon children's rights.[18] This has expressed itself legally in such areas as child advocacy and representation in court proceedings of different types.[19] A more recent development of great potential significance to the future may suggest, however, not that promoting children's rights to protection from parental discretion is an idea whose time has come, but that it is an idea whose brief time has just gone.[20] The spirit of so-called neo-conservatism visible in contemporary Anglo-North-American society affects perceptions of the family unit, relations between the State and the family, and between the child and the family, in ways which merit attention. This attitude may reverse the historic trend Professor Bromley observed from favouring parental rights to favouring welfare of the child.

Neo-conservatism may be described, certainly in the United States where it is most visible, as the response of liberals to their failure, despite winning strategic and doctrinal victories, to improve society. It expresses without bitterness the mellowing realisation of modern-minded pragmatists that there are inexorable forces that do not yield to enlightenment, but which mark the boundaries within which enlightenment may modestly prevail to achieve good.

The neo-conservative response to the failure of elaborate and costly family welfare programmes, supported by different levels of government, to arrest perceived family breakdown and violence, and to the role of welfare workers in achieving family dismemberment, has been to urge restriction of government involvement in families and in parental decision-making. The reaction to treatment of delinquency in the United States in many ways anticipated the evolution of neo-conservatism. In 1973 the sociologist Edwin Schur wrote that:

> " Much of the disenchantment with current delinquency policy arises from the simple fact that it doesn't work . . . neither the treatment reaction nor the reform response has provided any real basis for confidence that our measures are effective in preventing delinquent behaviour or rehabilitating youthful offenders. . . . Many observers are coming to believe that our present approaches to delinquency and juvenile justice are *basically* unsound: that the underlying assumptions are all

18 See John E. Coons and Robert H. Mnookin " Toward a Theory of Children's Rights " in Ian F. G. Baxter and Mary A. Eberts (eds.), *The Child And The Courts* (1978), p. 391.

19 See Bernard M. Dickens " Representing the Child in the Courts " in Ian F. G. Baxter and Mary A. Eberts, *ibid.*, p. 273.

20 Even more optimistic commentators recognise the conflict regarding the balance of power among infants, their parents and the State, and that prevalence of children's rights against parental preference is not assured; see A. J. Klienfeld, " The Balance of Power Among Infants, Their Parents And The State," (1970) 4 Family L.Q. 320, 410 and (1971) 5 Family L.Q. 64.

wrong, and that present programs are not just ineffective but positively harmful." [21]

The approach or philosophy resulting from this perception is called Radical Non-intervention. Like modern American neo-conservatism, which is associated with broader convictions of fundamentalist and Born-Again Christianity, radical non-intervention fits within a broader philosophical framework. Edwin Schur noted that: "Piecemeal socioeconomic reform will not greatly affect delinquency; there must be thoroughgoing changes in the structure and the values of our society." [22]

At the operational level, radical non-intervention paved the way regarding children for policies subsequently advanced by neo-conservatives for families. Edwin Schur's conclusion was that: "Thus, the basic injunction for public policy becomes: *leave kids alone wherever possible.* This effort partly involves mechanisms to divert children away from the courts but it goes further to include opposing various kinds of intervention by diverse social control and socializing agencies." [23]

The modern approach to families, and to the role of parental rights within families, is to leave them alone, and to oppose intervention by social control agencies, including the courts. The special value of the family in evolving neo-conservative philosophy appears to be that it is not only a unit whose support is difficult to oppose, but also that it is self-regulating and self-financing. The family does not require public officers to inspect and monitor its behaviour, and it functions according to its economic means, whether in affluence, comfort or poverty, without the State having to itemise its income and supervise its budget. It conforms to the principle of minimal public intervention. If it is a "welfare" family, however, dependent in whole or in part upon public subventions, it becomes amenable both to public inspection to ensure accountability, and to public discipline. This return to the independent family as the basic social unit which functions without State involvement reflects a shift in focus. It marks an evolution from seeing welfare officers as benign helpers and guides leading families out of distress into self-reliance, to seeing welfare officers as interfering and accident-prone bureaucrats whose meddlesome interventions perpetuate dependency and endanger the potential for autonomy.

The evolution of this attitude is apparent in the significant writ-

[21] Edwin M. Schur, *Radical Nonintervention: rethinking the delinquency problem* (1973), pp. 117–118.

[22] *Ibid.* at p. 155. See also Ronald Bayer, " Crime, Punishment and the Decline of Liberal Optimism " (1981) 27 *Crime & Delinquency* 169.

[23] *Ibid.* emphasis in original.

ings of Joseph Goldstein,[24] Anna Freud [25] and Albert Solnit.[26] The first book they wrote together was published in 1973, entitled *Beyond the Best Interests of the Child.* It was a spectacularly influential book, with an impact visible throughout the U.S., in England and in Canada. The title was drawn from the formula developed in the courts to determine the disposition of the child in the event of disputed custody at the breakdown of the parents' marriage, or, for instance, when a child's institutional placement was in issue. The formula replaced earlier concepts of parents' property rights, and stated that the court was to seek " the best interests of the child." In England, this is often described as " the welfare of the child." [27] In *Beyond the Best Interests of the Child,* Goldstein, Freud and Solnit creatively observed the merit and sensitivity of this formula, but also explored both its possible sterility and lack of guidance, and its euphoric pointing in the wrong direction. It suggests a scale of good-better-best; that what exists is good, it may become better, and courts must seek " the best." In reality, the authors pointed out that what exists is almost invariably bad, it is likely to become worse, and courts must strive to prevent the worst. Accordingly, legislation influenced by this first, seminal text tend to provide that " best interests " or " welfare " be interpreted to mean " least detrimental alternative." Least detriment occurs when the authors' guidelines for decision-makers are observed. These emphasise the significance of psychological rather than biological ties in the mind of the child whose detriment is to be minimised. They require safeguarding the child's need for continuity of relationships, a response reflecting the child's sense of time rather than the time scale adults find convenient, and recognition of the law's incapacity to supervise interpersonal relationships and to make long-range predictions.[28]

These perceptions have secured considerable advances in the legal management of child placement, although their implications

[24] Sterling Professor of Law, Yale Law School and Child Study Center; he is also a qualified psychoanalyst.

[25] Director of a child therapy clinic; psychoanalyst, daughter of Sigmund Freud.

[26] Sterling Professor of Pediatrics and Psychiatry, Yale Medical School, and Director, Child Study Center; widely experienced in psychoanalysis.

[27] See Olive M. Stone, " The Welfare of the Child " in Ian F. G. Baxter and Mary A. Eberts, note 18 above at p. 231.

[28] The Child Welfare Act 1978 of Ontario reflects these guidelines in providing in s. 1 (b) that " best interests of the child " must be found by regard to, *inter alia,* "... (ii) the child's opportunity to enjoy a parent-child relationship and to be a wanted and needed member within a family structure... (iv) the effect upon the child of any disruption of the child's sense of continuity . . . (vii) the effect upon the child of any delay in the final disposition in the proceedings."

have not been observed without criticism.[29] Through legislation and court decisions, interventions in families and in private inter-spousal agreements at marriage breakdown have become more sensitive to children's needs and perspectives, under the influence of *Beyond the Best Interests.* The new book by the same three authors appeared in 1979, and expresses its neo-conservative philosophy under the title *Before the Best Interests of the Child.* The book appears likely to attract as much attention as the predecessor, but not necessarily as much admiration. Its appearance compels critical regard to be paid to its underlying philosophy, and especially to ways that may be adopted of making its philosophy operative in administrative and judicial practice.

The message of *Before the Best Interests* is that there should be restraint in judicial and other State intervention to seek a child's best interests. Before the best interests of the child become open to judicial or administrative assessment, it must be proven by due process of law that the family has fallen short of legally set and pre-notified standards of child care. The first page of the book (not of the text, but literally of the book) states that: "So long as the child is part of a viable family, his own interests are merged with those of the other members. Only *after* the family fails in its function should the child's interests become a matter for State intrusion."

The major premise of this approach is that the family, directed, of course, by the parent or parents, should be proven to be dysfunctional before the child's interests can be isolated and protected. Implications of this philosophy appear to include that the State should not intervene if parents decide against their children having reasonably advised medical treatment when their lives are not jeopardised by its refusal, that the State should permit parents to decide to submit their children to non-therapeutic, irreversible surgical procedures, such as contraceptive sterilisation of mentally retarded adolescents, and that parental refusal to supply their child involved in a delinquency hearing with a lawyer, or refusal to seek a lawyer through legal aid, should be conclusive, and not be superseded by judicial order.[30] As the authors observe: "This ground recognizes that an integral part of the autonomy of parents is their authority and presumed capacity to determine whether and how to meet the

[29] See, for instance, the review of *Beyond the Best Interests of the Child* by Judge Nanette Dembitz of the Family Court of New York State, entitled "Beyond Any Discipline's Competence" (1974) 83 Yale L.J. 1304.

[30] Joseph Goldstein's general thinking on the role of lawyers for children was outlined in "Psychoanalysis and a Jurisprudence of Child Placement—with Special Emphasis on the Role of Legal Counsel for Children" in David N. Weisstub (ed.), *Law and Psychiatry II* (1979), p. 1; see also Bernard M. Dickens "Comments on Goldstein", *ibid.* at p. 22.

legal care needs of their child—just as they do with regard to his medical care needs." [31]

The idea that children and their futures should be at the disposal of their parents' discretion, and that the courts should be entitled to intervene in the exercise of discretion only when parents are clearly and convincingly shown by due process of law to be at fault, may appear an overreaction to instances of children being placed at disadvantage by judicial and administrative insensitivity and oppression of parental choice. However much the concept of parental autonomy may appeal to adherents of family solidarity and privacy, and to those sympathetic in principle to the prevalence of parental authority, the risk of injury and disadvantage to which this principle leaves children exposed may compel harshness of the principle to be mitigated in practice.[32]

To say this is by no means to dismiss or discredit the potential contribution of *Before the Best Interests of the Child* to our jurisprudence and administrative policy. The book is of immense value in clearly reasoning and articulating the first principles to be applied to family units and their children. The book creatively explores the point at which society's well-meaning urge to protect children may threaten the substance or at least the quality of family life, which society has no less strong an urge to protect. It compels us to face the possibility that liberal instincts to furnish protection may be, or may be perceived as being, totalitarian, and that identification of dysfunctional families may not be sufficiently tolerant of unorthodoxy or accommodating of parents who simply dissent from the prevailing norm.[33]

The thesis of optimal services for children, in health care, education, encouragement of individuality and, for instance, litigation is fundamentally challenged by the Goldstein, Freud and Solnit antithesis of minimal State intervention in families. The dilemma of synthesis is rendered more acute by recognising that both thesis and antithesis represent in themselves goals worthy of communal respect and advancement. The modern governmental dynamic has come to favour minimal intervention, however, since this better serves governmental goals of reducing public spending upon welfare programmes and services, and of reducing welfare dependency. The search for means of accommodation between the incompatible virtues of offering assistance and maintaining family independence compels us to face the implications of the underlying conflict.

[31] *Before the Best Interests of the Child* (1979), p. 112.

[32] See Bernard M. Dickens, note 30 above.

[33] Excesses of protectively intended intervention are discussed in Judith Areen, "Intervention Between Parent and Child: A Reappraisal of the State's Role in Child Negect and Abuse Cases" (1975) 63 Georgetown L.J. 887.

Society may preserve family integrity at a price its children may be called upon to pay.

The underlying dilemma of the emphasis of *Before the Best Interests* has been expressed by Joseph Goldstein himself in his earlier writing. He has explained that minors are not permitted to take decisions and risks for themselves, since they are poorly informed and inexperienced in the ways of the world and need the care of adults, which may appropriately be described as paternalistic, to protect them against their tendencies to make mistakes. Goldstein has expressed his basic postulates in three propositions. First, " To be a *child* is to be at risk, dependent, and without capacity or authority to decide what is ' best ' for oneself "; Secondly, " To be *adult* is to be a risktaker, independent, and with capacity and authority to decide and to do what is ' best ' for oneself "; and Thirdly, " To be an *adult who is a parent* is to be presumed in law to have the capacity, authority, and responsibility to determine and to do what is good for one's children." [34]

These postulates may be criticised for addressing only the contrast between a child and an adult. The period of transition from childhood to adulthood is adolescence, and Goldstein's theory seems not adequately to take account of its characteristics. This may not be a weakness in the theory, of course, but simply a limitation in the scope of the problem the latest book was primarily designed to address.[35] Adolescence is a time not only of personal turmoil and developmental change, but also a state beset by legal confusion. This is reflected in uneven legal provisions concerning the age of majority, the age of effective consent to sexual relations, the age of marriage with and without parental approval, the age of legal consumption of alcohol, of driving a motor vehicle (these last two not uncommonly coinciding in tragedy) and of giving autonomous consent to medical treatment.[36]

Without further criticising Goldstein's basic postulates, however, one may present them in sharper form to express the dilemma of parental autonomy over children. Children are prone to errors of comprehension and judgment and need to be protected against their mistakes. Adults have gained autonomy to suffer the consequences of their errors, and administrative or professional zeal to offer adults more than advice and guidance—that is, zeal to govern

---

[34] Joseph Goldstein, " Medical Care for the Child at Risk: On State Supervention of Parental Autonomy " (1977) 86 Yale L.J. 645; repeated in *Before the Best Interests*, p. 7.

[35] *Before the Best Interests*, note 31 above, considers adolescents at pp. 126–129.

[36] See generally the *Report of the Latey Committee on the Age of Majority*, Cmnd. 3342 (1967).

their actual conduct—may be unjustifiable paternalism.[37] Even mentally ill and handicapped adults are allowed a growing measure of autonomy under modern legislation, and lose liberty only at the point where they are positively dangerous to others, or to themselves through suicidal tendencies or excessive self-neglect.[38]

If Goldstein's first postulate means that "Children are not allowed to make mistakes," and his second means that "Adults are allowed to make mistakes," the third postulate means that "Parents are adults who are allowed to make mistakes regarding their children."

The question must therefore be asked: At what point in parental decision-making governing children should the State intervene? This issue will be explored primarily in the context of decisions concerning the medical care of children. Clearly, other areas would serve the purpose of illustration, such as parental decisions on education, on religious upbringing and on legal representation in delinquency, care and protection and custody and access disputes. The issue of the medical treatment of legal minors offers a richness of case law, however, particularly in the United States, which is not found regarding these other areas.

The modern function of parental rights, it is proposed, is not to enforce duties children owe their parents, or simply to enforce against third parties powers of custody and control parents enjoy over their children. It is to permit parents to discharge their duties to their children. These duties are not positively to do good, but to avoid harm. It is obvious that to the extent that ill-health and, for instance, illiteracy are considered harm, parents are bound by positive duties to provide health care and education. This proposition may be derived from an abundance of case law and legislation.[39] The duty to avoid harm is more elastic, however, since it affords license to control a child not for its benefit, but in non-beneficial or non-therapeutic ways falling short of causing or risking harm.[40] The issue to be critically addressed is the point at which an exercise of parental choice over a child's management and future is so potentially harmful to the welfare or interests of

---

37 Not all paternalism is unjustified, however; see Bernard Gert and Charles M. Culver, "Paternalistic Behaviour" (1976) 6 *Philosophy and Public Affairs* 45 and "The Justification of Paternalism" (1979) 89 *Ethics* 199.

38 Legal developments in the United States liberating the non-dangerous mentally ill and mentally handicapped were influenced by the decision in *Wyatt* v. *Stickney* (1972) 334 F.Supp. 1341, requiring placement of the impaired according to the "least restrictive alternative." This is comparable to the "least detrimental alternative" standard developed in *Beyond the Best Interests of the Child* (1973).

39 See generally Angela R. Holder, *Legal Issues in Pediatrics and Adolescent Medicine* (1977).

40 See, for instance, Bernard M. Dickens, note 17 above.

the child as to require state intervention and possibly a countermanding of parental choice.

Principles may be derived from a position of extremity. Where parents leave a child at risk of avoidable death, intervention is clearly justifiable. Legal doctrines of necessity to save human life and the quality of life, meaning physical and mental health, supersede laws prohibiting unauthorised surgical or other physical interventions,[41] and prohibiting unauthorised entry upon land,[42] such as where the endangered child is in custody. The focus of the law is upon preservation of life and health, to enable the child to grow into maturity and consequent autonomy. The law protects the present child, in order to protect the future adult the child is intended to survive to become. This indicates another means of expressing the modern function of parental rights. They exist to preserve and to prepare children for adulthood and emerging autonomy. A parental decision to take immediate non-emergency action which may deny the child an option to be exercised later by the child upon gaining maturity, may violate this function of parenthood. As such, it may not be a legitimate exercise of parental authority, and may present a limitation of parental rights. This is clearly demonstrated where a parental decision is concerned which may result in avoidable or premature termination of the child's life,[43] but is equally true at a less extreme level concerning decisions affecting the child's future options in life and life-style. The principle would apply to parental decisions on such matters as contraceptive or eugenic sterilisation, and, for instance, on committal to detention in a psychiatric facility.

Anglo-American case law has addressed these and related matters in a way which must be considered. Before judgments are selectively discussed, however, the interaction of substantive law and procedural law must be noted. The dichotomy of substance and procedure has been considered critical by Joseph Goldstein, who has laid emphasis upon the significance in decisions regarding children not of what is decided, but of who decides.[44] Since all decision-takers are risk-takers, who are prone to human error whether they be individual parents, public bureaucracies or quasi-

---

[41] See *R.* v. *Bourne* [1939] 1 K.B. 687, which has been widely followed in the Commonwealth and the United States; see Bernard M. Dickens and Rebecca J. Cook, "The Development of Commonwealth Abortion Laws" (1979) 28 I.C.L.Q. 424, 434 *et seq.*

[42] *Esso Petroleum Co. Ltd.* v. *Southport Corporation* [1956] A.C. 218.

[43] Goldstein, Freud and Solnit do not question the propriety of State intervention to protect a child's "chance for normal healthy growth or a life worth living"; see *Before the Best Interests*, note 31 above, Chap. 6, at p. 91.

[44] That is, in whose judgment a decision is "best" for a child; see, for instance, Goldstein note 34 above, at p. 651.

public (perhaps volunteer) agencies, the identification of who is allowed to decide is no less important in theory, and more important in practice, than how choice is to be exercised between options. The judgments reflect in different ways the significance of determinations of who are to be decision-makers, as well as of what decisions are made.

The leading English case on parental initiative to achieve sexual sterilisation of a minor child is *Re D (A minor)*.[45] In this case, the widowed mother had arranged the sterilisation of her 11-year-old daughter who was mentally impaired, in agreement with a physician. The girl was precocious in development and presented behaviour problems, causing her mother to fear that she would be seduced and become pregnant. There was medical evidence that any child the daughter might have could be abnormal, and that in any event the girl would be unable to cope with a family. The mother and a pediatrician agreed that she be sterilised. The girl gave no evidence of likely menstrual or other difficulties making sterilisation a therapeutic option for her, but was proposed to be sterilised on contraceptive and partly eugenic grounds. The chance intervention of an interested third party [46] led to wardship proceedings to challenge the sterilisation decision. In the Family Division, Heilbron J. discussed the proposal to undertake the sterilisation. The judge condemned it in clear terms. She said that: "The type of operation proposed is one which involves the deprivation of a basic human right, namely the right of a woman to reproduce, and therefore, it would, if performed on a woman for non-therapeutic reasons and without her consent, be a violation of such right." [47] The court was not saying that sterilisation should not be performed. The judge had noted evidence that the girl, although impaired, was likely to develop intellectually to a stage where she would be capable of independent social life, and marriage. The judgment required that any decision on sterilisation be postponed until the girl could take such part in it as would be effective, and probably decisive.

The judgment presents a limit of parental rights, in controlling a decision to permit non-therapeutic, irreversible surgery that would have appropriated beforehand a choice that the girl would have been able to make for herself, when she had achieved sufficient maturity. It also exposes a limit in the protective tests set by Goldstein, Freud and Solnit in *Before the Best Interests of the Child*. The authors are concerned with gross failures of parental care by

[45] *Re D. (A Minor) (Wardship: Sterilisation)* [1976] Fam. 185.

[46] An educational psychologist who assessed children's skills at the daughter's school.

[47] Note 45 above, at p. 193.

abandonment, sexual and other assaults against children, repeated failure to prevent children from suffering serious bodily injury, and parental refusals to authorise lifesaving medical care. These tests seem to lack the fine tuning required to deal with the situation presented by *Re D*, since they are directed primarily at decisions to remove children entirely from parental custody and control.[48] Further, they are concerned with parents whose treatment of their children falls short of legislated or judicially set minimum standards of care. They seem not to address parents whose well-meaning and conscientious initiatives are misguided or insensitive in ways denying children future rights. The tests set by *Before the Best Interests* are illustrated by failures to come up to standards, and do not consider deviations from norms of child-rearing by, for instance, overprotectiveness. They do not deal with causing harm to children by violating or pre-empting their human rights, such as their rights of reproduction.

Goldstein, Freud and Solnit say that " when death is not a likely consequence of exercising a medical choice, there would be no justification for governmental intrusion." [49] They apparently consider that the mother of D was proposing to act in a manner with which the courts should not have interfered. The trial judge found, however, a proposed deprivation and violation of the child's basic human rights, and intervened on that ground. This is consistent with a body of case law in the United States, where non-therapeutic sterilisation of mildly retarded minors has been prohibited. In the case in Indiana of *A. L.* v. *G. R. H.*, for instance, involving a mother's request for sterilisation of her 15-year-old retarded son who was showing increasing interest in girls, the court held that: " the common law does not invest parents with such power over their children even though they sincerely believe the child's adulthood would benefit therefrom." [50]

These cases parallel decisions concerning sterilisation of mentally retarded adults, where courts have been unprepared to allow the procedure in the absence of the clearest statutory authority.[51] Where sterilisation serves a therapeutic purpose, or retardation is severe and the medical prognosis is that it will be chronic, with the effect that the retardate will never be able to participate in any

---

48 *Re D.* resulted in wardship to prevent sterilisation, but the girl's mother was not deprived of her care and custody of D.

49 *Before the Best Interests of the Child*, note 31 above, at p. 92.

50 (1975) 325 N.E. 2d 501, 502.

51 See Stephen L. Isaacs, " The Law of Fertility Regulation in the United States: A 1980 Review " (1980) 19 J. of Family Law 65, and the cases given at note 62. See also *Guardianship of Eberhardy* (1980) 294 N.W. 2d 540.

meaningful way in a decision on sterilisation, parental or institutional preference may prevail.[52]

It must be said that a number of quite recent decisions by United States courts [53] and a Canadian court,[54] the former perhaps influenced by *Before the Best Interests*, have recognised power in courts to ratify parental decisions for sterilisation. These cases add an important element to the decision-making process, however, which was absent from the circumstances of the case *Re D*, which came to light and to court by fortuitous means and the personal tenacity of an interested third party.[55] The cases disallow purely private arrangements between parents and doctors to sterilise children for contraceptive or eugenic purposes. They require proposals for sterilisation to be presented to courts, and to be expressly approved before they can be implemented. Courts finding that they have a common law power to ratify parental preference may do so, but they have to be satisfied upon objective evidence that the procedure is justifiable in the best interests of the children. This provides some protection against the danger that parents may overreact to fears for their children, underestimate their children's capacity for intellectual and emotional growth and marriage, and fear being burdened themselves with the rearing of their grandchildren, who they believe may also be mentally impaired.

Courts can monitor whether the parental decision is in the best interests of the children, or primarily in the best interests of the parents. Retardation may be related, for instance, to genetic conditions causing infertility, so that eugenic and child-rearing fears of parents may be biologically ill-founded. The cause of mental handicap in the children may be traumatic rather than genetic, so that the condition would not be transmitted to children's children. Reliable means of contraception may be available, with options of selective legal abortion,[56] or of adoption of less impaired children. Courts may therefore seek responses to a check-list of questions before deciding to approve parental choice, concerning a child's capacity for instance for independence, marriage, child-rearing, and contraception, as well as concerning fertility and genetic trans-

---

52 State sterilisation statutes are reviewed in G. S. Neuwirth, P. A. Heisler and K. S. Goldrich, "Capacity, Competence, Consent: Voluntary Sterilization of the Mentally Retarded" (1974–75) 6 Columbia Human Rights L.R. 447.

53 See, *e.g. In the Matter of the Guardianship of Hayes* (1980) 608 P. 2d 635.

54 *In the Matter of Eve* (1980) 115 D.L.R. (3d) 283 (P.E.I.S.C. *in banco*).

55 Heilbron J. exonerated the Official Solicitor from responsibility to commence proceedings protective of such human rights, but noted that this may leave a gap in law enforcement; see note 45 above, at p. 197.

56 Although Canadian law has no eugenic indication for abortion; see Criminal Code, s. 251 and Bernard M. Dickens, "Eugenic Recognition in Canadian Law" (1975) 13 Osgoode Hall L.J. 547.

mission.[57] Private decisions of parents may be less objective in these regards. A clear need exists for legal provisions prohibiting non-therapeutic sterilisations of children, and non-consensual sterilisations of adults, unless courts have assessed medical answers to such a check-list of questions.[58]

United States courts apply this principle regarding another area where parental decision-makers may be caught in a conflict of interest, namely organ transplants and bone-marrow transplants between minors.[59] The conflict is not so much between interests of children and parents, but between a desperately ill child and another child of the same parents who could serve as a donor of histologically compatible body material for transplantation. Parental dedication and concern towards the ill child may cause them to be less circumspect regarding the welfare and protection of the healthy young potential donor, especially where they harbour unrealistic hopes that the healthy child's sacrifice can aid the siblings at risk of death. Suspected abuse of the bodies of healthy young donors over a decade ago,[60] including physically healthy mental retardates,[61] persuaded most Canadian provinces to prohibit any organ donations by minors and the mentally incompetent,[62] but this may be an overreaction.

A better solution was reached in the United States, where the possible psychological advantage to the donor child and the relatively low risk of bone-marrow and organ removal for transplantation has been recognised. The risk-to-benefit ratio for the child may be favourable, although donation from a healthy child is physiologically non-therapeutic, where the psychological and emotional dimensions of health are accommodated. In the 1972 Connecticut case of *Hart* v. *Brown* [63] concerning kidney transplantation between siblings, the court spoke of the parents' rights as decisions takers, but emphasised the public monitoring function over their decisions of the judiciary. The court held that:

> "To prohibit the natural parents and the guardian *ad litem* of the minor children the right to give their consent under these

[57] See, for instance, the conditions specified in the *Hayes* case, note 53 above.

[58] An additional inadequacy of the *Before the Best Interests* approach is that it might not only deny a child's right to such a hearing, but also deny legal representation to the child when such a hearing is legally mandated.

[59] See generally C. H. Baron, M. Botsford and G. F. Cole, "Live Organ and Tissue Transplants from Minor Donors in Massachusetts" (1975) 55 Boston Univ.L.R. 159.

[60] See *ibid.* at pp. 162, note 16 and 171, note 63.

[61] *Strunk* v. *Strunk* (1969) 445 S.W. 2d 145. In the case of *Re Richardson* (1973) 284 So. 2d 338, a Louisiana appeal court upheld judicial refusal to approve a transplant from a mentally retarded 17 year-old to his 32 year-old sister.

[62] See the Uniform Human Tissue Gift Act, Proceedings of the Uniform Law Conference of Canada 1971, pp. 76, 152.

[63] 289 A.2d 386.

> circumstances, *where there is supervision by this court and other persons in examining their judgment*, would be most unjust, inequitable and injudicious. Therefore, natural parents of a minor should have the right to give their consent to an isograft kidney transplantation procedure *when their motivation and reasoning are favourably reviewed by a community representation which includes a court of equity.*" [64]

Goldstein, Freud and Solnit criticise this requirement of public supervision of parental decisions, on the ground that neither doctors nor judges are trained or otherwise qualified to impose their own preferred value choices about what is good or right for such children or families.[65] That may be conceded without reducing the value of having more objective scrutiny, whether in a court or in another independent forum, of the factual and evaluative basis upon which parents reach decisions which may risk serious harm to their children. As in the case of sexual sterilisation, parental rights should exclude the enforcement of purely private decisions involving surgical interventions in healthy children under their control for the purpose of assisting other persons, if the risk is more than minimal; that is, if it exceeds that of blood-sampling, or perhaps of donation of a volume of blood assessed to be safe by reference to the donor's body-weight and normal health state.[66]

United States courts have become somewhat more active to protect minors against another form of parental medical decision-making which may affect their future in harmful ways, namely voluntary committal to mental health facilities.[67] Modern mental health laws favour voluntary or informal recourse to psychiatric care. This is consistent with routine health care, and assists the consensual nature of therapy. Coerced detention is reserved for those who are considered dangerous, to themselves or others, and is imposed on grounds of security rather than treatability.[68] Persons involuntarily detained on mental health grounds have access to

---

[64] *Ibid.* at p. 391 (emphasis added). In *Before the Best Interests* it is noted of this observation that although the judge "avoided tragic consequences for the Harts, he did set a precedent for unwarranted and undesirable intervention by the state": note 31 above, at pp. 107–108.

[65] Note 31 above, at p. 108.

[66] The legitimacy of measuring risk by a blood sampling standard draws support from legislative and judicial practice of permitting a parent to consent without more to the drawing of blood from a child for paternity testing for purposes of litigation; see *S.* v. *McC., W* v. *W* [1972] A.C. 24, especially Lord Reid at p. 43.

[67] Gerald P. Koocher *Children's Rights and the Mental Health Professions* (1976), and John P. Wilson *The Rights of Adolescents in the Mental Health System* (1978).

[68] See Bruce Ennis *Prisoners of Psychiatry: Mental Patients, Psychiatry and the Law* (1972), and Alan Dershowitz "Dangerousness As A Criterion For Confinement" (1974) 2 *Bulletin* (American Acad. Psychiatry and Law) 172.

means of review of the decision to detain them, and to retain them, in custody.[69] Beyond review provisions built into mental health legislation, they may ultimately bring habeas corpus proceedings. Voluntary patients require no such protections, of course, since they are in principle free to terminate treatment and leave a facility at will. If they are not free in this way, their status is changed to that of involuntary detainees, when review hearings and other procedural protections become available to them.

Adolescents are at a major disadvantage, however, when their parents voluntarily commit them to a psychiatric facility.[70] As "voluntary" patients they have no review or procedural protections, but they will not be released when their parents refuse to take them back home or to have them otherwise institutionalised or sent, for instance, to foster parents or a group home. They remain classified as "voluntary" patients, however, despite their own strong opposition to institutionalisation, because their parents possess legal rights to control their custody.

Parental motivation to commit to psychiatric care may be suspect when parents fear that their adolescent children are out of their control, mixing with the wrong crowd, or prone to crazy and unpredictable behaviour; that may reflect a generation gap rather than psychopathology. It is particularly suspect, however, when delinquent behaviour has occurred or is feared. Parents of a potential delinquent may fear suffering stigmatisation as inadequate or ineffective parents, whereas parents of a psychiatrically disturbed child may receive pity and sympathy. That is not to say, of course, that a psychiatric history is not itself stigmatising. The mark is borne by the patient, however, rather than by the parents or the family. An adolescent's educational opportunities, career opportunities and social and marital opportunities may be affected by a history of even voluntary psychiatric institutionalisation.

It may be understandable that parents prefer to consider their children, in crude language, to be mad rather than bad. A sizable body of literature reflects upon the way modern society applies psychiatric classifications to behaviour once considered sinful or evil.[71] Institutional psychiatry continues to struggle with such issues as whether, for instance, homosexuals are affected by a psychiatric disease, why in modern Western society women fighting against

---

[69] See David Baker "Ontario's Mental Health (Amendment) Act 1978" (1978) 2 Legal Medical Q. 177.

[70] See Thomas Szasz "The Child as Involuntary Mental Patient: The Threat of Child Therapy to the Child's Dignity, Privacy, and Self-Esteem" (1977) 14 San Diego L.R. 1005.

[71] Thomas Szasz has written widely on this theme, beginning with his book *The Myth of Mental Illness* (1961).

limited personal and career opportunities are more likely than men to be considered mentally ill, and to what extent extreme political dissidents closer to home than the Soviet Union, and adherents to unorthodox religious faiths, may be considered psychotics or pathologically disturbed. In short, the very credibility and legitimacy of psychiatry as a medical specialty are under challenge.[72] A result has been the refining of the criterion for involuntary detention on grounds of mental health to clear and convincing proof of dangerousness. This exposes the hazard to adolescents when their parents subvert this criterion and its standards by employing their power of custody to commit their non-dangerous children to psychiatric facilities as ostensible volunteers, on the basis of personal, unspecified and unsympathetic conclusions.

The problem of parental volunteering of children for mental health care is not easily accommodated by *Before the Best Interests of the Child.* The book urges minimal State intervention in parental choice. It does not address parental placement of children with State mental health agencies on a temporary basis,[73] nor such agencies' conditions of accepting children lodged with them. If parental autonomy is to prevail, the State must, it appears, accept any children parents choose to place with psychiatric facilities whom the staff believe they can help.

The issue came before the United States Supreme Court in the *Parham* case in 1979, arising in Georgia.[74] While the court was sympathetic to parental wishes to supply children with mental health services with a minimum of procedural preconditions, and quoted from Joseph Goldstein's writings to buttress this position,[75] it also acknowledged children's interests in liberty from detention and from irresistible treatment. The court accordingly felt it proper that voluntary committal be subject to due process requirements.[76] In fact, the court held that Georgia's voluntary commitment statute satisfied these requirements, since it provided for parental commitment to be subject to an initial psychiatric investigation by a neutral fact-finder, for instance a staff physician at the hospital, followed by periodic reviews of the child's condition, as if the child was an

[72] See Leon Eisenberg "Psychiatry and Society: A Sociobiologic Synthesis" (1977) 296 New England J. of Medicine 903.

[73] *Before the Best Interests* recognises that "intervention is justified only when one or both separating parents, whether married or unmarried, bring to the court their disagreement about the custody of their children"; note 31 above, at p. 31.

[74] *Parham* v. *J.R.* (1979) 99 S.Ct. 2493.

[75] The reference, at *ibid.* at p. 2505, was to Goldstein, note 34 above.

[76] *Before the Best Interests* was published after the Supreme Court wrote its judgment, but see Andrew S. Watson, "Children, Families, and Courts: *Before The Best Interests Of The Child* and *Parham* v. *J.R.*" (1980) 66 Virginia L.R. 653.

involuntary patient. Any provision less careful than this to protect children's independent interests would apparently have been unacceptable. Further, United States courts had already held that minors of an age and capacity voluntarily to admit themselves to psychiatric treatment, which they can do below the age of majority, have by the same token the legal power to leave such facilities, and cannot be detained as volunteers merely upon parental insistence.[77]

The effect of the *Parham* decision and recognition of adolescents' capacity of self discharge from facilities to which parents have had them committed imposes conditions and limits upon parental rights, in favour of children's liberties. There remains a serious problem, however, regarding parental opposition to policies of de-institutionalisation of mentally retarded children.[78] Their developmental progress had been indicated to be better in regular homes and ordinary schools where they interact with a range of normal children, and can learn from their conduct.[79] Parents may be apprehensive of being responsible for them at home, of inadequate community-based services, and of experiencing constraints upon their time and lifestyle. That conflict between interests of parents and children awaits resolution, but government restrictions upon funding of welfare services does nothing to ease the position.

The last case to be cited to illustrate problems of parental autonomy over children's interests is the most threatening, since it faithfully followed the thrust of Joseph Goldstein's reasoning, and has allowed parents to opt for the death through curable disease of a child having a good prospect of survival with surgical treatment. It has left commentators asking: What happened to the best interests of the child? [80]

Phillip Becker [81] was aged 11 in 1979 when litigation was presented on his behalf in California. He suffered from Down's Syndrome (mongolism) and was mentally retarded. His I.Q. measured slightly under 60, in the upper range of mild retardation. He could develop social and communication skills, and be quite independent in self-care. He was able to dress and care for himself and do domestic chores, he attended school and belonged to a Boy Scout troop, and was likely to be able to function in a sheltered workshop in the

[77] *Melville* v. *Sabbatino* (1973) 313 A. 2d 886. See generally H. Beyer and J. Wilson, "The Reluctant Volunteer: A Child's Right to Resist Commitment," in Gerald P. Koocher, note 67 above, at p. 133.

[78] See R. Frohboese and B. D. Sales, "Parental Opposition to Deinstitutionalization: A Challenge in Need of Attention and Resolution" (1980) 4 *Law and Human Behavior* 1.

[79] See R. Kugel and A. Shearer (eds.) *Changing Patterns in Residential Services for the Mentally Retarded (President's Committee on Mental Retardation)* (1976).

[80] See Donna Mitchell "In re Phillip B.: What Happened to the Best Interests of the Child?" (1980) 12 *Toledo L.R.* 151.

[81] See *Re Phillip B.* (1979) 156 Cal.Rptr. 48, *cert. denied* (1980) 100 S.Ct. 1597.

future, if he had a future. Phillip Becker was also affected, however, by a congenital heart defect, which in a normal child would have been correctable by relatively uncomplicated standard surgery. Without surgery, Phillip Becker might live up to 20 or more years, but progressive deterioration and damage to his lungs would cause him to become increasingly incapacitated and eventually bedridden. With surgery, he would enjoy a significant expansion of life, develop into a healthy adult, and have a reasonable capacity for enjoyment of life. Down's Syndrome children face above average risk of post-operative complications, however, and because of existing damage to Phillip Becker's heart, he bore a mortality risk in surgery in 1979 of 5 to 10 per cent. As surgery is withheld, the percentage risk of mortality rises, when surgery becomes contraindicated.

These facts may not lead to a clear-cut choice of treatment, and preferences either way may be defensible. Joseph Goldstein's emphasis is not only upon decisions, however, but also upon determination of decision-making people and procedures.[82] In the case of Phillip Becker,[83] he had never lived at home with his parents. He had been placed in a private care institution at birth, and had remained in a residential care facility up to and after the litigation concerning him. His parents visited him for several hours on average once every two months.[84] The Santa Clara County Juvenile Probation Department filed a petition to have him declared a dependent no longer of his parents but of the court, since the parents were withholding necessities of life, so that consent to surgery might be given *in loco parentis*. The supervisors of the care home where the boy lived considered that the operation should be performed.

The parents refused consent to surgery, and opposed the petition for the transfer of dependency and for surgical consent to be given on the apparent grounds [85] that:

(1) Since the boy's life was not a "life worth living," [86] he should not have his life prolonged by surgery;
(2) he would outlive his parents if the life-extending surgery

[82] See text at note 44, and Goldstein, note 34 above, at p. 651.

[83] Basic facts of the case, and references to the trial transcript, are presented in Donna Mitchell, note 80 above and by W. A. Moeller in "Notes: Domestic Relations—Custody—Refusal to Award Custody of Retarded Child to State Where Parents Would Not Permit Heart Surgery" (1980) 63 *Marquette L.R.* 511. The initial juvenile court proceedings were unreported.

[84] *Ibid.* at p. 523.

[85] See note 80 above, at p. 167.

[86] Goldstein, Freud and Solnit recognise the propriety of state intervention to protect "a life worth living"; see note 43 above, and *Before the Best Interests*, note 31 above, Chap. 6 at p. 91.

was performed, and they would be unable to supervise his placement and care; and

(3) the operation was too risky, and might result in death.

The California trial court concluded that it would be improper to intervene in the parental decision based on these reasons, and denied the petition. The State appellate court recognised the principle of parental autonomy, and dismissed the appeal. The United States Supreme Court declined to review the decision of the appellate court.

In the *Parham* case,[87] the United States Supreme Court observed the principles of judicial modesty urged in *Beyond the Best Interests of the Child* in stating that: "we do not accept the notion that the shortcomings of specialists can always be avoided by shifting the decision from a trained specialist using traditional tools of medical science to an untrained judge." [88] At the Phillip Becker trial, medical experts gave uncontradicted testimony that without surgery, death could result at any time after the next two years, but that surgery to repair the defect could be performed only within a short period of time. The trial judge observed, however, that medical experts have been wrong before,[89] and ignored the uncontradicted expert evidence in order to favour an absolute principle of parental decision-making. The trial transcript discloses the parents' lawyer saying that: "If I might paraphrase what I think seems the Beckers' position . . . it seems to be that it would be preferable that Phillip's life end early, instead of going through a full life with what is obviously an extremely serious handicap." [90]

The transcript also shows that the baby was initially placed in institutional care out of fear about how his presence at home could affect other children of the family, and that Mr. Becker expressed concern that if the boy survived, he would become a financial burden on his brothers.[91] The judge failed to observe any parental conflict of interest, however, in the decision the parents reached. There was no recognition of the judicial monitoring function where a conflict was possible, which was emphasised by the court in the sibling organ-transplant case of *Hart* v. *Brown*.[92]

In *Custody of a Minor* [93] in 1978, the Supreme Judicial Court of Massachusetts recognised the role of parental autonomy, but held that: "parental rights . . . do not clothe parents with life and death authority over their children." [94] The court removed legal

[87] Note 74, above.
[88] *Ibid.* at p. 2507.
[89] See W. A. Moeller, note 83 above at p. 516.
[90] *Ibid.* p. 518, note 35.
[91] *Ibid.* p. 522, note 56.
[92] Note 63 above; and see text at note 64.
[93] (1978) 379 N.E. 2d 1053.
[94] At p. 1063.

custody of a child from parents who were unwilling to continue medically advised chemotherapy for their child suffering from leukemia, and who wanted to treat him through prayer and dietary management. The court provided for medically orthodox treatment even though it involved risk, because the risk was minimal when compared to the risk of non-treatment. Without specifying what the resolution should have been on the facts of the case, that may appear a superior method of determining the case of Phillip Becker than the trial court applied, and appellate courts have considered adequate.

The Massachusetts Supreme Judicial Court in *Custody of a Minor* noted the competition of three sets of interests: the "natural rights" of the parents, the responsibilities of the State, and the personal needs or best interests of the child.[95] No violence need be done to parental rights to acknowledge that they are not absolute. The case of Phillip Becker gives disquieting modern support to the conclusion that before courts of law, they may be becoming so. The perspective appears to be advanced that the best interests of the child are to be found less by reference to objective criteria, where they exist, than by reference to subjective parental preference, even when parents are in a conflict of interest or have an adverse interest. Theoretical offensiveness of interfering with a parent-child bond was reduced in the *Becker* case, of course, since the boy had never lived with his parents and family, and his contact with them was minimal. The family prevailed, however, to deny him the reasonable prospect of continued life and enjoyment. It may be hoped that the case presents a high water-mark of parental autonomy, and not the governing approach courts will come to adopt.

Phillip Becker may not survive to reach an age of 14, 15 or 16, and if he does, he is unlikely to gain the intellectual competence to become what the common law describes as a mature minor. He may never be able to take advantage, therefore, of the mature minor rule, which is the last limitation upon parental rights to be considered here.

It has been noted that Lord Denning has properly described a parental right as: "a dwindling right which the courts will hesitate to enforce against the wishes of the child, the older he is. It starts with a right of control and ends with little more than [a right of] advice."[96]

Whatever parental rights may be against third parties, it is evident from case law and legislation[97] that the children central to those

[95] *Ibid.* at pp. 1061–1062.

[96] See note 3 above.

[97] The Family Law Reform Act 1969, s. 8 affords medical autonomy to a minor who has reached 16 years of age.

rights may resist them progressively as they advance to maturity. The House of Lords has found that constraints can be used to compel an infant or a young child to submit to a blood test, for instance for paternity testing,[98] but, by implication, an older child can effectively refuse a parental order to give blood. The more invasive the procedure and the older the minor, the greater will be the minor's right to resist and the less will be the parental right to insist. Parents cannot require, for instance, that their pregnant daughter should have an abortion, as the Maryland Supreme Court has confirmed in the case of *Re Smith*,[99] and a mentally normal girl could not be compelled to receive a contraceptive pill or intra-uterine device when her parents feared her pregnancy. The case of *Re D*,[1] excluding contraceptive or eugenic sexual sterilisation of a retarded girl, clearly excludes the procedure for one who is normal.

Equally, parents have little if any veto power over mature minors' fertility control. United States courts have excluded parental veto power over abortion decisions of competent minors,[2] and parents would have no greater power to prevent a competent minor's therapeutic abortion under the British Abortion Act 1967.[3] In Canada, the Criminal Code permits only therapeutic abortion,[4] and since parents have legal duties under the federal Criminal Code[5] and provincial child welfare legislation[6] to supply children with therapeutic services, no parental veto appears to exist. In the Supreme Court of British Columbia it was recognised in 1970 that in principle a physician can fit a 15-year-old girl with an intra-uterine device without parental consent or notification,[7] and in Britain in 1971 the Disciplinary Committee of the General Medical Council, after taking legal advice, declared the principle that physicians must respect confidentiality over contraceptive management of a patient even if he or she is aged, for instance, 15 years, and refrain from informing parents without the minor patient's prior approval.[8]

98 See *S.* v. *McC.*, *W.* v. *W.*, note 66 above.

99 (1972) 295 A. 2d 238.

1 Note 45 above.

2 *Planned Parenthood of Central Missouri* v. *Danforth* (1976) 428 U.S. 52, 74. The same judgment excluded a right of spousal veto.

3 It may be otherwise regarding abortion upon other than therapeutic grounds, but even then the mature minor rule may prevail to achieve adolescent autonomy. In *Paton* v. *B.P.A.S. Trustees* [1979] Q.B. 276, Sir George Baker P. noted only mental or physical incapacity as barring autonomy, at p. 281, although the case concerned a married woman whose husband was denied an abortion veto.

4 Criminal Code, s. 251 (4) (*c*).

5 *Ibid.* s. 197; see note 13, above.

6 See for instance Ontario's Child Welfare Act 1978, s. 19 (1) (*b*) (ix).

7 *Re "D" and Council of the College of Physicians and Surgeons of British Columbia* (1970) 11 D.L.R. (3d) 570; see especially at p. 577.

8 General Medical Council, Disciplinary Committee Minutes (1971), 108 Minutes of the G.M.C., pp. 58–59.

The modern function of parental rights is to prepare children and adolescents for maturity, and as minors come to achieve maturity and to exercise autonomy, this may be seen not as a limitation or defeat of parental control, but as a successful discharge of parental responsibility. It is not accidental that a common manifestation of maturity in minors lies in the area of fertility control and family planning, since this is the link through which they themselves decide to become parents, and to acquire the rights and responsibilities which attend upon that status. Where parents exercise choice over their children's survival, and over the quality of the lives they will grow up to lead, a need exists to have a means of public monitoring. Without questioning parental good intentions, one can see that cases exist which show that the latest proposals of Goldstein, Freud and Solnit, strongly favouring parental autonomy, should not drown other and opposing views giving emphasis to the rights of children themselves. The book *Before the Best Interests of the Child* offers a helpful first word to assist judicial and administrative analysis. It cannot necessarily serve, however, as the last word.

BERNARD M. DICKENS.*

---

* Ph.D., LL.D. Faculty of Law, University of Toronto. This paper was presented at a Special University Lecture in Laws at Queen Mary College, University of London, on February 17, 1981.

Part III
The Best Interest of the Child? (Concerning the Freud-Goldstein-Solnit Theory)

[7]

Freedom and the Welfare State: Child-Rearing, Parental Autonomy and State Intervention

By M. D. A. Freeman

Reader in English Law, University College London

Libertarianism is once again an intellectually respectable polictical ideology.[1] Not since Victorian times has the minimal state[2] enjoyed the airing it is currently getting. The writings of Hayek and Nozick mirror the political regimes on both sides of the Atlantic, though needless to say, their arguments are put with a good deal more sophistication than is found in the speeches of Reagan or Thatcher or any of their associates.[3] In *Anarchy, State and Utopia*,[4] Nozick argues from a restricted set of natural rights to the conclusion that most of what states do is *ultra vires*. This is the philosophy of extreme liberalism, of an individualism which treats all rights as if they were private property.[5] Nozick (and similar exponents of this liberalism) is opposed to the state imposition of restraints.[6] He can accept "the night-watchman state of classical liberal theory, limited to the functions of protecting all its citizens against violence, theft, and fraud, and to the enforcement of contracts, and so on," but not a state committed to a notion such as "social justice."[7]

Nozick makes only a cursory reference to the family and Goldstein, Freud and Solnit,[8] whose *Before the Best Interests of the Child*[9] is to be the pivot of this article, make absolutely no reference to the philosophy of Nozick or Hayek. Nozick's is true "grand theory": the Goldstein *et al.* project is a micro-study. Though less extreme than Nozick, *Before the Best Interests* belongs very much to the same tradition of libertarianism as *Anarchy, State and Utopia*. Goldstein *et al.* are most typical of a powerful lobby today which advocates parental autonomy in child-rearing. They argue for strict limitations upon state intervention in matters which intimately concern parent-child relations. Such interventionism is a characteristic of the growth of the Welfare State.[10] This article examines the appropriateness and viability of non-intervention in child-rearing practices. The question of the preservation of the

---

[1] A good introduction for the non-specialist is Alan Ryan, "The New Libertarians: A Gauntlet to Both Left and Right," *New Society*, June 11, 1981, pp. 437–430.

[2] See, particularly, Herbert Spencer's *The Man Versus The State*, reissued in 1969 with an introduction by Donald Macrae.

[3] See *Law, Legislation and Liberty*, Vol. 2, *The Mirage of Social Justice* (1976).

[4] *Anarchy, State and Utopia* (1974). His *Philosophical Explanations* (1981) does not continue the same themes.

[5] See, *e.g.* K. Joseph and J. Sumption, *Equality* (1979).

[6] *Op. cit.* note 4, p. 26.

[7] Such as found in the writings of that other guru of the 1970s, John Rawls (see his *Theory of Justice* (1971)).

[8] *Op. cit.* note 4, pp. 167–168.

[9] *Beyond the Best Interests of the Child* (Revised edition, 1979); and more particularly in *Before the Best Interests of the Child* (1979), upon which this article is largely focused.

[10] See B. Jordan, *Freedom and The Welfare State* (1976).

integrity of the family from intrusion by state agencies may well be a key social and legal issue in the coming decade.

The philosophy of minimum state intervention

The philosophy of minimum state intervention in the family was expressed most clearly in the United States Supreme Court in the case of *Prince* v. *Massachusetts* in 1944.[11] The case arose out of a conflict between Jehovah's Witnesses and state authority. It was a questionable attempt by the Commonwealth of Massachusetts to extend its child labour legislation to prevent a child selling religious literature on the streets. This is not the place to question what to Justice Rutledge was self-evident, *viz*: "the state's authority over children's activities is broader than over like actions of adults." More important is the judge's statement that: "it is cardinal with us that the custody, care and nurture of the child reside first in the parents, whose primary function and freedom include preparation for obligations the state can neither supply nor hinder. And it is in recognition of this that these decisions[12] have respected the private realm of family life which the state cannot enter." He conceded, though, that "the family [was] not beyond regulation in the public interest." Thus, the state could require, as it has done for a very long time, compulsory education and it could prohibit child labour, insist upon the vaccination of children and the like. He also thought that while parents could become martyrs themselves, they were not free "to make martyrs of their children before they have reached the age of full and legal discretion when they can make that choice for themselves."

Justice Rutledge's remarks have been regularly cited with approval in recent American jurisprudence. It is also given a similar accolade in Goldstein, Freud and Solnit's second monograph, *Before the Best Interests of the Child*.[13] In this is to be found the fullest statement of minimum state intervention in the affairs of the family. "The child's need for safety within the confines of the family must be met by law through its recognition of family privacy as the barrier to state intrusion upon parental autonomy in child rearing."[14] They treat the family as a private area outside the law. The purported justification for this position is both psychologically and philosophically grounded. Its basis is in part the authors' notion of psychological parenthood which they developed in their earlier *Beyond the Best Interests of the Child*.[15] This requires, as spelt out there, day-to-day interaction, companionship and shared experiences. But this psychological relationship requires "the privacy of family life, under guardianship by parents who are autonomous. The younger the child, the greater is his need for them. When family integrity is broken or weakened by state intrusion, his needs are thwarted and his belief that his parents are omniscient and all-powerful is shaken prematurely. The effect on the child's developmental progress is invariably detrimental."[16] It is, to say the least, questionable whether this is so but Goldstein and his colleagues dismiss, what I consider to be, the very persuasive evidence of Michael Rutter,[17] the Clarkes,[18] Barbara

[11] (1944); 321 U.S. 158.

[12] He referred to *Meyer* v. *Nebraska*, 262 U.S. 390, *Pierce* v. *Society of Sisters*, 268 U.S. 510 and *West Virginia State Board of Education* v. *Barnette*, 319 U.S. 624.

[13] *Op. cit.* p. 217.

[14] *Idem.* p. 9.

[15] See pp. 17–20. See also *Before the Best Interests of the Child*, pp. 40–57.

[16] *Before the Best Interests of the Child*, p. 9.

[17] *Maternal Deprivation Re-Assessed* (2nd ed., 1981).

[18] Ann M. Clarke and A. C. B. Clarke, *Early Experience: Myth and Evidence* (1976).

Tizard,[19] Jerome Kagan and his collaborators[20] as "simplistic."[21] At the very least the breaking of ties cannot be "invariably detrimental." If that were the case no state intervention into the family could ever be justified.

Goldstein *et al.* also adduce a philosophical rationale. A policy of minimum coercive intervention by the state accords with their "firm belief as citizens in individual freedom and human dignity."[22] These notions are superficially attractive. Unfortunately, in a world of basic structural inequalities individual freedom can be so exercised as to undermine not only the freedom of others but also their human dignity. The parent-child relationship is a microcosm of this imbalance. Bill Jordan puts this point well: "the case against intervention in family life often rests on the freedom of more powerful members (usually husbands in relation to wives and parents in relation to children) to exercise their power without restriction."[23] Not all who favour a non-interventionist stance belong to the radical right,[24] though critics and commentators often lump them all together. The Goldstein *et al.* reasoning is, however, common in neo-conservative thought. Doubt may be cast as to how tenable it is in practice. There is, Goldstein *et al.* argue, a further justification for their philosophy, *viz:*

> "the law does not have the capacity to supervise the fragile, complex interpersonal bonds between child and parent. As *parens patriae* the state is too crude an instrument to become an adequate substitute for flesh and blood parents. The legal system has neither the resources nor the sensitivity to respond to a growing child's ever-changing needs and demands. It does not have the capacity to deal on an individual basis with the consequences of its decisions, or to act with the deliberate speed that is required by a child's sense of time."[25]

Much of this is incontrovertible, though it should be said that the processes of the legal system could be speeded up. What is questionable, however, is their rather simplistic view of autonomy. To them it is "there," taken for granted and uproblematic. They ignore the ways in which the autonomy they value is constructed and regulated by legal processes. The law is a cultural underpinning of autonomy. Families (that is parents in our context) have as much autonomy as the law allows them. It gives and it withdraws. It is not surprising that Goldstein *et al.* do not consider laws regulating education or child labour.[26]

Goldstein and his colleagues are not alone in formulating a philosophy of minimum state intervention in family matters. Michael Wald[27] and Robert

---

[19] *Adoption: A Second Chance* (1977).

[20] J. Kagan, R. Kearsley and P. Zelazo, *Infancy; Its Place In Human Development* (1978).

[21] *Before the Best Interests of the Child*, p. 200.

[22] *Idem*. p. 12.

[23] *Op. cit.* note 10, p. 60.

[24] Typically represented today in the C. Brewer and J. Lait's polemic, *Can Social Work Survive?* (1980).

[25] *Before the Best Interests of the Child*, pp. 11–12.

[26] See, to like effect, J. Hodges, "Children and Parents: Who Chooses?" in *Politics and Power*, Vol. 3: *Sexual Politics, Feminism and Socialism* (1981), pp. 49–65.

[27] See "State Intervention on Behalf of 'Neglected' Children: A Search for Realistic Standards" (1975) 27 *Stanford Law Review* 985–1040 "State Intervention on Behalf of 'Neglected' Children: Standards For Removal of Children From Their Homes" (1976) 28 *Stanford Law Review* 623–706. See also "Thinking About Public Policy Toward Abuse and Neglect of Children" (1980) 78 *Michigan Law Review* 645.

Mnookin,[28] two prominent American child lawyers, have also questioned the wisdom of coercive state intervention, mainly on the ground that it does more harm than good. Radical criminologists, such as Edwin Schur[29] and Edwin Lemert[30] have also called for "radical" or "judicious" non-intervention, specifically in the area of juvenile delinquency, where Schur advocates "leaving the kids alone." Similar views have been expressed by the authors of two recent English publications, *Justice For Children*[31] and *In Whose Best Interests?*[32]

The roots of state intervention have been traced by a number of writers, notably Christopher Lasch in *Haven In a Heartless World,*[33] and Jacques Donzelot in *The Policing of Families.*[34] They show that intervention is neither straight-forwardly altruistic nor polictically neutral. I agree, and have argued elsewhere,[35] that non-intervention is basically the policy to pursue. As Burger C.J. said in the important United States Supreme Court case of *Parham* v. *J.R.* in 1979, "the statist notion that governmental power should supersede parental authority in *all* cases because *some* parents abuse and neglect children is repugnant . . ."[36] But the pursuit of a policy of non-intervention must not blind us to the fact that, for all its faults and imperfections, interference with child-rearing practices is sometimes imperative. The alternative is to throw out the baby with the bathwater. We are thus engaged in a line-drawing exercise.

The argument presented in this article is that Goldstein and his colleagues, who advocate the most restrictive grounds for intervention of any and whose views are highly influential, have drawn the line in the wrong place. If we are to err it should be on the side of protecting the child. Such a policy, plus an emphasis on controlling the controllers and giving parents and children adequate and speedy remedies against mistakes, inefficiency and maladministration is, it is argued, ultimately preferable to the somewhat dogmatic approach of the authors of *Before the Best Interests*. Given their psychological and philosophical premises their conclusions are inevitable. As indicated already, I am happy neither with their rejection of behavioural psychology nor their adoption of neo-conservative philosophical values. I therefore devote the bulk of this article to a critique of their proposals, but before doing so, I consider the positive side to their case. The issue, as already indicated, is not all black and white.

The case for non-intervention

At the crudest the case for non-intervention is that intervention does not work. It is worth looking at the effects of intervention on child abuse. There in no evidence that the increased control mechanisms of the last decade have conquered, or are likely to conquer, violence against children. An N.S.P.C.C. study[37] found that anxious

---

[28] "Foster Care; In Whose Best Interest?" (1973) 43 Harv. Educ. Rev. 599.

[29] *Radical Non-Intervention: Rethinking The Delinquency Problem* (1973).

[30] "Choice and Change in the Juvenile Court," (1976) 3 Br. J. of Law and Society 59–75. See also A. Morris, "Diversion of Juvenile Offenders From The Criminal Justice System" in N. Tutt (ed.), *Alternative Strategies For Coping with Crime* (1978), pp. 45–63.

[31] A. Morris, H. Giller, H. Geach and E. Szwed (1980).

[32] L. Taylor, R. Lacey and D. Bracken, Cobden Trust/Mind (1980).

[33] (1977).

[34] (1979). See, further, P. Hirst, "The Genesis of The Social" in *op. cit.* note 26, pp. 67–82.

[35] "The State: The Family and Law in the 'Eighties'" (1981) 11 *The Kingston Law Review* 129. *cf.* now M. Barrett and M. McIntosh, *The Anti-Social Family* (1982), pp. 95–126.

[36] (1979) 442 U.S. 584, below, p. 85.

[37] A. Skinner and R. Castle, *78 Battered Children: A Retrospective Study*, N.S.P.C.C., 1969.

visiting of families by social workers actually increases battering of children. A rebattering incidence of 60 per cent. in a sample of cases known to the agency does not compare favourably with the estimate of 25 to 30 per cent. rebattering where there has been no intervention. Bill Jordan's comment is worth producing: "In the tragic cases which have been so much publicised, the clients were not new referrals who had not been investigated quickly enough, but cases known to several departments (but the direct responsibility of social services) for a considerable period."[38] Goldstein and his colleagues are sensitive to much the same point: "by intrusion," they note, "the state may make a bad situation worse."[39] There is, of course, no guarantee that children removed from home will not suffer similar hardship, deprivation and cruelty elsewhere. It is striking, however, how little attention is given to cases of violence by substitute parents.[40] Compare the column inches given to the *Mehmedagi*[41] or the *Page*[42] cases with the *Frankland* case.[43] There a baby of six months was killed by his prospective adopters (parents chosen by professional social workers). It fits in well with the general "rescue"[44] idealogy associated with the 1975 Children Act that a case like this should be given relatively little attention.

A second argument supportive of non-interventionist policies concerns the vagueness of the standards conventionally used to measure parent conduct. Vague language invites unwarranted and arbitrary intervention. Where vague standards are used it is difficult to give parents advance warning of what is required of them. A firmly entrenched maxim of the criminal law is *nulla poena sine lege*. Since the consequences of falling foul of the standards in children's protective legislation is, or can be, little short of penal, similar considerations should apply. That is why Goldstein *et al.* insist, and rightly so, that parents should be given a fair warning, so that clear, precise standards should govern intervention. The obvious parallel is what H. L. A. Hart has called "the doctrine of fair opportunity" in criminal law.[45]

A cognate point is that vague standards can all too easily be employed to impose the standards of one section of the population on another. There are different types of parenting, as a cursory reading of the Newsons's studies of their Nottingham cohort demonstrates.[46] Patterns of disciplining, for example, are not uniform. Not only are there class differences but there are also regional and racial differences as well. Nor do the ethnic minorities constitute a homogeneous population: what constitutes good parenting amongst the Asian communities is very different from

---

[38] *Op. cit.* note 10, p. 166. The original was a speech at a B.A.S.W. Conference reported as "Is a Client A Fellow Citizen?" in *Social Work Today*, Vol. 6, no. 15 (1975), pp. 471–475.

[39] *Before the Best Interests of the Child*, p. 13.

[40] But note the *Richard Clark* case (child badly injured by foster parents). This case does not feature in Martin's excellent chapter (Chap. 9) of his edited collection, *Violence and The Family* (1978). Also the *Shirley Woodcock* case (*Community Care*, January 20, 1983, p. 3).

[41] London Borough of Southwark, June 1981 (given wide press coverage on June 11, 1981). See also M. D. A. Freeman, "A Second Maria: What Can We Learn From Inquiries Into Child Abuse Cases?" (1981) 145 J.P. 440.

[42] Essex C.C., March 1981.

[43] *The Times*, September 24, 1981.

[44] See R. Holman, *Inequality In Child Care*, C.P.A.G. Family Rights Group (2nd ed., 1981).

[45] *Punishment and Responsibility* (1968).

[46] *Patterns of Infant Care* (1963); *Four Years Old in an Urban Community* (1968); *Seven Years Old in The Home Environment* (1976).

that found in those of West Indian origin. There will often also be differences in attitudes of different castes and tribes and different Caribbean islands. Critics of the practices of intervention by agencies allege, sometimes with considerable justification, that these operate so as to impose middle-class and white standards of parenting on working-class parents and on the parents of black children.

These criticisms are directed particularly at the way in which names are placed on child abuse of "at risk" registers, at the way place of safety orders are sought and made and at the attitudes adopted towards the passing of resolutions assuming parental rights. Of the third of these examples (the section 3 resolution procedure) the authors of *Justice For Children* have persuasively written:

> "The actual mechanism by which a . . . resolution is obtained is very simple and depends very much on the quality of the individual social worker and local authority social services department. The criteria for obtaining a . . . resolution are often subjective: they depend on the social worker's perception of the family. This is shaped by a number of factors: the social worker's personality and training, the structure and morale of the social services department, and the social worker's relationship with the parent and child. There is no objective standard by which parents can be assessed as 'bad parents.' Such an assessment can be as much a product of a clash of personalities as of the parents' behaviour. Social enquiry reports are often scattered with such inexact terms as 'manipulative,' 'aggressive,' inadequate,' 'schizoid' and 'infantile.'

Even in trained hands psychological concepts can be misused, and there is even greater risk that this might happen when young and untrained social workers prepare reports."[47]

In the wake of the Maria Colwell scandal[48] in 1973–74 the number of place of safety orders has rocketed. In March 1973 there were approximately 214 place of safety orders in existence each week. By March 1977 this figure had more than trebled to reach 759. Only a small proportion of the orders end up as care orders (some no doubt are resolved by voluntary receptions—"going quietly" in criminal parlance) and this gives additional cause for concern. Not only are the civil liberties considerations disturbing but such a rupture of mother and child, particularly where the child is very young, can have deleterious effects on the bonding process.[49] Not uncommon now is the taking of babies at birth.[50] The moral propriety of these "pre-emptive strikes" may be questioned: since many of the babies are first babies it is difficult to see how such action may be legally justified.[51] The proportion of children in care for whom parental rights resolution are passed has also increased rapidly.[52]

---

[47] *Op. cit.* note 31, p. 112–113. See also A. Sutton, "Science In Court" in M. King (ed.), *Childhood, Welfare and Justice* (1981), pp. 45–104.

[48] See Field-Fisher Report, D.H.S.S., 1974. East Sussex C.C. also commissioned an inquiry and published a report (*Children At Risk*, 1975).

[49] See M. Lynch and J. Roberts, "Predicting Child Abuse: Signs of Bonding Failure In a Maternity Hospital" (1977) Br. Medical Journal 624.

[50] See A. Tredinnick and A. Fairburn, "Left Holding The Baby," *Community Care*, April 10, 1980, pp. 22–25. The research is commented upon in the same issue of *Community Care* at pp. 5–6.

[51] See M. D. A. Freeman, "Removing Babies At Birth: A Questionable Practice" (1980) 10 *Family Law* 131.

[52] In 1973 the proportion of children in care under s.1 of the 1948 Act in respect of whom parental rights had been assumed was 25.3 per cent: by 1979 it had risen to 40.1 per cent.

Case conferences and registers have mushroomed. But to what end is all this activity? Albert Solnit has written of there being too much reporting and too few services. He claims there is an "epidemic" of reporting.[53] It must be questioned whether registers are anything more than insurance policies for the social services departments. In what way do they meet the needs of families deemed to be "at risk?" Solnit, writing of the American experience, thought registers "were intended mainly to safeguard the conscience and legal vulnerability of our adult society."[54] Few, it is thought, would dissent from this assessment. There is no consistent policy as to which children are placed on registers. In addition to cases of confirmed abuse, suspected abuse and sexual abuse, registers include cases of children "at risk." Indeed, the majority of children on registers have had their names placed there because they are thought to be "at risk." But being "at risk" is not equivalent to suffering from chickenpox. It is, in other words, not an objective condition but is rather a label, a social construction.[55]

It very much depends upon how one interprets the phenomenon of child abuse as to which children are thought to be "at risk." If one adopts the dominant medical interpretation,[56] a psychopathological model of child abuse emerges and one looks to particular, though it must be confessed, heterogeneous traits[57] in parents and caretakers which are assumed to be causally linked to child abuse. It is common for medical definitions of deviance to be adopted even where, as here, there is no reliable evidence that biological variables cause the deviant behaviour in question or that medical treatment is any way efficacious. If one works within this paradigm, predictions become the key. Useful predictive studies have been carried out (by Margaret Lynch,[58] for example) but screening is fraught with ethical and methodological problems. Richard Light has shown a possible 85 per cent. rate of error.[59]

Social and environmental explanations of child abuse are also now common, notably in social work literature.[60] Writers refer to "multi-faceted deprivations of poverty,"[61] to bad housing, poor education, and similar deficiencies. These, it is

[53] See his "Too Much Reporting, Too Little Service: Roots and Prevention of Child Abuse," in G. Gerbner *et al.* (eds.), *Child Abuse* (1980), pp. 135–146.

[54] "Child Abuse: The Problem" in J. Eekelaar and S. Katz (eds.), *Family Violence* (1978), pp. 243, 246.

[55] See M. D. A. Freeman, "Child Welfare: Law and Control" in M. Partington and J. Jowell (eds.), *Welfare Law and Policy* (1979), p. 223.

[56] A good example is B. Steele and C. Pollock in R. Helfer and C. H. Kempe, *The Battered Child* (1974), p. 89.

[57] As to which see R. Geller, "Child Abuse as Psychopathology: A Sociological Critique and Reformulation" (1973) 43 Amer. J. of Orthopsychiatry 611.

[58] "Child Abuse–The Critical Path," *Journal of Maternal and Child Health*, July 1976, p. 25.

[59] "Abused and Neglected Children in America," Harvard Educational Review Report, 1974, p. 198. *cf.* on the other hand, J. Gray *et al.*, "Prediction and Prevention of Child Abuse and Neglect" (1977) *Child Abuse and Neglect* 1 (a popular account is R. Kempe and H. Kempe, *Child Abuse* (1978), Chap. 5). But their claim to predict with 76.5 per cent. accuracy is highly suspect since their whole notion of abuse is so all-encompassing. S. Montgomery's re-interpretation of their figures suggesting 8 per cent. accuracy is closer to the truth. See "Problems in the Perinatal Prediction of Child Abuse" (1982) 12 Br. J. of Social Work 189–196. Helfer's reply (1982) 12 Br. J. of Social Work 669 is most unconvincing.

[60] A good example is J. Garbarino's research. See (1976) 47 *Child Development* 178.

[61] *Per* D. Gil, "Unraveling Child Abuse" (1975) 45 Amer. J. of Orthopsychiatry, p. 346, 352.

said, lead to stress which is expressed by the use of physical force against children. In 1976, to take an example, one and a half million households lived in homes that were officially considered unfit for human habitation or were lacking the most basic amenities.[62] Are all these children potentially at risk? Should their names be included on registers? The government (or rather the last one, although it did not do much about it) accepts that families with young children should be transferred out of the "stressful conditions" of tower block life. It has nevertheless been estimated that some 300,000 children live in flats above the second floor.[63] Should their names all be suitably registered as "at risk" of abuse of one form or another?

But if the medical interpretation would require the children (say) of immature parents to be registered and the social interpretation would, *inter alia*, insist that all children living in bad housing conditions go on to the register, what can we say of the third interpretation? This[64] sees abuse as taking place in any cultural setting where a stratified relationship exists, where the victim is treated as an inferior, lacks personality and integrity is not accorded respect and rights. For, if this interpretation is right (and I would insist that it is at least part of the explanation) then all children are at risk of abuse and registers should contain the names of the whole child population. Take the example uncovered by Hugh Geach of a housing welfare officer in one London borough "who placed countless children on the register as his interpretation of 'at risk' included children who lived in council accommodation which was not kept up to his standards of cleanliness by the parents."[65] It is worrying to think that case conferences must have legitimated such a practice. Furthermore, once a family is labelled in a particular way, subsequent actions are often interpreted to fit those labels. If an "accident" occurs to a child "at risk," parents will not have much chance of successfully defending care proceedings (or for that matter a criminal prosecution). It was the American sociologist, John Lofland, who noted that "the *present* evil of current character must be related to *past* evil that can be discovered in biography."[66] Nor should it be thought that "accident" is a real and objective condition which exists independently of man's consciousness. What constitutes an accident is a product of a large number of situational contingencies.[67] Amidst all the glib talk of non-accidental injury, a real understanding involves not just the parents nor even their victim children[68] but also the officials, medical personnel, police, social workers and their response patterns in terms of their definitions of the situation.[69] This intervening defining process is not neutral and one factor which plays an important part is the stereotype resulting from defining the child as "at risk."

---

[62] *Housing Policy*, Technical Vol. III, Cmnd. 6851 (1977).

[63] "A Towering Problem for Children," *Community Care*, January 1979.

[64] See M. D. A. Freeman, *Violence in the Home—A Socio-Legal Study* (1979), p. 31. See also D. Gil, "Unraveling Child Abuse": *op. cit.* note 61 and "Social Violence in Families" in J. Eekelaar and S. Katz (eds.), *Family Violence* (1978), p. 14.

[65] *Child Abuse Registers—A Major Threat To Civil Liberties*, Justice for Children, 1980. Rumours also tend to be rife. See, *e.g.* Community Care, July 10, 1981 (rumour that East Sussex putting all children of former and present psychiatric patients on register denied). (A good general criticism is Nigel Parton, "Recording Concern—The Case Against Child Abuse Registers," *Social Work Today*, Vol. 11, No. 25 (February 26, 1980), pp. 12–14.)

[66] *Deviance and Identity* (1969), p. 150.

[67] *Op. cit.* note 55.

[68] M. D. A. Freeman, "What Do We Know of the Causes of Child Abuse?" (1977), 7 *Family Law* 182.

[69] See P. Berger and T. Luckmann, *The Social Construction of Reality* (1967).

Some of this could be more readily forgiven had the "safety first" policy been successful. The reports of inquiries make depressing reading: the communication problems have changed very little in the nine years since Maria Colwell. It comes as no surprise when we learn that the abuse registers are scarecely used. In Devon, for example, the Director of Social Services has recently written of "minimal" use by fieldworkers: "our own experience," he writes, "is a minute number of referrals are made each year—never more than five."[70] The situation in Newcastle is similar.[71] In Wandsworth 52 inquiries were made in 1980.[72] Case conference practice is hardly more successful, with conflicts between agencies still rife.[73] The ostensible reason for case conferences is to protect children but, as the Director if Social Services for Essex recently noted, "co-operation/co-ordination . . . is in danger of becoming the reason for [their] existence." He doubted whether "such activity improves services to the clients."[74]

I have deliberately concentrated on the problematic nature of intervention in an area which justifies intervention more than most. If these problems exist in relation to violence against children, how much greater are they in areas where the abuse itself is more difficult to define? Let us take the example of "emotional abuse." It is pertinent to do so for a recent D.H.S.S. Circular on *Child Abuse Registers* has proposed to extend the existing system to include "children who suffer severe mental or emotional abuse?"[75] Of course, emotional damage should be a basis for social work intervention in some cases. But what is "emotional abuse?" What evidence is to be required to substantiate such damage?

The danger is that intervention will be grounded on vague concepts such as "proper parental love" or "inadequate parental affection." As Michael Wald has argued, language like this (and it is commonly found in social welfare literature) "invites unwarranted or arbitary intervention. It could be applied to parents who travel a great deal, leaving their children with housekeepers, who send them to boarding school to get rid of them, or who are generally undemonstrative people."[76] Another critic is Harry Krause who insits that "emotional neglect" is hardly "susceptible to legally acceptable proof."[77] He is another to emphasise the difficulty of separating prejudices regarding lifestyles from it. In fact, the D.H.S.S. Circular wisely concentrates on damage to the child. But is this the way social workers and others concerned with the problem will see it? It is all too easy for agencies to concentrate on, and seek out, parental behaviour. And this would bring us back to the problem we have just considered.

This is not the only problem with a standard such as "emotional abuse." We do not know enough about child development to be able to evaluate the long-term consequences of current neglect. Nor do we know whether a child will suffer less emotional trauma when he is removed from a home where he has been suffering

[70] "Abuse Registers Scarcely Used." *Community Care*, March 19, 1981.

[71] *Idem.*

[72] *Idem.* See also "Slipshod Use of N.A.I. Registers by Councils." *Community Care*, August 13, 1981.

[73] "Case Conferences—Time for a Change?" *Community Care*, August 27, 1981, p. 16.

[74] Quoted *idem.* p. 17. See also C. Hallett and O. Stevenson, *Child Abuse—Aspects of Interprofessional Co-operation* (1980).

[75] LASSL (80) 4.

[76] "State Intervention on Behalf of "Neglected" Children: A Search for Realistic Standards" in M. Rosenheim (ed.), *Pursuing Justice for the Child* (1976), pp. 246, 261.

[77] *Family Law in a Nutshell* (1977), p. 236.

emotional deprivation. The removal may be equally damaging, the new home or homes equally bad or worse or as bad in other ways. Intervention becomes easier to justify where there is evidence of actual harm, demonstrated by, for example, the child's anxiety, depression or extreme aggression. The D.H.S.S. Circular makes no such proviso. It should be added that the coupling of actual harm in the way just suggested would not necessarily act as sufficient protection. Goldstein *et al.* properly point out that "observed behaviour" is not enough for assessing a child's mental state. What appears to be similar behaviour, whether as a symptom of illness or a sign of health, may for different reasons be a response to a wide range of different and even opposite phychic factors. And the same deep-seated emotional disturbances may lead to the most diverse manifestations of a child's behaviour.'[78] It is relatively easy to relate a child's physical injury to his parents' action. It is a considerably more complex process to link emotional damage with actions that may be called emotional abuse.

The importance of intervention and the limitations of the before the best interests thesis

Not even Goldstein and his colleagues, who adopt the most extreme position of all thinkers on the subject, believe in total laissez-faire policy. They accept without question compulsory immunisation programmes, the state's insistence on the education of children and they seem happy with limitations on child labour. These limitations upon parental freedom are all questionable, yet Goldstein *et al.*, natural conservatives that they are, accept these long-standing examples of the status quo as unproblematic.

I propose to consider the case for intervention by a close and critical examination of the principles underlying the grounds for intervention which Goldstein and his colleagues stipulate. It may be helpful to summarise these briefly. The first is that a parent has requested that the state place a child.[79] This ground would exist if separated parents failed to arrive at a custody decision themselves or either or both requested a voluntary termination of thir parental rights. A consequence of this is that court intervention would not be permitted where parents were in agreement as to the child's disposal, even where the court sensed or was convinced that the placement chosen by the parents was unsuitable. I find this limitation on a court's powers difficult to accept but will say little more about it here.[80]

Secondly, Goldstein *et al.* envisage that where familial bonds (psychological parentage) exist between long-term parental caretakers and children, a long-term caretaker might seek to become the legal parent or at any rate might refuse to relinquish the child to his parents or to a state agency. In such a situation, state intervention would be justifiable. "Under this ground," they argue, "the time for intervention is when both the child and caretaker have turned to and accept one another."[81] Although, we are told, "the complex process of forming psychological parent-child relationships is not beyond description (and they give one), its time-

[78] *Before the Best Interests of the Child*, pp. 75–76.

[79] *Idem.*, p. 31.

[80] The limitation is reminiscent of the authors' arguments about leaving decisions as to access to the custodial parent. See *Beyond the Interests of the Child*, p. 38.

[81] *Before the Best Interests of the Child*, p. 41. See, further, C. Curtis, "The Psychological Parent Doctrine in Custody Disputes between Foster Parents and Biological Parents" (1981) 16 Columbia J. of Law and Social Problems 149.

table cannot be set precisely."[82] Despite this, they argue that "parental rights must rest on objective data which are readily obtainable with the minimum of intrusion."[83] To this end they put forward statutory periods (12 months for a child up to three years at the time of placement and 24 months for a child of three years plus at the time of placement), which, they stress, are "time *with* (caretakers), not time *away* from [parents]."[84] They see these time spans coupled with the caretaker's wish to continue custody as reliable indicators for granting legal recognition to the new relationship and terminating the legal relationship between the children, absent parents and state agencies. To this end they make one exception. Older children (more than three at the time of placement and in continuous parents' care for three years at the time of placement) who had not been separated from parents because they inflicted or attempted to inflict serious bodily injury or because they were convicted of a serious sexual offence against the child concerned and whose parents were still their psychological parents would first be the subject of a "special hearing" designed to determine psychological parenthood and "whether [the child's] return to [his parents] would be the least detrimental alternative." They add: "in the event that such evidence is inconclusive, the child's relationship to his longtime caretakers should be given legal recognition."[85] Where termination takes place the authors see adoption as the best solution; failing this, they believe in what they call "*care with tenure*." Care with tenure is not spelt out: in conception it appears close to the, as yet unimplemented, notion of custodianship.[86] I am not happy with "*care with tenure*," partly because it is so imprecise (to what rights and duties does it give rise?)[87] but also on policy grounds which I have considered elsewhere.[88] All in all the process of divestment of parental rights looks ominously like the sort of administrative process (currently under greater scrutiny than heretofore)[89] with which we associate an assumption of parental rights. If anything the protection, the "due process," accorded parents is weaker than that in operation under section 3 procedure. It is surely strange also that the reason why a child is in care should count for absolutely nothing. There is surely a difference between a child voluntarily placed with foster parents and one taken from parents because of abuse of neglect. It is also notable that, even with older children, their wishes and feelings are imputed rather than sought out.

A third ground for intervention is "the death or disappearance of both parents, the only parent or the custodial parent—when coupled with their failure to make provision for their child's custody and care." This is "designed to provide the state with the authority to discover and to safeguard children for whom no day-to-day care arrangements have been made by parents who die, disappear, are imprisoned or hospitalised."[90] Our statutes deal with abandonment and voluntary reception into

[82] *Idem.* p. 42. [83] *Idem.* p. 45. [84] *Idem.* p. 48. [85] *Idem.* p. 49.

[86] See Children Act 1975, s.33. See, further M. D. A. Freeman, "Custodianship—New Concept, New Problems" (1976) 6 *Family Law* 57; "Custodianship and Wardship" (1977) 7 *Family Law* 116.

[87] See S. Maidment, "The Fragmentation of Parental Rights" (1981) Camb. L.J. 135, 152–155.

[88] M. D. A. Freeman, *The Children Act 1975* (1976).

[89] A Bill to transfer jurisdiction to the juvenile court made little progress in Parliament in 1982. See *Hansard*, H.C. Deb., Vol. 89, cols. 866–870. Another Bill did not get a second reading in January 1983.

[90] *Before The Best Interest of the Child*, p. 59.

care under section 2 of the Child Care Act 1980 deals with hospitalisation and similar emergencies.[91] Where the Goldstein *et al.* standard is new is in authorising intervention only if the absent parent failed to make provision for the care of the child. Further intervention would only be allowed if the parent substitute's actions brought him within another of the grounds for intervention.

The fourth ground is conviction of a sexual offence[92] against the child (or acquittal by reason of insanity). The ground is controversial because the authors insist on conviction of the parent in a criminal court as a pre-requisite to any intervention. There are any number of objections to this. The trend in the treatment of sexual abuse within the family is to see it as a social problem concerned with family dysfunction. There is a move away from penal responses.[93] It is recognised that the criminal law is a clumsy instrument. Yet Goldstein and his colleagues seem to want to reurn to it. Again, if we look at this from the perspective of the child, what does the proposed standard achieve? First, it will allow most sexual abuse to continue. As Appleton says, "what of the teenager who does not want to put her parent behind bars?"[94] Secondly, if intervention must await a conviction there will be inevitable delays in taking measures to protect children. Who gains from this? Thirdly, the narrowness of the test will mean that protective measures will be impossible where a conviction is not obtained because of a technicality or where sexual offences are committed by, for example, the mother's boyfriend. Fourthly, although Goldstein *et al.* are aware that "harm done by the inquiry may be more than that caused by not intruding,"[95] they are prepared to subject children to an involvement in the criminal process which is not attuned to their needs and which is likely to perpetrate greater harm to them than any juvenile court placement process. It is difficult to see, as Katz also notes,[96] how authors who express concern for family integrity and protection of the family from invasion of its privacy can possibly want to encourage the continued use of the criminal law and its processes to tackle incest and allied offences.

The fifth ground for intervention is "serious bodily injury inflicted by parents upon their child, an attempt to inflict such injury or the reported failure of parents to prevent their child from suffering such injury."[97] They define serious bodily injury narrowly. The ground is intended to:

> "provide protection to children who are brutally kicked, beaten or attacked by their parents. It is meant to safeguard children whose parents may have attempted to injure them, for example, by starvation, poisoning or strangling . . . It is designed to safeguard children from parents who prove to be incapable of preventing their child from repeatedly suffering serious bodily injury or being exposed to such harm."

Douglas Besharov[98] has rightly complained of the way Goldstein and his colleagues construct rigid one-dimensional rules. I think this is a good example. For, whilst they

[91] Children and Young Persons Act 1933, s.1; Child Care Act 1980, s.2.
[92] *Before the Best Interests of the Child*, p. 62.
[93] See H. Giarietto, "Humanistic Treatment of Father-Daughter Incest" in R. Helfer and C. H. Kempe, *Child Abuse and Neglect* (1976), Chap. 8. See also B.A.S.P.C.A.N., *Sexual Abuse of Children*, BASPCAN 1981.
[94] "Growing Up with Goldstein, Freud and Solnit" (1980) 58 *Texas Law Review* 1343.
[95] *Before the Best Interests of the Child*, p. 64.
[96] (1981) 45 *Albany Law Review* 525, 529.
[97] *Before the Best Interests of the Child*, p. 72.
[98] (1981) 34 *Vanderbilt Law Review* 481.

would limit intervention to "serious" injuries, thus ruling out of court a whole range of conduct which is deleterious to children, they have no doubt about their belief that, when serious bodily harm has been inflicted, parental rights should always be permanently terminated. "Parental maltreatment," they claim, "leaves psychological scars which endure long beyond any physical healing and preclude a child from regaining the feeling of being safe, wanted and cared for in his parents' presence—the very emotions on which his further development advances need to be based."[99] They believe that battered children should always be adopted. This is a totally inflexible position to take and it is difficult to see why they take it. Parents who batter their children can be helped to become adequate caretakers.[1] Children returned to parents who have battered them do not develop very differently from those placed in foster homes or, for that matter, from working-class children brought up by their own parents in comparable environments.[2]

But, if the consequences of battering are to be so drastic, why do so many forms of conduct fall short, on Goldstein *et al.'s* test, of warranting intervention at all? It seems strange that a parent who beats his child should risk losing him but one who chains his child to a bed or locks him in a cupboard or insists on dressing him in female clothes should be immune from state intervention.[3] Two further points should be made. First, although Goldstein and his colleagues specify in some detail what is meant by "serious" bodily injury they leave themselves open to a criticism they make of existing standards, that of vagueness. For what is "serious" injury? This surely depends upon values. What is a "brutal" assualt? Is the parent's motive relevant? Take the case of *R.* v. *Derrivière* in 1969.[4] A West Indian father whipped his 12-year-old son to punish him for coming home late. He was convicted of an assault occasioning actual bodily harm. He claimed that he was using a method of chastisement common among parents of his background. The court held that immigrant parents must conform to English standards (whatever they are)[5] in the correction of their children. Goldstein *et al.* would, I think, have itervened here. But would they intervene in the case cited by Wald in his critique of *Before The Best Interests?* His example is of a child "physically disciplined by a parent using a paddle in a manner sufficient to leave bruise marks and to cause the child pain in walking, but where it cannot be shown that the parent was attempting to cause more severe injuries."[6] It would seem not. How easy then would it be to lay down standards relating to corporal punishment, to give parents the "fair warning" that is thought so essential? Secondly, the reluctance of Goldstein and his colleagues to intervene in cases of less than serious injury may lead to danger signs not being picked up. As is

---

[99] *Before the Best Interests of the Child*, p. 73.

[1] See, *e.g.* the work of the Park Hospital in Oxford described by M. Lynch, "Family Unit In a Child's Psychiatric Hospital" (1975) 2 *British Medical Journal* 127 and by M. Lynch and C. Ounsted, "Residential Therapy—A Place of Safety" in R. Helfer and C. H. Kempe (eds.), *Child Abuse and Neglect* (1976), p. 206. See also A. H. Cohn and M. K. Miller, "Evaluating New Modes of Treatment for Child Abusers and Neglectors," (1977) 1 *Child Abuse and Neglect* 453.

[2] See E. Elmer, *Fragile Families, Troubled Children: The Aftermath of Infant Trauma* (1977). *cf.* now M. Lynch and J. Roberts, *Consequences of Child Abuse* (1982).

[3] See, further, M. Wald, "Thinking About Public Policy Toward Abuse and Neglect of Children" (1980) 78 *Michigan Law Review* 645, 665–666.

[4] (1969) 53 Cr.App.R. 637.

[5] See the Newson studies referred to, *op. cit.* note 46.

[6] *Op. cit.* note 103, p. 666.

well known, minor injuries often forewarn of more dangerous traumas.[7] It is a vicious circle for, as suggested in this article, intervention can cause an amplification of the deviance.

The sixth ground for intervention hinges on failure to take medical care, and is, I believe, the most controversial of all the suggested grounds. Goldstein *et al.* argue that intervention can be justified where there is a "refusal by parents to authorize medical care when (1) medical experts agree that treatment is non-experimental and appropriate for the child, and (2) denial of that treatment would result in death, and (3) the anticipated result of treatment is what society would want for every child—a chance for normal healthy growth or a life worth living."[8] They define adequate medical care in as narrow a way as possible: the child must be faced by death, not, for example, blindness; there must be medical consensus in the type of intervention and on the fact that it is therapeutic; and (dealing specifically but not exclusively with "defective newborns") the child must have a chance to live "a normal life or a life worth living."

This ground raises profound social, legal, medical and ethical issues. What, for example, is non-experimental treatment? Is a procedure experimental because it is not orthodox?[9] Suppose a child, or better still an adolescent, would like to take the risk of being cured by treatment which is still at the experimental stage. What is "a life worth living?" Whose decision should matters of life and death be? Goldstein and his colleagues insist that "when death is not a likely consequence of exercising a medical choice, there would be no justification for governmental intrusion. Where the question involves not a life-or-death choice but a preference for one style of life over another, the law must restrain courts and doctors from coercively imposing their personal preferences in the form of medical care upon non-consenting parents and their children."[10] There is surely a distinction, which they do not acknowledge, between giving parents some autonomy and allowing courts to review the decisions made by parents.

Goldstein *et al.* are critical of the Connecticut case of *Hart* v. *Brown*.[11] The case arose out of a decision by parents to save an eight-year-old daughter's life by a kidney transplant from her healthy twin sister. Acting on medical advice, the parents consented to surgery. The hospital would not operate without a court review. The court upheld the parents' decision though, as Goldstein *et al.* write, "not their autonomy to decide."[12] They are concerned that neither doctors nor judges are trained or in any other way qualified to impose their values about what is right for children or families in such situations. But this is surely not the point. In cases so fraught with emotion as an isograft kidney transplant there is a strong case for an objective review of the decision. Nor is it necessary for a judge (or doctor for that matter) merely to impose his own prejudices and views. There clearly ought to be guiding standards, acceptable to the community as a whole. It may be difficult to decide upon these but this should not discourage us from trying to formulate principles.

---

[7] See R. Bourne and E. Newberger, *Critical Perspectives on Child Abuse* (1979).

[8] *Before the Best Interests of the Child*, p. 91.

[9] See, *e.g.* the *Green* case (1979) 393 N.E. 2d. 836.

[10] *Before the Best Interests of the Child*, p. 92. See also Goldstein's earlier article "Medical Care for the Child at Risk" (1977) 86 *Yale Law Journal* 45.

[11] 289 A. 2d 386 (1972).

[12] *Before the Best Interests of the Child*, p. 107.

One final ground for intervention may briefly be disposed of. They recognise a child's need for legal assistance as constituting a ground for state intervention. This intervention would depend on a "request by parents who are unable to obtain legal assistance for their children, an adjudication of any ground for modifying or terminating parent-child relationships, or an emergency placement pending adjudication."[13] Once again children get little say as legal battles are polarised between their parents and the state.

Four case studies

In this section a number of cases from both sides of the Atlantic are examined to test out the thesis presented in *Before the Best Interests of the Child.*

Goldstein *et al.* make only a passing reference to the issue of sterilisation of a child as a result of a parental decision. "It may be," they write in a note, "that parental consent to surgery for the irreversible sterilization of a child ought not to be sufficient to authorize the operation without court review."[14] There follows a reference to *A.L.* v. *G.R.H.*[15] (an Indiana decision similar to the well-known English case of *Re D*,[16] and a discussion of *Stump* v. *Sparkman*,[17] which, for what it is worth, gets the decision wrong! If Goldstein *et al.* think that *A.L.* v. *G.R.H.* was correctly decided, their view of this case seems inconsistent with their general arguments. Let us, therefore, examine *Re D*, in which an application was made via wardship proceedings by an educational psychologist employed by a local authority to prevent an 11-year-old suffering from Sotos Syndrome from being sterilised. The proposed sterilisation was stopped. The case exposes the limitations of the Goldstein *et al.* approach. Their grounds for intervention are based on parental failures to meet particular standards. But the mother in *Re D* was not neglecting or inflicting injury on her daughter (or at least this is not how she saw it). If anything, she was trying to protect her daughter from dangers she thought she would lack the maturity to fend off. Bernard Dickens expresses this particularly well:

> "*Before the Best Interests*" tests seem to lack the fine tuning required to deal with the situation presented by *Re D*, since they are directed primarily at decisions to remove children entirely from parental custody and control. Further, they are concerned with parents whose treatment of their children falls short of legislated or judicially set minimum standards of care. They seem not to address parents whose well-meaning and conscientious initiatives are misguided or insensitive in ways denying children future rights. The tests set by *Before the Best Interests* are illustrated by failure to come up to the standards and do not consider deviations from norms of child-rearing by, for instance, over-protectiveness. They do not deal with causing harm to children by violating or pre-empting their human rights, such as their rights of reproduction."[18]

In a sense the problem can be generalised by noting that the *Before* guidelines are too clear-cut, too rigid, too polarised. Just as there are adults on the one hand and children on the other, so there are "black" decisions and "white" decisions. There is

[13] *Idem*, p. 111. See also Appendix II where there are additional grounds: note that the language of the grounds is not necessarily congruent with that in the main text of the book.

[14] *Idem*, p. 257.

[15] 325 N.E. 2d 501 (1975).

[16] [1976] Fam. 185.

[17] 98 S. Ct. 1099 (1978).

[18] "The Modern Function and Limits of Parental Rights" (1981) 97 L.Q.R. 462.

no understanding of grey areas, any more than there appears to be of the rights or wishes of adolescents.

The problem in *Re D* (and *A.L.* v. *G.R.H.*) can be seen in another context in the important recent United States Supreme Court case of *Parham* v. *J.R.*[19] The case concerned children committed to mental hospitals by their parents or legal guardians without the procedural protections which accompany other involuntary admissions. The court concluded that a parent or guardian might effect an admission to a mental hospital. It stated that "precedents permitted the parents to retain a substantial, if not the dominant, role in the decision, absent a finding of neglect or abuse," and favoured the "traditional presumption that the parents act in the best interests of the child."[20] Nevertheless, it recognised that the risk of error involved was suffficiently high to require a pre-admission inquiry by a neutral factfinder. It thought, however, that the admitting psychiatrist constituted an adequately neutral and independent decision-maker. The opinion was given shortly before the publication of *Before the Best Interests*. One commentator[21] thinks it regrettable that that book was not available to the court. An earlier article[22] of Joseph Goldstein's was, and was influential in the decision.[23] But the decision departs from the *Before the Best Interests* position to a considerable degree. It recognises, as after *Planned Parenthood* v. *Danforth*[24] it had to do, that children had interests in liberty from detention and treatment. It accepted as well that adolescents, capable of admitting themselves, also had the legal power to leave a mental hospital.

The decision in *Parham* v. *J.R.* is something of a compromise. It recognises the state's interest in avoiding unnecessary and destructive interventions.

> "The State in performing its voluntarily assumed mission also has a significant interest in not imposing unnecessary procedural obstacles that may discourage the mentally ill or their families from seeking needed psychiatric assistance. The *parens patriae* interest in helping parents care for the mental health of their children cannot be fulfilled if the parents are unwilling to take advantage of the opportunities because the admission process is too onerous, too embarrassing or too contentious."[25]

Indeed, as an author in the *Harvard Law Review*[26] noted, "the Court allowed minors to be institutionalised with fewer procedural safeguards than it has required for the termination of welfare benefits." Andrew Watson, the most loyal supporter of the *Before the Best Interests* thesis, would have preferred the court to have defined the admission process "solely as a therapeutic contact between family and doctor." He argues that "to conceptualise automatically hospital admission as a danger to the child's welfare . . . runs counter to the Court's preferences for parental privacy." He is concerned that protection of parental decision-making, rather than children's liberty interests, should have been "the opening question in *Parham*."[27] The dangers

[19] 442 U.S. 584 (1979).
[20] *Idem*. p. 604.
[21] Andrew Watson, "Children, Families and Courts: Before the Best Interests of the Child and *Parham* v. *J.R.*" (1980) 66 *Virginia Law Review* 653.
[22] "Medical Care for the Child at Risk" (1977) 86 Yale L.J. 645.
[23] Other psychological literature is also referred to in the opinions.
[24] 428 U.S. 52 (1976).
[25] *Loc.cit.* note 19, p. 605.
[26] 93 Harvard L.R. 1, 97–99 (1979).
[27] *Loc.cit.* note 21, p. 672.

inherent in this approach are profound. Szasz[28] in an authoritative article has depicted them. Analogies with tonsillectomies, appendectomies and other similar medical procedures (to which the court in *Parham* drew attention) are not apposite. For, as Watson concedes, "the child's medical symptoms (of mental illness) may stem from parental problems . . . and the child may serve as the scapegoat and a symbolic focus for intrafamily conflicts. This sort of admission," he continues, "differs from hospitalisation for other medical purposes because it presents the question under what circumstances the state should intervene into family psychological or social difficulties that hinder the development of the child."[29]

A third case which highlights the shortcomings in the Goldstein *et al.* approach is the sad saga of Phillip Becker (*Re Phillip B*).[30] The decision, faithful to the letter and I fear the spirit of Goldstein and his colleagues, has led one commentator[31] to ask poignantly: "what happened to the best interests of the child?" Perhaps they will be buried with Phillip Becker. Phillip Becker is (or was) a mongol. At the time of the litigation in 1979 he was 11. He was mentally retarded with an I.Q. of slightly under 60. He was capable of developing social and communication skills and could go some way towards looking after himself. He went to school, was a Boy Scout and, it was predicted, would be able to function in a sheltered workshop when (or if) he grew up. He also had a congenital heart defect which in a normal child would have been correctable by standard surgery. In a Down's Syndrome child there was a risk of post-operative complications. There was also a 5 to 10 per cent. risk of his dying in the course of surgery. Without surgery he would positively deteriorate. With surgery he would develop into a healthy adult with a reasonable capacity for enjoyment of life.

The Santa Clara County Juvenile Probation Department filed a petition to have him declared a dependant of the court so that he might receive the cardiac surgery to which his parents refused their consent. The action was dismissed by a judge who ruled that there was no clear and convincing evidence to sustain the petition. The Court of Appeal affirmed the dismissal and the the United States Supreme Court denied certiorari, thereby sanctioning a common law doctrine permitting parents to refuse non-emergency medical treatment to their unemancipated children. The parents' opposition to surgery was based on three grounds[32]: (i) since Phillip's life was not a "life worth living," he should not have his life prolonged by surgery; (ii) he would outlive them if surgery were performed and they would be unable to surpervise his placement and care; (iii) concern because the operation was too risky and Phillip might die.

It is difficult to see what legitimte claim Phillip's parents had to have their view heard, let alone accepted. Phillip never lived at home with his parents: he had always been in residential care. His parents visited him about every two months. The home where he lived thought the operation should be performed. This case was just the

---

[28] "The Child As Involuntary Mental Patient: The Threat of Child Therapy to the Child's Dignity, Privacy and Self-Esteem" (1977) 14 San Diego L.R. 1005. See also G. Koocher, *Children's Rights and the Mental Health Professions* (1976).

[29] *Loc. cit.* note 21, p. 676.

[30] 156 Cal. Rptr. 48 (1979), *cert. denied* (1980) 100 S. Ct. 1597.

[31] Donna Mitchell in "In re Phillip B.: What Happened to the Best Interests of the Child?" (1980) 12 Toledo L.R. 151. The case is also discussed by W. A. Moeller (1980) 63 Marquette L.R. 511.

[32] See D. Mitchell, *loc. cit.* note 31, p. 167.

sort of decision which ought to have been taken on the basis of an objective review: in fact it was taken by endorsing parental preferences where their interests should have counted for little. It is remarkable that in deciding as the courts did they were ignoring uncontradicted medical testimony to the effect that without the operation death could result in the near future; indeed, that surgery to repair the defect could only be performed within a short time if Phillip were to have any worthwhile existence. The case shows once again the inflexible and over-narrow grounds for intervention prescribed by Goldstein and his colleagues.

My final example brings me back to this country. The facts of *Re B*[33] (the "Alexandra" case) are relatively straightforward. Alexandra was born on July 28, 1981. She suffers form Down's Syndrome. She was also born with an intestinal blockage (duodenal artresia) which would be fatal unless it were operated upon. The parents took the view that it would be kinder to let her die. They therefore refused to consent to the operation. The doctors made contact with the local authority (the London Borough of Hammersmith and Fulham) which made the child a ward of court and asked Ewbank J. to give them care and control and to authorise them to allow the operation to be carried out. The judge made the necessary orders. When the child was transferred from the hospital where she was born to another hospital for the operation, the surgeon declined to operate when informed that the parents objected. The local authority, accordingly, returned to the judge. He, after hearing the parents, refused his consent. The local authority appealed to the Court of Appeal. Inquiries showed that other surgeons were prepared to perform the operation. It was reckoned that, if the operation proved successful, and the prognosis for such surgery is good, the child would have a life expectancy of 20 to 30 years. The Court of Appeal in Templeman L.J.'s words, saw the question for the Court as: "was it in the best interests of the child that she should be allowed to die or that the operation should be performed? . . . Was the child's life going to be so demonstrably awful that it should be condemned to die; or was the kind of life so imponderable that it would be wrong to condemn her to die?" He held that "it was wrong that the child's life should be terminated because, in addition to being a mongol, she had another disability. Accordingly, the court's duty was to decide that the child should be allowed to live."[34] Dunn L.J. thought Alexandra should be "put in the same position as any other mongol child."[35] The Court of Appeal thought Ewbank J.'s error was that he had been influenced by the views of the parents, instead of deciding what was in the best interests of the child.

The Goldstein, Freud and Solnit view on this case is I think, clear. They quote from Duff to the effect that: "families know their values, priorities and resources better than anyone else. Presumably they, with the doctor, can make the better choices as a private affair. Certainly, they, more than anyone else, must live with the consequences . . ."[36] Duff, writing with Campbell,[37] is very much of the same mind as the *Before the Best Interests* authors: "We also acknowledge," they say, 'that there are limits of support that society can or will give to assist handicapped persons and their families." This, unfortunately, is true. Goldstein *et al.*, accordingly, insist, with considerablejustification, that in the case of children who receive medical treatment

[33] [1981] 1 W.L.R. 1421. [34] *Idem.* p. 1424. [35] *Idem.* pp. 1424–1425.

[36] In Kelsey, "Shall These Children Live? A Conversation with Dr. Raymond S. Duff" (1975) 72 *Reflection* 4 at p. 7.

[37] "Moral and Ethical Dilemmas in the Special Care Nursery" (1973) 289 *New England Journal of Medicine* 890.

rejected by their parents, "the state must take upon itself the burden of providing the special, financial, physical and psychological resources essential to making real the value it prefers for the child it 'saves.'"[38] This, of course, may involve finding foster or adoptive parents: at the least it involves fully financing special care requirements.

This argument, that if the state is going to step in and override the parents' decision it must be prepared to shoulder the cost, has been much in evidence in Britain in the aftermath of *Re B*. Thus estimates of how much the care of Alexandra is going to cost the local authority have been given considerable attention in the press. But decisions such as those in this case must be decided on moral grounds, not economic ones. The case sparked off considerable controversy. The British Paediatric Association immediately took the line that parents must ultimately decide whether a severely handicapped baby is to be treated.[39] This view is consonant with the principles set out in the British Medical Association's *Handbook of Medical Ethics*. It is there stated in the paragraph on "severely malformed infants" that: "Adult patients can make their own decisions but for an infant the parents must ultimately decide." The principles do, however, go on to urge that doctors "attend primarily to the needs and rights of the individual infant."[40] The B.M.A. view is thus not all that clear-cut. An organisation (Prospect) has been formed to promote the rights of parents to make the decision when they want their severely handicapped newborn babies to be allowed to die.[41] One commentator in *The Times* has referred to the decision in *Re B* as "the cruel folly." "Those who call for legal intervention in preference to the quickly reached private decisions made between parents and trusted doctors seem to me," wrote Claire Tomalin, "to lack understanding of the moral capacities of ordinary people."[42] She calls for parents to be able to make their decisions "privately and peacefully and with people whose goodwill [they] can trust." It certainly seems that parental acceptance or rejection of a handicapped child influences doctors more than their own assessment of the child's quality of life. A recent survey of 280 consultant paediatricians showed that in cases where parents rejected the child, only 36 per cent. would recommend surgery for a Down's baby needing an intestinal operation to live but where the parents accepted the baby 64 per cent. would favour surgery.[43]

The Goldstein *et al.* view is thus not without support. The fault with the thesis (theirs and the more generalised line of argument pursued in the wake of *Re B* and the prosecution of Dr. Arthur[44]) is that the alternative is not between withholding medical assistance so that the child dies and being burdened with the care of the child, though critics of interventionism often insist it is. There is a third option—the termination of the parental relationship and with it parental rights, powers and duties. As Robertson has written[45]: "while parental discretion to terminate the

[38] *Before the Best Interests of the Child*, p. 97.
[39] *The Times*, August 19, 1981.
[40] (1981 ed.), paras. 5.11 and 5.12.
[41] *The Times*, September 14, 1981.
[42] Claire Tomalin, "Alexandra: The Cruel Folly," *The Times*, September 1, 1981.
[43] E. Harbridge, "Life or Death—Who Decides?" *Community Care*, November 19, 1981, pp. 4–5. Alexandra was recently returned to her parents. See *The Observer*, December 5, 1982.
[44] Charged with murder (the charge subsequently reduced to attempted murder—*The Times*, October 28, 1981). On the *Arthur* case, see I. Kennedy, *New Society*, January 7, 1982, pp. 13–15.
[45] "Involuntary Euthanasia of Defective Newborns" (1975) 27 *Stanford Law Review* 213, 263. See also P. Foot, "Euthanasia" (1977) 6 *Philosophy and Public Affairs* 85, and J. A. P. Davis, "Defective Children—Who Should Decide?" (1979) 9 *Family Law* 203–207.

parental relationship may be justified, it does not follow that parents should also have the right to decide whether the child lives or dies. Clearly, discretion to terminate a relationship of dependency does not mandate that one has the power to impose death on the terminated party."

There are both procedural and substantive problems at issue. Goldstein and his colleagues for obvious reasons concentrate on the procedural. Within outer and narrow limits they leave the decision to the parents and expect them to get some assistance from doctors. But neither parents nor doctors are dis-interested parties and they cannot accordingly be impartial. Each has a committed personal interest in the decision. Both, but particularly the parents, are emotionally involved. These are not the actors to take a rational decision. This is why I believe outside intervention is important and why I believe that courts are, to pinch a phrase, the least detrimental alternative.[46] This is not to look to the courts for "palm-tree" justice. Like Ian Kennedy[47] I believe that a code of principles should develop and I agree with him in thinking that their development and testing in real human cases in courts is preferable to legislation "in the cold" by Parliament. The clearer the principles become the less need there will be to refer cases to courts.

Can any guidance be offered on such principles? The formulation of these constitutes the substantive issue. The presumption must always favour life, unless it is proved otherwise. First, it may be worthwhile to classify different types of cases. A useful typology has been constructed by Ruddick.[48] First, there are, at one extreme, children who have no life possibilities at all. Karen Quinlan,[49] though not a child, came into this category. It may even be argued that she had no "life" to which she could be said to have a right. Alexandra, of course, had life possibilities.

Secondly, there will be children who, even with treatment, have no life possibilities acceptable to their parents or to parent substitutes, so that they will be institutionalised. This is to me the most difficult case. Ruddick can accept the decision of parents in such circumstances (he refers to cases of spina bifida) to refuse surgery. He writes: "Parents of spina bifida infants . . . may in their initial disappointment, resentment and guilt too quickly assume that (1) no acceptable individual parent substitute can be found and that (2) institutional life is unacceptable. But if," he continues, "afer suitable counseling and reflection, they refuse surgery for their infant, they do not violate our parent principle, even if death ensues."[50] Ruddick's "parent principle" is too narrow. In his words "it only requires that [parents] give serious thought to the future in the rearing of children."[51] Like Goldstein *et al.*, it puts a premium on parental preferences and neglects the interests and rights of children. It adopts as a value the view that no life is better than life in an institution.

---

[46] The phrase was, of course, coined by Goldstein, Freud and Solnit in *Beyond the Best Interests of the Child*, pp. 53 *et seq.*

[47] "Where Doctors and the Law Can Meet," *The Times*, September 8, 1981.

[48] "Parents, Children and Medical Decisions" in E. L. Bandman and B. Bandman (eds.), *Bioethics and Human Rights* (1978), p. 165. See also W. Ruddick in O. O'Neill and W. Ruddick, *Having Children* (1979), p. 123.

[49] 355 A. 2d 647 (1976). On the *Quinlan* case see I. Kennedy, "The Karen Quinlan Case: Problems and Proposals" (1976) 2 J. Med. Ethics 3. See also the informative symposium in (1977) 30 *Rutgers Law Review* 243–328, and M. Kohl, "Karen Quinlan: Human Rights and Wrongful Killings" in Bandman and Bandman (eds.), *op. cit.* note 48, p. 121.

[50] In E. L. Bandman and B. Bandman (eds.), *op. cit.* note 48, p. 169.

[51] *Idem.* p. 168.

Whilst it is difficult to compare and measure the two options, there are surely cogent arguments against.

The third type of case is very close to *Re B*. This concerns children, who, if treated, have independent life possibilities but none the parents can accept, even though there are foster parents who can accept and bring the child to accept them.

A fourth type of case concerns children with no independent life possibilities acceptable to both parent and child without treatment, but with some life possibilities with standard medical treatment. Examples are children with cleft palates and tumours.[52]

Our concern here is with the third type of case. Ruddick's typology is useful though his reasoning is not attractive. A useful distinction which carries us further is made by Angela Holder. She distinguishes between treatment which can cure the condition for which it is performed and that which cannot. She argues:

> "It seems to be legally mandatory for treatment to be instituted if it can cure the condition for which it is performed. If a Down's baby has an intestinal obstruction or . . . an infant has a fistula, either one of which can be cured by relatively simple surgical procedures *and* if those procedures would clearly be performed by court order if necessary on an otherwise normal newborn, then it is arguable that treatment is legally required.
>
> On the other hand, neurosurgery for a paralyzed newborn is by no means 'ordinary care,' since normal babies do not require it. Second, the condition for which surgery might be performed is not curable, and thus the operation may be regarded as both futile and one that would subject the baby to more pain than he would have felt if left alone. Third, if the child survives he may well have sufficient self-awareness to suffer the agonies of knowing his limitations and to be tormented by them. Thus, it may be possible to justify as good medical practice a determination that a child whose condition is incurable should not be subjected to surgery for that condition solely to keep him alive."[53]

Bernard Dickens amplifies this in the following useful way: "the mongoloid child with bowel obstruction may be in the same position as a normal child refused a necessary blood transfusion by parents who are Jehovah's Witnesses; the medical care in issue will restore normal function to the part of the child's body for which it is indicated, and cannot lawfully be withheld."[54]

These arguments are highly persuasive. They are not offered as a definitive blueprint but they open up a path for principled rather than ad hoc decision-making. There is a school of juristic thought, associated primarily with Ronald Dworkin,[55] which requires of judges that they search out the "right answer" by considering all the relevant principles. Although critical of much of Dworkin's thesis,[56] I believe he has much to offer us in the sort of "hard cases" which here concern us. I believe, to quote Dworkin, that decisions relating to defective newborns should be (Dworkin

52 The American cases of *Re Sampson* 278 N.E. 2d 918 (1972) and *Re Seiferth* 127 N.E. 2d 820 (1955) are commonly-quoted examples.

53 *Legal Issues in Pediatrics and Adolescent Medicine* (1977), p. 114.

54 *Medico-Legal Aspects of Family Law* (1979), p. 105.

55 *Taking Rights Seriously* (1977).

56 See Lord Lloyd (co-editor M. D. A. Freeman), *Introduction to Jurisprudence* (4th ed., 1979), p. 841.

will say "are") "generated by principle,"[57] that litigants (and in our case subjects of litigation) are "entitled" to the judge's "best judgment about what their rights are."[58] Dworkin admits that different judges can come to different conclusions "because a constitutional theory requires judgments about complex issues of institutional fit, as will as judgments about political and moral philosophy."[59] He insists that judges must rely not on their own political views but on their beliefs in "the soundness of those convictions."[60] These decisions are too important to be left to judges acting alone and what is required is informed and interdisciplinary debate as well as mutual respect between the professionals involved. Principles can only evolve in this way.

A concluding comment

In this paper I have examined the pros and cons of state intervention in the family. Much has been omitted. Elsewhere[61] I have traced the ways in which state intervention developed and the reasons why it did. It is clear to me that what has happened in the twentieth century is that the liberal state has provided itself with a system of indirect controls which preserves the appearance, even some of the reality, of private initiative within an overarching structure of professional supervision. As Lasch has written, the therapeutic apparatus leaves the family "always 'justified' in theory and always suspect in practice."[62] Although I do not think that Goldstein and his colleagues would agree with the language used, their thesis is an attempt to guard against further intrusion by the liberal state into the family.

My position, as expressed in this article, is to suggest that there are considerable problems in leaving the family alone. Victory for the family often means defeat for the children. It is, as I have indicated, a line-drawing exercise. Goldstein and his colleagues have erred in drawing the line too close to the parents' interests and too far from the children's. But the picture is not all black and white. Goldstein *et al.* seem to think in polar positions (you are, for example, either an adult or a child): I hope I do not. I recognise that intervention has its problems but I do not ignore its benefits. Intervention must be properly controlled. This requires an activist, committed judiciary capable of forging principles with the collaboration of other disciplines involved. One detects a laissez-faire attitude in our judges as well: this is the world of "social administration," not a "legal battlefield," said Lord Scarman in a recent case.[63] Perhaps cases like *Re D* and *Re B* offer hope for the future. I would like to think so. I cannot help thinking, however, that they, laden with emotion as they are, represent the exceptions rather than the rule. The judiciary must be prepared to control the controllers if intervention is ever to be acceptable. This, it may be thought, leads inevitably to one of the most commonly posed questions of all: *quis custodiet ipsos custodes?*[64] An answer to that thorny question is well beyond the scope of this article.

---

[57] *Op. cit.* note 55, p. 97.
[58] *Idem.* p. 104.
[59] *Idem.* p. 117. [60] *Idem.* p. 124. [61] *Op. cit.* p. 73, note 35.
[62] "Life in the Therapeutic State," New York Review of Books, Vol. XXVII, No. 10 (June 12, 1980), p. 24.
[63] *Lewisham L.B.C.* v. *Lewisham Juvenile Court* [1979] 2 W.L.R. 513, 538.
[64] *cf.* Lord Denning's Dimbleby Lecture, *Misuse of Power*, B.B.C., 1980 (or in *What Next in The Law?* (1982), Pt. 8).

[8]

"THERE IS A BOOK OUT . . .":*
AN ANALYSIS OF JUDICIAL ABSORPTION OF LEGISLATIVE FACTS

*Peggy C. Davis***

I. INTRODUCTION

CLASSICAL jurisprudence posited that law was found by judges through application of logic and adherence to fixed principles. This notion has been thoroughly repudiated. We now recognize that judges often must make law and that general knowledge is relied upon in the process. The application of law involves three elements: reason, precedent, *and* choice. Facts or theories about the state of the world commonly form the bases of choice.

More than forty years ago, the powerful insight that creation of law "must depend upon fact-finding"[1] led Professor Kenneth Culp Davis to articulate a valuable distinction between what he termed adjudicative and legislative facts. He observed:

> [When a court] finds facts concerning immediate parties — what the parties did, what the circumstances were — [it] is performing an adjudicative function, and the facts may conveniently be called adjudicative facts. When [a court] wrestles with a question of law or policy, it is acting legislatively, . . . and the facts which inform its

---

* Ross v. Hoffman, 33 Md. App. 333, 336–37, 364 A.2d 596, 599 (1976), *aff'd as modified*, 280 Md. 172, 372 A.2d 582 (1977). These words were uttered by a trial judge to introduce a theory, foreign to the record, but relied upon in making a custody award. *See infra* pp. 1595–96. They illustrate, in unselfconscious terms, the process of judicial absorption of legislative facts.

** Associate Professor of Law, New York University. B.A., 1964, Western College for Women; J.D., 1968, Harvard Law School. I am indebted to my colleagues, Anthony Amsterdam, Paul Chevigny, Randy Hertz, Lewis Kornhouser, Sylvia Law, and William Nelson, and to Professors Derrick Bell, Kenneth Culp Davis, Martha Minow, Robert Mnookin and Michael Wald for their thoughtful comments on early drafts of this work. I also acknowledge, with gratitude, support provided by the Filomen d'Agostino and Max E. Greenberg Research Fund of New York University School of Law.

[1] Davis, *An Approach to Problems of Evidence in the Administrative Process*, 55 HARV. L. REV. 364, 402 (1942). The insight is no longer controversial:

> It is conventional wisdom today to observe that judges not only are charged to find what the law is, but must regularly make new law when deciding upon the constitutional validity of a statute, interpreting a statute, or extending or restricting a common law rule. The very nature of the judicial process necessitates that judges be guided, as legislators are, by considerations of expediency and public policy. They must, in the nature of things, act either upon knowledge already possessed or upon assumptions, or upon investigation of the pertinent general facts, social, economic, political, or scientific.

E. CLEARY, MCCORMICK ON EVIDENCE § 331, at 928 (3d ed. 1984) (footnotes omitted).

> legislative judgment may conveniently be denominated legislative facts.[2]

At the time, Professor Davis did not seem to insist upon defining legislative factfinding as a variety of judicial notice.[3] However, the legislative fact concept has become firmly established within the judicial notice pigeonhole of evidence scholarship.[4]

With a few notable exceptions,[5] courts and legislatures have failed or refused to regulate the process that has come to be known as judicial notice of legislative facts.[6] As evidence scholars began to craft rules for the presentation of facts in litigation, the rules that emerged for judicial notice seemed suited to governance of adjudicative factfinding, but useless in the realm of legislative factfinding. The original version of the Uniform Rules of Evidence and the American Law Institute Code Rules permitted judicial notice only of facts that were *indisputable*.[7] In neither of these early codifications was it clear whether the rules were meant to preclude the common (and inevitable) practice of judicial reliance upon *disputable* facts to interpret or develop principles of law.[8] The more recent and now domi-

---

[2] Davis, *supra* note 1, at 402.

[3] *See id.* at 403 ("The courts have generally treated legislative facts differently from adjudicative facts, even though the distinction has not been clearly articulated and explanations have been beclouded by an erroneous use of the concept of judicial notice."); *id.* at 410 n.95.

[4] Professor Davis describes "The Two Worlds of Judicial Notice," legislative and adjudicative, as follows: "One world of judicial notice has to do with a judge's thinking about questions of law or policy. The other world of judicial notice has to do with finding the facts about a particular party. The two worlds are almost totally different, having hardly anything in common with each other." K. DAVIS, 3 ADMINISTRATIVE LAW TREATISE §15:4, at 146 (2d ed. 1980). For other evidence scholars' discussions of the legislative fact concept, see E. CLEARY at note 1 above, § 328, at 921, and 9 WIGMORE, ON EVIDENCE § 2565(b) (Chadbourne rev. ed. 1981).

[5] *See infra* pp. 1598–99.

[6] *See* K. DAVIS, *supra* note 4, at 146 ("Restrictions on use of legislative facts are almost nonexistent but when they exist they are loose and liberal.").

[7] *See* UNIF. R. EVID. 9–12 (1953) (superseded by UNIF. R. EVID. 201, 13A U.L.A. 60 (1986)); MODEL CODE OF EVIDENCE Rules 801–803 (1942).

[8] Professor Davis, noting the unworkability of these rules, commented:

> The central idea of the judicial notice provisions of the Model Code and of the Uniform Rules is that facts may not be noticed unless they are either indisputable or are contained in sources of indisputable accuracy. . . . [Yet] the facts that enter into [the courts'] thinking processes are frequently either highly disputable or inseparably fused with questionable or uncertain judgment. The courts often take judicial notice of legislative facts in circumstances in which they would not take judicial notice of adjudicative facts, but the Model Code and the Uniform Rules apply in the same way to all facts, without drawing the cardinal distinction between legislative and adjudicative facts.

Davis, *Judicial Notice*, 55 COLUM. L. REV. 945, 982–83 (1955). It is possible, however, that the drafters of these rules took the view that consideration of legislative facts was not a category of judicial notice, or that it was a part of the process of taking judicial notice of propositions of law. *See* McNaughton, *Judicial Notice — Excerpts Relating to the Morgan-Wigmore Controversy*, 14 VAND. L. REV. 779, 787 (1961). The latter view is consistent with the position of Professor Morgan, the Reporter of the American Law Institute Rules, concerning the fiction of known law. *See* Morgan, *Judicial Notice*, 57 HARV. L. REV. 269, 270–71 (1944). *But see* K.

nant Federal Rules of Evidence,[9] however, are explicit that the rule addressing judicial notice "governs only . . . adjudicative facts."[10]

The absence of traditions and procedures for regulating judicial notice of legislative facts provides the sitting judge with a dangerous freedom. Professor Morgan described that freedom in stark terms:

> [T]he judge is unrestricted in his investigation and conclusion. He may reject the propositions of either party or of both parties. He may consult the sources of pertinent data to which they refer, or he may refuse to do so. He may make an independent search for persuasive data or rest content with what he has or what the parties present. He may reach a conclusion in accord with the overwhelming weight of available data or against it . . . . In all this he is entitled to the assistance of the parties and their counsel . . . . But the parties do no more than to assist; they control no part of the process.[11]

The drafters of the Federal Rules of Evidence quoted this language with approval, concluding that "[t]his is the view which should govern judicial access to legislative facts."[12]

As a former judge who has experienced the freedom granted by this permissive view, I have had cause to doubt its wisdom. My doubts have grown out of very specific contexts. In a case that proved memorable for me, but was routine by any objective measure, I terminated the parental rights of a young mother, freeing her child for adoption against the mother's wishes and ending her rights to custody or contact with the child. A strong but not overwhelming record supported my decision. Mental health professionals who had examined the child recommended termination of parental rights. The decision was bolstered — perhaps clinched — by my own, independently acquired notions about child development and parental bonding. The mother's words upon announcement of my order were to this effect:

DAVIS, *supra* note 4, § 15:7, at 158 (arguing that the Advisory Committee misinterpreted Professor Morgan).

[9] The 1974 version of the Uniform Rules of Evidence, which superseded the 1953 version, is "almost identical to the . . . Federal Rules of Evidence." UNIF. R. EVID., 13A U.L.A. 2 historical note (1986). It has been adopted by the legislatures of 29 states and Puerto Rico. *Id.* at 1 (table of jurisdictions adopting the Uniform Rules of Evidence).

[10] FED. R. EVID. 201(a). This disinclination to regulate judicial incorporation of legislative facts has been uniform through time and across United States jurisdictions.

A review of legislation regarding judicial notice yields no basis for modification of Professor Davis' report that "as of 1980 no federal statute and no rule of civil or criminal procedure (other than what emerges from judicial opinions) governs judicial notice of legislative facts." K. DAVIS, *supra* note 4, § 15:1, at 135; *accord* J. WEINSTEIN & M. BERGER, 1 WEINSTEIN'S EVIDENCE ¶ 23–27 (1986) [hereinafter 1 WEINSTEIN'S EVIDENCE] (comparative table of state rules of evidence).

[11] Morgan, *supra* note 8, at 270–71 (1944).

[12] FED. R. EVID. 201 advisory committee's note.

> Why are you doing this?! You don't know what you are doing! I've been with kids all my life. I love my son. If he came home to me, I know that he would be just fine.

Indeed. If the decision turned upon my probably imperfect understanding of disputable principles of child development, should there not be a formal procedure for testing my premises?

My concern grew as I recognized that cases, like the one described above, in which extra-record sources informed a particular decision were dwarfed in significance by cases in which the same kind of extra-record information led courts to alter common law or to define the reach and import of a statute or a constitution.

This Article investigates the effects of judicial liberty in the determination of legislative facts. The investigation centers around analysis of judicial decisions that were influenced by a particular set of legislative "facts" — the psychological parent theories espoused by Joseph Goldstein, Anna Freud and Albert Solnit. It was undertaken to identify the ways in which judges find and use legislative facts; to discover whether there are patterns of misuse; and to document the effect of legislative facts upon the development of law. The investigation reveals that legislative facts do have a dramatic and broad effect upon the development of law. Yet, their legal enshrinement is casual and unselfconscious, and their assessment often superficial and skewed by litigation imbalances. These results cast serious doubt upon Professor Morgan's view that judicial lawmaking should be unrestrained in the investigation and incorporation of factual predicates. The Article addresses the deeply problematic nature of permissive legislative factfinding and seeks to offer a more constrained method by which judges may take notice of legislative facts.

Part II begins with a description of psychological parent theories and the manner in which they were introduced to the legal community. It then briefly explains the study underlying this Article and the methodology used to identify and evaluate the cases involved. Part III first examines the adjudicative uses of psychological parent theories and then examines the judicial lawmaking that these uses foreshadow, presenting cases that illustrate observed patterns in the development of common law, the interpretation of statutes, and the delineation of constitutional principles. Part IV summarizes the problems posed by discretionary legislative factfinding and presents suggestions for developing a tradition of care in the determination of facts.

II. The Focus of the Investigation: Judicial Absorption of Psychological Parent Theory

A. The Theories

In recent years, custody disputes between biological parents (and between nonparents) have been determined in accordance with the best interests of the child. Prior to the dissemination within legal circles of psychological parent theories, however, child placement law reflected skepticism within and without the mental health professions that the best interests of children could be determined by reliance on rules of thumb drawn from theories of child development. The law contained no rigid formulae for determining the best interests of children, but rather permitted consideration of the broadest variety of factors that might affect their welfare. In addition, the law embodied presumptions in favor of the preservation of biological parent/child bonds. These presumptions reflected a mix of policy judgments concerning the biological family: judgments as to the primary social status of biological family ties, the value of family autonomy, and the need to protect family privacy against intrusion by the state. The presumptions were firmly applied in cases arising between private citizens, and in cases pitting a parent against a nonparent. State laws, however, permitted official action to intervene in the biological family for reasons that varied in terms of the level of harm or risk to the child.

Psychological parent principles were first introduced in the legal literature in a 1963 *Yale Law Journal Note.*[13] The Note urged that the standard for determining custody disputes be changed. Instead of seeking to determine in a general way which custodial arrangement would serve the best interests of the child, the Note argued that courts should narrow the inquiry and adopt a "psychological best interest" test designed to identify and preserve "existing affection-relationship(s)."[14] It based its argument on a concept of psychological parenthood gleaned from the work of Anna Freud and from other scholarly works on separation and maternal bonding.[15] The Note described the premises of psychological parenthood in these terms:

> The mutual interaction between adult and child, which might be described in such terms as love, affection, basic trust, and confidence, is considered essential for the child's successful development, and is the basis of what may be termed psychological parenthood. It is this psychological parenthood, rather than the biological events which may precipitate such a relationship, which many psychologists identify as the *sine qua non* of successful personality development.[16]

After publication of the Yale Note, Joseph Goldstein, Anna Freud and Albert J. Solnit published a work designed to change the laws and practices affecting the custody and guardianship of children.[17]

---

[13] Note, *Alternatives to 'Parental Right' in Child Custody Disputes Involving Third Parties,* 73 YALE L.J. 151 (1963) [hereinafter *Yale* Note].

[14] *Id.* at 162 (citations omitted).

[15] *See id.* at 158 n.34.

[16] *Id.* at 158.

[17] J. GOLDSTEIN, A. FREUD & A. SOLNIT, BEYOND THE BEST INTERESTS OF THE CHILD

Beyond the Best Interests of the Child sought to ground decisionmaking in custody, adoption, neglect, and abuse proceedings in principles derived from the work and observations of psychoanalysis. The three scholars brought their professional prestige and the persuasive force of this brief, nontechnical, strongly written volume to the task of assuring that disputes over the custody of children be decided according to three principles. First, they argued that the disruption of established bonds between a child and its "psychological parent(s)" is inevitably destructive to the emotional health of the child.[18] The authors subsequently broadened this first principle to create a presumption — usually irrebuttable, despite the existence of competing considerations — that the interests of children are defeated by change in any custody arrangement that has existed for a year (in the case of younger children) or two (in the case of older children).[19] Second, Goldstein, Freud and Solnit urged that custody determinations be made in accordance with a "child's sense of time."[20] Third, the authors cautioned that the family unit consisting of psychological parent and child be protected against external interference.[21]

The authors apparently believed the evils of prevailing child placement policies too great and too urgent to await a legislative remedy. They announced that the principles advanced were "intended to provide a basis for critically evaluating *and revising the procedure and substance of court decisions*, as well as statutes."[22] In addition, the authors demonstrated means for altering the procedure and substance of court decisions. *Beyond the Best Interests of the Child* includes a reprint of a judicial decision that seems to follow established precedent closely. The decision is followed by a rewritten version, proposed by the authors, which reverses the outcome of the original "[o]n the basis of *knowledge* extrapolated from [the Goldstein, Freud and Solnit] guidelines."[23] The rewrite also incorporates psychological parent prin-

(1973). Dr. Solnit is affiliated with the Yale Child Study Center, Professor Goldstein, with the Yale Law School. *See id.* at ix.

[18] *See id.* at 31–34.

[19] J. GOLDSTEIN, A. FREUD & A. SOLNIT, BEFORE THE BEST INTERESTS OF THE CHILD 46–48 (1979).

[20] *SEE* BEYOND THE BEST INTERESTS OF THE CHILD, *supra* note 17, at 40–42. Positing that "children have a built-in time sense based on the urgency of their instinctual and emotional needs," the authors suggest that (1) an infant or toddler "cannot stretch his waiting more than a few days without feeling overwhelmed by the absence of parents," (2) "[f]or most children under the age of five years, an absence . . . for more than two months is equally beyond comprehension," and (3) for older, but preadolescent, children, absences of more than a year carry similarly "detrimental implications." *Id.* at 40–41.

[21] *See id.* at 49–52, 99, 105.

[22] *Id.* at 5 (emphasis added). These principles were based, not on empirical research, but "on psychoanalytic knowledge . . . reinforced by common sense." BEFORE THE BEST INTERESTS OF THE CHILD, *supra* note 19, at 4.

[23] BEYOND THE BEST INTERESTS OF THE CHILD, *supra* note 17, at 94 (emphasis added).

ciples into a rule of law, thereby ensuring that in future cases there would be no need for individualized evaluation and hence no risk of an outcome inconsistent with the authors' beliefs.

Goldstein, Freud and Solnit proposed a new legal framework for the determination of custody and the allocation of other parental rights. On the one hand, they advocated a strengthening of the presumption against the removal of children from the household except in cases of dire threat to their physical well being.[24] On the other hand, they advocated a weakening of the biological parent presumption in cases involving children of broken homes and children residing outside the biological family.[25] Children of divorce would be assigned to the custody of a psychological parent[26] who would be relieved of any legal obligation to permit contact with the noncustodial parent.[27] Similarly, children who had been in the care of nonparents for a period sufficient to give rise to a presumption of psychological attachment to the new caretakers[28] would be permanently placed with those caretakers.[29] The authors also urged that child placement decisionmaking be made, in most cases, solely on the basis of a judgment or presumption concerning bonding and without consideration of other factors.[30]

The psychological parent principles described above are not universally accepted among child development specialists. In 1975, a member of the Committee on the Family of the prestigious Group for the Advancement of Psychiatry[31] testified that the theory was contro-

---

[24] *Cf.* BEFORE THE BEST INTERESTS OF THE CHILD, *supra* note 19, at 4, 59–90 (arguing, on the principle of minimum state intervention, against disrupting ongoing family units).

[25] *See id.* at 31–33.

[26] *See id.*

[27] *See* BEYOND THE BEST INTERESTS OF THE CHILD, *supra* note 17, at 101.

[28] *See supra* p. 1544.

[29] *See* BEFORE THE BEST INTERESTS OF THE CHILD, *supra* note 19, at 39–51.

[30] *See id.* at 189; BEYOND THE BEST INTERESTS OF THE CHILD, *supra* note 17, at 53. The authors adopt the term "least detrimental alternative" in place of the traditional formulation "best interests of the child," and then define their preferred term as that choice "which maximizes . . . [the child's] opportunity for being wanted and for maintaining on a continuous basis a relationship with at least one adult who is or will become his psychological parent." *Id.* The flexibility that might be offered by the concept of "being wanted" is foreclosed by the authors' conviction that limitations upon the ability to make predictions with respect to human relationships and the power of the continuity factor are such that:

> We can predict that the adult most likely suited for this role [of making the child feel wanted] is the one, if there be one, with whom the child has already had and continues to have an affectionate bond rather than one of otherwise equal potential who is not yet in a primary relationship with the child.

Id. at 51. The authors "conclude that specific statutory periods [of continued custody], when coupled with the explicit wish of the longtime caretaker to become permanently responsible for a child's care, are the most reliable indicators and the least detrimental means that we have for giving the 'new' relationships full legal recognition." BEFORE THE BEST INTERESTS OF THE CHILD, *supra* note 19, at 42.

[31] COMMITTEE ON THE FAMILY, GROUP FOR THE ADVANCEMENT OF PSYCHIATRY, DIVORCE,

versial, and raised questions concerning the validity and implications of research and theoretical work that was reported in the 1930s and 1940s and subjected to serious challenge in succeeding decades.[32] Five years later, the Committee on the Family offered a competing approach to the determination of child placement questions in the divorce context, advocating a "family perspective on divorce and custody" and reporting that it found "no evidence for the existence of a single 'psychological parent' with whom the tie is critically more important than with the rest of the network."[33]

Psychological parent theory has, then, special characteristics that commend it as the focus of a study of legislative factfinding: its judicial acceptance calls into question a variety of settled legal rules, its use as a legislative fact has been actively encouraged, and it remains controversial. Moreover, the compelling facts of cases involving psychological parent theory highlight the significance of matters at issue in the debate between laissez-faire and controlled approaches to legislative factfinding.

B. The Methodology of the Study

Judicial opinions that address psychological parent principles are numerous, and refer in most cases directly to the *Yale* Note or to the work of Goldstein, Freud and Solnit, or indirectly to discussions of one or both of these works in other judicial opinions or in the legal literature.[34] The following Sections present the results of an analysis of cases decided between 1963 (the year of publication of the *Yale* Note) and 1984.

The method of this investigation was modest and straightforward. Opinions were collected by means of a computer search designed to capture cases in which either the work of Goldstein, Freud and Solnit or the YALE Note was referenced or in which psychological parenthood was discussed. The search yielded a total of 193 cases, out of which 179 opinions contained an adjudicative or legislative determi-

---

CHILD CUSTODY AND THE FAMILY 786 (Mental Health Materials Center No. 106, 1980) [hereinafter GAP REPORT].

[32] *See* Brief for the Appellants, app. at 247a–248a, Smith v. OFFER, 431 U.S. 816 (1977) (No. 76–180) (deposition of Dr. Henry Ulmann Grunebaum). For a thorough analysis of the bases of psychological parent theory and of questions concerning the validity of the Goldstein, Freud and Solnit proposals, see Garrison, *Why Terminate Parental Rights?*, 35 STAN. L. REV. 423, 455–74 (1983), and sources cited therein.

[33] GAP REPORT, *supra* note 31, at 872. This work was cited in none of the cases uncovered by this study. For reasons that are not entirely clear, it professes not to refute the applicability of psychological parent theories to child placement matters outside the divorce context. *See id.* at 871.

[34] *Cf. infra* note 45 (describing judicial use of legal literature to obtain social science information).

nation apparently influenced by psychological parent theory.[35] These 179 opinions were then categorized along the following nine dimensions: (1) whether expert evidence based on psychological parent theory was presented; (2) whether any such evidence was rebutted; (3) the type of case (for example, custody, termination of parental rights, neglect, abuse, or adoption); (4) whether the parties were institutional or individual; (5) whether the case-specific outcome was consistent with psychological parent theory; (6) whether a development in law based upon psychological parent theory was announced; (7) the category of any such legal development (common law, statutory definition or delineation of constitutional rights); (8) whether the court relied upon social science literature or legal commentary addressing psychological parent theory; and (9) whether the court explicitly addressed the issue of judicial notice of legislative or background facts. The analysis of the data was not statistical. Rather, it consisted of close readings and comparisons in an attempt to discern patterns relevant to the presentation and judicial use of psychological parent theory. It is hoped that this close look at the "legalization" of a single social science theory will be a useful addition to the existing anecdotal and theoretical literature describing judicial notice of nonadjudicative facts, and will broaden the base of support for reform.

III. The Results of the Investigation

In the cases reviewed for this study, psychological parent theories were used in four distinct ways. They served as background for the determination of case-specific, adjudicative facts. They also served as legislative facts to support an interpretation or declaration of a common law rule; to support an interpretation of a statute; and to determine the reach or definition of a constitutional provision. The following Sections will discuss each of these four uses in turn.

A. Psychological Parent Theories and Adjudicative Factfinding

When generalizations like the psychological parent theory serve as underlying premises for case-specific, factual determinations, they are sometimes referred to as background facts.[36] Background facts occupy a grey area between adjudicative and legislative factfinding, an area which has been the subject of considerable analytical confusion.

---

[35] In rare cases, briefs and other portions of the records of cases under study were available for consultation. In general, however, this study suffers from the limitations inherent in virtually exclusive reliance upon judicial opinions. Chief among these limitations is the inability to determine the extent to which judges relying upon social science literature did so as a result of independent research or as a result of Brandeis briefs. *Cf. infra* note 44.

[36] *See* McNaughton, *supra* note 8, at 789–90.

Background facts are characteristically derived both from record and extra-record sources. They are frequently "noticed," despite the absence of pertinent evidence, in an invisible process by which a judge or juror relies upon "beliefs (though they are not in evidence) which he reasonably thinks he shares with other intelligent persons as to the general nature of things — the meanings of ordinary words, typical modes of human behavior, causal relations between commonplace events, and the like."[37] Judicial (or jury) notice of background facts is pervasive, occurring "inconspicuously and interstitially"[38] as an inevitable part of the adjudicative decisionmaking process. On occasion the process is "flushed to the surface by a party and . . . subjected to the test of judicial notice in the traditional sense . . . and, if it fails that test, to the requirement of proof by formal evidence."[39] On such occasions, background facts become the subject of record evidence and thus are analytically indistinguishable from other subultimate, adjudicative facts. On other occasions, background facts are flushed to the surface but may not be subjected either to the test of indisputability or to the requirements of proof by formal evidence. On these occasions, they may be the subject of argument, Brandeis briefs, or independent judicial investigation.[40]

Functional definitions would lead us to classify background facts as adjudicative, for they are used to decide the facts at issue between the parties rather than to decide questions of law.[41] For purposes of this analysis, however, they are set apart with the recognition that they serve an adjudicative function, although they are sometimes "found" in accordance with the rules applicable to adjudicative factfinding and sometimes "noticed" in accordance with the rules (or license) applicable to legislative factfinding.

---

[37] *Id.* McNaughton's article continues in language that exemplifies the lack of academic interest in the reliability of the process:

> In most instances these beliefs, assumptions, preconceptions, are true in the sense relevant to the controversy. In most of the remaining instances, either the error or the issue is relatively trivial. And the remainder of instances illustrates a largely unavoidable characteristic of a factfinding system employing imperfect human beings. A trial, after all, is a human process, and the judge and jury must be accepted with their normal human characteristics. This assumes that any one of them will have beliefs which are at least partially wrong, that no two of them will share exactly the same beliefs, and that the reasoning processes of no two will operate in exactly the same way.

Id. at 790.

[38] *Id.* at 789.

[39] *Id.* at 790. The test of judicial notice in the traditional sense is a requirement of indisputability. *See* FED. R. EVID. 201(b) (stating that "a judicially noticed fact must be one not subject to reasonable dispute"). Background facts are, however, often disputable, and existing rules of evidence invariably prohibit judicial notice of disputable adjudicative facts. The analytic issues raised by notice of disputable background facts have never been adequately addressed.

[40] For an example of this method of determining background facts, see pp. 1598–99 below.

[41] Professor Davis resists this classification, arguing that "[g]eneral facts that are judicially noticed may help the court determine facts about a party, but the general facts do not for that reason become adjudicative facts." K. DAVIS, *supra* note 4, § 15:5, at 149.

Psychological parent theory has emerged in each of the characteristic modes of background factfinding described above. In some cases, judges simply referred to the theory as they had seen it described in general or social science literature,[42] or the theory formed the subject of argument or briefs. In other cases, the theory was the subject of case-specific expert testimony. In these cases, a psychiatrist or psychologist who had examined one or more of the parties, or who had simply reviewed the facts in a guardianship, visitation, or custody dispute, would rely on psychological parent principles to urge that the relationship between a particular child and particular adults was such that parental rights should be continued or terminated, visitation should be ordered or withheld, or custody should be granted or denied. Some experts in these situations discussed the theory upon which their testimony was based; others did not.[43] Some courts relied upon both record and extra-record[44] presentations of psychological parent theory, consulting general, legal,[45] or social science literature to support or refute expert testimony.

Background uses of psychological parent theory often appeared to be outcome determinative. Parties unable effectively to litigate the merits of the theory were therefore considerably disadvantaged. Moreover, case-specific expert evidence and judicial investigations of background facts often had significance beyond the litigation in which the facts were directly used. It was in the context of these seemingly narrow cases that trial and appellate courts became educated concerning psychological parent theories. This educational process facilitated the use of psychological parent theories to justify interpretations of common law, of constitutional principles, or of statutes. Indeed, it often happened that cases in which psychological parent evidence and literature were used in an adjudicative context themselves became vehicles for the development of law. Because of the potentially broad impact of background facts, the patterns and contexts in which they have been accepted or rejected deserves attention.

In sixty-two cases in which psychological parent theories were advanced as a basis for adjudicative factfinding, the likelihood of an

---

42 *See, e.g.*, Nathan M. v. Catholic Guardian Soc'y, 76 Misc. 2d 1003, 352 N.Y.S.2d 319 (Fam. Ct. 1973); *infra* note 102 (describing *Nathan M.*).

43 *See* Davis & Dudley, *Family Evaluation and the Development of Standards for Child Custody Determination*, 19 COLUM. J.L. & SOC. PROBS. 505 (1986) (arguing that rules and customs of litigation should encourage the articulation of theoretical premises that underlie expert opinions).

44 A study of appellate litigation revealed that forty percent of judicial citations to scientific literature were derived from independent research by the court. *See* T. MARVELL, APPELLATE COURTS AND LAWYERS 192 (1978). The proportion should be higher in the psychological parent cases, because they include trial and appellate matters, typically involve counsel with relatively few resources, and are often decided without presentation of briefs or trial memoranda.

45 The findings of this study are consistent with those of other studies in that they reveal a tendency of courts to turn to legal literature, particularly judicial opinions, for social science information. *See id.* at 184.

outcome consistent with the theories was better than two to one. Results compelled by psychological parent theories were ultimately achieved in forty-two[46] cases and rejected in twenty.[47] However, the

---

[46] In the following thirty cases, psychological parent theory was followed at the trial level. They include trial court decisions that relied upon psychological parent theories and appellate opinions reviewing such decisions with approval: Hudgins v. State, 418 So. 2d 913 (Ala. Civ. App. 1982); Herbert H. v. Warren B. (Guardianship of Phillip B.), 139 Cal. App. 3d 407, 188 Cal. Rptr. 781 (1983); Donald H. v. Gloradon M. (*In re* Lynna B.), 92 Cal. App. 3d 682, 155 Cal. Rptr. 256 (1979); Brownfield v. Brown (*In re* D.L.C.), 54 Cal. App. 3d 840, 126 Cal. Rptr. 863 (1976); *In re* Juvenile Appeal, 181 Conn. 638, 436 A.2d 290 (1980); Seymour v. Seymour, 180 Conn. 705, 433 A.2d 1005 (1980); Faria v. Faria, 38 Conn. Supp. 37, 456 A.2d 1205 (Super. Ct. 1982); *In re* J.O.L. II, 409 A.2d 1073 (D.C. 1979), *cert. granted*, 449 U.S. 818 (1980), *vacated*, 449 U.S. 989 (1980), *cert. denied*, 454 U.S. 832 (1981); *In re* Adoption of J.S.R., 374 A.2d 860 (D.C. 1977); People v. Al Saadon (*In re* Al Saadon), 78 Ill. App. 3d 319, 397 N.E.2d 178 (1979); Coffey v. Department of Social Servs., 41 Md. App. 340, 397 A.2d 233 (1979); Ross v. Hoffman, 33 Md. App. 333, 364 A.2d 596 (1976), *aff'd as modified* 280 Md. 152, 372 A.2d 582 (1977); Custody of a Minor, 383 Mass. 595, 421 N.E.2d 63 (1981); Custody of a Minor (No. 3), 16 Mass. App. Ct. 998, 454 N.E.2d 924 (1983); State v. Levey (*In re* Levey), 211 Neb. 66, 317 N.W.2d 760 (1982); Sorentino v. Family & Children's Soc'y (*Sorentino II*), 74 N.J. 313, 378 A.2d 18 (1976); *In re* J.R., 174 N.J. Super. 211, 416 A.2d 62 (App. Div. 1980), *cert. denied* 85 N.J. 102, 425 A.2d 266 (1980); D.Y.F.S. v. D.T. (*In re* Guardianship of J.A.T), 171 N.J. Super. 520, 410 A.2d 79 (Juv. & Dom. Rel. Div. 1979); *In re* Guardianship of D., 169 N.J. Super. 230, 404 A.2d 663 (Juv. & Dom. Rel. Div. 1979); Cook v. Brownfield (*In re* Doe), 98 N.M. 340, 648 P.2d 798, *cert. denied* 98 N.M. 336, 648 P.2d 794 (1982); Bennett v. Marrow, 59 A.D.2d 492, 399 N.Y.S.2d 697 (App. Div. 1977); *In re* Jonathan D., 97 Misc. 2d 859, 412 N.Y.S.2d 733 (Fam. Ct. 1978); Dodd v. Dodd, 93 Misc. 2d 641, 403 N.Y.S.2d 401 (Sup. Ct. 1978); Doe v. Doe, 92 Misc. 2d 184, 399 N.Y.S.2d 977 (Sup. Ct., Special Term 1977); *In re* Richard N., 88 Misc. 2d 721, 389 N.Y.S.2d 525 (Fam. Ct. 1976); *In re* Kimberly P., 84 Misc. 2d 887, 376 N.Y.S.2d 791 (Fam. Ct. 1975); State *ex rel.* Juvenile Dep't v. Johns (*In re* Johns), 42 Or. App. 39, 599 P.2d 1230 (1979); *In re* Tremayne Quame Idress R., 286 Pa. Super. 480, 429 A.2d 40 (1981); Mitchell v. Mitchell, 668 P.2d 561 (Utah 1983); Toombs v. Lynchburg Div. of Soc. Servs., 223 Va. 225, 288 S.E.2d 405 (1982).

An additional nine cases involved decisions based upon acceptance of psychological parent theories at the appellate level only: Ralph Edward B. v. State Dep't of Health (*In re* Adoption of Michelle Lee T.), 44 Cal. App. 3d 699, 117 Cal. Rptr. 856 (1975); *In re* Ross, 29 Ill. App. 3d 157, 329 N.E.2d 333 (1975); M.P. v. S.P., 169 N.J. Super. 425, 404 A.2d 1256 (App. Div. 1979); Hoy v. Willis, 165 N.J. Super. 265, 398 A.2d 109 (App. Div. 1978); *In re* Adoption of a Child by I.T., 164 N.J. Super. 476, 397 A.2d 341 (App. Div. 1978); *In re* Adoption of a Child by P., 114 N.J. Super. 584, 277 A.2d 566 (App. Div. 1971); Meirowitz v. Meirowitz, 96 A.D.2d 1030, 466 N.Y.S.2d 434 (App. Div. 1983); Mansukhani v. Pailing, 318 N.W.2d 748 (N.D. 1982); *In re* Hansen, 24 Wash. App. 27, 599 P.2d 1304 (1979).

In three cases, there was acceptance at the trial level with more limited acceptance on appeal: Z. v. San Bernadino County Welfare Dep't (*In re* B.G.), 11 Cal. 3d 679, 523 P.2d 244, 114 Cal. Rptr. 444 (1974); (Anonymous) v. Commissioner of Children & Youth Servs. (*In re* Juvenile Appeal), 177 Conn. 648, 420 A.2d 875 (1979); *In re* Welfare of Solomon, 291 N.W.2d 364 (Minn. 1980).

In those cases in which psychological parent theory is classified as having been followed, the evidence appears from the opinions reviewed to have been a major or determinative factor in the outcome of the child placement issue that was the subject of the litigation. Cases in which psychological parent principles were not central to the litigation were excluded from consideration.

[47] The following eleven cases involve rejections at the trial level or approval at the appellate level of such rejections: Yontef v. Yontef, 185 Conn. 275, 440 A.2d 899 (1981); L.B.T. v. E.,

success rate was notably higher than the rejection rate only in those cases in which psychological parent evidence was offered by a state agency in an action against a parent. In that category of cases the rate of success was remarkable: the results dictated by the theory were accepted in twenty-six cases[48] and rejected in six.[49] Among the cases in which parents were pitted against nonparents or nonparents were in competition, results dictated by the theory were accepted in nine[50]

---

318 N.W.2d 200 (Iowa 1982); Deel v. Deel, 113 Mich. App. 556, 317 N.W.2d 685 (1982); La Croix v. Deyo, 88 A.D.2d 1077, 452 N.Y.S.2d 726 (App. Div. 1982), *appeal dismissed*, La Croix v. Deyo, 57 N.Y.2d 759, 440 N.E.2d 1336, 454 N.Y.S.2d 989 (1982); Seneca v. Seneca, 94 Misc. 2d 418, 404 N.Y.S.2d 827 (Fam. Ct. 1978); Pierce v. Yerkovich, 80 Misc. 2d 613, 363 N.Y.S.2d 403 (Fam. Ct. 1974); Schneider v. S.L.M., 347 N.W.2d 126 (N.D. 1984); Gardebring v. Rizzo, 269 N.W.2d 104 (N.D. 1978); *In re* M., 65 Ohio Misc. 7, 416 N.E.2d 669 (C.P., Juv. Ct. Div. 1979); *In re* Marriage of Goldberg, 23 Or. App. 324, 542 P.2d 139 (1975); Palmer v. Tokarek, 279 Pa. Super. 458, 421 A.2d 289 (1980).

An additional seven cases involved trial level acceptance with rejection on appeal: Montgomery County Dep't of Social Servs. v. Sanders, 38 Md. App. 406, 381 A.2d 1154 (1977); State *ex rel.* Dep't of Human Servs. v. Minjares (*In re* Doe), 98 N.M. 367, 648 P.2d 1180 (Ct. App. 1981), *rev'd* 98 N.M. 198, 647 P.2d 400 (1982); Dickson v. Lascaris, 53 N.Y.2d 204, 423 N.E.2d 361, 440 N.Y.S.2d 884 (1981); *In re* Donna Dorene G., 52 N.Y.2d 890, 418 N.E.2d 1323, 437 N.Y.S.2d 304 (1981); *In re* Donna W., 325 Pa. Super. 39, 472 A.2d 635 (1984); *In re* J., 134 Vt. 480, 365 A.2d 521 (1976); Finney v. Finney, 619 S.W.2d 130 (Tenn. Ct. App. 1981), *modified on unrelated grounds sub nom.* State v. Hamilton, 688 S.W.2d 821, 824 (Tenn. 1985).

In one case the evidence was offered and rejected on appeal. *See* Commonwealth *ex rel.* Grimes v. Yack, 289 Pa. Super. 495, 433 A.2d 1363 (1981). In the final case, Smith v. OFFER, 431 U.S. 816 (1977), the reaction of the trial court was ambiguous, and the proposition in support of which the evidence was urged was ultimately rejected.

The cases in this category include rejections based upon a view that the theories are incorrect as well as rejections based upon either a view that they were outweighed by other considerations or that their acceptance was precluded by applicable law. The category therefore encompasses opinions that discuss psychological parent theory in seemingly favorable terms. The outcome of each of these cases is, however, directly inconsistent with the dictates of the theory.

48 *See Hudgins*, 418 So. 2d 913; *Herbert H.*, 139 Cal. App. 3d 407, 188 Cal. Rptr. 781; *Donald H.*, 92 Cal. App. 3d 682, 155 Cal. Rptr. 256; *Brownfield*, 54 Cal. App. 3d 840, 126 Cal. Rptr. 863; *Juvenile Appeal*, 181 Conn. 638, 436 A.2d 290; *(Anonymous)*, 177 Conn. 648, 420 A.2d 875; *J.O.L. II*, 409 A.2d 1073; *J.S.R.*, 374 A.2d 860; *Ross*, 29 Ill. App. 3d 157, 329 N.E.2d 333; *Al Saadon*, 78 Ill. App. 3d 319, 397 N.E.2d 178; *Coffey*, 41 Md. App. 340, 397 A.2d 233; *Custody of a Minor*, 383 Mass. 595, 421 N.E.2d 63; *Custody of a Minor (No. 3)*, 16 Mass. App. Ct. 998, 454 N.E.2d 924; *Solomon*, 291 N.W.2d 364; *Levey*, 211 Neb. 66, 317 N.W.2d 760; *Sorentino II*, 74 N.J. 313, 378 A.2d 18; *J.R.*, 174 N.J. Super. 211, 416 A.2d 62; *D.T.*, 171 N.J. Super. 520, 410 A.2d 79; *D.*, 169 N.J. Super. 230, 404 A.2d 663; *Hoy*, 165 N.J. Super. 265, 398 A.2d 109; *I.T.*, 109 N.J. Super. 476, 397 A.2d 341; *P.*, 114 N.J. Super. 584, 277 A.2d 566; *Jonathan D.*, 97 Misc. 2d 859, 412 N.Y.S.2d 733; *Richard N.*, 88 Misc. 2d 721, 389 N.Y.S.2d 525; *Kimberly P.*, 84 Misc. 2d 887, 376 N.Y.S.2d 791; *Toombs*, 223 Va. 225, 288 S.E.2d 405.

49 *See Sanders*, 38 Md. App. 406, 381 A.2d 1154; *Minjares*, 98 N.M. 367, 648 P.2d 1180; *Donna Dorene G.*, 52 N.Y.2d 890, 418 N.E.2d 1323, 437 N.Y.S. 2d 304; *M.*, 65 Ohio Misc. 7, 416 N.E.2d 669; *Donna W.*, 325 Pa. Super. 39, 472 A.2d 635; *J.*, 134 Vt. 480, 365 A.2d 521.

50 *See Z.*, 11 Cal. 3d 679, 523 P.2d 244, 114 Cal. Rptr. 444; *Ralph Edward B.*, 44 Cal. App. 3d 699, 117 Cal. Rptr. 856; *Hoffman*, 33 Md. App. 333, 364 A.2d 596; *Cook*, 98 N.M. 340, 648 P.2d 798; *Bennett*, 59 A.D.2d 492, 399 N.Y.S.2d 697; *Doe*, 92 Misc. 2d 184, 399

and rejected in seven.[51] In cases in which a parent was pitted against another parent, the theory was followed in seven[52] and rejected in six.[53]

No firm conclusions can be drawn from bare numerical comparisons within such a small data base. It is possible, of course, that the pattern results from the fact that public agency cases present stronger arguments for adherence to psychological parent principles. Such cases may involve more troubled biological families with more strained biological ties. Close analysis of the patterns of acceptance and rejection strongly suggests, however, that factors other than the condition of families under public supervision affected the courts' receptivity to psychological parent theory.

1. Full Acceptance of the Theory: The No-Apparent-Contest Cases. — Cases in which psychological parent theories were followed[54] typically involved the presentation of expert evidence premised upon or consistent with the Goldstein, Freud and Solnit theses. These cases typically lacked expert rebuttal evidence,[55] judicial consideration of

---

N.Y.S.2d 977; *Mansukhani*, 318 N.W.2d 748; *Tremayne Quame Idress R.*, 286 Pa. Super. 480, 429 A.2d 40; *Hansen*, 24 Wash. App. 27, 599 P.2d 1304.

[51] *See L.B.T.*, 318 N.W.2d 200; *Deel*, 113 Mich. App. 556, 317 N.W.2d 685; *La Croix*, 88 A.D.2d 1077, 452 N.Y.S.2d at 726; *Dickson*, 53 N.Y.2d 204, 423 N.E.2d 361, 440 N.Y.S.2d 884; *Schneider*, 347 N.W.2d 126; *Grimes*, 289 Pa. Super. 495, 433 A.2d 1363; *Palmer*, 279 Pa. Super. 458, 421 A.2d 289.

[52] *See Seymour*, 180 Conn. 705, 433 A.2d 1005; *Faria*, 38 Conn. Supp. 37, 456 A.2d 1205; *M.P.*, 169 N.J. Super. 425, 404 A.2d 1256; *Meirowitz*, 96 A.D.2d 1030, 466 N.Y.S.2d 434; *Dodd*, 93 Misc. 2d 641, 403 N.Y.S.2d 401; *Johns*, 42 Or. App. 39, 599 P.2d 1230; *Mitchell*, 668 P.2d 561.

[53] *See Yontef*, 185 Conn. 275, 440 A.2d 899; *Seneca*, 94 Misc. 2d 418, 404 N.Y.S.2d 827; *Pierce*, 80 Misc. 2d 613, 363 N.Y.S.2d 403; *Gardebring*, 269 N.W.2d 104; *Goldberg*, 23 Or. App. 324, 542 P.2d 139; *Finney*, 619 S.W.2d 130.

[54] *See supra* note 46.

[55] The fact of presentation of expert evidence inconsistent with the Goldstein, Freud and Solnit theories was clear in only nine of the cases reviewed. Four were cases pitting parent against parent; in two the psychological parent evidence was followed, *see Seymour*, 180 Conn. 705, 433 A.2d 1005; *Faria*, 38 Conn. Supp. 37, 456 A.2d 1205, and in two the rebuttal evidence was followed, *Pierce*, 80 Misc. 2d 613, 363 N.Y.S.2d 403; *Goldberg*, 23 Or. App. 324, 542 P.2d 139. Psychological parent evidence offered by agencies was rebutted in three cases; in two such cases the psychological parent evidence was followed, *see* Coffey v. Department of Social Servs., 41 Md. App. 340, 397 A.2d 233 (1979); Sorentino v. Family & Children's Soc'y (*Sorentino II*), 74 N.J. 313, 367 A.2d 1168 (1977), and in one the rebuttal evidence was followed, *see In re* Donna W., 325 Pa. Super. 39, 472 A.2d 635 (1984). Psychological parent evidence offered by a class of individuals in an action against a state agency was rebutted and was ultimately rejected in *Smith v. OFFER*, 431 U.S. 816 (1977). Evidence to rebut psychological parent theories was presented by a court-appointed expert in *Palmer*, 279 Pa. Super. 458, 421 A.2d 289, leading to rejection of the theories in a custody contest between a biological father and grandparents who had been long-term custodians.

the possibility of litigation imbalances,[56] or indications that the court was aware of competing expert perspectives.[57]

In re Kimberly P.[58] illustrates this pattern. The case involved the application of a biological mother to regain custody of a daughter who had been in a foster home for less than two years.[59] This voluntary foster placement had been triggered by behavioral problems experienced by the child after her father's death from cancer.[60] A court-solicited psychiatric report (from an agency that had previously recommended foster placement for the child) concluded, in terms suggesting familiarity and agreement with psychological parent theory, that the child should remain in the foster home.[61] The court discussed what it saw as a tension between its duty to further the child's best interests and the presumption favoring biological parents in custody matters. Then, relying upon the *Yale* Note and the expert testimony, the court concluded that the presumption had been overcome.[62] There was no competing expert evidence, no mention of the possibility of litigation imbalance, and no hint that the court entertained the possibility of expert disagreement.

2. *Rejection and Cautious Acceptance of the Theory: Searching Out and Hearing Both Sides.* — Rejection of the outcome dictated by psychological parent theory was, not surprisingly, more likely when courts considered expert evidence on both sides of the question.[63] Rejection occurred with greater frequency in cases involving disuptes between parents[64] and may have been facilitated by more equal liti-

[56] Discussion of litigation imbalances appeared in none of the cases categorized as having followed psychological parent theory. *But cf. In re* Jonathan D., 97 Misc. 2d 859, 865–66, 412 N.Y.S.2d 733, 737–38 (Fam. Ct. 1978) (discussing in general terms the disadvantages parents may suffer in dealing with child care agencies).

[57] In only one of the cases following psychological parent theory, Herbert H. v. Warren B. (Guardianship of Phillip B.), 139 Cal. App. 3d 407, 420–21, 188 Cal. Rptr. 781, 789–90 (1983), was conflict in the literature acknowledged. However, in *In re* Adoption of a Child by I.T., 164 N.J. Super. 476, 397 A.2d 341 (App. Div. 1978), an appellate court denied that controversy existed with respect to psychological parent theory, despite the trial judge's citation of competing views in the social science literature. The trial court noted indications of conflicting expert opinions in studies concerning the effects of separation upon children in circumstances comparable to those of the child at issue, 162 N.J. Super. at 603, 394 A.2d at 128. The appellate court, in contrast, appeared to deny the possibility of expert disagreement, expressing "little doubt" about the correctness of the expert's testimony, which the court found "in accord with [views] expressed by Goldstein, Freud and Solnit." 164 N.J. Super. at 489, 397 A.2d at 347.

[58] 84 Misc. 2d 887, 376 N.Y.S.2d 791 (Fam. Ct. 1975). Two similar cases also exhibit this pattern. For other illustrations of this pattern, see *In re* Adoption of J.S.R., 374 A.2d 860 (D.C. 1977), and *In re* Adoption of a Child by P., 114 N.J. Super. 584, 277 A.2d 566 (App. Div. 1971).

[59] *See* 84 Misc. 2d at 888, 376 N.Y.S.2d at 792.

[60] *See id.*

[61] *See id.* at 889, 376 N.Y.S.2d at 793.

[62] *See id.* at 891, 376 N.Y.S.2d at 795 (quoting the *Yale* Note, *supra* note 13, at 158–59).

[63] *See supra* note 55.

[64] *See supra* note 53.

gation resources in those cases.[65] Court opinions rejecting psychological parent theory were also likely to involve one or more of the following factors: judicial recognition of litigation imbalances,[66] judicial awareness of literature reflecting a conflict of relevant expert opinion,[67] and judicial resistance to nascent lawmaking.[68]

Pierce v. Yerkovich[69] illustrates rejection of the theory by a court exposed to a battle of experts. *Pierce* was a visitation dispute involving an unwed father whose efforts to maintain contact with his daughter had been resisted by the mother and stepfather. The court heard two psychiatrists, Dr. Solnit and Dr. Bernard F. Kalina. Dr. Kalina testified for the father that the denial of visitation would "have a negative effect . . . because the child would then feel rejected [by her father] and confused"; he was "firmly of the opinion that . . . visits [with the father] would be 'important for her whole growth, mental, physical and spiritual.'"[70] Dr. Solnit countered with views that coincided with those expressed in his book, *Beyond the Best Interests of the Child*.[71]

Having heard these diametrically opposed interpretations of the best interests of a single child, the trial court "totally reject[ed] the specious notion so ingenuously urged by Professor Solnit and his coauthors that the custodial parent should have the sole right to determine in the name of the best interests of the child whether the

---

65 Although battles of experts over psychological parent theory were rare, they occurred in a particularly small proportion of public agency cases. *See supra* note 55.

66 This factor was explicitly considered in four of the twenty cases in which courts declined to follow psychological parent theory. *See* Montgomery County Dep't of Social Servs. v. Sanders, 38 Md. App. 406, 423, 381 A.2d 1154, 1165 (1977); *In re* M., 65 Ohio Misc. 7, 13, 416 N.E.2d 669, 673 (C.P., Juv. Ct. Div. 1979); Commonwealth *ex rel.* Grimes v. Yack, 289 Pa. Super. 495, 528, 433 A.2d 1363, 1381 (1981); Palmer v. Tokarek, 279 Pa. Super. 458, 463, 421 A.2d 289, 292 (1980).

67 Awareness of conflicting expert literature was apparent in four of the twenty cases in which courts declined to follow psychological parent theory. *See* Smith v. OFFER, 431 U.S. 816, 844–45 n.52 (1977); Schneider v. S.L.M., 347 N.W.2d 126, 131 (N.D. 1984); *In re* Donna W., 325 Pa. Super. 39, 56–57, 472 A.2d 635, 644–45 (1984); *Grimes*, 289 Pa. Super. at 528, 433 A.2d at 1381.

68 Although psychological parent theories were rejected more than twice as frequently as they were followed, discussions of the risks of nascent lawmaking appeared in five cases in each category. In the "followed" category, they appeared in Seymour v. Seymour, 180 Conn. 705, 709–10, 433 A.2d 1005, 1007–08 (1980); Faria v. Faria, 38 Conn. Supp. 37, 40–41, 456 A.2d 1205, 1208 (Super. Ct. 1982); *In re* J.O.L. II, 409 A.2d 1073, 1075 (D.C. 1979); *In re* Welfare of Solomon, 291 N.W.2d 364, 367 (Minn. 1980); and *In re* Jonathan D., 97 Misc. 2d 859, 866–67, 412 N.Y.S.2d 733, 736 (Fam. Ct. 1978). In the "reject" category, they appeared in *Sanders*, 38 Md. App. 406, 420–21, 381 A.2d 1154, 1163–64; *Schneider*, 347 N.W.2d at 130; Gardebring v. Rizzo, 269 N.W.2d 104, 110 (N.D. 1978); *Donna W.*, 325 Pa. Super. at 58–59, 472 A.2d at 645; *In re* J., 134 Vt. 480, 484–85, 365 A.2d 521, 524.

69 80 Misc. 2d 613, 363 N.Y.S.2d 403 (Fam. Ct. 1974).

70 *Id.* at 621, 363 N.Y.S.2d at 410 (quoting testimony of Dr. Kalina).

71 *See id.* at 621 n.3, 363 N.Y.S.2d at 410 n.3.

noncustodial parent should be permitted or denied association with his own child."[72] Accordingly, the court ordered paternal visitation during one month each summer and during alternate weekends for the balance of each year.[73]

In re M.[74] illustrates judicial rejection of psychological parent theory, resulting, in part, from sensitivity to biases that affect the reliability of expert evidence offered by state agencies. Although the case pitted a parent, seemingly without expert resources, against an agency armed with expert evidence, it resulted in an exploration of psychological parent principles and a rejection of their broad or automatic application. The case concerned five siblings who had been placed in foster care upon findings of neglect "occasioned by repeated, brutal, physical assaults *on the mother* by [the father of the three youngest children]."[75] The mother had not abused the children in any way. Her efforts to secure the return of the three oldest children succeeded approximately four years after their placement,[76] but the foster care agency resisted her efforts to secure return of the youngest (twins who had been placed in infancy)[77] on the ground that their best interests lay in adoption by foster caretakers who had become their psychological parents. In support of this position, the agency offered "the expert testimony of caseworkers, a psychologist and a psychiatrist."[78]

The court acknowledged the prominence of the theory relied upon by the agency[79] and offered, without basis, its opinion that the theory did not apply in cases in which the child had had contact, through visitation, with the biological parent.[80] It did not, however, rest upon this opinion alone in returning the twins to the biological mother. In an apparent effort to test the validity of psychological parent theory, the court devised an experiment. It ordered changes in casework supervision and a program of increased visitation followed by a return of the children on a trial basis. Its final order and accompanying

---

72 *Id.* at 623, 363 N.Y.S.2d at 412.

73 *See id.* at 626, 363 N.Y.S.2d at 415. Goldstein, Freud and Solnit cite this case as an example of the risks involved in declining to follow their principles. The authors make the dubiously relevant observation that the child was abducted during a visit and not returned to its mother and stepfather. *See* BEYOND THE BEST INTERESTS OF THE CHILD, *supra* note 17, at 122–33 (epilogue). The child's whereabouts were discovered ten years later, at which time custody was continued with the father with visitation rights awarded to the mother. United Press Int'l, Aug. 28, 1984, a.m. cycle.

74 65 Ohio Misc. 7, 416 N.E.2d 669 (C.P., Juv. Ct. Div. 1979).

75 *Id.* at 8, 416 N.E.2d at 670 (emphasis added).

76 *See id.* at 8–9, 416 N.E.2d at 670–71.

77 *See id.*

78 *Id.* at 10, 416 N.E.2d at 671.

79 *See id.*

80 *See id.* at 11, 416 N.E.2d at 672.

opinion were issued with a report that the twins had "been in their mother's home for 18 months"[81] and were doing well.[82] Commenting upon its critical evaluation of the expert evidence, the court revealed a sensitivity to the manner in which expert evidence is developed in an adversary context: "The court does not lightly brush aside the recommendation of psychologists and psychiatrists. However, we are much aware of the dependence of these clinicians upon the reports of the social workers assigned to the case by the agency which is one of the adversaries in this custody dispute."[83]

Like *In re M.*, *Montgomery County Department of Social Services v. Sanders*[84] involved a foster placement based upon abusive behavior by the father and exemplary responses by the mother.[85] When the case came to trial, the plaintiff child care agency argued that, since the child had been in placement for more than six months, psychological parent theory precluded his return to his natural mother.[86] The *Sanders* appellate court recognized that special litigation imbalances often exist when an individual parent is pitted against a government agency. It was therefore skeptical of the unopposed expert evidence in support of application of psychological parent theory,[87] and declined to "place judicial imprimatur upon the socio-psychological concept of 'the psychological parent' . . . as *the* paramount factor in awarding custody."[88]

Concerns about litigation imbalance and expert bias combined with the availability of competing expert evidence to lead a Pennsylvania

[81] *Id.* at 14–15, 416 N.E.2d at 674.

[82] *See id.* at 15, 416 N.E.2d at 674.

[83] *Id.* at 13, 416 N.E.2d at 673.

[84] 38 Md. App. 406, 381 A.2d 1154 (1978).

[85] *See id.* at 408–11, 381 A.2d at 1157–58.

[86] *See id.* at 412–13, 381 A.2d at 1159.

[87] *See id.* at 422–23, 381 A.2d at 1164–65. The court stated:

> Reliance upon "the auxiliary services of psychiatrists, psychologists, and trained social workers . . . should not be too obsequious or routine or the experts too casual." *Ross v. Hoffman*, 280 Md. 172, 191, 372 A.2d 582, 594 (1977). Such reliance could lead the courts, in acts of misapplied psychology, to separate unjustly family members.
>
> > Particularly important is this caution where one or both parties may not have the means to retain their own experts and where publicly compensated experts or experts compensated by only one side have uncurbed leave to express opinions which may be subjective or are not narrowly controlled by the underlying facts. *Bennett v. Jeffreys*, 40 N.Y.2d [543,] 549, 356 N.E.2d [277,] 283, 387 N.Y.S.2d [821,] 827 [(1976)].
>
> Caution is particularly apropos in the case *sub judice*, where Mrs. Sanders was financially unable to match the weight of experts brought forth by the [government child care agency].

See id.

[88] *Id.* at 408, 381 A.2d at 1156–57 (emphasis in original) (quoting BEYOND THE BEST INTERESTS OF THE CHILD, *supra* note 17). The court was somewhat derisive of the agency position: "Seemingly, because Christopher was ignorant of [the] theory, he continued to call Rebecca Sanders 'mother' long after the [psychological parent theory] deadline had passed." *Id.* at 413, 381 A.2d at 1159.

trial court to reject psychological parent theory in a private custody case, *Palmer v. Tokarek*.[89] The appellate court, in affirming the trial court's rejection of psychological parent theory, quoted testimony by the experts that revealed different clinical views regarding the emotional resilience of children. The expert witnesses had addressed the likely effect of transferring custody of an eight-year-old boy from his grandparents, who had cared for him for all but a brief period since his birth, to his biological father. The grandparents' expert, Dr. Schachner, testified, consistently with the views of Goldstein, Freud and Solnit, that the psychological effects of a transfer would be sufficiently serious to preclude an award of custody to the father.[90] The court-appointed expert, Dr. Garrity, testified, in direct contradiction of the Goldstein, Freud and Solnit theories, that the boy could weather a change of custody.[91]

The trial and the appellate courts in *Palmer* both discounted the psychological parent theory offered by Dr. Schachner and awarded custody to the biological father. Yet neither opinion analyzed the empirical research or theories of child development to which one might turn to determine the "correctness" of the Garrity or Schachner views. This failure to evaluate the substance of expert views was typical of the trial and appellate opinions reviewed in this study. A court's awareness of *conflict among experts* with respect to psychological parent theory was often sufficient in itself to produce caution in approving or advocating its application. In *Palmer*, this awareness was gleaned from evaluation of expert evidence on both sides of the controversy. The Superior Court of Pennsylvania, also acting with the benefit of a record that included expert evidence on both sides of the issue, reacted similarly in *In re Donna W.*[92] The court criticized the trial court for giving too much heed to psychological parent theory and too little heed to principles of biological family integrity:

> One of the greatest mistakes we can make is to regard as simple what is complex. If psychiatrists and psychologists *knew* how to achieve a child's best interests, deciding child custody cases would be comparable to diagnosing and treating a known medical condition. But psychiatrists and psychologists don't know — as the record of their disagreement in this case amply demonstrates.[93]

---

[89] 279 Pa. Super. 458, 463, 421 A.2d 289, 292 (1980).

[90] *See id.* at 470, 421 A.2d at 295–96 ("In my professional opinion I think P.J. would respond traumatically in a very upset manner to a relation of custody in that direction. I believe that he would be very upset over the separation; he would become anxious, depressed, he would regress in terms of some childhood behaviors.")

[91] *See id.* at 471, 421 A.2d at 296 ("I don't feel . . . that [a change of custody] would create such trauma to his psyche that he would not recover from it.").

[92] 325 Pa. Super. 39, 472 A.2d 635 (1984).

[93] *Id.* at 58–59, 472 A.2d at 645 (emphasis in original).

Courts confronted with unrefuted or seemingly balanced expert evidence sometimes sought guidance from child development literature. In turning to these external sources, courts replicated the process by which they weighed conflicting expert evidence. Those courts that rejected psychological parent theory avoided substantive evaluation of the theory, asking only whether it was the subject of consensus or conflict. Thus, in rejecting a claim that a trial court had given too little heed to psychological parent principles and holding that "bonding is not necessarily the dispositive factor in determining [child placement matters],"[94] the North Dakota Supreme Court said: "'Some authorities, particularly those with a psychoanalytic orientation, take the position that continuity is absolutely critical, particularly in very early childhood . . . . Others dispute this, maintaining that children are developmentally much more resilient . . . . We are not required to settle this scientific dispute.'"[95]

We have observed that the *Sanders* court refused to "place judicial imprimatur upon the socio-psychological concept of 'the psychological parent.'"[96] This disapproval of nascent lawmaking is a theme that recurs in other opinions in which courts recognized the fallibility of psychological parent theory and circumscribed its use. The appellate court in *In re Donna W.* held that the trial judge had committed an "error of law" in applying a "psychological bonding presumption."[97] Connecticut courts have also taken the view that custody decision-making requires "flexible, individualized adjudication of the particular facts of each case without the constraint of objective guidelines."[98] They have resisted claims that psychological parent principles were given too little heed in matrimonial custody cases, saying "the concept of the psychological parent is not a fixed star by which custody decisions can invariably be guided."[99]

The tendency of some courts to eschew such formulae is significant because it implies recognition that judicial absorption of background facts may lead to judicial lawmaking and indicates an appreciation of

---

[94] Schneider v. S.L.M., 347 N.W.2d 126, 130 (N.D. 1984).

[95] *Id.* at 131 (emphasis omitted) (citing *In re* Tremayne Quame Idress R., 286 Pa. Super. 480, 495 n.6, 429 A.2d 40, 48 n.6 (1981)).

[96] Montgomery County Dep't of Social Servs. v. Sanders, 38 Md. App. 406, 408, 381 A.2d 1154, 1156 (1977).

[97] *See* 325 Pa. Super. at 59, 472 A.2d at 645. The court added that even if the trial court opinion were read to indicate that bonding was "heavily weighed" rather than raised to the level of a presumption, the appellate court would reject the judgment below, weigh the bonding factor less heavily, and order the institution of a procedure designed to lead to gradual return of the children to their natural mother. *See id.* at 59–63, 472 A.2d at 645–47. *Donna W.* is one of the very few cases in which psychological parent evidence offered by a state agency was rebutted by expert evidence. *See supra* note 55.

[98] Seymour v. Seymour, 180 Conn. 705, 710, 433 A.2d 1005, 1007 (1980).

[99] *Id.* at 711–12, 433 A.2d at 1008.

the significance and risks of such lawmaking.[100] In subsequent Sections, we will review cases in which this tendency was absent or was overcome — cases in which the theory was used as legislative fact to develop common law and constitutional and statutory interpretation.

B. A Subset of Cases Illustrating the Point of Slippage Between Adjudicative and Legislative Factfinding

In the State of New York, an unusually explicit dialogue occurred concerning the appropriateness of adjusting the law in response to psychological parent theory. On one side of the dialogue were trial courts, which recognized that "[t]his concept, of a psychological parent-child relationship, has gained increasingly greater acceptance in the courts where the phenomena have been observed at close hand and where psychiatric experts have testified to its being well grounded and significant."[101] On the other side were the appellate courts, which more easily resisted the pressure to conform law to psychological parent theory. This dialogue is revealing both for its articulation of judicial motivations and for its failure to articulate a theory that would justify and regulate the actions of judges who seek to change the law. It therefore provides a useful introduction to the succeeding analysis of legislative factfinding.

In an opinion dated October 31, 1973, a family court judge referred to a new approach to custody, citing a prepublication review of *Beyond the Best Interests of the Child* in the *New York Times*.[102] Discussion of the tensions between the theory and New York law had begun even earlier. *In re Catherine S.*[103] was a case in which nonparent custodians of approximately twenty months vied with the bi-

[100] These risks can run both ways, as was sometimes recognized in cases that followed psychological parent theory. One Washington court found relative rulelessness preferable to strict doctrinal rules because it allowed the courts to respond flexibly to changes in expert views. *See In re* Aschauer, 93 Wash. 2d 689, 697 n.5, 611 P.2d 1245, 1250 n.5 (1980) (en banc); *In re* J.O.L. II, 409 A.2d 1073, 1075 n.2 (D.C. 1979), *cert. granted*, 449 U.S. 818 (1980), *vacated*, 449 U.S. 989 (1980), *cert. denied*, 454 U.S. 832 (1981) ("'A norm is ill-suited for determining the future of a unique being whose adjustment is vital to the welfare of future generations. . . . [I]t is not asking too much to demand that a court, in making a determination as to the best interest of a child, make the determination upon specific evidence relating to that child alone. . . . [M]agic formulas have no place in decisions designed to salvage human values. . . ." (quoting Bazemore v. Davis, 394 A.2d 1377, 1383 (D.C. 1978))); L.B.T. v. E., 318 N.W.2d 200, 201–02 (Iowa 1982) (holding that psychological bonding is an important factor to weigh in the balance in adoption proceedings).

[101] Doe v. Doe, 92 Misc. 2d 184, 192, 399 N.Y.S.2d 977, 982 (Sup. Ct., Special Term 1977) (awarding custody to a stepmother as against a biological father and relying inter alia upon expert testimony that the stepmother was the psychological parent).

[102] *See* Nathan M. v. Catholic Guardian Soc'y, 76 Misc. 2d 1003, 1005–06, 352 N.Y.S.2d 319, 322–23 (Fam. Ct. 1973) (citing Kramer, *The 'Psychological Parent' is the Real Parent*, N. Y. Times, Oct. 7, 1973, (Magazine), at 70).

[103] 74 Misc. 2d 154, 347 N.Y.S.2d 470 (Fam. Ct. 1973).

ological parents for custody of a three-year-old child.[104] The parents asserted, with clear support from prior case law, that "without a finding that the natural parents are presently unfit, [the] court is without option and must return the child forthwith."[105] The trial judge, clearly influenced by psychological parent theory, resisted application of the New York rule of preference for fit biological parents. He framed a rhetorical question: "Are the parents entitled to the immediate return of the child because they are the natural parents regardless of the effect of such return upon the child?"[106] In response to the parents' characterization of the law, he cited dicta of the highest court of the state: "'[The requirement that] the nonparents . . . prove that the mother is unfit to have her child and that the latter's well-being requires its separation from its mother . . . does not mean the child's rights and interests are subordinated.'"[107] He interpreted this ambiguous bit of dicta broadly: "If we are not to completely subordinate the child's rights and interests we must also consider his emotional well-being and the effect of an immediate or even eventual return to the natural parents."[108]

The judge acknowledged that "New York [law had] . . . been more oriented toward the principle of 'parental right.'"[109] But to support an expansive reading of applicable law, he relied upon the views contained in the *Yale* Note,[110] and upon language from decisions in other jurisdictions[111] in which fit biological parents had been denied custody in contests with nonparents. The court saw in the out-of-state cases a recognition "that 'the best interests of the child' . . . are determinative,"[112] and read that recognition into New York law.

Interestingly, the court did not enter a final order awarding custody to the nonparents. It continued the custody of the nonparent contestants for a brief period, arranged a program of visitation with the parents and supervision by the probation department, and, upon receipt of a report favorable to the parents, transferred custody.[113] But despite the limited action taken in *Catherine S.*, the case was used in

---

[104] *See id.* at 155, 347 N.Y.S.2d at 471.

[105] *Id.* at 157, 347 N.Y.S.2d at 473. A finding of abandonment of the child would also have justified a denial of custody, but the facts of this case did not meet the stringent requirements for a finding of parental abandonment under New York law.

[106] *Id.*

[107] *Id.* at 158, 347 N.Y.S.2d at 473 (quoting Spence-Chapin Adoption Serv. v. Polk, 29 N.Y.2d 196, 204, 274 N.E.2d 431, 436, 324 N.Y.S.2d 937, 944 (1971)).

[108] *Id.*

[109] *Id.* at 159, 347 N.Y.S.2d at 475.

[110] *See id.* at 158–59, 347 N.Y.S.2d at 474.

[111] *See id.* at 160–61, 347 N.Y.S.2d at 475–76.

[112] *Id.* at 159, 347 N.Y.S.2d at 475.

[113] *See id.* at 162, 347 N.Y.S.2d at 477–78. Endorsements entered upon the court file indicate that the transition to parental custody was successfully completed.

subsequent cases to justify much broader applications of psychological parent principles.[114] Two months later, in *Confessora B. v. Ana L.*,[115] a judge referred to the deliberations of his colleague in *Catherine S.* in denying custody to a fit biological parent. He explained his action as follows:

> The court is indeed fortunate and deeply indebted to its learned colleague . . . for this is the very same issue to which he addresses himself in *Matter of Catherine S.* . . . His review of the numerous cases relating to this issue both in New York State and throughout the country, of articles dealing with child's rights and interests and the role of the court acting for the state as *parens patriae* and the works of notable psychoanalysts on what they consider the essential elements for a child's successful development and all other facets are thoroughly examined in his scholarly decision. This court unreservedly concurs in his opinion that the best interests of the child must in the final analysis be the deciding factor.[116]

The decision and affirmance of *Confessora B.* marked a shift in New York common law.

Catherine S. and *Confessora B.* were both custody cases. They did not involve attempts to sever altogether the relationship between parent and child and they were governed by common law. Trial judges who were persuaded by psychological parent theories, however, were often motivated to take the further step of applying them to impose the more drastic, statutorily controlled[117] remedy of terminating parental rights. In this context, a trial judge in *In re Patricia Ann W.*,[118] writing four years after *Catherine S.*, described a "tug-of-war"[119] that had developed between trial and appellate courts over the proper standards for interruption or termination of parental rights. The description makes clear that the conflict was between "sociological thinking" on the one hand and legal principles that were formerly held to be controlling on the other.[120] The court described a 1974

---

[114] *Compare Catherine S.*, 74 Misc. 2d 154, 347 N.Y.S.2d 470 *with In re* M., 65 Ohio Misc. 7, 416 N.E.2d 669 (C.P., Juv. Ct. Div. 1979). For a discussion of *In re M.*, see pp. 1555–56 above.

[115] 75 Misc. 2d 576, 348 N.Y.S.2d 21 (Fam. Ct. 1973), *aff'd sub nom.* Benitez v. Llano, 47 A.D.2d 566, 365 N.Y.S.2d 1016 (App. Div. 1975), *aff'd*, 39 N.Y.2d 758, 349 N.E.2d 876, 384 N.Y.S.2d 775 (1976).

[116] *Id.* at 579, 348 N.Y.S.2d at 25.

[117] *See* N.Y. Soc. Serv. Law § 384(b) (McKinney 1983 & Supp. 1987).

[118] 89 Misc. 2d 368, 392 N.Y.S.2d 180 (Fam. Ct. 1977).

[119] *Id.* at 372, 396 N.Y.S.2d at 183.

[120] The court stated:

> [B]ecause the law mandated return of a child to a parent not declared unfit, regardless of how long the child had lived with its nonblood psychological parents, terrible situations arose in which lives were literally wrecked by a failure to recognize the tremendous importance of persons who were parents in all respects other than ties of blood. . . .
>
> Because of certain changes in sociological thinking coupled with heightened public

case[121] in which the highest court of the state reaffirmed the principle that parental rights could not be terminated without findings of gross misconduct or a clear intention to abandon the child.[122] The judge found this reaffirmation "surprizing [sic]" despite its adherence to precedent, because it "stifl[ed] expectations that with lower courts following the 'psychological parent' school of thought" a relaxation of the stringency of prior judicial holdings might have been expected.[123] He traced "an emerging trend of judicial thinking . . . giving increased recognition to the 'psychological parent' school of thought" and described *Catherine S.*, *Confessora B.*, and subsequent cases as having "reorder[ed] judicial thinking."[124] On the basis of this "reordered thinking," the court determined in an interim opinion that it had the power to terminate parental rights in the interest of preserving a psychological bond, despite a clear absence of statutory grounds.[125] This was possible in the court's view because certain features of the statutory scheme had been "judicially erased."[126]

The tug-of-war between New York trial and appellate judges occurred in part because many appellate judges believed that only the legislature could make the changes in law required to permit adherence to psychological parent principles.[127] Trial judges occasionally reflected this view in their opinions,[128] sometimes rejecting psychological parent theory explicitly on this ground.[129] As previously cited

---

> awareness of this problem, informed prognostications as to future judicial actions now entertained the possibility that the courts would soon be able to consider the best interests of a child and his psychological parentage unfettered by heretofore controlling considerations of blood . . . .

Id. at 373–74, 392 N.Y.S.2d at 184.

121 *See* Susan W. v. Talbot G., 34 N.Y.2d 76, 312 N.E.2d 171, 356 N.Y.S.2d 34 (1974).

122 *See Patricia Ann W.*, 89 Misc. 2d at 374, 392 N.Y.S.2d at 184 (citation omitted) (describing *Susan W.*, 34 N.Y.2d at 80, 312 N.E.2d at 174, 356 N.Y.S.2d at 38).

123 *Id.*

124 *Id.* at 375, 392 N.Y.S.2d at 185.

125 *See id.* at 376, 392 N.Y.S.2d at 185. This assessment of the extent to which appellate thinking had been reordered was incorrect. For a discussion of subsequent developments in New York law, see pp. 1565–66, 1574–75 below.

126 *See Patricia Ann W.*, 89 Misc. 2d at 377, 392 N.Y.S.2d at 186.

127 *See id.* at 373, 392 N.Y.S.2d at 183.

128 *See, e.g.*, *In re* Raymond M., 81 Misc. 2d 70, 364 N.Y.S.2d 321 (Fam. Ct. 1975). The *Raymond M.* court acknowledged the urging of principles by "eminent authorities," citing BEYOND THE BEST INTERESTS OF THE CHILD, *supra* note 17, but says "without further legislative changes, the sole fact of a psychological attachment to a foster parent cannot control the determination of whether or not further efforts to encourage and strengthen the parental relationship" should have been required under existing law. *Id.* at 77, 364 N.Y.S.2d at 328. The case was, however, decided consistently with psychological parent principles.

129 *See, e.g.*, Schneider v. S.L.M., 347 N.W.2d 126 (N.D. 1984). The *Schneider* court stated:

> At the hearing various experts testified about the concept of bonding, the central concept in the book *Beyond the Best Interests of the Child* . . . . The court in its oral recitation stated that even though it had read *Beyond the Best Interests of the Child*, the thesis of

cases illustrate, however, most New York trial courts did what Goldstein, Freud and Solnit recommended: they applied the theory to "revis[e] the . . . substance of court decisions."[130] Moreover, they did so without pausing to consider whether, and on the basis of what sort of showing, a court is justified in creating or modifying legal doctrine to accommodate a social science theory. We will see that trial and appellate courts across the country reacted similarly.[131]

C. *Psychological Parent Theory and the Common Law: Evolution and Denial*

It is clear that judicial acceptance of psychological parent theory has altered the common law.[132] What is most striking is that these alterations were barely acknowledged. Indeed, courts openly acknowledged that common law doctrine might be changed or modified in response to psychological parent principles only in cases in which they declined to make changes requested by litigants.

We have considered factors that led courts faced with case-specific psychological parent evidence to resist nascent lawmaking. This phenomenon occurred when courts saw the theory as fallible or controversial and appreciated the advantages of individualized consideration of child placement issues.[133] Similarly, an awareness that the theory is controversial led two courts forthright to reject proposals to modify

---

> the book would not control the disposition of the case because the North Dakota Legislature had not adopted statutes similar to the ones discussed in the book.

Id. at 130.

130 BEYOND THE BEST INTERESTS OF THE CHILD, *supra* note 17, at 5.

131 The state supreme court in Gardebring v. Rizzo, 269 N.W.2d 104 (N.D. 1978), held, for example, that adoption of the Goldstein, Freud and Solnit position regarding visitation would require legislative action:

> The authors' goal of using "each child's placement as an occasion for protecting future generations of children by increasing the number of adults-to-be who are likely to be adequate parents" is . . . laudable. . . . The means suggested by the authors of reaching this goal contain many ideas which may be applied within the existing framework of law and many which represent such a shift in policy that they are better left to the Legislature.

Id. at 110 (quoting Jordana v. Corley, 220 N.W.2d 515, 523 (N.D. 1974)); *accord In re* J., 134 Vt. 480, 485, 365 A.2d 521, 524 (1976).

132 The cases reported here may not fully portray the common law changes that have resulted from acceptance of psychological parent principles. The cases upon which this study is based include only those in which explicit reference is made to Goldstein, Freud and Solnit or to the concept of the psychological parent. Analysis of these cases establishes a disinclination on the part of courts to acknowledge that changes in the common law are taking place or to discuss in detail the psychological principles by which they seem to be influenced. This finding suggests that courts are likely to modify common law on the basis of an acceptance of psychological parent principles without mentioning those principles or the sources from which they are derived. If this is so, then we can expect that additional common law changes were made but not captured in the data.

133 *See, e.g.*, cases discussed *supra* p. 1558 & n.98.

the common law. In response to a request that it modify its rule with respect to the status of biological parents in custody contests, a Missouri Court of Appeals noted that "[t]his court is not desirous or prepared to suggest abandonment of the 'parental right' doctrine . . . based upon limited sociological and psychological data which by its nature leaves unanswered the impact or importance of the biological or natural nexus between parent and child."[134] In a Pennsylvania case, the Regional Council of Child Psychiatry appeared as amicus curiae to urge a reform of child placement laws roughly consistent with the principles articulated in *Beyond the Best Interests of the Child*.[135] The court cited authorities on both sides of the psychological parent debate to indicate its belief that professional opinion was not uniform.[136] The court observed that "'[t]he relationship between parent and child should be broken only with the greatest reluctance,'"[137] and declined to modify "settled Pennsylvania law."[138]

Common law issues of first impression were often decided on the basis of psychological parent theory. These common law developments were generally announced in matter-of-fact terms, with little or no discussion of the theory, and with no acknowledgement that it might be controversial. A Connecticut court, for example, adopted a rule of statutory construction based upon the principles of nonintervention espoused by Goldstein, Freud and Solnit.[139] A New Jersey court, finding a constitutional right to counsel in neglect proceedings, cited *Beyond the Best Interests of the Child* in denying retroactive application of its ruling, based in part on the desirability of protecting the "psychological environment" of children whose cases had previously been determined.[140] An Illinois court applied the doctrine of laches to set aside an adoption decree, despite the absence of local precedent,[141] on the ground that the child would otherwise suffer a "[d]isruption of the continuity of relationship . . . [with] 'psychological parents' [that] is almost certain adversely to affect the child's devel-

---

[134] Frederick v. Frederick, 617 S.W.2d 629, 637 (Mo. App. 1981) (per curiam).

[135] *See* Commonwealth *ex rel.* Grimes v. Yack, 289 Pa. Super. 495, 525–27, 433 A.2d 1363, 1379–80 (1981). The case involved a revocation of consent to adoption of an infant, followed by a period of approximately 16 months during which the prospective adoptive parents refused to relinquish custody. *See id.* at 500–510, 433 A.2d at 1366–71. The issue was whether the child should be returned to the biological parents or adopted.

[136] *See id.* at 527–29, 433 A.2d at 1380–81.

[137] *Id.* at 530, 433 A.2d at 1382 (quoting K.N. v. Cades, 288 Pa. Super. 555, 556, 432 A.2d 1010, 1016 (1981)).

[138] *Id.* at 529–30, 433 A.2d at 1381–82.

[139] *See* Welfare Comm'r v. Anonymous (1976), 33 Conn. Supp. 100, 103–06, 364 A.2d 250, 252–53 (Super. Ct. 1976).

[140] *See* Crist v. New Jersey Div. of Youth & Family Servs., 128 N.J. Super. 402, 417, 320 A.2d 203, 211 (Law Div. 1974), *modified*, 135 N.J. Super. 573, 343 A.2d 815 (App. Div. 1975).

[141] *See* Rodriguez v. Koschny, 57 Ill. App. 3d 355, 360–61, 373 N.E.2d 47, 51 (1978).

opment."[142] The courts of California granted standing in custody[143] and paternity[144] disputes to any "person who, on a day-to-day basis, assumes the role of parent, seeking to fulfill both the child's physical needs and his psychological need for affection and care."[145] The Court of Appeals of New Mexico voided a contract in which a mother assigned custody to another on the condition that her parental rights be preserved, relying on a public policy favoring termination of parental rights "where it is shown . . . that a positive, nurturing parent-child relationship no longer exists, the child has been allowed to remain for an extended period of time in a foster home, and a psychological bond has been created between the child and the foster parents."[146] A dissenting Oregon opinion cited *Beyond the Best Interests of the Child* in support of common law recognition of the tort of maternal abandonment.[147] And an intermediate appellate court in Florida referred to psychological parent concepts in rejecting a presumption for fit, biological parents in favor of a best interests test.[148]

The salient characteristics of the common law cases — cursory treatment of psychological theories and an atmosphere of denial that any change in law was being introduced — are illustrated by *Bennett v. Jeffreys*.[149] In *Bennett*, a majority of the highest court of the State of New York was silent with respect to scientific literature, and reluctant to acknowledge the impact of its decision, as it made a significant, if temporary,[150] change in the common law of custody. Although New York appellate courts initially resisted trial level discussions of psychological parent theory,[151] the New York Court of Appeals in 1976 made a change in common law that was roughly consistent with psychological parent principles.[152] The case involved

---

[142] *Id.* at 362, 373 N.E.2d at 52.

[143] *See* Z. v. San Bernadino County Welfare Dep't (*In re* B.G.), 11 Cal. 3d 679, 692–93, 523 P.2d 244, 253–54, 114 Cal. Rptr. 444, 453–54 (1974).

[144] *See* Perez v. Department of Health, 71 Cal. App. 3d 923, 927, 138 Cal. Rptr. 32, 34 (1977).

[145] *Z.*, 11 Cal. 3d at 692 n.18, 523 P.2d at 253 n.18, 11 Cal. Rptr. at 453 n.18 (citing BEYOND THE BEST INTERESTS OF THE CHILD, *supra* note 17); *accord Perez*, 71 Cal. App. 3d at 926, 138 Cal. Rptr. at 33–34 (citing *Z.*).

[146] *In re* John Doe, 98 N.M. 340, 347, 648 P.2d 798, 805 (Ct. App. 1982). This court seemed to base its ruling less upon its own acceptance of psychological parent doctrine than upon the fact that the legislature had "recognize[d] that children may form strong psychological bonds with foster parents" and had drafted statutes governing analogous issues in light of that recognition. *See id.* at 346, 648 P.2d at 804.

[147] *See* Burnette v. Wahl, 284 Or. 705, 720–23, 588 P.2d 1105, 1114–15 (1978) (Lent, J., dissenting in part).

[148] *See* Gorman v. Gorman, 400 So. 2d 75, 78 (Fla. Dist. Ct. App. 1981).

[149] 40 N.Y.2d 543, 356 N.E..2d 277, 387 N.Y.S.2d 821 (1976).

[150] *See infra* note 163.

[151] *See supra* pp. 1561–63.

[152] *See* Bennett v. Jeffreys, 40 N.Y.2d 543, 356 N.E.2d 277, 387 N.Y.S.2d 821 (1976).

a child who had been informally placed in the care of a nonparent; it was a contest between the biological mother and the nonparent custodian. Under established New York common law, "only a finding of abandonment, surrender or neglect could defeat the presumption in favor of natural parents"[153] in such a contest, and the court conceded that no such finding applied.[154] Nevertheless, it remanded the case for a new hearing to determine which contestant could better meet the child's best interests.[155] It did so on the theory that the prolonged (more than seven-year) period of custody with the nonparent combined with other related factors to constitute an "extraordinary circumstance" that justified application of a best interests test in lieu of the biological parent presumption.[156] Despite the court's insistence that it was merely clearing up "confusion, sometimes in thought but most often only in language"[157] and reporting "a shifting of emphasis rather than a remaking of substance,"[158] it is reasonably clear that the court was, in fact, announcing a change in common law.[159] Although prior decisions had described instances of *parental unfitness* as "special and weighty circumstances"[160] or "dire circumstances or gross misconduct,"[161] the notion that custody might be denied on the basis of "extraordinary circumstances" other than unfitness or abandonment was new to New York jurisprudence. The court cited only one case, decided months earlier in a memorandum opinion, in which a biological parent had been denied custody in a contest with a nonparent on a basis other than formal surrender, abandonment, or unfitness.[162] A review of prior case law reveals that case to be unique. After the court's decision, New York law afforded a new, two-step decision procedure in contests between fit biological parents and others. If an "extraordinary circumstance" was found, then custody was awarded, without regard to biology, to the contestant deemed better able to serve the child's best interests.[163]

---

[153] *Id.* at 554, 356 N.E.2d at 286, 387 N.Y.S.2d at 830 (Fuchsberg, J., concurring).

[154] *See* 40 N.Y.2d at 544, 356 N.E.2d at 283, 387 N.Y.S.2d at 820.

[155] *See id.* at 550, 356 N.E.2d at 284–85, 387 N.Y.S.2d at 827–28.

[156] *Id.*

[157] *Id.* at 546, 356 N.E.2d at 281, 387 N.Y.S.2d at 824.

[158] *Id.* at 546, 356 N.E.2d at 281, 387 N.Y.S.2d at 825.

[159] *See* Note, *The Fundamental Right to Family Integrity and Its Role in New York Foster Care Adjudication*, 44 BROOKLYN L. REV. 63, 94 (1977).

[160] Kropp v. Shepsky, 305 N.Y. 465, 469, 113 N.E.2d 801, 804 (1953).

[161] Spence-Chapin Adoption Serv. v. Polk, 29 N.Y.2d 196, 199, 274 N.E.2d 431, 432, 324 N.Y.S.2d 937, 939 (1971).

[162] *See* Benitez v. Llano, 39 N.Y.2d 758, 349 N.E.2d 876, 384 N.Y.S.2d 775 (1976). In this case, the court affirmed an award of custody to a cousin with whom a child had lived for most of the child's life, noting that the child was "within months of attaining his legal maturity," *id.*, and declining to engage in analysis of the legal issues raised by the award.

[163] In a concurring opinion, a single justice announced his view, based explicitly upon BEYOND THE BEST INTERESTS OF THE CHILD, *supra* note 17, and authorities cited in the *Yale*

All but unacknowledged changes in common law are most strikingly illustrated by a case from the state of New Jersey that altered the status of parental rights under both common and statutory law. *Sorentino v. Family and Children's Society of Elizabeth (Sorentino I)*[164] involved a child who had been surrendered for adoption by a procedure held to be "a legal nullity"[165] because the mother was "coerced," subjected to "unwarranted pressures," and denied the benefits of procedural protections.[166] The Supreme Court observed that termination of parental rights could not occur under these circumstances "merely because it might be determined that the best interests of the child, in the ordinary sense, would be promoted by the adoption,"[167] and acknowledged that "[o]rdinarily" these circumstances would require a return of custody to the biological parents.[168] The court was unable to cite precedent for any other course; New Jersey law clearly prohibited termination of parental rights without a valid surrender or a finding that the biological parents had, in the language of the relevant statute, "forsaken parental obligations." Yet the court did not order return of the child. It noted, citing the *Yale* Note,

---

Note, *supra* note 13, that the best interest standard should govern in all custody disputes. *See* Bennett v. Jeffreys, 40 N.Y.2d 543, 553–54, 356 N.E.2d 277, 285–86, 387 N.Y.S.2d 811, 829–30 (Fuchsberg, J. concurring). The majority clearly wished to stake out different ground, noting that it "[p]articularly rejected . . . the notion . . . that third-party custodians may acquire some sort of squatter's rights in another's child." *Id.* at 552 n.2, 356 N.E.2d at 285 n.2, 387 N.Y.S.2d at 829 n.2. The extraordinary circumstance test stood, however, as a vehicle by which lower courts might overcome the biological parent presumption and follow psychological parent theory in the adjudication of New York custody disputes. The courts' freedom to do so was unquestioned in the custody context until five years later when, in Dickson v. Lascaris, 53 N.Y.2d 204, 423 N.E.2d 361, 440 N.Y.S.2d 884 (1981), the court, without further discussion of the psychological issues, undermined the *Bennett* precedent by holding that extraordinary circumstances were *not* present in a case involving a comparable period of parental absence and parental conduct more vulnerable to criticism than any attributed to Ms. Bennett. *See id.* at 211–12, 423 N.E.2d at 365, 440 N.Y.S.2d at 888 (Meyer, J., dissenting).

164 72 N.J. 127, 367 A.2d 1168 (1976).

165 *Id.* at 131, 367 A.2d at 1170.

166 *Id.* at 129, 367 A.2d at 1169. The mother was sixteen when she placed her newborn in foster care for a thirty-day period. When, at the end of that period, the mother returned to the foster care agency with her parents to retrieve her child:

> [A]s a result of ensuing unwarranted pressures exerted by the supervisor [of the foster care agency] . . . , of threats of harassment and litigation by him, and of his failure to inform her of options for care of the child other than an immediate choice either of irrevocable surrender for adoption or return of the child, she was coerced within a half-hour or so into signing a surrender of the child for adoption.

Id. The biological father then went to the agency "and told a representative he opposed the surrender and would contest it. He was told that as an unwed father he had no 'say-so.'" *Id.* (The mother and father were subsequently married. *See id.* at 134, 367 A.2d at 1171.) These factual findings and the legal conclusion that they rendered the surrender void were affirmed by an intermediate court and by the state supreme court. *See id.* at 130–31, 367 A.2d at 1169–70.

167 *Id.* at 131, 367 A.2d at 1170.

168 *Id.*

among other authorities, that there was a possibility of psychological injury to the child if custody were changed,[169] and turned to case law from another jurisdiction to find judicial recognition of the need to preserve established, nonbiological relationships.[170]

Although the higher court saw no error in the trial judge's finding that the biological mother's surrender was involuntary,[171] it held that the potential for serious psychological injury required a hearing and determination on "the issue of whether transferring the custody of the child to plaintiffs . . . will raise the probability of serious harm to the child."[172] In taking this course, the court authorized additional proceedings that would lead to a decision to terminate, on unprecedented bases, the custodial and guardianship rights of the biological parents. The proceedings authorized by the remand order were as new to New Jersey law as was the doctrine of extraordinary circumstances to New York law.

In addition to the hearing requirement, the *Sorentino I* court announced a second common law development, this one literally without comment. It held that because the biological parents sought to "change the status quo," they would "have the burden of proving by a preponderance of the credible evidence that the potentiality for serious psychological harm accompanying or resulting from such a

---

[169] *See id.*

[170] *See id.* (citing Commonwealth *ex rel.* Bankert v. Children's Servs., 224 Pa. Super. 556, 307 A.2d 411 (1973) (involving foster parents' challenge of an agency decision to transfer a child from their home to another foster home)). The *Sorentino I* court also cited two New Jersey adoption cases involving surrender documents that were found valid and enforceable. See *Sorentino I*, 72 N.J. at 130–32, 367 A.2d at 1169–71 (citing *In re* R.D., 127 N.J. Super. 311, 317 A.2d 382 (App. Div. 1974) (reversing a trial court finding that a surrender of parental rights had been coerced); *In re* Adoption of a Child by P., 114 N.J. Super. 584, 277 A.2d 566 (App. Div. 1971) (relying on psychological parent theory to approve an adoption under a best interests test)).

[171] *See Sorentino I*, 72 N.J. at 129, 367 A.2d at 1169.

[172] *Id.* at 133, 367 A.2d at 1171. The court acknowledged having previously held that "where a parent has not forsaken or surrendered his parental obligations, he or she cannot be cut off from the child . . . on the basis that 'the best interests and welfare' of the child call for such action." *Id.* at 132, 367 A.2d at 1170. In distinguishing its previous holding, however, the court claimed that prior case law indicated that termination was precluded by "a mere demonstration," *id.*, of best interests, and suggested that a stronger showing might dictate a different result: "The court cannot evade its responsibility, as *parens patriae* of all minor children, to preserve them from harm . . . . The possibility of serious psychological harm to the child in this case transcends all other considerations." *Id.* at 132, 367 A.2d at 1171 (citations omitted). A review of New Jersey case law revealed that although the doctrine of parens patriae had been *mentioned* in the context of cases decided consistently with established principles, *see P.*, 114 N.J. Super. 584, 277 A.2d 566; *In re* Mrs. M., 74 N.J. Super. 178, 181 A.2d 14 (App. Div. 1962); *In re* Adoption of a Child by Jacques, 48 N.J. Super. 523, 138 A.2d 581 (Ch. Div. 1958), it had never been invoked in support of an action inconsistent with established law. Use of the doctrine to trump settled law had, however, been suggested on one occasion in a dissenting opinion. *See* Small v. Rockfeld, 66 N.J. 231, 247, 330 A.2d 335, 348 (1974) (Conford, P.J.A.D., dissenting).

move will not become a reality."[173] The court did not cite Goldstein, Freud and Solnit in this or any other context. Yet *Beyond the Best Interests of the Child* is, perhaps, the single work to which it might have turned to support the proposition that the burden of proof in the *Sorentino I* situation should properly be placed upon the biological parents. In describing the way in which a somewhat similar case might have been decided under their guidelines, the authors said:

> [The judge] would have dismissed the action by the biological mother. He would have asserted that the law, in accord with a child's need for continuity, presumes . . . that the present, and now long-standing custody ought not to be disturbed.
>
> The court would place the burden to overcome that presumption squarely on the adult claimant who challenges the existing relationship.[174]

The significance of the New Jersey court's announcement of a new standard of proof to be used in this context is indicated only by the fact that it evoked dissent.[175]

The *Sorentino* litigation was not finished before the court found an intolerable tension between the common law principles it had announced and the statutory scheme within which questions concerning the adoptability of the Sorentino child had ultimately to be decided. We turn now to the effect that psychological parent theory had upon the interpretation of statutes, beginning with the end of the *Sorentino* saga.

D. Psychological Parent Theory and the Malleability of Statutory Language

1. Reinterpretation of Facially Neutral Statutes. — Because *Sorentino I* was decided in accordance with common law principles, the court was tied to no referents other than precedent on the one hand, and an emerging, haphazardly informed sense of societal best interests on the other. In the cases now to be considered, courts functioned within a statutory framework, with legislative intent providing a third (and obligatory) referent for judicial decisionmaking. Examination of these cases illustrates that judges convinced of the validity of psychological parent theory not only read ambiguous statutory language in ways that facilitated application of the theory, but also blinded themselves to statutory language that seemed to inhibit its application. This Section will review those decisions in which courts tended to

---

[173] *Sorentino I*, 72 N.J. at 133, 367 A.2d at 1171.

[174] BEYOND THE BEST INTERESTS OF THE CHILD, *supra* note 17, at 61–62. Goldstein, Freud and Solnit proposed similar guidelines in a model statute. *See id.* at 100.

[175] *See Sorentino I*, 72 N.J. at 134, 367 A.2d at 1171–72 (Conford, P.J.A.D, concurring and dissenting).

ignore or stretch statutory language to permit outcomes consistent with psychological parent theory. It will then consider cases in which those tendencies were resisted. Analysis of the latter cases reveals an appreciation of the social interests that might be compromised by adherence to psychological parent theory, skepticism concerning the merits of the theory, and a deferential attitude toward legislative prerogatives.

Sorentino II provides a striking example of statutory interpretation faithless to precedent and legislative text. Upon remand of *Sorentino I*, the trial judge heard testimony of the parties and their experts, concluded that "plaintiffs had failed to satisfy him by a fair preponderance of the credible testimony that transfer of the child would not raise the probability of serious harm to the child," and continued custody with the prospective adoptive parents.[176]

The biological parents appealed, claiming inter alia[177] that the decision on remand had been against the weight of the evidence. The state supreme court affirmed, accepting the trial judge's finding that defendants' experts were "persuasive and convincing" and deeming their testimony sufficient to dispose of plaintiffs' contention.[178] The court added, however, that the trial judge's decision had support not only from the trial record, but also from "medical and scientific authorities, and the legal literature on the subject."[179] The court went on to address the issue of adoption "in the interest of finalizing this child's status."[180] In doing so, it had to contend with a statutory prerequisite for adoption without parental consent: a finding of "'forsaken parental obligations.'"[181] The statute defined this phrase as "willful and continuous neglect or failure to perform the natural and regular obligations of care and support of a child,"[182] and the court had previously interpreted this definition to require "'a past course of conduct amounting to intended abandonment or very substantial neglect of both parental duties and claims, with no reasonable expectation of any reversal of that conduct in the near future.'"[183] In light

[176] Sorentino v. Family & Children's Soc'y of Elizabeth (*Sorentino II*), 74 N.J. 313, 378 A.2d 18 (1977).

[177] Their constitutional claim is discussed *infra*, note 267.

[178] *See Sorentino II*, 74 N.J. at 320, 378 A.2d at 21.

[179] *Id.*

[180] *Id.* at 321, 378 A.2d at 22. A separate proceeding in which the preadoptive parents sought an order of adoption had been stayed below, but a similar application had been made by motion directly to the supreme court during the course of the appeal of the termination proceeding. *See id.*

[181] *Id.* (quoting N.J. STAT. ANN. § 9:3-24C (West 1976) (since repealed)). The court acknowledged that other statutory grounds for termination were "not present in this case." *Id.* at 322, 378 A.2d at 22.

[182] N.J. STAT. ANN. § 9:13-18(d) (West 1976) (since repealed).

[183] 74 N.J. at 321, 378 A.2d at 22 (quoting *In re* Adoption of Children by D., 61 N.J. 89, 94–95, 293 A.2d 171, 173 (1972)).

of this statutory interpretation, the court also had to contend with its assumption in *Sorentino I* that parental obligations had in fact not been forsaken.[184]

The court never directly addressed the problems raised by either the statutory language or case precedent, but rather focused exclusively on the policy it thought the legislation designed to serve. It reasoned that the legislature was concerned with "maintenance of stable, continuing relationships between parent and child,"[185] but pointed out that "where that relationship does not exist, there can be no separation."[186] In that event, the court reasoned, "another important policy of the Act comes into play: the protection of the stability and permanence of the new familial grouping."[187] The court asserted that prior decisions by New Jersey courts had implemented these policy choices, noting that cases denying termination of parental rights had "encouraged the maintenance of an existing relationship," while prior decisions to "terminate[] parental rights on grounds of forsaken parental obligations ha[d] encouraged the establishment of a permanent home by protecting the child from interference from a parent with whom it ha[d] no relationship."[188] However, none of the cases cited by the court had held that termination might be ordered without a finding that the parent had willfully and continuously failed to perform parental obligations.[189]

The court then presented a less sympathetic characterization of the conduct of the biological parents than had been presented in *Sorentino I* and announced that "no policy of the Act would be ignored by the termination of plaintiffs' rights."[190] The case was remanded for consideration of the adoption petition consistent with this opinion.[191]

---

[184] The court "acknowledge[d] that in *Sorentino I* there was at least an implied determination that there was *then* no basis for terminating parental rights." *Id.* (emphasis in original).

[185] *Id.* at 322–23, 378 A.2d at 22.

[186] *Id.* at 323, 378 A.2d at 23.

[187] *Id.*

[188] *Id.* at 323–24, 378 A.2d at 23.

[189] Of the three cases cited to illustrate terminations that preserved psychological parent relationships, two involved legally valid surrenders and therefore did not involve the need for statutory findings against the biological parents to justify termination of parental rights. *See* Lavigne v. Family & Children's Soc'y, 11 N.J. 473, 95 A.2d 6 (1953); *In re* Adoption of Child by P., 114 N.J. Super. 584, 277 A.2d 566 (App. Div. 1971). The third case seemed to fall easily within the statutory language in that it involved a biological father who had no contact with his child for fourteen years after which he appeared to oppose a proceeding to change the child's name. *See In re* Adoption of a Child by Jacques, 48 N.J. Super. 523, 138 A.2d 581 (Ch. Div. 1958).

[190] *Sorentino II*, 74 N.J. at 324, 378 A.2d at 23.

[191] *See id.* at 326, 378 A.2d at 24. A New Jersey intermediate appellate court subsequently abandoned the language of the governing statute, and with it the process of searching for "some arguable basis of unfitness," concluding:

> [W]here . . . foster care has been permitted for so extended a period as to have resulted in the virtual creation of a new parent-child relationship . . . and a trial judge, with

Acceptance of psychological parent principles in *Sorentino II* played a leading role in the court's decision to redefine statutory grounds for termination of parental rights in the face of contrary statutory language and case law. In less extreme situations, acceptance of psychological parent principles tipped the scales in favor of statutory interpretations that, although more plausible than the *Sorentino II* interpretation, were nonetheless open to question. For example, the Supreme Court of Alaska relied in part upon psychological parent principles to hold that a stepchild was a "child of the marriage" with respect to whom an award of visitation might be authorized in a dissolution proceeding.[192] The Court noted that five of six sister jurisdictions considering the question had acted similarly "*notwithstanding the absence of clear statutory authorization.*"[193] It then acknowledged the influence of psychological parent theory upon these judicial determinations, saying that "courts authorizing stepparent visitation have done so on the premise that the stepparent has become a surrogate parent. This concept . . . [is] expressed in the journals as that of 'psychological parentage.'"[194]

Reliance upon psychological parent theory served in several cases to dilute legislative provisions apparently designed to facilitate return of foster children to their biological parents. The termination statute of Washington provides that the state must supply "all necessary services, reasonably available, capable of correcting . . . parental deficiencies within the foreseeable future" before the parental rights of a child in foster care may be terminated.[195] The Washington Supreme

> evidential justification, concludes that disruption of that new relationship . . . would damage the child, an order permanently terminating the biological parent-child relationship can be validly issued *despite the absence of present or past parental unfitness*. This holding is, in our view, entirely consistent with the practical effect of [*Sorentino II*].

In re Guardianship of J.R., 174 N.J. Super. 211, 416 A.2d 62 (App. Div.), *cert. denied*, 85 N.J. 102, 425 A.2d 266 (1980) (emphasis added).

192 Carter v. Brodrick, 644 P.2d 850, 853 & n.2 (Ala. 1982) (citing ALASKA STAT. § 09.55.205, *renumbered as* ALASKA STAT. § 25.24.150 (1983)). The court held that a child becomes a "child of the marriage" only with respect to those stepparents who stand in loco parentis by virtue of the quality of their relationship with the child. In these situations, the trial court may determine that it is in the best interests of the child to grant the stepparent visitation rights. *See id.*; *cf. In re* Halpern, 133 Cal. App. 3d 297, 310, 184 Cal. Rptr. 740, 747 (1982) (holding that visitation rights could be awarded upon an allegation that the party seeking them stood in loco parentis, a term deemed by the court to be synonymous with psychological parent); Stanley D. v. Deborah D., 124 N.H. 138, 467 A.2d 249, 250 (1983) (holding that a New Hampshire statute, referring simply to "the children," authorized an award of custody to a stepfather found to be a psychological parent). *See also*, In re Baby M., No. FM-25314-86E, slip op. at 1–3 (N.J. Super. Ct. March 31, 1987) (discussing the scope of parens patriae powers in a case governed neither by common law or statute).

193 *Carter*, 644 P.2d at 853 (emphasis added).

194 *Id.* The court cited a statement of the Goldstein, Freud and Solnit theories contained in a law review article and referred to another law review article and a student note discussing psychological parent principles. *See id.* at 853 n.2.

195 WASH. REV. CODE § 13.34.180 (4) (1985).

Court drew exclusively upon *Beyond the Best Interests of the Child* to hold that the "period of time which constitutes the foreseeable future, depends in part on the age of the child,"[196] quoting that work for the proposition that "three months may not be a long time for an adult decisionmaker. For a young child it may be forever."[197]

Another case, *In re Lynna B.*,[198] involved a statute under which termination of parental rights required a finding that the parent was "likely to fail in the future to . . . [p]rovide a home" for the child.[199] The court relied heavily on psychological parent principles in interpreting the statute and evaluating the evidence marshalled against its interpretation.[200] With respect to the ability of this mother, to whom two other children had been returned from foster care,[201] to provide a "home" for the third, the court said: "Appellant is now able to provide a 'house' for Lynna, but it would be paradoxical to require the child's return for this reason in spite of the finding that it would be detrimental to her. In using the word 'home,' the Legislature intended a broader meaning . . . ."[202]

In *In re Hansen*, another Washington court relied upon statutory language providing that "'the family unit should remain intact in the absence of compelling evidence to the contrary'"[203] to order the release of a child from foster care. The appellate court reversed, relying upon psychiatric evidence below and the psychological parent theory upon which that evidence seems to have been based to define "family unit" to mean *psychological* family unit.[204]

Courts did not invariably accept the invitation to interpret ambiguous or inhospitable statutory provisions to accommodate psychological parent theory. Although a number of New York courts went

---

[196] *In re* Hall, 99 Wash. 2d 842, 851, 664 P.2d 1245, 1250 (1983). The case involved a father who was to have been released in eight months from a work release facility. *See id.* at 844, 664 P.2d at 1246–47.

[197] *Id.* at 851, 664 P.2d at 1250.

[198] 92 Cal. App. 3d 682, 155 Cal. Rptr. 256 (1979).

[199] *Id.* at 698, 155 Cal. Rptr. at 264 (quoting CAL. CIV. CODE § 232(a)(7)).

[200] *See id.* at 697 & n.3, 155 Cal. Rptr at 263 & n.3 (detailing the testimony of a child psychiatrist on the "wanted child-psychological parent relationship" and quoting at length from BEYOND THE BEST INTERESTS OF THE CHILD).

[201] *See id.* at 692, 155 Cal. Rptr. at 260.

[202] *Id.* at 699, 155 Cal. Rptr. at 265. The court also held that it was not necessary to termination that each of four statutory prerequisites be present, although the four are listed in conjunctive form.

[203] 24 Wash. App. 27, 37, 599 P.2d 1304, 1310 (1979) (quoting WASH. REV. CODE § 13.34.020 (1985) (as then codified)).

[204] *See id.*; *see also In re* Diana P., 120 N.H. 791, 424 A.2d 178 (1980), *cert. denied sub nom.*, Beverly P. v. Anne B., 452 U.S. 964 (1981) (relying, in part, upon psychological parent theory to interpret ambiguous statutory language to authorize termination of parental rights at the request of foster parents and against the wishes of both the supervising foster care agency and the biological parent).

beyond interpretation — and arguably beyond redefinition — of statutory language to hold that the familial rights of a biological parent might be terminated *regardless of the absence of statutory grounds* when the child had formed a psychological bond with another,[205] the highest court of New York rejected this view. Its opinion contrasts sharply with the approach taken by the highest court of New Jersey,[206] and exemplifies judicial rejection of statutory constructions inspired by acceptance of psychological parent theory. Opinions rejecting statutory manipulations of this kind frequently appear in the data only because they provoked separate opinions, or reversed lower court opinions, urging that the statutes in question be interpreted to accommodate the theory.[207] To this extent, the cases represent additional examples of judicial willingness, albeit frustrated, to implement the theory in the face of ambiguous or arguably inconsistent statutory language. The majority opinions provide, on the other hand, insight into the conditions that produce a reluctance to construe statutes to implement the recommendations of Goldstein, Freud and Solnit.

The New York Court of Appeals revealed an appreciation of policy concerns inconsistent with psychological parent theory, noting that legislated constraints upon the power to terminate parental rights are more than technical rules:

> A child, of course, is not a parent's property, but neither is the child property of the State . . . . In many cases the State may, and under some legal systems undoubtedly does, find "better" parents for a child even though the natural parents may be willing and able to provide proper care. But it is fundamental to our legal and social system, that it is in the best interest of a child to be raised by his parents, unless the parents are unfit . . . .[208]

Other courts urged deference to the legislative function, stating or implying that statutory adoption of the theory could be unambiguously indicated and should not be presumed.[209] Finally, in at least one

---

205 See cases cited at notes 117–26 above.

206 *See supra* pp. 1569–71.

207 *See, e.g.*, Eason v. Welfare Comm'r, 171 Conn. 630, 370 A.2d 1082 (1976); *In re* Sanjivini K., 47 N.Y.2d 374, 391 N.E.2d 1317, 418 N.Y.S.2d 339 (1979); E. v. J.T., 578 P.2d 831 (Utah 1978).

208 *Sanjivini K.*, 47 N.Y.2d at 382, 391 N.E.2d at 1321, 418 N.Y.S.2d at 344.

209 *See Eason*, 171 Conn. at 634, 370 A.2d at 1085 ("If the legislature had intended to include a foster parent among the persons permitted the right to file an application . . . it could easily have done so."); *In re* Donna Dorene G., 52 N.Y.2d 890, 437 N.Y.S.2d 304, 418 N.E.2d 1323 (1981) (adopting the view of a dissenting justice below that "[t]he contention . . . that a meaningful relationship has been established between the child and the foster parents, is no basis for finding compliance with the statute"); *In re* Derek Denlow, 87 Misc. 2d 410, 422, 384 N.Y.S.2d 621, 631 (Fam. Ct. 1976) (holding that the child's need for stability "is quite beside the point where statutory standards must be satisfied as a basis of decision"); E. v. J.T., 578 P.2d 831 (Utah 1978) (holding that the existence of a psychological parent relationship between

case, the disinclination to interpret a statute to accommodate psychological parent theory seemed to result in part from skepticism concerning its validity.[210]

2. Judicial Resistance to Legislative Acceptance of Psychological Parent Theory. — The cases discussed in the preceding Section involved the influence of psychological parent theory upon interpretation of statutes that seemed inconsistent with the theory's teachings. We must also consider those cases in which courts were called upon to interpret statutes that reflect, in some measure, legislative acceptance of the theory.[211] Examination of these cases provides additional evidence that legal results in this area depend not only upon the language of the law but also upon the attitude of judges — determined within and without the litigation — toward psychological parent theory.

The phenomenon appears most clearly in cases involving conflict between a legislative preference for assuring continuity of care and a court's inclination to change custody on the basis of evidence that a long-term custodian had adopted a disapproved lifestyle. For example, *Whaley v. Whaley*[212] concerned the interpretation of a statute providing that prior custody awards may not be changed in the absence of newly available evidence establishing that "[t]he child's present environment endangers significantly his physical health or his mental, moral, or emotional development and [that] the harm likely to be caused by a change of environment is outweighed by the advantages of such change to the child."[213] Despite these statutory requirements, the trial court found it possible to order a change of custody on the ground that the established custodian was involved in a romantic relationship with a married man.[214] The appellate court reversed, citing *Beyond the Best Interests of the Child* and other works of Anna Freud[215] to argue that a more literal interpretation of the statute would protect against unnecessary disruption of a child's psychological bonds.[216]

---

the child and a foster parent may not be relied upon to establish abandonment on the part of the biological parent).

210 *See Derek Denlow*, 87 Misc. 2d at 422, 384 N.Y.S.2d at 631. ("[F]or most children in foster care the idea [that adoption is] in their best interests [is] in the minds of the social planners [but is] not necessarily true, nor always desirable.").

211 For an indication of the extent of such acceptance, see Taub, *Assessing the Impact of Goldstein, Freud and Solnit's Proposals: An Introductory Overview*, 12 N.Y.U. REV. L. & SOC. CHANGE 485 (1983–84) and Garrison, note 32 above, at 449–53.

212 61 Ohio App. 2d 111, 399 N.E.2d 1270 (1978).

213 *Id.* at 112–13, 399 N.E.2d at 1272–73 (citing OHIO REV. CODE ANN. § 3109.04(B) (Anderson 1980) (as then codified)).

214 *See id.* at 116–17, 399 N.E.2d at 1274 ("[I]f your moral judgment is that warped in my opinion at least, then I can't trust your judgment in other incidents." (emphasis omitted)).

215 *See id.* at 112–13, 399 N.E.2d at 1272.

216 *See id.* at 118, 399 N.E.2d at 1275.

Appellate courts were not, however, always in disagreement with trial courts that acted in the face of custodial situations involving disapproved lifestyles to dilute legislated standards designed to encourage continuity of care. Thus, a custodial change was approved by the highest court of Illinois despite statutory language similar to that found in the Ohio statute requiring evidence of harm to the children and despite an absence of evidence below that such harm had occurred.[217] Although psychological parent principles figured prominently in the reasoning of the Ohio appellate court in *Whaley*, they were left unmentioned by the Illinois court.

A conflict between intermediate and ultimate appellate courts in New Mexico illustrates judicial resistance to psychological parent theory in a different context, pitting legislation informed by psychological parent theory against a firm judicial commitment to principles of family autonomy. The New Mexico legislature had provided that parental rights might be terminated in the case of a foster child upon a showing, inter alia, that "the parent/child relationship has disintegrated" and that "a psychological parent/child relationship has developed between the foster family and the child."[218] A New Mexico court of appeals, reviewing this statute in 1981, chose to defend "the principle of priority of right of a parent to the custody of a child," apparently accepting its "premise that a blood relation and instinct will cause the parent to better love and care for the child than one not so related."[219] The court relied in part upon the trial testimony of a psychologist and in part upon "common sense" to find that the appellant mother had been denied the opportunity to form a bond with her child.[220] It then proceeded to hold that the parent/child relationship could not have disintegrated because it had not existed.[221] The state supreme court reversed the court of appeals' order on separate grounds.[222] Months after the reversal, the court of appeals

---

[217] *See* Jarrett v. Jarrett, 78 Ill. 2d 337, 400 N.E.2d 421 (1979), *cert. denied*, 449 U.S. 927 (1980). For interpretations of the Jarret court's response to the Illinois statute, compare Comment, *Modifying Child Custody Awards: A Substantial Change Under the Illinois Marriage and Dissolution of Marriage Act*, 1980 S. ILL. U.L.J. 439, which argues that the court's decision not to require evidence of actual harm undercuts the basic purpose and policy of the statute, with Note, *Modification of Child Custody Predicated on Cohabitation of the Custodial Parent*: Jarret v. Jarret, 1981 B.Y.U. L. REV. 169, which maintained that "[t]he decision to allow modification [of the custody award] when the children were endangered, rather than await evidence of actual harm, served the best interests of the children."

[218] N.M. STAT. ANN. § 40-7-4B(4)(b), (c) (1978) (repealed 1985), *reprinted in* State *ex rel.* Dep't of Human Servs. v. Minjares (*In re* Doe), 98 N.M. 367, 368, 648 P.2d 1180, 1181 (Ct. App. 1981), *rev'd* 98 N.M. 198, 647 P.2d 400 (1982).

[219] *Minjares*, 98 N.M. at 372, 648 P.2d at 1185.

[220] *See id.* at 371, 648 P.2d at 1184.

[221] *See id.* at 370, 648 P.2d at 1183.

[222] *See* State *ex rel.* Dep't of Human Servs. v. Minjares (*In re* Doe), 98 N.M. 198, 647 P.2d 400 (1982).

confronted the statute again,[223] and on this occasion, it found the statute unconstitutionally vague, arguing that the word "disintegrated" was of uncertain meaning.[224] A review of the briefs of the parties reveals no direct citation to Goldstein, Freud and Solnit nor to the body of legal commentary derivative of their work.[225] A dissenting judge noted, however, that a case cited by the state contained discussions of "the concepts of parental functions; the legal and emotional relationships between the child and the parents, the foster parents, and the state agency; and the psychological ties that are broken and formed between a child and its natural and foster parents."[226] The Supreme Court of New Mexico reversed, adopting the opinion of the dissenting judge.[227]

Although hostility to or ignorance of psychological parent theory affects judicial interpretation of statutes designed to implement the prescriptions of Goldstein, Freud and Solnit, courts may develop more sympathetic interpretations as they reconsider the theory in specific factual contexts. A pair of cases decided by the Supreme Court of Connecticut is illustrative. These cases involved a statute that resembles the New Mexico statute discussed above in that it permits termination of biological parents' rights upon a finding inter alia that "'there is no ongoing parent-child relationship.'"[228]

The first case of the pair involved a woman who worked to support a child and a severely disabled husband.[229] During her working hours, the child received care in the home of a babysitter. When the child was three years old, the mother was involuntarily committed to a mental institution because her acute hyperthyroidism was misdi-

[223] *See* State *ex rel.* Human Servs. Dep't v. Staples (*In re* Doe) (Ct. App. 1982), *rev'd, dissenting opinion adopted*, and *reprinted in* 100 N.M. 92, 93–97, 666 P.2d 771, 772–76 (Ct. App. 1983).

[224] *See* 100 N.M. at 93–95, 666 P.2d at 773. The majority indicated its appreciation of social values apart from the preservation of psychological bonds, saying "[i]t is generally desirable for a child to remain with the natural parent because the child's need for a normal family life will usually best be met in the natural home," and announced that its invalidation of the statute "preserves the unity of the family [and] bars the State from excessive interference with family autonomy." *Id.* at 95, 666 P.2d at 774.

[225] *See* Defendant-Appellant's Brief-in-Chief, Answer Brief by Plaintiff-Appellees, State *ex rel.* Human Servs. Dep't v. Staples (*In re* Doe), 100 N.M. 92, 666 P.2d 771 (Ct. App. 1983) (No. 5306).

[226] 100 N.M. at 97, 666 P.2d at 776 (Walters, C.J., dissenting) (citing Smith v. OFFER, 431 U.S. 816 (1977)).

[227] *See id.* at 92, 666 P.2d at 772. The resistance of the court of appeals to generous interpretation of the statute continues. In a recent case, it narrowed the reach of the statute by engrafting a clean hands doctrine. *See* Jacklin v. Dudley (*In re* Adoption of Doe, I and II), 101 N.M. 34, 677 P.2d 1070 (Ct. App.), *cert. denied*, 677 P.2d 624 (N.M. 1984).

[228] (Anonymous) v. Commissioner of Children & Youth Servs. (*In re* Juvenile Appeal), 177 Conn. 648, 668 n.14, 420 A.2d 875, 885 n.14 (1979) (quoting CONN. GEN. STAT. ANN. § 17-43a (West Supp. 1986) (as then codified)).

[229] *See id.* at 650, 420 A.2d at 877.

agnosed as a "mental disability."[230] During the seven months required for the mother to obtain her release, secure appropriate treatment, and recover sufficiently to care for her child, the child was adjudicated "uncared for" and placed in foster care in the babysitter's home.[231] Efforts to secure the child's return culminated in a court order, entered nearly two years after the mother's commitment, denying her petition to remove the child from foster care and granting an agency petition to terminate parental rights.[232] The court called upon to review this order appreciated that the expert evidence offered by the agency was not conclusive; it noted the concession of the agency's psychiatrist that "in a case such as this, the future is very difficult to predict, and that it is possible the child could successfully make a transition back to her mother's custody."[233] Although it upheld the decision to continue foster care,[234] the court interpreted the statute to preclude a termination of parental rights, holding that it "quite clearly does not authorize termination upon a showing of no *meaningful* relationship, but rather requires that there be *no* relationship."[235] The court suggested that, in providing for the termination of parental rights, the legislature had contemplated only a situation in which "the child has no present memories or feelings for the natural parent."[236]

Subsequently, the Connecticut Supreme Court confronted a case involving a mother with a less sympathetic history who had placed an infant and a child of three years in foster care.[237] After approximately two years, she was able to secure return of the older child.[238] However, with respect to the younger child, who had contact with his mother but reacted negatively to her visits,[239] the state supreme court affirmed the trial court's conclusion that the relationship was nonexistent, and that parental rights should be terminated.[240] Assuredly, the majority could have found a way to read the "slippery language"[241] segregating disintegrated and disrepaired relationships more narrowly in order to protect the biological mother's rights. Its

[230] *See id.* at 651, 420 A.2d at 877.

[231] *See id.* at 651–52, 420 A.2d at 877.

[232] *See id.* at 655, 420 A.2d at 879.

[233] *Id.* at 666, 420 A.2d at 884.

[234] *See id.* at 668, 420 A.2d at 885.

[235] *Id.* at 675, 420 A.2d at 888 (emphasis added).

[236] *Id.* at 670, 420 A.2d at 885–86.

[237] *See In re* Juvenile Appeal, 181 Conn. 638, 641, 436 A.2d 290, 292 (1980).

[238] *See id.* at 643, 436 A.2d at 293.

[239] *See id.* at 644 n.3, 436 A.2d at 293 n.3.

[240] *See id.* at 639, 645, 436 A.2d at 294. A dissenting judge acknowledged that "the real mischief [lay] in the slippery language of the statutory ground" but complained that the majority improperly disregarded the mother's visits with her son, her expressions of concern for him, and her attempts to obtain a revocation of his commitment. *See id.* at 648–49, 436 A.2d at 295 (Parskey, J., dissenting).

[241] *Id.* at 648, 436 A.2d at 295 (Parskey, J., dissenting).

failure to do so suggests confidence, faced with facts less wrenching than those of the first case, in the correctness of the psychological premises supporting broad termination powers. In contrast to its reference in the first case to the difficulties associated with expert predictions concerning human development, the court relied in the second upon a psychologist's conclusion (arguably irrelevant under a standard requiring the complete absence of a parental relationship) that the child had "a tenuous psychological bond with his family of origin"[242] and that there was "'no evidence of any psychological bonding between the child and the defendant.'"[243]

E. Psychological Parent Theory and the Constitution

We have seen that judges who must apply common law and statutes often interpret or adjust those rules to accommodate acceptance or rejection of psychological parent principles. Judges must also test rules against constitutional standards. The testing process and the constitutional standards themselves similarly reflect judges' exposure and reactions to psychological parent principles.

Biological parents enjoy the protection of the constitutional principle that responsibility for "the custody, care and nurture of the child reside[s] first in the parents, whose primary function and freedom include preparation for obligations the state can neither supply nor hinder."[244] This principle of autonomy establishes a "private realm of family life which the state cannot enter" without adequate justification.[245] As psychological parent theory influenced states to sanction more sweeping incursions upon traditional prerogatives of the biological family, litigants sought shelter in this realm of family autonomy, asking courts to determine whether particular placement laws and procedures could be justified against claims that constitutionally protected rights had been violated. The tests for adjudicating the constitutional validity of state action explicitly permit reliance upon extrajudicial facts that influenced, or might have influenced, the action. Thus, social science theories and findings may provide the rational basis or important or compelling interest needed to justify challenged state conduct. When the challenge is framed to pit ordinary rights against the prerogatives of the state, the simple assertion of a theory that rationalizes the state action may serve to meet the challenge. When the competing right is important or fundamental, as it is in most of the cases involved in this study, the constitutional analysis is more complex, involving evaluation of the efficacy of the action taken,

---

[242] 181 Conn. at 642, 436 A.2d at 292–93 (quoting a clinical psychologist).

[243] *Id.* at 642, 436 A.2d at 293.

[244] Prince v. Massachusetts, 321 U.S. 158, 166 (1944).

[245] *Id.*

its sweep, and the importance of the state interest, as against the appropriate reach of the competing right or liberty.

The principles advocated by Goldstein, Freud and Solnit can be marshalled either to support or to restrict the constitutional right of family autonomy. The authors state that "a child's need for continuity of care by autonomous parents requires acknowledging that parents should generally be entitled to raise their children as they think best, free of state interference."[246] On the other hand, they argue that "[t]o favor the biological parents [when the child has established a psychological bond with other adults] would impose an intolerable hardship on both the child and the psychological parents."[247] Nonetheless, courts have typically employed the Goldstein, Freud and Solnit theories to restrict rather than expand biological parents' rights.[248] In cases in which the state offered psychological parent principles to justify encroachment upon biological family autonomy, the work of Goldstein, Freud and Solnit often served to meet a constitutional challenge. However, courts have rarely broadened or strengthened principles of family autonomy as a result of accepting the view that children fare better when biological family environments are secure against unnecessary state intrusion. This observation suggests — as did analysis of the background fact cases — that decisions to implement the Goldstein, Freud and Solnit proposals might result from a resource imbalance between state officials (who typically argue the case for protecting psychological family bonds) and impoverished parents (who typically argue the case for protecting biological family bonds).[249]

1. Justifying the Adequacy of State Interests: Psychological Parent Theory Delivers a Double Blow. — Adjudicative and background findings commonly buttressed arguments for the validity of an allegedly unconstitutional invasion of biological family autonomy or integrity.[250] When this occurred, the litigant asserting a constitutional

---

[246] BEFORE THE BEST INTERESTS OF THE CHILD, *supra* note 19, at 4.

[247] BEYOND THE BEST INTERESTS OF THE CHILD, *supra* note 17, at 110.

[248] *See* Davis, *Use and Abuse of the Power to Sever Family Bonds*, 12 N.Y.U. REV. L. & SOC. CHANGE 557, 560–62 (1983–84).

[249] The data include one significant case in which the pattern of selective acceptance of psychological parent theory was broken. When — in the course of litigation seeking to extend special constitutional protection to the psychological family unit — competent arguments both for and against judicial incorporation of psychological parent principles were presented, the erosion of biological family rights was checked. *See* Smith v. OFFER, 431 U.S. 816 (1977); *infra* pp. 1588–91.

[250] Psychological parent principles were referred to in justifying state action in the face of claimed violations of rights of family autonomy in several cases. *See, e.g.*, Custody of a Minor (No. 3), 16 Mass. App. Ct. 998, 1000, 454 N.E.2d 924, 926 (1983) (upholding the constitutionality of an award of permanent custody to the Department of Public Welfare); Mills v. Atlantic City Dep't of Vital Statistics, 148 N.J. Super. 302, 372 A.2d 646 (Ch. Div. 1977) (upholding the constitutionality of a statute restricting adoptees' access to information concerning biological

right suffered a double blow. The strength of adverse trial evidence based on psychological parent theory would lead to a finding against the biological parent as to particular facts. When these background or adjudicative facts were established to the satisfaction of a trial or appellate tribunal, the tribunal was then more likely to accept generalized psychological parent principles as legislative facts. The legislative facts, in turn, served to support the constitutionality of rules and procedures by which the adjudicative facts had been weighed and their consequences determined. In these cases, relative resources and litigation advantages influenced not only the outcomes of particular controversies, but also the development of constitutional law.

In *Custody of a Minor*,[251] for example, the amount and the quality of available expert evidence apparently influenced both the outcome and the breadth of the court's holding. A biological mother claimed that she had been unconstitutionally denied custody of her son because the evidence offered at trial established neither that she was unfit nor that her custody would harm the boy.[252] The son was fifteen at the time of the challenged adjudication, and had been in substitute care for three years. His recently divorced mother, a native of Thailand, was experiencing serious financial difficulties and expecting her seventh child.[253] The boy's fifth grade teacher became concerned by his complaints of mistreatment, and initiated an investigation. The investigator found no neglect or abuse, but reported that the mother "'sees her children and her responsibility to them somewhat differently than one would wish.'"[254] The teacher arranged to have the boy live with her until the baby was born. When the mother tried to reclaim the child, he refused to leave the teacher's home. Court proceedings led to the boy's placement in temporary foster care with the teacher.[255] A psychologist reported that the boy was "very angry, disturbed, and mistrustful of his mother" as well as of the teacher and her family.[256] According to the trial judge, the psychologist also reported that the

---

parents); *In re* Ginnan, 101 Misc. 2d 853, 422 N.Y.S.2d 1003 (Fam. Ct. 1979) (upholding the constitutionality of a statute authorizing automatic termination of the parental rights of imprisoned felons); *infra* pp. 1581–85 (discussing cases).

251 383 Mass. 595, 421 N.E.2d 63 (1981).

252 *See id.* at 596, 421 N.E.2d at 64.

253 *See id.* at 596–600, 421 N.E.2d at 64–66.

254 *Id.* at 597, 421 N.E.2d at 64 (quoting the caseworker). The investigator also stated that the mother "'does not recognize [the children's] feelings, their desires, their separateness as individuals as much as she requires their obedience and their loyalty and dedication to the family unit.'" *Id.* (quoting the caseworker). The investigator therefore "recommended psychological evaluation of [the boy] regarding his feelings toward himself, and feelings of rejection toward his mother, his family, and his culture, which [the investigator] opined could have damaging repercussions for him if he did not receive help." *Id.* at 598, 421 N.E.2d at 64–65.

255 *See id.* at 598, 421 N.E.2d at 65.

256 *Id.* at 599, 421 N.E.2d at 65.

boy saw the foster parents as his "psychological parents" and that "'to take [him] out of the [foster] family would be psychologically devastating and deleterious to his emotional growth.'"[257] Although an investigation had found the mother's "home adequate and clean, and the other children supportive of [her],"[258] the trial court relied upon the psychologist's report and placed the boy permanently in the foster home.

The state supreme court reviewed this evidence with approval and affirmed.[259] In addressing the constitutional question raised by the mother, it embarked upon a process reminiscent of that by which statutes are reinterpreted to take account of psychological parent principles.[260] The court adopted the view that although the relevant statutes simply articulated a best interest standard,[261] the state could not lawfully deprive biological parents of custody without a finding of unfitness.[262] However, the court broadened its definition of unfitness: "A finding of parental unfitness may be predicated on the circumstances within a particular family, as they adversely affect the particular child, *without regard to the general quality of parental conduct per se*."[263] The court bolstered its determination by reference to its understanding of child development principles. It cited a second opinion of the same date, which took a similarly broad view of unfitness, referring to "a 'substantial and impressive consensus' among experts in the field of child development that 'disruption of the parent-child relationship carried significant risks' for the child."[264] The court then held that the trial court's findings in this case were "tantamount to a finding of unfitness in relation to the furtherance of this particular child's welfare."[265] The constitutional adequacy of a no-fault, or vir-

---

[257] *Id.* at 599–600, 421 N.E.2d at 65.

[258] *Id.* at 598–99, 421 N.E.2d at 65.

[259] *See id.* at 600–02, 421 N.E.2d at 66–67.

[260] *See supra* 1570–73.

[261] *See* Petition of the Dep't of Public Welfare to Dispense with Consent to Adoption, 383 Mass. 573, 421 N.E. 2d 28 (1981).

[262] *See* Custody of a Minor, 383 Mass. 595, 600, 421 N.E.2d 63, 66 (1981) (citing *Petition to Dispense with Consent to Adoption*, 383 Mass. 573, 421 N.E.2d 28).

[263] *Id.* at 600, 421 N.E.2d at 66 (emphasis added).

[264] *Petition to Dispense with Consent to Adoption*, 383 Mass. at 588, 421 N.E.2d at 36 (quoting Mnookin, *Child-Custody Adjudication: Judicial Functions in the Face of Indeterminacy*, 39 LAW & CONTEMP. PROBS., 226, 265 (Summer 1975)). The court also cites the *Yale* Note, four other articles in legal publications, and a Wisconsin opinion and its collected authorities. It mentions John Bowlby and Goldstein, Freud, and Solnit as experts who share the consensus view. *See id.* Although *Petition to Dispense with Consent to Adoption* was, like *Custody of a Minor*, driven by psychological parent evidence and theories, *see id.* at 587–92, 421 N.E.2d at 35–38, it involved an imprisoned former drug addict, *id.* at 574–76, 421 N.E.2d at 29–30, and, as a result, represents less of a departure from traditional definitions of unfitness. Moreover, the matter was remanded for further consideration of the fitness issue. *See id.* at 593–94, 421 N.E.2d at 39–40.

[265] 383 Mass. at 601, 421 N.E.2d at 67.

tually no-fault, termination of parental custody rights turned, therefore, on an application of psychological parent principles.

The court relied upon social science literature and expert evidence at trial to strike the constitutional balance between the state's right to promote what it regards as the psychological interests of a child and parental rights of custody and autonomy. Many psychologists and psychiatrists would disagree as to the wisdom of separating this boy from his mother and siblings. Had competing expert opinion been part of the record, the deliberations on the constitutional questions would have been enriched by consideration of the psychological processes of adolescence and the desirability of allowing children to work through, rather than escape, the parent/child conflict.[266] These additional considerations might have led the court to announce identical rulings concerning the meaning of unfitness and the reach of constitutional rights of biological family autonomy. They might, however, just as possibly have left the court disinclined to adopt, and to sustain against a constitutional challenge, a standard that facilitated state intervention to order placement in cases in which the biological parent was fit by traditional definitions but in which the relationship with a particular child was troubled.[267]

Brownfield v. Brown (In re D.L.C.)[268] also exemplifies the double-blow effect. The trial court decided to terminate biological parental rights on the basis of unrefuted expert evidence that a psychological parent relationship existed between the child and her foster parents and that severance of that relationship would cause "tremendous trauma."[269] The appellate court found this decision "[c]learly . . . supported by the evidence."[270] It then dismissed the constitutional question on similar grounds:

> [The] argument is that a mother's right to custody of her children is a fundamental right which can only be infringed if the state advances a compelling state interest and that in the instant case "there has been no demonstration that parental custody at this time will be detrimental

---

266 *See, e.g.*, Colon, *Family Ties and Child Placement*, 17 FAM. PROCESS 289, 290 (1978).

267 *Custody of a Minor* also illustrates an interplay between statutory and constitutional interpretation. Understandably, decisions to interpret a statute consistently with psychological parent principles were often accompanied by opinions that the statute, as interpreted, met constitutional muster. Both the statutory and the constitutional rulings in these decisions seem to depend on impressions created by the record and independently acquired information concerning the state of psychological knowledge. *Sorentino II* provides another example of this interplay. After finding that the facts of the case compelled it, in the interests of the child, to interpret the New Jersey termination statutes to accommodate psychological parent principles, the court easily found that its reinterpretation was constitutionally permissible. *See Sorentino II*, 74 N.J.2d 313, 319, 378 A.2d 18, 21 (1977).

268 54 Cal. App. 3d 840, 126 Cal. Rptr. 863 (1976).

269 *See id.* at 849, 126 Cal. Rptr. at 868.

270 *Id.*

> to the minor." Appellant's argument manifestly appears to be without merit. As stated above, the evidence presented at trial, primarily that of [a] psychiatrist . . . was that it would be detrimental to the child to return her to the custody of appellant. Appellant presented no contrary expert testimony.[271]

The sweep of the power of psychological parent principles to justify state action was demonstrated by two cases in which the parent conceded the necessity of state intervention, but argued that constitutional considerations required the state to adopt less drastic means than extinguishing parental rights. In both cases, the biological parents acknowledged the need for adoption or long term foster care of their children, but sought to preserve limited rights of visitation and communication. A double blow felled even these modest claims, as judicial exposure to expert evidence and psychological literature gave victory to the state on the facts and on the constitutional law.

In *Petition of the Department of Public Welfare to Dispense with Consent to Adoption*,[272] the Supreme Judicial Court of Massachusetts approved a probate decision denying the biological parents' request for an "open" adoption.[273] It found the probate decision fully supported by unrefuted expert evidence.[274] The court then considered the constitutional issue. Noting that many social science authorities did not fully endorse open adoption, it determined that the constitutional rights of the biological parents had not been violated and announced that "in cases dealing with child custody and adoption, 'the doctrine of least restrictive alternatives should not be uncritically applied.'"[275]

Coffey v. Department of Social Services of Baltimore City[276] raised similar issues but was unusual among cases involving termination of parental rights in that both the biological mother and the State presented expert evidence. In reviewing the evidence, the court noted the child's specific psychological problems and found that a majority of the expert evidence on the issue of visitation favored the State.[277] The court proceeded to rule that "appellant's substantive [constitutional] rights were not violated by application of a 'best interests of the child' standard,"[278] in place of more rigorous barriers to termi-

---

[271] *Id.* at 850, 126 Cal. Rptr. at 868.

[272] 383 Mass. 376, 419 N.E.2d 285 (1981).

[273] An open adoption is an adoption that does not entirely extinguish the rights of biological family members to ongoing contact with the child. *See id.* at 379 n.3, 419 N.E.2d at 287 n.3.

[274] *See id.* at 379 & n.4, 419 N.E.2d at 287 & n.4.

[275] *Id.* at 380, 419 N.E.2d at 287 (quoting Petition of the Dep't of Public Welfare to Dispense with Adoption, 376 Mass. 252, 266, 381 N.E.2d 565, 573 (1978)).

[276] 41 Md. App. 340, 397 A.2d 233 (1979).

[277] *See id.* at 342–45, 397 A.2d at 236–37.

[278] *Id.* at 355, 397 A.2d at 242.

nation of biological relationships. Accordingly, it upheld total severance of the parent/child relationship. In doing so, the court relied upon opinions from other jurisdictions that cited the work of Goldstein, Freud and Solnit[279] and upon the court's own belief that "experts in child psychology and psychiatry overwhelmingly agree that a stable home environment, and the security and continuity which flow from that condition are absolutely essential."[280] Thus, general expert views concerning continuity, drawn primarily from case law and other legal literature, and case-specific expert evidence presented by the state, overwhelmed the appellant's arguments that the state decision to sever parental bonds unnecessarily compromised family integrity, as they overwhelmed appellant's expert evidence that preservation of those bonds could work to further the best interests of the child.[281]

2. *Expanding Rights of Biological Family Autonomy: Psychological Parent Theory Strikes an Occasional Blow.* — We have reviewed a number of cases in which rights of biological family autonomy were diluted because of trial evidence and other information concerning the need for continuity of care by foster parents. As was indicated earlier in this Section,[282] there were very few cases in which those rights were bolstered by evidence concerning the need for continuity of relationships with biological families.

Among cases considered in this study, *In re Juvenile Appeal*[283] contains the strongest statement of constitutional protections against unwarranted removals of children from their biological homes. The case involved a family supported by public assistance and under the

---

[279] *See id.* at 356–57, 397 A.2d at 243 (citing *In re* Adoption of J.S.R., 374 A.2d 860 (D.C. 1977); *In re* Adoption of Tachick, 60 Wis. 2d 540, 210 N.W.2d 865 (1973)).

[280] *Id.* at 358, 397 A.2d at 244. In support of this conclusion, the court cited the views of Dr. Andrew Watson, psychiatrist and professor of law, Dr. Herbert Modlin of the Menninger Foundation, an article from legal literature written by a psychiatrist and a general family law treatise. *Id.* at 358 n.3, 397 A.2d at 244 n.3. The court did not provide the sources of the quotations from Drs. Watson and Modlin. The remaining citations were to H. CLARK, LAW OF DOMESTIC RELATIONS IN THE UNITED STATES 326 (1968) and Plant, *The Psychiatrist Views Children of Divorced Parents*, 10 LAW & CONTEM. PROBS. 807 (1944).

[281] As reliance upon psychological parent principles increased, it became increasingly likely that rights of custody or guardianship would be terminated without evidence of clear parental misconduct or deliberate abrogation of parental responsibility. Biological parents therefore complained that the standards to which they must adhere in order to preserve rights to custody and guardianship were unconstitutionally vague. In this context, too, the work of Goldstein, Freud and Solnit was part of the justification for state assertions of authority. This phenomenon is illustrated by *In re* J.O.L. II, 409 A.2d 1073, 1075 (D.C. 1979), *cert. granted*, 449 U.S. 818, *vacated*, 449 U.S. 989 (1980), *cert. denied*, 454 U.S. 832 (1981); *In re* Adoption of J.S.R., 374 A.2d 860, 862–63 (D.C. 1977); *In re* William L., 477 Pa. 322, 329–32, 383 A.2d 1228, 1231–33 (1978), *cert. denied* 439 U.S. 880 (1978); *In re* Aschauer, 93 Wash. 2d 689, 695–96, 611 P.2d 1245, 1249–50 (1980) (en banc). In *J.S.R.* and *William L.* the court also considered and rejected claims that substantive due process rights had been denied by the decision below.

[282] *See supra* p. 1580.

[283] 189 Conn. 276, 455 A.2d 1313 (1983).

supervision of a protective service worker who "considered the family situation 'marginal,' but noted that the [six] children were 'not abused [or] neglected'" and expressed the opinion "that the children were very happy and active, and that they had a 'very warm' relationship with their mother."[284] When an infant child of the family died of unexplained causes, the surviving children were placed in protective custody.[285] Neglect petitions were filed and hearings ensued to determine the appropriateness of continued orders of temporary foster care.[286] Three years and five months later, the Connecticut Supreme Court set aside the temporary custody orders, finding that "no substantial showing" had been made "that the . . . children were suffering from either serious physical illness or serious physical injury, or that they would be in immediate physical danger if they were returned to the defendant's home."[287]

The biological mother's victory was not total. Her constitutional challenge of the temporary commitment statute failed because the court interpreted that statute to require a more substantial showing of exigency than had been made or required below.[288] The court also rejected the mother's claim that the constitutionally appropriate burden of proof in cases of this kind was clear and convincing evidence rather than a fair preponderance of the evidence.[289] It did hold, however, that the fundamental character of the right at stake warranted placing upon the state the burden of establishing a need for placement.[290] In determining the constitutional issues, the court adhered to the requirements of a compelling state interest to which the state's means are narrowly tailored.[291] In announcing its adherence to this principle, the court referenced works of Goldstein, Freud and Solnit, a separate work by Goldstein, and other legal literature, noting that "[e]ven where the parent-child relationship is 'marginal,' it is usually in the best interests of the child to remain at home and still benefit from a family environment."[292]

---

[284] *Id.* at 278, 455 A.2d at 1315 (quoting testimony of caseworker).

[285] *See id.* at 279, 455 A.2d at 1315.

[286] *See id.* at 280–81, 455 A.2d at 1316–17. These neglect petitions:

> alleged, in addition to [the] unexplained death, that the defendant's apartment was dirty, that numerous roaches could be found there, that beer cans were to be found in the apartment, . . . that on one occasion the defendant may have been drunk, that a neighbor reported that the children once had been left alone all night, and that the two older children had occasionally come to school without having eaten breakfast.

Id. Nevertheless, the court stated that the "medical evidence at the hearing indicated no connection between [the infant's] death and either the defendant or the conditions in her home." *Id.* at 290, 455 A.2d at 1321.

[287] *Id.* at 289–90, 455 A.2d at 1321.

[288] *See id.* at 289, 455 A.2d at 1320.

[289] *See id.* at 296, 455 A.2d at 1323.

[290] *See id.* at 295, 455 A.2d at 1323.

[291] *See id.* at 285, 455 A.2d at 1318.

[292] *Id.* at 286, 455 A.2d at 1319. In addition to the Goldstein, Freud and Solnit works, the

Two other cases, *State ex rel. Human Services Department v. Staples* and *In re Juvenile Appeal*, stand virtually alone among the cases reviewed in concluding that encroachments upon family autonomy were constitutionally impermissible in the context of foster care or termination of parental rights.[293] In a third case, however, psychological parent principles led to an expansion of family autonomy rights in a different context. *Franz v. United States*[294] raised the question whether the relocation of three children by the federal witness protection program violated the constitutional rights of the children and their noncustodial biological father by denying the father the right to visit with and know the whereabouts of his children.[295] In confronting the preliminary question whether the right to preserve a noncustodial parent/child relationship was fundamental, the D.C. Circuit Court of Appeals found no controlling case law.[296] To "explore the concerns that underlie the constitutional protection traditionally accorded parental and filial bonds,"[297] the court therefore turned not only to constitutional jurisprudence but also to the literature of social theory and the social sciences. In support of the proposition that a child's "right to protection from interference in the [parent/child] relationship derives from the psychic importance to him of being raised by a loving, responsive, reliable adult,"[298] the court cited case law, legal commentary, and *Beyond the Best Interests of the Child*.[299] In asserting the importance of relationships between children and biological parents with whom they do not reside, the court, relying upon social science research concerning children of divorce, found "considerable evidence that the emotional stability of children of divorced parents is often tied to the quality of their continuing relationships with their non-custodial parent."[300] These factors contributed to the

---

court cited Goldstein, *Medical Care for the Child at Risk: On State Supervision of Parental Autonomy*, 86 YALE L.J. 645, 649 (1977); Wald, *State Intervention on Behalf of 'Neglected' Children: Standards for Removal of Children from Their Homes, Monitorinq the Status of Children in Foster Care, and Termination of Parental Riqhts*, 28 STAN. L. REV. 623 (1976), and Wald, *Thinking About Public Policy Toward Abuse and Neglect of Children: A Review of Before the Best Interests of the Child*, 78 MICH. L. REV. 645, 662 (1980).

[293] State *ex rel.* Human Services Department v. Staples (*In re* Doe) (Ct. App. 1982), *rev'd, dissenting opinion adopted and reprinted in* 100 N.M. 92, 93–97, 666 P.2d 771, 772–76 (1983), discussed *supra* pp. 1576–77, invalidated a termination of parental rights statute on the ground of unconstitutional vagueness. *Cf.* Custody of a Minor (No. 1), 377 Mass. 876, 882–86, 389 N.E.2d 68, 73–75 (1979) (citing BEYOND THE BEST INTERESTS OF THE CHILD for the proposition that "the interest of the child is thought to be best served in the stable, continuous environment of his own family," but holding that the procedures at issue did not violate the constitutional rights of biological families).

[294] 707 F.2d 582 (D.C. Cir. 1983).

[295] *See id.* at 585.

[296] *See id.* at 597.

[297] *Id.*

[298] *Id.* at 599.

[299] *See id.* at 599 n.73.

[300] *Id.* at 601.

court's conclusion that the plaintiffs' rights to maintain a noncustodial parent/child relationship were "roughly comparable to the interests of a parent and child in a viable nuclear family."[301] It followed that the government could justify its action only by a showing that it furthered a compelling interest by the least restrictive means available and that appropriate procedural protections had been taken.[302]

Since *Franz* involved an appeal from a pretrial dismissal, the court of appeals was unable to refer to expert or other trial evidence. The court's use of legal and social science literature, however, was extensive, and consistent with its articulated view that constitutional adjudication appropriately involves, at the frontiers of establishment of individual rights, attention to social "facts."[303]

3. Assessing Constitutional Claims Premised Exclusively Upon the Psychological Parent Relationship: Psychological Parent Theory in a Fair Fight. — The most radical argument for incorporating psychological parent principles into legal doctrine is that the "psychological family" deserves some or all of the constitutional protection traditionally afforded to the biological family. This argument was considered in four of the cases under review, the most significant of which was *Smith v. Organization of Foster Families for Equality & Reform (OFFER),*[304] in which foster parents in the state of New York sought additional procedural safeguards against removal or reassignment of children for whom they had cared for a year or more. Analysis of *OFFER* supports the hypothesis that litigation imbalances facilitate judicial lawmaking responsive to psychological parent theories urged by the stronger side.

OFFER was assertively litigated by all sides. Although the issues raised in the case put the interests of biological and psychological parents in conflict, they did not pit the state against biological parents. After hearing both the strengths and the weaknesses of psychological parent theory, the Supreme Court declined the invitation to use the theory as a basis for recognizing a new sphere of psychological family rights. The Court's opinion supports the conclusion, drawn from the common law and statutory cases reviewed above, that legislative facts influence judicial decisionmaking even when the Court denies their impact. The *OFFER* plaintiffs' "basic contention . . . [was] that when a child has lived in a foster home for a year or more, a psychological tie is created between the child and the foster parents which consti-

---

301 *Id.* at 602. The court later rooted this interest constitutionally by "finding that the plaintiffs' stake in one another's companionship must be deemed a 'fundamental liberty interest.'" *Id.* at 603.

302 *See id.* at 602.

303 *See id.* at 599 n.72. It is not possible to determine from the court's opinion whether this review was undertaken by the court independently or with the participation of the parties.

304 431 U.S. 816 (1977).

tutes the foster family the true 'psychological family' of the child."[305] Relying heavily upon *Beyond the Best Interests of the Child,* the plaintiffs argued that this psychological unit "has a [fourteenth amendment] 'liberty interest' in . . . survival as a family."[306] Justice Stewart, joined in concurrence by Chief Justice Burger and Justice Rehnquist, disagreed, writing that "the interests asserted by . . . [the foster parents] are not of a kind that the Due Process Clause of the Fourteenth Amendment protects."[307] The majority held that the challenged procedures violated no due process rights, but treated the unusual and difficult questions of the constitutional rights of the foster parents more gingerly. The Court acknowledged that the Constitution protects liberty interests arising out of nonbiological family relationships, such as marriage,[308] but held that the foster parent relationship gives rise only to limited entitlements. The Court reasoned that the foster parent relationship, as designed by the state, furthers a legitimate purpose — provision of temporary foster care — in a manner that limits the reasonable expectations of the foster parent.[309] It observed that any liberty interest that might result from the fostering relationship "must be substantially attenuated" if it conflicts with liberty interests of the biological family.[310] With respect to the psychological issues, the Court said:

> The briefs dispute at some length the validity of the "psychological parent" theory propounded in . . . Beyond the Best Interests of the Child. . . . *That book* on which appellee foster parents relied to some extent in the District Court, *is indeed controversial*. . . . But this case turns, not on the disputed validity of any particular psychological theory, but on the legal consequences of the undisputed fact that the emotional ties between foster parent and foster child are in many cases quite close, and undoubtedly in some as close as those existing in biological families.[311]

This denigration of the issue is not entirely convincing. It begs the question whether state prerogatives and the liberty interests of biological families might be trumped if it were established that a transfer of custody would seriously and permanently harm the child. Such a demonstration by the plaintiffs might well have led the Court to define the liberty interest in maintaining the biological family more narrowly and to hold that the state has a duty to protect more fully against harm to the child. If this is so, then much turned upon the Court's

[305] *Id.* at 839.
[306] *Id.*
[307] *Id.* at 858 (Stewart, J., concurring).
[308] *See* 431 U.S. at 843–44.
[309] *See id.* at 845–46.
[310] *Id.* at 846–47.
[311] *Id.* at 844 n.52 (emphasis added).

judgment that the views of Goldstein, Freud and Solnit are "controversial." The process by which the Court made this judgment therefore deserves attention.

The Court described the debate over psychological parent theory as having been carried out in the briefs on"the parties.[312] All parties were strongly represented in the Supreme Court and at trial,[313] and the debate over psychology was fought to a draw at each level.[314] In addition to thorough Brandeis briefs of the psychological literature, the parties provided the trial court with affidavits of eminent experts both supporting and attacking psychological parent theory. Moreover, in the Supreme Court, amici on each side briefed the psychological issues from the perspective of various disciplines and interest groups.[315]

Although both the trial and the appellate benches sidestepped the psychological issue,[316] the trial panel found a constitutional basis for enhancing procedural protections against "the trauma of separation,"[317] while the Supreme Court found the State's procedures adequate.[318] The difference may be attributed not only to the Supreme Court's greater skepticism concerning psychological parent theory, but also to changes in the circumstances of the named plaintiffs during the course of appellate proceedings. The district court confronted three ongoing foster families, each threatened with or having recently experienced interruption of a long-term fostering relationship.[319] The plaintiffs' claim was premised upon a prediction that safeguarding the foster family unit was necessary to the children's emotional health. At the Supreme Court, however, this premise had been undercut with respect to two of the three named plaintiffs: one set of foster children had been reunited with the biological mother and was reported to be adjusting successfully, and another foster family had been disrupted by the separation of the foster parents.[320]

---

[312] *See id.* at 844 n.52.

[313] *See* Chambers & Wald, Smith v. OFFER, in IN THE INTEREST OF CHILDREN 67 (R. Mnookin ed. 1985).

[314] *See OFFER*, 431 U.S. at 844 n.52; OFFER, 418 F. Supp. 277, 282 (S.D.N.Y. 1976).

[315] *See* 431 U.S. at 818.

[316] *See id.* at 844 n.52; ***Dumpson***, 418 F. Supp. at 282.

[317] 418 F. Supp. at 283. The court acted not on the basis of a privacy interest inhering in the foster family, but rather on the ground that the children had a constitutional right to a full hearing before being subjected to a "grievous loss." *Id.* at 282 (quoting Joint Anti-Fascist Comm. v. McGrath, 341 U.S. 123, 168 (1951) (Frankfurter, J., concurring)).

Other courts have also explored the possibility that the constitutional rights of children embrace rights of continued association with psychological parents. *See, e.g., In re* Roy, 90 Misc. 2d 35, 393 N.Y.S.2d 515 (Fam. Ct. 1977); *In re* Jennifer "S," 69 Misc. 2d 942, 330 N.Y.S.2d 872 (Surrogate's Ct. 1972).

[318] *See OFFER*, 431 U.S. at 847.

[319] *See* ***Dumpson***, 418 F. Supp. at 280.

[320] *See OFFER*, 431 U.S. at 819 n.1. The child of the disrupted foster family had been

The Supreme Court also seems to have been influenced by its skepticism concerning broader social issues. The Court reviewed competing descriptions by litigants and amici of the foster care system as well as descriptions contained in "empirical criticism of the system presented in the record of this case and confirmed by published studies of foster care."[321] One group saw the system as "a class-based intrusion into the family life of the poor";[322] others saw it as a de facto system of long-term care made ineffective by a pretense that care was inevitably temporary.[323] The State of New York, meanwhile, asserted that the system worked reasonably to provide temporary care "'intended to lead to the future reunion of the child with his natural parent or parents, or if such a reunion is not possible, to legal adoption and the establishment of a new permanent home for the child.'"[324] In language that reflects an awareness of the limitations of factfinding within the litigation model, the Court concluded that while "there are elements of truth in both pictures . . . neither represents the whole truth about the system."[325] After having devoted six pages to a review of various proffered characterizations of the system,[326] the Court suggested that the inquiry had been irrelevant.[327]

In this regard, as with the Court's treatment of psychological parent theory, it appears significant that the parties litigated the empirical issues to a draw of sorts; yet it is wrong to suggest that the struggle over those issues was irrelevant to the outcome. Had the Court been convinced that foster care agencies systematically undermine the rights of biological parents, it might have accepted the concurring justices' view that recognition of a liberty interest in the preservation of the foster family should be denied outright.[328] On the

---

placed in a residential treatment center. He was visited by the foster father but not by the foster mother, who had left the home, taking her biological child but leaving the foster child. *See id.*

[321] *Id.* at 833.

[322] *Id.*

[323] *See id.* at 835–38.

[324] *Id.* at 833 (quoting Brief for Appellants at 3, Smith v. OFFER, 431 U.S. 816 (1977) (No. 76-180)).

[325] *Id.* at 838 n.41.

[326] *See id.* at 833–38.

[327] The Court stated that:

> The parties and *amici* devote much of their discussion to these criticisms of foster care, and we present this summary in the view that some understanding of those criticisms is necessary for a full appreciation of the complex and controversial system with which this lawsuit is concerned. But the issue presented by the case is a narrow one. Arguments asserting the need for reform of New York's statutory scheme are properly addressed to the New York Legislature. The relief sought in this case is entirely procedural. Our task is only to determine whether the District Court correctly held that the present procedures preceding the removal from a foster home of children resident there a year or more are constitutionally inadequate.

Id. at 838 (footnotes omitted).

[328] *See supra* p. 1589.

other hand, had it been convinced that the overwhelming majority of foster children suffer severe and lasting emotional harm as a result of arbitrary transfers among foster homes and from foster care to detrimental biological family environments, it might well have accorded constitutional protection to the foster family unit.

As Kenneth Culp Davis reminds us, perceptions about social facts regularly tip the balance between competing constitutional rights or affect the definition of legitimate state interests and individual rights.[329] To borrow one of Professor Davis' examples, if a "generally black picture of police conduct"[330] contributed substantially to the *Miranda* articulation of fifth amendment rights,[331] a convincing picture of the foster care system as exploiting biological family rights, or destroying the potential for healthy development of children in care, might have affected the definition of rights of family integrity and autonomy. The *OFFER* litigation illustrates the irony of legislative factfinding: although assertive litigation of legislative facts is commonly outcome determinative, forthright judicial consideration of legislative facts is consistently avoided, even in the most sophisticated forums.[332]

---

[329] *See* Davis, *Facts in Lawmaking*, 80 COLUM. L. REV. 931, 933–35 (1980). Professor Davis argued, for example, that a determination that "'a positive correlation exists between group size and the quality of both group performance and group productivity'" was crucial to adjudication of the constitutionality of the five-person jury, *id.* at 934–45 (quoting Ballew v. Georgia, 435 U.S. 223, 232–33 (1978)); that findings regarding prevailing police practices were crucial to the definition of detainee rights in Miranda v. Arizona, 384 U.S. 436 (1966), *see* Davis, *supra*, at 935; and that the decisions in Paris Adult Theatre I v. Slaton, 413 U.S. 49 (1973), and Carey v. Population Servs. Int'l, 431 U.S. 678 (1977), were driven by evidence concerning the relationship between pornography and unlawful behavior and the relationship between the availability of contraceptives and early sexual behavior, respectively, *see* Davis, *supra*, at 938–39.

Davis also argued that Caban v. Mohammed, 441 U.S. 380 (1979), which struck down legislation that permitted the termination of the parental rights of fathers, but not of mothers, without a showing of unfitness, rested on the "factual impression" that "mothers and fathers of illegitimate children do not significantly differ from each other in their relationships with and attitudes toward their children." Davis, *supra*, at 933. This argument raises the question whether the values of individualized decisionmaking and the avoidance of sexual stereotypes and role regulation would have supported the decision regardless of general facts concerning the relationships between mothers and fathers and their children.

[330] Miranda v. Arizona, 384 U.S. 436, 515 (1966) (Harlan, J., dissenting).

[331] *See* Davis, *supra* note 329, at 935.

[332] Because the *OFFER* decision came at a time when the use of psychological parent theory to modify legal rules was in a relatively early stage, it may have inhibited litigation of the constitutional status of psychological families in other courts and the publication of detailed opinions concerning the creation of constitutional rights based upon psychological family relationships. The highest courts of two states addressed the issue, however. *See* Eason v. Welfare Comm'r, 171 Conn. 630, 637, 370 A.2d 1082, 1086 (1976), *cert. denied sub nom.* Easey v. Mohoney, 432 U.S. 907 (1977) (rejecting a constitutional claim comparable to that subsequently asserted by the *OFFER* plaintiffs); *In re* E.G. & K.B., 268 N.W.2d 420, 422 (Minn. 1978) (relying upon the reasoning of *OFFER* to decide, at the urging of a biological mother and the Minnesota Chippewa Tribe as amicus curiae, that a foster parent had no constitutional right to

IV. The Processes of Absorption and Evaluation

Professor E.F. Roberts has said that "judicial notice is the art of thinking as practiced within the legal system."[333] Roberts recommended study of the decisions of a single state court over time "to render articulate the thinking processes inherent in its decisions."[334] This Article takes a more modest approach, with a similar, albeit narrower, goal. It follows the trail of judges who have revealed, through some explicit reference, that a particular theory figured in their deliberations. In doing so, it attempts to discover how and what they learned about the theory and how the theory influenced the outcomes of cases and the development of precedent.

Psychological parent theory is complex and richly illuminating. Its presentation in legal circles has brought attention to important factors that had previously been ignored or undervalued in child placement decisionmaking. Cautious judicial use of the theory is to be applauded.[335] But the uses uncovered by this study were often incautious. Courts have frequently accepted the theory on the basis of one-sided presentations,[336] rendering case-specific results of its acceptance questionable.[337] Developments in the law based upon psychological parent theories have been far reaching, yet they too have resulted from one-sided deliberations. Moreover, they have resulted from deliberations in which the evolution of law was denied. In so easily accepting psychological parent theory while disregarding competing theories and the consequences of doctrinal evolution, courts have altered common law rules,[338] ignored or transformed statutory language,[339] given constitutional sanction to significant state incursions upon family autonomy, and diluted constitutional standards of scrutiny with respect to rights of biological family autonomy.[340] At the

---

intervene in a neglect proceeding in which the mother sought clarification of visitation rights and ultimate return of the child). In a third case, *In re* Adoption of Alex J. McFadyen III., 108 Ill. App. 3d 329, 438 N.E.2d 1362 (1982), it was claimed that constitutional rights of family autonomy inhered in the psychological and social relationship between a man and his wife's child, who was the product of artificial insemination. *Id.* at 332, 438 N.E.2d at 1364. The constitutional claim was held to have been waived. *See id.* at 338, 438 N.E.2d at 1368.

333 Roberts, *Preliminary Notes Toward a Study of Judicial Notice*, 52 Cornell L. Q. 210, 236 (1967) (emphasis omitted); *cf.* J. Thayer, A Preliminary Treatise on Evidence at the Common Law 279 (1898) ("The subject of judicial notice . . . belongs to the general topic of legal or judicial reasoning. It is, indeed, woven into the very texture of the judicial function.").

334 Roberts, *supra* note 333, at 238.

335 For an example of cautious use of the information and theories offered by Goldstein, Freud and Solnit, see *supra* p. 1558.

336 *See supra* p. 1552 & n.55.

337 *See, e.g., supra* pp. 1552–53, 1581–82.

338 *See supra* pp. 1563–69.

339 *See supra* pp. 1561–62, 1570–73.

340 *See supra* pp. 1580–85.

same time, full implementation of *legislated* responses to psychological parent theory has been delayed by judicial rejection or misunderstanding of the theories.[341] The sweeping effects of the various judicial reactions to this single theory raise grave questions about how judges absorb and evaluate social science theories.

A. The Process of Absorption

1. Screening Expert Evidence: An Overlooked Opportunity. — Courts often screen scientific evidence, allowing consideration only of evidence "deduced from a well-recognized scientific principle"[342] or, in the case of more novel scientific evidence, deduced from a principle "sufficiently established to have gained general acceptance in the particular field in which it belongs."[343] In none of the opinions reviewed for this study did a court screen expert testimony that presented, or was based upon, psychological parent theory to determine whether it is generally accepted within the disciplines of psychiatry and psychology. This is not surprising. It has been persuasively argued that broad use of the general acceptance test imposes unnecessarily "drastic constraints on the admissibility of scientific evidence."[344] Moreover, courts commonly apply the general acceptance test only to theories and methods that lead to empirical conclusions in the physical sciences, not to theories, like psychological parent theory, that are used to interpret or predict behavior.[345] Subjecting psychological parent theory to a general acceptance analysis would, however, educate courts about the theory's limitations and thereby provide a safeguard against overreliance.[346]

Some scholars[347] have pointed out that courts may obtain many of the benefits of the general acceptance test by applying rules of evidence (often characterized, somewhat misleadingly, as "relevance rules") that require courts to determine whether proffered evidence would be helpful to the trier of fact[348] or prejudicial.[349] In the course

---

341 *See supra* pp. 1575–79.

342 Frye v. United States, 293 F.2d 1013, 1014 (D.C. Cir. 1923).

343 *Id.*

344 E. CLEARY, *supra* note 1, § 203, at 608.

345 The general acceptance test has, however, been debated and sometimes applied with respect to rape trauma and battered wife and premenstrual syndromes. *See, e.g.*, *In re* Irvin, 31 Bankr. 251, 261 (1983) (rejecting premenstrual syndrome as a defense).

346 It is also possible that aspects of psychological parent theory would not survive a general acceptance test. Goldstein, Freud and Solnit themselves have characterized their position on parental visitation as "controversial" and "resisted" in a passage that references both legal and social science literature. BEYOND THE BEST INTERESTS OF THE CHILD, *supra* note 17, at 116.

347 *See, e.g.*, McCormick, *Scientific Evidence: Defining a New Approach to Admissibility*, 67 IOWA L. REV. 879 (1982).

348 *See, e.g.*, FED. R. EVID. 702.

349 *See, e.g.*, FED. R. EVID. 403.

of such a "relevance rules" inquiry, a court would consider whether psychological parent theory, for example, is commonly accepted within relevant disciplines. But the focus of a "relevance rules" inquiry is broader. It also involves consideration of (1) the universality of the theory (Do *all* children enjoy constructive bonds with custodians of a year or more?); (2) the extent to which the theory obscures important variables (Does it apply to a child of fourteen who spent ten years in a healthy custodial relationship followed by four years with a less responsive and nurturing caretaker?); (3) the extent to which the theory diverts attention from the unique characteristics of the parties before the court (Will a judge or jury see the strength and value of older ties or the deficiencies of the present caretaker after a solemn, expert formula has been offered?); and (4) the availability of a pool of experts from whom analyses of the theory might be elicited (Do experts able to put the evidence in perspective and avoid its overvaluation exist, and does the opposing party have the resources to produce them?).[350] Formal consideration of the helpfulness of psychological parent evidence and the risk of prejudicial impact upon the trier of fact would enhance the likelihood of a balanced presentation of case-specific, expert evidence. Balanced presentations of case-specific evidence would, in turn, facilitate balanced consideration of psychological parent theory as legislative fact.

2. *Controlling Resort to Extra-Record Sources: An Opportunity Mishandled.* — Psychological parent theory reached the courts through both expert testimony and social science and legal literature. Discussions of the appropriateness of judicial resort to extra-record literature exist within the body of cases considered for this study, but they are few, and they are brief. Moreover, they inevitably adopt one of two equally unsatisfactory extremes. Courts that acknowledge the value of judicial resort to extra-record literature fail to appreciate the need to regulate the process. Conversely, courts that appreciate the risks inherent in unregulated, extra-record legislative fact-gathering fail to appreciate the value and the inevitability of the process. They therefore impose controls so rigid that open use of extra-record information is precluded.

Ross v. Hoffman[351] illustrates both the haphazard way in which extra-record literature infects judicial decisionmaking and the reluctance of judges to control the process. The trial judge's deliberations proceeded as follows:

---

[350] On the question of resources, "the trial court's authority to call experts of its own choosing might . . . come into play." McCormick, *supra* note 347, at 911; *cf.* FED. R. EVID. 706. For a detailed argument that this kind of analysis adequately assures that new scientific techniques will be used cautiously and effectively in litigation, see McCormick, note 347 above, at 908–15.

[351] 33 Md. App. 333, 364 A.2d 596 (1976), *aff'd as modified* 280 Md. 172, 372 A.2d 582 (1977).

> After reviewing the evidence adduced by the parties, the chancellor [who had decided this custody matter below] explained that his reasoning had, to some extent, been influenced by certain educational background factors to which he had been exposed extra-judicially, as that term applies to the evidentiary confines of this case. He said:
>
> > "Now, very briefly, there is a book out, which is widely read, by three very well respected professional doctors, Drs. Goldstein, Freud and Solnick [sic], called 'Beyond the Best Interests of the Child' and in that book they point out that whether any adult becomes a psychological parent over the child is based upon a day-to-day interaction, companionship and shared experiences. And if you look at it from that view, Mrs. Hoffman has had this advantage."[352]

On appeal, Ross complained about the chancellor's reliance upon psychological parent theory, arguing that she had had no notice that the theory was at issue and no opportunity to refute it.[353] Intermediate and ultimate appellate courts both dismissed her protest. These courts found "no error in the fact that a trial judge continues his general education by reading, or that his reasoning is influenced by such education or by his experiences during his lifetime."[354]

In two of the remaining three cases discussing judicial absorption of extra-record literature, courts disapproved of the process in terms that suggest rigid adherence to the rules applicable to judicial notice of adjudicative facts.[355] The Supreme Court of Vermont held that a

---

[352] 33 Md. App. at 336–37, 364 A.2d at 599. The chancellor had also heard expert testimony that supported an award of custody to Ross, partly on a theory of bonding.

[353] *See id.* at 338, 364 A.2d at 600.

[354] *Id.* ("To expect either judge or juror to erase from memory all that he has read or experienced, not specifically related to the facts of a case, before deciding a case is an absurdity so apparent as to deserve no rebuttal . . . . [W]e commend . . . [the chancellor] both for recognizing and expressing that which helped him to decide.").

[355] In a third case, questionable use was made of the California Evidence Code provision that a court may take judicial notice of "[f]acts and propositions that are of such common knowledge within the territorial jurisdiction of the court that they cannot reasonably be the subject of dispute" or "are not reasonably subject to dispute and are capable of immediate and accurate determination by resort to sources of reasonably indisputable accuracy." CAL. EVID. CODE § 452(g), (h) (West 1966). In determining whether to take judicial notice, a court may consult "[a]ny source of pertinent information, including the advice of persons learned in the subject matter . . ., whether or not furnished by a party." *Id.* § 454(a)(1). When a California trial court denied an adoption petition solely because the applicants, who were long-term custodians, were elderly, an appellate court reversed, relying upon these provisions to take "judicial notice of a recent authoritative work on child placement . . . . 'Beyond the Best Interests of the Child' by Goldstein, Freud & Solnit" which concluded that "changes or interruptions in . . . [a custodial] relationship cause the child to regress 'along the whole line of his affections, skills, achievements, and social adaptation.'" Ralph Edward B. v. State Dep't of Health (*In re* Adoption of Michelle Lee T.), 44 Cal. App. 3d 699, 706, 117 Cal. Rptr. 856, 859–60 (1975) (citations omitted). The question whether this conclusion is "reasonably subject to dispute" was not discussed.

trial court's reliance upon extra-judicial presentations of the psychological parent theory constituted reversible error:

> In its findings of facts and conclusions of law, the court relied heavily on a child psychology treatise, quoting from it extensively. This treatise was not introduced into evidence, nor otherwise made a part of the record . . . . The parties . . . were denied the opportunity for cross-examination, rebuttal, or the introduction of further testimony, particularly relative to the conclusion that the appellant was no longer the psychological parent of her children, and . . . such is error.[356]

A Tennessee court ruled similarly in *Finney v. Finney*[357]:

> The Trial Judge based his custody award, at least in part, on the fact that "all of the studies that I have seen indicate that for a child this young, . . . [it] can be very harmful . . . for the custody to be changed [and for] the psychological parent not to continue to have the child. . . ." We have searched this record and our search fails to disclose any such psychological data or studies. Psychological data or studies referred to by the Trial Judge are not such facts as may be judicially noticed. . . . The Trial Court's judgment must be based on evidence in the record or on matters of which judicial notice can be taken.[358]

When we consider the chancellor in *Ross* who admitted his reliance on "a book out . . . by three very well respected professional doctors,"[359] we might conclude that he did no more than to rely inevitably upon what he knew to decide the case at hand, understanding that "no judge or administrator can possibly think about any question of fact, law, policy or discretion without using extrarecord facts."[360] But extra-record facts are not equal. Some, like the definition of the word "the,"[361] are inevitable to human intercourse and uncontroversial. Their acceptance warrants neither regulation nor concern. The same cannot be said when a judge accepts a background fact that is articulable, disputable, and important to the resolution of a central issue of the litigation. Judicial absorption of background facts of this kind should be controlled. The Vermont and Tennessee appellate courts have imposed controls, but do not distinguish among legislative, background and adjudicative factfinding. Consequently, their controls are inadequate to any but the adjudicative context. To say that "[t]he

[356] *In re* J., 134 Vt. 480, 481, 365 A.2d 521, 522 (1976).

[357] 619 S.W.2d 130 (Tenn. Ct. App. 1981), *modified on unrelated grounds sub nom.* State v. Hamilton, 688 S.W.2d 821 (Tenn. 1985).

[358] 619 S.W.2d at 133–34 (citations omitted).

[359] Ross v. Hoffman, 33 Md. App. 333, 336, 364 A.2d 596, 599 (1976), *aff'd*, 280 Md. 172, 372 A.2d 582 (1977).

[360] K. DAVIS, *supra* note 4, § 15:1, at 133.

[361] *See* Davis, *A System of Judicial Notice Based on Fairness and Convenience*, in PERSPECTIVES OF LAW 69, 73–74 (1964).

Trial Court's judgment must be based on evidence in the record or on matters of which judicial notice can be taken"[362] is to state a truism with respect to most adjudicative facts. But all legislative facts, and many background facts, depend upon extra-record sources and are properly determined without the requirement of indisputability that the Tennessee court apparently thought a prerequisite to judicial notice.[363]

It is unwise either to leave judges "unrestricted" in the investigation and determination of legislative and background facts[364] or to impose upon those processes the restraints that apply to judicial notice of ordinary, adjudicative facts. This study provides the bearings by which to chart a middle course. Techniques are required for evaluation of propositions that inform judicial deliberations concerning questions of law or serve as background for resolution of adjudicative facts. Regular application of these techniques is the means to develop a tradition of care with respect to heretofore unregulated aspects of judicial notice.

B. Techniques of Evaluation

1. Seeking Out Both Sides. — Critical evaluation of psychological parent theory was more likely when both sides of the question were presented by the parties. When it becomes clear that disputable background or legislative facts will be important to the outcome of litigation, judges should encourage the parties to participate in consideration of those facts. *Bulova Watch Co. v. Hattori & Co.*[365] provides a model of this kind of judicial behavior. But the results of this study and the dearth of judicial opinions addressing legislative factfinding indicate that this model is not the norm.

In *Bulova Watch*, the court relied heavily on its own research into the history and structure of multinational corporations in general and Japanese multinationals in particular.[366] The court did not, however, exclude the parties from its investigative and decisionmaking process. The opinion cautioned that "[t]here is always a danger in the superficial sociological musings of lawyers and judges," but recognized that "resort to less well known and accepted sources of data . . . for *legislative and general evidential hypothesis purposes* must be accepted because it is essential to the judicial process." In anticipation of the issuance of a judgment dependent on "extensive judicial notice . . .

---

[362] *Finney*, 619 S.W.2d at 134 (citation omitted).

[363] *See supra* pp. 1540–41, 1548. *Adoption of Michelle Lee T.*, discussed in note 355 above, provides evidence that the need to notice disputable adjudicative and background facts will lead to distortion of the disputability rule.

[364] *See supra* p. 1541.

[365] 508 F. Supp. 1322 (E.D.N.Y. 1981).

[366] *See id.* at 1335–40.

based partly upon the court's own research," the judge "invited the parties to be heard on the 'propriety of taking judicial notice and the tenor of the matter noticed.'" Surely, as the court observed, this procedure "has the advantage of reducing the possibility of egregious errors by the court and increases the probability that the parties may believe they were fairly treated."[367] At the same time, the procedure is grounded in a sophisticated understanding of the nature of legislative and background facts and therefore avoids the error of imposing procedural strictures that are appropriate only to adjudicative fact-finding. It does not require that information concerning legislative or background facts be placed in evidence, and it clearly recognizes that courts may properly notice disputable facts "for legislative [purposes] and [as] general evidential hypothes[es]."[368]

Litigation imbalances affect the evaluation of psychological parent theory whether the facts in dispute are regarded as adjudicative and litigated through expert testimony,[369] or as legislative and decided by some sort of judicial notice.[370] In the cases reviewed for this study, courts gave the theory more careful consideration when litigation resources were balanced, or judges were sensitive to litigation imbalances and willing to correct for them.[371] The process of seeking out both sides requires that courts be both sensitive to any resource disparity that impairs the ability of a party effectively to litigate legislative and background facts and willing to protect against the disparity's prejudicial impact.

Although use of the techniques and screening devices described above should assure care and equity vis-a-vis the parties in the investigation and determination of background facts, additional measures are required when questions of legislative fact are at issue. In the latter context, appreciation of both sides of the issue may require an inquiry that extends beyond the rights and interests of the parties. When judges determine legislative facts, they develop principles that have significance for non-parties. Such judicial lawmaking is neither wrong nor avoidable,[372] but its proper execution requires a factfinding

---

[367] *Id.* at 1322, 1328–29; *accord* 1 WEINSTEIN'S EVIDENCE, *supra* note 10, at ¶ 201[05].

[368] 508 F. Supp. at 1328.

[369] *See supra* pp. 1552–59.

[370] *See supra* pp. 1580–85.

[371] *See supra* pp. 1553–58.

[372]

> [W]hether or not a type of legislation which would eliminate the need for judicial lawmaking is desirable or possible, precious little of such legislation is to be found on the books today. On the contrary, the weight of the traditional common law ideology, and the techniques of American political and legislative machinery, have joined forces to multiply the instances wherein legislators give judges no better guidance than adjectives such as "just," "reasonable," "fair," "convenient," "adequate" or "proper." And the greater the strategic value of a given provision, the greater the likelihood that the legislative

process structured to facilitate consideration of points of view that the litigants may not adequately represent. Informed legislative factfinding may require assignment of experts answerable only to the court,[373] solicitation of amicus curiae briefs from non-party individuals or organizations likely to be affected by the precedent being developed, or appointment of experts or counsel assigned to represent issues rather than individuals.[374]

2. *Owning Up to the Legislative Function.* — Careful legislative factfinding requires the application of two additional techniques unrelated to assurance of equity between the parties. The first is simple acknowledgement of the legislative functions of judges. To a striking extent, courts that were clearly engaged in changing law insisted that they were merely applying established law, and courts confronted with social facts bearing upon choices among competing legal theories insisted that those facts were irrelevant to the "legal" issue at hand.[375]

This is not a new story. Consider a twenty-five-year-old version: "[a]ppellate lawmaking . . . is still typically covert and indirective, still half-apologetic and guilt-laden."[376] "Even today 'when a judge invents his own law and concocts his version of the facts, he will not fail to profess obedience to the accepted tradition.' He still purports to be finding the very law which he has himself laboriously rebraided."[377] The conclusion has not changed. So long as courts deny they are making law, they "perpetuate . . . confusion and becloud every effort to contribute to the technology of judicial lawmaking as a consciously undertaken and responsible discipline, subject to criticism (including judicial self-criticism) addressed to the real grounds of the decision."[378]

In making this point, one need not deny that judges are legitimately concerned with avoiding unnecessary encroachments upon the legislative domain or the appearance thereof. Limited lawmaking powers are, however, essential to the judicial process.[379] Inordinate denial of the exercise of those powers is counterproductive. What we

> majority for its adoption will be gathered through the use of "neutral" words which do not prejudge the issue.

Pekelis, *The Case for a Jurisprudence of Welfare*, 6 LAW. GUILD REV. 611, 617 (1946).

373 Proposals for science advisors to the judiciary have been numerous. *See, e.g.*, those cited in Monahan & Walker, *Social Authority: Obtaining, Evaluating, and Establishing Social Science in Law*, 134 U. PA. L. REV. 477, 509–10 n.116 (1986).

374 For an argument that this unusual approach should have been taken at trial in the *OFFER* litigation, discussed above at notes 304–32, see Guggenheim, *The Right to be Represented But Not Heard: Reflections on Legal Representation for Children*, 59 N.Y.U. L. REV. 76, 143–47 (1984).

375 *See supra* pp. 1563–71, 1591–92.

376 Levy, *Realist Jurisprudence and Prospective Overruling*, 109 U. PA. L. REV. 1, 2 (1960).

377 *Id.* at 4 (quoting E. CAHN, THE SENSE OF INJUSTICE 143 (1949)).

378 *Id.* at 3.

379 *See* Bulova Watch Co. v. Hattori & Co., 508 F. Supp. 1322, 1328 (E.D.N.Y. 1981).

require is clarity about the inevitability of their exercise and rigorous attention to the limitations that should surround it.

In only one of the cases reviewed for this study did a judge acknowledge that he was on the frontiers of legal doctrine and offer a coherent theory concerning the relevance of legislative facts to the task of interpreting and extending that doctrine.[380] The prerequisite for appropriate regulation of judicial notice of legislative facts is more frequent acknowledgment that judicial lawmaking occurs and that it is influenced by real or supposed facts.

3. Marking the Point of Slippage Between Adjudicative and Legislative Factfinding. — Sensitivity to the line between legislative and adjudicative factfinding is as critical to responsible lawmaking as is acknowledgement of the legislative function. When courts own up to the possibility of making law in response to social and scientific facts, they are more likely both to hesitate to change or embellish legal rules and to proceed responsibly when changes are called for. For example, a court applying a statute that permits termination of parental rights whenever adoption is in the best interests of the child may believe that adoption is in the best interests of a particular child who has been in foster care for five years. That court may *choose* whether simply to free the child for adoption or to announce a presumption that it is in the best interests of all children to be freed for adoption if they are out of parental custody for an equivalent period. Some of the opinions studied for this Article showed awareness of these alternatives and restraint with respect to "legislative" use of the theory.[381] This restraint is appropriate. Development of rules of law in response to perceived social or scientific truths must always proceed cautiously. Case-specific facts may serve to test a fallible theory within the context of each determination. When courts may apply scientific learning without announcing novel propositions of law, they should hesitate to venture into the realm of legislative factfinding. Thus, in the case of psychological parent theory, individualized analysis may serve to check unwarranted or overbroad application, while the theory serves to emphasize the risks of separation trauma among other factors relevant to the best interests of children.

When courts could not apply psychological parent theory without working a change in the law, they too often proceeded to effect the change without carefully considering either the soundness of the theory

---

[380] *See* Franz v. United States, 707 F.2d 582 (D.C. Cir. 1983); *supra* pp. 1587–88. The New York opinions discussed above at notes 101–26 acknowledge reliance upon psychological parent theory in the context of developing the law. However, the common law opinions stop short of forthright recognition that the law is being changed, and the opinions involving statutory questions fail to articulate a coherent theory by which the law might change in the manner indicated by psychological parent theory.

[381] *See supra* pp. 1558–59, 1564.

or the impact of its application beyond the facts of the case at hand.[382] This tendency is unfortunate. The evidence in a particular case may argue strongly for a legal principle that would ease the burden or win the day for the more persuasive side. But the apparent strength of the evidence may result from a litigation imbalance. Expert witnesses may have overstated premises as a result of their conviction concerning case-specific conclusions. And it is unlikely that the experts will have considered or communicated the implications of broad application of those premises.

A controversial theory may appropriately serve as background for drawing factual conclusions in the course of applying an established rule of law, yet use of the same theory as a legislative fact may be entirely unwarranted. Thus, in deciding what course the best interests of a particular child require, it may be appropriate to consider the views of an expert who believes that separation from long-term caretakers always, almost always, or even occasionally causes irreparable psychological damage. In the context of announcing law, however, the court should supplement that evidence with close examination of the social function served by a tradition of assigning responsibility on the basis of biological parentage (and the social costs of diluting the effect of that assignment), and recognize that scientific consensus concerning the expert's causal judgment may be lacking or temporary.

The process by which judges learn from individual cases and, from that learning, announce or argue for changes in the law is valuable. It will be more valuable to the extent that judges correct for distortions that are possible when legislative facts are gathered in the context of narrowly focused litigation, and protect against the risk of making bad — or inappropriately broad — law in compelling cases.

V. Legislative Measures to Foster a Tradition of Care

This Article began with the observation that courts and legislatures have not significantly regulated the process of judicial notice of legislative facts.[383] The results of this study lend force to the complaints of commentators who have opposed this rulelessness.[384] Commentary

[382] *See, e.g., supra* pp. 1559–62, 1565–71.

[383] *See supra* pp. 1540–41.

[384] *See, e.g.*, Note, *Social and Economic Facts — Appraisal of Suggested Techniques for Presenting Them to the Courts*, 61 Harv. L. Rev. 692 (1948). The Note author observed:

> Failure to provide some satisfactory method for bringing factual premises of law before both trial and appellate judges throws the court back upon its own resources — at best, individual research independent of the parties in the guise of judicial notice; at worst, an uninformed guess as to common usage or other economic and social realities. However, once it is recognized that there are occasions when a judge must be a fact finder in order to be an adequate lawmaker, the means for remedying this failure would seem capable of evolution from the traditional procedures, practices and techniques now used to gather and present adjudicative facts.

Id. at 702.

decrying rulelessness has failed to stimulate development of a tradition of care in legislative factfinding. But modest legislative measures may succeed where scholarship has failed.

Judicial notice of legislative and background facts is a process that includes many kinds of judicial behavior, some of which are rarely acknowledged and little understood. It is unwise to attempt to force judicial behavior in this arena into a rigid pattern. It is, however, equally unwise to permit it to proceed unconsciously and without even the most general guiding principles. Some device is needed to focus the attention of judges and litigants upon the possibility that background and legislative fact issues will arise; to encourage judges and litigants to address these issues directly rather than leave them sub rosa; and to suggest, in broad outline, means for assuring that judicial notice is undertaken in a manner that assures fairness and informed deliberation. The laissez-faire policy with respect to judicial notice of background and legislative facts has failed. Rules of evidence should meet this important issue with something other than silence.[385]

Although modern rules of evidence are silent regarding judicial notice of legislative facts, the commentary that typically accompanies these rules recognizes the process and acknowledges the legitimacy of considering reliable, but disputable, matters of fact in "construing statutes, determining constitutional issues, and formulating rules of law."[386] In some jurisdictions, the authority to take notice of background facts is similarly recognized.[387] The simple act of recognizing these judicial powers in the text of rules respecting judicial notice would encourage forthrightness and care in their use.

An additional legislative step also is desirable. The litigator or judge who senses that judicial notice of a disputable proposition may figure significantly in a pending matter should have an acknowledged method of addressing the issue. This, too, could be accomplished by simply codifying an authority that no one disputes: the authority of a court to entertain or solicit special briefs, argument, affidavits or depositions of experts, or, in the rare case, hearings, as to the propriety of taking judicial notice of a disputable fact. A trial court's decision whether to exercise this authority should be reviewable and informed by standards. The rules themselves might provide such standards, or standards might evolve as acknowledgment and enhanced visibility of the process leads to its review and discussion in judicial opinions. But legislative controls should in either event be loose — in acknowledgment of, and without complaint against, the "creative nature of the judicial function."[388] Their enactment would stimulate a period

[385] *See supra* pp. 1540–41.

[386] CAL. EVID. CODE § 450 comment (West 1966).

[387] *See. e.g.*, FED. R. EVID. 201 advisory committee's note.

[388] Pekelis, *supra* note 372, at 611.

of percolation during which "exploratory consideration and experimentation"[389] in courts at each level within an enacting jurisdiction might finally produce principled resolution of the complex difficulties associated with the uncharted worlds of judicial notice.

---

[389] Estreicher & Sexton, *A Managerial Theory of the Supreme Court's Responsibilities: An Empirical Study*, 59 N.Y.U. L. REV. 681 (1984).

[9]

BOOKS

BEYOND THE BEST INTERESTS OF THE CHILD. By Joseph Goldstein, Anna Freud and Albert J. Solnit. New York: The Free Press (MacMillan Publishing Co.), 1973. Pp. xiv, 170. $7.95 hardcover; $1.95 paperback.

Identifying just principles for minimizing and resolving disputes over child custody remains one of the law's knots. King Solomon's renowned gambit for resolving the claims of two women to a newborn child[1] was in fact the easy case: only one of the two contenders had a just claim; only one of the two contenders was prepared to be responsible; and in that first of reported cases, the judge had the advantage of surprise. Yet where each potential custodian has a claim, where each is equally prepared (or unprepared) to sacrifice his interests for the child, and where the rules of decision are known in advance and thus susceptible to manipulation, justice for adult and child is much harder to achieve. Only with difficulty has the law advanced the rules regarding child-possession beyond the law of land-possession or slave-possession. Even in acknowledging that the "best interests of the child" are its central concern, the law has made false promises, both beyond its capacity and camouflage for rules that most strongly respond to the presumed interests of the competing adults.

In *Beyond the Best Interests of the Child*, three distinguished social science professionals have crafted out of evident compassion for the child a brief yet subtle program for the law's resolution of these difficult cases. Anna Freud and Albert J. Solnit are pre-eminent figures in child psychoanalysis and psychiatry, respectively, who insist that law recognize both what is known about child development and, as importantly, what is not known and cannot be predicted with certainty. Joseph Goldstein, a distinguished professor of law who has also acquired professional psychoanalytic training, seems ideally placed for the arduous task of smelting sound legal policy from the social science ore. Their book, warmly hailed by an impressive array of judges, child welfare professionals and others concerned with children, insists that the child's perspective must be controlling in any judicial proceedings to decide custody issues.

Even if the full force of their recommendations does not prevail, the symbolic importance of their commitment to the child's side and the fresh view that they give of the law's impact and failings are sufficient to require that their book be read. Yet their commitment carries with it possibly unavoidable overstatement. The book views child development from a questionably narrow

1. I KINGS 3:16-28.

stance. As a plan for concrete action, it is compromised by partisanship and apparent failure to relate its insights to the realities of an operating legal system; it fails to consider the way in which radically new rules may shape parental behavior and the incidence of litigation, and takes insufficient account of the limited capacity of a legal system staffed by fallible humans to administer them.

The beginning chapters describe with elegant brevity the existing psychiatric understanding regarding child-parent relationships and child development, and define a variety of concepts important to the authors' themes. The central thoughts are that the child's development depends upon the continuity and character of his relationship with the adult he perceives as his parent, *and that this perception rather than the fact of biological parenthood is the basis of their relationship.* This adult is described by the authors as the child's "psychological parent"—one who wants a relationship of enduring character with the child, and who through a course of continuing care and concern for the child comes to be regarded by him as "parent" and thus serves as the touchstone for his maturation and development.

> Whether any adult becomes the psychological parent of a child is based thus on day-to-day interaction, companionship, and shared experiences. The role can be fulfilled either by a biological parent or by an adoptive parent or by any other caring adult—but never by an absent, inactive adult, whatever his biological or legal relationship to the child may be. (P. 19.)

Once such a relationship is formed, it ought not to be disturbed absent the most serious provocation.[2]

From this conjunction of need for continuity and importance of perceived relationships, the authors develop guidelines of major force for all child placement decisions. First, such decisions must safeguard the child's need for continuity of existing relationships. This need varies in character as the child grows but is always present in an intensity unlikely to be appreciated by adults; adults' formal relationships are not ordinarily subject to severance by others, their dependence on those relationships is not usually pervasive, and their capacity for rational manipulation of the environment and postponement of gratification is usually high. That prior relationships should be given significant force is no doubt unsurprising, but in the authors' view such a relationship once established must be made controlling. As importantly, they view the

2. Thus, when a child of divorce has been placed with one parent and, over time, is integrated into a new home, death of the custodial parent ought not entitle the surviving biological parent automatically to assume custody of the child as against the surviving step-parent. The potential for harm to the child (and the family in which it has been living) is transparent. Students of Professor Goldstein developed this aspect of the idea some years ago in a widely cited note, *Alternatives to "Parental Right" in Child Custody Disputes Including Third Parties*, 73 YALE L.J. 151 (1963), but it is still far from universally accepted. *See, e.g.*, Quaresmo v. Schwab, 44 App. Div. 2d 568, 353 N.Y.S. 2d 48 (1974).

anxiety engendered by the prospect of legal interference as equally objectionable; "each child placement [must] be final and unconditional and . . . pending final placement a child must not be shifted to accord with each tentative decision." (P. 35.) And, consequently, the child should not be subjected to legal regimes, such as enforcible rights of visitation, which increase the likelihood of future legal actions. Placement orders must be absolute, subject neither to modification nor to conditions enforcible by courts. For a divorcing couple, this would require sole custody to be given one of the two parents, with the other retaining no legal right to the child's company nor voice in his upbringing.

Second, placement decisions must reflect the child's, not the adult's, sense of time. Unlike adults, children can not readily manage delay; a delay of one month for a two-year-old corresponds in relative terms to perhaps a year's time for a young adult. The younger the child, the quicker the process by which memory of prior relationships is suppressed in favor of replacement relationships—whose loss, in turn, would compound the emotional harm uprooting has caused. "[T]o avoid irreparable psychological injury, placement, whenever in dispute, must be treated as the emergency that it is for the child." (P. 43). The consequences: limited time for the hearing of disputes; sharply limited and expedited appeals; and the suggestion that success on appeal should entitle the appellant to no more than an opportunity to show that intervention in the child's *current* placement is required at the time of rehearing.[3]

Finally, the authors strike a cautionary note: child placement decisions must take into account the law's incapacity to supervise interpersonal relationships and social science's incapacity to make behavior predictions. Law "may be able to destroy human relationships, but it does not have the power to compel them to develop" (p. 50); psychoanalysis can identify existing capacities for parenthood, assess existing relationships, and demonstrate the harm often wrought by interruptions in continuity or extended uncertainty, but it cannot predict the future of any particular relationship. Consequently, the law should take an openly modest stance in resolving child placement disputes, letting well enough alone unless the need or inevitability of change is made clear and then—for such a child is "already a victim of his environmental circumstances [and] . . . greatly at risk" (p. 54)—selecting "that placement which is the least detrimental among available alternatives for the child." (P. 62.) Rather than make the unattainable false promise of "best interests," the authors choose to focus our attention on "the need to salvage as much as possible out of an unsatisfactory situation," our limited capacity to make valid predictions, and the limited choices generally open to us for achieving our goals. (p. 63).

These guidelines (if not all the conclusions drawn from them) are the

3. *Cf.* State *ex rel.* Lewis v. Lutheran Social Services, 405 U.S. 1051 (1972).

work's contribution. They have not previously been stated, at least with such cogent force. And they warrant the most careful attention by legislators, judges and lawyers. Modesty in intervention, speed and finality are all qualities presently lacking from the law's endeavors in child placement.[4] There is ample demonstration here of the need and basis for each in the learnings of psychoanalytic science. Limited and controversial as some of the propositions made in the name of behavioral science may be, the findings relied upon here are bedrock, not seriously disputed among the contending schools and camps, or by skeptical outsiders.[5]

The emphasis on psychological rather than biological relationships in disputed cases seems equally sound, provided that the importance of environment and the possible psychological advantages of biological relationships are not overlooked. The losses that a child faces through removal from his accustomed home are imperfectly accounted for if only the "parent" is looked to; the change may equally involve siblings, friends, community, house, toys, clothes—every aspect of his existence—and a change in parent figure that did not also involve these changes would not present as intense a threat. So, too, biological ties, if not interfered with, encourage the development of psychological relationships. A mother's hormonal response to childbirth may foster attachment; mother and father both are prepared for attachment by the unfolding of pregnancy, and may be aided by their realization that the child is their biological continuation. This sense of continuity and heritage is valuable from the child's perspective, if it strengthens parental ties.

We doubt the authors would disagree with these observations, although their stress on cases in which biological cues have failed tends to submerge them.[6] Similarly, the success of adoption—prime evidence for the "psychological parent" notion—ought not be permitted to obscure the greater risk faced by any child whose psychological and biological parents are not identical. Such a child will seek (or ignore, or reject) roots in more than one family. Even well-adjusted adopted children yearn to know their natural parents as part of their developing sense of identity. And their adoptive parents may experience attachment to them somewhat differently than to a natural child. For instance, emotional problems frequently arise when parents adopt a child and subsequently succeed in having one of their own; often they try to maintain an

4. While the book and this review are chiefly directed to legal roles, the point has equal bearing on child welfare workers. Speed and urgency are radical notions for a placement bureaucracy. *Cf.* N.Y. State Assembly Committee on Social Services, Report of the Temporary Sub-Committee on Adoption Practices (1970).

5. Ellsworth & Levy, *Legislative Reform of Child Custody Adjudication*, 4 LAW & SOC. REV. 167 (1969).

6. To return for a moment to the Solomonic judgment: on reflection it seems irrelevant to the justice of the result whether the woman who volunteered to give up the child to avoid its dismemberment was its biological mother or the competitor; common sense acquaintance with human behavior prepares us to believe that she was its mother, but the important point lay in her present and probable future relationship with the child, shown by her willingness to sacrifice herself for it.

identity of feeling towards each child which is not possible or realistic to have. Obviously, these considerations are not arguments against adoption. The differences are subtle, vary from person to person in unpredictable ways, and in any event are not susceptible of management by law. But they do suggest that the basis for recognition of the natural parent's claim to initial custody of his child is stronger than mere convenience, as the authors at times appear to suggest.

To take the argument one step further, we think that the authors introduce political premises which receive no support from the findings of psychoanalysis or psychiatry when they insist that the natural parent has no claim independent of his child's interests, that he has no "right." The point is strikingly made by repetitive characterization of the birth certificate as an "allocation," as if it were more than an (optional) record-keeping device and as if placement at birth involved a social judgment that *could* be made in any way. This characterization is effective only as a rhetorical device. The parents' claim is honored, not only out of concern for the child or even diffidence regarding present ability to determine its interests, but also in recognition of interests that the biological parents enjoy, which must somehow be compromised before any intervention can be justified. The failure to acknowledge this independent parental, perhaps more properly custodial, claim flaws the analysis.

Anticipating this criticism, the authors assert a value preference for abstention, "to safeguard the right of parents to raise their children as they see fit, free of government intrusion, except in cases of neglect[7] and abandonment"

7. The concept of neglect is central to the authors' thesis, since it defines one of the few circumstances in which state intervention into family life is authorized. Perhaps the most regrettable of the omissions of this book is its failure to bring the authors' perceptions and knowledge to bear on defining this most troublesome term. Although in some respects they seem to believe that wide ranges of "parental" behavior disserve the developing child (pp. 15-21), they contribute no more toward a definition of neglect than the observation that the present definition is unsatisfactorily diffuse. (P. 105). It is hard to imagine a question for which the risk of judicial misadventure is as high. *See* Burt, *Forcing Protection on Children and Their Parents*, 69 MICH. L. REV. 1274-81 (1971); *cf. In re* Raya, 255 Cal. App. 2d 260, 63 Cal. Rptr. 252 (1967). Portraying the child as they do—a fragile creature, particularly subject to parental influence in determining his future for good or for ill—the authors risk encouraging such misadventures.

For example, suppose a state agency exercising both child protection and adoption placement functions brings a neglect proceeding against the impoverished, unwed mother of a recently born child, proposing to place the child for adoption in a suburban, childless, two-adult home. Under the authors' scheme, the state need establish only that the child is "unwanted" and that its current placement is not the least detrimental available. "Unwanted" is not defined, but a wanted child is one who receives continuous affection and nourishment and "feels . . . valued . . ." (p. 10); the least detrimental alternative is the one that maximizes the opportunity for being wanted and maintaining on a continuous and permanent basis a relationship with an adult who will "through interaction, companionship, interplay and mutuality fulfill the child's psychological need for a parent as well as the child's physical needs." (P. 10.) The authors are emphatically for nonintervention; but picture this language as the subject of litigation, or in the hands of any ordinary judge. Its indefiniteness requires the most excruciating inquiry in every case and risks decision on the basis of prejudice rather than rational judgment; precise rules, at cost to *some* children, would at least make clear the cases in which intervention was not to be sought.

(pp. 7, 105 ff.), but purport to found this preference upon the child's need for continuity rather than any independent claim that the parent may have. That does not suffice. The point is a subtle, but important one. The authors assert the primacy of the state and its planning function, which for them is hedged by "preferences" for privacy and recognition of limitations on our present capacity to plan. But government is more effectively limited by recognizing that the parents' claim is not a mere derivation of what the interests of the child require or what is least detrimental to the child. Rather, the parents' claim reflects an independent assertion of personal rights and instinct, of a liberty which a state subject to constitutional restraint is required to recognize.[8] While we agree with the authors' view that children's claims are to be preferred to adults' in situations of balanced conflict, it does not follow that the adults have no respectable, independent legal claim. To substitute blind adherence to "children's right" for blind adherence to "natural parents' right" would mark little improvement, and in hands less sophisticated or self-effacing than the authors' could easily unloose rather than contain the floods of state intervention.[9] Indeed, children have an interest in their parents' claims. For parents truly to give to an infant or small child, they must also be given to; emphasizing only the child's interests or rights may lead in the end to poorer care. That the children have claims is indisputable, and the importance and nature of those claims is forcefully revealed by the analysis; that the adults concerned have none involves different judgments, unrelated to behavioral science analysis and not at all necessary to this work.

For the child who has two existing or probable future relationships, the child of divorcing parents, the case for rejecting parental claims seems especially weak. Referring to asserted Japanese practice,[10] the authors propose that the courts act only choose the single parent who will have entire control over the child's life, finally and without possibility of modification save in cases of established abuse or neglect. (P. 38 and note). In legal perspective,

8. Stanley v. Illinois, 405 U.S. 645 (1972). *See also* Wisconsin v. Yoder, 405 U.S. 205 (1971).

9. *See* note 7 *supra*.

10. The reference is an example of legal documentation which too often seems slight. The authors quote a Japanese custody statute that limits judicial authority in contested cases to assigning custodial authority to one or the other parent. The statute is presented, however, without an explication of development or context that would help to understand its full meaning. Thus, no indication is given of the effect, if any, of parental *agreement* on visitation or other custodial matters of joint interest. Professor Michiko Ariga, a respected authority on Japanese law, has stated to one of us conversationally that although such agreements are not directly enforced, they are available for defensive use—for example, to resist enforcement of a claim to child support payments withheld because visitation has been denied, or to resist prosecution for asserted "trespass" in exercising visitation privileges. Such recognition of contractually-established visitation rights would be an incentive to agreement, but would apparently be unacceptable to the authors.

Further, even if our understanding of the legal rules were complete, we could hardly believe those rules importable without change unless we first understood the cultural and social context within which they operate. Japanese attitudes towards family relations and the importance of conciliation in interpersonal dispute are probably different enough from our own to make transplantation risky.

the other parent would become a stranger to his child, save, perhaps, for an obligation of support the nature or justice of which is nowhere examined.

We are entirely unpersuaded, both for parent and for child, that the law must turn its face from one of the divorcing parents. Even assuming the child's interests should control, the social science data to support the proposition that a single official parent is preferable to two seems remarkably weak. The authors simply observe:

> Unlike adults, children lack the capacity to [maintain positive emotional ties with unrelated or hostile adults]. They will freely love more than one adult only if the individuals in question feel positively to one another. Failing this, children may become prey to severe and crippling loyalty conflicts. (P. 12.)

To be the child of a mother and father who dislike one another is, to be sure, an unfortunate life experience; and parents who would subject their children to conflicting loyalties, whether or not they remain married, are less than adequate to their task. Nonetheless, given a child with existing relationships to *both*, we know of no studies which show that the legal death of one parent, the complete subordination of the child to the other's possibly distorted view, is invariably the preferable step for its future development.

Undoubtedly, the particular facts of some cases make it unwise to provide for visitation rights.[11] A judge who has read this book will be aided in identifying those cases. But there are also cases in which such factors as the child's age, the non-custodial parent's other strengths, the importance of providing an opportunity for tempering the distortions likely in the custodial parent's household, or the custodial parent's demand for occasional "time off," may counsel provision for regular visitation despite the risks. In an era of increasing incidence of divorce, the child has many models available to him for coping with the strains. The non-custodial parent, and the child's relationship with him, cannot be wished away by the law,[12] particularly with respect to the increasing number of families in which both parents have been actively involved in day-to-day child care; the risks in permitting one parent the power to impose that wish may be at least as severe for the child as the risks in legal recognition of the continuing relationship.[13]

---

11. *Cf.* Kesseler v. Kesseler, 10 N.Y. 2d 445, 180 N.E. 2d 402, 225 N.Y.S. 2d 1 (1962).

12. The difficulty of "banishing" a natural parent has long been recognized. *E.g.*, J. Bowlby, Child Care and the Growth of Love (1965 ed.). An example encountered by one of us in practice was Tony, a bright but disturbed twelve-year-old who had lived in several foster homes. Although his current foster parents cared deeply for him, he could not tolerate separation from his mother—even though she openly resisted the agency's efforts to maintain a thread of contact between them. (Tony's father had completely disappeared.) He often ran away from his foster parents and found his way to her; she returned him within a day or two each time. No court order could have kept Tony from his mother, as long as he could hope to find her.

13. A child of divorce deserves the chance to build on whatever strengths exist in his relationships with both parents. Even in cases in which a child can salvage little or nothing positive for his development from the non-custodial parent, direct coping with the

The authors state that their proposition is simply one of legal controls—a preference that legal process not be invoked more than the bare minimum necessary to resolve the initial dispute. Where neither parent is clearly more qualified, they suggest, the choice should be made by lot or any other impartially arbitrary means. The point is to keep the uncertainties and strains of litigation to a minimum; and the underlying belief is that parents otherwise disposed to be civilized will work these matters out privately, without need for judicial determination or enforcement. As a technique for selection, the proposal is striking in its originality, and if limited to the cases of actual litigation out of which the authors' concerns arise would merit serious consideration. How better to dramatize to the contending parents the disfavor with which such disputes are viewed and law's limited tools for resolving them?

At just this point, unfortunately, the authors commit compound failures of analysis. They take multi-hearing litigation about custody and visitation as paradigmatic, although such trouble cases are clearly exceptional; and they do not consider the impact of their proposals beyond those cases, on the future shape of planning and litigation in matters which do not presently rise to contest. Their reliance on agreement is unquestionably sound; many lawyers insist that their first duty in any case in which custody might become an issue is to keep their clients out of court. But what would the effect of an agreement be under the authors' scheme? Would it confer a private right of visitation, as it apparently does in Japan, unenforceable by injunction but available as a defense against trespass actions or against claims for support when visitation has been withheld?[14] Or, as seems likely, do they envision an entirely precatory document?

Our guess is that litigation about custody is more likely to rise than fall with the adoption of rules favoring an either/or regime. The emotional hurts attending divorce have not disappeared with the wide-spread acceptance of no-fault divorce laws; and there is some basis for belief that the wounded spouse and his lawyer-champion, deprived of the direct if unedifying revenge of a fault divorce contest, are repairing to child custody as the remaining

---

reality of his parent may serve him better than the unrealistic fantasies he might otherwise substitute. Kapit, *Help for Child of Separation and Divorce*, in CHILDREN OF SEPARATION AND DIVORCE 214 (I. STUART & L. ABT eds. 1972). Moreover, the parent who would deny the non-custodial parent visitation privileges may not be as strong or well-qualified as he imagines; the relief that visitation provides can as easily forestall serious difficulty as its strains can engender it. A good example is Mrs. B, whose husband was treated by one of us. According to her husband, she was disinterested in making arrangements for him to visit their children. Her psychological strength to cope with them, however, was limited. On occasion she felt overwhelmed, and would then call him and ask for a few days relief, lest she harm them. However, she would not accept regular visitation privileges for him without a court order. *See also*, C. FOOTE, R. LEVY & F. SANDER, CASES AND MATERIALS ON FAMILY LAW 866-895 (1965).

14. *See* note 10 *supra*.

"fault" battlefield.[15] The temptation for viciousness is surely increased when the odds are heightened by narrow restriction of the possible outcomes; it strains human capacities to trust a spouse accorded custody in such a context voluntarily to permit her former spouse's relationship with their child to continue. Law may not influence human behavior much; but when it places an efficient instrument for revenge at hand, it is hard to believe that the instrument will not be both used and feared, with unfortunately predictable impact on litigation incidence and character.

One case of which we are aware provides a concrete example. Mrs. C's first husband was a devout and orthodox practitioner of their mutual religion who agreed to their divorce and Mrs. C's custody of their children only on the conditions that he could exercise frequent visitation rights (including all important religious holidays) and that she would rear them in strict adherence to religious precepts. Mrs. C would not herself have chosen such an upbringing, which included a parochial education for her children, but she agreed, and both she and her former husband have honored that agreement, which is enforcible in its major parts. Especially now that she is remarried to someone who shares her beliefs, she would prefer to change these arrangements; she finds them inconvenient and fears that her children's view of the world is being restricted. At the same time, however, she acknowledges that the children are fundamentally healthy, and have strong and apparently successful relationships with both their parents, and with their new step-father as well. And since litigation to change the conditions of custody might be more disturbing to the children and their present relationships, even if success were assured, she and her new husband have permitted matters to remain as they are. The reader of domestic relations cases will recognize in this situation the scenario for a bitter and destructive custody dispute. Mrs. C and her first husband avoided that outcome, we are persuaded, *only* because compromise of the deeply held feelings of both was available and enforceable. Were Mrs. C now free to abandon her undertaking, she would do so; and Mr. C, aware of that, would never have accepted her custody voluntarily. Whichever parent had received sole custody in a contest under the authors' scheme,[16]

15. Sass, *The Iowa No-Fault Dissolution of Marriage Law in Action*, 18 S. DAK. L. REV. 629, 650, 652 (1973) (Questions 4 & 5).

16. Not to be overlooked is the possibility that the more responsible parent, faced with an either/or situation most likely to be resolved by bitter dispute, will "responsibly" attempt to prolong the marriage or withdraw from litigating custody rather than impose that harm. Prolongation of the marriage could be more damaging to the children's well-being than a divorce; "almost every serious researcher in American family behavior has suggested that the effects of continued home conflict might be more serious for the children than the divorce itself." W. GOODE, WOMEN IN DIVORCE 309 (1956, paperback ed.). Nor is withdrawal from conflict clearly for the best; the modern-day parent, eschewing litigation, would be acting as the victor in King Solomon's court did, but without the advantage of having the judge present to reward his self-sacrifice. Even a parent unprepared to take custody may forward his children's interests by asserting his presently recognized claim to visitation. For example, Mr. A, seen in therapy by one of us, considered his wife to be psychotic and believed that he stayed with her as long as

and putting aside the destruction done by its searing if momentary bitterness, their children would have lost a strong relationship, one which has benefited them despite their parents' differences. Legal recognition of the claim may be more important for such parents and their children than the gains to be achieved by curbing that fringe of parents willing to tear their children apart in public feuding.

All the foregoing is wholly apart from the claim each parent has, unless somehow forfeited or overcome, to continued association with his child. Where both parents meet the (quite properly) limited standard for fitness for their parental role, and the child has an existing relationship with both at the time of divorce, nothing the authors suggest comes close to establishing a basis for disregarding that claim. The child cannot be cut in half; it must go to one parent at a time and for a variety of reasons that usually means more time with one than the other. But that the second parent has no claim for time does not at all follow. One must know the incidence of abuse of visitation rights before the judgment can be confidently made that they must be abolished.

This criticism, we should stress, does not impair other conclusions bearing on the custody process—in particular, that custody proceedings be treated as emergency matters, independent of the underlying divorce; that any decree or agreement be made final, subject to modification only by the voluntary action of the parties or on a showing of facts which would warrant intervention as an original matter; and that the principal determinant of the custody award be the least detrimental alternative, stressing strength and continuity in the psychological relationships the child enjoys.[17] While not forbidding judicial enforcement of visitation rights or other rights of control conferred upon the second parent, the law might with less harmful effect discourage judicial recourse, as by penalties for obvious harassment or inhibitions upon repetitive suits. Perhaps, in truth, these remedies would not be very effective; few invoke them even now, whether out of respect for their children or for the expense involved one cannot say. Yet the analysis to support casting them aside simply has not been made.

If one turns to settings, like King Solomon's, in which only one of the contending adults makes a claim characterized by an existing or probably future psychological relationship, the work's insights become more successful.

---

he did to protect their son's life. Although he stated that she was negligent in caring for the boy, whose school reported that he seemed extremely fearful of her, Mr. A feared court action and even withdrew from visitation when his wife made that difficult during their initial separation. He looked forward to divorce as an occasion that would define his visitation rights and permit him to resume his protective role. While Mr. A had neither the desire, the strength, or the resources for custody, his child faced greater risk to his emotional health without some input from his father. Mr. A felt he needed court support to enable him to continue his involvement with his son against his wife's opposition, and she needed to know that visitation was his *right* in order to be able to tolerate it.

17. Detriment inheres in food supply and living conditions, too; in close cases, a decision for economy might be the most appropriate.

Painful as the conclusion may be for his prior caretakers, a child who has established himself in a new and "fit" household, and signals his wish to remain, will often be disserved by removal from that setting. The time taken for this establishment varies with age, a few months for an infant, longer for a school age child; but every child will reach a point at which he regards his present environment as "his," from which he can be separated only at a severe cost. The authors bite the bullet on this one: even where the child's placement is entirely involuntary, the product of wartime coercion, hospital error—or, one surmises, sale of a kidnapped child on the "black market"[18]—they deem it impermissible for the law to interfere with the existing custodial relationship. And more: to foster psychological parenthood, the law must insist upon speed and finality in such matters as adoption, so that adults concerned are not tempted to regard custody decisions as provisional and so withhold from the child the emotional commitment that will best foster his growth.

Here, too, we believe that substantial risks are created to legitimate interests of children and adults by concentration on the fringe case, and by disregard for the impact of new rules on adult conduct. For instance, the authors devote considerable space to a poignant series of decisions involving Stacey Rothman, whose mother gave her up to foster care at the age of one and then, when the child was eight, sought to reclaim her. The court at first ordered Stacey's return, although it noted that her mother agreed to a program of gradual transition; after the transition provided for did not take hold, the court, in a second decision, restored the right of custody to Stacey's foster mother. The authors insist that the right of the foster mother ought never to have been questioned. Granted the mother had the best of reasons for initially severing her relationship with her child—a mental illness that required hospital care—clearly the result is the right one. It requires no great psychological insight to see that after spending seven-eighths of her life in another family, Stacey would view the woman of that household as her mother and removal to Mrs. Rothman's care as a terrible threat; particularly so if her foster mother, encouraged by the passage of time and a darling "daughter," had promoted those views.[19]

18. *Cf.* PEOPLE MAGAZINE, March 18, 1974, at 38.

19. Rothman v. Jewish Child Care Ass'n., 1 N.Y.L.J. Nov. 5, 1971, and Nov. 1, 1972 (N.Y. Sup. Ct.). This effect is unavoidable and essential for the emotional health of a child in long term foster care. Removal of a child in long term foster care from her foster parents because they are acquiring emotional ties is indeed barbaric, as the authors state (pp. 24, 39 & nn.); *see also* Note, *The Rights of Foster Parents to the Children in Their Care*, 50 CHI-KENT L. REV. 86 (1973). We note, however, that in cases which do not now get litigated in courts—say, long term care by uncles and grandmothers in cultures typified by family relationships more extended than common for middle class whites, or care by boarding schools and nannies—children seem able to maintain relationships with usually absent parents and to return comfortably to their care when the occasion arises. To what extent these seemingly healthy adaptations are supported by a legal regime in which the child is the parent's by "right" is, again, a question the authors do not address.

More to the point from our perspective are cases like *Painter v. Bannister.*[20] There, Harold Painter, overcome for the moment by the sudden death of his wife, asked her parents to look after their five-year-old son Mark for a time. In some respects the Bannisters may not have been the best choice—they disapproved of Mr. Painter and his way of living, and were themselves upset by their daughter's death, as they had been by her marriage. But they were nonetheless family, and it is to family that people are accustomed to turn in such moments. Professional foster care, Mr. Painter knew from personal experience, was likely to be more traumatic for Mark. With his grandparents, Mark would not suffer a *complete* change of environment; Mark knew them and what their part of the world was like. Just as children find babysitting in their own home less threatening than a night without their own parents in a strange house, Mark could adjust to a painful situation more easily with the Bannisters than in any other substitute home.

Unlike Mrs. Rothman, Mr. Painter kept in contact with Mark; unlike Stacey, Mark was five, when placement was made; and "only" a year-and-a-half intervened before Mr. Painter returned to reclaim Mark for his home. As is well known, the Bannisters resisted; they produced credible psychiatric testimony that Mark now regarded Mr. Bannister as his psychological father and would be set back by removal "at this time"; and whether because it believed that testimony or preferred Midwestern solidity to West Coast bohemianism, the Iowa Supreme Court directed that Mark remain.

To our view, this victory for the psychological parent theory is problematic. Two years after this litigation was begun, Mark returned to his father at his own wish, with his grandparents' acquiescence, if not agreement.[21] Mark's relationship with his father was not dead and, indeed, it would have been a sign of mental illness, not health, had Mark regarded Mr. Bannister as his *real* father, however much strength he drew from their relationship. Had the Iowa Supreme Court purported finally to sever Mark's legal relationship with his father by decreeing an adoption, as it did not, it would have been taking a course that was *not* the "least detrimental" to the child.[22]

The authors make their problem too simple, indeed almost a caricature, by the unstated assumption that their proposed rules would have no influence either on the conduct of parents placing their children in foster care or on the conduct of foster parents in carrying out that high responsibility. Determining the "least detrimental alternative" for the child is in fact a highly

20. 258 Iowa 1390, 140 N.W.2d 152 (1966), *cert. denied*, 385 U.S. 949 (1967). The authors discuss the case briefly in a footnote.

21. C. FOOTE, R. LEVY & F. SANDER, SUPPLEMENT TO CASES AND MATERIALS ON FAMILY LAW 59 (1971).

22. In *Rothman*, too, the court did not sever the child-parent tie, but merely awarded the present right of custody to the foster parents. Query the justice *to the child* of the further step, once her present custody is safeguarded from involuntary change. *See* note 12 and accompanying text, *supra*.

complex matter. On the one hand, the present rules may make it too easy for parents to initiate separations from their dependent children: Harold Painter's separation from Mark may have been unnecessary. The introduction of some measure of insecurity for the parent could be defended on the ground that that would give him pause before acting, and thus force him to examine more closely his resources for coping and the possible harms of separation.[23] On the other hand, this book's recommendations seem to make that insecurity complete.

If Harold Painter had known in advance that he would be unable to protect his relationship with Mark, even after the most agonizing appraisal of the need for interim separation, we fear the outcome would have been poorer care for Mark. One result might have been to force him to keep Mark, although virtually disabled as a father. Or, concluding that Mark's placement was unavoidable, he might have felt forced to look elsewhere than to the Bannisters for aid. He could no longer have put his trust in an agreement for return, even one which responsibly set a time limit for return and specified contacts to be maintained in the interim; he would fear that if psychological relationships developed between Mark and his foster parents the "conditions" on the agreement would become unenforceable. That rule strikes us as an invitation to ugly litigation, if not to deliberate choice for placement of homes where psychological relationships are unlikely to develop. We wonder whether other grandparents or temporary custodians who now work to maintain their charges' real or imagined relationship with absent parents, and promptly return the children when the parents reappear, would be tempted by the "psychological parent" rule to impose themselves upon the children and to resist returning the children when that demand was made. Tempted not only because the rule promises that often seductive result, but more importantly, because it makes full emotional commitment to the child—the effort to adopt him in the psychological sense—seem the only moral course to take.[24]

23. This argument was suggested to us by our friend Professor Robert A. Burt of the University of Michigan. Letter of May 16, 1974. We owe thanks, too, to Professor David Rothman of Columbia University and his wife Sheila for their many helpful comments.

24. The authors view as encouraging, and a welcome link to the past, Chapsky v. Woods, 26 Kan. 650 (1889), a decision written by Mr. Justice Brewer while he was still sitting on the Kansas Supreme Court (pp. 82-85). The case sustained a child's surrogate parents against her father's claim for custody many years after he had placed her with them. Putting aside the aura of indenture surrounding the father's action and the court's general disapproval of his conduct and character, the case might be read—as the authors read it—to support a psychological parenthood theory. Tracing the decision down through the pages of Sheppard's, however, one is struck by the vehemence with which this reading of Kansas law has been rejected; and, more, by the impression, which would be interesting to try to confirm, that in the years since this decision Kansas has seen more, and more bitter, child custody litigation than other states whose rules are more clearly protective of parental right. *See, e.g., Re* Vallimont, 182 Kan. 334, 321 P. 2d 190 (1958); *In re* Jackson, 164 Kan. 391, 190 P.2d 426 (1948); Jones v. Jones, 155 Kan. 213, 124 P.2d 457 (1942); *but see* Hodson v. Shaw, 128 Kan. 787, 280 P. 761 (1929) (ten

At the least, one would expect an assessment of these possibilities. And the trouble cases generated by the present rules are not the place one would look for that data. Psychoanalytic science has often been criticized for the skewed character of its data base. Such criticisms probably do not apply to the very basic developmental propositions put forward in this book, and in many respects the authors seem commendably aware of the limitations on knowledge in this area. But the criticisms do apply to the legal data base the authors have chosen. The trouble cases are indeed extreme, and with lawyers' craft can be met without impairing the smooth flow of transactions which now never reach litigation and would not so disturb us if they did. How much of an incursion on parental right can be sustained without harming children who, as a consequence of the authors' proposed rules, will not be placed, or who will be placed (as Mark Painter might have been) into inferior settings, requires more subtle analysis than this work sustains.

It would have been interesting, in this light, to know the authors' views of some recent changes in New York law regarding adoption and foster care, changes which they must regard as pointing in a welcome direction.[25] For the preceding several decades, New York had been an extraordinarily strong adherent of the "natural parent's right" theory of child placement. Unless proved unfit, a difficult showing to make, a parent was entitled to the custody of his child against all comers. Even after seven years of foster care, as the first decision in the *Rothman* series held, a fit parent was entitled to the return of her child upon demand. The second *Rothman* case arose, indeed, only because Mrs. Rothman was willing—foolishly or wisely—to undertake gradual change; at law, she might have demanded, and would have received, immediate custody of her child. Similarly, under New York's prior law, foster parents had no interest in the custody of their foster child; their relationship with the child was subject to summary termination by the agency (or themselves), and they would be afforded no standing to participate in any judicial proceedings concerning placement. Adoption rules were equally one-sided; the natural parent's right to retract her consent before final entry of the decree was virtually unfettered. To be sure—again, a point very easy to miss in one's horror at the few cases in which the option *was* exercised—these rights were rarely availed of. Still, under pressure of the belief that the parent's interest rises to important constitutional status, the New York courts

years in custody; father a former felon). This withdrawal from Justice Brewer's sweeping words might be explained by the hypothesis that his successors were less sensitive to children's claims than he; but if the pace and bitterness of litigation did increase, his successors may equally have been responding to that.

25. It is unrealistic to expect much attention to the detail of the law in a brief and Olympian work such as this, but the omission is a regrettable one. These changes were occurring just as the *Rothman* case was proceeding through the courts and seem a direct response to the authors' concerns. *Compare* note 10 *supra*.

had invariably held for the natural parent or against the foster parent in those few cases in which the issue was presented.[26]

The past few years have seen the emergence of a complex network of statutes all apparently intended to increase the likelihood that a child placed for adoption or foster care will remain in that setting despite its parents' subsequent change of heart. The new laws provide mechanisms by which consent to adoption may be made irrevocable and, in addition, sharply limit the circumstances in which consent may be revoked when those mechanisms are not used. Consent becomes final thirty days after the child is placed for adoption (in the case of a private placement) or with an agency; even during that period, the law now requires, attempted revocation merely raises the question of what custody arrangement will be in the child's best interests. The statute explicitly states that no preference is to be given the natural parent in that determination. If he is able to establish fraud, coercion, or duress, however, these rules do not apply.[27] The overall impact is certain to reduce still further the already limited incidence of attempted revocation; while not fully satisfying the authors' tests, the laws surely tend in that direction and, in practical terms, may well suffice.

The New York law regarding foster care has been steadily moving in the direction of recognizing parental interests in foster parents and facilitating severance of formal connections with absent natural parents. Thus, while New York still does not permit severance of child-parent relationships immediately upon a finding of neglect or abuse,[28] a subsequent action to terminate the relationship no longer requires a showing that the responsible child-care agency worked diligently but unsuccessfully with the parents to repair the relationship; a sound reason for determining not to work with them toward that end now suffices as an alternate ground.[29] More importantly, once a

26. *See, e.g.*, People *ex rel.* Kropp v. Shepsky, 305 N.Y. 465 (1953) (custody); People *ex rel.* Scarpetta v. Spence-Chapin Adoption Serv., 28 N.Y.2d 185, 269 N.E.2d 787, 321 N.Y.S.2d 65 (1971) (adoption consent); *In re* Jewish Child Care Ass'n, 5 N.Y.2d 222, 156 N.E.2d 700, 183 N.Y.S.2d 65 (1959) (foster care).

27. N.Y. Dom. Rel. Law § 115-b (McKinney 1964); N.Y. Soc. Serv. Law § 384 (McKinney Supp. 1973).

28. N.Y. Fam. Ct. Act § 1051. The authors appear to believe that this relief should be available, and invoked, whenever removal is the "least detrimental alternative." They appear to consider that termination would almost invariably be *less* detrimental than temporary removal during which the parents undergo some form of rehabilitation. To be sure, their view is that removal should rarely if ever occur at all; and it is probably true that family therapy will work best for a family that remains together, rather than one from which the source of stress has been removed. Yet, it seems to us, this is another situation in which disregarding the parental interests is simply too brutal. More important, the situation is one in which the risks of unchecked arbitrariness run very high. In a human world, decisions regarding neglect and abuse too often threaten to reflect class prejudices or personal background rather than assessment of a child's needs. *See* note 7 *supra*. Permitting parents a last clear chance to reform is, in the circumstances, a wise legislative judgment. It both respects the parent's interests, reduces somewhat the consequences of an erroneous finding of neglect, and, so far as the law can, denies the court the simple solution of "capital" punishment.

29. N.Y. Family Ct. Act § 614 (McKinney 1963); *see* note 25 *supra*.

child has been with the same foster parents for two years, they acquire a quasi-parental interest that grants them priority in adoption, standing in any proceedings concerning the child's custody, and the right to seek initiation of proceedings to terminate the natural parents' custody.[30]

One suspects the authors would find these latter provisions insufficient, a compromise sacrificial of children's interests and hence unacceptable. The uniform time period the legislature has provided, two years, is too long for young children; perhaps, in their view, for all. They would object to the suspense in which foster parents must wait while the initial period runs, and the resulting harm to the developing child. And they would surely protest the possibility that children might be returned, even after that period had elapsed.

Yet even this mild statutory change should permit studies of the sort we find lacking in this work, and subsequent assessment of the impact of its proposals. One area for study should be the statutes' impact on parents' use of foster care: as the risks to the parent of putting his child in foster care increase, will resort to foster placement diminish? That would not in itself be a regrettable effect, if less detrimental alternatives are chosen; but some parents, still unable to avoid giving their child up for a time, might be expected instead to seek congregate care, usually inferior for the child. Informal (non-agency) foster care, to which the New York statutes do not presently apply, might also be expected to increase.

A second area of research should be the effect of the change on foster parents. The authors distinguish between foster care anticipated from the outset to be long-term, and foster care for brief, emergency periods and apparently feel, as we do, that the latter serves valuable functions that should be preserved. The two-year period under the New York laws seems intended to mark the line between the functions, however crudely; the authors suggest no similar test. Rather, they seem to ask individually, and after-the-fact, whether the particular child in question formed a psychological attachment to its foster parents before return was sought. If the cut-and-dry New York provision encourages foster parents to promote formation of psychological relationships even during the initial period,[31] thus interfering with the emergency rationale, we would suppose the authors' proposal to have an even stronger effect. It then seems important to know (1) whether the New York provisions are seen by foster parents as a back road to adoption, (2) what impact their view of possible future adoption has on the progress of their relationship with the foster child, and (3) what, if any, techniques can successfully be used to protect the designedly emergency placement. Again, this inquiry must be undertaken not only for the natural parents but for their

30. N.Y. Soc. Serv. Law § 392 (McKinney Supp. 1973).

31. The authors would agree that while psychological relationships inevitably form at *some* time for the child, manipulation by adults can delay or promote their growth.

child, who might be placed at serious risk if they concluded that the dangers of placing him in foster care were too high.

A related question is the impact of the new laws on child welfare agencies, which for some populations are encountering severe difficulties in securing children to meet the demand for adoption. Do they now more freely encourage would-be adoptive parents to undertake foster care, the reverse of the earlier practice of insisting that foster placement forbid eventual adoption of the child placed? In their dealings with parents seeking foster care, are they able to expose and handle adequately what are now possibly conflicting interests? Finally, down the road a little, is the effect of the change to quiet or to exacerbate the problems of transfer? The prior rule against adoption by foster parents, misguided as its application may have been to relationships long-term in fact, was defensible as an inhibition to destructive litigation. The new statutes encourage foster parents and natural parents to fight, and the authors' proposals—pregnant with expert dispute regarding the existence and quality of asserted "psychological parenthood"—offer an even stronger incentive. Is it clear, in King Solomon's sense, who will be acting for the child in this case? We fear that it will be the responsible parents who are tempted to withdraw; when they do not, the want of clarity in the outcome will encourage litigation.

The problem is compounded, in our view, by failure of an unarticulated premise that long and short term foster care can be reliably distinguished at the outset. Regrettably, that is not the case. The major cause of child placement is poverty or some condition related to it; and the intention of the placing parent is frequently only to seek temporary relief from the (often unshared) burdens of child-rearing in the face of some emergency. These parents cannot afford the wages of a housekeeper who might maintain the children in their familiar environment and thus reduce the risk of psychological harm or major new attachments, even in the parents' absence. Provision of in-home services to avoid the necessity of foster care would be a more satisfactory step than termination of parental rights in many cases where foster care is now sought, and would avoid the risk of unconscious discrimination against the poor that seems to us inherent in the authors' prescriptions. Nor is it enough to make homemaker services available at low or no charge; ways must be found to bring them to the attention of the community and to make use of these services realistic for one-adult or two-worker families, whose schedules may appear too inflexible for the demands of the welfare bureaucracy.

One possible response to some of these questions lies in counsel for the child, a procedural measure that the authors strongly (and rightly, in our view) favor. The child has an indisputable interest in the outcome of the proceedings: since his liberty is at stake, in a significant sense, our traditions command that he be represented, independently of others whose interests may conflict with his. It would be a mistake, however, to put too much hope in this measure. In the first instance, it will not prevent litigation. It may tend to aggravate it, since counsel, in order to justify himself, will feel called upon to make his own contribution to the proceedings, enlarging the issues and hence the opportunity for crossfire and delay. Most important, how will counsel inform himself of his role? Counsel qualified for such delicate proceedings are scarce and expensive. The proposal seems to require that counsel in effect duplicate the entire inquiry to determine the "least detrimental alternative"—his litigating position. And counsel will encounter difficulty in taking any kind of instructions from his "incompetent" client.[32] Perhaps the most appropriate form of assistance would be provided by a social agency associated with the court—a measure many courts already employ, but without consistent success given the development over the long term of inevitable resource deficiencies and closer relationships between court and reporting agency than between the agency and its "clients." Uncomfortable as we are in the role of nay-sayers to the authors' high-minded arguments, something is to be said for the simplifying virtues of presumptions and of legislative categories for avoiding destructive litigation *in the large*. We grant, however, that unfortunate spill-over may occasionally occur, and that some flexibility must remain to account for it.

One other measure strikes us as central: steps must be taken at the moment children enter another's care to assure that the consequences of that transition are known, and the bargain must then be enforced. Assume that temporary foster care is to remain available, but that parental vacillation or long-term commitment to another's care will not be tolerated; that neglectful parents whose child is removed from their home may be given a chance at rehabilitation, but only that, at which they must succeed. It then becomes essential to identify at the outset of foster care what conditions parents must meet if their children are to be returned to them, by what time they must be reclaimed, *and* that return is a matter of right if these conditions are met. The authors, coming to the trouble cases long after foster care began, never really focus on the transactions with which it begins. They seem to assume that a case will cleanly identify itself as long-term or emergent at the outset, after which solution is simple. But that identification will not occur without

32. In the juvenile delinquency setting, serious commentators have been so impressed by the potential conflicts between determination of a client's best interest and representation of them as to suggest that each child must have *two* representatives, a guardian as well as a litigating counsel. Paulsen, *Juvenile Courts and the Legacy of '67*, 43 Ind. L.J. 527, 536-540 (1968).

procedures, and with the risks of overreaching and undercomprehension that inhere in agency and court relationships with the poor and ill who are the usual clients of foster care services, those procedures must be straight-forward and certain. A system that creates a reasonable plan for continuing parental contact and hinges the custody outcome upon the parents' adherence to that plan is, in our view, far more acceptable than one that only asks, at a later time, whether dependency relationships have in fact been formed.

All of the foregoing, like the book under review, assumes that willing foster parents, interested in adoption or its equivalent and fully qualified for child rearing, are in the wings. Regrettably, this is infrequently the case. The proportion of foster parents who fail to behave responsibly towards their wards is substantial; nor are they legally obliged to continue their relationship with a child even after it has matured into psychological dependency. Agency supervision of the quality of foster care is too often deficient. When foster parents have been unavailable or unsuccessful, return of a child to his biological parents who want him will be the least detrimental for him. The authors seem to suggest imposing responsibility as well as opportunity on foster parents; the idea warrants the most serious consideration. Again, the process of identifying foster parents who will accept this expectation of them underscores the importance of early and rigorous definition of the circumstances in which a child may be returned to his original home. One would wish neither to waste such a resource, nor to condemn these adults to the hurt of removal from their homes of a child they had expected to keep.

In sum, we view much of what the authors say as extraordinarily helpful. The exhortation that courts would ordinarily do best to leave well enough alone—to distrust their capacities for bettering even apparently harmful family situations, and consequently to follow a policy of repose—is forcefully grounded and long overdue. But lawyers who understand and accept the authors' imperative concerns, whose highest value now in custody matters is keeping their clients out of court, may come to question this book for its failures to consider both the values—values *to children* as well as to their parents—of planning and compromise, and the impact of changed law upon behavior that does not presently come to court or find reflection in trouble cases.[33] The book takes only the first, creative step towards important legal growth. So understood, its insights may mark the spot from which further analysis will occur. But initial creativity, the bold shift of perspective, must

33. These failures are sharply reflected in the proposed model child placement code, said to embody the "concepts, guidelines, and conclusions" of the work, and which forms its penultimate chapter. The authors themselves seem to acknowledge its difficulties by their failure to refer to it or illustrate its workings, even once in any other part of the book. It is hard to imagine that others will take it seriously if they do not.

be channeled and refined before effective legal regimes can be shaped from it. That job remains to be done.

PETER L. STRAUSS

Professor of Law
Columbia Law School

JOANNA B. STRAUSS

Assoc. Staff Member
Postgraduate Center for Mental Health

Part IV
Judge Posner's Proposition and the Economics of Adoption

[10]

THE REGULATION OF THE MARKET IN ADOPTIONS†

Richard A. Posner*

I. The Shortage of Babies for Adoption

Whenever critics of the law-and-economics movement want an example of its excesses they point to what is popularly known as the "baby selling article," which Dr. Elisabeth Landes and I wrote almost a decade ago.[1] The article is usually, although incorrectly, described as advocating a free market in babies. Worse, an official of a national adoption organization wrote me recently (and more important, the *Wall Street Journal*) that, as he understood the article, I advocate allowing the wealthy parents of a child who needs a liver transplant to buy a child and "harvest" its liver for their own child. In fact, Dr. Landes and I had stated in the article: "Laws forbidding child abuse and neglect would continue to be fully applicable to adoptive parents even if baby sales were permitted."[2]

Another profound misconception about the article is that in discussing the

---

* Judge, U.S. Court of Appeals for the Seventh Circuit; Senior Lecturer, University of Chicago Law School. This is the revised text of a lecture given in the Distinguished Lecture Series of Boston University Law School on October 10, 1986. The comments of Gary Becker, and the comments and assistance of Richard Porter, are gratefully acknowledged.

[1] Landes & Posner, *The Economics of the Baby Shortage*, 7 J. Legal Stud. 323 (1978). For a briefer treatment of the subject see R. Posner, Economic Analysis of Law § 5.4, at 139-43 (3d ed. 1986). For discussions of the "baby selling" article by the popular press see, e.g., Barrett, *Influential Ideas: A Movement Called 'Law and Economics' Sways Legal Circles*, Wall St. J., Aug. 4, 1986, at 1, col. 1, 16, col. 2; McDaniel, *Free-Market Jurist*, Newsweek, June 10, 1985, at 93-94; Caplan, *Meet Richard Posner, the Judge Who Would Sell Homeless Babies*, Washington Post Nat'l Weekly Ed. (Commentary), Oct. 29, 1984, at 23, col. 1. For temperate scholarly criticism of the Landes-Posner article see Prichard, *A Market for Babies?*, 34 U. Toronto L.J. 341, 347-57 (1984); for intemperate see Kelman, *Consumption Theory, Production Theory and the Ideology of the Coase Theorem*, 52 S. Cal. L. Rev. 669, 688 n.51 (1979) (commenting on my discussion of baby selling in Economic Analysis of Law, and calling it, without elaboration, "irrational and immoral," a "parody of Jonathan Swift's 'Modest Proposal' ").

[2] Landes & Posner, *supra* note 1, at 344. The letter, by William L. Pierce, President of the National Committee for Adoption, was published in the Wall Street Journal of Aug. 22, 1986, at 16, col. 1. In further correspondence with me, Pierce stated that he had never read my article with Dr. Landes and that his understanding of my position came from accounts in the popular press, such as Barrett's article cited in note 1, *supra*. Letter from William L. Pierce to Richard A. Posner (August 4, 1986).

pros and cons of using the market to equilibrate the demand for and supply of babies for adoption, Dr. Landes and I were proposing a radical break with existing ethical norms. Actually, wholly apart from the black market in babies for adoption, the market *is* used, though in a stunted form, to allocate babies for adoption. Adoption agencies charge fees, often stiff ones, to adoptive parents, and part of the agencies' fee income goes to pay the medical expenses and other maintenance expenses of the natural mother; thus the adoptive parents pay the natural mother, albeit indirectly and at a regulated price, to give up her child.[3] In "independent" adoptions, which are arranged through a lawyer or obstetrician, the element of sale is even more transparent, and indeed the system of independent adoption is often referred to as the "gray market." Dr. Landes and I were simply trying to consider how changes in the law might make the existing market in babies for adoption operate more efficiently—and more equitably.

Writing a second article on "baby selling" is not likely to dispel misconceptions harbored by people who feel free to criticize the first article without having read it and are therefore unlikely to read the second either. My purpose is different. The social problem that impelled Dr. Landes and me to write our article remains serious, and this article is addressed to those willing to think about possible solutions in a rational manner.

Some critics of our article apparently believe we wrote it as an exercise in mechanical extrapolation from the economic analysis of conventional markets. According to one of the least controversial concepts in normative economics—Pareto superiority—a transaction that makes at least one person better off and no one worse off increases social welfare, and is therefore efficient. A voluntary exchange is such a transaction, since the parties would not make it if they did not think it would make both of them better off. Therefore (it might seem) the exchange of money for a baby is efficient. But this last step does not follow from the first two.[4] A baby is a member of society too. If the transaction diminishes its welfare, the transaction is not Pareto-superior. If it diminishes the baby's welfare by more than it increases the transactors' welfare, the transaction is not efficient even under a less demanding definition of efficiency. These points are fundamental to an economic analysis of family law,[5] but they do not establish the irrelevance of

---

[3] To simplify the analysis, I shall abstract from the issue of the natural father's rights. To the extent that the father is thought to have a legal right in the child, the transaction costs of baby selling are, obviously, increased.

The fees charged by the agencies are of course regulated. *See In re* Baby Girl D., 517 A.2d 925 (Pa. 1986). If they were not, and if the agencies acted as profit maximizers, the baby shortage would disappear.

[4] We noted this in our earlier article, *see* Landes & Posner, *supra* note 1, at 342, but I shall now drop this refrain to spare the reader.

[5] *See generally* R. POSNER, *supra* note 1, ch. 5. What if, in Mr. Pierce's "harvest" example, *supra* note 2, the transplant would increase the net utility of the rich baby and its parents by more than it would decrease the net utility of the poor baby and its

economics to adoption. Economics is not just about the exchange of objects. Labor economics, and more recently family or household economics, are important fields of economic inquiry even though they deal with the exchange of, and not merely between, human beings. The purpose of our article was not to make an extrapolation at once mechanical and unsound from the market in goods to the market in in babies but to use the analytical tools of economics to explore a pressing social problem—the imbalance between the demand for and supply of babies for adoption.

On the demand side, many married couples are unable to have children and want to adopt them. Recent advances in the treatment of fertility problems appear to have been offset by the growing tendency of women to marry later and postpone childbearing to their thirties, when they are likelier to have fertility problems and will have less time to do something about them (whether the something is medical treatment or joining the queue for adoption). Childless couples who try to adopt through an adoption agency find that they must join a long queue and that even then they may be ineligible to adopt—not because they would be unfit parents but because the agencies, having a very limited supply of babies, set demanding (and sometimes arbitrary) criteria of age, income, race, and religion to limit demand to supply. Few healthy white infants are placed through adoption agencies today; I postpone discussion of the special problems involved in placing other children for adoption.

A couple may try to go the independent adoption route, but this route is haphazard and disorganized, and information about babies available for adoption through it is hard to come by. Some states, moreover, have outlawed independent adoptions.[6] It goes without saying that both adoption

parents? Would the sale then be efficient? These questions pose dilemmas at the heart of ethical debate over utilitarianism and cognate normative concepts such as wealth maximization. *See, e.g.*, Laycock, *The Ultimate Unity of Rights and Utilities*, 64 TEX. L. REV. 407 (1985); Posner, *Wealth Maximization Revisited*, 2 NOTRE DAME J. L., ETHICS & PUB. POL'Y 85, 100-05 (1985); Thomson, *The Trolley Problem*, 94 YALE L.J. 1395 (1985). These are, however, academic questions, because child abuse laws protect children from being killed or injured by their parents, whether natural or adoptive, and whether to reduce or increase welfare in its broadest utilitarian sense. Just as economists who study labor markets normally do not urge the repeal of the thirteenth amendment, which prohibits involuntary servitude, even though under some conditions such servitude might be efficient, Dr. Landes and I did not and do not advocate any relaxation of child abuse laws.

[6] On the varying pattern of state regulation of independent adoption see Note, *Independent Adoption: The Inadequacies of State Law*, 63 WASH. U.L.Q. 753, 755-56 (1985); Note, *Independent Adoption: Regulating the Middleman*, 24 WASHBURN L.J. 327, 345-56 (1985). On the practice of independent adoption agencies see Galen, *Baby Brokers: How Far Can a Lawyer Go?*, 9 NAT'L L.J. no. 22, at 1 (Feb. 9, 1987).

As stunted as the independent adoption system is, it offers a dramatic example of the superiority of market to administrative methods of allocating resources. One commentator, after noting the arbitrary restrictions that adoption agencies impose, points out another serious problem with adoption agencies:

through an agency and independent adoption favor the wealthy and well connected. The final alternative is the black market, a form of independent adoption. The black market is by definition illegal,[7] and illegality forces price up and quality down and makes prospective buyers uneasy. Long queues, shortages, uncertain quality, a black market—these are the classic symptoms of excess demand, whether in the baby market or the Soviet food market.

The difficulty of satisfying the potential demand for babies for adoption would be easier to accept if the supply of babies were inherently quite limited in relation to the demand, as it would be if premarital sex were rare—for the usual source of babies for adoption is illegitimate births. But sex outside marriage is rampant in our society. Although the widespread use of contraceptives reduces the fraction of sexual encounters that result in unwanted conception, the reduction is not so great as one might imagine. Because the probability of conception is reduced, the "costs" of sex (one cost being unwanted conception) are also reduced. The reduction in cost can be expected to increase, and undoubtedly has increased, the amount of premarital sexual activity. For although there are effective methods of contraception, people are often careless about using them; and some people have greater moral inhibitions about contraception than about premarital sex. So even though the fraction of pregnancies is reduced, when it is multiplied by the larger number of sexual encounters the number of undesired pregnancies may not be reduced greatly or even at all.[8] Furthermore,

---

> The harsh interrogation method employed by most agencies also alienates expectant mothers. Approximately four out of five women who consult agencies decide against adoption and raise their own children. Yet, most women who consult independent placement attorneys ultimately place their children for adoption. The difference lies in the fact that agency workers often appear unsympathetic and offer these prospective mothers only economical medical care, while the intermediaries are usually more considerate and provide the best of hospital accommodations.
>
> Consequently, in states that allow independent placements to flourish, the ratio of adoptions to total population is substantially higher than in states that discourage or prohibit independent placements. In Connecticut, the number of state-wide adoptions dropped almost ninety percent in the thirteen-year span following the state's prohibition of all forms of direct and intermediary placement. Understandably, the adoption agencies have frequently sponsored national legislation to eliminate independent placements in an effort to gain control over all non-relative arrangements.

Krones, *Stimulation of Independent Adoptions—A Sensible Approach to Eradicating the Baby Black Market*, 6 ORANGE COUNTY B. J. 192, 200-01 (1979) (footnotes omitted). *See also* Leavitt, *The Model Adoption Act: Return to a Balanced View of Adoption*, 19 FAM. L.Q. 141 (1985).

[7] Although only about half the states have laws specifically aimed at the black market in babies for adoption, see Katz, *Surrogate Motherhood and the Baby-selling Laws*, 20 COLUM. J.L. & SOC. PROBS. 1, 8 n.34 (1986), a free market in babies would run afoul of restrictions on adoptions in every state.

[8] Dr. Landes and I presented figures showing that the number of illegitimate births

because the stigma of illegitimacy, for both parents and children, has also lessened, a smaller fraction of babies born out of wedlock is put up for adoption. The decline in that stigma is also partly responsible for the increase in premarital sex and the casual attitude of many engaged in it about contraception. And more than a change in moral attitudes is involved. The welfare system enables indigent single women and girls, who might otherwise be forced to give up their children for adoption, to keep them.

The supply of babies for adoption has been dramatically affected by the increase in abortions since the Supreme Court's decision in *Roe v. Wade*.[9] The number of reported legal abortions rose from nearly 600,000 in 1972 (before *Roe*) to almost 1,300,000 in 1983, the last year for which reliable figures are available.[10] Of course, even if abortion were illegal, there would still be many abortions, and of the additional babies born many would be retained by the mother. Nevertheless the supply of babies for adoption would be greater. Because of *Roe v. Wade*, the state cannot compel a woman determined to have an abortion to have the baby and give it up for adoption, but it does not follow that the woman should not be given incentives to do so. For many women, abortion is a last resort; indeed, most supporters of a right to abortion insist that this is generally the case. Thus, for little more than the maintenance and medical expenses of pregnancy plus any lost earnings, and often for less, many women might be induced to forgo an abortion and give up the baby for adoption. Dr. Landes and I proposed authorizing some adoption agencies, on an experimental basis, to use a part of their adoption fees to pay women contemplating abortion to forgo the abortion, have the baby, and put it up for adoption through the agency.[11] I

---

in the United States had risen from 183,000 in 1957 to 407,000 in 1973. Landes & Posner, *supra* note 1, at 325 n.6. By 1984 this figure had risen to 770,355. *See* NAT'L CENTER FOR HEALTH STATISTICS, MONTHLY VITAL STATISTICS REPORT, vol. 35 no. 4 Supp., ADVANCE REPORT OF FINAL NATALITY STATISTICS, 1984, 31 tab. 18 (July 18, 1986).

[9] 410 U.S. 113 (1973).

[10] *See* CENTERS FOR DISEASE CONTROL, U.S. PUB. HEALTH SERV., ABORTION SURVEILLANCE 1983, tab. 1 (not yet published).

[11] *See* Landes & Posner, *supra* note 1, at 347-48. An alternative to the scheme Dr. Landes and I suggest would be to subsidize adoption; this is proposed in Comment, *Funded Adoption: A "Viable" Alternative to Adoption*, 1979 B.Y.U. L. REV. 363 (1979). It is an odd proposal, however. The imbalance in the baby market comes not from insufficient, but from excess, demand; subsidizing adoption would make the demand even greater. What is needed is a mechanism for getting more money into the hands of women facing a choice between having an abortion, on the one hand, and carrying the baby to term and then putting it up for adoption, on the other. The Comment does recommend that the program of funded adoption include payment for maternal health care, but it would be a lot simpler (and require no public funding) to let the adoptive parents make a transfer payment to the natural mother via the adoption agency. Although the general case for subsidized adoption is weak, there is

continue to believe that this would be a good experiment. Dr. Landes and I did not in 1978 and I do not today advocate the wholesale and immediate abolition of laws forbidding the sale of babies for adoption.

One problem we did not consider was the age of consent for giving up a child for adoption in exchange for money. If a young girl, say a fourteen-year-old, becomes pregnant, should she be considered competent to decide among abortion, sale, and perhaps other alternatives? I would elide this difficult issue by confining the experiment to pregnant women eighteen or older.[12]

Because no one to my knowledge proposes the "deregulation" of the adoption market beyond the limited experimental step just mentioned, debate about a free market in babies is academic. But that should not be an objection to an article published in an academic journal. In the remainder of this article I shall describe briefly how such a market might operate, under what regulatory constraints, and with what likely consequences, and in doing so will try to respond to the most frequently expressed objections to allowing the market to function in this area.

II. Characteristics of and Desirable Constraints on the Baby Market

A. *The Question of Price*

For heuristic purposes (only!) it is useful to analogize the sale of babies to the sale of an ordinary good, such as an automobile or a television set. We observe, for example, that although the supply of automobiles and of television sets is rationed by price, not all the automobiles and television sets are owned by wealthy people. On the contrary, the free market in these goods has lowered prices, through competition and innovation, to the point where the goods are available to a lot more people than in highly controlled economies such as that of the Soviet Union. There is even less reason for thinking that if babies could be sold to adoptive parents the wealthy would come to monopolize babies. Wealthy people (other than those few who owe their wealth to savings or inheritance rather than to a high income) have high costs of time. It therefore costs them more to raise a child—child rearing still being a time-intensive activity—than it costs the nonwealthy. As a result, wealthy couples tend to have few rather than many children.[13] This pattern would not change if babies could be bought. Moreover, since most people

a stronger case for subsidizing the adoption of children for whom the market demand is weak—children who are nonwhite, or handicapped, or no longer infants. I come back to this issue in Part IIA.

[12] This is probably three-fourths of all women who have abortions, for only 27.1% are 19 or under. *See* Centers for Disease Control, *supra* note 10, tab. 1.

[13] *See* G. Becker, A Treatise on the Family 98, 102 (1981).

have a strong preference for natural, as distinct from adopted, children, wealthy couples able to have natural children are unlikely (to say the least) to substitute adopted ones.

It is also unlikely that allowing people to bid for babies with dollars would drive up the price of babies, thereby allocating the supply to wealthy demanders. Today we observe a high black-market price conjoined with an artificially low price for babies obtained from adoption agencies and through lawful independent adoptions. The "blended" or average price is hard to calculate; but probably it is very high. The low price in the lawful market is deceptive. It ignores the considerable queuing costs—most people would pay a considerable premium to get their adopted baby now, not five or ten years from now. And for people unable to maneuver successfully in the complex market created by the laws against baby selling, the price is infinite. Quality-adjusted prices in free markets normally are lower than black market prices, and there is no reason to doubt that this would be true in a free market for adoptions. Thus, while it is possible that "[i]nherent in the baby black market is the unfairness that results from the fact that only the affluent can afford to pay the enormous fees necessary to procure a baby,"[14] the words "black market" ought to be italicized. It is not the free market, but unwarranted restrictions on the operation of that market, that has raised the black market price of babies beyond the reach of ordinary people.

Thus far I have implicitly been speaking only of the market for healthy white infants. There is no shortage of nonwhite and of handicapped infants, and of any children who are no longer infants, available for adoption. Such children are substitutes for healthy white infants, and the higher the price of the latter, the greater will be the demand for the former. The network of regulations that has driven up the full price (including such nonmonetary components of price as delay) of adopting a healthy, white infant may have increased the willingness of childless couples to consider adopting a child of a type not in short supply, though how much (if at all) no one knows. The present system is, in any event, a grossly inefficient, as well as covert, method of encouraging the adoption of the hard-to-place child. If society wants to subsidize these unfortunate children, the burden of the subsidies should be borne, if not by the natural parents of these children, then by the taxpaying population at large—rather than by just the nation's childless white couples, who under the present unsystematic system bear the lion's share of the burden by being denied the benefits of an efficient method of allocating healthy white infants for adoption in the hope that this will induce them to adopt nonwhite, handicapped, or older children.

B. *The Question of Quality*

As soon as one mentions quality, people's hackles rise and they remind you that one is talking about a traffic in human beings, not in inanimate

[14] Katz, *supra* note 7, at 15 (footnote omitted).

objects. The observation is pertinent, and at least five limitations might have to be placed on the operation of the market in babies for adoption. The first, already mentioned and already in place, is that the buyers can have no right to abuse the thing bought, as they would if the thing were a piece of steel or electronics. This really should go without saying. The laws against child abuse have never distinguished among different methods of acquiring custody of the child. Natural parents are not permitted to abuse a child because they are natural rather than adoptive parents; and people who acquire their children illegally through the black market are no more exempt from the child-abuse laws than people with illegal income are exempt from paying income tax on it. If I were arrested for torturing my cat and charged with violation of the laws forbidding cruelty to animals, it would be no defense that I had bought the cat for forty dollars.

If the laws against child abuse were perfectly efficacious, nothing more would have to be said on the subject. But they are not. The abuse occurs in secret, and the victim may be too young and too dependent to bring it to the attention of the authorities—or indeed to know what is going on. In addition, many child abusers may be so mentally or psychologically abnormal that they cannot be deterred even by very harsh penalties. In such a setting, preventive as well as punitive measures may be justified. Today, all adoptive parents are, in theory anyway, screened for fitness. Adoption agencies are charged with this responsibility, and if we moved toward a freer market in babies the agencies could be given the additional function of investigating and certifying prospective purchasers, who would pay the price of the service.

But let us not make too much of screening. The idea that a significant number of people are lurking about who if given the chance would buy babies for criminal purposes is a bogeyman. Most child abuse occurs as a result either of stresses arising from the experience of parenthood or from the sexual maturing of the child; it is not planned in advance when a baby is conceived or when steps are initiated to adopt a baby.[15] As I will note in a moment, a market in babies for adoption should only be allowed to operate with regard to infants; a couple should not be allowed to sell its thirteen-year-old daughter for immoral (or any other) purposes.

Moreover, since we do not screen natural parents, and any proposal to do so would be met with justifiable protests against governmental intrusion into private matters, the case for screening adoptive parents can hardly be considered self-evident. Maybe, since people like their own children more than strangers' children, the child molester is less likely to molest his own children than other people's children. But people who adopt children do so not out of a mild affection toward children in general, which might easily be

---

[15] On the character and causes of child abuse see, e.g., A. COHN, AN APPROACH TO PREVENTING CHILD ABUSE 3-7, 15-17 (National Committee for Prevention of Child Abuse, 1981), and studies cited therein.

overborne by a tendency to abuse children, but in the hope of creating the same close bonds of affection with the adopted child as natural parents have with their children. Allowing price to play a bigger role in adoptions is not likely to change this. But whether screening adoptive parents is a good or a bad idea is not the issue in this article. Whatever screening is deemed necessary for persons who adopt through an agency or by independent adoption would also be necessary for persons who adopted children in a free(r) market. Freeing the adoption market from price regulation would leave the case for or against screening largely, perhaps entirely, unaffected.

The third limitation on a baby market concerns remedies for breach of contract. In an ordinary market a buyer can both reject defective goods and, if the seller refuses to deliver and damages would be an inadequate remedy for the refusal, get specific performance of the contract. Natural parents are not permitted to reject their baby, either when it is born or afterward, because it turns out to be handicapped or otherwise not in conformity with their expectations; no more should adoptive parents who buy their babies.[16] Nor should the adoptive parents be able to force the natural mother to surrender the baby to them if she changes her mind, unless some competent authority determines that the baby would be better off adopted. For the welfare of the baby must be considered along with that of the contracting parties. Refusing to grant specific performance in circumstances in which it appears that forcing the sale to go through would harm the baby is consistent with the basic equity principle that the third-party effects of equitable remedies must be considered in deciding whether to grant such a remedy or confine the plaintiff to damage remedies. The child is an interested third party whose welfare would be disserved by a mechanical application of the remedies available to buyers in the market for inanimate goods.

For the same reason (the child's welfare) neither natural nor adopting parents should be allowed to sell their children after infancy, that is, after the child has established a bond with its parents. Nor should the natural mother be allowed to take back the baby after adoption, any more than a seller of a conventional good or service can (except in extraordinary circumstances) rescind the sale after delivery and payment in accordance with his contract with the buyer, unless, once again, a competent authority decides that the baby's welfare would be increased. I shall not try to resolve the question whether, in any of these remedial settings, the welfare of the child should be paramount or should be balanced with that of the adult parties.[17]

[16] *Cf.* Burr v. Board of County Comm'rs, 23 Ohio St. 3d 69, 491 N.E.2d 1101 (1986), where the adopting parents were awarded damages because the adoption agency had intended to induce reliance on its material misrepresentations of fact about the child, and the parents did reasonably rely, to their detriment, on the misrepresentations. For a discussion of the remedial problem see Note, *Rumpelstiltskin Revisited: The Inalienable Rights of Surrogate Mothers*, 99 HARV. L. REV. 1936 (1986), which discusses the constitutionality of specific performance in breach of contract suits against surrogate mothers.

[17] *See supra* note 5.

The last limitation on the baby market that I shall discuss relates to eugenic breeding.[18] Although prospects still seem remote, one can imagine an entrepreneur in the baby market trying to breed a race of *Übermenschen* who would command premium prices. The external effects of such an endeavor could be very harmful, and would provide an appropriate basis for governmental regulation.

I am not so sanguine about the operation of a baby market, even with the limitations I have discussed, that I am prepared to advocate the complete and immediate repeal of the laws forbidding the sale of babies for adoption. That such a market might give somewhat greater scope for child abusers and might encourage weird and potentially quite harmful experiments in eugenic breeding should be enough to give anyone pause. But to concentrate entirely on the downside would be a mistake. One million abortions a year is a serious social problem regardless of where one stands on the underlying ethical issues; so is a flourishing black market in babies combined with a severe shortage in the lawful market.

The severity of the shortage is, admittedly, a matter of fair debate. In our 1978 article Dr. Landes and I estimated that about 130,000 married couples who at present are childless might adopt a child under free-market conditions.[19] More recent research suggests this estimate is reasonable. A study conducted by the National Center for Health Statistics found that 46% of the estimated 274,000 currently married women who are between 30 and 44 years of age and sterile have adopted a child.[20] If all those who have not adopted would like to, and would be willing to pay a free-market price, then the 148,000 married couples in the relevant population who have not yet adopted a child are unsatisfied demanders. But some unknown fraction of this number either do not want to have children at all or do not want to have adopted children. Dr. Landes and I noted that 96% of couples marrying in 1975 in which the wife was between 18 and 24 years old expected to have a child.[21] Since most people who marry young do not know whether they have a fertility problem, it seems a fair guess that almost all of the 274,000 married couples who are sterile planned when they got married to have children, and hence that most of the 148,000 who have not yet adopted a child would like, or at some time in the past would have liked, to adopt a child. Of course,

---

[18] *See generally* Smith, *Genetics, Eugenics, and Public Policy*, 1985 S. ILL. L.J. 435, 447-53 (describing artificial insemination, *in vitro* fertilization and embryo implants, cloning, and parthenogenesis, and discussing the constitutionality of eugenics legislation).

[19] Landes & Posner, *supra* note 1, at 336.

[20] *See* Bachrach, *Adoption as a Means of Family Formation: Data from the National Survey of Family Growth*, 45 J. MARRIAGE & FAM. 859, 862 & tab. 2 (1983).

[21] Landes & Posner, *supra* note 1, at 336. The figure was the same in 1983. *See* U.S. BUREAU OF THE CENSUS, STATISTICAL ABSTRACT OF THE U.S.: 1986, 64 tab. 98 (106th ed. 1985).

wanting something and being willing to pay for it are two different things, and it might seem that many childless couples would be unwilling or unable to pay for a baby if they had to pay free market prices. But this seems unlikely. The purchase price on the free market would probably be lower than under the present system (for reasons discussed earlier), and in any event only a small fraction of the total cost (even discounted to present value) of raising a child. Bear in mind, too, that adoptive parents save the medical and opportunity costs of pregnancy. Marrying couples who expected to have a child, notwithstanding the cost, are unlikely to be deterred by the small, probably zero or even negative, incremental cost of adopting a child in a free market.

True, some couples decide after marriage that they don't want to have a child. This is particularly likely if the couple anticipates a high probability of divorce. About half of American marriages end in divorce, and some of these divorces are anticipated before children enter the picture. Another consideration is that some couples do not consider an adopted child a good substitute for the natural child they cannot have, and they may therefore decide to remain childless even if the price of an adopted child is low and the quality high.[22] Although these factors suggest a downward adjustment in my estimates, there are three offsetting factors to consider. First, some unknown fraction of adoptions is of babies bought in the black market, and the part of the demand for a good that is satisfied in a black market reflects the shortage in the lawful market. Second, the 148,000 figure excludes married couples who become sterile after having one or more children and who would like to adopt. In fact, 20% of married couples who become sterile after having one child go on to adopt a child, and 42% of married couples with one child say that they would adopt a second child if they became sterile.[23] Finally, and bearing particularly on the experiment that Dr. Landes and I proposed, ten times as many premarital pregnancies end in "pregnancy loss" (miscarriage, stillbirth, and no doubt the biggest category, abortion) as in putting the baby up for adoption.[24]

[22] The potential importance of this point is brought out by a 1977 study that found that, of then-married women who had no children and wanted to have one or more, only 62% said they would adopt a child. *See* Bonham, *Who Adopts: The Relationship of Adoption and Social-Demographic Characteristics of Women*, 39 J. MARRIAGE & FAM. 295, 300 tab. 3 (1977). If 46% of sterile couples have adopted a child, Bachrach, *supra* note 20, and 62% would like to, it might seem that the fraction of unsatisfied demanders (to be multiplied by 274,000 to yield an estimate of their number) would be 16% rather than 54%. But apart from other factors mentioned in the text, a statement of nonintention to adopt a child may simply reflect awareness of the obstacles to adoption under the present system. As we shall see, the nonintending 38% (100% − 62%) is almost twice the percentage of couples who become sterile after having one child and then adopt—suggesting a very large unsatisfied demand among this group.

[23] *See id.*; Bachrach, *supra* note 20.

[24] *See* Bachrach, *Adoption Plans, Adopted Children, and Adoptive Mothers*, 48 J. MARRIAGE & FAM. 243, 251 tab. 6 (1986).

One reason people fear the operation of a free market in babies for adoption is that they extrapolate from experience with the illegal market. Critics who suggest that baby selling offers the promise of huge profits to middlemen—the dreaded "baby brokers"—fail to distinguish between an illegal market, in which sellers demand a heavy premium (an apparent, though not real, profit) in order to defray the expected costs of punishment, and a legal market, in which the premium is eliminated. Seemingly exorbitant profits, low quality, poor information, involvement of criminal elements—these widely asserted characteristics of the black market in babies[25] are no more indicative of the behavior of a lawful market than the tactics of the bootleggers and rum-runners during Prohibition were indicative of the behavior of the liquor industry after Prohibition was repealed.

III. The Objection from Symbolism and the Issue of Semantics

Even if partial deregulation of the baby market might make practical utilitarian sense along the lines just suggested, some will resist on symbolic grounds. If we acknowledge that babies can be sold, the argument goes, we open the door to all sorts of monstrous institutions—including slavery. We regularly resist this type of argument in analogous contexts, and I have difficulty understanding why it stubbornly persists in this one. Some people argue that military conscription is wrong because it legitimates government coercion of the civilian labor force, or because it is a form of slavery; others that the sale of blood should be forbidden because it treats human life as a commodity; others that medicine should be socialized so that the wealthy can't use their wealth to increase their chances of a long and healthy life, relative to the poor; others that parents should not be allowed to spank their children because that is treating the children like slaves; others that capital punishment should be outlawed because it implicates the state in murder. The common thread in these arguments is the reprobating of social practices not because of any demonstrable or even probable bad effects, but because the practices have a symbolic affinity with practices that do have horrible effects. Allowing parents to sell their children into slavery would be a monstrous idea. Allowing the prospective mother of an illegitimate child to receive money in exchange for giving up the child for adoption, when described in shorthand as "baby selling," seems to many people uncomfortably close to the type of real baby selling that is found in slave societies—that was found in the slave societies of the South before the Civil War. No doubt it requires more thought than most people are willing to give to the problem to hold these quite different concepts separate in their minds. But if

---

[25] *See, e.g.*, Grove, *Independent Adoption: The Case for the Gray Market*, 13 Vill. L. Rev. 116, 118-21 (1967). There are few data on the operation of the black market, and none later than the mid-1970s. See references in R. Posner, *supra* note 1, at 139 n.3, and in *Black-Market Adoptions*, 22 Cath. Law. 48 (1976).

they are not held separate we may find ourselves condemned to perpetuate the painful spectacle of mass abortion and illegitimacy in a society in which, to a significant extent, children are not available for adoption by persons unwilling to violate the law.

One should always be suspicious of arguments against the market when they are made by people who have no desire to participate in it themselves, people who want to restrict the availability of goods to other people. Most people who invoke vague symbols in opposition to "baby selling" have no interest in or expectation of either adopting a child or conceiving one out of wedlock. They have little empathy with the needs of people who find themselves involuntarily childless or involuntarily pregnant.

The opponents of "baby selling" are unwilling to acknowledge that what we have today, even apart from the black market, is closer to a free market in babies than a free market in babies would be to slavery or torture (always bearing in mind that a free market in an economic sense is one in which due consideration is given the welfare of affected third parties, here the babies themselves). As I said at the outset, adoption agencies do lawfully "sell" babies, and many charge thousands of dollars. Moreover, in independent adoptions, the mother herself may "sell" her baby, for it is not considered unlawful to use a part of the fee paid by the adoptive parents to defray the medical and other maintenance costs of the mother during pregnancy. It seems that to obtain lawfully a healthy, white infant (rarely available through adoption agencies), a couple must be prepared to lay out at least $5,000.[26] Black-market prices of $25,000, even $50,000, have been rumored, but the equilibrium baby price in a free market (by which I do not mean an entirely unregulated market, for I suggested in Part II of this paper that the market should be regulated in various ways) might not exceed $5,000. As a matter of fact, though baby selling is everywhere unlawful, almost half the states have no specific restrictions on fees payable for adoption, and in many other states the restrictions are porous.[27] No doubt many lawful and semi-lawful "baby sales" are taking place today at approximately free-market prices.

Two other important examples of legal baby selling should be mentioned.[28] One is the "family compact" doctrine, which allows a woman to enter into an enforceable contract to give up her baby for adoption by a close

---

[26] *See* Pesmen, *Bizarre Sector of the Economy Awaits Adoptive Couples Here*, Crain's Chi. Bus., Sept. 1, 1986, at 27, col. 1.

[27] *See* W. MEEZAN, S. KATZ & E. RUSSO, ADOPTIONS WITHOUT AGENCIES: A STUDY OF INDEPENDENT ADOPTION 182-85 (1978).

[28] *See generally* Note, *Developing a Concept of the Modern "Family": A Proposed Uniform Surrogate Parenthood Act*, 73 GEO. L.J. 1283, 1289-92 (1985) (discussing whether and in what circumstances surrogate mother arrangements violate laws against baby selling); Cohen, *Surrogate Mothers: Whose Baby Is It?*, 10 AM. J. L. & MED. 243 (1984) (discussing the legality and judicial enforcement of surrogate mother contracts).

relative. The other is surrogate motherhood, by which (at least in some states) a married couple in which the wife is infertile can make an enforceable contract with another woman whereby the latter agrees to be artificially inseminated with the husband's sperm and to carry the baby to term and give it up to the couple. In the first case the close family relative "buys" the baby, in the second the father (and his wife) "buys out" the natural mother's "share" in their joint product.

So we have legal baby selling today; the question of public policy is not whether baby selling should be forbidden or allowed but how extensively it should be regulated. I simply think it should be regulated less stringently than is done today.

Part V
Child Custody on Divorce

[11]

Child of Divorce: An Overview

Judith S. Wallerstein, Ph.D.

Children of divorce represent a diverse population at risk for subsequent psychological problems, whose interests are insufficiently understood or protected by the legal system or the mental health community. Although many children weather the stress of marital breakdown without psychopathological sequelae, a significant number show lasting difficulties. Information concerning the psychological adaptation of these children has increased rapidly during the past decade, but it remains unequal to the task of guiding family policy in this arena. Current knowledge identifies child gender and developmental stage as crucial factors that interact with the chronic stresses of postdivorce family life to produce short- and long-range impediments to the maturation of these vulnerable young people. There is a critical need to facilitate understanding and cooperation between the behavioral sciences and the legal profession on behalf of children in divorced families. The major research tasks relevant to enlightened public policy lie ahead.

INTRODUCTION

The child is the hidden client in the divorce proceeding. Children are rarely seen by the attorney or by the judge. Little in their professional education equips either the attorney or the judge to interview the child or to query the parent regarding the child, or even to direct the parent knowledgeably to a careful consideration of the child's needs and concerns. Nor is there specialized training that would prepare the judge for the complex, arduous tasks of determining the best interests of the child amid a mass of conflicting arguments and diverse perspectives, or of weighing the urgency of the child's condition and circumstances. Children are seen infrequently by mediators in private practice or court-related services. Few mediators are trained

---

Judith S. Wallerstein, Ph.D., is the Executive Director of the Center for the Family in Transition, Corte Madera, California, Principal Investigator for the California Children of Divorce Study, and Senior Lecturer at the University of California at Berkeley, School of Social Welfare and School of Law. *Correspondence and reprint requests should be addressed to Judith S. Wallerstein, Ph.D., Center for the Family in Transition, 5725 Paradise Drive, Corte Madera, CA 94925.* This work is supported by the San Francisco Foundation, the Zellerbach Family Fund, and the Marion E. Kenworthy-Sarah H. Swift Foundation.

Behavioral Sciences & the Law, Vol. 4, No. 2, pp. 105–118 (1986)
 CCC 0735–3936/86/020105–14$04.00

in the assessment of children, and many oppose the inclusion of children in the negotiation process.

It is generally assumed that parents will speak on behalf of their children. However, we have observed that the capacity of parents to separate their own needs and wishes from those of their children is often limited at the time of the marital rupture and during its immediate or extended aftermath (Wallerstein, 1985c). As a result, at the critical time of decision making regarding their future, many children are invisible or are represented by parents whose parenting capacity and judgment may be gravely impaired and whose customary sensitivity to their children's needs may be temporarily dulled by their intense feelings and conflicts during the crisis.

Yet, ironically and tragically, the person most likely to be affected by the divorce itself and the settlement that frames the postdivorce years may well be the child. Divorce for the middle-class American child represents the single most acutely stressful event of his or her growing up years. For a significant number of children the developmental effects of marital unhappiness and divorce last for many years and may be not only prolonged but may be enduring.

Children have been excluded as subjects from a great deal of research that bears directly on child-related issues and public policy. For example, studies that have been widely invoked to support the presumption of joint custody have not included an assessment of the children. The influential work of Roman and Haddad (1978) and of Ilfield and Alexander (1982) falls into this category. An extensive review of the joint custody research calls attention not only to the paucity of research altogether in this important public domain, but specifically to the very limited knowledge about the key figure of the child in the joint custody arrangement (Clingempeel & Reppucci, 1982). As a result, except for the work of a few researchers (Luepnitz, 1982; McKinnon & Wallerstein, 1986; Steinman, 1981, 1986; Steinman, Zemmelman, & Knoblauch, 1985), each of whom studied a small group of families, the characteristics of children who are likely to benefit from joint custody versus those for whom this arrangement might be detrimental have scarcely been examined directly. There is, in fact, no body of scientific knowledge that supports either a presumption of joint custody or the imposition of joint physical custody over the objection of one parent. Nevertheless, joint custody has been introduced in legislation in a majority of the states within the recent decade and has been accorded presumptive status in several leading states.

Similarly, research concerning the impact of parental conflict on the child's psychological and moral development has been meager despite widespread public concern both with family violence and with the mounting incidence of litigation over issues of custody and visitation. Curiously, although it is reasonable to assume that psychopathology in one or both parents is highly correlated with chronic marital or postdivorce conflict, interparental conflict has been treated as an independent factor as if it were unrelated to other aspects of the parents' personalities and relationships. Additionally, the experience of the child who witnesses interparental quarreling or violence is likely to differ considerably from the experience of the child who stands at the center of the parental dispute. Yet, these different experiences have been poorly distinguished. Moreover, all of these experiences are likely to differ in their impact on the child depending on its age and sex, the patterning, duration and intensity of the conflict, the psychological functioning of the child and the parent, the overall cast of the parent-child relationship, and whether the child participates in the fighting, or remains neutral and strongly rejects a participatory role despite parental blandishments or threats. Yet, only very recently have we begun to acquire a body of direct observations about the children who are at the center of unremitting, chronic custody and visitation disputes (Campbell & Johnston, 1986; Johnston, Campbell, & Mayes, 1985; Johnston, Campbell, & Tall, 1985)or about the impact of the court proceedings on the disputing family (Hauser, 1985). The total sum of these studies, themes evident in an earlier comprehensive review (Emery, 1982), remains far below that required in order to guide social policy or clinical practice.

Despite the accumulating reports of the difficulty that many children in divorced families experience, society has been reluctant to regard children of divorce as a special group at risk. Notwithstanding the magnitude of the population affected and the widespread implications for public policy and law, community attention has been limited, research that includes the direct assessment of children has been poorly supported. New legislation and new programs have often reflected the narrow priorities of parents or of the judiciary rather than the needs of children, and appropriate social, psychological, and economic measures have only begun to develop.

INCIDENCE OF DIVORCE

The trends that have been extrapolated from the 1980 census translate into startling expectations for American families. It is estimated currently that 45% of all children born in the early 1980s will experience their parents' divorce, 35% will experience a remarriage, and 20% will experience a second divorce (Norton, 1985). In 1981, approximately 22.5 million young people, or 36% of all American children under 18, were living in a family other than the traditional two-parent family. This group included 11.4 million children living with their mothers only; 1.2 million living with fathers only; 6.4 million living with one biological parent and one stepparent; and the remainder living with adoptive parents, grandparents, or in foster homes. For black children, living with two parents is already less common than living with one parent (Zill, 1983).

Psychopathological Sequelae

Although many children weather the stress of marital discord and family breakup without psychopathological sequelae, a significant number are identified within a troubled population. Children of divorce are significantly overrepresented in outpatient psychiatric, family agency, and private practice populations compared with children in the general population (Gardner, 1976; Kalter, 1977). The best predictors of mental health referrals for school age children are parental divorce or parental loss as a result of death (Felner, Stolberg, & Cowen, 1975). A significant survey of adolescents whose parents had separated and divorced by the time the children were seven-years old found that 30% of these children had received psychiatric or psychological therapy by the time they reached adolescence, compared with 10% of adolescents in intact families (Zill, 1983).

Several studies suggest that children of divorce show lower achievement and experience greater difficulty in learning than do their classmates from two-parent families. Several large scale surveys report a higher incidence of disrupted learning, erratic attendance, higher dropout rates, increased tardiness, and deteriorated social behavior among boys from single-parent families (Brown, 1980; Guidubaldi et al., 1983). Another survey revealed that 15% of teenagers living with divorced mothers had been expelled or suspended from school at some time between elementary school and high school, whereas only 3% of teenagers from low-conflict, intact families had sustained a similar experience (Zill, 1983). At the other end of the developmental ladder, a study of kindergarten children shows that single-parent status resulting from divorce predicts significantly lower academic and lower social competence at school entry independent of socioeconomic status (Guidubaldi et al., 1984). Also relevant to the children's experience is the fact that divorced adults use inpatient and outpatient mental health services at a significantly higher rate than adults in intact marriages (Bloom, White, & Asher, 1979).

THE AMBIANCE OF THE SEPARATION PERIOD

Within the past decade we have acquired a much greater understanding of the nature of the separation and divorcing process and the responses of children and adults to the marital rupture. Earlier there had been insufficient recognition of the disabling impact of divorce on the psychological functioning of the adult. Many adults who can live alongside each other for years without open anger become openly hostile as the marriage ends. Others who suffer from chronic moderate depression may become severely depressed or agitated. In the majority of households, feelings of bitterness and scenes of conflict increase. Much of the anger and depression among the parents reflects the fact that in a family with children, the decision to divorce is rarely mutual. Of the 60 couples who were studied over many years in the California Children of Divorce study, only one couple agreed together to dissolve their marriage. Most often the divorce is sought by one spouse and opposed or reluctantly accepted by the other. The profound narcissistic injury and psychic pain engendered by the one-sided decision and the pattern of the separation itself set the stage for the interaction at the time of the divorce and during the years that follow.

Perhaps of central importance from the child's perspective is the bizarre but short-lived behavior frequently exhibited by the parents, such as verbal accusations and threats, rage (which may be accompanied by violence), depression, and, sometimes, suicidal ideation. A marriage that has been humdrum for years is likely to spring to life with the decision to divorce, and the unrestrained expression of aggressive and sexual impulses and intense feelings tends to dominate households that were accustomed to a more circumspect way of life prior to the divorce decision.

DIMINISHED CAPACITY TO PARENT FOLLOWING MARITAL RUPTURE

The acute phase of the divorce is characterized by diminished physical and psychological availability of the parents. Newly employed parents are likely to leave children alone after school or for long periods with new sitters in a strange setting. Sometimes the burden of work for the parent is such that very young children prepare their own lunches, get themselves to school, and put themselves to bed. The practical changes of life take an immense toll by reducing the time and attention available for children and so increasing the child's anxiety and anger.

New relationships become important and demand considerable time. The flurry of social or sexual activity that often immediately follows the marital rupture is likely to absorb weekend time and evenings. At the outset the visiting and noncustodial parent's house is often inadequate for extended visits, and early visits tend to be uneasy, tense, or on the run. Also, new partners, some of whom have children, are likely to be present during these early visits, and children may feel aggrieved because their access to the parent has been blocked.

The household disorder that prevails in the aftermath of divorce, the rising tempers in both mother and child, especially between mothers and small sons, eventuates in a sense of reduced competence and a greater helplessness in the mother, provoking a continuing cycle of mutually destructive behaviors (Hetherington, 1979). Further cause for household deterioration can be found in the mother's fear of rejection by her children. Wishing to avoid reproach for the divorce and fearful of evoking the children's anger, the mother may retreat from requiring certain standards of behavior or meeting ordinary household standards. As a result, there is mounting disorder, less discipline, less caretaking, and the anxiety driven sense among the children that the divorce has led to the loss of not one, but both parents (Wallerstein and Kelly, 1980).

CHANGES IN PARENT-CHILD RELATIONSHIP

The Visiting Relationship

During the extended aftermath of the divorce, the relationships between parents and children undergo many significant changes. Because close to 90% of children in divorced families reside with their mothers, the visiting relationship is critical to child and parent. Our evidence is that the visiting parent-child relationship is likely to differ markedly from the preexisting relationship during the marriage. Poor, even impoverished parent-child relationships may improve, while others that had been close and affectionate during the marriage may dwindle unexpectedly. It may be that the most difficult and challenging psychological task for parent and child within the postdivorce family is to transplant the parent-child relationship that develops within the rich soil of family life into the strange, relatively impoverished and very limited ground that even a generous, regular visiting schedule provides. It is no surprise that a great many parent-child relationships fail to survive the shock of a move and fail additionally to take root outside the family. For the visiting relationship, it should be clearly understood, is *a new relationship* that is created at the time of the marital rupture and has no true counterpart within the intact family. The processes by which this new relationship are established and maintained are complex, and they entail many difficulties that have been insufficiently acknowledged by attorneys, the courts, clinicians, or the divorcing families themselves (Wallerstein, 1985c).

Visiting carries a heavy emotional overload. The visit usually requires a return of the departed parent to the family residence, a brief meeting between the adults, and some verbal interchange around logistics. Often at such brief meetings the adult reexperiences intensely the hopes and dreams of the marriage, combined with the angers, the disappointments, the sorrows, the justifications for the divorce. For many people such meetings engender intolerable stress. Although the tensions which are stirred by the visit are likely in most families to diminish over time, many adults become discouraged and yield to the impulse to stay away. Others become depressed, not only at returning to the family residence, but at each successive separation from the children. Eventually they restrict their visiting or give it up altogether. Others, feeling guilty for having left, find that each visit with the children renews and sharpens their guilt, especially if the child has been left in the care of a troubled or depressed parent. There is, in fact, no other family relationship that depends so heavily on voluntary association, and that is so poorly supported by the social milieu. The visiting relationship must be flexible, to adapt to the changing developmental needs, aspirations, and goals of the child and the parent, and it must withstand the impact of the inevitable frustrations and resentments that arise in the course of the youngster's growing up years (Wallerstein, 1985c).

The Custodial Parent-Child Relationship

Similarly, the custodial parent and child move into new roles with each other. Many youngsters, some very young, become very close to their mothers and act as proud helpers and confidantes. Others move precipitously away from a closer involvement out of fear of engulfment. The 10-year study of the California Children of Divorce found that preschool children of a decade later were very close to the mother and profoundly appreciative of her efforts on their behalf (Wallerstein, 1984). These youngsters were also concerned about the mother's loneliness and the emotional toll of being a single parent. Their concerns were reinforced as these young adolescents thought ahead to the time of leaving home. The concern about growing up and leaving mother alone—husbandless and childless—was a repeated theme in postdivorce households where the mother had not remarried (Wallerstein, 1985b).

For the oldest children, a frequent pattern was that of heavy reliance by the custodial parent on the competent child to participate actively in the household and in the decision making of daily living. Young people worked hard and long, and their contributions were substantial. As parents and children joined to deal with the problems and routines of life, they were brought together in new ways that directly helped the parent and also promoted emotional, psychological, and intellectual growth in the children. A significant group of these young people report resentment at having to take on so much responsibility at the time of the breakup and during the extended aftermath.

Regarding the divorce as a voluntary decision of the parents, these youngsters felt that they were forced to bear the brunt of their parents' mistaken marriage and that they have been unjustly required to take responsibility at home for disturbed or incompetent parents, or for parents who themselves were free to enjoy an active social and sexual life. A significant number of young people at the 10-year followup expressed anger at their parents because they, the children, had had to give up so much of their play time and school time in order to care for their parents, for the younger children, and to assure the continuity of the household (Wallerstein, 1985b).

THE OVERBURDENED CHILD

Our society has been slow to recognize that one consequence of the erosion of the supporting structure of the family is that the burden of supporting themselves, as well as supporting troubled parents, often falls heavily on the children. I have reported the disruption of the childrearing functions of the family within a significant number of postdivorce households (Wallerstein, 1985a). One effect is the overburdening of a significant number of children who are unable to maintain their developmental course because the responsibilities they carry for themselves and for others are too arduous and long lasting. Several groups of youngsters in different circumstances fall under this overburdened rubric. These include: (a) Children who take on responsibility for their own physical care and upbringing which taxes them beyond their capacities. Such children remain responsible over the years, often beginning at very early ages, for their own routine care, including meal time and bedtime. (b) Youngsters who acquire special psychological significance in response to the regressed need of one or both troubled parents. These children shoulder responsibility for maintaining the psychological functioning of one or both parents, or of the family, and this responsibility is beyond their capacity. (c) Children who are the targets of continued litigation between their parents out of the loneliness and emotional dependence of one or both parents. Often the disputing parent is fighting for the child's presence and the key psychological and social role that the child has come to play. The child's roles are many and varied. These roles, as they relate to the troubled parent, include those of mentor, of sibling, of ally, of parent, of friend, of concubine. Their function includes warding off loneliness, despair, even suicide. Unfortunately, even when disputes are formally settled, these youngsters often suffer from mediated agreements or court orders that fail to consider their interests adequately, attempting primarily to compromise the parents' conflicting demands or, more accurately, to meet both parents' regressed needs for the presence of the child (Wallerstein, 1985a).

Initial Responses

Many children are relatively content and even well-parented in families where one or both parents are unhappy (Wallerstein & Kelly, 1980). Few youngsters experience relief with the divorce decision and those who do are usually older and have witnessed physical violence or open conflict between their parents. The child's early responses are governed neither by an understanding of issues leading to the divorce nor by the fact that divorce has a high incidence in the community. To the child, divorce signifies the collapse of the structure that provides support and protection. The child reacts as to the anticipated cutting of his or her lifeline (Wallerstein & Kelly, 1980).

The initial responses of children and adolescents to a marital separation are compounded by realistic fears and by fantasies about catastrophes which they fear that the divorce will bring in its wake. Children suffer from a pervasive sense of vulnerability as they feel that the protective and nurturant function of the family has given way. They grieve over the loss of the noncustodial parent, over the loss of the intact family, and often over the multiple losses of neighborhood, friends, and school. Children also worry about their distressed parents. They are concerned about who will take care of the parent who has left and whether the custodial parent will be able to manage alone. They experience intense anger toward one or both parents whom they hold responsible for disrupting the family. Some of their anger is reactive and defends them against their own feelings of powerlessness, concern about being lost in the shuffle, and fear that their own needs will be disregarded as the parents give priority to their own wishes and needs. Some children, especially young children, suffer from guilt over fantasied misdeeds which they feel may have contributed to the family quarrels and led to the divorce. Others feel that it is their responsibility to mend the broken marriage (Wallerstein & Kelly, 1980).

The responses of the child must also be considered within the social context of the divorce and in particular within the loneliness and social isolation that so many children experience. Children face the tensions and sorrows of divorce with little help from anybody else. Fewer than 10% of children in the California Children of Divorce study had any help at the time of the crisis from adults outside the family although many people, including neighbors, pediatricians, ministers, rabbis, and family friends, knew the family and the children (Wallerstein & Kelly, 1980).

Sex Differences

Boys are reported to be more vulnerable than girls to the acute stress of the marital rupture, as well as to the more chronic stresses of the transitional phase in the preschool and latency ages. Major differences between preschool boys and girls in a wide range of cognitive, social, and developmental measures have been reported (Hetherington, Cox, & Cox, 1982). Boys from divorced families perform less well on a range of learning measures than boys in intact families, although girls from divorced families are indistinguishable from their peers in intact families on the same measures (Guidubaldi et al., 1983).

Sex differences also emerged in the California Children of Divorce study. While boys and girls did not differ in their overall psychological adjustment at the time of the marital breakup, at 18 months later the boys' psychological adjustment had deteriorated markedly, whereas that of the girls had greatly improved, making for a growing gap between the two groups (Wallerstein & Kelly, 1980). Other evidence shows that marital turmoil has a greater impact on boys than on girls, both in divorced families and in intact, discordant families (Block, Block, & Morrison, 1981; Emery & O'Leary, 1982; Rutter, 1970).

How much of this differential effect between the sexes is mediated by the mother having custody is unknown. The Texas custody research project compared a small group of latency-aged children in the custody of the same-sex parent with a matched group in the custody of the opposite-sex parent and with a matched group of children in intact families. The result suggested that the sex of the custodial parent has a direct bearing on the child's social adjustment. Children in the custody of the same sex parent showed more maturity, greater sociability, more independence, and less demanding behavior than did children in the custody of the opposite sex parent (Santrock & Warshak, 1979; Warshak & Stantrock, 1983).

A confounding set of observations is reported from the 10-year followup study of the California Children of Divorce project. Findings here suggest that girls from divorced families may have a more stormy adolescence and a more conflict-ridden entry into young adulthood than their male counterparts. A significant number of young women were caught up in a web of short-lived relationships, and they described themselves as fearful of commitment, anticipating infidelity and betrayal (Wallerstein, 1985b). It may be that boys, especially young boys, have a more difficult time immediately following the divorce, but that girls find adolescence a particularly hazardous time.

Developmental Factors

Developmental factors are critical in the responses of children and adolescents at the time of the marital rupture. Despite significant individual differences in the child, in the family, and in parent-child relations, the child's age and developmental stage appear to be the most important factors governing the initial response. The child's dominant needs, his or her capacity to perceive and understand family events, the central psychological preoccupation and conflict, the available repertoire of defense and coping strategies, and the dominant patterning of relationships and expectations all reflect the child's age and developmental stage.

A major finding in divorce research has been the common patterns of response within different age groups (Wallerstein & Kelly, 1980). The age groups which share significant commonalities in perceptions, responses, underlying fantasies, and behaviors are the preschool ages 3–5, early school age or early latency ages 5½–8, later school age or latency ages 8–11, and, finally, adolescent ages 12–18

(Kelly & Wallerstein, 1976; Wallerstein & Kelly, 1974; 1975; 1976; 1980). These responses, falling as they do into age-related groupings, may reflect children's reactions to acute stress, generally, and not only to marital rupture.

Observations about preschool children derived from longitudinal studies in two widely different regions, namely, Virginia and northern California, are remarkably similar in their findings (Hetherington, 1979; Hetherington, Cox, & Cox, 1978, 1982; Wallerstein & Kelly, 1975; 1980). Preschool children are likely to show regression following one parent's departure from the household. The regression usually occurs in the most recent developmental achievement of the child. Intensified fears are frequent and are evoked by routine separations from the custodial parent during the day and at bedtime. Sleep disturbances are also frequent. The preoccupying fantasy of many of the little children is fear of abandonment by both parents. Yearning for the departed parent is intense. Young children are likely to become irritable and demanding and to behave aggressively with parents, with younger siblings, and with peers.

Children in the 5- to 8-year-old group are likely to show open grieving. They are preoccupied with feelings of concern and longing for the departed parent. Many share the terrifying fantasy of replacement. "Will my daddy get a new dog, a new mommy, a new little boy?" were the comments of several boys in this age group. Little girls wove elaborate Madame Butterfly fantasies, asserting that the departed father would some day return to them, that he loved them "the best." Many of the children in this age group could not believe that the divorce would endure. About half suffered a precipitous decline in their school work (Kelly & Wallerstein, 1976).

In the 8½- to 12-year-old group, the central response often seems to be intense anger at one or both parents for causing the divorce. In addition, these children suffer from grief over the loss of the intact family, from anxiety, loneliness, and the humiliating sense of their own powerlessness. Youngsters in this age group often see one parent as the "good" parent and the other as "bad," and they appear especially vulnerable to the blandishments of one or the other parent to engage in marital battles. Children in later latency also have a high potential for assuming a helpful and empathic role in the care of a needy parent. School performance and peer relationships suffer a decline in approximately one-half of these children (Wallerstein & Kelly, 1976).

Contrary to community expectations, adolescents are very vulnerable to their parents' divorce. The precipitation of acute depression, accompanied by suicidal preoccupation and acting out, is frequent enough to be alarming. Anger can be intense. Several instances have been reported of direct violent attacks on custodial parents by young adolescents who had not previously shown such behavior (Springer & Wallerstein, 1983). Preoccupied with issues of morality, adolescents may judge the parents' conduct during the marriage and the divorce, and they may identify with one parent and do battle against the other. A good number become anxious about their own future entry into adulthood, concerned that they may experience marital failure like their parents (Wallerstein & Kelly, 1974). Researchers have also called attention to the adolescents' impressive capacity to grow in maturity and independence as they respond to the family crisis and the parents' need for help (Weiss, 1979).

OUTCOME AFTER SEVERAL YEARS

The child's early response to divorce should be distinguished from the impact of the many family changes on the child's development and psychological adjustment. No single theme appeared among those children who enhanced or continued their good developmental progress after the divorce crisis had finally ended. Nor was there a single theme which appeared among those whose functioning deteriorated moderately or markedly. Instead, a set of complex configurations was found (Wallerstein & Kelly, 1980), in which the relevant components appear to include (1) the extent to which the parent has been able to resolve and put aside conflict and angers and to make use of the relief from conflict provided by the divorce (Emery, 1982; Jacobson, 1978); (2) the course of the custodial parent's handling of the child and the resumption or improvement of parenting within the home (Hess & Camara, 1979); (3) the extent to which the child does not feel rejected by the noncustodial or visiting parent and the extent to which this relationship has continued regularly and kept pace with the child's growth; (4) the extent to which the divorce has helped to attenuate or dilute a psychopathological parent-child relationship; (5) the range of assets and deficits which the child brought to the divorce, including both the child's history in the predivorce family and his or her capacities in the present, particularly intelligence, the capacity for fantasy, social maturity, and the ability to turn to peers and adults; (6) the availability to the child of a supportive human network (Tessman, 1977); (7) the absence in the child of continued anger and depression; and (8) the sex and age of the child at the marital rupture and the remarriage (Hetherington, 1980).

When parents undertake the divorce throughtfully after careful consideration of alternatives, when they have anticipated the psychological, social, and economic consequences for all involved and have provided adequately for the economic security of the child, when they have arranged to maintain good parent-child relationships, then the children are not likely to suffer developmental interference or enduring psychological distress. Alternatively, if the divorce is undertaken in ways that humiliate or enrage a partner, if anger and unhappiness dominate the postdivorce relationship, if the children experience economic deprivation and diminished educational and social opportunities, if they are co-opted by the parents as allies, fought over, or viewed as extensions of the adults, if the child's relationship with one or both parents is impoverished and disrupted, and if the child feels rejected, then the most likely outcome for the children is developmental interference, depression, or both (Wallerstein & Kelly, 1980).

Long-Range Outcomes

Preliminary reports from a 10-year followup of the California Children of Divorce population suggest that outcomes assessed a decade later may be at considerable variance with earlier findings (Wallerstein, 1984; 1985b). These later responses may represent delayed responses to marital breakdown, or responses associated primarily with the impact of the new developmental stage and the new tasks associated with that stage that have been complicated by the child's past or current experiences within the divorced or remarried family. It appears, however, that young people entering adulthood who were aged 9–18 at the initial marital rupture carry with them the sense that their childhood was under the shadow of the parental divorce and that they have, as a result, suffered long-standing deprivation. They look back with nostalgia and longing to the intact family of their memory and their fantasy, although they have come to terms with what they regard as the incompatability of their parents and the inevitability of their parents' divorce. Perhaps most striking is the finding that a significant number of these young people have remained or perhaps become increasingly apprehensive about repeating their parents' marital failure during their own lives. The women entering young adulthood were especially frightened of betrayal in love and marriage and fearful, therefore, of commitment to a relationship despite their strong yearning for a lasting, faithful marriage.

The younger children appeared considerably less worried about their futures, less burdened by memories of unhappiness in the failed marriage, and less preoccupied with the sense that they need, at all costs, to avoid divorce for themselves and their yet unborn children. These youngsters who had been of preschool age at the marital rupture of their parents claimed little or no conscious memory of the intense conflict that prevailed in their families, although records from the project of 10 years earlier clearly document the presence of the children during many angry, even violent scenes. It was also surprising to find that, in contrast to the older group, these young people were more likely to accept the possibility of divorce in their own future as an unpleasant but far from inevitable aspect of their future lives. They were, in effect, more hopeful in the present and more optimistic about the future than the older youngsters. Since psychological theory and clinical wisdom have emphasized the vulnerability of the very young children, it may be, if these findings are widely replicated, that older children, by virtue of their greater capacity to remember the unhappiness of the marital rupture, are more likely to suffer more intensely and over a longer period of time with the unhappy memories and a sense of foreboding over their own future.

CONCLUSIONS

The problems that marital rupture poses to children are grave and potentially enduring. The initial responses of children and parents at the height of the crisis during the separation are serious. They need to be addressed at that time through a range of intervention programs that can relieve suffering and ameliorate or prevent the consolidation of psychological dysfunction. In the long term, however, the central hazards to the psychological health of children are not the result of the divorce, per se, but rather in the diminished or disrupted parenting that so often follows in the wake of marital breakdown, in the parental conflicts that can persist and become chronic within the post-divorce family, in the flawed or tragic role models provided by parents who fail over many years to reconstitute or to stabilize their lives, in the diminished quality of life, the multiple dislocations, the economic deprivation, and the sharply curtailed educational and social opportunities for the children that represent the legacy of divorce in so many post-divorce homes.

Although policy makers, legislators, and judges have increasingly sought support from the findings of behavioral science and guidance from the mental health professions, the accumulation of psychological knowledge has not kept up with the rapid evolution of family law. Knowledge about children and parent-child relationships in the post-divorce family is still fragmentary and insufficient to support many of the legislative changes in family policy that have found powerful adherents. The subtleties of psychological thinking and shadings of individual difference that are so critical to the perspective of the behavioral scientist translate poorly into the arenas of court and legislature. The several years of followup required to assess the impact of changed circumstances or altered family structure are ill suited to the pressured agendas of the political and judicial process. Despite the widespread acknowledgment given to the important interface between family law and mental health, the major task of building cooperation and mutual understanding on a firm basis of empirical knowledge and shared values still lies ahead.

REFERENCES

Block, J.H., Block, J., & Morrison, A. (1981). Parental agreement-disagreement on child rearing orientations and gender-related personality correlates in children. *Child Development, 52*, 965-974.

Bloom, B.L., White, S.W., & Asher, S.J. (1979). Marital disruption as a stressful life event. In G. Levinger and O.C. Moles (Eds.), *Divorce and Separation: Context, Causes, and Consequences* (pp. 184–200). New York: Basic Books.

Brown, B.F. (1980). A study of the school needs of children in one-parent families. *The Phi Delta Kappan*, April (pp. 537–540).

Campbell, L., & Johnston, J.R. (1986). Impasse-Directed Mediation With High Conflict Families in Custody Disputes. *Behavioral Sciences and the Law*, 4(2) (Child of Divorce).

Clingempeel, W.G., and Reppucci, N.D. (1982). Joint custody after divorce: Major issues and goals for research. *Psychological Bulletin, 92*, 102–127.

Emery, R.E. (1982). Interparental conflict and children of discord and divorce. *Psychological Bulletin, 92*, 310–330.

Emergy, R.E., & O'Leary, K.D. (1982). Children's perceptions of marital discord and behavior problems of boys and girls. *Journal of Abnormal Child Psychology, 10*, 11–24.

Felner, R.D., Stolberg, A.L., & Cowen, E.L. (1975). Crisis events and school mental health referral patterns of young children. *Journal of Consulting and Clinical Psychology, 43*, 305–310.

Gardner, R.A. (1976). *Psychotherapy and Children of Divorce*. New York: Jason Aronson.

Guidubaldi, J. et al. (1983). The impact of parental divorce on children: Report of the nationwide NASP study. *School Psychology Review, 12*, 300–323.

Guidubaldi, J. et al. (1984). The legacy of parental divorce: A nationwide study of family status and selected mediating variables on children's academic and social competencies. In B.B. Lahey and A.E. Kazdin (Eds.), *Advances in Clinical Child Psychology* (pp. 109–151), Vol. 7. New York: Plenum Press.

Hauser, B.B. (1985). Custody in dispute: Legal and psychological profiles of contesting families. *Journal of the American Academy of Child Psychiatry, 24(5)*, 575–582.

Hess, R.D., & Camara, K.A. (1979). Post-divorce relationships as mediating factors in the consequences of divorce for children. *Journal of Social Issues, 35*, 79–96.

Hetherington, E. (1979). Divorce: A child's perspective. *American Psychologist, 34*, 851–858.

Hetherington, E. (1980). Divorce, a child's perspective. In S. Chess and A. Thomas (Eds.), *Annual Progress in Child Psychiatry and Child Development*. New York: Brunner/Mazel. 277–291.

Hetherington, E., Cox, M., & Cox, R. (1978). The aftermath of divorce. In H. Stevens and M. Mathews (Eds.); *Mother-Child Relations* (pp. 149–176). Washington, D.C.: National Association for Education of Young Children.

Hetherington, E., Cox, M., & Cox, R. (1982). Effects of divorce on parents and children. In M.E.

Lamb (Ed.), *Nontraditional Families: Parenting and Child Development* (pp. 233–285). Hillsdale, N.J.: Lawrence Erlbaum Associates.

Ilfeld, F.W., Jr., & Alexander, J.R. (1982). Does joint custody work? A first look at outcome data of relitigation. *American Journal of Psychiatry, 139*, 62–66.

Jacobson, D.S. (1978). The impact of marital separation/divorce on children: II. Interparental hostility and child adjustment. *Journal of Divorce*, 2, 3–20.

Johnston, J.R., Campbell, L.E.G., & Mayes, S.S. (1985). Latency children in post-separation and divorce disputes. *Journal of the American Academy of Child Psychiatry, 24(5)*, 563–574.

Johnston, J.R., Campbell, L.E.G., & Tall, M.C. (1985). Impasses to the resolution of custody and visitation disputes. *American Journal of Orthopsychiatry, 55*, 112–129.

Kalter, N. (1977). Children of divorce in an outpatient psychiatric population. *American Journal of Orthopsychiatry, 47*, 40–51.

Kelly, J.B., & Wallerstein, J.S. (1976). The effects of parental divorce: Experiences of the child in early latency. *American Journal of Orthopsychiatry*, 46(1), 20–32.

Luepnitz, D. (1982). *Child Custody: A Study of Families After Divorce*. Lexington, MA. Lexington Books.

McKinnon, R., & Wallerstein, J.S. (1986). Joint custody and the preschool child. *Behavioral Sciences and the Law*, 4(2).

Norton, A.J. (1985) Assistant Chief of the Population Division of the United States Bureau of the Census. Personal communication.

Roman, M. & Haddad, W. (1978). *The Disposable Parent*. New York: Holt, Rinehart, and Winston.

Rutter, M. (1970). Sex differences in children's response to family stress. In E.J. Anthony and C. Koupernik (Eds.), *The Child in His Family* (pp. 165–196). New York: John Wiley and Sons, 165–196.

Santrock, J.W., & Warshak, R.A. (1979). Father custody and social development in boys and girls. *Journal of Social Issues, 35*, 112–125.

Springer, C., & Wallerstein, J.S. (1983). Young adolescents' responses to their parents' divorces. In L.A. Kurdek (Ed.), *Children and Divorce* (pp. 15–27). San Francisco: Jossey-Bass.

Steinman, S.B. (1981). The experience of children in a joint custody arrangement: A report of a study. *American Journal of Orthopsychiatry, 51*, 403–414.

Steinman, S.B. (1986). Studies on joint custody. *Behavioral Sciences and the Law, 4(2)*.

Steinman, S.B., Zemmelman, S.E., & Knoblauch, T.M. (1985). A study of parents who sought joint custody following divorce: Who reaches agreement and sustains joint custody and who returns to court. *Journal of the American Academy of Child Psychiatry, 24*, 554–562.

Tessman, L.H. (1977). *Children of Parting Parents*. New York: Jason Aronson.

Wallerstein, J.S. (1984). Children of divorce: Preliminary report of a ten-year follow-up of young children. *American Journal of Orthopsychiatry, 54(3)*, 444–458.

Wallerstein, J.S. (1985a). The overburdened child: Some long-term sequelae of divorce. *Social Work, 30(2)*, 116–123.

Wallerstein, J.S. (1985b). Children of divorce: Preliminary report of a ten-year follow-up of older children and adolescents. *Journal of the American Academy of Child Psychiatry, 24(5)*, 545–553.

Wallerstein, J.S. (1985c). Parent-child relationships following divorce. In E.J. Anthony & G. Pollock (Eds.), *Clinical Aspects of Parenthood*. Boston: Little, Brown & Co.

Wallerstein, J.S., & Kelly, J.B. (1974). The effects of parental divorce: The adolescent experience. In J. Anthony and C. Koupernik (Eds.), *The Child in His Family: Children at Psychiatric Risk* (pp. 479–505), Vol. 3. New York: Wiley and Sons, Inc.

Wallerstein, J.S., & Kelly, J.B. (1975). The effects of parental divorce: The experiences of the preschool child. *Journal of the American Academy of Child Psychiatry, 14(4)*, 600–616.

Wallerstein, J.S., & Kelly, J.B. (1976). The effects of parental divorce: Experiences of the child in later latency. *American Journal of Orthopsychiatry, 47(1)*, 4–22.

Wallerstein, J.S., & Kelly, J.B. (1980). *Surviving the Breakup: How Children and Parents Cope With Divorce*. New York: Basic Books.

Warshak, R.A., & Santrock, J.W. (1983). The impact of divorce in father-custody and mother-custody homes: The child's perspective. In L.A. Kurdek (Ed.), *Children and Divorce*. San Francisco: Jossey-Bass, 29–46.

Weiss, R.S. (1979) *Going It Alone*. New York: Basic Books.

Zill, N. (1983). Divorce, marital conflict, and children's mental health: Research findings and policy recommendations. Testimony before Subcommittee on Family and Human Services, United States Senate Subcommittee on Labor and Human Resources. March 22.

[12]

THE CHILDREN OF ARMAGEDDON: PROBLEMS OF CUSTODY FOLLOWING DIVORCE

Andrew S. Watson, M.D.*

Some of the more spectacular legal cases of recent years have involved disputes over the custody of children following divorce. The facts of these cases are so latent with the stuff of emotional conflict, that their every detail is reported in the press.[1] They have resulted in much editorializing, a multitude of law review notes,[2] and occasionally in energetic activity by various organizations and individuals involved with child care.[3] These cases are important to the children involved because of the very disturbing effects that such an experience has upon them.[4] Their conflicts are revealed in such things as school failure, delinquency, various psycho-physiologic disorders, and multitude of emotional syndromes which cause them to come to the attention of psychotherapists.[5] Analysis of these cases is valuable for what it reveals of many unresolved issues regarding the law of the family. This law bears the stamp of many conflicting values from the past, randomly and often illogically mixed with newer views about the rights of children.

Since the historical background of this conflict has been well covered by others,[6] a few summary remarks will suffice. Originally, children were treated as having essentially the status of paternal chattel. Just as households were under the dominance of feudal barons and their underlings, so children owed their services to their fathers. Wives and mothers held a similar status, and in all disputes reparding the custody of the child the father's interests were paramount.[7] More recently, the concept evolved that fathers could not rear children appropriately (and often did not wish to do so) and that therefore disposition should be made inevitably to the mother because of the "essential" nature of her participation in child caring. This rather categorical presumption

---

* Professor of Law and Professor of Psychiatry, University of Michigan.

1. *See, e.g., Civil Rights: Color and Custody*, TIME, Nov. 1, 1968, at 70. *See also* Painter v. Bannister, 258 Iowa 1390, 140 N.W.2d 152 (1966), *cert. denied*, 385 U.S. 949 (1966); In re Ernst, 373 Mich. 337, 129 N.W.2d 430 (1964).

2. *See* Levine, *Child Custody: Iowa Corn and the Avant Garde*, 1 FAM. L.Q. 3 (1967); Walker, *Measuring the Child's Best Interests—A Study of Incomplete Considerations*, 44 DENVER L.J. 132-46 (1967); Coyne, *Who Will Speak for the Child?*, 383 ANNALS 34-47 (1969).

3. N. LITTNER, SOME TRAUMATIC EFFECTS OF SEPARATION AND PLACEMENT (1956).

4. *See, e.g.*, L. DESPERT, CHILDREN OF DIVORCE (1962); W. GOODE, AFTER DIVORCE (1956).

5. McDermott, *Parental Divorce in Early Childhood*, 124 AM. J. PSYCHIATRY 1424-32 (1968).

6. *See* Foster & Freed, *Child Custody* (pt. 1), 39 N.Y.U.L. REV. 423 (1964); Bennett, *Child Custody: Considerations in Granting the Award Between Adversely Claiming Parents*, 36 S. CAL. L. REV. 255-56 (1963).

7. For several discussions of this problem *see* J. GOLDSTEIN & J. KATZ, THE FAMILY AND THE LAW 324-35 (1965).

was not without considerable merit, especially as it related to younger children. In more recent times, when conflicts arose over whether or not mother-substitutes might prevail over the natural mother and her interests, the feeling was that "blood is thicker than water" and therefore the best care would be given by the natural mother. Only very recently has the concept emerged that society's true interest in children is best promulgated by assuring that they be reared in the most effective way possible so far as *their* needs are concerned. Since healthy citizens are fundamental to the survival of any society, appropriate and effective rearing of children becomes a matter of great social concern. Without articulating its meaning, "the best interests of the child" has slowly evolved into the major basis for custodial disposition following divorce. (It also has been used in other legal considerations of children, as for example in the juvenile court.)[8] In short, there has been a marked change in the dispositional philosophy regarding children altering their status from that of chattels to that of individuals with rights of their own which need detailed and sophisticated implementation. It is obvious to all who have looked at the concept however, that its precise meaning and content remain to be defined.

Most of the judgments involving post-divorce disposition of children arrive at their conclusions with little data presented to indicate how they were accomplished. Though such conclusions are generally asserted with vigor, they must be taken primarily on the basis of faith.[9] This paucity of illuminating evidence is probably due to the difficulty of the task. Similarly, there has been little assistance from statutory law in this regard. While statutes may set forth the goal, the criteria for establishing the best interests of the child are conspicuous by their absence.

There are several controversial questions regarding custodial disposition which will not specifically be explored in this paper. One such issue is that of the child's religious education.[10] As will be discussed below, it is this author's opinion that many of these considerations may be subsumed easily and appropriately under the question of the best interest of the child. Perhaps the only issue which may be an exception is raised in the occasional situation where a parent, through circumstances totally beyond his control, will have to be absent temporarily from his child-caring role. This will necessitate a difficult decision for the court since, in the meantime, the child may well have established close, intense, and healthy relationships with others.[11]

8. J. GOLDSTEIN & J. KATZ, THE FAMILY AND THE LAW (1965).

9. Boone v. Boone, 150 F.2d 153 (D.C. Cir. 1945) (The court of appeals reversed Waddlington, noting that the trial judge should have gotten expert assistance to aid in determining the children's interests); Adams v. Adams, 206 Ga. 881, 59 S.E.2d 366 (1950); Brewer v. Macaluso, 221 So. 2d 243 (La. Ct. App. 1969); Keys v. Keys, 252 Mis. 138, 171 So. 2d 489 (1965); Beck v. Beck, 175 Neb. 108, 120 N.W.2d 585 (1963).

10. J. GOLDSTEIN & J. KATZ, *supra* note 7, at 216-19.

11. *See, e.g.*, Painter v. Bannister, *supra* note 1 where this appears to have been the situation.

For purposes of the discussion below, the dispositional standard utilized and explored will be that of "the psychological best interest of the child." This test has been well discussed and legitimated in an excellent note in the *Yale Law Journal*,[12] and the present article will attempt to extend the views taken there. It will set forth in more detail the psychological issues which underlie this standard.

"The psychological best interest of the child test" has the virtue of making it possible to deal with all of the intrapsychic as well as extrapsychic factors which are critical to a child's development.[13] With the exception of the conflict between parental rights which will arise occasionally under the circumstances mentioned above, it would appear that this may be an absolute assertion. Thus, if the psychological best interest of the child is properly estimated and implemented there will be no element of his needs left unattended.

Current Status

If the courts adopt the standard of the "psychological best interest of the child," do the legal and medical procedures used currently provide sufficient information to apply this test? It appears that, at the present time, the information elicited in the course of trials involving custody is largely dependant upon the skill of the advocates, and only cases involving relatively wealthy clients receive the attention which brings forth the detailed information needed to make such a sophisticated judgment. Most custodial questions are settled by the parties with inadequate attention paid to the child's best interest. The appropriateness of the decision turns mainly on the wisdom of the divorcing parents. While one can get little hard data on this point, clinical observation suggests that these decisions are not always made in the best psychological interest of the child. In those cases where there are vigorously contending adversaries, some kind of psychiatric or social work evidence will often be presented. Though this does not guarantee wise decisions, at least some reasonably reliable information about the behavior of the individuals will be brought into the case. The usefulness of such expert information will depend on which expert is chosen as well as upon the skill with which the advocate utilizes the information. Quite often, an expert will not be fully nor appropriately utilized; and valuable information which might have been elicited does not emerge.

Another important issue which will determine whether or not appropriate resolution of a child's needs will be carried out relates to the "matrix of

12. Note, *Alternatives to 'Parental Right' in Child Custody Disputes Involving Third Parties*, 73 YALE L.J. 151-70 (1963).

13. Fain, *The Role and Responsibility of the Lawyer in Custody Cases*, 1 FAM. L.Q. 36 (1967).

tension" that exists between the divorcing spouses. When there has been more or less mutual agreement to separate and divorce, there is little motive for fighting over anything, especially custody of the children. On the other hand, if the battles which characterized the marital relationship during the years are continued, there will be little likelihood of parental objectivity during the divorce proceedings and later.[14] In other words, the nature of the past parental relationship will be critical to the future stability of the dispositional decision. Tensions generated between the spouses during the custodial procedure will redound inevitably to the future, and perhaps permanent, disadvantage of the child. For this reason it is extremely important that custodial procedures avoid all friction-producing actions excepting those absolutely essential to the determination. For example, a father intensively abraded by his former wife during the course of the proceedings might well be effectively removed from his children as a paternal identification figure for months or years. Since this is contrary to the desired result, careful attention must be given to the manner in which these procedures are carried out.

Another important question which has been raised is whether or not the adversary proceeding distorts the information utilized to make the custodial decision.[15] Though it is again difficult to answer this question from appellate opinions, the fragmentary information usually contained therein suggests that an inaccurate picture often emerges. This is either due to an imbalance in the advocacy powers of counsel, or to the fact that information has been distorted during its appellate handling. First-hand observation of these procedures leads me freely to the conclusion that the almost routine distortion which occurs comes from the simple fact that the main object of concern, the child, is without counsel. This creates an important kind of distortion.

In custody battles involving third parties, an early need arises for counsel to prove his client is "good" while the opponent is "bad". This totally ignores the principle issue, which is the relative importance of both parties to the child and his needs. Thus, a series of exaggerations and distortions is created by wrenching information out of its social and family context. Additionally, frequent efforts are made to demonstrate that one party or the other has some "emotional difficulty" which, *per se*, should eliminate him from eligibility as a parent. This kind of effort does not accurately deal with the child's best interest and often causes serious difficulties for him which stem from the parties' own needs to adapt themselves to the trauma developed during the trial.

Many judges will openly acknowledge that they attempt to achieve resolution in difficult custody battles by merely facilitating the passage of

14. Barnett, *Emotional Problems Encountered in Divorce Cases—A Seminar*, 3 J. FAM. L. 208, 223 (1963).

15. *Supra* note 12, at 169.

time. If children are approaching the age when the court can permit them to make the decision, it merely avoids making its own decision until that age is reached and the matter can be taken out of its hands. This is similar to the courts' inclination to force counsel to achieve some custodial agreement between themselves.[16] While there is virtue in a decision which does reflect the views of both parties as well as the best interest of the child, to trust this matter solely to adversary counsel is truly to abandon responsibility for the child's needs. I have known cases which dallied on for years while judge and counsel alike hoped for this kind of resolution. Although this goal was ultimately achieved, it was at the child's expense. The grown-ups effectively avoided their conflicts in this manner; but this approach left the children in limbo.

One covert goal often seen in these hearings is to use the child custody issue as a lever against some economic consideration. The promise to fight over custody, with its attendant re-dredging of all manner of embarrassing things, can often cause a parent to relinquish other considerations, such as economic ones. Of course this is not made explicit in most records, but discussion with counsel and reference to the clinical histories found in any child treatment center reveal this often to be the case. Clearly, such behavior comes close to active abandonment of ethical propriety insofar as the child's interests are concerned. One often hears counsel cynically remark "it is amazing how custodial claims can be shifted by relinquishment of an appropriate number of dollars." While there can be no doubt that this happens, to handle a parent's conflicting motives in this way can have only negative effects on the child's interests in the case.

Another dispositional matter often used for similar covert purposes is the question of visitation rights. The bloody fight over the rights of parents versus the needs of the children may be focused on this issue. It is an ideal place to reincarnate the punitive attitudes of one parent or the other, or to re-mobilize moralizing in relation to past behavior.[17] While there is the usual mouthing of platitudes about the needs of children, the ubiquitous inclination to look upon marriage relationships as matters to be handled in purely moralistic ways is hard to resist. It is not uncommon for these attitudes to creep into case decisions, and certainly many of these decisions cannot be understood without paying cognizance to such intentions.

In encountering the kinds of issues about which children are brought to judges for adjudication, any sensitive observer will have little difficulty in appreciating the nature of the struggle which is taking place before him. It

16. Rothenberg, *The Lawyer's Role in Child Custody Disputes*, 23 N.Y. Co. B.J. 95, 98-99 (1966).

17. Note, *A Fit Parent May Be Deprived of Custody of His Child if the Best Interest and Welfare of the Child Would Be Served by Allowing Another Person to Raise Him*, 4 HOUSTON L. REV. 131, 137 (1966).

would indeed take the wisdom of a Solomon to think of a solution which would at one and the same time be in the child's best interest and also resolve the combat between the parents. We can readily sympathize, therefore, with the judge's desire to somehow avoid decision. While this human inclination is easily understood, when carried out, it always redounds to the disadvantage of the child and highlights his need for counsel in his own behalf. Otherwise the conservatism of the judge might join with the hidden intentions of adversary counsel and result in a prolonged stalemate.

Perhaps by examining some of the reasons for the ongoing friction between former spouses, we will be better able to resolve that friction so that some kind of permanent dispositional adjustment can be worked out. All those who study marital relationships agree in the observation that the choice of marriage partners conforms to the psychological needs of both spouses. Psychiatric literature is now filled with descriptions of the multiform and paradoxical nature of these choices.[18] Such selections reflect the hopes as well as the vulnerabilities for a happy psychological resolution between the parties. In essence, a successful marriage is one in which both parties, confronting each other, press one or other toward the full exploitation and implementation of their personality characteristics.[19] This same psychological confrontation, if it does not lead toward personality growth, results in a progressive and permanent impasse. If one accepts this dynamic concept as true, it should be clear that there is no place for the concept of a "good" or a "bad" partner in the marriage. Instead, we should see that the bilateral and interlocking inability to resolve and respond to the growth potential has brought about the stymied development we call marriage failure.

What, then, is the effect of the "fault" concept in divorce actions? One inevitable necessity is that the husband or the wife must be viewed as "bad" for the purposes of the divorce. From the outset, this is psychologically inaccurate. Since there are elements present in any marriage relationship which could be viewed as "bad" in the abstract, the fault concept provides an omnipresent coercion lever to be used during litigation. Psychological attributes, once positively adaptive to the marital pair, are now modified through the definitional process of litigation, into negative ones. This fact arouses anxiety (probably in both parties) which predictably causes defensive retaliation in one or both of the spouses.

While the adult may occasionally be able to sustain such assaults on his personality, children are not so fortunate. Accepting the fact that children

18. *See, e.g.*, Watson, *The Conjoint Psychotherapy of Marriage Partners*, 33 AM. J. ORTHOPSYCHIATRY 912-13 (1963); N. ACKERMAN, PSYCHODYNAMICS OF FAMILY LIFE (1958); Jackson, *Family Rules*, 12 ARCH. GEN. PSYCHIATRY 589-94 (1965); S. ROSENBAUM & I. ALGER, THE MARRIAGE RELATIONSHIP (1968); E. BERNE, GAMES PEOPLE PLAY (1964); V. EISENSTEIN, NEUROTIC INTERACTIONS IN MARRIAGE (1956).

19. A. WATSON, PSYCHIATRY FOR LAWYERS 273-74 (1968).

need continuing relationships with both mother and father, they are now in the unenviable position of having one of their parents progressively defined as bad. This, coupled with frequent tactics of harassment, puts the children in a position of progressively deeper ambiguity and emotional ambivalence towards their parents. The parents must also suffer. If they are sufficiently "disturbed" and they "know" of their own participation in the marriage difficulty, they may be deeply upset by the necessity to participate in what they accurately perceive as a fraudulent and erroneous definition of the facts in their marriage. I recall one such patient who could hardly tolerate the divorce procedure and went into a profound depression because she had to participate in defining her husband as having been "cruel" to her. While he had not met her needs adequately from the psychological standpoint, to attribute consciously motivated cruelty to him was grossly inaccurate. The woman knew this, and her own sense of integrity and justice made it nearly impossible to go through the procedure. Right up to the last moment before the divorce hearing, it was not clear that she would be able to tolerate the guilt raised by this legal necessity. While she had typical mixed feelings about dissolving her marriage, it was primarily this definitional factor which caused the hesitation.

The fact that one or both parents continues to battle over problems of child care and visitation itself provides evidence of some weight about the nature of their concern for their children.[20] If it is true that children need both parents, then either parent's effort to thwart this need or in any way make it difficult or impossible, should be taken as evidence of parental apathy. Needless to say, such behavior is only useful evidence if the judge accepts the psychological facts about child needs. Once more this makes the child's welfare vulnerable to the judge's understanding of such matters. Unfortunately, one cannot rely upon this kind of judicial wisdom.

Judicial Attitudes

Occasionally, in discussions involving custody and other family law matters, there are bursts of wisdom about methods for handling such procedures.[21] When they occur, the tools to effect substantial change become available. As in all areas of the law, however, there is a great distance between the writings of law professors and the opinions of appellate judges, and the practices in the trial court. Probably one of the most frequently demonstrated judicial attitudes is the tendency to moralize. Judges, perhaps somewhat more than other human beings, tend to believe that if they inveigh against something strongly enough, change will ensue. It rarely works. All too often, judicial moralizing only reiterates that which has been repeatedly stated to the parties

20. *Supra* note 12, at 166, n.63.

21. *See* 1 *Portrait of the Judge as Popular Author: An Appeal for Anonymity and Restraint in Domestic Relations Opinions*, 1 FAM. L.Q. 77, 77-82 (Dec. 1967).

before, and it only helps the listener to turn off his hearing, insuring a negative result.

Another attitude often found among judges is a powerful desire to be "completely correct" in their decisions. While this goal is highly desirable, when it is linked to a feeling of inadequacy whenever perfection is not achieved, it may result in decision-making paralysis. This is because psychologically, failure to achieve perfection can be warded off by taking no action at all. To complicate matters, this usually is not an entirely conscious process. If it were, it could be handled readily. Instead, the vacillation will be camouflaged and rationalized by a multitude of "explanations" which are always available for use in such situations. This inclination does not distinguish judges from most other human beings, but in their decision-making role this tendency has serious social repercussions.

Another characteristic frequently found in the courts which hear custody cases is a considerable lack of understanding about the way children grow up and develop psychologically. While this lack of knowledge is not surprising,[22] it has serious consequences relative to the decision-making process. Unfortunately, judges must frequently weigh extremely complicated issues, including technical information from expert witnesses, without appropriate training for doing so. Although law-trained people often harbor the belief that they can analyze virtually anything without prior experience in the matter (and to a high degree they can!), understanding and manipulating behavioral science data clearly demands some degree of training. For this reason, judicial ignorance of human psychological behavior is bound to cause results in custody cases leaving much to be desired.

Occasionally, one encounters judicial attitudes (it would be more correct to call them neuroses) which cause the judge to follow a line of decision-making ending in catastrophe. In one case I encountered, a couple, long locked in mortal combat, finally obtained a divorce. The judge who granted the divorce was unusually perceptive of the human elements in the case and was able to handle them with skill and patience. Though the divorce had been highly complicated because of the emotional problems of both spouses, the judge managed to avoid the kinds of psychological impasses which so often cause great difficulty. Property settlement was made and so was custodial disposition. However, immediately after the decree the husband proceeded to initiate a multitude of harassing actions which postponed the settlement and challenged the custody of the children. None of the issues was new, but they clearly reflected the husband's continuing desire to attack his wife for real and imagined wounds to his pride. The judge fielded these harassments effectively, although at one point it was necessary to put the husband in jail for contempt

22. Watson, *The Quest for Professional Competence: Psychological Aspects of Legal Education*, 37 CIN. L. REV. 93 (1968).

in order to settle who was to make the legal decisions! This brought the husband swiftly back to appropriate behavior.

Sadly for the outcome of this case, the process of judicial administration caused it to be rotated to another judge's docket. The second judge, lacking the capacity to understand the psychological characteristics of the issues before him, proceeded to acquiesce to the husband's multitudinous legal harassments of his former wife. He consented to hear challenge after challenge to the original opinion, which resulted in examination of the children by a multitude of experts on the question of their appropriate custodial placement. These maneuvers, originating from hostility toward the wife but implemented through "appropriate" legal actions, caused a progressive deterioration in the mother's emotional capacity to deal with the children's lives. The judge, attempting to resolve the deep emotional chasm between the couple by judicial fiat, moralistically ordered the wife to prove to him that she was not trying to alienate the children from their father by permitting the father to visit the children in her home every Sunday afternoon! This order, given the personality characteristics of these two parties, was tantamount to lighting a fuse in a powder keg. Although therapists, lawyers, and other legal personnel struggled vigorously to ward off the impending explosion, all was to no avail. The judge had ordered the visits and so it was. When the husband arrived on Sunday afternoon, true to the storm signals which had been wildly flown by the distressed ex-wife, she emptied a revolver through the front door. Miraculously the husband escaped with a mere scratch. While the denouement of this case is not yet in, it should be amply clear that judicial dictum does not resolve emotional disorder nor can it magically regulate the lives of children. These actions by the second judge, all of which were contrary to the earnest recommendations of many therapists, leads one to fear for the future of the children, long subjected to traumatic manipulation by the father, aided and abetted by inappropriate legal procedures. Sadly, this is not an isolated nor rare case. One would hope that in time, judges would learn that situations such as these need to be resolved within the framework of psychological reality as well as consistently with legal requirements.

Another characteristic of current dispositional procedure which may be criticized is the fact that any custodial disposition may be freely challenged and disrupted. This has serious and detrimental effects on the custodian, who must remain ever alert to defend against such legal onslaughts.[23] Parents lose spontaneity with their children when they feel they must constantly anticipate the court's reaction to their activities with their children. Since spontaneity in relationships between parents and children is highly important, the end result of this situation is detrimental to the children. Of course, there is also high economic cost to these ongoing defensive maneuvers. Since lawyers charge for

23. Philips, *Mental Hygiene, Divorce and the Law*, 3 J. FAM. L. 63, 67-68 (1963).

the handling of these procedures, it is a source of constant financial as well as emotional strain on the parties.

The most serious aspect of these vacillating and dilatory tactics is the effect they have on the children. As will be noted, one of the critical aspects of a child's development is the need for stability in order to develop a sense of identity. When a child is kept suspended, never quite knowing what will happen to him next, he must likewise suspend the shaping of his personality. This is a devastating result and probably represents one of the greatest risks which current procedures pose for children.[24]

Role Demands on Lawyers

If it is decided to utilize the psychological best interest of the child standard it will place some very explicit role demands upon lawyers. As an officer of the court, counsel will have (and indeed has) a clear and affirmative duty to reach toward this goal.[25] Likewise, he must avoid procedures and petitions which will be obstructive of this purpose. Not only is this the duty of counsel for the ultimate custodial party, but it is also the role of the lawyer for the opposing party, who must similarly direct his efforts to this end. For example, utilization of the custody issue as a lever for other issues would have to cease. Under current custodial procedure, this would appear to be the only way to assure that the child's best interests will be fostered.

What is counsel to do if his client refuses to go along with this approach to custodial disposition? It would seem sufficiently clear that in such cases he would have an affirmative duty to refuse demands from his client which run counter to the psychological best interests of the child. It would become another of the areas in which counsel must vigorously control his client. Lawyers seem to have no hesitation to exercise this control in most areas of law and with most clients; and one would hope they could do so here. Public policy certainly dictates that the attorney vigorously press for the appropriate resolution vis-à-vis the child. This means there would be situations where counsel must refuse to intervene on behalf of his client in regard to issues which would upset custodial tranquility.[26] This will raise a multitude of technical problems relating to the lawyer-client relationship. Counsel will no doubt experience a certain amount of anxiety, especially if his client is an aggressive and a valuable one. Because the client will have the capacity to stimulate this kind of anxiety, anger toward that client will be stirred up which

24. *See* A. WATSON, *supra* note 19 for discussions of the need for stability of identification objects at various stages of psychological development; McDermott, *supra* note 5; *see, e.g.*, Gay & Tonge, *The Late Effects of Loss of Parents in Childhood*, 113 BRIT. J. PSYCHIATRY 753-59 (1967).

25. *See, e.g.*, Fain, *supra* note 13, at 37; J. POLIER, THE RULE OF LAW AND THE ROLE OF PSYCHIATRY 111-13 (1968); Rothenberg, *supra* note 16, at 95-100.

26. Fain, *supra* note 13, at 45.

must be muted or at least modulated. The presence of these powerful emotions can lead counsel either to vigorous and angry rejection of his client or, conversely, to a tendency to surrender his position and withdraw from an objective determination of the appropriate solution.[27]

In proper perspective, counsel should view his client's attitude toward custodial disposition as something he must actively help to shape. This might mean a conscientious job of persuading his client toward the correct disposition, or conceivably he might need to help his client obtain proper therapeutic assistance which will help direct him toward an appropriate resolution. These observations presume, of course, that counsel has the ability to work toward a sensible resolution for the appropriate disposition of children.

In this regard, one must again note that lawyers have a conspicuous lack of understanding of the behavioral sciences. This is not attributable to neglect on their parts, for legal education and training do little to facilitate the gaining of such knowledge. As I have said elsewhere, legal education tends to blunt native ability so far as psychological sensitivity is concerned.[28] Together with this functional "blindness," there is a strong inclination for lawyers to be oblivious to the emotional results of their procedures. They appear to believe that they can conduct a vigorous adversary contest and then have the contestants return to some kind of working rapport. Such contests in child custody cases will most surely produce wounds which do not heal adequately to assure a good subsequent working relationship between the parents.

If judges are to handle custodial disputes effectively, they must give very careful consideration to the techniques they use. The not uncommon and often inviting temptation to moralize with one or the other parent must be avoided if the contestants are to be assisted in fulfilling their ongoing parental duties. For many judges this will be an almost insurmountable task.[29] Judges should use their considerable authority to help the parents press toward a progressive understanding of their importance in handling child-rearing problems.[30] It is now a familiar observation that judicial decisions in this area will tax a judge's emotional maturity to the ultimate. Inevitably, he must find against one party or the other. This causes emotional pain in the parties before him with which he will surely identify. This may often cause a judge to become evasive and circuitous in his ruling, and he may use language in his opinion which will ultimately mislead the parties in ways detrimental to the child. Painful "explanations" and justifications for action are frequently found in these opinions, which more accurately reflect the judge's own emotional dilemmas

27. Barnett, *supra* note 14, at 217.

28. WATSON, *supra* note 19, at 116-22.

29. Paulsen, *Juvenile Courts, Family Courts, and the Poor Man*, 54 CALIF. L. REV. 695, 712-13 (1966).

30. Hansen, *The Role and Rights of Children in Divorce Actions*, 6 J. FAM. L. 10-12 (1966).

than the issues in the case. On occasion, one has the impression that the whole opinion is a long rationalization to help the judges make the decisions that they may be compelled to make for other reasons than those they state.[31] In this they deserve sympathy, even though they often spread confusion. Judges receive little training to prepare them for this kind of difficulty.[32]

Thus far I have described some of the role demands upon lawyers if they are to carry out custodial procedures adequately. Because of these intrinsic role difficulties, I do not believe that we may rely on counsel's capacity to fulfill them at the present time. Statutes have always been devised to bolster dispositional goals with procedural limitations and controls. This provides individual lawyers with something to fall back upon and even to utilize in a rationalizing way, to justify to themselves action which they may find painful to carry out.[33] This kind of remedy is greatly needed in relation to custodial disposition.

The most important single safeguard which could be utilized to assure the psychological best interest of the child, in a custody action, would be to provide counsel to represent him.[34] This has already been accomplished in several jurisdictions. In the state of Wisconsin, under the leadership of Judge Hanson and others, there has been developed "a ten point listing of the rights of children in divorce."[35] This is directed toward assuring that all relevant matters will be adequately evaluated during the custodial disposition and includes counsel to represent the child during divorce actions. Similarly, in the New York family courts and others, children may be represented by law guardians to assure that their needs will be met.[36] The goal of these proceedings is to assure that children get adequate protection during the

31. In re Ernst, *supra* note 1, at 338-39, 129 N.W.2d at 431 (1964):

As 1964 has brought another change in our personnel, a little child may lead the remaining parent-minded distinguished from child-minded Brethren from out of that legal fog into which they stray when a child custody case arrives here. That child could be little Gerri Ernst. And if Gerri, armed as she is with innocence and supreme legal right, cannot get through to such Brethren as her case comes to decision, then the probate and circuit judges of Michigan by what they have done and are now doing ultimately will get across to all of us an indelible fact; a fact which, no matter how long judicial ears are covered and judicial gaze is averted no member of the court can ignore much longer.

32. *See, e.g.*, H. CECIL, A CHILD DIVIDED (1966). This book, though it does not deal with a custody problem *per se*, humorously describes the psychological discomforts of a judge when dealing with problems involving children. The author, himself a judge, has many whimsical insights into the difficulties of his role; *see also* Oster, *Custody Proceedings: A Study of Vague and Indefinite Standards*, 5 J. FAM. L. 23 (1965).

33. Rothenberg, *supra* note 16.

34. Coyne, *supra* note 2, at 45-47.

35. Hansen, *supra* note 30, at 5-7.

36. *See, e.g.*, Paulsen, *supra* note 29, at 702-06. Though the N.Y. Family Court could be used for dealing with custody disputes it appears that it is little used for that purpose. *See also* Kay, *A Family Court: The California Proposal*, 56 CAL. L. REV. 1236-37 (1968).

divorce actions. With all of the intrinsic conflicts that counsel appears to have when he represents an individual parent, it seems clear that the safest way to assure the child's best interest is to see to it that he has personal representation. Thus, a totally independent child-oriented course of exploration may be followed to insure that the important aspects of his needs are adequately attended.

All recognize that it takes more than a judicial decree to assure that children will get what they need following a divorce. This led Dr. Lawrence Kubie to make a most ingenious suggestion. He urges that for all children for whom post-divorce custody arrangements must be made, a committee chosen by the parents to decide questions on which the parents are unable to agree be appointed by the court. This committee would always be available to the parents for settling relevant questions and to carry out friendly persuasion with them on behalf of the children. It may be chosen from friends, clergy, or any other persons who have an interest in the children and who enjoy the respect of both parents.[37] This seems a most logical approach to the problem and should be possible to arrange for every family where it is needed.

The Substantive Test: "Psychological Best Interest of the Child

It is of course necessary to attempt to ascertain the meaning of "psychological best interest of the child." While there have been many statements that this is the desired standard in custodial dispositions, generally it appears as a conclusion and as an article of faith. Few appellate opinions have given any details as to its meaning.[38] It seems quite clear that the psychological best interest of the child test is an organizing concept which can relate and integrate all relevant data in relation to custodial disposition.[39] These data fall into several general catagories.

Social Environment

First of all let us eqamine the issues of what might broadly be called the social environment. One aspect of the child's environment is his school needs. While generally the neighborhood school will be adequate, occasionally, because of the presence of emotional disturbance or a particular intellectual deficiency, a special kind of educational experience may be indicated. This need will be reflected in past academic performance, from the results of psychological and psychiatric examination, and through the impressions of teachers skilled in making these kinds of diagnostic judgements.

Occasionally the issue of material need is raised. Though the child's

37. Kubie, *Provisions for the Care of Children of Divorced Parents: A New Legal Instrument*, 73 Yale L.J. 1197-1200 (1964).

38. Oster, *supra* note 32, at 21-38.

39. *Supra* note 12.

general situation will usually reflect the manner in which his past needs have been satisfied, it is usually argued that he should be kept in a home situation which will, so far as possible, continue his prior standard of living. While there is truth to the idea that continuity and stability are desirable, material needs beyond those required for supporting survival are not among the more crucial ones.[40] So long as there is sufficient satisfaction of simple needs for food, clothing, etc., the child may readily adjust to the situation. This is especially true of the young child. With older children there is probably somewhat more difficulty in fitting into a new mode of living, and marked alternation of life style could stimulate strong emotional reaction. This is not to say that visible equity in family property distribution is not important. In fact the main impact that the material need question may have on the children (beyond subsistence) relates to what it reveals of "fairness" as mother, father, and the court demonstrate it. How the material need question is adjudicated can also have indirect effects on subsequent parental involvment with the children. If they are unfairly handled, it can stimulate open or latent resentments which will disturb appropriate involvement with one or the other parent.

One crucial need of all children is adequate social stimulation. By this is meant sufficient opportunity for ongoing relationships with other children, and confrontation with progressively more complex social experiences which facilitate individual maturation and development. Occasionally, judges will comment about what an appropriate environment should consist of, and it should be remembered that this is a value judgment—and a highly questionable one at that.[41] The critical point is that children should encounter the full spectrum of situations with which they are likely to deal as adults. In this day of rapid social change, it surely means that children from all sectors of society should interact socially on a day to day basis, so that each can learn to fit into the community as it really is. Children must also have continuous living contact with adults of both sexes so that the characteristics of adult male and female roles may be seen and learned adequately.

Sometimes, a child may need some special kind of therapy. This might be physical and/or psychological and it is important that he be in a situation where it may be obtained. While good physical care can be found nearly anywhere, psychological care is not as easy to locate, and there are places in the United States where it would be totally unavailable. Such considerations might be important in deciding where a child should live.

The next set of child needs relates to the quantity and quality of "parenting". This is probably the most critical issue to determine since the healthy growth and identification of children is totally or nearly totally

40. Oster, *supra* note 32, at 35-36.

41. *See, e.g.*, Painter v. Bannister, supra note 1, at ——, 140 N.W.2d at 155-56; Levine, *Child Custody: Iowa Corn and the Avant Garde*, 1 FAM. L.Q. 7 (1967).

dependent upon the presence of a father and a mother who are objects of affection and the source of much learning.[42] Effective parents have the capacity to become deeply involved with their children as they provide for their daily needs. They are able to derive deep satisfaction from vicariously living through, with their children, the various stages of development and maturation. They must see themselves in the role of parents and enjoy what they see.[43]

Whether or not "parents" are the biological ones or are persons who have served in the parental role for a protracted period of time, may be an issue which arises for consideration.[44] The impact and effects of parent substitution will vary from age group to age group. For example, children below the age of six months may be moved from one parent to another with very little or no difficulty. Between the first and the seventh or eighth years of life such moves are much more difficult and when a substitute has served in the parent role for a protracted period of time, the return of the child to his natural parent may be extremely disruptive. Nevertheless, it will probably be necessary in some cases to return a child to a natural parent following long care by a parental substitute. In such a situation the intention to carry out the best interest of the child will come under great duress. (For example, both parents may be hospitalized for a prolonged period of time for tuberculosis or some other chronic illness. Or a parent may be in military service and need to have someone else care for his children.[45]) Here there may be conflicting policies, and probably concerns for justice under law will cause the child-needs to become secondary.

Another set of factors which must be evaluated relates to the child's own psychic status. This must be ascertained by direct observation of the child as well as through a review of his past history. Psychological needs vary according to a child's level of maturity. They relate to his capacity to understand the world around him and to his ability to make various kinds of adjustments. Very young children below the age of 6 months may change their home situations with little or no intrapsychic stress so long as they are well cared for. Similarly, those entering adolescence have a greater capacity for adjustment. The kind of psychological adaptive mechanisms which the child utilizes should also be carefully examined. He may be developing specific psychological defenses in response to one or the other parent, and, depending on what he needs for appropriate development, custodial placement should reflect these psychological facts.

As noted above, children must have adult models with whom to identify.

42. A. FREUD, SAFEGUARDING THE EMOTIONAL HEALTH OF OUR CHILDREN (1955).

43. Benedek, *Parenthood as a Developmental Phase*, 7 J. AM. PSYCHOANALYTIC ASSOC. 389-417 (1959).

44. *Supra* note 12.

45. *Id.* at 159-62 and accompanying footnotes.

Which parent they need most will vary according to age and, of course, according to the sex of the child. It has become traditional for mothers to be the parent of first choice for children below the age of adolescence. This is psychologically sound provided that the mother is emotionally capable. With the onset of adolescence, however, the like-sexed parent becomes more important since learning to become male or female is the principle psychological task for that age group. This means that with boys there should be a higher incidence of placement with fathers if the needs of male children are to be met. This no doubt will necessitate a marked change in viewpoint for most courts.[46]

For older children especially, the law quite typically attempts to find out what his preferences are so far as where he will live. In psychological terms, this reflects his orientation toward those whom he loves. It is just this particular point which will cause considerable trauma when parents separate and divorce. It inevitably causes a division of loyalty in the children and this must be carefully assayed if wise decisions are to be made. Visitation arrangements should reflect these considerations and every effort should be made to provide the child with as much contact as possible with both of his parents, provided this does not augment internal conflicts.

The older the child, the more he will have developed his own value systems and value orientations. Sometimes there will be conflicts in these systems caused by the family tensions incident to the marriage breakdown. Children should be helped as much as possible to find the situations in which these tensions might be mitigated. Frequently, this goal can be implemented through various alterations in custodial arrangements.

Finally, some children may have particular intrapsychic needs which are a product of their biological condition at birth. For example, if a child has suffered brain damage which causes retardation, this will necessitate certain psychic adaptations. This fact will probably itself result in certain needs which should be reflected in the custodial situation. These should be taken into account when the court makes disposition. While these problems are not common, their occasional presence necessitates special arrangements.[47]

There are certain characteristics about the needs of children which must be viewed in terms of their psychological-process implications. The fact is that there can be no psychological pharmacopoeia to which we may turn for explicit answers. A child's needs are in a constant state of dynamic alteration. They modify with age, both as a function of physiological maturation and in response to the day-by-day experiences of the child. Each experience leaves its

46. For discussions on this point *see* O. English & C. Foster, Fathers are Parents Too (1951); 1 H. Deutsch, The Psychology of Women 7, 174 (1944); E. Erikson, Identity Youth and Crisis ch. III (1968); S. Brody, Patterns of Mothering 88-89, 356-57 (1956); A. Watson, *supra* note 19.

47. Phillips, *supra* note 23 at 63-70.

memory traces which subsequently modify perceptions and experiences. For this reason, plans for children must keep these omnipresent changes in mind.

It should be clear by now that an individual's mind always reflects his past experiences. This "genetic" concept of personality development is a foundation-stone of all contemporary psychological theories. It is the reflection of a "feedback system" in which every stimulus causes a response which modifies the individual's reaction to subsequent stimulii.[48] This view about the shaping of human behavior has long been reflected in aphorisms like "as the twig is bent so doth it incline." Another aspect of behavior which is undergoing constant change relates to the child's ability to control his impulse life. Starting from the infant's biological requirement of having needs rather quickly satisfied, he must learn to put off and control his responses so they fit not only internal need but external limitation. This is a crucial part of behavior modification, and custodial arrangements must reflect these dynamic changes. Firm controls must progressively give way to freedom so that the child may more fully experience, and experiment with, his life.[49]

The next quality in a child's environment needed as a substratum for maturation, is a condition of approximate stability. Every human being is born in a state which might be analogized to a huge computer before it has been programmed. His enormous potential depends entirely on the nature of the programming he receives, especially during the early years of life. Since the programming process takes so many years to accomplish, a basic requirement for successful growth and development is a high degree of stability in the environment. Just as one would not mount a computer on a foundation constantly subject to powerful vibration, nor leave it exposed to inclement weather, so the human child must be reared in a stable and adequately protected environment if he is not to be seriously harmed. Programming must be carried on in a regular and predictable fashion with consistent information being fed in, so that the child can progressively develop effective and satisfying patterns of behavior.[50] The learning must be in terms which are consistent with the situation in which the child is reared, and must accurately reflect his environment. Such stability gives a child the kind of predictive capability with which he can learn to master inner impulses and to relate them to the external world. The cause and effect of life relationships may then be ascertained and managed. In the view of most child psychiatrists, stability of the environment is far more crucial than its precise nature and content. The one thing with which children have most difficulty coping is unpredictable variation, and this is especially critical between the ages of two and adolescence. With adolescents, if they have had a more or less healthy

48. A. WATSON, *supra* note 19, at 139-41.

49. A. WATSON, *supra* note 19, at 76-88.

50. J. RICHMOND & E. LIPTON, *Studies on Mental Health of Children with Specific Implications for Pediatricians*, PREVENTION OF MENTAL DISORDERS IN CHILDREN 95-121 (1961).

and stable environment up to that time, they will have developed a fair amount of resiliency and a considerable capacity to understand alterations in their surroundings.

Another inevitable effect the divorce will have upon children is the precipitation of a grief response. No matter how the custodial arrangements are made, there is an inevitable deprivation which the child will have to sustain. Though in the long run his lot may have considerably improved, he cannot but face the fact that at that particular moment in time, he has lost the advantage of an intact family. While there may have been an absent parent for a long time before the divorce occurred, the divorce brings with it a finality which dashes any hopes for restoration of family wholeness.[51] Awareness of this fact will precipitate any or all of the possible grief responses in the child. He may become depressed, a more healthy and open kind of grieving. He may become "bad". Or he may fail in such life tasks as school performance. Any system which adequately takes the child's interests into account should give him some kind of assistance with this grieving process. At the very least he must be given clear awareness of what his status is and what he may reasonably rely upon for the future.

Another problem which confronts the courts when deciding questions of custody is the relative importance of blood relationships vis-à-vis the care and nutrative support which might have been provided by others. Clearly, a parent-child relationship of biological origin has the highest potential for providing the child-needs set forth above. The reasons for this are psychologically complex. Though this has been long known in an intuitive way, the precise nature of these ties has only recently been described scientifically. Evidence suggests that it is highly unlikely there is a "maternal instinct". Rather, the relationship between mother and child appears to be the complicated product of a whole series of physiological feedback mechanisms which have evolved to assure a mother's interest in her child.[52] Inevitably the mother must have a relationship to her baby at the time of its delivery. (Provided she has not been drugged into total obliviousness.) In addition to all of the psychological images a woman develops during her upbringing which make it important to her to become a mother, she also has physiological needs which must be met at the time of delivery. For example, in order for her physiological status to return to a more or less normal condition, her uterus must strongly contract after the delivery is completed. Otherwise she may bleed to death. Appropriately, her physiology is so arranged that the infant's sucking at her breast will stimulate the needed uterine contraction. The recent trend toward giving the baby to the mother immediately after delivery helps to stimulate these physiological reactions. Her fondling of the baby is not only

51. This is discussed in A. FREUD, *supra* note 42, at 11-14; Barker, *The Child and Divorce*, 37 J.B. ASS'N KANS. 97-102 (1968).

52. J. RICHMOND & E. LIPTON, *supra* note 50, at 108-10.

good for it, but it also aids her own physiological responses. Obviously this normal chain of events has been radically modified by the usual contemporary obstetrical procedures. However, efforts are made to emulate the natural course of events. For example, the injection of Pitocin just after delivery, causes the needed uterine contraction. Similarly, the discomfort from breast engorgement is alleviated by nursing. These feedback systems build up a psycho-physiological interdependence between the mother and child which draws them ever more complexly into an intimate, mutual need-satisfaction relationship. This is the bonding process whereby the natural mother, if she participates in it has a large initial advantage over anyone else. If this chain of natural events is interrupted, the substitute mother may assume the psychological status of the real one. However, both the child and the substitute mother will have slightly different kinds of emotional anchorages during the very early period of the relationship.

While these physiological involvements are more concrete and crucial during the early months and years of life, they will have their analogues during later development. For example, a person who cares for an ill child over a protracted period of time may develop the same kind of close involvement with him. Men who teach male children various skills develop such closeness. These kinds of psychological ties, extended over time, may become fully substitutive for the original parental ones. Their intensity and strength relate to the time in the child's life they were introduced and how long they have persisted.

It should be amply clear by now, that whenever one considers the psychological best interest of the child test, (or any other dispositional standard for that matter) one is engaged in a process of predicting. It should be said at the outset, that we are on treacherous ground so far as hard data is concerned. Though the literature is replete with studies of the various factors which relate to a child's successful maturation, none of it is without the vulnerability of methodological inadequacy. These inadequacies are not due necessarily to the naivete of the observers although that is sometimes the case. They are caused both by the complexity of the subject, as well as by the fact that we do not experiment with human beings. For this reason, any view put forward by the behavioral scientist can be speedily set aside on the ground that it lacks "scientific certainty". Let us hasten to note, however, that this kind of information is considerably more "hard" than the hunches of philosophers or the theoretical predilections of judges. It would seem short-sighted, therefore, were courts to ignore the widely held consensus of professional opinion about certain aspects of child rearing. It should be emphasized that until more complete and detailed records about child custodial disposition are maintained, we are not likely to know any more about predictive accuracy than we now do. It is startling to discover that most records concerning custodial disposition are in such condition that one cannot even be sure precisely what predictions were made! Although it may well run against their grain to do so, the judges and clinicians involved in these cases, should force themselves (and be forced?) to set down in the record why the particular result was reached. Such information should then be systematically collected, so that future studies can determine the accuracy of these dispositions.

THE DETERMINATION OF THE PSYCHOLOGICAL BEST INTEREST OF THE CHILD

Clearly, the first order of concern should be to improve communication between those who possess and provide information about child rearing, and the courts which must utilize it. Each side of this communication axis deals with highly technical considerations which must be fully understood by the other party. Thus, psychiatrists, social workers or psychologists who seek to provide relevant information for the court's decision making, should know something about the legal issues and values with which the court must deal. All too often, these persons have no awareness whatsoever about the judicial process which must be followed. If there is to be a contest and the information must be presented as expert testimony, then the person who is to provide it must know something about the gamesmanship of the evidentiary process. If he does not, it is predictable that he will find himself in such discomfort as to assure that information forthcoming will be grossly distorted.[53] This calls for modification of the educational experience of both the behavioral expert and the lawyer; and, although it will take some time to fully accomplish it, several highly productive innovations are beginning to reach toward this goal.[54]

If the information needed to make a wise decision is to be garnered according to the standard set forth above, the examining expert must have access to all relevant parties and information. This may raise difficult procedural questions. For example, what if one of the parties does not care to engage in this evaluation process? Under the New York statute, which gives both parties the *option* of participation, it is clear that the procedure is not utilized as often as it should be.[55] This suggests that if we wish to implement fully the psychological best interest of the child standard, it must be possible to force all parties to participate, or permit the court to draw negative inferences from their refusal. Unwillingness to participate in the examination

53. *See* A. WATSON, *Communication Between Psychiatrists and Lawyers* 185-98 in 1 INTERNATIONAL PSYCHIATRY CLINICS (1964); Barnett, *supra* note 14 at 224-25; Walker, *supra* note 2, at 143.

54. *See* George, *The Team Approach to Family Law Teaching*, 1 FAM. L.Q. 64-68 (1967); Levy, *The Perilous Necessity: Non-Legal Materials in a Family Law Course*, 15 J. LEGAL ED. 413-18 (1963); Suarez, *Reciprocal Education—A Key to the Psychiatrico-Legal Dilemma*, 17 J. LEGAL ED. 316 (1965).

55. Paulsen, *supra* note 29, at 698.

should be prima facie evidence that the party does not have the child's best interest as a goal.

Another procedural question of importance relates to the problem of who shall carry out the examination of the parties. Should this be done by one expert or by a group of experts? There is the clear possibility for contest about who the expert shall be. Because of this, the court must maintain at least enough control over the process to assure that an adequate job is done. Therefore, if the parties wish to have several experts carry out the procedure, it should be permissible so long as it is done adequately and without incurring detrimental effects. I have observed that multiple experts are often used covertly to delay the litigation. This maneuver is always possible so long as one party may challenge the findings of an expert by simply seeking the opinion of another. If a contestant has enough money to afford this form of delaying tactic, it may be continued indefinitely. I know of cases in which the examination process has been carried out three, four or five times. This would suggest that there is a point at which the court must decide that no further examination may be made and that it have the capacity and knowledge to do this accurately. This type of situation is almost prototypical of those which cause great disturbance to children. While children may have some vague notion of what is going on, the main message they get is that their status is vague and will continue to be so. This again underscores the importance of the judge's possessing sufficient skill and understanding about behavioral science so that he can comfortably and with finality make his decision. At the present time too many judges are reluctant to act, and so they let matters take their own course. The examinations go on *ad infinitum* to the severe detriment of the children involved.

What should the examination entail? Obviously, all of the potential parenting persons have to be examined in relation to their psychological relationship to the children. An adequate clinical psychiatric examination of these individuals will take approximately one to three hours per person. While such a clinical examination is usually adequate, on some occasions it might be necessary to supplement this with psychological tests. Often, due to the sparse number of psychiatrists, such evaluations are made by social workers who possess skill and understanding in the dynamics of parent-child relationships.

The examination of children is somewhat more difficult. The younger the child, the more skill that is required to carry out a psychological examination. Because young children are not able to describe their feelings, their evaluation is ordinarily conducted in the context of "play". The play is then "interpreted" by the expert who goes behind its manifest meaning in order to discover the child's attitudes about himself and his home situation. This clinical examination will often be supplemented by psychological testing which once more construes the surface content for its underlying symbolized meaning. This would take about two to five hours with the child. Further, one or two hours will be spent going over background material such as school records, school observations, and comments made by others who know the child well. This information is studied for the insights it provides of the child's adaptive patterns and the reflections of his needs. Following these studies the report will be written.

All of these observations and conclusions must be organized and presented in a form that will withstand the legal validating procedure of cross-examination. Clearly, the lawyers involved must have the capacity to elicit the appropriate material from the experts and then subject it to appropriate examination and cross-examination procedures. Not only must all of the relevant material be elicited, but it must be presented in a clear and communicative form. This need will tax the technical and ethical capacities of all concerned. It is not difficult to embroil the legally uninitiated expert into all kinds of logical inconsistencies once he is on the witness stand. These inconsistencies often reflect the expert's lack of legal gamesmanship rather than any intrinsic errors in his material. Therefore, the presentation of expert testimony in these custodial cases must be well controlled by the courts if accuracy and good judgment are to prevail.

It should be acknowledged that the evaluation procedure described above is an expensive one that can be employed only in locations where experts are available. As such, the courts are faced with the following questions may viable alternatives be developed? What may be done in the absence of appropriate experts? It is this author's opinion that if a court does not have the capacity to make skillful determinations concerning expert opinions, it should not invest time and money in measures which are predictably inadequate. All too often, the courts will employ any "expert" at all. I would say categorically that those psychiatrists who are capable only of pasting diagnostic labels on their cases, and who do not have the ability to delineate and formulate the psychodynamic patterns of behavior of the parents and the child, have no utility whatsoever for the court.[56] The parties would do better to save their money than to embark upon that kind of examination. In locations where there is a shortage of skilled experts, some type of central diagnostic center might be set up. In these days of rapid travel, distance is of relatively little consequence. A skillful diagnostic formulation is of such importance to these custodial decisions that it is well worth a considerable investment to solve any logistical problems which arise.

RECOMMENDATIONS.

Let us now enumerate those changes which would best potentiate the "psychological best interest of the child" following divorce.

1. The obvious and principle goal is to assure a correct initial decision which

56. *See, e.g.*, A. WATSON, *supra* note 19, at ch. XI; J. RUBIN, *The Psychiatric Report*, READINGS IN LAW AND PSYCHIATRY 69-73 (1968).

can be safeguarded against capricious modification. In other words, to foster the principle of stability, a good decision should be made and it should be difficult or impossible for any party to modify that decision. Statutory re-definition should be carried out so that a child's custodial situation cannot be readily challenged in the service of covert tactical goals by any party.

2. A procedure must be established which assures that the child's interests are effectively advocated during the divorce proceedings. Because of this author's skepticism regarding the ethical commitments of the parties' counsel, it must be secured by appointing, for the child, counsel who will skillfully and tactfully represent his interests. It seems clear that the court must maintain an interest in this throughout the procedure, in order to insure that such counsel does his job effectively. If counsel for one of the parents is more effective than the child's, so that issues are not properly brought forward on behalf of the child, then the court must see to it that balance is re-established. This is best accomplished by assuring legal skill and effectiveness when the appointment is made. For this purpose the court should have a large pool of lawyers, experienced in this type of case, from which it can make its appointments. This would also tend to progressively upgrade the skills required of that group for dealing with the complex issues involved in custodial actions.

3. One issue which counsel for the children must closely watch is the matter of delay in the resolution of custody. While substantive protection is important, so detrimental is delay in the disposition of the child that counsel must vigorously press the court in order to avoid it. This is at least equal in importance to the right of a "speedy trial" guaranteed in criminal procedures, for time is often even of more critical importance for children than it is for adults. Vigorous counsel and an alert judge must see that it is not lost.

4. The judge should assure that all relevant parties to the custody action are adequately evaluated psychologically. In the event that one of the parents resists, they must be advised that failure to participate will be construed as evidence of distinterest in the child. Anything short of this will markedly diminish the accuracy of the decision-making.

5. This article has already commented upon the effects of a poor evaluation of the potential custodians. If the diagnostic personnel do not carry their examinations far enough to establish a psychodynamically relevant formulation about the parties involved, the information is not "expert" and has no value at all. It is submitted that under those circumstances, the court might just as well fall back on its own intuitive judgments and save the money involved in the evaluation. Similarly, when the court's staff is so heavily burdened that it cannot adequately evaluate all of the cases referred to it, it should make the strategic decision to handle some cases effectively, rather than all of them inadequately; the latter strategy results in almost total waste of staff talents. Hopefully, professional personnel would refuse to be pressed

into such wasteful and unprofessional behavior; realistically, however, such personnel sometimes need moral support to perform in this way.

6. The children's lawyer must also assure that, depending upon their age and emotional maturity, the children know as much about the procedure as possible. He should seek and take advice from the psychological evaluators about how best to carry this out. Counsel might, if necessary, employ one of them to assist the children in comprehending the divorce and the evaluative process, and to thus better understand their own plight. Everything possible should be done to assure that the children fully comprehend their changed and changing status. Lawyers should learn never to underestimate a child's capacity to fantasize all sorts of bizarre facts concerning such disturbing events as a divorce. For example, it is not at all uncommon for children to believe that their behavior had something to do with the dissolution of their parents' marriage. Children cannot emotionally afford to continue such a fantasy since it inevitably leads to some kind of maturational inhibition or inappropriate behavior aimed at undoing their "badness". The child's lawyer as a matter of duty, should do what he can to ward off this potential danger in every way possible.

7. Another matter with which the child's lawyer should deal involves making the custodial arrangements as satisfying as possible for both parents: for in the last analysis, it is the parents who will be primarily responsible for how well the custodial arrangements work. There will be many wounds from the past which need to heal, and parents often attempt to use the children for balm. The child's counsel should make such efforts as he can to help parents work out their problems and frustrations, since all such efforts redound to the young client's advantage. This may involve helping the parents to secure some form of psychological assistance in order to unlock pernicious conflicts over the children.[57]

8. Another procedure which the children's lawyer might do well to seek is to have the divorce heard "in chambers." While this is done occasionally in some jurisdictions, the practice ought to be widened extensively. There is no reason for maintaining the public cockpit aspects in these procedures, since they do nothing but harm. Nor should this change be merely nominal; for that kind of sham only discredits the law.[58] I have heard counsel describe the advantage of having their clients "blow off steam," but this is useful only if the parties understand what they are doing. I have never personally seen lawyers handle these public explosions in any way which would even remotely redound to the psychological advantage of their clients. If these procedures were held in private, it would greatly enhance their usefulness for more constructive discussion.[59] In England a very high percentage of contested

57. Rothenberg, *supra* note 16, at 99.

58. Paulsen, *supra* note 29, at 694-716.

59. Rothenberg, *supra* note 16, at 99.

divorce actions are carried out "in chambers." Whenever the judge feels that there would be psychological disadvantage to raising a public spectacle in pursuit of proof of "fault," he merely orders his bailiff to hang a sign on the court room door saying "The Court is in Chambers" which automatically bars everyone from the courtroom except relevant parties and their counsel. Such a procedure would be very useful in promoting the child's best interest. It would permit the court to obtain more objective data since it would greatly diminish covert revenge maneuvers.

9. Another desirable step for promoting the child's psychological best interests would be to modify the judiciary. Though judges widely acknowledge that handling these cases is one of the more painful and difficult tasks they must perform, little has been done to correct the situation. It would seem entirely possible to appoint behavioral science "judges" to sit with the divorce court judge when he is hearing a case involving child custody. The need for positive expert assistance in these cases has already been suggested to the Law Commission in England by Mr. John Hall of St. John's College, Cambridge, in his report of February, 1968.[60] Such a "judge" could bring to bear on the decision-making process the insights of the psychological sciences, thus increasing the likelihood that all appropriate information relating to the child's disposition would be included. Consequently, the decision could be more wisely made while improving the chances for an appropriate disposition of the children. This procedure would also have secondary advantages. The presence of both legal and psychological experts on the bench would immediately begin to cross-educate the parties to the decision-making process. Each would progressively learn from the other the problems involved in the judicial handling of these matters. Not only would it increase effectiveness in the instant case, but skills would progressively be increased with the passage of time.

In England, where all juvenile and most family problems are handled initially in Magistrate Courts, the Magistrates who sit on those benches have obligatory supplemental training in the behavioral sciences. This is based on the assumption that there are many special kinds of problems relating to the law involving family problems, and an ordinary magistrate is not usually equipped to handle them.

10. The next recommendation is Professor Kubie's idea of a "committee for each child who is in custody."[61] The most important issue to which this idea attends is the fact that children's daily problems often require instant attention. The disturbances of children in custody cannot be put off until one can gain the attention of a court or an administrative agent such as the "friend of the court". It must be recognized that delay inevitably results in

60. Hall, *Family Law: Arrangements for the Care and Upbringing of Children (Sec. 33 of the Matrimonial Causes Act 1965)*, 2 LONDON LAW COMMISSION 39–40 (1968).

61. Kubie, *supra* note 37.

such psychological beclouding that it becomes difficult, if not impossible, to ascertain precisely what is going on. In any event, the issue will be so far out of touch from the child's immediate emotional reality that the delay might have a detrimental effect on his development. By appointing a committee of interested persons who will be immediately available, there is somebody to whom either the parent or the child may turn to explore and hopefully resolve any acute problem. Since the committee is chosen by both parents, there is a built-in reliance on their views. When it carries the added authority of the court's approval, this exerts a subtle pressure upon the parents to take the committee's advice without carrying the matter on to court. It permits the elaboration of numerous face-saving maneuvers by the parents and, in the end, issues can be expeditiously handled in ways which are of great emotional advantage to the child. The committee would take on some aspects of legal guardianship. It would have the persuasive authority to bring about many decisions on behalf of the child even while the court stood available to resolve any impasses. When and if an issue did come to hearing after consideration by the committee, the court would immediately be in possession of a great deal of relatively objective information about the events which it must litigate. Thus, the committee could also act as an informed "referee" for the court.

Similarly, this device provides an excellent buffer for the legal system. It would keep many symbolic battles out of the courtroom and prevent such issues from being solidified into decisions which themselves might prove ultimately detrimental. Needless to say, it would save the court a great deal of work, and the parties considerable expenditure for legal fees. While I do not know whether this procedure has ever been invoked, it clearly should be. There appears to be no obstacle to a particular court moving in this direction at any time.

11. The next consideration is the question of review of custodial decisions. As noted above, at the present time there is little to prevent any party from initiating judicial reconsideration of the custodial decision. There can be little doubt that many if not most of these petitions are related to continued in-fighting between the parents. It is felt that statutes should be developed to assure that once the carefully considered custodial decision is made, it will be extremely difficult to reopen the issue. The court, on its own initiative, could then maintain a strong and resistant barrier between the child and continuing litigation. After a relatively brief time, perhaps six to nine months, no challenge to the custodial decision should be possible except where substantial evidence indicates that the child stands in some sort of jeopardy. Such an initial procedure should be *ex parte*, between the court and the petitioner, without any need for the custodian to defend. This would keep a multitude of potential harassments at arms length, and thus greatly help the custodian to maintain a spontaneous and normal relationship with the child.

In the last two sessions of the Michigan State Legislature, a statute has been under consideration as a substitute for the typical habeas corpus procedure used to modify a child's custodial status following divorce. The proposed amendments would alter the divorce statute so that it would function similarly to the English Matrimonial Causes Act of 1965, which requires a showing of adequate custodial arrangements before a final divorce decree may be entered. This procedure was opposed by several judges on the grounds that it would interfere with reconciliation attempts through premature solidification of the battle lines between the warring spouses, cause duplication of proceedings, and also occasionally produce abortive results if a divorce were not granted.[62] Since I have high regard for the judges who voiced this opposition, I assume these challenges to be well-grounded. However, there was general agreement among most who were involved that some cutoff date for challenge should exist under the proposed legislation. Once the arrangements have been made and the cutoff date passed, the decision may not be re-opened without great procedural difficulty. The proposed Michigan statute also attempts to set forth some explicit criteria as guidelines for the best interest of the child.[63] While these amendments have not yet been passed, the

---

62. Letter from Judge Victor J. Baum to State Representative Dennis O. Cawthorne, April 11, 1968, which analysed the shortcomings of House Bills 2841 and 2842 (Child Custody Act of 1968).

63. SUBSTITUTE FOR HOUSE BILL NO. 2842

A bill relating to civil procedures for determination of the custody of children: to provide standards for courts in awarding child custody in actions for child custody, divorce, separate maintenance and annulment; and to repeal certain acts and parts of acts.

THE PEOPLE OF THE STATE OF MICHIGAN ENACT:

Sec. 1. This act shall be known and may be cited as the "child custody act of 1968."

Sec. 2. The courts shall follow the procedure prescribed by this act without unnecessary delay to the end that final determinations of child custody may be made as quickly as is reasonably possible consistent with the best interests of a child. An application for a writ of habeas corpus to obtain custody of a child shall not be entertained if the applicant did not file an action under this act, unless it appears that the remedy under this act would be inadequate or ineffective to determine the matter of child custody.

Sec. 3. (1) Except as otherwise provided by law, an award of the custody of a child under age 18 shall be made only in an action brought in the circuit court for the county where the child is found. An action may be brought by a parent, relative or legal guardian of the child, or on leave of the court by any other person or agency claiming an interest in the welfare of the child. An adoptive parent after a final order of adoption is considered a parent. The natural parent shall then be considered "any other person" under this section. This act shall not be used to attack collaterally adoption orders.

(2) If a divorce, separate maintenance or annulment action is pending in this state, or if custody of a child was previously ordered in such an action in this state, custody shall not be determined under this act but in such action.

(3) The court, in its discretion, and at any stage of the proceedings, may appoint an attorney for the child and assess a reasonable attorney fee as part of the costs.

Sec. 4. The procedure in the action shall be the same as provided by statute or

atmosphere for so doing appears to be favorable, and there is a strong likelihood of future enactment.

12. Some reconsideration of the legal presumptions regarding custodial disposition appears to be appropriate. Instead of favoring the mother as custodian for all children, the presumption should probably be limited to children under ten. Similarly, there should be the presumption in favor of the mother for all female children. Natural parents should have a presumption in their favor except in situations where there has been a parent-substitute of long duration. In regard to defining "long", this might be articulated in appropriate operational terms such as "parental substitution of sufficient duration to have caused the child to regard the substitute person as his parent." (In regard to this presumption, there will no doubt have to be some exceptions, such as in those cases in which a parent has been removed from his child through no fault of his own.) There should be a presumption in favor of fathers for boys over age 15, if he is able to care for them. No presumption whatsoever should exist in relation to religious preference. With the exception of the last mentioned one, the presumptions above could be rebuttable, and perhaps the grounds for rebuttal might also be spelled out. Possibly some of these elements could be included in the preamble to any statute on post-divorce custodial disposition.

---

court rule for other actions in circuit court, except as hereinafter provided. A defendant shall answer within a time ordered by the court but not later than 5 days after personal service of the summons and a copy of the complaint upon him in this state. Questions of law and fact shall be determined by the court without a jury.

Sec. 5. After the answer is filed or defendant is in default:

(a) The court shall order the matter to be heard at a time stated not later than 45 days from the date of the filing of the answer or default by the defendant, and make an order adjudicating whether or not the child is uncared for forthwith after the hearing.

(b) The court may order an investigation and report as to the welfare and custody of the child, if good cause appears therefor, to be made by the friend of the court, an investigator or professional personnel attached to the court. Copies of the report shall be mailed to all parties, whether or not in default or to their counsel of record within 14 days after receipt of the order by the person directed to make the investigation, unless the time is extended for good cause shown. The report may be received in evidence if no objection is made, or when objection is made, if the persons making the report are available for cross-examination as to any matter reported.

(c) The court shall issue an order requiring any person who has custody or control of the child to appear personally at the hearing, and may order that such person bring the child before the court at the hearing unless the best interests of the child require otherwise. The court may notify any other person of the time and place of the hearing prior to the hearing, and may order the appearance of any other person at the hearing. The court may authorize the payment of necessary travel expenses incurred by persons ordered or otherwise required to appear at the hearing.

Sec. 6. The court shall give priority to hearings and other proceedings under this act over all other matters before it, except those involving contested child custody proceedings and persons who are in confinement under criminal or civil process.

13. Another way in which the psychological best interest of the child could be greatly potentiated relates to the education of lawyers who handle these matters. There is probably no other area of law in which basic knowledge of human behavior is more important. Although this information should hopefully be included in the education of all lawyers, it is crucial for those working in family law. Information about child development and personality theory is essential to understanding fully the processes so visible in this type of case. While ideally this should be a part of pre-legal training, the absence

---

Sec. 7. The hearings shall not take place without the presence of 1 or both of the parents, the legal guardian, or a guardian ad litem appointed by the court to protect the best interests of the child.

Sec. 8. The court may hear the testimony of any person or expert produced by any party or upon the court's own motion whose skill, insight, knowledge and experience is such that his testimony is relevant to a just and reasonable determination of the custody issue.

Sec. 9. The court shall not change the custodial environment of a child as it was established prior to commencement of the action, except in case of the death of a parent or unless the plaintiff proves by clear and convincing evidence, or if plaintiff is a parent, by preponderance of the evidence, that the child is uncared for. However, if the plaintiff was the established custodian in such environment, the court shall grant custody to him unless the defendant proves by clear and convincing evidence that the child is uncared for by the plaintiff.

Sec. 10. The custodial environment of a child as used in Section 9 is established if over an appreciable time the child naturally looks to the custodian in such environment for guidance, discipline, the necessities of life and parental comfort. The age of the child, the physical environment and the inclination of the custodian and the child as to permanency of the relationship shall also be considered.

Sec. 11. A child is uncared for if:

(a) It has been abandoned. Abandonment may be physical or psychological, and includes (i) leaving the child in destitute circumstances, whereby it is homeless or in a state of want or suffering due to lack of sufficient shelter, food, clothing or medical or surgical care, (ii) leaving the child without proper shelter, food or clothing, or the means to provide them, (iii) failing to visit or have personal contact with the child for a period of 1 year, (iv) habitually making grossly insufficient contribution to the child's psychological, social and emotional growth and development, or (v) the custodian being imprisoned for a crime or being committed as mentally deficient or mentally ill for such time that the child will be deprived of a normal home for a critical period of time.

(b) It has been abused. Abuse may be physical or psychological, and includes (i) cruelty, (ii) misusage, (iii) gross and continued failure to supply the child adequately with shelter, food, clothing, medical or surgical care or education though financially able or offered financial means to do so, (iv) wilful failure or refusal to provide special care made essential by the child's physical or mental condition, or (v) exposure of the child to circumstances in which he suffers or is likely to suffer serious harm from improper guardianship, including inadequate or improper moral supervision or guidance, of the person in whose custody he is at the time of the commencement of the action.

Sec. 12. A child adjudicated to be uncared for shall be permanently removed from the control of those with whom it is found at the commencement of the action and shall become a ward of the court. The court may make arrangements for the temporary care of the child.

of explicit pre-law requirements makes it necessary to include this knowledge in the law school curriculum. In the past, family law courses were absolutely devoid of such information. However in the last several years, textbooks have been developed which go far toward remedying this serious omission.[64] In addition to the psychological content which has been fed into family law courses, there have also been other courses added to the curriculum which present general material about human behavior. Several textbooks for utilization in such courses have also been published recently.[65]

There is a similar need on the part of psychiatrists, social workers, and psychologists working in this area of law to be educated about some of the

---

Sec. 13. (1) The court, as soon as practicable, shall determine and order custody for the child as follows:

(a) When the dispute involves only the parents, the best interests of the child shall control.

(b) The permanence, as a family unit, of the existing or proposed home or homes of the child.

(c) The emotional, ethical and economic stability of such home or homes.

(d) The mental and physical health of all individuals involved.

(e) The home, school and community record and adjustment of the child.

(f) The reasonable preference of the child, if first deemed by the court to be of sufficient age to express it.

(g) Any other factor or factors considered by the court to be relevant to a particular child custody dispute.

Sec. 14. Reasonable visitation rights may be awarded to parents or to any person interested in the welfare of the child unless such rights will be detrimental to the best interests of the child.

Sec. 15. When the court has ordered permanent custody of a child no change in custody shall be made unless a new action is begun and new grounds for judicial intervention established as provided by Section 9, except that custody may be ordered in a subsequent divorce, separate maintenance or annulment action. Although the parties and the county where the child is found remain the same, the proceeding shall not be treated as a modification of the original judgment but as a new action.

Sec. 16. In an appeal to the court of appeals, that court, upon its own motion, or the motion of any party, may dismiss an appeal, assess punitive damages not exceeding the actual damages and expenses incurred by the opposing party including reasonable attorney fees, or take other disciplinary action, when it is determined that an appeal or any of the proceedings therein was vexatious because:

(a) The appeal was taken for purposes of hindrance or delay or without any reasonable basis for belief that there was a meritorious issue to be determined on appeal.

(b) Any motion, argument, petition, brief or appendix filed in the case was grossly lacking in the requirements of propriety or grossly disregarded the requirements of a fair presention of the issues to the court.

Sec. 17. Act No. 192 of the Public Acts of 1873, being section 722.541 of the Compiled Laws of 1948, is repealed.

64. C. FOOTE, R.J. LEVY & F. SANDER, CASES AND MATERIALS ON FAMILY LAW (1966); J. GOLDSTEIN & J. KATZ, *supra* note 7.

65. R. ALLEN, E. FERSTER & J. RUBIN, READINGS IN LAW AND PSYCHIATRY (1968); J. KATZ, J. GOLDSTEIN & A. DERSHOWITZ, PSYCHOANALYSIS, PSYCHIATRY AND LAW (1967); A. WATSON, *supra* note 19, at 38.

fundamental legal matters which arise in family law cases. While there have been occasional courses offered to these professionals, nowhere do they learn enough to assure that they will come into court or write their opinions with adequate legal knowledge about how their information will be used. This, too, should be remedied, since failure of communication between these two professional groups can only increase the hazards for children.

14. Finally, some means must be developed to assure that visitation activities are handled in a way less likely to place the children in a cross-fire. Instead of viewing this as a matter of right to the parents, the issue should be reversed so that it becomes the right of children to have ongoing relationships with both his parents unless there is a serious and damaging reason for not doing so. It has been recommended to the Law Commission in England that custody should be vested in both parents if they are "fit."[66] As noted above, every child has the need to identify with members of both sexes. Girls must learn how to become women, but they must also understand how to relate to men. Boys have to develop masculinity, while they learn to understand the ways of women. The first and crucial lessons in this area are learned from the father and mother, and for this reason every effort should be made to assure that this access continues. Indeed, there should be a very substantial presumption regarding this right, requiring very considerable evidence to rebut it.

No matter what type of parents the child has, sooner or later he must see them in accurate perspective and eliminate whatever fantasies he may have had about them. This may not be accomplished *en vacuo* and can only come about through continued and intensive contact. Indeed, the loss of easy access to both parents is one of the principle tragedies of the disrupted marriage so far as children are concerned. For this reason, there should be few reasons for blocking the children's contacts with both parents, and orders to that effect should be made rarely and only with a strong showing of detriment. While there will be some distress caused by movement back and forth between the parents, in the end such movement is necessary to growth. Every effort should be made to facilitate visitation; clearly, this is one of the places where the Kubie committee idea could be invaluable. These friends, chosen by both parties, could help to work out, or at least modulate, the parental stresses that visitations may precipitate, so that such visits can continue. At the very least, visitation should not be the subject of continuing litigation. Under the protection of a statute which would limit the options for challenging custodial orders, visitation should be regarded as inevitable. The child's counsel should work vigorously with the family committee in order to help the parents accept this as something which their child desperately needs. Any procedure which suggests otherwise should be viewed as contrary to the psychological best interests of the child.

66. Hall, *supra* note 60 at 38.

CONCLUSION

Hopefully, the discussion in this paper has added to the content of the concept of the "best psychological interests of the child." While many of the questions found in this area of the law may not be explicitly answered at the present time, if these questions are kept in the forefront of discussion, while relevant information is considered and collected, we may hopefully be better able to answer them in the near future. Court administrators should attempt a more systematic collection of the data about child custody placements, and competent behavioral scientists should be set to the task of analyzing them. Then and only then may we establish the kinds of procedures and statutes which will truly protect children in the context of divorce actions. Deeply disturbing at best and extremely tragic at worst, this is an area for mental health practice as well as for preventive law.

[13]

Custody Investigations as Evidence in Divorce Cases

ROBERT J. LEVY*

> [T]here is a growing conviction that persons with specialized training and experience such as social workers are better qualified to determine what is in the best interests of the child than even the best intentioned judge.[1]

> The most fundamental problem with the so-called "home study" in child custody litigation is that it is neither limited to the home, nor is it a study. Rather, high sounding protestations to the contrary notwithstanding, the "home study" is usually merely one untrained person's opinion based upon individual prejudices superimposed upon a collection of hearsay devoid of any objective standards. Such sham results in an effective usurpation of judicial discretion by officious intermeddlers whose unfettered judgment is protected by overworked judges seeking the expedient way to rely upon their employees and functionaires. . . .
>
> If ever the Rona Barretts of the United States are seeking a new career, the expertise as *gossips* most certainly could be put to immediate use as Court-appointed investigators conducting "home studies."[2]

The term "custody investigation" commonly signifies an out-of-court exploration of and written report about the circumstances of children who are the subjects of judicial custody awards in divorce cases. Investigations usually provide social, psychological, and economic data about the children as well as a variety of information about the adults who are litigating the right to the children's custody. The investigation

*Mr. Levy is a professor of law at the University of Minnesota.

1. Annot., 35 A.L.R.2d 629, 631, 632 (1954). The remark has been quoted in the following articles: Note, *The Family in the Courts*, 17 U. Pitt. L. Rev. 206, 250 (1956); Foster & Freed, *Child Custody (Pt. 2)*, 39 N.Y.U.L. Rev. 615, (1964); Okpaku, *Psychology, Impediment or Aid in Child Custody Cases?*, 29 Rutgers L. Rev. 1117 n.3 (1976); Gozansky, *Court-Ordered Investigations in Child Custody Cases*, 12 Willamette L. Rev. 511 (1976).

2. Wolf, What Is Wrong with Home Studies, Speech Delivered to the Family Law Section, American Bar Association, New Orleans, La. (Aug. 11, 1981).

is commonly conducted by a social worker employed by the divorce court's own social service arm or by an employee of a local welfare department or social service agency. Although investigations are ordered in a variety of litigation contexts, this article is devoted to practices in the most common procedural context: when the investigation is ordered in the course of the initial skirmishes of divorce litigation.[3]

Typically, but not exclusively, investigations are ordered at the divorce's "temporary hearing" (as it is described in Minnesota), the first judicial encounter of the spouses after the action is filed, one that occurs if the spouses and their lawyers cannot agree as to the financial or custodial arrangements to govern their postseparation but predivorce living arrangements.[4] At temporary hearings, a referee (a judge in rural counties) commonly issues a variety of temporary (*"pendente lite"*) orders, governing such matters as temporary support and alimony, custody to one spouse and visitation for the other. In addition, at the request of one of the spouses, or on his own initiative after reading the parties' affidavits and/or hearing the testimony, the referee may order the spouses to go immediately to a caseworker for the initial (or "intake") interview of a custody investigation.[5] In almost every investigation, the caseworker interviews the parents and the children, may visit the home of each parent, may interview a parent's therapist or the children's teachers, may refer the parents and/or the children for psychological or psychiatric assessment, and makes inquiries about the family from friends and neighbors. The result, in almost every case, is a written report which is delivered to the judge and sometimes to the spouses or their lawyers.[6]

---

3. This article is based largely on the research on custody investigations in Hennepin County (Minneapolis), Minnesota, the state's major population center, which formed the basis for a much larger study of custody investigations. *See* Levy, *Custody Investigations in Divorce Cases*, 1985 AM. B. FOUND. RES. J. 713 [hereinafter cited as Levy, *Custody Investigations*]. Quotations are reprinted with the permission of the American Bar Foundation.

4. In 1970 in Hennepin County, a "temporary hearing" was held in 73 percent of the divorce actions. Most of the custody investigations conducted that year were ordered at the temporary hearing. The eighty-four cases which included investigations that year were some 4 percent of the divorce actions with children that terminated in a decree. The fifty-five investigation cases in Ramsey County (St. Paul) that year represented a 5.7 percent of the divorce actions with children that terminated in a decree. In 1980 in Ramsey County, the only county where such data have been collected, investigations were conducted in 7.2 percent of a considerably smaller (by more than 13 percent) number of divorces with children.

5. I will refer to the investigator as a caseworker. Usually, but not exclusively, reports are conducted by personnel trained as social workers. For a description of the training of the Hennepin County custody investigation staff, see Levy, *Custody Investigations*, 736–38.

6. The description here, and in subsequent pages, of typical custody investigation practice and reports is taken from my investigation of the Minnesota experience. *See* note 3 *supra*. The few appellate decisions from other jurisdictions which describe investigation practice suggest that the style and the problems may be similar in other

A variety of "nonadversarial" techniques have become popular in recent years to supplement traditional courtroom fact-finding. A "*guardian ad litem*" for the children is sometimes appointed;[7] some judges appoint an attorney for children whose parents cannot agree as to a postdivorce custodian.[8] Mediation has become common. But custody investigations of the traditional kind continue to be popular. In Hennepin County, Minnesota, for example, the number of investigations quadrupled during the decade following 1970 and may have grown at the same rate in the five years since;[9] a recent empirical investigation of the role of the "attorney for the child" in a jurisdiction where such appointments are made, examining in-depth attitudes of eighteen lawyers who had participated in some thirty-five divorce cases, disclosed that in thirty of those cases a custody investigation had been ordered by the judge prior to appointing counsel for the child;[10] the number of appellate cases from all jurisdictions raising custody investigation issues has grown significantly;[11] the Uniform Marriage and Divorce Act, promulgated in 1970, for the first time provided state legislatures with a model for custody investigation regulation—and the Act's provision has been enacted in a number of states and has received appellate court attention.[12]

Judges have enthusiastically relied upon out-of-court caseworker custody investigations in divorce cases for a complex of reasons which they have often identified in appellate decisions and in the trade literature: custody decisions are too important to be treated in the same

states. *See, e.g.*, Denningham v. Denningham, 49 Md. App. 328, 431 A.2d 755 (1981), *cert. denied*, 455 U.S. 990 (1982) (refusal of trial judge to show investigation report to husband who was appearing *pro se* was unconstitutional but harmless error); Ziehm v. Ziehm, 433 A.2d 725 (Me. 1981) (statute regulating custody investigations prescribes practices similar to those followed in Minnesota in 1970). *See also* Pearson & Ring, *Judicial Decision-Making in Contested Custody Cases*, 21 J. FAM. L. 703, 723 (1983) (Colorado trial judges interviewed for study of social service and judicial practices in contested custody cases where close to half the sample of cases included a custody investigation "were especially critical of the private psychological reports that were extremely jargon-ridden and evaluative"). *See also* text accompanying note 49 *infra*.

7. *See, e.g.*, WIS. STAT. ANN. § 767.045 (West 1981); Haugen v. Haugen, 82 Wis. 2d 411, 262 N.W.2d 769 (1978).

8. *See* Landsman & Minow, *Lawyering for the Child: Principles of Representation in Custody and Visitation Disputes Arising from Divorce*, 87 YALE L.J. 1126 (1980).

9. *See* Levy, *Custody Investigations*, 716–17.

10. *See* note 6 *supra*.

11. The term "custody investigation" was mentioned in 960 West Publishing Company key number paragraphs between 1951 and 1960 and in 3,464 key number paragraphs during the period 1961–70—an increase of 361 percent. The term was mentioned in 8,227 key number paragraphs during the period 1970–80, an increase of 238 percent from the previous decade. *See also* Pearson & Ring, *supra* note 6, at 713 (custody investigation ordered in almost all contested cases in Denver County during 1973–77, in less than 50 percent of the cases in the two other counties).

12. *See* UNIFORM MARRIAGE AND DIVORCE ACT § 405 (1970). *See also In re* Kramer, 177 Mont. 61, 580 P.2d 439 (1978); *In re* Waggener, 13 Wash. App. 911, 538 P.2d 845 (1975).

fashion as ordinary adversary litigation—in which the parties have uncontrolled discretion as to what testimony is presented to the decision maker; a neutral expert, removed from the emotional turmoil of the dispute and the partisan advocacy of the lawyers, can provide more reliable information to the judge than the embattled spouses are likely to provide;[13] the information essential to custody decision making tends to be more psychological than in other litigation contexts and therefore more suited to written reports by psychological experts than to testimony in a courtroom. The themes were articulated nicely by Professor Gellhorn when he argued for the creation of a family court for New York City:

> Present procedures are inadequate for dealing with [the parent-child relationships of custody cases.] [T]he adversary method is a painfully slow way of developing the mass of factual detail out of which such attitudes can be made apparent . . . [T]he conduct of adversary judicial proceedings intensifies the hostilities and further obscures the picture . . . [T]he court needs the advice of experts in the field of human emotions . . . .
>
> Social investigation into family situations is by now a well-established technique. It is used in connection with probation and parole as applied to adult offenders. It is used in connection with the investigation and determination of treatment in the Children's Court. . . . The common element in these activities is their use of the basic premises of psychology and psychiatry as the core of what may be called a science of the dynamics of personality and of interpersonal relations. It may be acknowledged that this new science is not fully developed; that there are deep cleavages in theoretical approach and differences in clinical method. But there are broad areas of agreement which transcend most of the differences and controversies . . . This kind of knowledge is, at least in theory, a central part of the professional training of probation officers as well as social workers. . . .
>
> A judge who is a wise man can certainly formulate a conclusion about many of [the facts] from observation of parties in the light of the full factual report. But there is serious doubt whether observation can be fair and effective where, without further aids, it consists solely of impressions in the unnatural atmosphere of a courtroom, during the course of contentious proceedings in the outcome of which the parties have an almost violent interest. . . . [Lawyers and judges] should . . . have the benefit of investigations by persons who, because they do have the requisite knowledge, will be able to appreciate and search out those facts.[14]

---

13. *See, e.g., In re* Waggener, 13 Wash. App. 911, 914–15, 538 P.2d 845, 848 (1975), concluding that the provisions of the Uniform Marriage and Divorce Act designed to guarantee the spouses' confrontation rights where an investigation has been conducted "evidence a clear legislative purpose to substantially diminish the adversary nature of the traditional custody proceedings which had preceded enactment of the new law. . . . Considered in their entirety these [custody] provisions persuade us the legislative purpose is to avoid custody determinations based solely on the evidence—often partisan—produced by the adversaries, and to avoid a result dictated by the skill of the advocates or the strategy employed by counsel."

14. Gellhorn, Children and Families in the Courts of New York City, Report by a Special Committee of the Association of the Bar of the City of New York at 310–11, 314 (1954).

But many judges and academics who have advocated reliance upon such nonadversarial methods have been unwilling to acknowledge that the intellectual justifications for, as well as the typical practice methods of, custody investigations can be traced to the juvenile court movement, to that "child-saving," interventionist style which in recent years has drawn so much deserved criticism.[15] Since custody investigations can be identified as one of the nonadversarial methods of "Child Savers, Inc.—Divorce Division,"[16] then, when we examine the quality of custody investigations and devise procedural techniques to regulate their use, we should be attentive to the risks to children and to family privacy and autonomy posed by their interventionist potential.

Part I of this article describes the procedural contexts in which custody investigations are used and what those contexts suggest as to their regulation; Part II explores the law of custody investigations; Part III provides data about the actual content of custody investigations in one county in Minnesota during the year 1970; and Part IV recommends new procedural protections against the risks to families and to the judicial process that the empirical survey indicates custody investigations regularly pose.

Part I

Custody investigation "law" is usually made when a disappointed spouse seeks appellate review of a trial judge's adverse custody disposition. Such cases are typified by Mr. and Mrs. H-1's divorce.[17] Two months after Mrs. H-1 signed a divorce complaint, in September 1969, and following a temporary hearing, the trial judge issued a temporary order which included a provision—to which the parties probably agreed[18]—requiring a custody investigation. If the *H-1* case conformed to Hennepin County practice, the parties' attorneys were permitted to read

---

15. *See, e.g.*, Feld, *Juvenile Court Legislative Reform and the Serious Young Offender: Dismantling the "Rehabilitative Ideal,"* 65 MINN. L. REV. 167 (1981). The history is traced in Levy, *Custody Investigations*, 718–28.

16. *Id.* at 719.

17. The cases described here were the first of each type to appear in Hennepin County when the reports for 1970 were arranged alphabetically. For a description of the numbering system, *see* Levy, *Custody Investigations*, 714 n.3.

18. *See* Stanford v. Stanford, 266 Minn. 250, 123 N.W.2d 187 (1963). Requiring the spouses to consent may not always guarantee that the investigation will be truly voluntary. *See, e.g.*, Withrow v. Withrow, 212 La. 427, 31 So. 2d 849 (1947) (trial judge stated that under the evidence neither spouse should get custody and requested permission to order an independent investigation; when plaintiff refused consent, custody was awarded to defendant). *See also* Comment, 24 U. CHI. L. REV. 349 (1957); Duro v. Duro, 392 Mass. 574, 577 n.7, 467 N.E.2d 165, 168 n.7 (1984) (mother withdrew motion to recuse judge who had received *ex parte* report about mother from court probation officer because judge had been assigned to case for two years and judge " 'is the law. [The judge] is higher than any of us around here.' ").

the caseworker's report in his courthouse office a few days prior to trial but were not permitted to copy it. During the trial, the judge probably had the investigator's documentary file and case dictation at the bench; but neither lawyer would have thought to ask to see the file (as distinct from the report itself) and the judge probably would have refused such a request if made.[19] The caseworker probably did not testify.[20] The report may have been consulted by the judge during the trial even if not introduced into evidence by either party. The trial judge awarded custody of three of the four H-1 children to Mr. H-1; the oldest, a thirteen-year-old girl, permitted to choose her custodian, decided to live with her mother.

In cases like *H-1*, the custody investigation becomes part of a record in adversary litigation. The caseworker can be subpoenaed to be sure he attends the trial; the caseworker can be cross-examined. The lawyers would have to be concerned only about whether calling the caseworker as a witness, or cross-examining him vigorously, might offend the judge (who is, after all, the caseworker's nominal employer). These are risks, to be sure, but only somewhat more substantial than those that lawyers weigh in every trial. The spouse denied custody by the trial judge can seek appellate review of the decision on the merits as well as review of any accompanying procedural or evidentiary issues concerning the investigation. Thus, the losing party, Mrs. H-1, would have been able to complain that the report did not fairly assess the children's situation, to contend, perhaps, that she should have been permitted to cross-examine the caseworker—claims incidental to her basic contention that she should have been awarded custody of the younger children. The appellate court reviewing such contested cases would be in a position to establish and enforce basic procedural and evidentiary constraints upon caseworkers and the permissible scope of investigation reports in contested cases. In addition, the quality of the report and the credibility of the caseworker would be subject to the relatively neutral judgment of a trial judge and an appellate panel. A pattern of shoddy reports in contested cases would be difficult to hide for very long.

But most custody investigations are conducted for cases which never come to trial. Indeed, in 1970 only 26 percent of Hennepin County custody investigations were conducted for cases like *H-1*. Much more common that year were cases like the H-2's "default" divorce. Again, the custody investigation was ordered at the temporary hearing. After the report was finished, the disputed issues

19. Uniform Marriage and Divorce Act § 405(c) (1970) requires disclosure of the file to both parties. *See also* notes 28 and 36 *infra* and accompanying text.

20. *But see* Uniform Marriage and Divorce Act § 405(c) (1970) (right to cross-examine caseworker may not be waived prior to hearing). *See also* notes 28 and 30 *infra* and accompanying text.

were apparently negotiated and the parties signed what in Minnesota is called a "stipulation"[21] which included a provision giving custody of the children to Mrs. H-2. Mrs. H-2's attorney then placed the divorce action on the "default" calendar. Mrs. H-2's lawyer "proved up" divorce grounds and her right to custody of the children as the caseworker had recommended. Neither Mr. H-2 nor his attorney was present; the "trial" was probably over in about ten minutes.

Procedural and evidentiary requirements imposed upon custody investigations by appellate courts in contested cases have very little to do with the *H-2* divorce—because it eventually became an informal and consensual proceeding. In the *H-2* case, in all likelihood, the spouses did try to estimate, after reading the report or hearing about it from their attorneys, whether and how he or she might be able to minimize or reinforce the report's factual assertions and recommendations if the case were to go to trial. But, by and large, in these cases the investigation simply adds a "bargaining chip" to the spouses' negotiation—one whose impact is uncertain even after it is placed on the table. Additional uncertainty is created before the report is delivered. But once the recommendations are known, the report's "winner" gains substantial negotiating leverage. To be sure, attorneys who know the caseworkers conducting investigations and their "batting averages" are in a position to predict how influential the report is likely to be in a trial; and a lawyer might advise a client to go to trial despite an adverse report.[22] Nonetheless, the negative impact on the "loser's" bargaining position must be substantial.[23]

21. The "stipulation" is correctly named because it is a document filed in a lawsuit that specifies the issues the litigants will not contest. In fact, the document resembles what lawyers in other states would call a separation agreement.

22. In the *H-1* case, the impact on the judge of the wife's adultery outweighed the recommendation by the caseworker that the wife be given custody of the three younger children. *See* note 42 *infra* and accompanying text.

Overall, in cases where the report made a specific recommendation, the children were a little more likely to end up in the custody of the recommended parent in cases like *H-2* than they were in cases like *H-1*. Thirty-six of forty-two recommendations, 86 percent, were followed in negotiated cases; but only ten of eighteen recommendations, 55 percent, were followed by the judge in contested cases. (The comparison is somewhat inappropriate because we do not know what the judge would have done if the negotiated cases had been litigated.) Recommendations that the temporary custodian be awarded custody were much more likely to be followed than recommendations of other possible custodians. More than 75 percent of the reports recommended that the temporary custodian be awarded permanent custody. *See* Levy, *Custody Investigations*, 731 n.68.

23. Many of the lawyers who are regulars in the divorce court must have some idea of the caseworkers' "batting averages" in different kinds of cases, *see* note 22 *supra*, and would guide clients in accord with their implications. Yet predictions as to a judge's response to a report must leave some uncertainty; room for bargaining remains despite the fact that a substantial bargaining "endowment" is given to the spouse recommended by the caseworker. *See* Mnookin & Kornhauser, *Bargaining in the Shadow of the Law: The Case of Divorce*, 88 YALE L.J. 950 (1979).

The advantages and disadvantages of having custody investigation reports available for use in negotiated settlements such as the *H-2* case have not been explored adequately—because appellate judges and statutory drafters have assumed, quite incorrectly, that the custody investigation world is populated exclusively by *H-1* cases.

Part II

The Uniform Marriage and Divorce Act, promulgated by the National Conference of Commissioners on Uniform State Laws in 1970, codified and regularized custody investigation practice for cases which reach trial—at least in those states which have adopted the Act. Ignoring for the moment some procedural safeguards discussed below, the Act's provisions are fairly consistent with pre-Act appellate doctrine in most states. The traditional rule has been that in the absence of a governing statute, an investigation can be ordered only if both spouses have consented—although the principle has been clouded by appellate opinions which have failed to distinguish clearly between an investigation order and admission of the report into evidence at the trial.[24] The Uniform Act is considerably less constraining: the judge may order an investigation if only one of the parents requests it or if the proceeding is "contested."[25] Appellate courts in both common-law and Uniform Act jurisdictions have customarily upheld a trial judge's discretionary *refusal* to order an investigation despite a request for one by a parent.[26]

At least some of the older opinions assumed that spouses who consent to the investigation have also stipulated to admissibility, even to nondisclosure to the spouses, of the investigator's report.[27] But the

That reports are in fact influential is indicated by anecdotal information from lawyers as to an important role played by custody investigations—to allow lawyers to dampen a client's enthusiasm for a custody contest without offending the client.

Some of the cases in which investigations are conducted are settled following an informal mediation with the judge who has had access to the investigation report. The potential impact of the report under these circumstances is analyzed in Levy, *Custody Investigations*, 731–32.

24. *See generally* Annot. 35 A.L.R.2d 629 (1954); Foote, Levy & Sander, Cases and Materials on Family Law 937 (3d ed. 1985). *See, e.g.*, Nichols v. Nichols, 106 Mich. App. 584, 308 N.W.2d 291 (1981) (judge may consult report prepared by "friend of court" but, if the case goes to trial, a decision must be based on admissible evidence only); Adams v. Adams, 100 Mich. App. 1, 298 N.W.2d 871 (1980) (report from agency in another state). *See* especially the line of Minnesota cases ending with Stanford v. Stanford, 266 Minn. 250, 123 N.W.2d 187 (1963). For some indication that the consent rule may not significantly limit trial court discretion to order investigations, *see* note 18 *supra*.

25. *See* Uniform Marriage and Divorce Act § 405(a) (1970).

26. *See, e.g.*, Lepper v. Lepper, 495 N.E.2d 820 (Ind. App. 1986); Hollo v. Hollo, 131 Ill. App. 3d 119, 474 N.E.2d 827 (1985); Meyer v. Meyer, 375 N.W.2d 820 (Minn. App. 1985).

27. *Compare* Kesseler v. Kesseler, 10 N.Y.2d 445, 225 N.Y.S.2d 1, 180 N.E.2d 402 (1962) (where agreement for custody investigation failed to mention disclosure, judge

Uniform Act carefully distinguishes between the investigation itself and whether the report can be used at the trial: the report cannot be admitted in evidence unless the caseworker and the court have adhered to pretrial procedures designed to protect the spouses' opportunity to review the report and to cross-examine the investigator if a trial should occur.[28] But even in states which have not adopted the Uniform Act (with occasional inconsistencies and obfuscations), the appellate decisions usually condemn trial court efforts to insulate the report's contents or the reporter from the spouses or from their lawyers' cross-examination. Indeed, the more recent decisions have been so uniform that continuing failures by divorce court judges to require confrontation of the caseworker suggests that those "child saver" genes, which lead them enthusiastically to order investigations, exercise as well a powerful influence on their decisions about the necessity for procedural protections for the spouses.[29]

Trial judges who deny the spouses the right to cross-examine the caseworker are not always reversed. The complaining party may have "waived" his confrontation right;[30] on many occasions, appellate courts

---

not required to allow spouses to see report or cross-examine caseworker) *with* Krebs v. Krebs, 83 A.D.2d 989, 443 N.Y.S.2d 530 (1981) (custody decision reversed where record showed that trial judge relied upon but did not give husband opportunity to review investigation report) *and* DiStefano v. DiStefano, 51 A.D. 885, 380 N.Y.S.2d 394 (1976) (same).

28. *See* UNIFORM MARRIAGE AND DIVORCE ACT § 405(b) (1970): "If the requirements of subsection (c) are fulfilled, the investigator's report may be received in evidence at the hearing." Subsection (c) requires the court to mail the investigator's report to counsel and to a party if not represented by counsel at least ten days prior to the hearing. It also requires that counsel or the parties be given the investigator's file "of underlying data, and reports, complete texts of diagnostic reports made to the investigator pursuant to the provisions of subsection (b), and the names and addresses of all persons whom the investigator has consulted." See also the "no waiver of crossexamination until trial" requirement of subsection (c), discussed in note 30 *infra*.

The states which have adopted the Uniform Act have not always followed its recommendations. *See, e.g.*, 40 ILL. STAT. ANN. § 605(c) (1980) ("court shall not examine the investigator's report and it shall only be used for impeachment purposes"). *See In re* Marriage of Auer, 86 Ill. App. 3d 84, 407 N.E.2d 1034 (1980). In Missouri, the Act's report admissibility clause was eliminated. An investigation can be ordered but the caseworker must testify orally. *See* FOOTE, LEVY & SANDER, *supra* note 24.

29. *See, e.g.*, Duro v. Duro, 392 Mass. 574, 467 N.E.2d 165 (1984) (one of several reporting statutes which does not mention need to disclose report to litigants interpreted to require such disclosure in light of constitutional requirements); Ohmer v. Superior Court, 148 Cal. App. 3d 661, 196 Cal. Rptr. 224 (1983) (cross-examination of investigating officer required unless, as in this case, spouse has waived right); Ziehm v. Ziehm, 433 A.2d 725 (Me. 1981) (statute authorizing custody investigation reports constitutional because spouses given reasonable right to cross-examine caseworker); Nichols v. Nichols, 106 Mich. App. 584, 308 N.W.2d 291 (1981); Denningham v. Denningham, 49 Md. App. 328, 431 A.2d 755 (1981), *cert. denied*, 455 U.S. 990 (1982) (unconstitutional to deny husband who was not represented by lawyer opportunity to review caseworker's report personally, but harmless error). *See also* note 36 *infra* and accompanying text.

30. *See, e.g.*, Ohmer v. Superior Court, 148 Cal. App. 3d 661, 196 Cal. Rptr. 224 (1983) (local rule made custody investigation available only if spouses waived right to confront investigator); Kern v. Kern, 333 So. 2d 17 (Fla. 1976) (spouses could have called case-

have held that failure to afford the spouses an opportunity to cross-examine the caseworker was "harmless error."[31] It seems very likely that holdings such as these reflect not only the appellate courts' attitudes about extrajudicial investigations, but as well the judges' response to the merits of the trial judge's decision in each case. Indeed, a review of the appellate decisions in one jurisdiction concluded: "Worst of all—for litigants, for the regulation of investigations, and for the legal process—custody investigation rules rapidly became a legal volleyball, bouncing back and forth from decision to decision, applied here to affirm and there to reverse a trial judge's disposition whenever it suited the Justices' own nisi prius preferences."[32]

The proper scope of the waiver and harmless error rules should depend, at least in part, on the nature and importance of the procedural right which has been violated. If the right to confront the caseworker is of constitutional dimension, behavior by a litigant sufficient to constitute waiver may well have to be more deliberate, more clearly evidenced, than would otherwise be necessary.[33] Although the United States Supreme Court has not treated kindly the claim of convicted criminal defendants to a right to confront probation officers who have prepared "presentence investigations,"[34] state supreme courts have

worker for cross-examination but failed to do so). *But see* Flickinger v. Flickinger, 494 S.W.2d 388 (Mo. App. 1973) (counsel's stipulation that investigation be made and filed with court does not waive objection to hearsay matters in report because any other result would abdicate trial court's powers to the investigating officer); Walter v. Walter, 61 Ill. App. 2d 476, 209 N.E.2d 691 (1965) (waiver by counsel of objection to investigation cannot bind the child, whose interest is the main subject of the proceeding). *See also* note 35 *infra* and accompanying text.

UNIFORM MARRIAGE AND DIVORCE ACT § 405(c) (1970) tried to protect spouses from nonvoluntary waivers by providing that the right to cross-examine the caseworker may not be waived prior to the hearing. Subsection (b) requires that this procedural rule be followed as a prerequisite to the report's admissibility. *But see* 1984 Minn. Laws 635, 4 (eliminating this provision from Minnesota's version of the Uniform Act).

31. *See, e.g.*, SanFilipo v. SanFilipo, 637 S.W.2d 77 (Mo. App. 1982) (trial judge's use of inadmissible report not reversible error because other evidence amply supported judge's custody decision); Theeke v. Theeke, 105 Ill. App. 3d 119, 433 N.E.2d 1311 (1981) (same). *But see* Coble v. Coble, 323 Pa. Super. 445, 470 A.2d 1002 (1984) (denial of cross-examination of caseworker not harmless error where trial judge had relied upon report in making decision). *See generally* TRAYNOR, THE RIDDLE OF HARMLESS ERROR (1970).

32. Levy, The Law of Custody Investigation: Procedural Principle v. Dispositional Discretion, 3–5 (mimeograph 1982) (survey of Minnesota law from 1952 to 1980).

33. For the intricacies of evolving United States Supreme Court doctrine concerning prejudice to criminal defendants in the context of waiver and harmless error, see the following authorities: Berger, *The Supreme Court and Defense Counsel: Old Roads, New Paths—A Dead End?*, 86 COLUM. L. REV. 9 (1986) (ineffective assistance of counsel); Dix, *Waiver in Criminal Procedure: A Brief for More Careful Analysis*, 55 TEX. L. REV. 193 ("voluntary" waiver of right to counsel); Goldberg, *Constitutional Error: Constitutional Sneak Thief*, 71 J. CRIM. L. & CRIM. 421 (1980) (harmless error).

34. *See* Williams v. People, 337 U.S. 241 (1949). For a report on the strength of "informality" in adult corrections procedures and a powerful argument for formal hearing controls, *see* Fennell & Hall, *Due Process at Sentencing: An Empirical and Legal Anal-*

often spoken the language of "Fourteenth Amendment procedural due process" in custody investigation cases:

> These decisions [requiring confrontation of the investigating caseworker] merely make manifest one of the cornerstones of our system of justice: the right of the parties to be aware of all of the evidence considered by the trier of fact in making an adjudicatory determination and to have the opportunity to challenge and answer that evidence. "Due process" encompasses that principle and requires that if a court bases its custody decision, even in part, on an independent report, the parties—or their attorneys—must be given the opportunity to examine the report and must be allowed the opportunity to cross-examine the investigator and to produce outside witnesses to establish any inaccuracies the report may contain. However sensitive the material may be, a party has the right to know what evidence is being considered by the court in judging his cause. A custody case can no more be tried and decided upon secret *ex parte* evidence than any other proceeding.[35]

The constitutional issue is not likely to be resolved finally in a direct appeal by a disappointed litigant so long as appellate courts insist as a matter of state law that investigators cannot be shielded from traditional adversary testing of their observations and conclusions. But if appellate judges continue to be concerned more with whether the child was awarded to the parent they consider the right custodian than with the process by which the choice was made, they are likely to make liberal use of harmless error notions. Consistent supervision of how caseworkers conduct custody investigations in uncontested cases and how trial judges use them in trials is likely to suffer. Yet appellate judges are certainly aware that uncertainty may be as harmful to a child as being awarded to the less qualified parent; and frequent retrials of the contested cases may not be worth their financial and emotional cost. Thus, the proper scope of the harmless error doctrine may well depend upon what a reliable evaluation of the general quality of custody investigation reports shows. The same is true of procedural safeguards for those custody contests (the great majority, remember) which are

---

ysis of the Disclosure of Presentence Reports in Federal Courts, 93 HARV. L. REV. 1613 (1980). Of course, a defendant objecting to being sentenced on the basis of an undisclosed report to the judge by a probation officer has already been convicted; the custody investigation, on the other hand, is used to determine the merits of the litigation.

35. Denningham v. Denningham, 49 Md. App. 328, 431 A.2d 755 (1981), *cert. denied*, 455 U.S. 990 (1982) (constitutional error but harmless). *But see* Hall v. Luick, 461 A.2d 248 (Pa. Super. 1983) (case remanded for new hearing at which caseworker could be cross-examined; dictum that waiver inapplicable to custody cases). *Cf.* Duro v. Duro, 392 Mass. 574, 467 N.E.2d 165 (1984) (statute interpreted to require confrontation, thus avoiding constitutional issue; case remanded for new hearing because impossible to tell the extent to which trial judge was influenced by *ex parte* contacts with probation officer). *See also* M. v. K., 186 N.J. Super. 363, 452 A.2d 704 (1982) (statutory privilege for communications with marriage counselor cannot be applied to deny trial judge right to reports from such counselor in custody litigation because doing so would deny constitutional rights to child subject to the custody award).

settled before trial but after an investigation has been conducted and a report prepared.[36] If the general quality of custody investigations is poor, lawyers and judges (appellate as well as trial) should rely upon them less, and adequate procedural safeguards should be created. Factual inquiry as to the nature and quality of custody investigation reports is obviously essential.

Part III

Unfortunately, the evidence from the Hennepin County, Minnesota, custody investigation reports prepared during 1970 suggests that assumptions that caseworkers will be impartial and their reports careful and reliable are often unwarranted. Some of the reports, it is true, were modest, thoughtful and, insofar as it was possible to check their facts, careful and accurate. But such conclusions could not be drawn about all, or even most, of the reports.

A. Fact "Shaping" and Fact Suppression

In virtually none of the cases was it possible for a neutral decision maker to determine independently whether the investigator's custody recommendation followed logically and necessarily from the facts reported. In some of the cases, "by the time information-gathering was complete, the [investigator] had already decided which parent would make the better custodian—and the report became a 'brief,' defending a decision made in some other ('clinical') fashion."[37] Consider two (fairly dramatic) illustrations. *H-7* was a contested case. A two-year-old girl was living in a suburban home with her great-grandmother (whose age was never disclosed) five days a week; her twenty-three-year-old, previously divorced mother worked at a variety of jobs (during the study as a cocktail waitress four nights a week) and lived by herself in an apartment in the city. When the study began, the caseworker was not enthusiastic about the mother's custodial qualifications. In an initial interview, according to the caseworker's "running dictation,"[38]

36. *See* note 28 *supra*. Recently proposed (but not enacted) legislation in New York would have allowed attorneys to see "underlying data and reports" used in the preparation of the custody investigation report only "upon a showing of good cause." *See* Symposium: *Children, Divorce and the Legal System: The Direction for Reform*, 19 COLUM. J.L.& SOC. PROBS. 105, 136 (1985), quoting the proposed statutory language and the commentary of the New York Law Revision Commission which had recommended the legislation. The "good cause" limitation was designed to avoid "pro forma requests for the underlying work product, which may be intrusive and obstructive to the evaluation process." *Id.* at 153. For the need to see what the caseworker has discovered but not always reported or reported accurately, see pp. 161–62 *infra*.

37. *See* Levy, *Custody Investigations*, 740.

38. The phrase describes the caseworker's diary of all contacts made during the course of the investigation. Only a few cases included such diaries.

Mr. H-7 disclosed that his wife had "run away" three times without the child since their separation, on one occasion to the West Coast for several months. The caseworker seemed concerned:

> Mr. H-7 comes across as sincerely interested in his daughter, has rearranged his occupation so he can care for her and/or visit her regularly. . . . Mrs. H-7's plans seems even less definite—and/or straightforward. . . . I feel the need for another interview with Mrs. H-7 to ascertain some facts now in question and to explore counseling with her. . . .[39]

During the course of the investigation the caseworker counseled the mother, obtained the mother's agreement to seek further counseling from a social agency,[40] and somehow concluded that the mother should be awarded the child's custody. In the report, most of the issues relevant to a custodial choice were explored—and all doubts resolved in the mother's favor. The report gave little weight to possible adverse effects of the existing physical separation of mother and daughter. Although "observation [of the child] was not extensive, nonetheless sufficient to confirm she is well cared for and loved in her great-grandmother's home." The caseworker did not observe the child in the presence of either parent. The caseworker predicted (without providing any supporting evidence) that the mother would assume physical custody of the child in her own apartment as soon as her finances would permit—"probably within a month." The father's plan for custodial care was disparaged although the report gave no indication of a serious effort to compare it with the mother's "less definite" plans. Evidence to support the choice of the great-grandmother was not provided: no description was given of the great-grandmother or her child care skills.[41]

Even more important, the caseworker failed to report relevant information in his possession. The report did indicate that the mother had been hospitalized by a psychiatrist thirteen months previously—with a throwaway line about the problem: "Dr. ______ provided counseling, largely around problems centering in the marriage relationship. A request for an evaluation of Mrs. H-7 has been requested of Dr. ______, but has not been received as of this writing." The report did not indicate that the hospitalization had been for "weight loss and depression," that the psychiatrist had reported that the mother had indicated that she had great "conflicts about taking care of her [child] and was 'running around,' " and that the psychiatrist's diagnosis had been "reactive depression superimposed on a sociopathic personality." Obviously, the child's presence in her great-grandmother's home

39. This quotation is from the caseworker's "running dictation."

40. The mother's amenability to counseling and agreement to be counseled may well explain the caseworker's recommendation better than the reasons given in the report. *See* Levy, *Custody Investigations*, 741, 769–70. *See also* p. 165 *infra*.

41. Statements from the report which provides the evidence for these conclusions may be found in Levy, *Custody Investigations*, 741–42.

for most of each week could be viewed very differently against a background which included this information. Significantly, the psychiatrist's letter made it clear that he had received the caseworker's November 19 letter on November 21; and the report, due at least five days before the adjourned court hearing on December 3, was dated November 20, the day after the request to the psychiatrist was mailed. The report, then, was designed to reinforce Mrs. H-7's claim to custody if the case were to be tried. It is not necessary, and may not even be possible, to question the caseworker's judgment "on the merits"; but the caseworker's tactics cannot be condoned.

Fact suppression also occurred occasionally because the caseworker seemed to want to minimize unpleasantness. Thus, in *H-1*, the caseworker recommended that the wife be granted custody of the couple's children despite the fact that she had been discovered having sexual intercourse with another man. The caseworker did mention that the husband, "critical of Mrs. H-1 and her past behavior," had kept his wife "under surveillance and he has along with some of his friends found his wife and another gentleman in bed . . ."[42] Yet the caseworker failed to disclose the details of a "venereal disease issue" which would certainly have helped the wife's custody claim—and thus the success of his recommendation. The caseworker reported:

> Both Mr. and Mrs. H-1 accuse each other of infecting the other with gonorrhea. I have spoken with a neutral doctor relative to this disease, as well as receiving a report from each of their doctors. It seems to be a matter of judgment as to who was first responsible for this disease. Both parents make an issue of this fact and are attempting to use this to prove their case.

But the facts were much less ambiguous and more favorable to the wife, as the caseworker had discovered a month previously. The wife's internist had reported:

> Mrs. H-1 was seen in our office [last summer] . . . Prior to this visit I had received a phone call from a man stating that he was her husband. He told me that he had a diagnosed case of gonorrhea which he had picked up on a recent trip . . . I was, therefore, alerted to the possibility that the patient did indeed have gonorrhea. A smear and culture confirmed the diagnosis. . . .
>
> As is usual in cases of this type to preserve the marital situation, the diagnosis was not given to the patient until [later when] she returned and asked me directly . . . She was told the culture did show gonorrhea . . . The reason for her sudden concern was the fact that her husband had told her that she had a venereal disease. . . .
>
> I have subsequently received another phone call, again purportedly from the husband of Mrs. H-1, asking me to give a statement in an impending

42. The caseworker did not mention that the husband and his friends had broken in on the couple in the middle of the night—although this information should have helped the wife's case. The incident was explored eventually when the judge had to determine whether evidence about the incident was admissible at the trial over the wife's objection.

> divorce suit stating the fact that she did have gonorrhea. I reminded the caller of the details of the previous call I had received and that I could not under oath refrain from telling the full story. His reply was that only a statement of her condition would be asked, nothing more. My response . . . was . . . that this would not represent the true sequence of events. . . .

In cases like *H-7* and *H-1*, the report's description of relevant facts is simply unreliable. In other cases there was clear evidence that the caseworker had "shaped" the report to produce a work product favorable to a judge or referee who had already made up his mind.[43] Because the caseworkers seldom kept supporting documents or a "running file," how common such fact suppression was cannot be determined. It is true that the spouses' lawyers may know or be able to discover in a particular case whether the report is unreliable in this fashion. But the confidence of attorneys in the accuracy of fact finding in the reports, which is essential to their utility for settlements, cannot be maintained if fact suppression is known to occur.

B. Value Impositions

In some of the cases, the investigators obviously imposed upon the divorcing spouses their own personal and idiosyncratic child care and personal behavioral values in making custodial recommendations.[44] Although the "maternal presumption" was consistently emphasized by one of the caseworkers, in most cases

> the presumption appeared to be a tool, a contention to be hauled out when it might add persuasiveness to a recommendation of the mother as custodian. As a result, those reports which rely heavily upon the presumption appear to lawyer-readers, accustomed to assessing whether conclusions follow from factual premises, to be unpersuasive and unsatisfactory.[45]

The investigators were much more consistent when addressing issues of extramarital sexual practices by custodial mothers. Here there was close to an automatic disqualification:

> Since Mrs. H-24 has not yet clarified her thinking as to her relationship with Mr. ________vs. the care and welfare of the children, I am not convinced custody should automatically be awarded to the mother at this time due to their young ages. It is therefore recommended custody of [the children] remain with the father with liberal visitation rights by the mother.

---

43. *See* Levy, *Custody Investigations*, 748.

44. *Id.* at 749–51. Some reports "hinted at an even more disquieting use of differential standards for minority race families and racially mixed couples." *Id.* at 752 n.137. In *H-9*, the report "commented that the wife, a young woman who had emigrated from Germany after her marriage to a soldier from Minnesota, was living with an 'age 27, young, a divorced negro man. This was verified during an unannounced home visit.' . . . The caseworker emphasized the wife's 'independent and defiant nature' and 'rebellious attitude' when threatened that she would lose custody of her son 'when she became involved in racially mixed relationships,' and reported that the wife 'stubbornly stayed with her decision to seek divorce and make friends of her own choosing.' " *Id.* at 752 n.137.

45. *Id.* at 758.

> Contact of the children with Mr. _______ is considered not to be in the children's best interest.[46]

The caseworkers' application of a "disqualification for sexual misconduct" causes grave discomfort. By 1970 the sexual revolution was in full swing and the Minnesota Supreme Court had recognized its implications for custody decision making.[47] The caseworker's emphasis on the mothers' sexual practices appeared to be "something of a rearguard action to preserve disappearing moral standards and to punish deviants."[48] Equally important, an exclusion for sexual misconduct which can be applied in a discretionary manner substantially increases the caseworker's real authority. Whether the caseworker investigates the behavior, decides to report it, and to emphasize it in the report may play a very important role in the outcome—whether it is negotiated or litigated. "The risks of 'moral imperialism' are obvious and substantial."[49]

C. Use of Psychological Criteria

The Hennepin County reports regularly emphasized what mght be called psychodynamic interpretations.[50] The initial concern is that many of these interpretations are not subject to easy or convincing rebuttal. Consider only one of many examples:

> One of the intangibles that helps to understand the comparative quality of parenthood is how each parent conveys the "person" of a child. Given, roughly, the same level of articulateness, parents reveal their knowledge and awareness of a child, the degree and kind of involvement with him, in their description of him and references to him.
>
> In this respect, I received a clearer picture and more definite impression of [the child] from her father than I was able to get from her mother. . . . The psychological evaluation of this couple suggests that both of them have yet to resolve emotional conflicts related to their own parents. This being the case, it is important to arrive at some determination of which is the least hampered by that in fulfilling the parental role. It would appear that Mr. H-65 is more able to function as a responsible parent, in spite of unresolved parental conflict, than is Mrs. H-65 at the present time.
>
> The mother's past and recent preoccupation with her own needs precludes an effective attention to the needs of her child at this point.[51]

---

46. *Id.* at 761.

47. *See* Reiland v. Reiland, 280 Minn. 444, 160 N.W.2d 30 (1968) (mother should have been awarded custody despite her sexual misconduct; for such evidence to be admissible, it must be shown to have a direct bearing on the welfare of the child).

48. Levy, *Custody Investigations*, 763.

49. *Id.*

50. The Ramsey County reports were much less "psychological" than those in Hennepin County. *Id.* at 734 n.78. But the Hennepin County style seems to be more common. *See, e.g.*, Pearson & Ring, *supra* note 6; Ash & Guyer, *In the Shadow of Solomon's Sword: The Functions of Psychiatric Evaluation in Contested Custody and Visitation Cases*, J. AM. ACAD. CHILD PSYCH. (forthcoming).

51. *H-65. Id.* at 767.

Such amorphous judgments add substantially to the power of the caseworker to influence the negotiation because they make it more difficult for lawyers to predict how influential the report will be with the judge if the case goes to trial.

More than a few of the psychodynamic interpretations seemed to reflect current fashions or fads in the therapy community:

> Mr. H-45 is contesting custody because he feels Mrs. H-45 rejects [the five-year-old daughter, oldest of three children] to some degree, has failed to provide adequate care and supervision of the children, and is in general not a very nice person. . . .
>
> Mrs. H-45 alleges that Mr. H-45's time spent with the children during the marriage was somewhat limited. She feels he has a good relationship with the children and is good with them when he does spend time with them, however, she does not feel they are his primary interest. This counselor would share in the feeling that Mr. H-45 might have difficulty sacrificing going to school in order to spend more time with the children, should this become necessary. Mr. H-45 acknowledges he has not spent as much time as he would have liked to with the children but feels he has a good relationship with them. . . .
>
> Mr. H-45 also has warmth and concern for the children, but may have difficulty giving them priority above his own desires and may also have difficulty in forming close, meaningful relationships with them. His plan for custody appears to necessitate a considerable amount of time during which the children would be in the care of others. . . .[52]

Is there any basis for believing that this caseworker's apparent commitment to the importance of "close, meaningful relationships" between parents and children should be imposed upon Mr. H-45? There is no community consensus that such relationships are essential to successful adulthood. Nor is there agreement that a parent should give a child "priority above [the parent's] own desires." Perhaps parents should deal with their personalities, behaviors, lifestyles, their relationships with each other and with their children—all of which, as far as we know, may bear importantly on how kids develop—with the therapists with whom they assume voluntary contractual relationships. But it is quite a different matter to allow such concerns and values to help to determine authoritarian (judicial) disposition of a child's custody based upon the recommendation of an assigned caseworker.

Unhappily, psychodynamic interpretations also seemed sometimes to mask in the language of therapy and family dynamics the investigator's personal and idiosyncratic values.[53] A caseworker could recommend against a sexually active mother, not because of her morals, but because she "has not yet clarified her thinking as to her relationship with Mr. _______vs. the care and welfare of the children";[54] or the

52. *Id.* at 768–69.
53. *Id.* at 769.
54. *H-24*, quoted in the text accompanying note 46 *supra*.

recommendation might favor a sexually active mother, despite the fact that "her need for self indulgence may work to the detriment of her children," because her sexual activities might have been a way of "retaliating" for her husband's "passivity and fiscal irresponsibility."[55] The language can add to the report's persuasiveness by putting a mental health veneer on otherwise unremarkable parental situations or behaviors.

The "psychological style" regularly encouraged reliance by the caseworkers on psychological tests and this practice added substantially to report unreliability. The caseworkers were especially misleading when they misused for individual diagnosis and prediction the statistical profile results of *pro forma* administrations of the Minnesota Multiphasic Personality Inventory, a standard nonprojective personality test.[56] Finally, the psychological style seemed from time to time to bias investigators to favor the parent who was willing to agree to or seemed more amenable to counseling.[57]

In sum, the Hennepin County investigators did not distinguish themselves in their use of psychological and family relationship material and criteria.[58]

Part IV

Procedural controls must be instituted. In fact, the evidence from the Hennepin County reports might persuade a state legislature to refuse to establish a formal custody investigation bureaucracy if one were not already in place.[59] Yet many legislators may deem the case settlement potential of investigations[60] too important to forego them even though they pose substantial risks; or judges may insist upon having them available as a check against their personal instincts about the correct

55. *H-35*, quoted in Levy, *Custody Investigations*, 765.

56. *Id.* at 775–78.

57. *Id.* at 770–71. The Hennepin County reports also indicate that the investigations were occasionally used for juvenile-court-like child protection (or "child saving") purposes. Thus, the divorcing parents and children subjected to custody investigations may also be subjected to significant authoritarian impositions on their privacy during and after their divorce. The facts are reported and the practices criticized. Levy, *Custody Investigations*, 782–84.

58. The relatively bare conclusions in these paragraphs are supported by much more substantial evidence from the reports themselves than is provided in this article. *Id.* at 776. Anyone who doubts the conclusions reported here should consult my full description of the evidence.

59. *See* New York Assembly Judiciary Committee, Child Custody Mediation Legislation: Analysis of Hearing Testimony 20 (mimeograph Oct. 1986) (reporting rejection of New York Legislative Revision Commission Bill, mentioned in note 36 *supra*, in part because the custody investigation provisions pose "a danger to individual and family autonomy").

60. For a description of how investigations settle custody contests, and the risks involved, *see id.* at 778–82.

outcome in contested cases. But if custody investigations are to be conducted, it is irresponsible not to develop regular procedures which will help to preclude the demonstrated evils of the Hennepin County program. Judges should be denied discretion to order an investigation unless both spouses agree to it. Because most investigations are used by the spouses rather than by the judge in litigation, at a minimum the investigator should be required to keep "running dictation"[61] of all contacts with informants and a file of all documents pertaining to the investigation. The "record" should be provided automatically to the spouses and their attorneys. With this information the litigants should be in a better position to estimate the reliability of the investigator's report and its likely impact on the judge if the case is litigated.

Perhaps more important than any procedural safeguard is the message to attorneys these data convey: beware of nonadversary experts bearing fact-finding gifts. Be prepared to doubt, to question, to investigate, and, if necessary, to cross-examine. That custody investigations appear often to be unreliable is not a reason to settle fewer custody cases; but it is a reason to protect your client by developing the facts of the case thoroughly.

61. *See* note 38 *supra* and accompanying text.

Part VI
The Child Support Obligation and One Paragraph on 'Illegitimacy'

[14]

MEN WHO KNOW THEY ARE WATCHED: SOME BENEFITS AND COSTS OF JAILING FOR NONPAYMENT OF SUPPORT

*David L. Chambers**†

Suppose that by some mysterious process the police in your town received each Monday a list of all the robberies and burglaries committed during the preceding week and the names of the persons who committed them. Suppose further that the list itself was admissible in evidence at trial and generally led to conviction. And suppose finally that persons considering committing offenses knew that the police had such a list and used it, relentlessly tracking down the miscreants named on it. Under such circumstances, one would probably expect that many potential offenders in the town with the magical list would resist the temptation to rob or burgle stores.

For one offense, such a list does exist. For over fifty years, each county government in Michigan has maintained an agency called the Friend of the Court that is responsible for receiving all child-support payments from parents under orders of support after a divorce or adjudication of paternity. The agency knows on Monday if the parent under an order of support failed to make a payment the preceding Friday, and the parent under an order of support, almost always the father, knows that the agency knows. He is also aware

---

* Professor of Law, The University of Michigan. A.B. 1962, Princeton University; LL.B. 1965, Harvard University.—Ed.

 This article reports part of the findings of a study of child support conducted over a five-year period. The full results should be available in 1978. A grant from the National Science Foundation provided funds for several stages of the study, including the stage reported here. Additional funds were provided by the Center for Studies in Criminal Justice at The University of Chicago and the William W. Cook Research Funds of The University of Michigan Law School.

The study would have been impossible without the active cooperation of the Friends of the Court in the 28 counties we examined. To them, and especially to Robert Standal of Genesee County and Richard Benedek of Washtenaw County, I am immensely grateful. I am also grateful to the score of persons who have worked on the project at various times. Three require special mention here: Ray M. Shortridge, who served as my research associate from 1974 to 1976, and who shaped and oversaw the execution of much of the 28 county phase of the study; Terry K. Adams, who served as research associate in earlier phases and has advised me throughout; and Priscilla Cheever, who has performed nearly all of the computer work for the last several phases of the project. William Birdsall, economist on the faculty of The University of Michigan School of Social Work, assisted me greatly by his comments on the drafts of this article.

that, if he does not make the payment, he stands a risk of being arrested by the agency's own deputized officers and sentenced to jail by a judge for civil contempt for failing to obey the court order. Each year Michigan judges sentence thousands of men for nonsupport—in 1974 around 4000, and probably more today. On any given day in several Michigan counties, the number of men in the local jail under sentence for nonsupport commonly exceeds the number under sentence for all other jailable offenses combined.

How do fathers behave in places with such a list and an ardent enforcement staff? If all fathers who can pay do so without prodding because of their affection for their children, even an omniscient and industrious police force would have no effect on payments. Nor would the police have an effect if those men who do not pay are men so angry or bitter that even fear of jailing would serve as an inadequate prod.[1] Unless love or anger is so powerful, however, one would expect that knowledge that an agency is aware of their nonpayment would cause some fathers to pay who otherwise would not, and the additional knowledge that the agency acts forcefully against nonpayment would lead even more to pay. The system should have effects.

For five years, a number of associates and I have been recording and analyzing data from the files of Michigan's Friends of the Court. We find, sad to say, that love alone fails to propel most parents into regular payment. On the other hand, we find that a well-oiled enforcement process capped by a substantial reliance on jail seems to lead significant numbers of men to pay who otherwise would not, although we cannot say with certainty whether the link between payments and jail is through fear of being jailed or some more subtle process of conveying through the use of jail the seriousness of a social obligation.

How we reached our conclusions about jail's effects on payments is the subject of this essay. For readers unfamiliar with research on deterrence, I hope the study can serve, as it has for the author, as a palatable introduction to a form of inquiry often reported in unnecessarily obscure terms. For those familar with such research, the study may still have value, for the nature of the offense and the

1. The angriest account of the divorce process from a male perspective that I have read is M. Franks, How To Avoid Alimony (1975), an altogether nasty book. A fine, tempered book is J. Epstein, Divorced in America (1974). An early study of women after divorce that remains impressive and timely despite its age is W. Goode, Women in Divorce (1965), originally published as W. Goode, After Divorce (1956).

thoroughness of the public records have permitted us to measure the effects of a jailing policy with considerably greater precision than is usually possible. For both groups, the study may reveal a process—the enforcement of child support—about which most people know very little.

Many states are moving swiftly to improve their systems for collecting child support in welfare cases. They are doing so to conform to recent federal legislation that conditions full reimbursement of welfare costs to the states on their making much more organized efforts than in the past to secure and enforce support orders against absent fathers.[2] Our findings, if read too hastily, might lead some people to conclude that payment levels can be improved simply by jailing a large number of nonpayers. Our findings do not support this conclusion; rather, they suggest that jailing makes a significant difference in collections if, but only if, it is coupled with a well-organized and visible system of other efforts to collect. There are no easy shortcuts.

More than money is at stake when we jail people. After reporting our findings on the deterrent effects of jailing, we will share some of our doubts about the wisdom of relying heavily on jail even if it does yield more dollars than it costs. We will then examine briefly an alternative to the use of jail that may be more effective even when measured solely by the return in dollars collected.

I. The Nature of the Research

Research on deterrence often focuses on persons on whom a particular sanction has been imposed to learn whether they commit the same acts again. Parts of our research included such an inquiry, but in this article we do not report on these men. Here we will deal with the effects of the use and threat of jail on the whole population who may commit an offense, the so-called "general deterrent" or "general preventive" effects. We will look, that is, at how the punishment of some fathers affects the behavior of all fathers, including those who are never arrested or jailed. Measuring these effects is a vexing task.[3] When large numbers of men who have been

2. See Title IV(D) of the Social Security Act, 42 U.S.C. §§ 651-660 (Supp. V 1975). Throughout this article, the term "welfare" refers to the program of Aid to Families with Dependent Children established by Title IV of the Social Security Act.

3. Among lawyers and social scientists, three persons have been largely responsible for providing a theoretical foundation for deterrent research and for cataloguing its pitfalls. The first is Johannes Andenaes of the University of Oslo. *See, e.g.*, Andenaes, *General Prevention—Illusion or Reality*, 43 J. Crim. L.C. & P.S. 176

jailed make lump-sum payments immediately preceding their release and immediately after release begin a period of regular payments for the first time in years, we can be fairly confident in most cases of a causal link between the jailing and the payments. When we look, however, at the records of men never jailed and find steady payments year after year, we cannot say anything about whether fear of jail, rather than affection for the child or something else, produced their payments.

To look for such "general deterrent" effects of jailing on the behavior of a group who might commit an offense, social scientists typically use either of two risky methods of inquiry.[4] Under one method, a single place—a state, a county—is followed through time to examine the relationship between changes in the incidence of the undesired behavior and changes in the rates of imposing certain sanctions. As the jail rate or hanging rate increases, does the crime rate decline? This was the method employed by Isaac Ehrlich in his recent and much-discussed study of the general deterrent effects of the death penalty.[5] Under the other model, several places—several states or counties—are examined, typically during a common period of time, in an effort to see whether the places that jail or execute more offenders have a lower incidence of the undesired behavior. Thorsten Sellin employed this method in an earlier and no less celebrated study of the death penalty.[6] It is also the method used in the study reported here.

That the two death penalty studies reached opposite conclusions on the same issue suggests the difficulties deterrence research en-

---

(1952); Andenaes, *General Deterrence Revisited: Research and Policy Implications*, 66 J. CRIM. L. & C. 338 (1975). The other two are Franklin Zimring and Gordon Hawkins, authors of F. ZIMRING & G. HAWKINS, DETERRENCE—THE LEGAL THREAT IN CRIME CONTROL (1973). Economists have also become interested in deterrence research. *See, e.g.*, Becker, *Crime and Punishment: An Economic Approach*, 76 J. POL. ECON. 169 (1968); AMERICAN ENTERPRISE INSTITUTE FOR PUBLIC POLICY RESEARCH, ECONOMICS OF CRIME AND PUNISHMENT (Rothenberg ed. 1973).

4. *See* F. ZIMRING & G. HAWKINS, *supra* note 3, at 249-93.

5. Ehrlich, *The Deterrent Effect of Capital Punishment: A Question of Life and Death*, 65 AM. ECON. REV. 397 (1975). A series of responses and comments to Ehrlich have been published recently in the *Yale Law Journal*. *See* Baldus & Cole, *A Comparison of the Work of Thorsten Sellin and Isaac Ehrlich on the Deterrent Effect of Capital Punishment*, 85 YALE L.J. 170 (1975); Bowers & Pierce, *The Illusion of Deterrence in Isaac Ehrlich's Research on Capital Punishment*, 85 YALE L.J. 187 (1975); Ehrlich, *Deterrence: Evidence and Inference*, 85 YALE L.J. 209 (1975); Ehrlich, *Rejoinder*, 85 YALE L.J. 368 (1976); Peck, *The Deterrent Effect of Capital Punishment: Ehrlich and His Critics*, 85 YALE L.J. 359 (1976). *See also* Zeisel, *The Deterrent Effects of the Death Penalty: Facts v. Faiths*, 1976 SUP. CT. REV. 317.

6. T. SELLIN, THE DEATH PENALTY (1959).

counters. All such research depends upon accurate counts of comparable data. It must begin with reasonably precise figures, either across locations or through time, of the incidence of the undesired behavior and of the sanction the impact of which one is seeking to gauge. Usually the frequency of imposing a certain sanction can be counted by poring through court records, but for many offenses, such as drug sales or larceny, it is much more difficult to determine the actual incidence of the undesired behavior. Figures on citizen complaints or police arrests may reflect quite unevenly across time or locations the actual incidence of the behavior.

After obtaining accurate information about the crime and the punishment, one can see whether there is less of the undesired behavior in places that make substantial use of penal sanctions. Half the job remains, however, for one must then determine whether the relation between sanction and conduct is actually a mirage:[7] whether, that is, some aspect of the enforcement process other than the incidence of sentences to jail—for example, the swiftness in sending reminders that payments are due—more adequately or wholly explains the relation between punishment and crime. Or, apart from any aspects of the enforcement process, perhaps what appear to be the effects of enforcement are properly attributable to differences in the characteristics of the population or to changes in the same population over time, differences that might affect attitudes toward the conduct or responsiveness to the same enforcement efforts. It is this latter part of the undertaking that has most bedeviled researchers into deterrence and has most bedeviled us.

II. The Twenty-Eight County Study

A. *Michigan's Friends of the Court and the Enforcement of Support*

Among American jurisdictions, Michigan's Friend-of-the-Court system is quite unusual. In most states, if a parent under an order of support fails to make payments, the custodial parent discovers that, unless she is a recipient of welfare benefits, there is no agency comparable to the Friend of the Court to which she can turn for assistance in enforcing the order. She must hire her own attorney to search for the father and bring him to court by civil processes. In Michigan, by contrast, a Friend of the Court in each county oversees all aspects of the child-support process in divorce, separate

7. The opposite phenomenon can also occur: a relationship between crime and punishment does not appear initially but emerges after controlling for other variables.

maintenance, and paternity cases.[8] The agency begins each case by gathering financial information from the parents and advising the judge on the appropriate size of the support order. After an order is entered, it collects all payments and forwards them to the appropriate receiver, either the custodial parent or the welfare department. Finally, it pursues the parents who fail to pay. In nearly all cases in which a support order is entered, payments are handled through the agency. Its responsibilities extend equally to welfare and non-welfare cases.

To carry out these tasks, a few small counties have only one or two full-time employees. By contrast, the Friend of the Court in Wayne County, the core of the Detroit metropolitan area, has a staff of over three hundred. Most agencies of any size have computerized payment records and full-time enforcing officers, many of them deputized by the county sheriff, who go into the field to arrest men who have not paid.

Jailing plays a part in this process because the willful or negligent failure to make payments ordered by the court is treated as a form of contempt that, by special state statute, can lead to a sentence in jail of up to one year, subject to earlier release upon the defendant's paying his full arrearage or working out some lesser arrangement satisfactory to the court.[9] Most men jailed do in fact purchase their early release by paying an amount less than full arrearage.

The steps taken before jailing and the extent of reliance on jail vary from county to county, but in every county the agency mails warning letters to delinquent fathers, and nearly all agencies issue orders to show cause directing the men to appear in court to explain their delinquency. Even in the counties that rely most upon jailing, the number of collection efforts short of jail dwarfs the number of sentences; in one that we examined particularly closely, for example, warnings mailed to men in the caseload exceeded jail sentences imposed by twenty-five fold. For men who fail to appear in response to warnings and orders to show cause, the agency staff secures and, in many counties, serves arrest warrants and then acts as prosecutor before the courts in delinquency hearings. After a hearing, if the man is sentenced, the same staff arranges deals with jailed men who wish to secure their early release from jail on payment of less than the full arrearage.

8. Michigan's legislature authorized the creation of Friends of the Court in 1919, 1919 Mich. Pub. Acts 412, and then made them mandatory in 1921, 1921 Mich. Pub. Acts 147. The provisions of current law that provide for Friends of the Court and fix their duties are found in MICH. COMP. LAWS § 552.251-.255 (1970).

9. *See* MICH. COMP. LAWS § 552.201 (1970).

Our study of jailing for nonsupport was undertaken because we found that rather like the biologist's fruitfly or guinea pig, nonsupport lends itself to closer inquiry than is possible with most other forms of behavior treated as criminal. As watchdogs over custody and support, the agencies maintain records of every aspect of the process: their files include information on family characteristics, weekly payments, and enforcement efforts. Their records and their cooperation made our inquiry possible.

B. *The Research Design and Findings*

As our first step, we drew a random sample of divorce cases in each of twenty-eight Michigan counties. The counties we picked were those in the southern half of Michigan that had reported caseloads of at least 1,000 in 1973.[10] Stretching from the eastern to western edges of the state, the counties contained all the cities in the state with 1970 populations of more than 50,000 and included all but one of the counties with populations of more than 100,000. On the other hand, four of the counties had populations under 50,000 and ten had populations under 80,000. Our research thus examined data sources ranging from the intensely urban southeastern corner through counties of farms and small towns.

The samples we drew in each county averaged 430 cases, for a total across the twenty-eight counties of about 12,000 cases. In each county, we drew a random[11] selection of all cases in which a final decree of divorce had been entered and an order of support had been in effect during the entire period we measured. Thus men paying every week were included, as well as men whose cases had been open for many years but who had never paid anything. For each case in each county, we recorded only a few pieces of information: the amount each person paid, the total amount he was under an order to pay during a fixed period, and whether the children covered by the support order were currently receiving welfare benefits. In most

10. The counties studied were Allegan, Barry, Bay, Berrien, Branch, Calhoun, Cass, Eaton, Genesee, Gratiot, Ingham, Jackson, Kalamazoo, Kent, Lapeer, Lenawee, Livingston, Macomb, Midland, Monroe, Oakland, Saginaw, St. Clair, St. Joseph, Shiawassee, Van Buren, Washtenaw, and Wayne. Two other counties, Muskegon and Ottawa, had caseloads meeting the numerical criterion we set. However, scheduling difficulties prevented our studying their files.

11. In all but a few counties, payment records were maintained in alphabetical order. To produce our random samples for these counties, we simply determined the size of the caseload and selected an interval (*e.g.*, every seventh case or every twelfth case) that would permit us to cull about 450 cases by moving once through the alphabet.

counties the period we used was calendar 1974 or a one-year period including some months in 1974, depending on the way the counties' bookkeeping records were kept. From this information, we computed how much each man had paid of all that he was supposed to have paid during the period—his batting average, so to speak.[12]

We then computed three payment figures for each county: the overall average of the individual payment rates within the county, a figure that is close, though not identical, to the portion collected by the county of all the dollars it was supposed to collect;[13] the portion of men in the county paying nearly nothing during the period (we put into this group men paying 10% or less of the ordered amount); and the portion of men paying everything due or close to everything due (we put into this group men paying 80% or more of everything due).

Checking the records of a county for any given one-year period, one would probably expect to find that most men either paid nothing or paid regularly, leaving few men in the middle. And in fact that is what we did find. The striking differences among our counties were in the portions of payers at the bottom and the top. Across the counties, the proportion of men in the high-paying bracket varied from one-third to two-thirds of the caseload; the proportion in the low-paying bracket ranged from one-tenth to one-half. Accordingly, across the counties the average portion paid by men of their amounts due varied widely—from a low in two counties of only 45% and

---

12. In most counties, we used the following formula: $\frac{d}{tw}$, where d = dollars paid during period, t = number of weeks in period, and w = weekly order in dollars. In some counties, where the records provided only a running total of the arrearage and no total of the dollars paid during a period, we used a different formula: $\frac{tw - (a_2 - a_1)}{tw}$ where a_2 = arrearage at end of period, a_1 = arrearage at beginning of period, and t and w represent the same values as above. So long as there were no artificial adjustments in the arrearage during the period, the two formulae yield identical results. Because there were in fact some such alterations in the arrearage not reflecting actual payments, usually to the payer's advantage (for example, when a credit was given because the noncustodial parent kept the children for an extended visit), we made a small adjustment downward in the payment figures for the counties in which we had to use the second formula. The adjustment was based on our experience in two counties, Washtenaw and Genesee, in which we had computed individual payment records by both formulae.

13. The figures would be identical if all orders were of the same size. Within our samples in Genesee and Washtenaw, there were, of course, variations in the size of orders, and there was in fact a very slight positive correlation between order size and payment rate, so that it is probable that the figure we use, the mean of individual payment rates, is quite close to (but slightly lower than) the portion the agency collected of everything due under all its orders.

46% of the ordered amounts to a high in two other counties of 85% and 87% of everything due. Nearly half the counties collected between 61% and 70% of the amounts due. Table 1 reveals the distribution of collections in the counties. We found that the portion at the bottom and the top correlated so overwhelmingly with the mean level of payments that we have used the county's mean for reporting almost all of our findings.[14]

TABLE 1

MEAN PORTIONS COLLECTED OF EVERYTHING DUE FROM DIVORCED PERSONS UNDER ORDERS OF SUPPORT IN TWENTY-EIGHT MICHIGAN COUNTIES DURING SURVEY PERIOD, 1974-1975

Counties Collecting a Mean of	No. of Counties	% of Counties in this Range	% of Fathers Paying 10% or Less	% of Fathers Paying 80% or More
41-50% of amount due	2	7%	47%	32%
51-60% of amount due	5	18%	38%	42%
61-70% of amount due	13	47%	24%	50%
71-80% of amount due	6	21%	16%	60%
81-90% of amount due	2	7%	8%	72%
	28	100%	25% (mean)	51% (mean)

When we speak, as we will shortly, of some counties as high-collecting, we need to remember that, even in the two counties with the highest mean payments, nearly 30% of the men paid less than 80% of the total amount due.[15] Thus, even in the high-collecting counties, many women and children already in precarious financial condition[16] went without needed income. Throughout, when we speak of high collections, we intend solely to convey relative levels of payment.

After determining the levels of collections for each county, our goal was to determine why some counties collected so much more

14. The product-moment correlation between the overall mean and the portion of the caseload paying less than 10% of everything due was —.935. The product-moment correlation between the mean and the portion of the caseload paying more than 80% was +.899.

15. In 1974, unemployment was at disastrously high levels throughout Michigan. Our findings suggest that nearly all the counties would have somewhat higher collection rates during periods of lower unemployment. *See* note 25 *infra*.

16. *See generally* W. GOODE, *supra* note 1; H. ROSS & I. SAWHILL, WOMEN IN TRANSITION (1975).

than others, despite the fact that all counties had Friends of the Court charged with enforcing orders. We were primarily interested in measuring the impact of the use of jailing as a technique of enforcement. To this end, we counted for each county the number of persons sentenced to jail during calendar year 1974. A few Friends of the Court maintained their own logs of all persons sentenced; more frequently we were forced to turn to the logs of the judges of each Circuit Court and scour the year's records of all court business for postings of sentences for nonsupport.

We found, as we had expected, a range of reliance on jail in 1974 from almost no jailings in a few counties up through several hundred jailings in a few others. Table 2 reveals the frequency of sentences to jail in absolute numbers and in terms of the rate of jailing for every 10,000 persons in the county (a figure that closely parallels the number of jailings as a portion of the Friend of the Court caseload).[17] Nearly all the Friends of the Court reported that the numbers jailed in 1974 had been much the same in the immediately preceding year or two.

TABLE 2

INCIDENCE IN TWENTY-EIGHT MICHIGAN COUNTIES OF SENTENCES TO JAIL FOR CONTEMPT OF COURT FOR FAILURE TO PAY SUPPORT IN 1974

Number of Men Sentenced to Jail for Nonpayment in 1974	Number of Counties	Per cent of Counties
Under 10 men	6	21%
11-30 men	9	32%
31-100 men	7	25%
100-300 men	3	11%
Over 300 men	3	11%
	28	100%
Number of Sentences to Jail for Nonsupport in 1974 Per 10,000 Persons in County* (1970 census)		
0-1 per 10,000	8	29%
2-3 per 10,000	8	29%
4-6 per 10,000	6	21%
7-10 per 10,000	3	11%
11 or more per 10,000	3	11%
	28	101%

Total Sentences to Jail in 28 Counties (1974)—3046 men (of a total caseload of around 290,000)

* Roughly equivalent to the number of jailings for every 250 persons in the Friend-of-the-Court caseload in 1974. *See* note 14 *supra*.

17. The size of the caseloads of the Friends of the Court and the populations of the counties correlate very highly, largely because the divorce rate varies remarkably little among the Michigan counties in our sample. In fact, the correlation is

We found a substantial positive correlation (+0.492) between the counties' rates of jailings and their rates of collections: in general, the more they jailed, the more they collected.[18] But this finding, though striking, was the merest beginning. Our task then was to develop measures of all the other factors that might also affect performance and then learn whether the apparent relationship between jailing and collections still held.

As a starting point, it was possible that jailing had a relation to collections through a more subtle link than the bare jail rate alone. For example, men might have been affected not by the mere incidence of jailing but rather by the sentencing rate among those summoned to appear at a hearing for nonpayment, or they might have been affected by some combination of the sentencing rate and the length of sentences commonly imposed. We accordingly developed indices to test for these possible causal links.

It was also possible that the jailing rate had nothing directly to do with payment rates at all. Counties that jailed more might well have had enforcement agencies that tried harder in other respects—sent more warnings, held more hearings, used larger enforcement staffs—and one or more of these other factors and not the jailing rate might actually best explain variations in performance. Accordingly, we gathered as much information as we could about all aspects of the counties' collections and enforcement systems—staff-caseload ratios, the use of computerized records, the rate of use of orders to show cause, and so forth.

so high that we were unable to test whether awareness of the possibility of jail, and thus the deterrent effect, depends on the size of the caseload or on the population. Within the counties in our study, the ratio of the county's population (in 1970) to number of men (or families) making up the caseload (in 1974) ranged from about 35:1 to 40:1. Thus our figure of the "number of jailings per 10,000 population" is roughly equivalent to the "number of jailings per 250 men in the caseload." We have consistently used the population figure as the denominator because in a few counties we were never confident that we had a precise count of the caseload of orders still in effect.

18. Here is another view of the relationship between collections and the rate of jailing:

RELATION OF JAILING TO COLLECTIONS IN TWENTY-EIGHT MICHIGAN COUNTIES

Number of Jailings per 10,000 persons in County:	Number of Counties:	Mean rate of collections: (mean of average portion collected of amounts due)
0-1 per 10,000	8	.60
2-3 per 10,000	8	.63
4-6 per 10,000	6	.67
7 or more per 10,000	6	.75
	28	.655 (mean)

Additional factors had to be taken into account. Payment performance could be affected by factors that varied from county to county but had no direct connection with the enforcement system. More fathers might have paid in County A than in County B—and a higher proportion of nonpayers jailed—because the people in County A felt more strongly about obligations of support or about their general obligations to obey the law or to adhere to social convention. Lacking county-by-county polls of citizen attitudes, we coded a wide range of possible, but quite indirect, indicators of attitude, such as the portion of county population living in a rural setting, total population and population density, conservative voting patterns, general crime rates, and formal church membership. We also recorded the results of our own survey of the attitudes of each county's Friend of the Court toward the functions of the enforcement process and toward possible legislative changes in the enforcement system.

We lastly coded information about income and unemployment rates because it was plausible, indeed likely, that men in all counties were not equally able to pay. For this we drew on 1970 census information about median incomes and portions of the population above and below various income levels and on census and Michigan Employment Security Commission figures regarding levels of unemployment.

It was during the phase of the study that we sought to control for the multitude of factors apart from jailing that might have affected payments that we skated on thinnest ice. We ourselves had computed parents' payment rates and developed confidence in our accuracy. We had similarly counted with care the exact number of men sentenced to jail during a common time period. But for the remaining factors other than the incidence of jailing that might have affected payment rates, we encountered the problems that have plagued all social scientists performing research on deterrence.[19]

Certain problems stood out above the others. First, for many plausible factors that might have affected payments—especially, as we have said, those bearing on people's attitudes toward their obligations—we often had to resort to the most oblique sorts of evidence. Even unemployment data was available only for residents of each county as a whole and so may not have accurately reflected actual rates of unemployment among men under orders of support.

19. *See* F. Zimring & G. Hawkins, *supra* note 3, at 264-66, 269; Baldus & Cole, *supra* note 5, at 177-83.

Secondly, when there was information that we could code, we had to worry about the comparability of the information across counties. For example, the seemingly simple task of counting the size of county "enforcement staffs" forced us to grapple with many different definitions given the term "enforcement" by the agency heads we interviewed and with multiple uses of individual staff members.

Finally, some sorts of information that were available and reliable displayed so little variation among the counties that we were unable to assess the significance of certain elements of the enforcement process or of the demography of the population of supporting fathers. For example, in setting orders, the counties made use of quite similar schedules that took into account men's earnings and the number of dependent children. (In nearly all, for example, the size of the support order for a family with two children was about one-third of the father's take-home earnings.) Because of the similarity across counties, we were unable to test for differences in collections that might have accrued from larger or smaller orders in relation to incomes.

After gathering all the relevant information that we could, we used multiple regression analysis to determine which factors best accounted for the differences in collections among the counties. Regression analysis is a technique used by social scientists and others to estimate the relationship between factors through the use of numerical data.[20] Complex in formula, yet readily accessible through computer programs, it permits one to estimate the relation between some phenomenon one wishes to understand (here, the level of payments across counties) and other measured factors that might have a bearing on that phenomenon (jailings, median incomes, and so forth). It permits learning the direction and strength of the relationships among the factors used in the analysis.

When we completed a long series of analyses of our own data, three factors stood out among all others as powerfully related to the levels of collections of support. The first was an aspect of the enforcement process: fourteen aggressive Friends of the Court, which we will call "self-starting," watched for a few weeks of missed payments or the accumulation of an arrearage of a certain number of dollars (say $100) and then sent a warning notice to the nonpaying parent. These counties that had a practice in nonwelfare cases of initiating enforcement efforts without waiting for complaints from

20. An explanation of regression analysis readily accessible to most lawyers is Finkelstein, *Regression Models in Administrative Proceedings*, 86 HARV. L. REV. 1442 (1973). A helpful basic text is H. BLALOCK, SOCIAL STATISTICS (1960).

the mothers collected more than those that relied on complaints.[21] The second significant factor was the rate of jailing. Even after controlling for other factors, counties that jailed more men in relation to their population still collected more. The third factor was population—the larger the county, the lower the collections. For example, none of the seven highest collecting counties had populations greater than 70,000. Nine of the ten lowest collecting counties had populations greater than 100,000.[22] Table 3 summarizes our findings with regard to these three factors, doing so at the cost of simplifying for display the true variations in population and rates of jailing.

These three factors were interrelated to some degree. The self-starting enforcement policy brings more men into the enforcement system, which in turn brings more men before judges for possible sentencing; similarly, large counties were somewhat less likely to be self-starters. Nonetheless, each of the three factors had independent explanatory importance. The three principal factors alone account for about 60% of the variation in payment rates among the counties.[23] Put another way, if you knew any Michigan county's population, whether its agency was self-starting, and its frequency of jailing, you could within our sample predict, typically within a few percentage points, how much the county actually collected of the total amount owed.[24]

21. In the regression analysis we used a simple binary variable that captured whether or not the agency had an established practice in nonwelfare cases of initiating enforcement efforts without awaiting complaints.

22. Not surprisingly, the relation between population and collections is not what social scientists would call "linear." A rise in county population from 30,000 to 130,000 will have far more impact on collections than a rise from 1,030,000 to 1,130,000. In our analysis, we used the $\log_{10}$ of population as a more plausible indicator of the relation of population to performance.

23. A list of all variables analyzed may be obtained by writing the author directly. In a regression analysis with the three factors only, the three explained 62.4% of the variance (unadjusted) and 57.7% of the variance (adjusted). See Appendix at the end of the article.

When we created a binary variable that contrasted all counties that were self-starting and high-jailing (four or more jailings per 10,000 population) with all other counties not having both enforcement policies, we accounted for 71.9% of the variance (unadjusted) and 69.7% (adjusted) with this variable and the population variable alone. See Appendix at the end of the article.

24. When we calculated what a county should be expected to collect within our sample using the regression coefficients for population, the jail rate and the "self-starting" factor, the actual collections varied from the predicted collections by more than six percentage points for only nine counties. For eleven counties, the prediction was off by less than three percentage points. Only one county, our highest collecting county, collected over ten percentage points more than would be predicted. That county impressed us even before surveying its records as the most thoroughly organized of all. Conversely, only one county, one of our two lowest collecting, collected more than ten percentage points less than was predicted. This county seemed about the least well organized for collections. It was the only county in our sample with a

TABLE 3

INTERRELATION OF THREE MOST IMPORTANT FACTORS RELATING TO COLLECTIONS IN TWENTY-EIGHT MICHIGAN COUNTIES

How much the county jails, whether Friend of the Court initiates enforcement without awaiting complaints, and county population

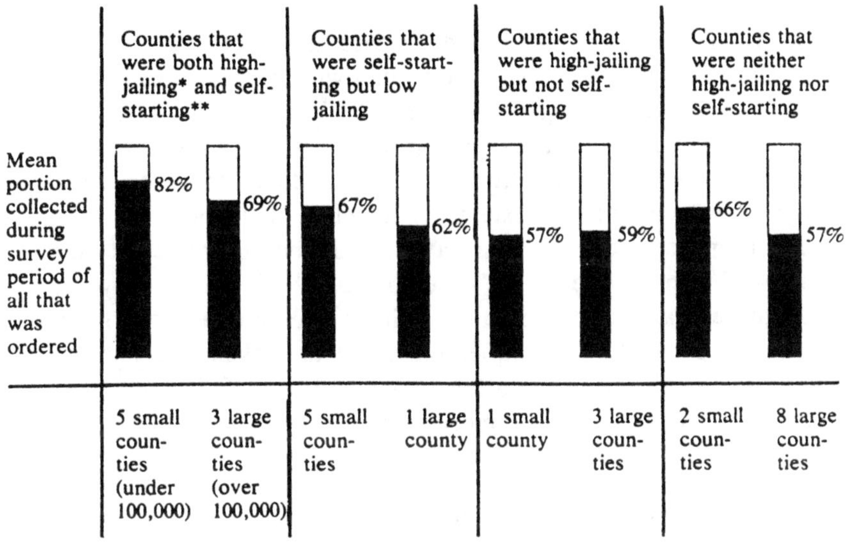

Mean collections:

13 small counties (under 100,000)—72%
15 large counties (over 100,000)—60%
12 high-jailing counties*—71%
16 low-jailing counties—61%
14 self-starting counties**—71%
14 non-self-starting counties—60%
5 small, high-jailing, self-starting counties—82%
8 large, low-jailing, non-self-starting counties—57%

* A high-jailing county, for our purposes, was one that jailed 4 or more men for nonsupport during 1974 for each 10,000 persons in the county population in 1970. The mean jailing rate for the high-jailing counties was 6.0 per 10,000. The mean rate for the low-jailing counties was 1.7 per 10,000. See further explanation in Appendix A.

** A self-starting county was a county that had had for some years a policy of initiating enforcement efforts in delinquent nonwelfare cases without waiting for complaints.

One other factor helps slightly in explaining differences in collections. When unemployment rates are higher, collections are lower. It is not, of course, surprising that payments should be lower in places where unemployment is high. It was surprising to us only

population over 100,000 whose agency head had only a part-time appointment. Later in this article, we discuss Washtenaw County, a low-jailing, non-self-starting county. The ill-organized county to which we are referring in this footnote is not Washtenaw.

that unemployment rates did not account for more of the differences among the counties. By adding in the unemployment factor, we could account for differences among the counties only to a slightly greater degree than we could using the three dominant factors alone.[25] An appendix at the end of this article provides for the reader who is interested more detailed statistical information on the findings.

The rate of jailing makes a difference in collections, but how much of a difference? Table 3 and our own analysis indicate that, for purposes of measuring the difference, it makes little sense to separate the jail rate from the factor of a self-starting enforcement process. The two work together.[26] Counties that have both a high jail rate and a self-starting system collect more than those that have neither and more than those that have one or the other but not both. And those that have one or the other but not both collect only very slightly more than those that have neither. When they are linked together and population and unemployment are taken into account, counties with both a high jailing rate and a self-starting policy collected an average of 25% more per case than was collected by the counties that did not have both.[27]

C. *The Significance of a Self-Starting Enforcement Process, the Rate of Jailing, and Population*

We have dismembered a complex and emotional process—the payments of divorced parents toward the support of their children.

25. The mean and median unemployment rate in our 28 counties was 10%. In nine of our counties the rate was 12.0% or more. In only eight was the rate less than 8.0%. Oddly, these rates were not useful in accounting for any of the difference, whereas the 1970 rates, when unemployment rates were lower but still checkered, were able to explain some of the variance in county collections.

With the four variables we could explain 65.6% of the variance (unadjusted) and 59.7% (adjusted). The addition of unemployment figures does produce a re-alignment of the ranking of important factors: population and the jail rate are now somewhat more significant than "self-starting" enforcement. See details in the Appendix at the end of the article.

26. As explained in note 23 *supra*, a single variable that combines the "self-starting" factor with the jail rate accounts for more of the variance than the sum of the two taken individually.

27. In a regression on the performance index using as controls (1) the variable that combined "self-starting" and the jail rate into a single binary factor, (2) $\log_{10}$ population, and (3) the unemployment rate, the combined self-start/jailing factor had a coefficient of 14.77. Since the performance index is coded in percentage collected, the coefficient of 14.77 indicates that a county that had both a self-starting system and a high rate should collect after controls 14.77 percentage points more than those that did not have both. Since the mean collection rate among our counties was 65%, an added 14.8 percentage points collected would represent about a 25% increase in collections for counties pushed from a mean collection rate of several percentage points below 65% to a mean rate of several points above.

Payments go down with a larger population, up with a self-triggering warning system, down with more unemployment, and up with more jailings. Though our findings have surface plausibility, those who cherish life's complexity will be pleased that, when we peered deeper into our pool of data, we found the waters muddier than they initially appeared. The significance of the unemployment rate does seem to signify just what one would expect: those who are not working are likely to pay less or not at all. The significance of the three more powerful factors is less clear, however.

Our finding that counties with Friends of the Court that initiate enforcement without awaiting complaints collected more money than other counties is, at first glance, hardly perplexing. One anomaly nonetheless persists about this "self-starting" factor. We defined a "self-starting" county as one in which the Friend of the Court initiated enforcement efforts in nonwelfare cases without awaiting complaints from the custodial parent. We excluded welfare cases from the definition because all Friends of the Court had self-triggering systems for initiating enforcement in welfare cases, since the custodial parent in welfare cases is not the receiver of support payments and often does not know whether payments are being made. Given our definition, one would have expected that, when we analyzed the welfare cases from our samples in the 28 counties, the "self-starting" factor would not have helped sort the high- and low-collecting counties. In fact, however, the "self-starting" factor is nearly as significant an explanatory factor of the variations in the collections in the welfare cases as it is in the caseload as a whole, suggesting that the counties that are self-starting simply collect support in both welfare and nonwelfare cases more effectively, for reasons related to but distinct from the self-starting attribute alone. Several other attributes of the enforcement process—efficiency of bookkeeping, size of the enforcement staff in relation to caseload, and so forth—correlate mildly with performance and with the self-starting factor. It appears that "self-starting" may simply capture best the sum of the attributes of an efficient and persistent organization.

That organization to collect and the rate of jailing work hand in hand is also unsurprising. Under a self-starting enforcement system more men who falter are told to "pay up." The high rate of jailing seems to add, "and we really mean it." All rather tidy. We had expected, however, that the rate of jailing would not have been the only way to say "we really mean it," but at least within our study no other aggressive aspect of the enforcement system served anywhere nearly as well to explain the differences in overall collections.

We looked, for example, at the use of orders to show cause, the orders to appear at hearings that are issued when men fail to respond to warning letters. We had a reasonably accurate count of such orders during the same period for which we counted jailings, and we found that counties varied widely in their rate of use of such orders and in the ratio of orders to subsequent sentences to jail. We had hypothesized that the rate of orders themselves, with their stern directive to appear in court, might well have served as a more effective indication than the sentencing rate itself of the seriousness of the enforcement agency. We found, however, that neither the rate of orders to show cause nor any combination of the show-cause rate and jail rate (to measure the conviction rate among those ordered to appear at hearings) helped sort the higher from the lower collecting counties nearly as well as the jail-rate alone.[28] Within the range of measures that were readily available to us, the incidence of that which men actually fear—jail itself[29]—appears to communicate most effectively the necessity of paying their support obligations.

It is possible, nonetheless, that some unmeasured aspect of the enforcement process short of jailing better explains what the jailing rate appears to explain. We were, for example, unable to count the number of warning letters mailed in the twenty-eight counties during 1974 or any other year. We thus could not calculate the rate at which the agency sent warnings either in relation to the number of cases in the caseload or in relation to the number of cases with payments in arrears at some point during the year. The only information we could obtain about the average time between the development of an arrearage and the mailing of a warning was the agency head's statements regarding the policy of the office. While we believe it highly probable that our "self-starting" factor would correlate strongly and positively with each of these measures had we been able to develop them, the self-starting factor's form is not subtle—every county either was or was not "self-starting" in our definition. There were no gradations. It is thus possible that one or more of these other dimensions of the enforcement process would account

28. Whereas the product-moment correlation of the jail rate and the collections rate was +.492, the correlation between the order-to-show-cause rate and the collections rate was only +.121. When used with other variables or combined into other indices with the jailing rate, the show-cause rate offered virtually no explanatory power. Similarly, the combination of the sentencing rate with mean sentence length provided far less explanation of variations in payments than the sentencing rate alone and offered no significant explanatory power when used in a regression run with the jail rate as one of the other independent variables.

29. We used the jail rate in unaltered form and in logarithmic form, with closely similar results. See Appendix at the end of the article.

for all or some part of the differences in collections that we have attributed to the rate of jailing.

A problem for analysis would persist even if we were to find within our twenty-eight counties that the jailing rate added nothing to the explanation of the variations in collections among counties, but that measures of milder enforcement efforts were powerful explainers of variation. Since the form letters of warning in nearly all counties carried threats of judicial action that many men probably read as a threat of jailing, a finding that nonpenal enforcement efforts, but not the jail rate, were a significant explainer of performance could have either of two very different meanings: it could mean that the threat of jail was truly irrelevant and that men can be propelled toward payments by reminders alone, or it could mean that letters threatening judicial action are sufficient in themselves to create the fear of jail, regardless of the actual rate of jailing. If the latter were the case, then, even though the actual jail rate was not a factor in collections, collections might well still decline if jail were removed as a legally permissible sanction and parents under orders of support learned of the change in the law.

The final significant factor apparently affecting collections was the county's population. Our findings suggest that, if two counties have a self-starting system of enforcement, jail at the same rate, and have the same rate of unemployment, the county with fewer residents[30] will still collect more money. Why should this be so? The lower collections in highly populated areas cannot be attributed to higher poverty there. On the contrary, the portions of the population living in poverty were higher, and median incomes appreciably lower, in the smaller Michigan counties than in the larger ones.[31]

The relevance of high population seems rather to lie either in attitudes of city dwellers about obligations to pay or, more likely, in a greater insulation of city dwellers from the enforcement process. In several of the small counties but none of the large, the director of the Friend of the Court knew personally most of the men in his county's caseload, a fact that probably affected some of the men

30. Since the counties in our sample vary little in geographic area, absolute population and population density correlated overwhelmingly.

31. For example, in the six counties in our sample with the smallest population, the median income (in 1970) and the unemployment rates during the months we surveyed averaged $9600 and 12.5% respectively. By contrast, during the same periods median income and unemployment for the six largest counties averaged $11,900 and 10.8% respectively. Similarly, in the six smallest counties the average portion of families living on incomes below the poverty line was 8.6%, whereas the average portion in the six largest was 5.9%.

under orders. I walked with one agency head into a coffee shop on the town square in his county seat. He exchanged good-morning banter with several persons and then leaned over to me and whispered, "Now I'm not telling you who, but three of the men in here with us now are under orders in my office." The difference for the parent under an order in the smaller county is probably not merely that someone whose esteem he may value knows whether he is paying. It is also likely that he believes—correctly—that he is easily located. Staffs of the Friend of the Court in populous counties often reported severe problems of finding nonpayers, even when the defaulters had remained within the county.

III. A Peek Inside: How Does Awareness of the Possibility of Jailing Affect Payments Within a County?

Within our samples, ardent agencies collect more than the less vigilant. But how does this ardor exert its effect? Even in places with the laxest enforcement some men pay all the time. Even in places with the most terrorizing enforcement some men never pay at all.

Among questions that the reader may already be asking is whether the difference between the higher-collecting counties and the lower-collecting counties lies solely in the jailed men themselves: the high-collecting counties jail more men, jailed men pay better after release than they did before, and unjailed men pay at about the same mean rate in all counties. And if a fresh inspiration of those actually jailed does not account for the differences in collections among counties, how does the prospect of jailing work its black magic on the men who are never jailed?

We cannot fully answer these questions, but our close inquiry into two counties, one an ardent enforcer and the other not, permits us to say a good deal more than we otherwise could. When the remainder of our study is published, much of it will deal with the men within these two counties—their families, their financial situations, their payments, their treatment at the hands of the agency and the court, and their responses to all manner of enforcement efforts. Here we will address a couple of the questions especially invited by the discussion of general deterrence.

One of the two counties, Genesee County, where Flint is located, had a population in 1970 of 444,000. Its Friend of the Court has long had a "self-starting" enforcement process, and its courts have long favored jail to punish defaulters. During 1974, Genesee County judges imprisoned 224 men for failing to pay support, a rate of 5 per 10,000 persons in the county, making Genesee one of the high-jailing counties. In a random sample we drew of over 400 divorced men whose cases were open in 1970, the men had paid an average of 74% of the total amount due over the lives of their decrees up to the point that we coded, a mean of seven years. Only 14% of the men had paid less than 10% of all amounts due under their decrees.

The other county, Washtenaw County, the county of Ann Arbor and Ypsilanti, was rather different. For most of this last decade, its Friend of the Court has expended a higher portion of its budget than any other Michigan county on social workers and other professionals concerned with marital counseling and child-custody matters.[32] A much smaller portion of staff efforts was addressed to collections. Thus, it is perhaps not surprising, even if somewhat disheartening, that a random sample of about 400 men under support decrees in Washtenaw had paid on the average only 56% of everything due, over 25% less than the average portion paid by the Genesee men. This was true despite the fact that median earnings are higher in Washtenaw, unemployment lower, and the county population only slightly more than half as large.[33] Over twice as many Washtenaw men (30%) had paid less than 10% of their amounts due.

The enforcement systems in the two counties differed greatly. Two such differences are familiar to the reader. For several years up to and including the years we studied, Washtenaw had not been a "self-starting" county: a woman not receiving welfare benefits had to phone in a complaint before a form notice of arrearage was sent to the father and had to complain again, this time in writing, before a nonresponding father was sent an order to show cause. Moreover, though many Washtenaw men in the caseload had been arrested for nonsupport, often through the serving of a warrant when arrested for an altogether different offense like a traffic violation, Washtenaw's judges jailed far fewer persons for nonsupport. In the year that Genesee's judges sentenced 224 men, Washtenaw's sentenced only five.

32. The special orientation of Washtenaw's Friend of the Court is indicated by the scholarly writing that the head of the agency, Richard Benedek, has undertaken with his wife, Elissa, a psychiatrist. *See, e.g.*, Benedek & Benedek, *Postdivorce Visitation: A Child's Right*, 16 J. AM. ACAD. CHILD. PSYCH. 256 (1977).

33. Median income in Washtenaw in 1970 was $12,300, whereas it was $11,300 in Genesee; unemployment during the months we surveyed was under 5% in Washtenaw but over 11% in Genesee. In 1970, Washtenaw had a population of 234,000; Genesee a population of 444,000.

A. *The Role of the Jailed Men*

It is possible that men who are never jailed pay at nearly identical average rates in both high- and low-collecting counties and that the only reason one group of counties collects more is that men actually jailed, much more numerous in that group of counties than the other, are frightened into paying more regularly. This explanation, while plausible, does not appear to hold for our counties. The margin of difference in collections between the self-starting, high-jailing counties and others is too great to be accounted for by the small portion of the men in those counties who have both been jailed and begun and continued to pay after release.[34]

Moreover, it is simply not the case that the never-jailed men in the higher-jailing counties are unaffected by the policy around them and pay at essentially the rate of the never-jailed men in the low-collecting counties. Everyone pays better in Genesee. Men sentenced, men arrested but never sentenced, and men never arrested all pay, as groups, significantly better in Genesee than their counterparts in Washtenaw.[35] Whatever it is about the system in Genesee that induces men to pay reaches the jailed and unjailed men with similar effect.

34. During the one-year period we studied in the 28 counties, only a small portion of the men in the sample, even in the counties that jailed most heavily, had been jailed in the recent past. Even if we assume that this previously jailed group paid at the unlikely mean rate of 60% during the year we surveyed and further assume that had they not been jailed they would have all paid nothing (equally unlikely), their numbers are not substantial enough to have boosted the collective average of the whole county by more than a third of the difference we have computed to be the effect of the jailing policy.

As a matter of fact, in Genesee, the payment rate for our sample of jailed men was .33 in the year after their release; a comparable sample of jailed men in Macomb County paid at a rate of .50. In the case of Genesee, the portion of the jailed men who maintained payments declined even further with the passage of time after release.

35. Our comparative data on Genesee and Washtenaw Counties, in table form, is as follows:

COMPARISON OF PAYMENTS OF MEN
IN TWO COUNTIES WHO WERE AND WERE NOT
EVER ARRESTED OR SENTENCED FOR NONPAYMENT
(Random Sample of Divorce Cases)

		Washtenaw County		*Genesee County*
	N	Average Payment Rate Over Life of Decree	N	Average Payment Rate Over Life of Decree
Men Sentenced to Jail	8	.31	60	.55
Men Arrested but Never Sentenced	75	.46	57	.73
Men Who Were Never Arrested or Sentenced	327	.60	292	.80
	410	.57	409	.74

Why do the men who are arrested or sentenced pay so much better in Genesee than in Washtenaw? One might have expected that jail would be equally chastening in both counties. Again, we cannot be completely certain of the reason. A partial answer may lie in the fact that the men arrested in Genesee had a smaller arrearage at the time of arrest. Men chastened earlier may respond better. Or, perhaps, as economists would predict, many jailed men ask themselves after release much the same question that the canny nonpayer asks who has never been jailed: not "how painful is jail?", but "how likely is it that I will soon (again) be arrested?" In Genesee, but not Washtenaw, the agency moved quickly against previously sentenced men who did not begin to pay. Indeed, when a Genesee man was in jail for the first time he would likely note that a significant portion of the other men there with him were persons who had been sentenced for nonsupport before;[36] only one person in our Washtenaw sample had been sentenced twice. To be sure, people who have been jailed are not in an identical position with the never-jailed—once jailed, a man no longer has to imagine the discomfort or embarrassment of jail—but the tendency to regard the jailed and never-jailed men as different species, though inviting, is misguided.

B. *The Effects of Enforcement on Payments over Time*

As time passes after the entry of an order of support, some men cease to pay, some begin to pay, and some pay at the same rate. A comparison of the patterns of payment performance of fathers in Genesee and Washtenaw over the lives of their decrees sheds more light on the effects of a zealous enforcement process. Consider first Table 4, which shows for our random samples of men in each county the portion of men paying nearly nothing, paying nearly

36. In a sample we drew in Genesee County of 191 men jailed in 1969 and in the first nine months of 1970, more than a quarter had been previously sentenced for nonsupport. On any given day, the portion of men in jail for nonsupport who had been previously sentenced was likely to have been even higher because the previously jailed men were typically held for longer terms.

TABLE 4

COMPARISON OF PAYMENT RATES IN GENESEE AND WASHTENAW COUNTIES THROUGH SIXTH YEAR OF ORDER (FOR CASES OPEN FOR AT LEAST THAT LONG)

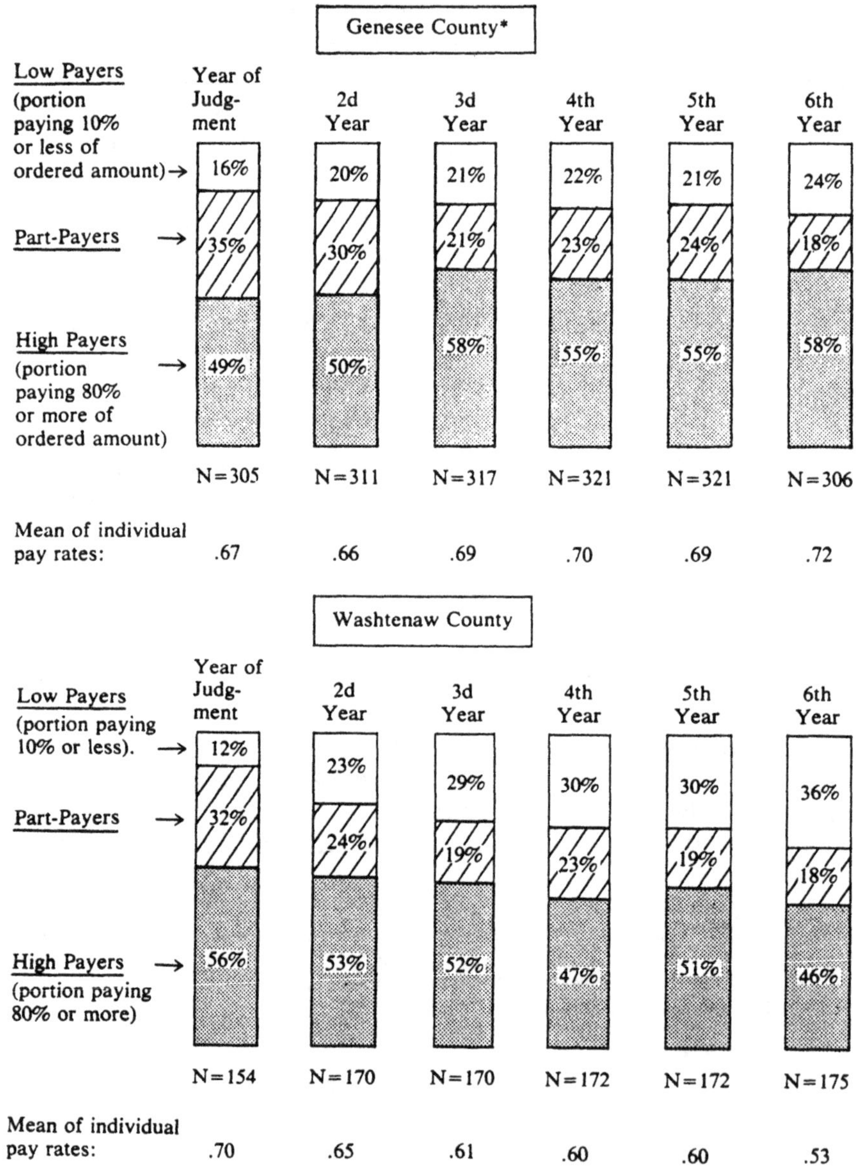

* In this table, we have made an adjustment for a small group of low-paying cases opened prior to 1966, when the Friend of the Court in Genesee put its payment

everything, or paying somewhere in between year by year after the entry of the decree.

In the first year in each county most men pay either nearly everything or nearly nothing, and over the years, quite predictably, more and more men are found at the extremes. The difference between the two counties, subtle but distinct, lies in the portions paying at high and low rates. In Genesee in the first year, of every twelve men, six are high payers and two are low payers. By the sixth year, seven are high payers and three are low payers.[37] The mean level of payments rises slightly over the years, up to .72. In Washtenaw, the pattern is better than Genesee in the beginning but worse at the end. In the first year, seven of every twelve men are high payers and only between one and two are low payers. By the sixth year, however, the portion of high payers has declined to five of twelve and the portion of low payers has risen to over four in twelve. The mean level of payments in Washtenaw falls somewhat every year, ending at .57. Were we able to control for population and unemployment, the earlier results suggest that Washtenaw, both smaller and with less unemployment, would appear even worse.

The distribution of payments in the two counties over time suggests that in each county a substantial number of men consciously or unconsciously test the enforcement system in the early years. In Genesee a significant number are "burned" and move toward full payments. In Washtenaw, many who paid nearly in full or in part in the first year move toward nonpayment after finding either that a period of haphazard payments is ignored or followed by hollow threats or that, even if they are arrested, they are soon released and forgotten. Our findings regarding the use of warning letters and the responses to warnings in Genesee corroborate these conclusions.

Standing next to Genesee's system, Washtenaw's may seem largely ineffectual. In fact, however, the presence in Washtenaw of a full-time agency has significant effects on collections that can be appreciated by comparing Genesee and Washtenaw with a jurisdiction in

---

records on computer. By examining all orders set by the courts in 1960 and 1963, we have determined that about 7% of cases opened in those years had been closed by 1966 for consistent nonpayment without request for enforcement. In the adjustments we have made, we have increased the total cases to reflect an additional number of cases presumably closed and placed all such assumed closed cases in the "no payments" column. The effect is slight. For the six years reprinted here, the actual number of files prior to the adjustment is 15 fewer than reported above in the first and last years and 16 fewer than reported above for the years in between.

37. The patterns in each county were actually somewhat more complex than these figures suggest since the figures represent only net movement. Few men, however, shifted from one bracket to another and back again.

which there is no systematic enforcement system at all. In the mid-1960s, Kenneth Eckhardt conducted a study of child-support collections in Dane County, Wisconsin.[38] This county, containing both the state capital and the main campus of the state university, was as prosperous as Washtenaw and Genesee and was substantially smaller than Genesee in its population.[39] In Dane, though an office of the court collected child-support payments and forwarded them to the wife, the agency played no routine role in enforcing orders and had no staff devoted to reminding men of their default. The mother who was not receiving payments had to find an attorney and pursue private remedies. Most defaulters were left completely alone. On the other hand, substantial numbers of men were prosecuted and jailed for nonpayment not as a capstone of a well-focused effort to enforce support but largely, it appeared, as a part of the enforcement of other laws: most of the jailed men seem to have been wanted by the prosecutor for committing other offenses not as easily proved.[40]

Table 5 contains information on the payment levels in the Wisconsin county and how they changed over time. The differences from our Michigan counties are startling. In Dane, as in our Michigan counties, a large portion of the men paid nearly all amounts due in the first year, but, whereas this full-paying group shrank only slightly over time in Washtenaw and grew over time in Genesee, the full-paying group in Dane shrank steadily and rapidly. By the sixth year only 17% of the caseload was paying in full. Moreover, the portion of men paying nothing began at a much higher level in Dane—nearly 40% paid nothing in the first year, in contrast to the nonpayment rate in the first year of around 15% in each of the two Michigan counties. By the sixth year, the group paying nothing in Wisconsin grew to 71% of the caseload.

---

38. K. Eckhardt, Social Change, Legal Controls, and Child Support: A Study in the Sociology of Law (unpublished dissertation, University of Wisconsin 1965). Parts of the results of his study are also to be found in Eckhardt, *Deviance, Visibility and Legal Action: The Duty To Support*, 15 Soc. Prob. 470 (1968).

39. 1970 Census Figures

	Dane County, Wisconsin	Genesee County, Michigan	Washtenaw County, Michigan
Population	290,000	444,000	234,000
Per cent of labor force unemployed	2.9%	5.3%	5.0%
Median family income	$11,300	$11,300	$12,300
Portion of workers-white collar	59%	38%	56%

See United States Bureau of the Census, County and City Data Book, 1972 at 234, 236-37, 522, 524-25 (1973).

40. K. Eckhardt, *supra* note 38, at 261-65.

TABLE 5

DISTRIBUTION OF PAYMENTS BY DIVORCED FATHERS IN DANE COUNTY, WISCONSIN THROUGH SIXTH YEAR AFTER DIVORCE*

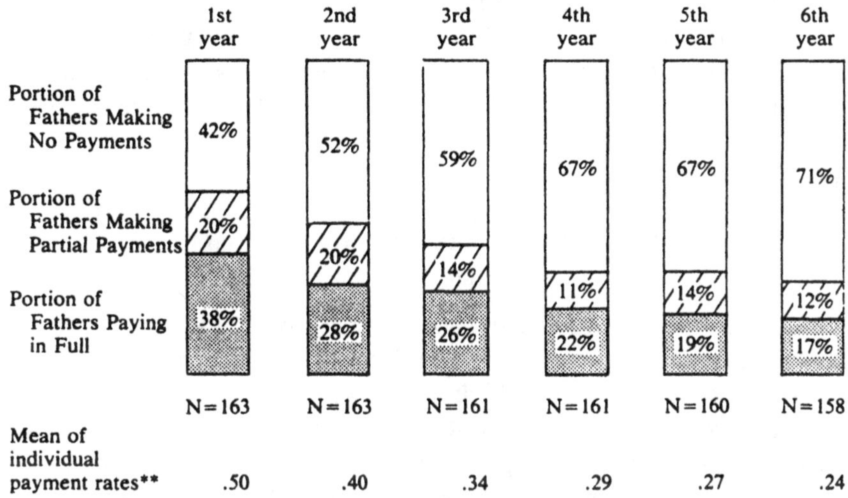

* Data from K. Eckhardt, *Social Change, Legal Controls and Child Support: A Study in the Sociology of Law* 226 (unpublished dissertation, University of Wisconsin 1965).

** Computed by ascribing 100% as payment rate of full payers, 0% as payment rate of nonpayers, and 60% as the rate of partial payers.

Because of the similar socioeconomic conditions in the three counties, two conclusions are invited by a comparison of their rates of collections. The first is that the presence of a full-time enforcement agency in Washtenaw, ready, if requested, to make efforts at enforcement, exerts significant and sustained effects on many fathers' payments throughout the lives of their orders.

Our conclusion that even a minimal, full-time enforcement system such as Washtenaw's Friend of the Court has a significant impact on collections is corroborated by the information collected annually by the Department of Health, Education, and Welfare on support payments in welfare cases in each of the fifty states, many of which, until recently, made no organized effort to collect support even in welfare cases. Year after year, up through the mid-1970s, Michigan apparently collected an average of more per case than any other state in the country.[41]

41. *See, e.g.*, STAFF OF THE SENATE COMM. ON FINANCE, 94TH CONG., 1ST SESS., CHILD SUPPORT: DATA AND MATERIALS 151 (Comm. Print 1975). Washington and

The second conclusion suggested by comparing the Michigan and Wisconsin data concerns the effects of jail as an instrument of enforcement. We found within Michigan that, in the absence of a self-starting enforcement system, a heavy jailing rate makes little difference in collections. The experience of the Wisconsin county, collecting so little but jailing as many men as Genesee, bolsters our own tentative conclusion about the futility of jail as an instrument of collection unless it is perceived by potential offenders as likely to occur to them, a belief that apparently arises not from the mere occurrence of jail but from an effective reminder system well marked with road signs pointing toward confinement.

IV. Implications of the Study for Collection of Child Support

An aggressive enforcement system, capped by jailing, induces many men to pay who otherwise would not. Working men who willfully refuse to support their children are widely considered immoral. On these two grounds alone, most Americans would probably consider jailing for nonsupport justifiable, even desirable. Before embracing jail too warmly, however, several further questions need answers: Do the dollar costs of a self-starting enforcement policy that relies in part on the use of jail exceed the dollars in added returns? Are there other costs to a jailing policy that cast doubt on the wisdom of relying on it? And finally, are there alternative systems not relying on jailing that can yield results that are as good as or better than those generated by jailing?

A. *The Dollar Costs and Benefits of Ardent Enforcement*

The answer to the first question—do dollar costs of especially aggressive enforcement exceed dollar benefits—seems to be a clear "no." The financial costs of a self-starting, high-jailing system—of extra enforcement officers, extra court time, jail operations, and so forth—are considerable, but the additional amount of support collected is simply greater. As we discussed above, within the Michigan study, counties with both a self-starting enforcement policy and a substantial reliance on jailing collected on average 25% more than counties that did not have both, after controlling for population and unemployment. Thus, in Genesee County the marginal dollar costs of the arresting, jailing, and self-starting policy in 1974 might

California also have highly organized systems for collection in welfare cases. Because some data are missing, it is possible that in some years Washington collected as much or more on the average as Michigan.

conceivably have been as high as $500,000,[42] but the amount of collections attributable to these enforcement efforts might have been nearly $3.5 million of the more than $17.3 million collected by the agency that year.[43]

We have so far been comparing costs and benefits among counties with full-time agencies, some more strident than others. If we compare instead the probable costs and returns of two jurisdictions, one having a full-time aggressive agency and the other having no agency at all and leaving each parent to private devices, by hypothesis, the savings in enforcement costs would be even greater for the latter. Yet, as the Dane County, Wisconsin, study suggests,[44] we would almost certainly find that the foregone collections would be vastly greater yet.[45]

Our calculations do not include conceivably determinable losses of wages by the men jailed or losses of tax revenues from them, but these losses, while not trivial, need not necessarily be great. If, as

42. More work remains to be done by us on the marginal costs of a jailing policy. As usual, numerous factors complicate the calculations. For example, each Genesee judge spent a few hours a week on child-support cases, but removal of these cases from the dockets would not have led to a reduction in the number of judges. The long average jail terms in Genesee must have inflated enforcement costs, but a portion of these costs were probably avoidable without any loss in collections since, within the counties in our study, neither the length of the sentence nor the amount of time served affected county collections. Our calculation that Genesee incurred marginal costs of $500,000 in order to sustain an aggressive, high-jailing system is based on a generous estimate of the expenses. *Viz.*, we assumed that a shift to a passive enforcement system would have allowed a reduction of one-half in the size of the enforcement staff and a savings of $100,000 in court time. We further assumed that the average jail term served would be 60 days (far longer than that in most high-collecting counties) and that the costs of jailing were $10 per inmate per day, the figure used by the Genesee sheriff in preparing his 1974 budget. Even with these highly inflated figures, costs barely totaled $400,000, while in 1974 Genesee's Friend of the Court collected $17.3 million.

43. Given our finding that a high-jailing, self-starting enforcement system boosts collections by roughly 25%, *see* text at note 27 *supra*, Genesee's collections in 1974 would have been about $13.8 million, rather than the $17.3 million actually collected, but for this system.

44. *See* text at and following notes 38-40 *supra*.

45. *See also* COMPTROLLER GENERAL OF THE UNITED STATES, COLLECTION OF CHILD SUPPORT UNDER THE PROGRAM OF AID TO FAMILIES WITH DEPENDENT CHILDREN (1972) (report to the House Committee on Ways and Means).

A study of child-support collections that has been done for the Department of Health, Education and Welfare in five places with ardent enforcement procedures in welfare cases (including Genesee County, Michigan) found that in all of them the returns in dollars collected vastly exceeded the dollar cost of the enforcement efforts. *See* U.S. DEPT. OF HEALTH, EDUCATION AND WELFARE, ABSENT PARENT CHILD SUPPORT COST-BENEFIT ANALYSIS (1975). The study was conducted by Arthur Young & Company. This study did not compute the costs of jailing. On the other hand, it included all the costs of a bookkeeping and enforcement system in both divorce and paternity cases.

other parts of our study suggest, the deterrent effect of the sentencing rate turns not at all on the length of sentences imposed nor on the number of days served (some of the highest-collecting counties imposed the shortest sentences), most men could be held only a day or two with loss of little, if any, of the general deterrent effect.

We must remember when we are comparing costs and benefits that we are often referring to costs to the taxpayers to produce benefits to individual families. Only in welfare cases does the government both bear the costs and reap the gains and, even in the welfare setting, federal, state, and local governments bear uneven shares of the costs in relation to their shares of the returns.[46] In nonwelfare cases, dollars collected by the state are sent on to the custodial parent. At any given time, most divorced parents with children are not receiving welfare benefits. Across our twenty-eight counties, an average of 30% of the families were receiving welfare at the time we sampled. For the 70% of families not on welfare, the relevant cost-benefit question differs from that appropriately asked when the government is collecting for itself: in a society that normally relies on private ordering, the question is whether public enforcement offers values over private enforcement sufficient to justify the expenditure of public funds. Because public enforcement is so much more effective and because so many dollars are at stake for the benefit of children, most Americans would probably answer "yes," but reaching such an answer does require more than simply counting dollars.[47]

B. *Other Costs of a Jailing Policy*

Even if a jailing policy yields more dollars than it costs, there may well be other reasons for doubting the wisdom of reliance on jail as an instrument of enforcement. An initial doubt about jailing for nonsupport is jurisprudential in nature. We might well decide that even willful nonsupport is not one of those forms of human misbehavior appropriately dealt with by criminal sanctions. Though not one of the "victimless" offenses, it is nonetheless an intra-family offense often signifying the continuation after divorce of patterns of behavior that were a part of the marital relationship: withholding as a technique of communication. Divorced men often "forget" to pay

46. *See, e.g.*, Title IV(D) of the Social Security Act, 42 U.S.C. §§ 655, 658 (Supp. V 1975).

47. To some degree the costs of public enforcement can be passed on to the "consumer." In Michigan, for example, each person subject to an order of support is charged $18 a year to offset part of the agency's operating expenses.

not out of vicious disregard for their children but from more prosaic human failings of jealousy or anger. Divorced women may similarly "forget" that Tuesday was the day the father was coming to visit the children. Citing the "emotional stress" of the post-divorce period and child support's connection with "an intimate personal relationship," the Committee on One-Parent Families of Britain's Department of Health and Social Security thus recently recommended that Parliament eliminate jail as a permissible sanction for nonsupport.[48]

Although the British Committee apparently assumed, contrary to our findings in Michigan, that neither jailing nor the threat of jailing produces beneficial effects on parents' payments, the Committee's judgment about the inappropriateness of penal sanctions in this context has appeal nonetheless. To be sure, the fact that behavior occurs between family members should not by itself place it beyond the reach of the criminal law. Few would recommend removing penalties for the killing of one spouse by another, even though it is connected with "an intimate personal relationship" and committed under "emotional stress." To most people, however, killing and nonpayment of support are simply not of the same order of seriousness. Thus, recognizing the emotional stress that lies behind the failure of many men to pay support may undercut our sense that the act should be considered criminal and the offender marked with our most severe form of public condemnation, even though the same degree of stress would alter only slightly our sense of the heinousness of murder.

Examining the men who end up in jail provides a second source of misgivings about using it widely. Most of us have probably growled over news accounts of a physician or insurance agent earning $60,000 but failing to make his support payments. Well, few doctors or insurance agents languish in Michigan jails for failing to pay child support. The hundreds of men found in Michigan's jails on any given day typically have unsteady work histories as unskilled workers. A high portion have alcohol problems.[49]

---

48. 1 DEPARTMENT OF HEALTH AND SOCIAL SECURITY, REPORT OF THE COMMITTEE ON ONE-PARENT FAMILIES 128-32 (1974).

49. In our sample of 191 men sentenced to jail in Genesee County in 1969 and 1970, over two-thirds had indications in their file—wife's complaints, arrests for alcohol offenses—of some sort of alcohol program. Half of this group had two or more such indications in their files. In a mail survey of the 28 Friends of the Court in our study, 18 answered a question asking whether there were any "recurrent patterns" among the men sentenced to jail for nonsupport in their county: 13 of these mentioned alcoholism or alcohol problems as one recurrent characteristic among their jailed men.

The agencies do not wink at nonpayment by the doctor; rather, the doctors who fail to pay are more likely, if jail is imminent, to have access to sufficient cash to appease the agency. Several aspects of the skewed population in the jails should give us pause. To the extent that we punish the unskilled worker in order to produce higher payments from thousands of higher-income fathers, we are repeating a familiar and dubious pattern in our society that finds its analogues in the use of jailing for street-corner gambling as well as in medical experimentation on prison inmates. To the extent that we punish the blue-collar workers because we are angry at them themselves, our anger is sometimes misplaced. While most of the men jailed could, in the literal sense, have paid more than they did, many see themselves, with some justification, as barely making do, scraping the sides of the bowl of thin gruel provided the least-skilled workers in our society. We blame such men and their supposedly footloose ways for the rise in the welfare rolls, just as some persons in the eighteenth century viewed those who did not pay their bills as a cause of the decay of civilized society. Jailing for nonsupport is a twentieth-century form of jailing for debt.[50]

A third and more tangible reason for avoiding criminal sanctions for nonpayment of support is the conditions of our jails. America's county jails are among our most vicious institutions of incarceration.[51] Often jammed with far more inmates than they were built to hold, they rely on forced inactivity and breed bodily and sexual assault. The character of our jails should be seen as particularly troublesome in this setting when we recall the high level of jailing in many of Michigan's counties. Judges sentence close to 4,000 Michigan men each year for nonsupport. In several counties their numbers outstrip by far the number of men sentenced to jail for drunken driving or larceny offenses. It is probable that each year at least 1,000 more Michigan men under support orders spend a day or so in jail under arrest without later being sentenced. While many sentenced men serve no more than a day or two, it is still alarming that we label as criminal one in ten or one in twelve of all divorced noncustodial

50. *See* P. ROCK, MAKING MEN PAY 307-16 (1973) (tracing the use of jailing for debt in 18th and 19th century England).

51. "Life in many institutions is at best barren and futile, at worst unspeakably brutal and degrading . . . . No part of corrections is weaker than the local facilities that handle persons awaiting trial and serving short sentences." PRESIDENT'S COMMISSION ON LAW ENFORCEMENT AND ADMINISTRATION OF JUSTICE, THE CHALLENGE OF CRIME IN A FREE SOCIETY 159, 178 (1967).

See also R. GOLDFARB, JAILS: THE ULTIMATE GHETTO (1975); Mattick, *The Contemporary Jails of the United States: An Unknown and Neglected Area of Jus-*

parents at some point during the life of their support orders.[52] Studies in other settings have shown well the long-term scars that can develop from labeling people as criminal deviants.[53] If Michigan's aggressiveness were replicated in the rest of the country, as might conceivably occur under the new pressures for collection the federal government is applying in welfare cases, we could find courts sentencing 100,000 American parents for nonpayment of support each year.

Frequently men who have been jailed flee the county upon release.[54] We have little way of measuring how many other men, never jailed, leave because they fear that jail may befall them, although that group also appears to be substantial in number.[55] Since those who leave because of such fears may well be men with a strong desire not to pay, it is unclear how many of them would have continued a relationship with their children if they had remained in the county. Jailing may nonetheless damage the quality of the relationship between parent and child, even when the father does continue to visit and pays support regularly. What is the impact of an ever-present threat of jail on the relationship between a noncustodial par-

---

tice in HANDBOOK IN CRIMINOLOGY 777 (D. Glaser ed. 1974). County jails typically include a mix of persons under sentence for misdemeanors (such as drunkenness) and persons awaiting trial for serious felonies who cannot make bail.

52. In Genesee, approximately one of every seven men in the active caseload in 1970 had been sentenced to jail at least once. Table 2 in the text shows that in 28 Michigan counties 3046 men, or 1.05%, from a total caseload of about 290,000 were sentenced to jail in 1974. However, the number of men in the caseload who have ever been jailed is much higher, since most men sentenced in one year remain in the caseload for succeeding years. A case typically will last 12 to 15 years, from divorce to the 18th birthday of the youngest child.

53. *See* H. BECKER, OUTSIDERS: STUDIES IN THE SOCIOLOGY OF DEVIANCE 31 (1963): "One of the most crucial steps in the process of building a stable pattern of deviant behavior is likely to be the experience of being caught and publicly labeled as a deviant." *See also* R. SCOTT & J. DOUGLAS, THEORETICAL PERSPECTIVES ON DEVIANCE (1972); THE LABELLING OF DEVIANCE: EVALUATING A PERSPECTIVE (W. Gove ed. 1975).

54. In a sample we drew of 191 men sentenced to jail in Genesee County during 1969 and 1970, over one-third (61 of the 172 whose records were complete and whose cases remained open for another year) fled town within a year after their release from jail. We use the verb "flee" here because the payment rate in the year after the release of those jailed persons who leave town is so low (.09) in comparison to those jailed persons who stay (.48) that, for most, avoidance of jail seems to have been a primary motive for their leaving town.

55. In our random sample of 411 divorced families in Genesee County, 70 fathers appear from our records to have moved away from the county after divorce. If this group had paid at roughly the same rate as those who stayed, we could make no inferences about their motive for leaving. In fact, this group paid so much less well than those who appear to have stayed (a mean payment rate of .35 as opposed to a mean of .82) that it seems highly probable that many left to avoid the enforcement system.

ent and his child? How, that is, does a parent begin to behave toward a child to whom he feels tied not by affection alone but at least in part by fear? Can jail's distant possibility make even more tense the already awkward visits between parent and child after divorce? Can it aggravate the injuries to the child's development?

Since little research exists on the impact on children's development of various patterns of relations between the child and noncustodial parent after divorce,[56] it is hazardous to speculate on the particular effects that the prospects of jailing could have. In many cases, perhaps most, my worries may well be groundless. Many fathers may be induced into regular payments in part through vague awareness of the jailing policy but form a habit of payment so routine that they soon cease altogether to be affected by the dire consequences of ceasing to pay. For them, the jailing policy may indirectly improve rather than corrode the relation with their children by removing friction between the divorced parents over erratic payments.

C. *An Alternative to Jail: Deductions from Wages*

Even if one concluded that the benefits of a jailing policy greatly exceeded all these possible social costs, jailing might still be wisely avoided or curtailed if an alternative method of enforcement exists that can produce as much or more money with lower costs. Such an alternative may well be available. In the United States, child support and taxes are the only personal financial obligations routinely enforced by public agencies. For the collection of income and Social Security taxes, Americans are well accustomed to the withholding of wages. "Wage assignments" for child support operate similarly when imposed on an employer and are authorized by law in Michigan and several other states. In most states, including Michigan, however, courts may not impose a wage assignment except on a person already in default,[57] and in all states a wage assignment ends

56. Parts of the results of a University of California at Berkeley study of children of divorce will be appearing in the summer of 1977. Kelly & Wallerstein, *Part-Time Parent, Part-Time Child: Visiting After Divorce*, J. OF CLINICAL CHILD PSYCH. (Summer 1977). See also Benedek & Benedek, *supra* note 32.

57. *Compare* MD. ANN. CODE art. 27, § 88 (1976) *and* MICH. COMP. LAWS § 522.203 (1970) (both requiring default before imposing a wage assignment) *with* WIS. STAT. § 247.265 (1973) (permitting wage assignment to be imposed "at any time.") *See also* 42 U.S.C. § 659 (Supp. V 1975), by which Congress recently provided that wage assignments for support of children would be honored for employees of the United States government as if the United States were a private employer. Thus, if state law permitted, a United States employee could be subject to an involuntary wage assignment without proof of default.

when a person ceases to work for the employer against whom it was ordered.

If a federal system were established under which withholding occurred from the first moment of an order and traveled with a person wherever he took work within the country, the need for much of the current enforcement system would largely disappear. To effectuate this network, the federal government would need to create a national computerized system tied to the man's Social Security number. Employers would be required to make a check on a new employee through a Social Security office to learn whether support payments were to be withheld from his wages. Under such a system, the frequency of payments would be nearly perfect except by the unemployed,[58] the self-employed, and those able to evade the floating wage assignment by falsifying their social security numbers or by colluding with the employer.[59]

A compulsory deduction system would, to be sure, have many troublesome aspects. It would be cumbersome to administer, a fountain of details inviting errors. Unlike income-tax withholding, deductions for child support would be required only for certain employees, who would not look any different at the time of hiring from other new employees. Unlike income taxes, support payments would generally have to be funneled to a recipient other than the federal government, a process likely to take several weeks, even months.[60] At varying intervals, as children reached majority, the amount to be withheld would change.

58. No sanctions should ever be imposed on unemployed men without other income. In Genesee, many unemployed men were jailed after a finding that they could have been working, a chimerical finding in a nation with over 7% unemployment. A few men are willing to starve themselves to avoid paying support, but their numbers are worth neither the effort to ferret them out, nor the injustice to those who are unemployed for reasons beyond their control.

59. An additional advantage of the assignment system is that it would allow the court to fix orders in terms of a percentage of the individual's net earnings, rather than following the universal practice of defining the order as a fixed dollar amount based on the individual's income at the time of the divorce. Although courts have the power to modify an order to reflect changes in earnings, the procedure is cumbersome and in many places infrequently used.

60. Presently, employers pay Social Security taxes quarterly. If, under the system envisioned here, employers had to forward support withholdings only once a quarter, some support payments would remain in the employers' accounts for over three months. Even if employers were required to forward payments weekly, the forwarding would likely be to a single federal office, which would in turn forward the amount either to the custodial parent, to a welfare department, or to another forwarding agency such as a Friend of the Court. The record of sloth and error in the Social Security Administration's handling of old-age and disability benefits is hardly encouraging.

The drawbacks of a compulsory wage-assignment system would not be solely ones of administration. Such a system would also curtail individual liberty. Many people feel strongly about their right to decide for themselves what to do with their earnings. They would resent involuntary wage assignments for child support as much as they would resent involuntary deductions for their utility bills, even though they would agree that it was reprehensible not to pay their bills. Whether seen as a right or an obligation, many noncustodial parents attach importance to their weekly voluntary writing of a support check, viewing it as a means to demonstrate their love for their children.[61]

A wage-assignment system would also involve another sort of federal intrusion on privacy. We can appropriately worry about a federal computer system carrying detailed information about the failed marriages of millions of citizens. Indeed, the employers would invariably learn through the system that their employee was divorced or the parent of an illegitimate child. Today, agencies often hesitate to impose wage assignments in cases in which they fear that the father is likely to be fired because his employer either does not want the bother of making an additional deduction or thinks ill of a person who is divorced or the parent of a "bastard." This troublesome problem of employer attitude could well continue under the system proposed here.

For all these reasons, it is easily understandable why only a bare majority of the Friends of the Court indicated in a mailed survey that they would favor a change in Michigan law to permit the imposition of a wage assignment at the moment the support order first takes effect, despite the fact that, as a group, they are strongly committed to improving collections of support.[62] In the end, however, the issue is not the evil of such a wage deduction system in the abstract. Rather, it is whether it is better or worse than the sin-based system that we have now—the system in which we dangle before men the opportunity not to pay, often so inviting because of the pain of continued recollection of the old family and the burdens of new ex-

61. This observation is based on field interviews with staff members of Genesee County's Friend of the Court during the summers of 1972 and 1973. From those interviews, we also learned that men often view the wage assignment with disfavor because it curtails their bargaining power in the post-divorce period. In the absence of a wage assignment, they can retaliate by slowing up on payments when the custodial parent reneges on visitation. When a wage assignment is in effect, they can retaliate in the same way only by quitting their job.

62. Twenty-three Friends of the Court among the 28 in our study responded to our questionnaire. Of the 23, 12 favored such a change in the law, one was neutral and 10 opposed.

penses, and, then, when men respond to the opportunity, clap them into jail.

If state and federal governments remain committed to compelling long-absent parents to support their children and determined to enforce the obligation aggressively, I for one would choose the compulsory deduction system over the system now found in Michigan. The deduction system would be my preference not so much because it would almost certainly lead to even higher collections than Michigan obtains today, but rather because of the doubts I have expressed about the justness of a jail-based system and about the atmosphere that system creates. The choice may seem easier because the new system does not yet exist. It is, however, hard to believe that a new system, however intrusive, could be as distasteful as one that depends heavily on imprisonment and the fear of imprisonment. If you have any doubts in this regard, turn yourself in for a weekend at your nearest county jail.

Another alternative to the heavy use of jail exists. It is simply for states to create efficient full-time enforcement offices, comparable to Friends of the Court, with courts empowered to use sentences to jail but rarely actually doing so. Remember that in eight of our counties, the judges jailed few people but the full-time agencies in each still collected vastly more than Dane County, Wisconsin. To those to whom jail is repugnant or at least distasteful, this is a possible middle ground that could lead to much higher collections in the many places that now leave mothers not receiving welfare to the same inadequate private remedies available in Dane.

V. The Implications of the Study for Efforts To Control Other Forms of Undesirable Behavior

If the use of jail deters nonpayment of support, can we conclude that it will similarly deter rape or armed robbery? Of course not. We can expect that jail will have a greater effect when men know that all their actions are observed. Most armed robbers and rapists hope that their identity will remain unknown. Most shoplifters and heroin sellers hope that even the offense itself will never be detected by anyone interested in securing an arrest. In the case of child support in Michigan the fact of the offense and the identity of the perpetrator are always known. Thus the very factor that made our study possible—the all-knowing files of the Friend of the Court—makes our findings ungeneralizable to most other forms of conduct.[63]

63. For a provocative discussion of the quite different problems of deterring

In addition, each form of behavior has its own psychological setting. Persons considering aggressive sexual or physical assaults, even if they know that their identities will be learned, may well be typically less responsive to the threat of incarceration. Nonpayment is not an irreversible act committed in the heat of passion. However angry a man may be at his former wife, a "sudden" decision on Tuesday not to pay can be fully undone and punishment avoided on Wednesday or even a week from Wednesday, after reflecting on the consequences of default.

Most men do not, of course, deliberate each week about payment or nonpayment. Penal sanctions may operate in a much more subtle way to reinforce a person's sense of how much importance the community attaches to a certain form of behavior. In the context of child support, we have been unable to determine the contribution of jailing to this socialization process, and our inability to measure this and compare it with other forms of behavior further reduces the utility of our study for understanding such other forms of behavior.

Despite all these cautions, the study does seem to confirm one commonplace prediction: swift and certain punishment can reduce the incidence of some forms of undesired conduct so long as potential offenders perceive a clear link between their own behavior and a system that leads to punishment. If a policeman is watching and customers know it, fewer candy bars are stolen. The sad finding of our study has been that, in the absence of sanctions, so many fathers fail to pay. The striking finding has been the effectiveness of enforcement agencies in many Michigan counties in creating a sense of a policeman at the elbow.

"street crime," see N. Morris & G. Hawkins, The Honest Politician's Guide to Crime Control (1970); J. Wilson, Thinking About Crime (1975).

APPENDIX

Regression Analysis of Factors Accounting for Differences in Rates of Collections Among Twenty-Eight Counties.

The measure of county performance used in the study was the mean for each county of the individual payment rates for each person in the sample for the period sampled. That measure is referred to here as the "Mean Payment Rate." For the manner in which the individual rate was computed, see note 12 *supra*. This measure was used as the dependent variable here either in its natural form, its log to base 10, or its "Logit" form, as indicated.

A list of around 40 control variables tested in the analysis can be obtained directly from the author. Below are the controls used in the analyses reported here:

1. *Self-Starting Factor.* A binary variable that records whether (coded 1) or not (coded 0) the county has used for several years an enforcement system in which the agency initiates enforcement in nonwelfare cases without awaiting complaints from the mother.

2. *Jailing Rate.* The number of sentences to jail in 1974 for contempt of court for nonpayment of support for each 10,000 persons in the county population. As explained in note 17 *supra*, this rate closely parallels the rate of jailing for each 250 men in the county caseload.

3. *Population.* The $\log_{10}$ of the county's population from the 1970 decennial census.

4. *Unemployment Rate.* The unemployment rate in the civilian labor force according to the 1970 census. A further explanation of our use of the unemployment figures is found in note 25 *supra*.

5. *High-Jail/Self-Start Factor.* A combination of factors 1 and 2 above into a binary variable that coded whether or not a county was both high jailing and "self-starting". Those counties that had both a jail rate of 4 or more per 10,000 and a self-starting system were contrasted with all other counties. The selected rate of 4 per 10,000 divided our counties approximately at the median and had no other conceptual foundation.

6. *Jail x Self-Start Factor.* Factor 1 above multiplied by Factor 2. The multiplication produced a 0 for all counties without a self-starting policy (regardless of their jailing rate) and their jailing rate (from 1 to 17) for all counties that did have a self-starting policy.

A. Regression on the "Mean Payment Rate"

1. *With three variables that explain most variance*:

	B	Beta	T-Ratio	Significance Level
Self-starting Factor	8.62	+0.41	2.89	<.01
Jailing Rate	0.92	+0.35	2.64	<.02
Log_{10} Population	−7.91	−0.34	2.53	<.02

Fraction of explained variance: 62.6 per cent (unadjusted)
57.9 per cent (adjusted)

2. *With four variables that explain most variance*:

	B	Beta	T-Ratio	Significance Level
Self-starting Factor	7.00	+0.33	2.25	<.05
Jailing Rate	0.96	+0.37	2.82	<.01
Log_{10} Population	−8.64	−0.38	1.48	<.20
Unemployment Rate	−2.35	−0.19	2.80	<.01

Fraction of explained variance: 65.8 per cent (unadjusted)
59.9 per cent (adjusted)

3. *With the "High-Jail/Self-Start Factor"*:

	B	Beta	T-Ratio	Significance Level
High-Jail/Self-Start Factor	14.8	+.64	6.36	<.01
Log_{10} Population	−10.8	−.47	4.72	<.01
Unemployment Rate	−2.65	−.22	2.20	<.05

Fraction of explained variance: 76.5 per cent (unadjusted)
73.6 per cent (adjusted)

4. *With the "Jail x Self-Start Factor"*:

	B	Beta	T-Ratio	Significance Level
Jail × Self-Start Factor	+1.33	+.55	4.30	<.01
Log_{10} Population	−9.96	−.43	3.50	<.01
Unemployment Rate	−1.94	−.16	1.25	—

Fraction of explained variance: 64.4 per cent (unadjusted)
60.1 per cent (adjusted)

B. Regression on Log_{10} "Mean Payment Rate"

With principal variables in log form:

	B	Beta	T-Ratio	Significance Level
Self-starting Factor	0.047	+0.33	2.06	<.05
Log_{10} Jail Rate	0.052	+0.31	2.20	<.05
Log_{10} Population	−0.059	−0.38	2.69	<.01
Log_{10} Unemployment	−0.240	−0.23	1.62	<.20

Fraction of explained variance: 62.1 per cent (unadjusted)
55.5 per cent (adjusted)

C. Regression on "Mean Payment Rate" in modified "Logit" form

$$\text{Log}_{10} \frac{\text{Mean Payment Rate}}{\text{1-Mean Payment Rate}}$$

With principal measures in log form:

	B	Beta	T-Ratio	Significance Level
Self-Starting Factor	+0.13	+0.30	1.91	<.10
Log_{10} Jail Rate	0.19	0.38	2.75	<.01
Log_{10} Population	−0.18	−0.37	2.67	<.01
Log_{10} Unemployment	−0.79	−0.24	1.88	<.10

Fraction of explained variance: 63.9 per cent (unadjusted)
57.7 per cent (adjusted)

[15]

CHILD SUPPORT REASSESSED: LIMITS OF PRIVATE RESPONSIBILITY AND THE PUBLIC INTEREST†

*Harry D. Krause**

I. The Setting

Looking back at twenty-some years of work with the legal parent-and-child relationship and, more specifically, the child support obligation,[1] I am increasingly concerned about current trends. Tension is mounting between (1) society's continuing need for a functioning family infrastructure, (2) the "me-generation's" emphasis on the individual's *rights* ("liberty and happiness"), (3) traditional financial responsibility for dependents (spouse and children), and (4) the care-giving capacity of the one-parent family. These tensions have become greater than the loosened framework of the modern family (or less formal, more casual relationships now competing with marriage) can reasonably handle.

At least since President Johnson, politicians have concerned themselves with the "breakdown" of the American family and have emphasized the importance of family policy.[2] Even sharper ideological

---

† *This article was originally presented at a symposium,* Divorce Reform in Retrospect, *sponsored by the Earl Warren Legal Institute, University of California at Berkeley, and the Institute for Research on Women and Gender, Stanford University, November 4-5, 1988. This paper also will be published by the Yale University Press as part of a collection edited by Professor Stephen D. Sugarman. My thanks go to participants in that conference, especially to Professor Stephen D. Sugarman and Frank Zimring, for constructive criticism and thoughtful suggestions, and to Marion Benfield as well as Eva and Peter Krause for their comments on earlier drafts.

* *Max L. Rowe Professor of Law, University of Illinois. A.B. 1954; J.D. 1958, University of Michigan.*

1. *See* H. Krause, Child Support in America: The Legal Perspective (1981) [hereinafter Child Support]; H. Krause, Illegitimacy: Law and Social Policy (1971) [hereinafter Illegitimacy]; Krause, *Equal Protection for the Illegitimate,* 65 Mich. L. Rev. 477 (1967) [hereinafter *Equal Protection*]; Krause, *Bringing the Bastard into the Great Society—A Proposed Uniform Act on Legitimacy,* 44 Tex. L. Rev. 829 (1966) [hereinafter *Uniform Act*].

2. President Reagan issued an executive order to assess the impact of federal activity on the family. Exec. Order No. 12,606, 3 C.F.R. 241 (1987 comp.), *reprinted in* 5 U.S.C. § 601 note at 139-40 (Supp. V 1987) [hereinafter Exec. Order]. The order asked:

(a) Does this action by government strengthen or erode the stability of the family and, particularly, the marital commitment?
(b) Does this action strengthen or erode the authority and rights of parents in the education, nurture, and supervision of their children?
(c) Does this action help the family perform its functions, or does it substitute governmental activity for the function?

disagreement now divides the political right and left.[3] They have one thing in common: neither side's proposals are likely to reconstitute the "American family," whatever that was.[4] Standing alone, current proposals to grant pregnancy leave[5] or to subsidize day care[6] are inadequate to that task—as inadequate as are calls to return to a moral past[7] that has been superseded by new facts.[8]

In the 1970s, divorce reform and child support reform seemed revo-

---

(d) Does this action by government increase or decrease family earnings? Do the proposed benefits of this action justify the impact on the family budget?
(e) Can this activity be carried out by a lower level of government or by the family itself?
(f) What message, intended or otherwise, does this program send to the public concerning the status of the family?
(g) What message does it send to young people concerning the relationship between their behavior, their personal responsibility, and the norms of our society?

Id. at 242, 5 U.S.C. § 601 note at 139.

3. In the fall of 1988, presidential candidates competed hotly on family issues, such as day care. All-but-forgotten presidential aspirants called for an increase in the American birthrate, *e.g.*, N.Y. Times, Oct. 24, 1987, at 9, col. 1 (Reverend Pat Robertson), and pregnancy leave (Representative Pat Schroeder's proposal is still pending in Congress). Senator Pat Moynihan's 1988 welfare reform shows a family and child support enforcement focus. *See, e.g.*, *Welfare: Reform or Replacement? (Child Support Enforcement—II: Hearings Before the Subcomm. on Social Security and Family Policy of the Senate Comm. on Finance*, 100th Cong., 1st Sess. (1987). The party platforms reflected different approaches to the problem of child care. N.Y. Times, Aug. 17, 1988, § A, at 20, col. 1. The Republicans:

> In returning to our traditional commitment to children, the Republican Party proposes a radically different approach: establish a toddler tax credit for preschool children as proposed by Vice President Bush, available to all families of modest means, to help them support and care for their children in a manner best suited to their families' values and traditions . . . .

Id.

The Democrats:

> We believe that Government should set the standard in recognizing that worker productivity is enhanced . . . by major increases in assistance making child care more available and affordable to low and middle income families, helping states build a strong child care infrastructure, setting minimum standards for health, safety and quality . . . .

N.Y. Times, Aug. 17, 1988, § A, at 20, col. 2; *see also Governor Michael Dukakis on Family Policy*, AM. FAM., Oct. 1988, at 5; Moritz, *Family Policy in the 1988 Campaign: More Than Patronage and Promise?*, AM. FAM., Oct. 1988, at 3; Rovner, *Democrats Lining Up Behind "Family" Banner*, 46 CONG. Q. WEEKLY REP. 183 (1988); *Vice President George Bush on Family Policy*, AM. FAM., Oct. 1988, at 4.

4. Consider *82 Key Statistics on Work and Family Issues*, Nat'l Rep. on Work & Fam. (BNA) Spec. Rep. No. 9 (Sept. 1988).

5. *See, e.g.*, S. REP. NO. 447, 100th Cong., 2d Sess. (1988). Compare the minority view of Senator Quayle. *Id.* at 64-69. *See Parental Leave Bill Put on Fast Track in Congress by House and Senate Sponsors*, 2 Nat'l Rep. on Work & Fam. (BNA) No. 5, at 1 (Feb. 17, 1989); Rovner, *Child-Care Debate Intensifies As ABC Bill Is Approved*, 47 CONG. Q. WEEKLY REP. 585 (1989).

6. *See, e.g.*, Besharov & Tramontozzi, *The Costs of Federal Child Care Assistance*, AM. FAM., Sept. 1988, at 10; *Bush Calls for $330 Million Package of Child Care Initiatives and Tax Credits*, 2 Nat'l Rep. on Work & Fam. (BNA) No. 5, at 1 (Feb. 17, 1989). Proposals remain active: Rovner, *Partisan Bidding War Erupts over Aid to Poor Children*, 47 CONG. Q. WEEKLY REP. 653 (1989); Rovner, *Senate's Child-Care Measure Would Broaden U.S. Role*, 47 CONG. Q. WEEKLY REP. 1543 (1989).

7. *See, e.g.*, Working Group on the Family, The Family: Preserving America's Future (Nov. 1986) (unpublished report transmitted with letter dated Dec. 2, 1986, from Gary L. Bauer, Under Secretary of the United States Department of Education, to President Reagan) (on permanent file with the *University of Illinois Law Review*); *cf.* Exec. Order, *supra* note 2.

8. *See, e.g.*, Chambers, *The "Legalization" of the Family: Toward a Policy of Supportive Neutrality*, 18 J.L. REFORM 805 (1985). *But see* Burt, *Coercive Freedom: A Response to Professor Chambers*, 18 J.L. REFORM 829 (1985).

lutionary. Looking back, those "reforms" amended traditional approaches and brought adjustments, but left in place many traditional concepts—perhaps too many. True, no-fault divorce ended the state's role in the divorce decision, but divorce by consent had been available all along.[9] Moreover, the state soon reasserted its interest by reregulating the financial consequences of divorce, which strengthened the legal meaning of marriage where it matters: after divorce. The (consequent?) increase in premarital, nonmarital, and postdivorce cohabitation,[10] has led to the demand—somewhat successful in several states—that cohabitation give rise to legally enforceable economic rights and obligations parallel to marriage.[11] And the enormous increase in births to unmarried mothers—which strained the welfare system to the breaking point—has led to the multibillion dollar, government-assisted child support enforcement industry.

Child support is my immediate topic. I shall put aside exciting, related questions regarding the continued legitimacy of interspousal support liability in the ongoing marriage and after divorce. I shall put aside concerns as to what reasonably should be the treatment of property accumulation in the modern marriage.[12] My focus will be on the rationale of the parental child support obligation (1) in the ongoing family, (2) after divorce, and (3) when the absent parent has never participated in a family or a similar social setting.

The very success of the federal child support enforcement legislation[13] (four billion dollars are now collected annually[14]), raises provocative new questions. What level of support obligation is consistent with modern perceptions of family ties? Is the father's demotion from cherished patriarch to absent parent entirely irrelevant to his obligations? Should a "second class" (noncustodial) parent pay "first class" support? Is the "mere existence of a biological link" enough?[15] How much support is enough? Will rigid enforcement of high levels of child support, along with the risk of easy divorce and consequent de facto termination of the father-child relationship, deter responsible men from fathering children? Do we need a better balance between individual and social responsibility—in the children's *and* in society's best interests?

---

9. *See generally* M. RHEINSTEIN, MARRIAGE STABILITY, DIVORCE, AND THE LAW ch. 4 (1972).

10. *See* U.S. DEP'T OF COMMERCE, BUREAU OF THE CENSUS, CURRENT POPULATION REPORTS, POPULATION CHARACTERISTICS, SERIES P-20, NO. 433, MARITAL STATUS AND LIVING ARRANGEMENTS: MARCH 1988 (1989).

11. *E.g.*, Krause, *Legal Position: Unmarried Couples*, 34 AM. J. COMP. L. 533 (Supp. 1986).

12. For example, is marital community property an idea that came 100 years too late? *See* Glendon, *Is There a Future For Separate Property?*, 8 FAM. L.Q. 315, 322-25 (1974).

13. The federal child support enforcement legislation is discussed *infra* Part III.A. to III.D.

14. *See infra* Part III.A.

15. Lehr v. Robertson, 463 U.S. 248, 261-62 (1983).

II. The Past: Little Interest in Child Support

In 1934, the American Law Institute's (ALI's) *Restatement of Conflict of Laws* characterized support obligations and their enforcement as "of no special interest to other states." The Restatement continued "[s]ince the duty is not imposed primarily for the benefit of an individual, it is not enforceable elsewhere . . . ."[16]

Twenty-five years ago, child support was not a public issue. Absent parents were not pursued. Even for a legally established child support obligation, the absent father could all but choose not to pay. The obligation was rarely enforced effectively—especially not across state lines. Paternity—where in doubt—was rarely ascertained.[17] Dominant social work doctrine proclaimed that the father should *not* be brought face-to-face with his (theoretical) support obligation, because enforcement might inconvenience the mother. In any event, since the AFDC system was paying for the child, support enforcement seemed quite unnecessary.[18] Feeble attempts to bring deserting fathers to accept responsibility were discounted with the argument that the funds thus collected would not benefit the children, because collections would only be offset against AFDC entitlements.[19] Some went further and suggested that child support enforcement actually harmed the fragile black family structure by driving away fathers—fathers who liked the social tie but not the financial responsibility.[20] When Congress enacted the federal child support enforcement legislation in the mid-1970s, opposition came from many respected quarters—including even the League of Women Voters—and

16. Restatement of Conflict of Laws § 458 comment a, at 548 (1934).

17. Illegitimacy, *supra* note 1, at 106-08.

18. *See* Stack & Semmel, *The Concept of Family in the Poor Black Community*, in Staff of Subcomm. on Fiscal Policy of the Joint Economic Comm., 93d Cong., 1st Sess., Studies in Public Welfare, Paper No. 12, The Family, Poverty, and Welfare Programs: Household Patterns and Government Policies pt. II, at 275 (Comm. Print 1973) (R. Lerman ed.) [hereinafter Studies in Public Welfare]; *cf.* H. Krause, Family Law: Cases, Comments, and Questions 935-36 (2d ed. 1983) (quoting G. Cooper & P. Dodyk, Income Maintenance 285 (1973)):

> Though consanguinity has been traditionally recognized as an acceptable basis for the allocation of support costs, that criterion is markedly discordant with the ability-to-pay notions which determine so much of the modern allocation of public costs. Particularly where an extended net of liable relatives is recognized under state law, the wisdom of departing from the normal general-revenue tax base may be questioned. Indeed, even where one is dealing with the relation of father to son, one finds the reports replete with cases in which the biological nexus is paralleled by no ties of familiarity, affection or support,—cases which raise grave doubt as to the ultimate significance of simple blood relationship for the problems at hand.
>
> Moreover, whatever the conclusions one may reach on such matters, one must contend with the fact that reluctance to precipitate enforcement of support obligations causes many applicants to refrain from seeking public assistance. The aversion to trenching upon the already stretched resources of another household has caused many, particularly among the elderly, to prefer private penury to public assistance. Whatever the gain derived from reliance upon support obligations, its cost is some degree of frustration of the central purpose of public assistance.

19. Sugarman, Roe v. Norton: *Coerced Maternal Cooperation*, in R. Mnookin, In the Interest of Children: Advocacy, Law Reform, and Public Policy 365, 415-17 (1985).

20. *See* Stack & Semmel, *supra* note 18.

remained strong for a time.[21]

To be sure, not all the blame rested on social workers. When a welfare-related support action *was* brought, judges often saw fit to impose only token obligations, such as $10 per month. In short, despite widespread enactment of the *Uniform Reciprocal Enforcement of Support Acts* of 1950, 1958, and 1968, and explicit references to child support collection in early AFDC legislation,[22] *in practice* American law remained deeply insensitive to the enforcement of child support obligations.

Indeed, only thirty-five years ago, American law provided a shaky basis for imposing a child support obligation on the father. An illustrative New Jersey case involved a medical necessity and arose within an *ongoing* family. Here are a few words from that case:

> Suffice it to say that it appears that the question to be resolved here has not yet been passed on in the court of last resort, but that there are divergent views at law and in equity as to the fundamental nature of a parent's obligation to maintain an infant child awaiting decision.[23]

In the 1750s, Blackstone had said:

> The duty of parents to provide for the *maintenance* of their children, is a principle of natural law . . . . By begetting them, therefore, they have entered into a voluntary obligation, to endeavour, as far as in them lies, that the life which they have bestowed shall be supported and preserved. And thus the children will have a perfect *right* of receiving maintenance from their parents.
>
> . . . .
>
> . . . [A]nd the manner, in which this obligation shall be performed, is thus pointed out. The father, and mother, grandfather, and grandmother of poor impotent persons shall maintain them at their own charges, if of sufficient ability, . . . and if a parent runs away, and leaves his children, the churchwardens and overseers of the parish shall seize his rents, goods, and chattels, and dispose of them toward their relief.[24]

III. The Present: Enforcement!

Looking now at Blackstone's last sentence, we see the federal child support enforcement legislation and corresponding state law reforms. The intermediate past has been overcome.

---

21. Child Support, *supra* note 1, at 285-306.

22. Congress added 42 U.S.C. § 602(a)(11) (requiring notice to state child support collection agency of AFDC benefits) in 1950.

23. Greenspan v. Slate, 12 N.J. 426, 437, 97 A.2d 390, 395 (1953).

24. 1 W. Blackstone, Commentaries on the Laws of England *447-48 (footnotes omitted).

A. *The Federal Enforcement Initiative of 1974*

The Office of Child Support Enforcement (OCSE) of the United States Department of Health and Human Services provides the following statistics for 1987: (1) 812,661 support orders were entered; (2) 268,766 paternities were established; (3) nearly 1.4 million parent-locate requests were filed, and eighty percent were filled within two weeks; (4) nearly four billion support dollars were collected, bringing to twenty-three billion dollars the total collected since the inception of the program twelve years before; and (5) on average, one dollar was spent to collect $3.68.[25]

When Congress enacted the sweeping legislation to strengthen enforcement of child support obligations across the nation, the primary goal was to reduce the federal cost of the AFDC program. Since then, the scope and purpose of the enforcement program have been broadened. It was recognized early that the objective of reducing the cost of AFDC programs could be secured more successfully if potential recipients were kept off welfare by extending the support enforcement program to them. But the program now reaches well beyond this group: support enforcement is available to anyone for a reasonable fee.[26] In terms of "middle class" family support, this has made a significant difference—more than one-half of total collections are going to children who are not on welfare.[27]

State authority and state laws remain primary vehicles, but state enforcement agencies—now commonly known as "IV-D agencies," reflecting their location in title 42 of the United States Code—must meet standards imposed by federal law. OCSE is the stimulator, overseer, and financier of state collection systems. The "stick" waved at the states is loss of some of their federal AFDC funding. The "carrot" is federal funding for a considerable portion of the states' support enforcement programs, but only if they meet federal standards.

25. *Twelfth Annual Report Released to Congress*, CHILD SUPPORT REP., Aug. 1988, at 3 [hereinafter *Report*].

26. *See* CHILD SUPPORT, *supra* note 1, at 323-30, discussing the drawn-out controversy over the non-AFDC support collection feature of the enforcement legislation. It is well worth emphasizing the significance of the extension of the federal support enforcement legislation beyond the welfare context. The provisions concerning non-AFDC support enforcement alleviate the all-too-common lot of the abandoned mother who has sufficient productive capacity and pride to keep herself and her children above the welfare eligibility line, but whose earning capacity may have been impaired by a role-divided marriage and now is restricted by the custodial services she renders her children. While the typical father's earnings enable him to make a reasonable contribution to child support, he does not earn enough to do so without pain. Thus, unless seriously encouraged, many fathers are unwilling to make their proper contributions. These contributions, though significant in terms of their children's needs, too often are not large enough to make it economical to involve lawyers in repeated enforcement forays under the cumbersome and correspondingly expensive traditional child support enforcement procedures.

27. 1 U.S. DEP'T OF HEALTH & HUMAN SERVS., OFFICE OF CHILD SUPPORT ENFORCEMENT, TWELFTH ANNUAL REPORT TO CONGRESS FOR THE PERIOD ENDING SEPTEMBER 30, 1987 7 (1988)[hereinafter REPORT TO CONGRESS]; 2 *id.* tables 3, 5.

B. The Federal Enforcement Process

To summarize:[28] federal law requires state AFDC agencies to collect data, use the social security numbers of all AFDC applicants as identification, notify state child support enforcement agencies when benefits are granted to eligible children, and open their records to support enforcement officials. Applicants must assign their rights to uncollected child support to the state and must agree to cooperate in locating absent parents, in establishing paternity, in obtaining support judgments if none are outstanding, and in securing payments. In case of an applicant's unjustified failure to cooperate, AFDC benefits are withheld from the applicant, though not from children.

The states maintain parent locator services equipped to search state and local records for information regarding the whereabouts of absent parents. OCSE maintains a sophisticated, computerized federal parent locator service based in Washington, D.C. with access to social security, internal revenue, and nearly all other federal information resources, except census records. When the absent (or alleged) parent is located, the state establishes paternity (if necessary and possible), obtains a support judgment, and enforces the obligation through either in-state or interstate proceedings. All states must cooperate fully with their sister states. Access to federal courts is provided, if necessary, and so is collection by the Internal Revenue Service. After collection, the state disburses child support payments, keeping detailed records and reporting to OCSE. To encourage local participation in child support enforcement, the state turns a portion of the proceeds over to the collecting unit of the local government.

C. The 1984 Child Support Amendments: Mandatory Withholding and Discretionary Guidelines

In 1984, significant federal amendments asked the states to sharpen their laws and strengthen enforcement powers.[29] State laws now must require employers to withhold child support from the paychecks of parents delinquent for one month.[30] State laws must provide for the imposition of liens against the property of defaulting support obligors, and credit companies may be informed of unpaid child support in excess of

28. The federal enforcement legislation is codified at 42 U.S.C. §§ 651-665 (1982). The text following this note briefly summarizes the federal enforcement process. For more detailed explanations, see CHILD SUPPORT, *supra* note 1, at 307-87; M. HENRY & V. SCHWARTZ, A GUIDE FOR JUDGES IN CHILD SUPPORT ENFORCEMENT (M. Reynolds 2d ed. 1987); M. HENRY & B. SCHWARTZ, ESSENTIALS FOR ATTORNEYS IN CHILD SUPPORT ENFORCEMENT (M. Reynolds ed. 1986).

29. Child Support Enforcement Amendments of 1984, Pub. L. No. 98-378, 98 Stat. 1305 (codified as amended in scattered sections of 42 U.S.C.) [hereinafter 1984 Amendments]; *see also* H.R. REP. NO. 527, 98th Cong., 1st Sess. (1983). The text following this note summarizes important provisions of the 1984 amendments.

30. The 1988 amendments require immediate withholding by 1994 *See infra* Part III.D.

$1,000.[31] Unpaid support obligations must be deducted from federal and state income tax refunds. Expedited hearings—judicial or administrative—are required in support cases. Following, extending, and anticipating various United States Supreme Court decisions,[32] statutes of limitation for the establishment of paternity must allow at least eighteen years after a child's birth for suit. To give families receiving welfare some direct benefit from the father's support payments, the first fifty dollars per month are now paid directly to the family and not deducted from the family's welfare check.

The 1984 amendments announced that Washington will play a more active role in defining standards for acceptable state law on these questions. The amendment achieves one important objective—long and effectively championed by David Chambers:[33] more effective methods of support enforcement will become the rule, specifically wage deduction to avoid default, rather than (often counterproductive) jail and loss of job after default.

At least as importantly, the 1984 amendments require states to establish discretionary guidelines for child support awards. Toward that end, the amendments provide:

> (a) Each State, as a condition for having its State plan approved under this part, must establish guidelines for child support award amounts within the State. The guidelines may be established by law or by judicial or administrative action.
>
> (b) The guidelines established pursuant to subsection (a) shall be made available to all judges and other officials who have the power to determine child support awards within such State, but need not be binding upon such judges or other officials.
>
> (c) The Secretary shall furnish technical assistance to the States for establishing the guidelines, and each State shall furnish the Secretary with copies of its guidelines.
>
> (b) [sic] The amendment made by subsection (a) shall become effective on October 1, 1987.[34]

In response to the House Ways and Means Committee's request, a national panel was set up to advise the states upon support guidelines.[35]

---

31. By August of 1988, eight states routinely reported child support debt to credit bureaus. *States Report Child Support Debts to Credit Bureaus*, CHILD SUPPORT REP., Aug. 1988, at 1.

32. Clark v. Jeter, 108 S. Ct. 1910 (1988); Paulussen v. Herion, 475 U.S. 557 (1986); Pickett v. Brown, 462 U.S. 1 (1983); Mills v. Habluetzel, 456 U.S. 91 (1982).

33. D. CHAMBERS, MAKING FATHERS PAY: THE ENFORCEMENT OF CHILD SUPPORT (1979).

34. 1984 Amendments, *supra* note 29, § 17, 98 Stat. at 1321-22 (codified as amended at 42 U.S.C.A. § 667 (West Supp. 1989)).

35. H.R. REP. NO. 527, 98th Cong., 1st Sess. 48 (1983):

> The Committee recommends that the report include a full and complete summary of the opinions and recommendations of an advisory panel to be comprised of at least one person who is representative of parents entitled to receive child support on behalf of their children, at least one person who is representative of absent parents obligated to pay child support, and at least two people with professional expertise in child support issues in the fields of law and economics, at least one person who is a member of the judiciary, at least one person who is a member of a

That Panel comprised a divorced women's advocate, a divorced men's advocate, a state support enforcement director, a child support judge, a state legislator, a court systems child support administrator, an economics professor, and a law professor (myself). After long debate and much compromise, we endorsed the following basic principles:

> (1) Both parents share legal responsibility for supporting their children. The economic responsibility should be divided in proportion to their available income.
>
> (2) The subsistence needs of each parent should be taken into account in setting child support, but in virtually no event should the child support obligation be set at zero.
>
> (3) Child support must cover a child's basic needs as a first priority, but, to the extent either parent enjoys a higher than subsistence level standard of living, the child is entitled to share the benefit of that improved standard.
>
> (4) Each child of a given parent has an equal right to share in that parent's income, subject to factors such as age of the child, income of each parent, income of current spouses, and the presence of other dependents.
>
> (5) Each child is entitled to determination of support without respect to the marital status of the parents at the time of the child's birth. Consequently, any guideline should be equally applicable to determining child support related to paternity determinations, separations, and divorces.
>
> (6) Application of a guideline should be sexually non-discriminatory. Specifically, it should be applied without regard to the gender of the custodial parent.
>
> (7) A guideline should not create extraneous negative effects on the major life decisions of either parent. In particular, the guideline should avoid creating economic disincentives for remarriage or labor force participation.
>
> (8) A guideline should encourage the involvement of both parents in the child's upbringing. It should take into account the financial support provided directly by parents in shared physical custody or extended visitation arrangements, recognizing that even a fifty percent sharing of physical custody does not necessarily obviate the child support obligation.[36]

The establishment by the states of reasonable guidelines for setting child support obligations will assure less arbitrary and diverse conceptions of the needs of the child and the father's ability to pay than have been applied in the past. The states' responses to the federal mandate are

---

State legislature, and at least one person with expertise in the administration of child support enforcement programs.

36. R. Williams, Development of Guidelines for Child Support Orders: Final Report I-4 (1987).

being evaluated.[37] For now I refer and defer to the analyses of others, and add only one point: more consistent and coherent results would be achieved if federal (not state-by-state) standards would set a national standard, with adjustments for regional variations in the cost of living. With the movement to OCSE-sponsored national support enforcement, continued federal deference to state-by-state discretion seems misplaced.

The 1984 amendments injected federal initiative and authority more deeply into matters that previously had been viewed as reserved to the states. Nevertheless, when Congress signalled this policy by passing a sense-of-congress resolution, it still insisted that "*state and local governments* must focus on the vital issues of child support, child custody, visitation rights, and other related domestic issues."[38] Specifically:

(a) The Congress finds that—

(1) the divorce rate in the United States has reached alarming proportions and the number of children being raised in single parent families has grown accordingly;

(2) there is a critical lack of child support enforcement, which Congress has undertaken to address through the child support enforcement program;

(3) Congress is strengthening that program to recognize the needs of all children;

(4) related domestic issues, such as visitation rights and child custody, are often intricately intertwined with the child support problem and have received inadequate consideration; and

(5) these related issues remain within the jurisdiction of State and local governments, but have a critical impact on the health and welfare of the children of the Nation.

(b) It is the sense of Congress that—

(1) State and local governments must focus on the vital issues of child support, child custody, visitation rights, and other related domestic issues that are properly within the jurisdictions of such governments;

(2) all individuals involved in the domestic relations process should recognize the seriousness of these matters to the health and welfare of our Nation's children and assign them the highest priority; and

(3) a mutual recognition of the needs of all parties involved in

37. *See* Brackney, *Recent Development—Battling Inconsistency and Inadequacy: Child Support Guidelines in the States*, 11 HARV. WOMEN'S L.J. 197 (1988); Dodson, *A Guide to the Guidelines: New Child Support Rules Are Helping Custodial Parents Bridge the Financial Gap*, FAM. ADVOC., Spring 1988, at 4; M. Minow & D. Rhode, On Divorce Reform: Reforming the Questions, Questioning the Reformers 21-27 (Draft Oct. 1988) (unpublished paper presented at a symposium, *Divorce Reform in Retrospect*, sponsored by the Earl Warren Legal Institute, University of California at Berkeley, and the Institute for Research on Women and Gender, Stanford University, Nov. 4-5, 1988, to be published by the Yale University Press as part of a collection edited by Stephen D. Sugarman) (on permanent file with the *University of Illinois Law Review*).

38. 1984 Amendments, *supra* note 29, § 23(b)(1), 98 Stat. at 1330.

divorce actions will greatly enhance the health and welfare of America's children and families.[39]

D. The 1988 Child Support Amendments

The 1988 child support amendments[40] provide that, beginning in 1994, for all new or modified support orders, child support payments are to be withheld from absent parents' wages automatically and without regard to whether they are in arrears. Support guidelines must be used to determine child support obligations, and child support orders are to be reviewed every three years. Federal standards for the establishment of paternity must be met, and the federal government will pay ninety percent of the cost of laboratory tests to establish paternity. Moreover, such tests may be required by the contesting party.[41] The legislation also mandates automatic tracking and monitoring systems, provides additional sources for the parent location service, and authorizes the establishment of a commission on interstate child support.

E. How Much Room Is Left for Improved Enforcement?

Room for improvement remains. There are unexplained, wide variations in collection performance from one state to another, arising from incomplete federal, state, and local implementation.[42] Better collection figures can and will come out of administrative improvements, stimulated by federal pressure. In August 1988, Wayne Stanton, the Director of OCSE, admonished:

> While collections have increased, child support agencies must become even more proficient at using every tool available to collect support from parents who are now simply walking away from their children. Much more State attention must be paid to collection efforts, such as using liens on personal and real property, as well as reporting delinquents to credit bureaus to cloud their credit.[43]

Despite OCSE's proud macrorecord described earlier, dismal microstatistics involving child support collections have been reported in numerous studies, prominently Professor Weitzman's[44] and Professors

39. *Id.* § 23, 98 Stat. at 1329-30.

40. Family Support Act of 1988, Pub. L. No. 102-485, 100 Stat. 2343 (to be codified in scattered section of 42 U.S.C.). For a summary and text of the 1988 amendments, see 15 Fam. L. Rep. (BNA) 1047-48, 2001-08 (1988). The text following this footnote briefly summarizes important provisions of those amendments.

41. This paternity establishment provision comes 15 years after it was proposed to the Senate Finance Committee. *See* ILLEGITIMACY, *supra* note 1, at 133-37; H. KRAUSE, FAMILY LAW: CASES, COMMENTS AND QUESTIONS 875-76 (2d ed. 1983). Then, the proposal was enacted by the Senate, but not by the House, and dropped in conference.

42. *See* 2 REPORT TO CONGRESS, *supra* note 27, tables 58-71.

43. *Report, supra* note 25, at 3 (quoting Director Stanton).

44. L. WEITZMAN, THE DIVORCE REVOLUTION: THE UNEXPECTED SOCIAL AND ECONOMIC CONSEQUENCES FOR WOMEN AND CHILDREN IN AMERICA (1985); *see Review Symposium on Weitzman's* Divorce Revolution, 1986 AM. B. FOUND. RES. J. 757 [hereinafter *Review Symposium*].

Bruch's and Wikler's.[45] These studies focus not on how much more is now being collected, but show that in the samples the authors studied, a lot of child support remains uncollected. OCSE reports that "[t]he aggregate amount of child support payments due for 1985 alone was $10.9 billion but payments actually received amounted to only $7.2 billion."[46]

F. Why Is That Support Not Collected?

To concentrate on the really hard cases, we might put aside the cases in which the custodial parent supports the child adequately and, for reasons of her own, does not wish to impose on the absent parent. Ignoring such cases leaves only two alternative explanations of inadequate support. One is that the state makes an inadequate effort to enforce existing law, law that increasingly is up to the task. But as implementation of existing law is—as it surely will be—perfected, only one explanation why absent fathers do not pay will remain: they do not have the money to render adequate child support. Even now, I suspect that a large number of defaulting fathers do not have (and never had) the missing money. Many a defaulting father's obligation, even if originally assessed fairly, does not correspond to his current economic circumstances, and current law or practice does not afford him an adequate opportunity to effect an appropriate modification.[47]

Looking carefully at statistics and reality, it is reasonable to conclude that many fathers are not alone able to provide the support their children need to get a decent start in life, even if many try.[48] And to the extent we are now driven to see child support enforcement as the sole solution to child poverty, we are as wrong as those in the 1960s who saw the AFDC program as the sole appropriate source of support for female-headed families. To refresh my memory, I occasionally go to our local courts—in a relatively affluent midwestern community, nothing like the big city courts I also have studied—and spend a few hours seeing the parade of unemployed, and often unemployable, teenagers being confronted with unmeetable financial obligations, arising, ironically, out of constitutionally protected conduct.[49] For those who have not seen these

45. Bruch & Wikler, *The Economic Consequences*, JUV. & FAM. CT. J., Fall 1985, at 5.

46. 1 REPORT TO CONGRESS, *supra* note 27, at 5.

47. CHILD SUPPORT, *supra* note 1, at 431.

48. *See* U.S. DEP'T OF COMMERCE, BUREAU OF THE CENSUS, CURRENT POPULATION REPORTS, HOUSEHOLD ECONOMIC STUDIES, SERIES P-70, NO. 13, WHO'S HELPING OUT? SUPPORT NETWORKS AMONG AMERICAN FAMILIES (1988).

49. The study shows that half of the teen fathers lived with their child at least for some time after the baby's birth. However, only one third of the fathers married the mother of the baby within twelve months of conception. The study also shows that teenage fathers who were married prior to conception were the least likely to have completed high school: 62 percent of those fathers dropped out of school compared to about 37 percent of those whose first birth was conceived outside of marriage whether they subsequently married or not.

Teenage Fatherhood, AM. FAM., Mar. 1988, at 19; *see generally* J. SMOLLAR & T. OOMS, YOUNG UNWED FATHERS: RESEARCH REVIEW, POLICY DILEMMAS AND OPTIONS 52-53 (1987).

proceedings, David Chambers has described them graphically.[50]

I fear that our current emphasis on enforcing the father's obligation is clouding our judgment as to how much money we can realistically expect the father to provide. Looking more carefully at detailed collection statistics at the bottom of the social pyramid, the fact is that at the AFDC level we currently spend nearly as much on collection as we collect—and in many states more.[51] Child support collection actually has been turned into an income transfer program from poor fathers to lawyers and welfare bureaucrats—something I had hoped we would avoid.[52]

On the fix-it-fast level, I have suggested that we institute facilitated, semiautomatic modification of prospective support payments to reflect the typical low-income father's often quickly changing ability to pay.[53] That would reduce or eliminate the accumulation of the hopeless arrears many fathers owe the government—by that I mean arrears that, short of winning the lottery, the father has no hope of ever being able to pay. We should consider reinstituting forgiveness of such arrears, at least in the context of bankruptcy.[54] Nor am I completely at ease with the work product of our National Panel on Child Support Guidelines.[55] These issues continue to concern me, but not here and not now.[56]

---

50. D. CHAMBERS, *supra* note 33, at 3-9, 253. Senator Moynihan has a more "optimistic" perception of the situation:

> This is a matter to be pressed *to* the point of punitiveness. . . . Hunt, hound, harass: the absent father is rarely really absent, especially the teenage father, but merely unwilling or not required to acknowledge his children's presence. The Child Support Enforcement program has the great virtue of paying for itself as well as having the inestimable advantage of linking the issue of welfare dependency to the more general issue of women's entitlements. . . . And for the too-much-pitied unemployed teenage male there would be nothing wrong with a federal work program— compulsory when a court has previously ordered him to support his children—with the wages shared between father and mother. This latter is not likely to get started or to work very well if it does. The disorder of the times would likely enough defeat it. But it does make a statement about legitimacy: there must be an acknowledged providing male.

D. MOYNIHAN, FAMILY AND NATION 180-81 (1986).

51. 2 REPORT TO CONGRESS, *supra* note 27, table 49; *see also* L. LOYACONO & S. SMITH, STATE BUDGET IMPLICATIONS: CHILD SUPPORT ENFORCEMENT apps. B & C (1988). Below "par" AFDC cost effectiveness ratios for 1987 are reported for New Hampshire (.83), Delaware (.92), Maryland (.96), New York (.74), Nebraska (.85), Florida (.81), Kentucky (.93), Louisiana (.90), Tennessee (.97), Virginia (.59), Arizona (.53), New Mexico (.95), Oklahoma (.97), Texas (.84), Colorado (.94), Alaska (.75), Nevada (.62), the District of Columbia (.53), Guam (.73), Puerto Rico (.52), and the Virgin Islands (.28). *Id.* In assessing the true meaning of "cost-benefit effectiveness," many caveats are in order. *See* CHILD SUPPORT, *supra* note 1, at 422-31, 446-55.

52. Krause, *Reflections on Child Support*, 1983 U. ILL. L. REV. 99, 106-11.

53. H. KRAUSE, *supra* note 41, at 897-99; H. KRAUSE, FAMILY LAW: CASES, COMMENTS, AND QUESTIONS 897-99 (2d ed. 1983) (quoting Krause, *Automatic Adjustment Clauses in Support Agreements or Decrees*, 1 FAIR SHARE 3-4 (1981).

54. *Child Support Enforcement Program Reform Proposals: Hearings Before the Senate Comm. on Finance*, 98th Cong., 2d Sess. 454, 458, 460 (1984) [hereinafter *Hearings*] (statement of Harry D. Krause, Professor of Law, University of Illinois). *Contra* Bruch, *Developing Standards for Child Support Payments: A Critique of Current Practice*, 16 U.C. DAVIS L. REV. 49, 62 (1982).

55. *See supra* text accompanying note 36.

56. We could debate at length the relative effectiveness of specific enforcement techniques, from wage withholding to extradition and imprisonment. *See* D. CHAMBERS, *supra* note 33; CHILD SUPPORT, *supra* note 1, at 81-84. We could discuss the United States Supreme Court's recent struggle with contempt sanctions, civil or criminal, in Hicks *ex rel.* Feiock v. Feiock, 108 S. Ct. 1423 (1988). But I think that the "better enforcement" debate is all but over. With mandated, formula-

Summing up what I see, the "next issues" in child support include (1) the reality that many defaulting fathers simply do not have what it takes to support their children—as enforcement becomes comprehensive, fewer defaults will be due to irresponsibility, (2) my growing (if heretical) notion that it may not be fair to ask all absent fathers to foot the entire bill, and (3) the need to understand that children have a direct claim on society at large, along with their parallel claim on their parents. Let me now risk offering some caveats about overemphasizing the paternal support responsibility.

IV. The Future

A. Toward a Better Balance Between Private and Public Responsibility: The Impecunious Father and His Welfare Child

In August 1988, the Census Bureau reported that, in 1987, the poverty rate (income below $11,612 for a family of four) for all children stood at 20.6%. Forty-nine percent of black children under the age of six were poor—one in two![57] I happily stipulate that the poverty measurement is subject to numerous doubts, ranging from its unrealistic derivation (three times a basic food basket) to its perverse disregard of the value of in-kind programs, such as food stamps, subsidized housing, medical care, and school lunches. Still, the poverty figure does provide a rough measure of well-being or its opposite. AFDC, in most states, does not come close to meeting this minimum. In 1987, Alabama provided $147 per month for a family of four, and Mississippi provided $144.[58]

Our success in child support enforcement has not significantly improved the poorest children's lot! And it cannot, until we share between the poorest fathers and the taxpayer the cost of supporting all children at a responsible minimum level. My, I think not extravagant, recommendation when the 1984 amendments were proposed was that the welfare father's child support payments should not be deducted from his children's public welfare check until the father's payments have moved his children up to the poverty level.[59] Instead, we got the current fifty-dollar-per-

based setting of support obligations, with payroll deduction of support owed, and with computer-provided nationwide access to support-owing parents, the law now provides an effective arsenal for imposing the obligation as well as collecting child support. Continuing complaints that child support collections remain inadequate can no longer expect much response from better enforcement law, although there is always room for improvement.

57. Champaign-Urbana News-Gazette, Aug. 31, 1988, at 1, col. 1. (42.7% of black children under the age of 18 were poor); *see also* N.Y. Times, Sept. 3, 1988, § 1, at 22, col. 1.

58. N.Y. Times, Apr. 12, 1987, § 4, at 5, col. 2, lists maximum fiscal 1987 monthly benefits for a family of four as of January 1987. Given in parentheticals are the figures as a percent of estimated median monthly income for a family of four. The highest paying states were Alaska: $833 (23%); California: $734 (26%); New York: $706 (26%); Connecticut: $688 (21%); Wisconsin: $649 (25%). The lowest paying states were: Mississippi: $144 (7.3%); Alabama: $147 (6.6%); Tennessee: $189 (8.5%); Texas: $221 (8.5%); Arkansas: $224 (11.6%).

59. *Hearings*, *supra* note 54, at 454, 464-66 (statement of Harry D. Krause, Professor of Law, University of Illinois); *see also* CHILD SUPPORT, *supra* note 1, at 456-65.

month disregard[60]—a "foot in the door," but hardly enough in terms of the children's realistic needs.[61]

The concrete reality of child poverty speaks for itself, but who is listening? Along with the rest of our economy and shifting ideology, children have been "privatized." Why? The perception has taken hold that the absent father is solely responsible for support of his children, and that if he does not pay enough, he is irresponsible, but worse, no one else is responsible. The realities predicted for the future, however, increasingly point away from the father.

In the so-called single-parent family, one parent (typically the mother) with one or more children constitutes a household unit. Either she is divorced, or she has never had a legal (and often not much of a personal) tie with the other parent. Increasingly, this is the social setting in which a significant proportion of our next generation is raised.[62] But easy-come, easy-go marriage and casual cohabitation and procreation are on a collision course with the economic and social needs of children. This may sound like a moral value judgment, but it is a pragmatic assessment. The last two decades of piecemeal adaptations of traditional law to a changing society are not meeting the challenge. If the traditional social structure—the traditional, ongoing two-parent family—no longer exists, can its ghost support traditional financial responsibility?

Senator Moynihan points out that by the year 2000:

> [W]e project that about three-quarters of American families will be of the "traditional" sort, whereas in 1960 nearly nine of ten families could be so described. In less than two generations the proportion of families headed by single persons will have doubled. . . .
>
> In the final two decades of the century we project the number of families will increase from 59.5 million to 72.5 million, which is to say a net of 13 million families. But of these additional households, only 5.9 million are expected to be "traditional" husband-wife families. Female-headed families will account for 5.8 million of the net increase, and male-headed families for 1.3 million. Put another way, in the period 1980-2000 the number of female-headed families will increase at more than five times the rate of husband-wife families.[63]

Can we afford to continue treating a phenomenon as widespread as one-parent child rearing as deviant? Can all problems attending one-parent child rearing be corrected simply by strict enforcement of child sup-

60. For more detail, see Disregard of Child Support Payments, 53 Fed. Reg. 21,642 (1988) (codified in scattered sections of 45 C.F.R. pts. 302 & 303).

61. Even this small step has proved to be expensive. The $50 disregard reduced the overall savings to the taxpayer from a high near $250 million in 1984 to less than $25 million in 1987, and more than tripled the federal program deficit to about $300 million in the same period. 1 REPORT TO CONGRESS, *supra* note 27, at 12.

62. *Cf.* Bowen v. Gilliard, 483 U.S. 587 (1987) (AFDC provision which attributes child support benefits to the family unit is not unconstitutional).

63. D. MOYNIHAN, *supra* note 50, at 147.

port obligations? Can we continue to limit social intervention to the prevention of outright starvation—at a level well below our official definition of a minimum standard? Are we dealing only with the failure of private responsibility?

As much and as long as I have worked to raise child support consciousness and have been criticized for that,[64] I now find it remarkable—even a little frightening—that the absent welfare father's child support obligation has become so fast, so deeply, the only true faith. Arguably, this was due in no small measure to an unlikely—if unwitting—political alliance between women's groups and a basically conservative, antiwelfare legislative constituency, the latter drawing its support from many real and more perceived excesses of the Great Society of the 1960s and 1970s. Whatever the reason, and putting it very bluntly, in the late 1980s the emphasis seems to be more on immorality—the culpability of the father—than on the needs of the child. This has dissipated any sense of urgency for legislative action to secure the financial welfare of children. By voting for tougher child support enforcement, legislators, state and federal, can congratulate themselves that something has been done for children—and at no public cost. In sum, our current intense preoccupation with the absent father's fault and irresponsibility has displaced awareness of the reality of the limited resources of many absent fathers. It has made much more difficult a responsible dialogue over public responsibility. Our justified insistence on the enforcement of the father's unmet legal obligation has unjustifiably eclipsed our need to understand that, ultimately, the adequate support of children is a public necessity.

B. The Rationale of the Parental Child Support Obligation

On a more fundamental level than sheer inability to pay, I now want to have another look at the current validity of the traditional parental child support obligation. As Mary Ann Glendon,[65] Martha Minow,[66] Herbert Jacob,[67] and many others have pointed out, the dominant dilemma is that family loyalties today are less close than they used to be. Consequently, family responsibilities are understood as less binding than they were even a generation ago. But in contradiction to these facts of

64. *E.g.*, Gray, Book Review, 46 N.Y.U. L. REV. 1228, 1233 (1971) (reviewing ILLEGITIMACY, *supra* note 1):

> Professor Krause . . . errs in suggesting that poor illegitimate children can be benefited by a systematic effort to force their fathers to pay support. . . . First, such a program would not create more stable families. Rather, the effect would be to encourage fathers to desert their illegitimate children entirely. Second, many children would not benefit financially even if fathers did pay, since the support payments would be deducted from any welfare benefits.

65. Glendon, *Modern Marriage Law and Its Underlying Assumptions: The New Marriage and the New Property*, 13 FAM. L.Q. 441 (1980).

66. Minow, *The Properties of Family and the Families of Property* (Book Review), 92 YALE L.J. 376, 379-81 (1982) (reviewing M. GLENDON, THE NEW FAMILY AND THE NEW PROPERTY (1981)).

67. Jacob, *The Changing Landscape of Family Policy and Law* (Book Review), 21 LAW & SOC'Y REV. 744 (1988).

modern life, recent child support doctrine reflects a sharpening of traditional values and concepts governing family responsibility.

I do not have a clear answer to the question of what is the most intelligent legal response to still evolving new perceptions of the family and new sexual-procreative lifestyles. But I am fairly sure that now, after divorce reform, the answer must involve a radical redefinition of society's economic and social involvement with the parent-and-child relationship.

1. Tradition: Social and Economic Reciprocity

When Blackstone formulated the support obligation for the common law world,[68] he was looking at a world that was centered on the ongoing family. Divorce did not exist—even if the law did not entirely comport with London reality.

Choosing to rest most of his case on natural law and what we now call sociobiology,[69] Blackstone did not say that the support obligation he saw was founded on the reciprocal relationship of parent and child in the ongoing family, but I think it was. This reciprocity had an economic and a social component.

Economically, the support-obligated parent was entitled to the child's earnings until the child reached majority.[70] More importantly, economic reciprocity extended to the parent's old age.[71] Support received by the young child morally and legally obligated the adult child to support the aged parent. Before we had social security, child support was an "investment" the parent made, to be recovered if needed. The law took this reciprocity quite literally: a child who unjustifiably had not been supported when young was absolved from the obligation later to support the parent.[72]

Socially, parent and child reciprocity involved an ongoing family life. Supporting parents had the emotional satisfaction of seeing their offspring grow up. They shaped their child's life. And their financial responsibilities were fairly minimal. Blackstone said:

> No person is bound to provide a maintenance for his issue, unless where the children are impotent and unable to work, either through infancy, disease, or accident, and then is only obliged to find them with necessaries, the penalty on refusal being no more

---

68. 1 W. BLACKSTONE, *supra* note 24, at *447-48.

69. *See* J. BECKSTROM, EVOLUTIONARY JURISPRUDENCE: PROSPECTS AND LIMITATIONS ON THE USE OF MODERN DARWINISM THROUGHOUT THE LEGAL PROCESS 50-53 (1989); J. BECKSTROM, SOCIOBIOLOGY AND THE LAW: THE BIOLOGY OF ALTRUISM IN THE COURTROOM OF THE FUTURE (1985).

70. 1 W. BLACKSTONE, *supra* note 24, at *453.

71. An Act for the Relief of the Poor, 43 Eliz., ch. 2, § VII (1601); 1 W. BLACKSTONE, *supra* note 24, at *453-54; *cf.* Swoap v. Superior Court, 10 Cal. 3d 490, 516 P.2d 840, 111 Cal. Rptr. 136 (1973) (statute requiring children to reimburse state for aid paid to parents is not unconstitutional); *see also* Garrett, *Filial Responsibility Laws*, 18 J. FAM. L. 793 (1979-80).

72. *See, e.g.*, Cannon v. Juras, 15 Or. App. 265, 515 P.2d 428 (Ct. App. 1973) (facts did not establish abandonment which would absolve son from support of his mother).

than 20*s*. a month. For the policy of our laws, which are ever watchful to promote industry, did not mean to compel a father to maintain his idle and lazy children in ease and indolence: but thought it unjust to oblige the parent, against his will, to provide them with superfluities, and other indulgences of fortune; imagining they might trust to the impulse of nature, if the children were deserving of such favors.[73]

In short, the father did not owe much beyond food and clothing, and even that not for long. Today's "budget busters" were not yet in the picture. Long before medical bills could have seriously accumulated, the child would have died under then prevailing standards of medical care. Education, if there was any, consisted of one-room schools. The main expense of schooling was the loss to the family of the child's earnings or potential contribution around the farm or in the family business. Today, ineligible for loans or tax breaks, middle class parents often expend $20,000 per year for seven years—four years of undergraduate college followed by three years of law school—and that after having invested upwards of another $100,000 in the same child before it turned eighteen.[74]

2. *Modern Reality: Illegitimacy, Divorce, and De Facto Loss of Parental Rights*

Today, fathers increasingly have assumed an active parental role in the ongoing family. In stark contrast, the typical custody adjudication on divorce terminates the father's parental status,[75] at least in any meaningful sense.[76] This de facto termination of parental status comes at the very time we impose on the absent parent a child support obligation that typically is potentially far larger than what he might have shouldered, or was legally obligated to provide, in the ongoing family. *Married* parents

73. 1 W. BLACKSTONE, *supra* note 24, at *449 (footnotes omitted).

74. The New York Times reports:

> A middle-income couple with two children will face total costs of about $130,000 per child in 1988 dollars by the time both children are 18 years old, said Thomas Espenshade, a senior fellow at the Urban Institute, a research organization in Washington, D.C. If the children go to college, the costs will significantly increase. "Most prospective parents grossly underestimate the financial obligations of parenthood," Mr. Espenshade said.

N.Y. Times, Feb. 20, 1988, § 1, at 34, col. 1. ("Planners advise parents to begin saving for a child's college education as soon as possible. For a child born in 1988, four years at a public university might cost about $120,000 in tuition and other expenses," *Id.*). "A study by the College Board indicates that from 1981 to 1987, the cost of attending a private university increased 81 percent, while median family income rose 40 percent." N.Y. Times, Mar. 23, 1988, § B, at 8, col. 1.

75. The traditional presumption that favors giving custody to the mother is dying a very slow death. The great majority of custody dispositions still go to the mother. H. KRAUSE, *supra* note 41, at 727-35.

76. Even in trend-setting California, the flirtation with joint custody seems to be ebbing. On September 27, 1988, Governor George Deukmejian signed a new law that declares that California has "neither a preference nor a presumption for or against joint legal custody, joint physical custody, or sole custody, but allows the court and the family the widest discretion to choose a parenting plan which is in the best interests of the child or children." Sherman, *Doubts Grow on Joint Custody*, Nat'l L.J., Oct. 24, 1988, at 3, col. 1 (quoting California law).

do not legally owe their children a lifestyle that is consistent with their income and station in life. They may choose to rear their children in any reasonable way they see fit. When the parents separate, the practicalities change. The decision-making power now is exercised by the custodial parent who, more often than not, is not the paying parent. In that situation, the custodial parent's reasonable choice of lifestyle largely controls. Without custodial control, the noncustodial parent may thus find himself (and in the future, herself) paying amounts well in excess of those the law would require him to provide if he had custody of his children. Further down the scale, unwed fathers typically never had, and even today rarely obtain, a social relationship with the children they are asked to support. Yet an Illinois court recently ordered an unmarried father to provide a college education for his nonmarital child,[77] whereas the married father in the ongoing marriage has no such obligation.[78]

The point is that the absent parent may fairly claim that he is not getting his "money's worth" for the support he is obligated to pay, not on the economic and not on the social level. Today's enlarged child support obligation does not resemble what Blackstone was talking about.

Of course, times do change and traditional concepts take on new meanings. If the original rationale no longer holds, this does not mean that a newer rationale might not support what we want to do. Let us consider this next.

3. *The Weakened Rationale of the Absent Parent's Support Obligation*

I see a contradiction between lifting all "prior restraint"—social and criminal sanctions[79]—on consensual nonmarital sexual activity and then insisting on strict enforcement of a civil liability that often amounts to eighteen years of potentially extreme restriction on the accidental (or in any event, absent) parent's lifestyle. I see an equally important contradiction on divorce, when we terminate the noncustodial parent's parental interest de facto and impose on him a greater and less flexible support obligation than the burden he shouldered in the ongoing family.

In other words, it does not seem at all obvious that the same (or a greater) level of parental responsibility that makes sense in the ongoing family should be grafted (1) onto consanguinity based on what is understood as permissible recreational sex, or (2) onto the essentially terminated postdivorce relationship between the typical father and his child.

Please do not misunderstand, I was among the first to insist that

77. Rawles v. Hartman, 172 Ill. App. 3d 931, 527 N.E.2d 680 (App. Ct. 1988), *leave to appeal denied*, 123 Ill. 2d 566, 535 N.E.2d 410 (1989).

78. *See* Kujawinski v. Kujawinski, 71 Ill. 2d 563, 578-80, 376 N.E.2d 1382, 1389-90 (1978); *see generally* Moore, *Parents' Support Obligations to Their Adult Children*, 19 AKRON L. REV. 183 (1985).

79. *E.g.*, Doe v. Duling, 603 F. Supp. 960 (E.D. Va. 1985) (Virginia fornication and cohabitation statutes declared unconstitutional).

financial responsibility be placed on absent fathers[80] and would be among the last to suggest that there be no responsibility. I am searching now for a level of responsibility that is commensurate with the social reality of the situation.

In a related context—where the unwed father seeks to assert his custodial right—the United States Supreme Court has seen fit to weave a pattern of preference for the social parent-and-child relationship. The biological father has been dealt "odd man out." The Court's crucial phrase is: "[T]he mere existence of a biological link does not merit equivalent constitutional protection."[81]

Consanguinity has a basic place in our culture and law, but does not give all the answers.[82] In the Supreme Court's considered view, the absence of a social relationship is sufficient to deny the biological, but unwed, father a right to object to his child's adoption. Some adaptation is needed to bring this perception to bear on our—one might say mirror-image—context. Just possibly, however, the mere existence of a biological link without a social link, should similarly be deemed insufficient to justify imposing an unmitigated support obligation on the absent, especially the involuntarily absent father. Conversely, as David Chambers suggests,[83] perhaps it is time to impose support obligations on stepparents, on those who have the social relationship although they lack the

80. *See Equal Protection*, *supra* note 1, at 504-06; *Uniform Act*, *supra* note 1, at 859.

81. Lehr v. Robertson, 463 U.S. 248, 261 (1983), and, very recently, consider Michael H. v. Gerald D., 109 S. Ct. 2333 (1989). In *Lehr*, the Court elaborated:

> The intangible fibers that connect parent and child have infinite variety. They are woven throughout the fabric of our society, providing it with strength, beauty, and flexibility. It is self-evident that they are sufficiently vital to merit constitutional protection in appropriate cases. In deciding whether this is such a case, however, we must consider the broad framework that has traditionally been used to resolve the legal problems arising from the parent-child relationship.
>
> . . . .
>
> The difference between the developed parent-child relationship that was implicated in *Stanley* and *Caban*, and the potential relationship involved in *Quilloin* and this case, is both clear and significant. When an unwed father demonstrates a full commitment to the responsibilities of parenthood by "com[ing] forward to participate in the rearing of his child," his interest in personal contact with his child acquires substantial protection under the Due Process Clause. At that point it may be said that he "act[s] as a father toward his children." *But the mere existence of a biological link does not merit equivalent constitutional protection*. The actions of judges neither create nor sever genetic bonds. "[T]he importance of the familial relationship, to the individuals involved and to the society, stems from the emotional attachments that derive from the intimacy of daily association, and from the role it plays in 'promot[ing] a way of life' through the instruction of children as well as from the fact of blood relationship."
>
> The significance of the biological connection is that it offers the natural father an opportunity that no other male possesses to develop a relationship with his offspring. If he grasps that opportunity and *accepts some measure of responsibility for the child's future*, he may enjoy the blessings of the parent-child relationship and make uniquely valuable contributions to the child's development. If he fails to do so, the Federal Constitution will not automatically compel a State to listen to his opinion of where the child's best interests lie.

Lehr, 463 U.S. at 256, 261-62 (citations omitted and emphasis added).

82. For the Court's most recent opinion on related issues, see Michael H. v. Gerald D., 109 S. Ct. 2333 (1989).

83. D. Chambers, Stepparents, Biologic Parents, and the Law's Perceptions of "Family" After Divorce (Conference Draft Oct. 28, 1988) (unpublished paper presented at a symposium, *Divorce Reform in Retrospect*, sponsored by the Earl Warren Legal Institute, University of California at Berkeley, and the Institute for Research on Women and Gender, Stanford University, Nov. 4-5,

biological.[84]

The correlation, in fact, between a father's willingness to pay support and the quality of his personal relationship with his child has been pointed out by Judith Wallerstein and Shauna Corbin.[85] In terms of law, I think that it may be time to reflect the involuntarily lacking or impaired social relationship in the duty to support.

The absent parent's support obligation should be pegged at a level at which the cost of family failure—whether through divorce or because a family was not established in the first place—is shared equally by father and mother. Of course, I say nothing different here than what has been said so insistently by many advocates of the ex-wife and mother—and said with the greatest popular publicity by Professor Weitzman.[86] So far we all agree. The problem is in the detail. What is a fair definition of equal cost, of equal sacrifice, to come out of family breakdown?

Even if many aspects of Professor Weitzman's influential study have been questioned,[87] the basic findings are obviously accurate. There *are* irresponsible fathers, and there *is* considerable economic suffering by divorced wives and their children. That is not news. Accordingly, it is not at all my intention to cast doubt on or to belittle the mother's side of the story.[88] My argument goes to maintaining a balance. Let us also look fairly at the responsible father's side of the case.

Professor Weitzman's oft-repeated[89] core charge that the father's standard of living after divorce goes up by forty-two percent, whereas the ex-wife's and the children's standard goes down by seventy-three percent,[90] is open to critical evaluation on a variety of levels. But I do not want to bog down in that dispute. I simply want to establish the obvious: the fractured family has three sides, child, mother, and father. With all my prior work having been on the side of child support enforcement, I never have wasted sympathy on the absent father. But now that national support enforcement has alleviated the traditional nonenforcement scandal, I have come to think that sympathetic consideration for the responsible father may not be wasted, but deserved.

What I suggest we seek is a fair equalization of the cost of the alter-

---

1988, to be published by the Yale University Press as part of a collection edited by Stephen D. Sugarman) (on permanent file with the *University of Illinois Law Review*).

84. *See* Ramsey & Masson, *Stepparent Support of Stepchildren: A Comparative Analysis of Policies and Problems in the American and English Experience*, 36 SYRACUSE L. REV. 659 (1985).

85. *See* Wallerstein & Corbin, *Father-Child Relationships After Divorce: Child Support and Educational Opportunity*, 20 FAM. L.Q. 109, 115 (1986); *see also* Pearson & Thoennes, *Supporting Children After Divorce: The Influence of Custody on Support Levels and Payments*, 22 FAM. L.Q. 319 (1988).

86. *See* L. WEITZMAN, *supra* note 44; Abraham, *The Divorce Revolution Revisited: A Counter-Revoluntionary Critique*, 3 AM. J. FAM. L. 87 (1989).

87. *See, e.g.*, *Review Symposium*, *supra* note 44.

88. *See, e.g.*, Hunter, *Child Support Law and Policy: The Systematic Imposition of Costs on Women*, 6 HARV. WOMEN'S L.J. 1 (1983).

89. *See, e.g.*, Moss, *No-Fault Divorce Hurts*, A.B.A. J., Dec. 1986, at 36.

90. L. WEITZMAN, *supra* note 44, at 337-43.

native family behavior that has come to pass for normal, or at least acceptable, in our increasingly value-free social environment. I do not plan to develop here any specific adjustments to the child support formulas that have been enacted by the states in response to the federal mandate—and for which I may have some small measure of responsibility. Let us first consider whether there really is a third set of equities in the picture. If we accept the principle, specifics will readily suggest themselves for a "social relationship factor" in the definition of appropriate child support.

The connection between visitation and child support has been noticed even by the support-enforcement-minded Congress:

> The Congress finds that . . . related domestic issues, such as child visitation and child custody, are often intricately intertwined with the child support problem and have received inadequate consideration . . . . It is the sense of Congress that . . . State and local governments must focus on the vital issues of child support, child custody, visitation rights . . . .[91]

The states have not yet done so. So far, even when deprived of custody and visitation, the father finds little sympathy in the courts or legislatures when he argues that he should be allowed to retaliate by withholding child support.[92] And the counterargument is well taken: the child is not denying visitation, and the child should not suffer for the mother's disregard of a visitation order. Accordingly, courts have kept enforcement of child support and the issue of visitation separate,[93] with rare exceptions in unusual cases[94] and even more unusual statutes.[95]

And indeed, what about the child? I certainly do not want to short-

---

91. 1984 Amendments, *supra* note 29, § 23, 98 Stat. at 1329-30.

92. R. Horowitz & G. Dodson, Child Support, Custody and Visitation: A Report to State Child Support Commissions (July 1985) (unpublished paper prepared for the American Bar Association National Legal Resource Center for Child Advocacy and Protection, Child Support Project) (on permanent file with the *University of Illinois Law Review*).

93. *See* CHILD SUPPORT, *supra* note 1, at 58, 67.

94. *See In re* Marriage of Boudreaux, 201 Cal. App. 3d 447, 247 Cal. Rptr. 234 (Ct. App. 1988) (where visitation rights are intentionally sabotaged, noncustodial parent may seek modification of original child support to enforce visitation); Washington *ex rel.* Burton v. Leyser, 196 Cal. App. 3d 451, 241 Cal. Rptr. 812 (Ct. App. 1987) (custodial parent who concealed herself and her children from noncustodial parent could not recover child support arrearages for period of concealment); Biamby v. Biamby, 114 A.D.2d 830, 494 N.Y.S.2d 741 (App. Div. 1985) (trial court erroneously granted unpaid child support in light of interference with visitation rights); Hoyle v. Wilson, 746 S.W.2d 665 (Tenn.) (custodial spouse denied child support payments for period she disappeared with the children), *reh'g denied*, 14 Fam. L. Rep. 1259 (Tenn. 1988); Rohr v. Rohr, 709 P.2d 382 (Utah 1985) (wilful failure to pay child support justified lower court's refusal to modify custody and visitation rights).

95. MO. ANN. STAT. § 452.340.6 (Vernon Supp. 1989):

> 6. A court may abate, in whole or in part, any future obligation of support or may transfer the custody of one or more children if it finds:
>
> (1) That a custodial parent has, without good cause, failed to provide visitation or temporary custody to the noncustodial parent pursuant to the terms of a decree of dissolution, legal separation or modifications thereof; and
>
> (2) That the noncustodial parent is current in payment of all support obligations pursuant to the terms of a decree of dissolution, legal separation or modifications thereof. The court may also award reasonable attorney fees to the prevailing party.

change the child. But along with the need to pick up responsibility for the child of the father who is unable to pay, I think that there is a pragmatic 1980s rationale for reconsidering the level of personal sacrifice the absent father is asked to make for a child that is his in a biological sense only.

To be sure, the lack of a social link between father and child—or social reciprocity as I called it earlier—has somewhat different implications in the case of the unwed father who has not lived with the child's mother than it does in the case of a divorced father who has lost custody. The latter more often maintains some social link through visitation. But the difference is one of degree only.

V. Society's Responsibility

A. *Debt, Self-Interest, and the Social Security System*

Former Secretary Bowen of the Department of Health and Human Services said:

> Providing financial support for children is first and foremost a parental responsibility. A successful child support enforcement program enhances the lives of children who because of divorce, separation, or out-of-wedlock birth live with only one parent. Furthermore, collecting child support payments saves hundreds of millions for taxpayers who must provide for families on welfare.[96]

As I see it, Secretary Bowen's view of the matter is correct, but incomplete. Why should any part of the child support burden be put on society? The answer is that economic reciprocity, as once it existed in the old-fashioned family and helped to justify parental responsibility, today furnishes a pragmatic rationale for taxpayer subsidy. The modern system of social security provides old age support for all retired workers and their spouses, regardless of whether they "invested" in children. Retirees who had no children are equally entitled to social security benefits—equally with those who shared their earnings with their children and had a hard time of it. To the argument that nonparents contributed to the system and that is the basis of their claim, my answer is that their contributions were paid out long ago to retire their own parents. The fact is that the pensions nonparents expect to receive will be paid to them by other people's children—other people's children who have been forced by taxation to substitute them for their own parents.

I am not quarrelling with the concept of social insurance. Nor am I advocating that childless retirees be cut off. We must also understand, however, that children are only in part the private folly of their parents. Taxation has removed old age provision from the family context. Taxation has nationalized that part of children's future earnings that might have gone to fund the retirement of their own parents. In exchange, the

96. *Report*, *supra* note 25, at 3 (quoting Secretary Bowen).

taxpayer should reciprocate by bearing an appropriate share of the cost of supporting those who will later bear the burden of old age support for all.

In short, I think that society owes a more active role in supporting the rearing of children. Social recognition of this as a debt, not as reluctant charity, seems to me as important as what we have already accomplished: raising the absent father's consciousness of his debt.

Drawing the elderly into this discussion has another dimension. In terms of family law, the elderly are becoming "obsolete."[97] Today's elderly no longer look first for help to their children, they look to the social security system, private pension plans, Medicare, Medicaid, home care, institutionalization, and other social provisions and services. In law even more than in fact, the extended family has given way to the nuclear family, even as—in fact but not yet in law—the nuclear family is giving way to the single-parent family.

Has society gone too far in the direction of accepting responsibility for the elderly[98] and fallen too short in what it does for children? The New York Times reports: "In the first half of the 1980's, the nation's elderly saw their median income rise by about 16 percent while that of the rest of the population either rose slightly, stayed about the same or fell."[99]

The economic share of children has been slipping. Senator Moynihan says: "There are some 12 million poor children in the nation but for one reason or another, 5 million get nothing. A half century after the enactment of Social Security, we look up to find that insensate numbers of children are poor and that young children have seven times the poverty rate of the elderly."[100]

---

97. Except for vestigial mention in relative responsibility laws, Schneider, *Moral Discourse and the Transformation of American Family Law*, 83 MICH. L. REV. 1803, 1813 & n.31 (1985), scattered attempts to resuscitate such laws, Byrd, *Relative Responsibility Extended: Requirement of Adult Children to Pay for Their Indigent Parent's Medical Needs*, 22 FAM. L.Q. 87 (1988); Garrett, *supra* note 71, a successful movement to allow grandparents visitation with their grandchildren, H. KRAUSE, *supra* note 41, at 792-98, 1149-50, and one attempt to impose support liability on grandparents, WIS. STAT. ANN. § 49.90(1m)(a) 1 (West 1987) (effective Jan. 1, 1990), the law has all but excised the elderly from the family.

98. Life is not all roses for all elderly persons. Lawrence Swedley of the National Council of Senior Citizens provides the following data:

> Fewer than half of all older people receive private or public pensions. For men, the median private pension is $3,190 a year; for women, it's $1,940. Social Security is the major source of income for the elderly, making up 38 percent on average. It is all that stands between nearly one-third of the elderly and poverty. The median annual benefit is $6,150. While 67 percent of retirees have income from assets, that constitutes just 26 percent of aggregate income. Median income for households headed by a person older than 65 is $14,334 (1987 Census). For single individuals, median income is $8,205. Lastly, even with the added protection Medicare will now provide against "catastrophic" costs, in 1989 beneficiaries will spend about $1,525 out of their own pockets on health care. For an average retiree, that doesn't leave too much for basic needs—let alone bonbons.

Letter to the Editor, N.Y. Times, Nov. 2, 1988, at A26, col. 4.

99. N.Y. Times, Apr. 23, 1987, at C1, col. 5.

100. N.Y. Times, Jan. 24, 1987, at 1, col. 1; *see also* D. MOYNIHAN, *supra* note 50, at 94-96; Chakravarty & Weisman, *Consuming Our Children?*, FORBES, Nov. 14, 1988, at 222.

A partnership in child support is the appropriate goal. Martha Minow and Deborah Rhode say that "child support is a public concern, discharged primarily by parents but enforced and supplemented when necessary by the state, through judicial enforcement, social welfare programs, tax subsidies, and so forth."[101] David Chambers and I have thought for some time that in a few decades, our society may conclude that the enforcement of individual parental child support obligations, at least at full support levels, may no longer be good social policy.[102]

In democratic western European welfare states, society insists on, but assists with, child support.[103] Typically, those systems accept the two most burdensome aspects of child support, health care and higher education, as primarily social, rather than private, responsibilities. Yet even the duties of providing sustenance and personal care are tempered by children's allowances, subsidized day care arrangements, and subsidized housing.[104]

Abstract fairness in defining support obligations is not the only issue. A practical concern is that reproduction rates may drop to levels endangering our economy and the social security system. For women, the instability of modern marriage has raised to nearly unacceptable levels the economic risk of choosing the home and children over a career. For responsible men, rigorous child support enforcement may turn out to be a deterrent to "assisting" in the "production" of children. Given effective birth control, ready access to abortion, and the mutual risk of easy divorce, increasing numbers of couples even now choose to remain childless. Most already limit reproduction under the pressure resulting from both parties' pursuit of individual careers and the increasing expense of rearing a modern child. The time may be approaching when the

---

101. M. Minow & D. Rhode, *supra* note 37, at 19 (citing Minow, *Rights for the Next Generation: A Feminist Approach to Children's Rights*, 9 HARV. WOMEN'S L.J. 1 (1986)).

102. CHILD SUPPORT, *supra* note 1, at 299; *see* Chambers, *Comment—The Coming Curtailment of Compulsory Child Support*, 80 MICH. L. REV. 1614 (1982).

103. *See* A. KAHN & S. KAMERMAN, INCOME TRANSFERS FOR FAMILIES WITH CHILDREN: AN EIGHT-COUNTRY STUDY (1983); Kamerman & Kahn, *What Europe Does for Single-Parent Families*, PUB. INTEREST, Fall 1988, at 70; S. Kamerman & A. Kahn, Family Policy: Has the U.S. Learned From Europe? (Apr. 28, 1986) (unpublished paper prepared for the Ford Foundation Seminar on Comparative Social Policy, Columbia University, Apr. 9, 1986) (on permanent file with the *University of Illinois Law Review*); *see also Family Allowances*, 12 ANN. REV. POPULATION L. 1985 § 420 (1988). Despite budget woes, the debate in Britain is over *raising* child benefits. *See The Aid of the Family*, ECONOMIST, Oct. 22, 1988, at 19.

104. *Cf.* M. RHEINSTEIN, *supra* note 9, at 425 (footnote omitted):

> The impact of social welfare measures upon family stability is potentially enormous. Through well-considered use they could constitute an effective device of rational family policy and prove much more effective than manipulation of the laws on divorce. But much research is needed to render these tools more effective and to avoid adverse consequences.
>
> So far little is known either about the effects upon family stability of those legislative and other measures which have been taken in numerous foreign countries but for which the United States does not, or not yet, have exact counterparts. The most conspicuous of these devices is the system of family allowances, which in 1959 existed in no less than thirty-eight countries, among them Canada. Mostly such legislation has been motivated by a desire to reverse a declining trend in the birthrate or simply to encourage fertility. In the Federal Republic of Germany general considerations of social welfare have been emphasized.

opportunity cost of child rearing becomes prohibitive. Rational men and women may then choose not to have children, unless their economic security is assured by society at large. At that point, mothers and fathers who care or who have cared for children may have to be rewarded for their parenting services by meaningful tax reductions[105] and subsidies financed by an equalization-of-burdens levy on those who choose not to (or for any reason are unable to) accept the social responsibility of bearing, rearing, and supporting children.[106]

Our society's de facto delegation of the child-raising chore to the lower economic strata (especially unmarried, divorced, and unemployed women without adequate income)[107] requires a greater awareness on the part of couples with double incomes and no kids (so-called DINKS) that their own future is in jeopardy. They should be asked whether they want to live in the kind of society that will be formed by an ever-increasing proportion of social outcasts—the inevitable product of continued disregard for the social and educational needs of the already twenty-five percent of all (and fifty percent of black) children who even now survive under the poverty line.[108] If that question elicits no constructive response, they should be told that their own retirement is directly in jeopardy. Only a healthy, educated, and willing working generation will generate the necessary income to provide retirement for their predecessors in the workplace. In short, *having* children is not just a private matter—and neither is *not* having children!

The problem of our neglected and impoverished children is not simply the result of the failure of private responsibility. The problem we face cannot be corrected solely by enforcement of private monetary responsibility. We should take from parents what they can pay, but not more than they fairly should pay. Society cannot continue to limit social intervention to bare survival at a level well below our official definition of a

105. Family policy and tax policy remain unreconciled, their interrelationship often unrecognized. For a summary review, see H. KRAUSE, *supra* note 41, at 280-92. Detailed analysis of the problem is provided by Bittker, *Federal Income Taxation and the Family*, 27 STAN. L. REV. 1389 (1975); McIntyre & Oldman, *Taxation of the Family in a Comprehensive and Simplified Income Tax*, 90 HARV. L. REV. 1573 (1977); *see also* STAFF OF HOUSE SELECT COMM. ON CHILDREN, YOUTH, AND FAMILIES, 99TH CONG., 1ST SESS., A FAMILY TAX REPORT CARD: ROUND II (Comm. Print 1985).

106. This is not even a new idea. 1 PLATO, LAWS bk. IV, at 313 (R. Bury trans. 1926) (circa 347 B.C.) suggested:

> [H]e . . . that disobeys and does not marry when thirty-five years old shall pay a yearly fine of such and such an amount,—lest he imagine that single life brings him gain and ease,—and he shall have no share in the honours which are paid from time to time by the younger men in the State to their seniors.

Much later, "Hartford taxed 'lone-men' twenty shillings a week 'for the selfish luxury of solitary living.'" 2 G. HOWARD, A HISTORY OF MATRIMONIAL INSTITUTIONS 153 (1904) (quoting from A. EARLE, CUSTOMS AND FASHIONS IN OLD NEW ENGLAND 37 (1893)).

107. Harvard's Joint Center for Housing Studies reports that "the median income of a single parent under 25 was $6,223 in 1988, down 15 percent in inflation-adjusted terms from 1974." Champaign-Urbana News-Gazette, June 22, 1989, at B9, col. 4.

108. N.Y. Times, Mar. 15, 1989, at A16, col. 4 (quoting The Family Support Administration of the Department of Health and Human Services).

minimum standard. Adequate financial and social support will turn a child from a social liability into a social asset. All of us must assume a fair share of the burden of decently raising the next generation. We are not doing that.[109]

B. The Custodial Parent's Need for Services

Money is not everything. Improved standards of economic assistance, in terms of a partnership between public aid and the child's parents, are but one aspect of a new public approach giving priority to the best interests of the child. We also should take a critical look at the relationship between the child and the custodial parent, and at the manner in which the mother takes care of her fatherless child. We cannot expect the absent parent to carry faithfully a full load of child support and refuse to look at the expenditure side. This has two aspects.

First, in fairness to the child and in analogy to the paying parent whose lifestyle is, in the best interest of his child, subjected to intensive scrutiny and often severe curtailment, the custodial parent should be held accountable that the money paid for the child's support actually goes to the child's support.

Second, honest concern for child welfare reasonably requires a routine check into the fitness for child rearing of single-parent homes—or, indeed, any home—without the implication of punishment or moral condemnation. Unlike some current child neglect laws, new laws should allow for the genuine cultural diversity and divergent lifestyles that legitimately coexist in our society. We must develop new concepts of sharing caretaking responsibility between parent and assistance institutions. But a line against the inadequate parent must be drawn where the essential interests of the child are in jeopardy.

I learned long ago that the politics of this area are fierce and angry[110]—all the more so because help for the child would have a statistically disproportionate impact in the African-American community.[111] But we must not be distracted by statistical appearances. For the sake of the children, I still think we must intervene in settings that are clearly

---

109. *See* Whitman, *The Hollow Promise*, U.S. NEWS & WORLD REP., Nov. 7, 1988, at 41.

110. *See* Gray, *supra* note 64, at 1233-34:

> Professor Krause's naive view of the role of law in the lives of poor families is reflected in his argument that poor children could be helped by a stricter enforcement of child neglect and dependency laws. He is apparently aware that neglect laws are generally vague and irrationally punitive statutes which are often applied by biased and poorly trained judges who, in any event, lack any resources with which to actually help poor children. Nevertheless, the author suggests that increased state intrusion into the lives of poor families is needed to protect their children. . . . The validity of this conclusion is, to say the least, doubtful. . . . Rather, public interferences in the lives of poor families tends to destroy the very family structure (although not a white, middle class one) which Professor Krause is at pains to encourage.

111. 15.3 million children live in one-parent households, and 1.9 million more live with neither parent. From 1980 to 1988, the proportion of white children in one-parent households rose from 15% to 19%; among blacks, from 46% to 54%; and among Hispanics, from 21% to 30%. Wash. Post, Feb. 16, 1989, at A7.

inadequate for rearing children[112]—in settings that violate the civil rights of children.[113] Even if cocaine addicts had a right to their addiction, should they have the right to pass it on?[114] Should not children have a constitutional right not to be homeless,[115] not to live in welfare hotels,[116] not in Manhattan,[117] and not to be born drugged?[118] But here goes another article.[119]

---

112. I am not alone. *See Bringing Children Out of the Shadows* (Book Review), CARNEGIE Q., Spring 1988, at 1, 7 (reviewing and quoting from L. SCHORR, WITHIN OUR REACH: BREAKING THE CYCLE OF DISADVANTAGE (1988)):

> Summarizing her arguments, Schorr presents "five pillars" on which, she believes, a "new national commitment of consequence" with "staying power" must stand:
>
> First, the public must accept the evidence that favorable outcomes among high-risk children can be achieved by systematic intervention early in life. Interventions, to be effective, must offer a "broad spectrum" of services and continuity of care to families and children in the context of the community in which they live. These programs must have skilled staff that can develop "reciprocal" relationships of trust and respect.
>
> Second, the public must understand that "intensive and sometimes costly" preventive care for vulnerable families and children represents a sound allocation of resources. Such assistance, she maintains, is cheaper by far than the price society already pays for neglected health, unemployment, and crime. Americans, in other words, must "recognize that investments to improve the futures of disadvantaged children represent a joining of compassion with long-term self-interest."

113. *Cf.* Garrison, *Why Terminate Parental Rights?*, 35 STAN. L. REV. 423, 436-37 (1983) (parental visitation rights for children in foster care); Sherman, *Keeping Baby Safe From Mom*, Nat'l L.J., Oct. 3, 1988, at 1, col. 1 (making pregnant women legally responsible for their fetuses).

114. For medical studies of such phenomena, see Chasnoff, Griffith, MacGregor, Dirkes & Burns, *Temporal Patterns of Cocaine Use in Pregnancy*, 261 J. A.M.A. 1741 (1989); Novick, Berns, Stricof, Stevens, Pass & Wethers, *HIV Seroprevalence in Newborns in New York State*, 261 J. A.M.A. 1745 (1989).

115. "A report by the National Academy of Sciences called the growing number of homeless children a 'national disgrace'." N.Y. Times, Sept. 20, 1988, at A1, col. 1. "The Report estimates that on any given night families with 100,000 children are homeless." *Id.*

> The report itself was written in the bland, moderate style typical of the academy, a private organization that advises the Government on policy issues in science and health. It analyzed the causes of homelessness and the health problems associated with it, and it recommended Federal action to improve health services, housing and income levels to reduce homelessness. But a more strongly worded supplementary statement, endorsed by 10 of the 13 experts on the panel that wrote the report complained that the report was "too limited" in its language and approach.

Id.

116. *Lost Generation in Welfare Hotels: Growing Up With Drugs and Despair*, N.Y. Times, Feb. 22, 1988, at 1, col. 1. A New York City plan calls for the closing of welfare hotels sheltering homeless families. As a result, "[s]ince Aug. 1, [1988,] city officials said, 720 families have been moved out of welfare homes; 2,586 families remain in 41 welfare hotels." N.Y. Times, Mar. 3, 1989, at B3, col. 1.

117. *Cf.* Shapiro v. Thompson, 394 U.S. 618 (1969) (statute denying welfare benefits to residents of state for less than one year declared unconstitutional).

118. There is a delicate balance to be struck between the reproductive rights and lifestyle of the mother and the fundamental rights of the child. The choice is between education and coercion. At a November 1988 health law conference in Boston, I heard Professor Martha Field eloquently rejecting coercion in favor of education. I would much prefer that route myself, but education has been tried. It is not working. *See* Field, *Controlling the Woman to Protect the Fetus*, 17 LAW MED. & HEALTH CARE 114 (1989). A summary of recent fetal abuse cases and controversy is presented by Jost, *Mother Versus Child*, A.B.A. J., Apr. 1989, at 84; *see also* Sherman, *supra* note 113.

119. *See* Krause, *Child Welfare, Parental Responsibility, and the State*, in PUBLIC WELFARE, *supra* note 18, pt. II, at 255, 266-73.

C. *What Can We Do in the High-Deficit Late 1980s?*

Quite immediately, we should focus tax rates and reductions on dependent children, not on joint returns triggered by a marriage certificate.[120] Driven originally by state law definitions of community income,[121] family tax relief has come primarily through income splitting by way of the joint return. The value of exemptions for dependents, even with a recent increase, pales by comparison. Wholly in line with this emphasis on the joint return, the recent family tax reform debate has long focused on the so-called marriage penalty, the difference between income tax owed by married and unmarried couples in the same or similar circumstances—demonstrating the self-centered political power of childless couples.[122] That debate culminated in a two-earner bonus provided under the Economic Recovery Tax Act of 1981.[123] That has been superseded by newer legislation, not least because the marriage penalty has been rendered less important by new nearly flat income tax rates.[124]

The real problem has been and remains: tax law has used marriage, not children, as the tax significant event. This approach has always been in conflict with the underlying justification of income taxation—ability to pay. Many modern forms of marriage have no bearing on ability to pay—or, more typically, marriage (or unwed cohabitation) reduces expenses through economies of scale and thus increases ability to pay.

For years, the marriage penalty debate has focused on the very reasonable question of why, for tax purposes, the married, two-earner, equal career partnership established for emotional and sexual satisfaction should not be equated with the unmarried, two-earner, equal career partnership established for the same purpose. Seen from that perspective, the marriage penalty complaint has obvious merit, even if the Internal Revenue Service and the courts have not agreed.[125] But this was the wrong question.

Properly, the question should be why our tax law does not make a distinction between (1) the two-earner, equal career partnership, married or unmarried, and (2) the wholly or partially role-divided family established for the purpose of raising children.

To both the wrong and the right questions, the appropriate answer

---

120. *See supra* note 105.

121. J. Cribbett & C. Johnson, Principles of the Law of Property 96-97 (3d ed. 1989).

122. An early analysis and the history of the marriage penalty are in *American Families: Trends and Pressures, 1973: Hearings Before the Subcomm. on Children and Youth of the Senate Comm. on Labor and Public Welfare*, 93d Cong., 1st Sess. 204, 204-11 (1973) (statement of Dr. Harvey E. Brazer, Professor of Economics and Research Associate, Institute of Policy Studies, University of Michigan).

123. I.R.C. § 221(a)-(b) (1982) (repealed 1986).

124. *See* McIntyre, *Rosen's Marriage Tax Computations: What Do They Mean?*, 41 Nat'l Tax J. 257 (1988); Rosen, *The Marriage Tax Is Down But Not Out*, 40 Nat'l Tax J. 567 (1987).

125. *See* Druker v. Commissioner, 697 F.2d 46 (2d Cir. 1982) (marriage penalty is not unconstitutional); Barter v. United States, 550 F.2d 1239 (7th Cir. 1977) (same), *cert. denied*, 434 U.S. 1012 (1978).

is clear: married and unmarried DINKS should indeed be treated alike. We should discontinue the tax preference (or penalty) triggered by the technicality of legal marriage. Instead, tax recognition and relief should be focused on children, where they are (affecting ability to pay), and where they were (affecting the "former" mother's ability to earn in step with her childless sister). That is, if our society (as I think it does) considers expenses for child rearing on a higher level of social utility than, say, love boat cruises.

Where tax reductions have no effect, we should provide subsidies. We must ensure appropriate and necessary flexibility at the workplace for those who choose to parent, in terms of constructive day care for the children of full-time workers and part-time work without loss of long-run opportunity for those who choose to care for their children themselves. We must change employment practices to assist reentry into the economy of those who have parented, for their sake and that of the economy. A network of laws designed for full-time workers and based on workplace seniority now discourages needed change.

As for the argument that the federal budget will not stand for such new burdens, the good news is that the deficit, and ultimately perhaps the underlying debt, will soon be absorbed by the rapidly growing Social Security surplus, scheduled to be collected under laws now in place.[126] Even now, the budget is balanced in terms of current tax receipts and expenditures. The current deficit is only interest on the national debt[127]—nearly two-thirds of which was borrowed in the last eight years.[128]

Besides, there is misspent welfare money even in the current budget. I reject the usual military target—defense is not welfare and furnishes no useful comparison. However, the taxpayer supplies more than twenty-five billion "welfare" dollars each year for "farmers,"[129] and not just to the romantic family farm of American history. The principal recipients

126. Senator Moynihan summarizes the figures:

> The current [Social Security] reserve is approaching $100 billion. Between now and the year 2000 it will grow to $1.4 trillion. (As of 1987, the entire assets of private pension funds were about $1.49 billion.) This revenue stream must be deposited with the Treasury. If at the end of the day the Treasury has more money on hand than it needs, it simply retires privately held debt. . . . The national debt begins to shrink. Our present deficit "path" takes us, in theory at least, to a zero deficit by 1993. If that happens, the revenue stream from Social Security will be sufficient to begin retiring debt by 1994. As public debt declines, private savings increase. By 2010 the Social Security reserve is projected to be nearly $4.5 trillion. ($4,600,000,000!) If we wanted to go all the way, we could probably have zero national debt by that time.

N.Y. Times, May 23, 1988, at A19, col. 2.

127. *Interest on U.S. Debt to Top Budgets' $150 Billion Deficit*, N.Y. Times, Oct. 8, 1988, at 1, col. 4.

128. Champaign-Urbana News-Gazette, Sept. 18, 1988, at B-1, col. 1.

129. "According to Agriculture Department finance officers, commodity price support operations rose to a record $25.8 billion in 1986." Champaign-Urbana News-Gazette, Nov. 26, 1988, at 1, col. 3. Bovard, *Farm Policy Follies*, PUB. INTEREST, Spring 1989, at 75, calculates:

> American consumers pay over $10 billion more for their food than they would in a free market. For the same aggregate cost, the government could give every full-time subsidized farmer two new Mercedes each year. With the $250 billion that government and consumers have spent on

of this "welfare" are agribusiness corporations[130] and adult individuals who have made bad business decisions—typically by borrowing irrational amounts to speculate in farmland.

The point is that we really can afford a major effort in this area. Can we afford not to step in? Recently, Justice Brennan wrote:

> In The Republic and in The Laws, Plato offered a vision of a unified society, where the needs of children are met not by parents but by the Government, and where no intermediate forms of association stand between the individual and the State. The vision is a brilliant one, but it is not our own.[131]

Indeed it is not. We seem to be moving not toward a "unified society," but toward a fractured society in which the needs of children are "met not by parents" *and not* "by the government."[132]

At the welfare level, appropriate concern for the child requires a much more effective public contribution in terms of services and dollars to assure basic necessities and give the child a fairer start in life. At the well-off level, the argument is irrelevant—actor Hurt is not hurt by paying $65,000 in annual child support for his six-year-old son, and the child has enough, even if the mother wants more.[133]

At the upper middle income level, the taxpayer would be wise to consider whether a proper public recognition of the social value of parenthood would not be the assumption of nonroutine health and higher education costs that now beggar responsible parents—and that contribute to many responsible would-be parents' decisions not to have children.

Above the welfare level and below the upper middle income level, my argument concerns the enormously wide strata of those whom we like to flatter with the designation "middle class," but who all too often

---

farm subsidies since 1980, Uncle Sam could have bought every farm, barn, and tractor in thirty-four states.

130. "In 1983, the nation's 24,000 superfarms with over $500,000 in annual sales received an average of $26,805 in direct government payments, while the smallest farms averaged $1,211." *Should We Save the Family Farm?*, REP. FROM INST. FOR PHIL. & PUB. POL'Y, Summer 1988, at 1, 5 (quoting from W. GALSTON, A TOUGH ROW TO HOE: THE 1985 FARM BILL AND BEYOND (1985)). In an ironic foreign policy twist, we provide the Soviet economy a price for our food exports that is below our own production cost. This does major harm to unsubsidized farmers in friendly countries, for instance, Australia.

131. Bowen v. Gilliard, 483 U.S. 587, 632 (1987) (Brennan, J., dissenting) (citation omitted).

132. *Cf.* C. MURRAY, LOSING GROUND: AMERICAN SOCIAL POLICY, 1950-1980, at 227-28 (1984), advocating:

> scrapping the entire federal welfare and income-support structure for working-aged persons, including AFDC, Medicaid, Food Stamps, Unemployment Insurance, Worker's Compensation, subsidized housing, disability insurance, and the rest. It would leave the working-aged persons with no recourse whatsoever except the job market, family members, friends, and public or private locally funded services. It is the Alexandrian solution: cut the knot, for there is no way to untie it.

Though pointing in the opposite political direction, Dr. Murray's medicine smacks of the infantile 1960s—if we trash what there is, the millennium will emerge. Senator Moynihan has explained what will emerge in 12 years. *See supra* text accompanying note 63.

133. N.Y. Times, June 25, 1989, at 7, col. 3; *id.*, June 28, 1989, at B3, col. 1.

are but a notch removed from what we have come to call the "working poor." At that level, sympathetic concern with the financial plight of parents who are doing what they can and the argument for a better balanced role division between parents and public have their greatest strength.

VI. Summary

Where we now are going is wrong. While very impressive progress in child support collection from absent parents has been made, the very progress seems to have led us to overestimate, and consequently overemphasize, financial support that can be obtained from absent parents. Perhaps we also ask too much from those who have lost their social relationship with their child. Finally, it seems that we overestimate, and consequently overemphasize, the parental rights of the care-taking parent past the point where the latter's conduct conflicts with the best interests of the child. These three misunderstandings are displacing public consciousness of our shared responsibility for the unprecedented havoc that is threatening much of our next generation.

My thesis is simple: children have a right to a decent start in life. This right is the obligation of the father and equally of the mother, and in recognition of a primary and direct responsibility, equally the obligation of society.

(1) The absent parent owes support commensurate with (a) his or her ability to pay, (b) the marital and sexual realities and expectations our society encourages or tolerates, and (c) his or her past and present social relationship with the child.

(2) The custodial parent owes services and care in an environment conducive to the child's short- and long-term best interests, (a) commensurate with his or her means, and (b) subject to an objective minimum standard.

(3) Society has a direct duty to the child to make up any shortfall, (a) on the absent parent's side, by provision of money, and (b) on the custodial parent's side, by intervention when care is not provided at a level called for by a minimal definition of the child's best interests.

Name Index

www.ingramcontent.com/pod-product-compliance
Lightning Source LLC
LaVergne TN
LVHW081342011026
849161LV00013BB/2991
9780814746318